COMPILATION OF SELECTED
UNITED STATES COAST GUARD AND
MARITIME TRANSPORTATION RELATED
LAWS
VOLUME 1
TITLE 14 UNITED STATES CODE – COAST GUARD
TITLE 46 UNITED STATES CODE — SHIPPING
SUBTITLES I AND II

As amended through Public Law 118-233, enacted January 4, 2025; except for

Public Law 118-159.

Prepared By M. TWINCHEK

2025

Forward

T his Compilation of Selected United States Coast Guard and Maritime Transportation Related Laws is a resource for those interested in U.S. laws governing the Coast Guard. This compilation includes laws governing United States Coast Guard and its establishment; the Coast Guard Academy; water pollution; lifesaving; ports and waterways; merchant marines; and other aspects of the United States Coast Guard.

The materials included comes from publicly available, open source information, prepared for the public by the Office of the Legislative Counsel of the U.S. House of Representatives and the Office of the Law Revision Counsel.

Items listed as a Statute Compilation do not appear in the U.S. Code or that have been classified to a title of the U.S. Code that has not been enacted into positive law. Each Statute Compilation incorporates the amendments made to the underlying statute since it was originally enacted and are current as of the date noted.

This compilation is not an official document and should not be cited as evidence of any law. The official version of Federal law is found in the United States Statutes at Large and in the U.S. Code, the legal effect of which is established in sections 112 and 204, respectively, of title 1, United States Code.

A special thanks is extended to the Office of Law Revision Counsel and the House Office of the Legislative Counsel for providing the U.S. Code and statute compilations; and to the Government Publications Office for hosting and making these available for use to the public. An additional thank you is offered to the staff of the House and Senate Committees who were gracious in responding to inquiries and providing background information on the legislation included. Questions and comments may be

directed to:
   M. Twinchek
   Email: mtwinchek@outlook.com

Contents

SELECTED PROVISIONS OF
TITLE 14 U.S.C. — COAST GUARD

CURRENT THROUGH PUBLIC LAW 118-233, EXCEPT FOR
PUBLIC LAW 118-159

SUBTITLE I
ESTABLISHMENT, POWERS, DUTIES, AND ADMINISTRATION

4

TITLE 14—COAST GUARD

This title was enacted by act Aug. 4, 1949, ch. 393, §1, 63 Stat. 495

SUBTITLE I—ESTABLISHMENT, POWERS, DUTIES, AND ADMINISTRATION

CHAPTER 1—ESTABLISHMENT AND DUTIES

Sec.

§101. ESTABLISHMENT OF COAST GUARD

The Coast Guard, established January 28, 1915, shall be a military service and a branch of the armed forces of the United States at all times.

(Aug. 4, 1949, ch. 393, 63 Stat. 496, §1; Pub. L. 94–546, §1(1), Oct. 18, 1976, 90 Stat. 2519; Pub. L. 107–296, title XVII, §1704(a), Nov. 25, 2002, 116 Stat. 2314; Pub. L. 112–213, title II, §217(1), Dec. 20, 2012, 126 Stat. 1555; renumbered §101, Pub. L. 115–282, title I, §103(b), Dec. 4, 2018, 132 Stat. 4195.)

§102. PRIMARY DUTIES

The Coast Guard shall—

(1) enforce or assist in the enforcement of all applicable Federal laws on, under, and over the high seas and waters subject to the jurisdiction of the United States;

(2) engage in maritime air surveillance or interdiction to enforce or assist in the enforcement of the laws of the United States;

(3) administer laws and promulgate and enforce regulations for the promotion of safety of life and property on and under the high seas and waters subject to the jurisdiction of the United States, covering all matters not specifically delegated by law to some other executive department;

(4) develop, establish, maintain, and operate, with due regard to the requirements of national defense, aids to maritime navigation, icebreaking facilities, and rescue facilities for the promotion of safety on, under, and over the high seas and waters subject to the jurisdiction of the United States;

(5) pursuant to international agreements, develop, establish, maintain, and operate icebreaking facilities on, under, and over waters other than the high seas and waters subject to the jurisdiction of the United States;

(6) engage in oceanographic research of the high seas and in waters subject to the jurisdiction of the United States; and

(7) maintain a state of readiness to assist in the defense of the United States, including when functioning as a specialized service in the Navy pursuant to section 103.

(Aug. 4, 1949, ch. 393, 63 Stat. 496, §2; Pub. L. 87–396, §1, Oct. 5, 1961, 75 Stat. 827; Pub. L. 91–278, §1(1), June 12, 1970, 84 Stat. 304; Pub. L. 93–519, Dec. 13, 1974, 88 Stat. 1659; Pub. L. 99–640, §6, Nov. 10, 1986, 100 Stat. 3547; Pub. L. 100–448, §17, Sept. 28, 1988, 102 Stat. 1845; Pub. L. 100–690, title VII, §7403, Nov. 18, 1988, 102 Stat. 4484; Pub. L. 112–213, title II, §217(1), Dec. 20, 2012, 126 Stat. 1556; renumbered §102 and amended Pub. L. 115–282, title I, §103(b), title III, §302, Dec. 4, 2018, 132 Stat. 4195, 4243.)

§103. DEPARTMENT IN WHICH THE COAST GUARD OPERATES

(a) IN GENERAL.—The Coast Guard shall be a service in the Department of Homeland Security, except when operating as a service in the Navy.

(b) TRANSFERS.—Upon the declaration of war if Congress so directs in the declaration or when the President directs, the Coast Guard shall operate as a service in the Navy, and shall so continue until the President, by Executive order, transfers the Coast Guard back to the Department of Homeland Security. While operating as a service in the Navy, the Coast Guard shall be subject to the orders of the Secretary of the Navy, who may order changes in Coast Guard operations to render them uniform, to the extent such Secretary deems advisable, with Navy operations.

(c) OPERATION AS A SERVICE IN THE NAVY.—Whenever the Coast Guard operates as a service in the Navy—

(1) applicable appropriations of the Navy Department shall be available for the expense of the Coast Guard;

(2) applicable appropriations of the Coast Guard shall be available for transfer to the Navy Department;

(3) precedence between commissioned officers of corresponding grades in the Coast Guard and the Navy shall be determined by the date of rank stated by their commissions in those grades;

(4) personnel of the Coast Guard shall be eligible to receive gratuities, medals, and other insignia of honor on the same basis as personnel in the naval service or serving in any capacity with the Navy; and

(5) the Secretary may place on furlough any officer of the Coast Guard and officers on furlough shall receive one half of the pay to which they would be entitled if on leave of absence, but officers of the Coast Guard Reserve shall not be so placed on furlough.

(Aug. 4, 1949, ch. 393, 63 Stat. 496, §3; Pub. L. 94–546, §1(2), Oct. 18, 1976, 90 Stat. 2519; Pub. L. 107–296, title XVII, §1704(a), Nov. 25, 2002, 116 Stat. 2314; Pub. L. 109–241, title II, §211, July 11, 2006, 120 Stat. 523; Pub. L. 112–213, title II, §217(1), Dec. 20, 2012, 126 Stat. 1556; renumbered §103, Pub. L. 115–282, title I, §103(b), Dec. 4, 2018, 132 Stat. 4195.)

§104. REMOVING RESTRICTIONS

Any law removing for the duration of a war or national emergency proclaimed by the President any restriction contained in any then-existing law as applied to the Navy, including, but not limited to, restrictions relating to the manner in which purchases may be made and contracts awarded, fiscal operations, and personnel, shall, in the same manner and to the same extent, remove such restrictions as applied to the Coast Guard.

(Aug. 4, 1949, ch. 393, 63 Stat. 550, §652; renumbered §104, Pub. L. 115–282, title I, §103(b), Dec. 4, 2018, 132 Stat. 4195.)

§105. SECRETARY DEFINED

In this title, the term "Secretary" means the Secretary of the respective department in which the Coast Guard is operating.

(Aug. 4, 1949, ch. 393, 63 Stat. 497, §4; May 5, 1950, ch. 169, §14(u), 64 Stat. 148; Pub. L. 89–444, §1(1), June 9, 1966, 80 Stat. 195; Pub. L. 112–213, title II, §217(1), Dec. 20, 2012, 126 Stat. 1557, renumbered §105, Pub. L. 115–282, title I, §103(b), Dec. 4, 2018, 132 Stat. 4195.)

§106. COMMANDANT DEFINED

In this title, the term "Commandant" means the Commandant of the Coast Guard.

(Added Pub. L. 115–232, div. C, title XXXV, §3531(a), Aug. 13, 2018, 132 Stat. 2320, §5; renumbered §106, Pub. L. 115–282, title I, §103(b), Dec. 4, 2018, 132 Stat. 4195.)

CHAPTER 3—COMPOSITION AND ORGANIZATION

§301. GRADES AND RATINGS

In the Coast Guard there shall be admirals (two); vice admirals; rear admirals; rear admirals (lower half); captains; commanders; lieutenant commanders; lieutenants; lieutenants (junior grade); ensigns; chief warrant officers; cadets; warrant officers; and enlisted members. Enlisted members shall be distributed in ratings established by the Secretary.

(Aug. 4, 1949, ch. 393, 63 Stat. 497, §41; Aug. 10, 1956, ch. 1041, §§6, 53, 70A Stat. 620, 679; Pub. L. 86–474, §1(1), May 14, 1960, 74 Stat. 144; Pub. L. 92–451, §1(1), Oct. 2, 1972, 86 Stat. 755; Pub. L. 97–417, §2(1), Jan. 4, 1983, 96 Stat. 2085; Pub. L. 98–557, §15(a)(3)(B), (C), Oct. 30, 1984, 98 Stat. 2865; Pub. L. 99–145, title V, §514(a)(2), Nov. 8, 1985, 99 Stat. 628; Pub. L. 103–337, div. A, title V, §541(f)(4), Oct. 5, 1994, 108 Stat. 2766; Pub. L. 114–120, title II, §201(a), Feb. 8, 2016, 130 Stat. 33; renumbered §301, Pub. L. 115–282, title I, §104(b), Dec. 4, 2018, 132 Stat. 4196.)

§302. COMMANDANT; APPOINTMENT

The President may appoint, by and with the advice and consent of the Senate, one Commandant for a period of four years, who may be reappointed for further periods of four years, who shall act as Chief of the Coast Guard. The term of an appointment, and any reappointment, shall begin on June 1 of the appropriate year and end on May 31 of the appropriate year, except that, in the event of death, retirement, resignation, or reassignment, or when the needs of the Service demand, the Secretary may alter the date on which a term begins or ends if the alteration does not result in the term exceeding a period of 4 years. The Commandant shall be appointed from the officers on the active duty promotion list serving above the grade of captain who have completed at least ten years of active service as a commissioned officer in the Coast Guard. The Commandant while so serving shall have the grade of admiral.

(Aug. 4, 1949, ch. 393, 63 Stat. 498, §44; Pub. L. 86–474, §1(3), May 14, 1960, 74 Stat. 144; Pub. L. 88–130, §1(3), Sept. 24, 1963, 77 Stat. 175; Pub. L. 89–444, §1(3), June 9, 1966, 80 Stat. 195; Pub. L. 92–451, §1(3), Oct. 2, 1972, 86 Stat. 755; Pub. L. 113–281, title II, §202, Dec. 18, 2014, 128 Stat. 3024; renumbered §302, Pub. L. 115–282, title I, §104(b), Dec. 4, 2018, 132 Stat. 4196.)

§303. Retirement of Commandant or Vice Commandant

(a)(1) A Commandant who is not reappointed shall be retired with the grade of admiral at the expiration of the appointed term, except as provided in section 306(d) of this title.

(2) A Vice Commandant who is retired while serving as Vice Commandant, after serving not less than 2 years as Vice Commandant, shall be retired with the grade of admiral, except as provided in section 306(d).

(b) A Commandant or Vice Commandant who is retired for physical disability shall be placed on the retired list with the grade of admiral.

(c) An officer who is retired prior to the expiration of the officer's term, while serving as Commandant or as an officer serving as Vice Commandant who has served less than 2 years as Vice Commandant, may, in the discretion of the President, be retired with the grade of admiral.

(d) Retirement under this section is subject to section 2501(a) of this title.

(Aug. 4, 1949, ch. 393, 63 Stat. 499, §46; Pub. L. 86–474, §1(5), May 14, 1960, 74 Stat. 144; Pub. L. 88–130, §1(4), Sept. 24, 1963, 77 Stat. 175; Pub. L. 89–444, §1(4), (5), June 9, 1966, 80 Stat. 195; Pub. L. 97–295, §2(1), Oct. 12, 1982, 96 Stat. 1301; Pub. L. 99–348, title II, §205(b)(1), July 1, 1986, 100 Stat. 699; Pub. L. 103–206, title II, §204(a), Dec. 20, 1993, 107 Stat. 2421; Pub. L. 114–120, title II, §209(2), Feb. 8, 2016, 130 Stat. 40; Pub. L. 115–232, div. C, title XXXV, §3528(a), Aug. 13, 2018, 132 Stat. 2318; renumbered §303 and amended Pub. L. 115–282, title I, §§104(b), 123(b)(2), Dec. 4, 2018, 132 Stat. 4196, 4240; Pub. L. 116–283, div. G, title LVXXXII [LXXXII], §8201(a), Jan. 1, 2021, 134 Stat. 4641; Pub. L. 117–263, div. K, title CXII, §11240, Dec. 23, 2022, 136 Stat. 4039.)

§304. Vice Commandant; appointment

The President may appoint, by and with the advice and consent of the Senate, one Vice Commandant who shall rank next after the Commandant, shall perform such duties as the Commandant may prescribe and shall act as Commandant during the absence or disability of the Commandant or in the event that there is a vacancy in the office of Commandant. The Vice Commandant shall be selected from the officers on the active duty promotion list serving above the grade of captain. The Commandant shall make recommendation for such appointment. The Vice Commandant shall, while so serving, have the grade of admiral with pay and allowances of that grade. The appointment and grade of a Vice Commandant shall be effective on the date the officer assumes that duty, and shall terminate on the date the officer is detached from that duty, except as provided in section 306(d) of this title.

(Aug. 4, 1949, ch. 393, 63 Stat. 499, §47; Pub. L. 86–474, §1(6), May 14, 1960, 74 Stat. 144; Pub. L. 88–130, §1(5), (6), Sept. 24, 1963, 77 Stat. 175; Pub. L. 89–444, §1(6), (7), June 9, 1966, 80 Stat. 195; Pub. L. 92–451, §1(4), Oct. 2, 1972, 86 Stat. 755; Pub. L. 97–295, §2(2), Oct. 12, 1982, 96 Stat. 1301; Pub. L. 99–348, title II, §205(b)(2), July 1, 1986, 100 Stat. 700; Pub. L. 103–206, title II, §204(b)(1), Dec. 20, 1993, 107 Stat. 2421; Pub. L. 111–281, title V, §511(f)(1), (g), Oct. 15, 2010, 124 Stat. 2952, 2953; Pub. L. 114–120, title II, §§201(b), 209(3), Feb. 8, 2016, 130 Stat. 33, 40; renumbered §304 and amended Pub. L. 115–282, title I, §§104(b), 123(b)(2), Dec. 4, 2018, 132 Stat. 4196, 4240.)

§305. VICE ADMIRALS

(a)(1) The President may—

(A) designate, within the Coast Guard, no more than five positions of importance and responsibility that shall be held by officers who, while so serving—

(i) shall have the grade of vice admiral, with the pay and allowances of that grade; and

(ii) shall perform such duties as the Commandant may prescribe, except that if the President designates five such positions, one position shall be the Chief of Staff of the Coast Guard; and

(B) designate, within the executive branch, other than within the Coast Guard or the National Oceanic and Atmospheric Administration, positions of importance and responsibility that shall be held by officers who, while so serving, shall have the grade of vice admiral, with the pay and allowances of that grade.

(2) The President may appoint, by and with the advice and consent of the Senate, and reappoint, by and with the advice and consent of the Senate, to any such position an officer of the Coast Guard who is serving on active duty above the grade of captain. The Commandant shall make recommendations for such appointments.

(3)(A) Except as provided in subparagraph (B), one of the vice admirals designated under paragraph (1)(A) must have at least 10 years experience in vessel inspection, marine casualty investigations, mariner licensing, or an equivalent technical expertise in the design and construction of commercial vessels, with at least 4 years of leadership experience at a staff or unit carrying out marine safety functions and shall serve as the principal advisor to the Commandant on these issues.

(B) The requirements of subparagraph (A) do not apply to such vice admiral if the subordinate officer serving in the grade of rear admiral with responsibilities for marine safety, security, and stewardship possesses that experience.

(4) Prior to making a recommendation to the President for the nomination of an officer for appointment to a position of importance and responsibility under this section, which appointment would result in the initial appointment of the officer concerned in the grade of vice admiral, the Commandant shall consider all officers determined to be among the best qualified for such position.

(b)(1) The appointment and the grade of vice admiral shall be effective on the date the officer assumes that duty and, except as provided in paragraph (2) of this subsection or in section 306(d) of this title, shall terminate on the date the officer is detached from that duty.

(2) An officer who is appointed to a position designated under subsection (a) shall

continue to hold the grade of vice admiral—

(A) while under orders transferring the officer to another position designated under subsection (a), beginning on the date the officer is detached from that duty and terminating on the date before the day the officer assumes the subsequent duty, but not for more than 60 days;

(B) while hospitalized, beginning on the day of the hospitalization and ending on the day the officer is discharged from the hospital, but not for more than 180 days;

(C) at the discretion of the Secretary, while awaiting orders after being relieved from the position, beginning on the day the officer is relieved from the position, but not for more than 60 days; and

(D) while awaiting retirement, beginning on the date the officer is detached from duty and ending on the day before the officer's retirement, but not for more than 60 days.

(c)(1) An appointment of an officer under subsection (a) does not vacate the permanent grade held by the officer.

(2) An officer serving in a grade above rear admiral who holds the permanent grade of rear admiral (lower half) shall be considered for promotion to the permanent grade of rear admiral as if the officer was serving in the officer's permanent grade.

(d) Whenever a vacancy occurs in a position designated under subsection (a), the Commandant shall inform the President of the qualifications needed by an officer serving in that position or office to carry out effectively the duties and responsibilities of that position or office.

(Added Pub. L. 92–451, §1(5), Oct. 2, 1972, 86 Stat. 755, §50; amended Pub. L. 103–206, title II, §204(c), Dec. 20, 1993, 107 Stat. 2421; Pub. L. 111–281, title V, §511(a), Oct. 15, 2010, 124 Stat. 2951; Pub. L. 111–330, §1(5), Dec. 22, 2010, 124 Stat. 3569; Pub. L. 114–120, title II, §202, Feb. 8, 2016, 130 Stat. 33; renumbered §305 and amended Pub. L. 115–282, title I, §§104(b), 123(b)(2), Dec. 4, 2018, 132 Stat. 4196, 4240; Pub. L. 116–283, div. A, title V, §551(b)(2), Jan. 1, 2021, 134 Stat. 3630.)

§306. RETIREMENT

(a) An officer, other than the Commandant or Vice Commandant, who, while serving in the grade of admiral or vice admiral, is retired for physical disability shall be placed on the retired list with the highest grade in which that officer served satisfactorily, as determined under section 2501 of this title.

(b) An officer, other than the Commandant or Vice Commandant, who is retired while serving in the grade of admiral or vice admiral, or who, after serving at least 2½ years in the grade of admiral or vice admiral, is retired while serving in a lower grade, may in the discretion of the President, be retired with the highest grade in which that officer served satisfactorily, as determined under section 2501 of this title.

(c) An officer, other than the Commandant or Vice Commandant, who, after serving less than 2½ years in the grade of admiral or vice admiral, is retired while serving in a lower grade, shall be retired in his permanent grade if performance of duties in such grade is determined to have been satisfactory pursuant to section 2501 of this title.

(d) An officer serving in the grade of admiral or vice admiral shall continue to hold that grade—

(1) while being processed for physical disability retirement, beginning on the day of the processing and ending on the day that officer is retired, but not for more than 180 days; and

(2) while awaiting retirement, beginning on the day that officer is relieved from the position of Commandant, Vice Commandant, or Vice Admiral and ending on the day before the officer's retirement, but not for more than 60 days.

(Added Pub. L. 92–451, §1(5), Oct. 2, 1972, 86 Stat. 755, §51; amended Pub. L. 99–348, title II, §205(b)(3), July 1, 1986, 100 Stat. 700; Pub. L. 103–206, title II, §§204(d), 205(c), Dec. 20, 1993, 107 Stat. 2421, 2422; Pub. L. 111–281, title V, §511(c), Oct. 15, 2010, 124 Stat. 2952; Pub. L. 114–120, title II, §201(c), Feb. 8, 2016, 130 Stat. 33; Pub. L. 115–232, div. C, title XXXV, §3528(b), Aug. 13, 2018, 132 Stat. 2318; renumbered §306, Pub. L. 115–282, title I, §104(b), Dec. 4, 2018, 132 Stat. 4196; Pub. L. 116–283, div. G, title LVXXXII [LXXXII], §8201(b), Jan. 1, 2021, 134 Stat. 4641.)

§307. VICE ADMIRALS AND ADMIRAL, CONTINUITY OF GRADE

The continuity of an officer's precedence on the active duty promotion list, date of rank, grade, pay, and allowances as a vice admiral or admiral shall not be interrupted by the termination of an appointment for the purpose of reappointment to another position as a vice admiral or admiral.

(Added Pub. L. 97–322, title I, §115(a)(1), Oct. 15, 1982, 96 Stat. 1585, §52; amended Pub. L. 101–225, title II, §203(1), Dec. 12, 1989, 103 Stat. 1911; Pub. L. 111–281, title V, §511(d), (f)(2), Oct. 15, 2010, 124 Stat. 2952, 2953; renumbered §307, Pub. L. 115–282, title I, §104(b), Dec. 4, 2018, 132 Stat. 4196.)

§308. CHIEF ACQUISITION OFFICER

(a) IN GENERAL.—There shall be in the Coast Guard a Chief Acquisition Officer selected by the Commandant who shall be a Rear Admiral or civilian from the Senior Executive Service (career reserved) and who meets the qualifications set forth under subsection (b). The Chief Acquisition Officer shall serve at the Assistant Commandant level and have acquisition management as that individual's primary duty.

(b) QUALIFICATIONS.—

(1) The Chief Acquisition Officer and any flag officer serving in the Acquisition Directorate shall be an acquisition professional with a Level III acquisition management certification and must have at least 10 years experience in an acquisition position, of which at least 4 years were spent as—

(A) the program executive officer;

(B) the program manager of a Level 1 or Level 2 acquisition project or program;

(C) the deputy program manager of a Level 1 or Level 2 acquisition;

(D) the project manager of a Level 1 or Level 2 acquisition; or

(E) any other acquisition position of significant responsibility in which the primary duties are supervisory or management duties.

(2) The Commandant shall periodically publish a list of the positions designated under paragraph (1).

(3) In this subsection each of the terms "Level 1 acquisition" and "Level 2 acquisition" has the meaning that term has in chapter 11 of this title.

(c) FUNCTIONS OF THE CHIEF ACQUISITION OFFICER.—The functions of the Chief Acquisition Officer include—

(1) monitoring the performance of acquisition projects and programs on the basis of applicable performance measurements and advising the Commandant, through the chain of command, regarding the appropriate business strategy to achieve the missions of the Coast Guard;

(2) maximizing the use of full and open competition at the prime contract and subcontract levels in the acquisition of property, capabilities, assets, and services by the Coast Guard by establishing policies, procedures, and practices that ensure that the Coast Guard receives a sufficient number of sealed bids or competitive proposals from responsible sources to fulfill the Government's requirements, including performance and delivery schedules, at the lowest cost or best value considering the nature of the property, capability, asset, or service procured;

(3) making acquisition decisions in concurrence with the technical authority, or technical authorities, of the Coast Guard, as designated by the Commandant, consistent with all other applicable laws and decisions establishing procedures within the Coast Guard;

(4) ensuring the use of detailed performance specifications in instances in which performance-based contracting is used;

(5) managing the direction of acquisition policy for the Coast Guard, including implementation of the unique acquisition policies, regulations, and standards of the Coast Guard;

(6) developing and maintaining an acquisition career management program in the Coast Guard to ensure that there is an adequate acquisition workforce;

(7) assessing the requirements established for Coast Guard personnel regarding knowledge and skill in acquisition resources and management and the adequacy of such requirements for facilitating the achievement of the performance goals established for acquisition management;

(8) developing strategies and specific plans for hiring, training, and professional development;

(9) reporting to the Commandant, through the chain of command, on the progress made in improving acquisition management capability; and

(10)(A) keeping the Commandant informed of the progress of major acquisition programs (as that term is defined in section 1171);

(B) informing the Commandant on a continuing basis of any developments on such programs that may require new or revisited trade-offs among cost, schedule, technical feasibility, and performance, including—

(i) significant cost growth or schedule slippage; and

(ii) requirements creep (as that term is defined in section 3104(c)(1) of title 10); and

(C) ensuring that the views of the Commandant regarding such programs on cost, schedule, technical feasibility, and performance trade-offs are strongly considered by program managers and program executive officers in all phases of the acquisition process.

(Added Pub. L. 111–281, title IV, §401(a), Oct. 15, 2010, 124 Stat. 2929, §56; amended Pub. L. 114–328, div. A, title VIII, §899(a), Dec. 23, 2016, 130 Stat. 2332; renumbered §308 and amended Pub. L. 115–282, title I, §§104(b), 123(b)(2), (c)(4), Dec. 4, 2018, 132 Stat. 4196, 4240, 4241; Pub. L. 117–81, div. A, title XVII, §1702(d)(1), Dec. 27, 2021, 135 Stat. 2156.)

§309. OFFICE OF THE COAST GUARD RESERVE; DIRECTOR

(a) ESTABLISHMENT OF OFFICE; DIRECTOR.—There is in the executive part of the Coast Guard an Office of the Coast Guard Reserve. The head of the Office is the Director of the Coast Guard Reserve. The Director of the Coast Guard Reserve is the principal adviser to the Commandant on Coast Guard Reserve matters and may have such additional functions as the Commandant may direct.

(b) APPOINTMENT.—The President, by and with the advice and consent of the Senate, shall appoint the Director of the Coast Guard Reserve, from officers of the Coast Guard who—

(1) have had at least 10 years of commissioned service;

(2) are in a grade above captain; and

(3) have been recommended by the Secretary of Homeland Security.

(c) TERM.—(1) The Director of the Coast Guard Reserve holds office for a term determined by the President, normally two years, but not more than four years. An officer may be removed from the position of Director for cause at any time.

(2) The Director of the Coast Guard Reserve, while so serving, holds a grade above Captain, without vacating the officer's permanent grade.

(d) BUDGET.—The Director of the Coast Guard Reserve is the official within the executive part of the Coast Guard who, subject to the authority, direction, and control of the Secretary of Homeland Security and the Commandant, is responsible for preparation, justification, and execution of the personnel, operation and maintenance, and construction budgets for the Coast Guard Reserve. As such, the Director of the Coast Guard Reserve is the director and functional manager of appropriations made for the Coast Guard Reserve in those areas.

(e) ANNUAL REPORT.—The Director of the Coast Guard Reserve shall submit to the Secretary of Homeland Security and the Secretary of Defense an annual report on the state of the Coast Guard Reserve and the ability of the Coast Guard Reserve to meet its missions. The report shall be prepared in conjunction with the Commandant and may be submitted in classified and unclassified versions.

(Added Pub. L. 106–65, div. A, title V, §557(a), Oct. 5, 1999, 113 Stat. 619, §53; amended Pub. L. 107–296, title XVII, §1704(a), Nov. 25, 2002, 116 Stat. 2314; renumbered §309, Pub. L. 115–282, title I, §104(b), Dec. 4, 2018, 132 Stat. 4196.)

§310. CHIEF OF STAFF TO PRESIDENT: APPOINTMENT

The President, by and with the advice and consent of the Senate, may appoint a flag officer of the Coast Guard as the Chief of Staff to the President.

(Added Pub. L. 109–163, div. A, title V, §597(a), Jan. 6, 2006, 119 Stat. 3283, §54; renumbered §310, Pub. L. 115–282, title I, §104(b), Dec. 4, 2018, 132 Stat. 4196.)

§311. CAPTAINS OF THE PORT

Any officer, including any petty officer, may be designated by the Commandant as captain of the port or ports or adjacent high seas or waters over which the United States has jurisdiction, as the Commandant deems necessary to facilitate execution of Coast Guard duties.

(Added Pub. L. 115–282, title I, §104(c)(1)(A), Dec. 4, 2018, 132 Stat. 4198.)

§312. PREVENTION AND RESPONSE WORKFORCES

(a) CAREER PATHS.—The Secretary, acting through the Commandant, shall ensure that appropriate career paths for civilian and military Coast Guard personnel who wish to pursue career paths in prevention or response positions are identified in terms of the education, training, experience, and assignments necessary for career progression of civilians and members of the Armed Forces to the most senior prevention or response positions, as appropriate. The Secretary shall make available published information on such career paths.

(b) QUALIFICATIONS FOR CERTAIN ASSIGNMENTS.—An officer, member, or civilian employee of the Coast Guard assigned as a—

(1) marine inspector shall have the training, experience, and qualifications equivalent to that required for a similar position at a classification society recognized by the Secretary under section 3316 of title 46 for the type of vessel, system, or equipment that is inspected;

(2) marine casualty investigator shall have the training, experience, and qualifications in investigation, marine casualty reconstruction, evidence collection and preservation, human factors, and documentation using best investigation practices by Federal and non-Federal entities;

(3) marine safety engineer shall have knowledge, skill, and practical experience in—

(A) the construction and operation of commercial vessels;

(B) judging the character, strength, stability, and safety qualities of such vessels and their equipment; or

(C) the qualifications and training of vessel personnel;

(4) waterways operations manager shall have knowledge, skill, and practical experience with respect to maritime transportation system management; or

(5) port and facility safety and security specialist shall have knowledge, skill, and practical experience with respect to the safety, security, and environmental protection responsibilities associated with maritime ports and facilities.

(c) APPRENTICESHIP REQUIREMENT TO QUALIFY FOR CERTAIN CAREERS.—The Commandant may require an officer, member, or employee of the Coast Guard in training for a specialized prevention or response career path to serve an apprenticeship under the guidance of a qualified individual. However, an individual in training to become a marine inspector, marine casualty investigator, marine safety engineer, waterways operations manager, or port and facility safety and security specialist shall serve a minimum of one-year as an apprentice unless the Commandant authorizes a shorter period for certain qualifications.

(d) MANAGEMENT INFORMATION SYSTEM.—The Secretary, acting through the Commandant, shall establish a management information system for the prevention and response workforces that shall provide, at a minimum, the following standardized information on individuals serving in those workforces:

(1) Qualifications, assignment history, and tenure in assignments.

(2) Promotion rates for military and civilian personnel.

(e) SECTOR CHIEF OF PREVENTION.—There shall be in each Coast Guard sector a Chief of Prevention who shall be at least a Lieutenant Commander or civilian employee within the grade GS–13 of the General Schedule, and who shall be a—

(1) marine inspector, qualified to inspect vessels, vessel systems, and equipment commonly found in the sector; and

(2) qualified marine casualty investigator, marine safety engineer, waterways operations manager, or port and facility safety and security specialist.

(f) SIGNATORIES OF LETTER OF QUALIFICATION FOR CERTAIN PREVENTION PERSONNEL.—Each individual signing a letter of qualification for marine safety personnel must hold a letter of qualification for the type being certified.

(g) SECTOR CHIEF OF RESPONSE.—There shall be in each Coast Guard sector a Chief of Response who shall be at least a Lieutenant Commander or civilian employee within the grade GS–13 of the General Schedule in each Coast Guard sector.

(Added Pub. L. 111–281, title V, §521(a), Oct. 15, 2010, 124 Stat. 2953, §57; amended Pub. L. 113–281, title II, §§203, 221(b)(1)(B), Dec. 18, 2014, 128 Stat. 3024, 3038; renumbered §312, Pub. L. 115–282, title I, §104(b), Dec. 4, 2018, 132 Stat. 4196; Pub. L. 116–283, div. G, title LVXXXV [LXXXV], §§8504(a), 8505(a)(1), Jan. 1, 2021, 134 Stat. 4747.)

§313. CENTERS OF EXPERTISE FOR COAST GUARD PREVENTION AND RESPONSE

(a) ESTABLISHMENT.—The Commandant may establish and operate one or more centers of expertise for prevention and response missions of the Coast Guard (in this section referred to as a "center").

(b) MISSIONS.—Any center established under subsection (a) shall—

(1) promote, facilitate, and conduct—

(A) education;

(B) training; and

(C) activities authorized under section 504(a)(4);

(2) be a repository of information on operations, practices, and resources related to the mission for which the center was established; and

(3) perform and support the mission for which the center was established.

(c) JOINT OPERATION WITH EDUCATIONAL INSTITUTION AUTHORIZED.—The Commandant may enter into an agreement with an appropriate official of an institution of higher education to—

(1) provide for joint operation of a center; and

(2) provide necessary administrative services for a center, including administration and allocation of funds.

(d) ACCEPTANCE OF DONATIONS.—

(1) Except as provided in paragraph (2), the Commandant may accept, on behalf of a center, donations to be used to defray the costs of the center or to enhance the operation of the center. Those donations may be accepted from any State or local government, any foreign government, any foundation or other charitable organization (including any that is organized or operates under the laws of a foreign country), or any individual.

(2) The Commandant may not accept a donation under paragraph (1) if the acceptance of the donation would compromise or appear to compromise—

(A) the ability of the Coast Guard or the department in which the Coast Guard is operating, any employee of the Coast Guard or the department, or any member of the Armed Forces to carry out any responsibility or duty in a fair and objective manner; or

(B) the integrity of any program of the Coast Guard, the department in which the Coast Guard is operating, or of any individual involved in such a program.

(3) The Commandant shall prescribe written guidance setting forth the criteria to be used in determining whether or not the acceptance of a donation from a foreign source would have a result described in paragraph (2).

(Added Pub. L. 111–281, title V, §521(a), Oct. 15, 2010, 124 Stat. 2955, §58; amended Pub. L. 113–281, title II, §204, Dec. 18, 2014, 128 Stat. 3025; Pub. L. 115–232, div. C, title XXXV, §3531(c)(1), Aug. 13, 2018, 132 Stat. 2320; renumbered §313 and amended Pub. L. 115–282, title I, §§104(b), 123(b)(2), Dec. 4, 2018, 132 Stat. 4196, 4240; Pub. L. 116–283, div. G, title LVXXXV [LXXXV], §8505(a)(2), Jan. 1, 2021, 134 Stat. 4747.)

§314. MARINE INDUSTRY TRAINING PROGRAM

The Commandant shall, by policy, establish a program under which an officer, member, or employee of the Coast Guard may be assigned to a private entity to further the institutional interests of the Coast Guard with regard to marine safety, including for the purpose of providing training to an officer, member, or employee. Policies to carry out the program—

(1) with regard to an employee of the Coast Guard, shall include provisions, consistent with sections 3702 through 3704 of title 5, as to matters concerning—

(A) the duration and termination of assignments;

(B) reimbursements; and

(C) status, entitlements, benefits, and obligations of program participants; and

(2) shall require the Commandant, before approving the assignment of an officer, member, or employee of the Coast Guard to a private entity, to determine that the

assignment is an effective use of the Coast Guard's funds, taking into account the best interests of the Coast Guard and the costs and benefits of alternative methods of achieving the same results and objectives.

(Added Pub. L. 111–281, title V, §521(a), Oct. 15, 2010, 124 Stat. 2956, §59; amended Pub. L. 113–281, title II, §221(a)(1), Dec. 18, 2014, 128 Stat. 3037; renumbered §314, Pub. L. 115–282, title I, §104(b), Dec. 4, 2018, 132 Stat. 4196.)

§315. TRAINING FOR CONGRESSIONAL AFFAIRS PERSONNEL

(a) IN GENERAL.—The Commandant shall develop a training course, which shall be administered in person, on the workings of Congress for any member of the Coast Guard selected for a position as a fellow, liaison, counsel, or administrative staff for the Coast Guard Office of Congressional and Governmental Affairs or as any Coast Guard district or area governmental affairs officer.

(b) COURSE SUBJECT MATTER.—

(1) IN GENERAL.—The training course required under this section shall provide an overview and introduction to Congress and the Federal legislative process, including—

(A) the congressional budget process;

(B) the congressional appropriations process;

(C) the congressional authorization process;

(D) the Senate advice and consent process for Presidential nominees;

(E) the Senate advice and consent process for treaty ratification;

(F) the roles of Members of Congress and congressional staff in the legislative process;

(G) the concept and underlying purposes of congressional oversight within the governance framework of separation of powers;

(H) the roles of Coast Guard fellows, liaisons, counsels, governmental affairs officers, the Coast Guard Office of Program Review, the Coast Guard Headquarters program offices, and any other entity the Commandant considers relevant; and

(I) the roles and responsibilities of Coast Guard public affairs and external communications personnel with respect to Members of Congress and the staff of such Members necessary to enhance communication between Coast Guard units, sectors, and districts and Member offices and committees of jurisdiction so as to ensure visibility of Coast Guard activities.

(2) DETAIL WITHIN COAST GUARD OFFICE OF BUDGET AND PROGRAMS.—

(A) IN GENERAL.—At the written request of a receiving congressional office, the training course required under this section shall include a multi-day detail within the Coast Guard Office of Budget and Programs to ensure adequate exposure to Coast Guard policy, oversight, and requests from Congress.

(B) NONCONSECUTIVE DETAIL PERMITTED.—A detail under this paragraph is not required to be consecutive with the balance of the training.

(c) COMPLETION OF REQUIRED TRAINING.—A member of the Coast Guard selected for a position described in subsection (a) shall complete the training required by this section

before the date on which such member reports for duty for such position.
(Added Pub. L. 114–120, title II, §214(b)(1), Feb. 8, 2016, 130 Stat. 43, §60; amended Pub. L. 114–328, div. C, title XXXV, §3503(a), Dec. 23, 2016, 130 Stat. 2775; Pub. L. 115–232, div. C, title XXXV, §3532, Aug. 13, 2018, 132 Stat. 2321; renumbered §315, Pub. L. 115–282, title I, §104(b), Dec. 4, 2018, 132 Stat. 4196; Pub. L. 117–263, div. K, title CXII, §11251(a), Dec. 23, 2022, 136 Stat. 4052.)

§316. National Coast Guard Museum

(a) Establishment.—The Commandant may establish, accept, operate, maintain and support the Museum, on lands which will be federally owned and administered by the Coast Guard, and are located in New London, Connecticut.

(b) Use of Funds.—

(1) The Secretary shall not expend any funds appropriated to the Coast Guard on the construction of any museum established under this section.

(2) Subject to the availability of appropriations, the Secretary may expend funds appropriated to the Coast Guard on the engineering and design of a Museum.

(3) The priority for the use of funds appropriated to the Coast Guard shall be to preserve, protect, and display historic Coast Guard artifacts, including the design, fabrication, and installation of exhibits or displays in which such artifacts are included.

(c) Funding Plan.—Not later than 2 years after the date of the enactment of the Elijah E. Cummings Coast Guard Authorization Act of 2020 and at least 90 days before the date on which the Commandant accepts the Museum under subsection (f), the Commandant shall submit to the Committee on Commerce, Science, and Transportation of the Senate and the Committee on Transportation and Infrastructure of the House of Representatives a plan for constructing, operating, and maintaining such Museum, including—

(1) estimated planning, engineering, design, construction, operation, and maintenance costs;

(2) the extent to which appropriated, nonappropriated, and non-Federal funds will be used for such purposes, including the extent to which there is any shortfall in funding for engineering, design, or construction;

(3) an explanation of any environmental remediation issues related to the land associated with the Museum; and

(4) a certification by a third party entity qualified to undertake such a certification process that the estimates provided pursuant to paragraphs (1) and (2) are reasonable and realistic.

(d) Construction.—

(1) The Association may construct the Museum described in subsection (a).

(2) The Museum shall be designed and constructed in compliance with the International Building Code 2018, and construction performed on Federal land under this section shall be exempt from State and local requirements for building or demolition permits.

(e) Agreements.—Under such terms and conditions as the Commandant considers appropriate, notwithstanding section 504, and until the Commandant accepts the Museum under subsection (f), the Commandant may—

(1) license Federal land to the Association for the purpose of constructing the Museum described in subsection (a); and

(2)(A) at a nominal charge, lease the Museum from the Association for activities and operations related to the Museum; and

(B) authorize the Association to generate revenue from the use of the Museum.

(f) ACCEPTANCE.—Not earlier than 90 days after the Commandant submits the plan under subsection (c), the Commandant shall accept the Museum from the Association and all right, title, and interest in and to the Museum shall vest in the United States when—

(1) the Association demonstrates, in a manner acceptable to the Commandant, that the Museum meets the design and construction requirements of subsection (d); and

(2) all financial obligations of the Association incident to the National Coast Guard Museum have been satisfied.

(g) SERVICES.—The Commandant may solicit from the Association and accept services from nonprofit entities, including services related to activities for construction of the Museum.

(h) AUTHORITY.—The Commandant may not establish a Museum except as set forth in this section.

(i) DEFINITIONS.—In this section:

(1) MUSEUM.—The term "Museum" means the National Coast Guard Museum.

(2) ASSOCIATION.—The term "Association" means the National Coast Guard Museum Association.

(Added Pub. L. 108–293, title II, §213(a), Aug. 9, 2004, 118 Stat. 1037, §98; amended Pub. L. 114–120, title II, §219, Feb. 8, 2016, 130 Stat. 48; renumbered §316 and amended Pub. L. 115–282, title I, §104(b), title III, §303, Dec. 4, 2018, 132 Stat. 4196, 4243; Pub. L. 116–283, div. G, title LVXXXIV [LXXXIV], §8439(a), Jan. 1, 2021, 134 Stat. 4737; Pub. L. 117–263, div. K, title CXII, §11259, Dec. 23, 2022, 136 Stat. 4058.)

§317. UNITED STATES COAST GUARD BAND; COMPOSITION; DIRECTOR

(a) The United States Coast Guard Band shall be composed of a director and other personnel in such numbers and grades as the Secretary determines to be necessary.

(b) The Secretary may designate as the director any individual determined by the Secretary to possess the necessary qualifications. Upon the recommendation of the Secretary, an individual so designated may be appointed by the President, by and with the advice and consent of the Senate, to a commissioned grade in the Regular Coast Guard.

(c) The initial appointment to a commissioned grade of an individual designated as director of the Coast Guard Band shall be in the grade determined by the Secretary to be most appropriate to the qualifications and experience of the appointed individual.

(d) An individual who is designated and commissioned under this section shall not be included on the active duty promotion list. He shall be promoted under section 2126 of this title. However, the grade of the director may not be higher than captain.

(e) The Secretary may revoke any designation as director of the Coast Guard Band. When an individual's designation is revoked, his appointment to commissioned grade under this section terminates and he is entitled, at his option—

(1) to be discharged from the Coast Guard; or

(2) to revert to the grade and status he held at the time of his designation as director.

(Added Pub. L. 89–189, §1(1), Sept. 17, 1965, 79 Stat. 820, §336; amended Pub. L. 102–587, title V, §5201, Nov. 4, 1992, 106 Stat. 5071; Pub. L. 107–295, title III, §311, Nov. 25, 2002, 116 Stat. 2102; Pub. L. 109–241, title II, §204(a), July 11, 2006, 120 Stat. 520; renumbered §317 and amended Pub. L. 115–282, title I, §§104(b), 123(b)(2), Dec. 4, 2018, 132 Stat. 4196, 4240.)

§318. ENVIRONMENTAL COMPLIANCE AND RESTORATION PROGRAM

(a) DEFINITIONS.—For the purposes of this section—

(1) "environment", "facility", "person", "release", "removal", "remedial", and "response" have the same meaning they have in section 101 of the Comprehensive Environmental Response, Compensation, and Liability Act (42 U.S.C. 9601);

(2) "hazardous substance" has the same meaning it has in section 101 of the Comprehensive Environmental Response, Compensation, and Liability Act (42 U.S.C. 9601), except that it also includes the meaning given "oil" in section 311 of the Federal Water Pollution Control Act (33 U.S.C. 1321); and

(3) "pollutant" has the same meaning it has in section 502 of the Federal Water Pollution Control Act (33 U.S.C. 1362).

(b) PROGRAM.—

(1) The Secretary shall carry out a program of environmental compliance and restoration at current and former Coast Guard facilities.

(2) Program goals include:

(A) Identifying, investigating, and cleaning up contamination from hazardous substances and pollutants.

(B) Correcting other environmental damage that poses an imminent and substantial danger to the public health or welfare or to the environment.

(C) Demolishing and removing unsafe buildings and structures, including buildings and structures at former Coast Guard facilities.

(D) Preventing contamination from hazardous substances and pollutants at current Coast Guard facilities.

(3)(A) The Secretary shall respond to releases of hazardous substances and pollutants—

(i) at each Coast Guard facility the United States owns, leases, or otherwise possesses;

(ii) at each Coast Guard facility the United States owned, leased, or otherwise possessed when the actions leading to contamination from hazardous substances or pollutants occurred; and

(iii) on each vessel the Coast Guard owns or operates.

(B) Subparagraph (A) of this paragraph does not apply to a removal or remedial action when a potentially responsible person responds under section 122 of the Comprehensive Environmental Response, Compensation, and Liability Act (42 U.S.C. 9622).

(C) The Secretary shall pay a fee or charge imposed by a State authority for permit services for disposing of hazardous substances or pollutants from Coast Guard facilities to the same extent that nongovernmental entities are required to pay for permit services. This subparagraph does not apply to a payment that is the responsibility of a lessee, contractor, or other private person.

(4) The Secretary may agree with another Federal agency for that agency to assist in carrying out the Secretary's responsibilities under this section. The Secretary may enter into contracts, cooperative agreements, and grant agreements with State and local governments to assist in carrying out the Secretary's responsibilities under this section. Services that may be obtained under this paragraph include identifying, investigating, and cleaning up off-site contamination that may have resulted from the release of a hazardous substance or pollutant at a Coast Guard facility.

(5) Section 119 of the Comprehensive Environmental Response, Compensation, and Liability Act (42 U.S.C. 9619) applies to response action contractors that carry out response actions under this section. The Coast Guard shall indemnify response action contractors to the extent that adequate insurance is not generally available at a fair price at the time the contractor enters into the contract to cover the contractor's reasonable, potential, long-term liability.

(c) AMOUNTS RECOVERED FOR RESPONSE ACTIONS.—

(1) All sums appropriated to carry out the Coast Guard's environmental compliance and restoration functions under this section or another law shall be credited or transferred to an appropriate Coast Guard account, as determined by the Commandant and remain available until expended.

(2) Funds may be obligated or expended from such account to carry out the Coast Guard's environmental compliance and restoration functions under this section or another law.

(3) In proposing the budget for any fiscal year under section 1105 of title 31, the President shall set forth separately the amount requested for the Coast Guard's environmental compliance and restoration activities under this section or another law.

(4) Amounts recovered under section 107 of the Comprehensive Environmental Response, Compensation, and Liability Act (42 U.S.C. 9607) for the Secretary's response actions at current and former Coast Guard facilities shall be credited to an appropriate Coast Guard account, as determined by the Commandant.

(d) ANNUAL LIST OF PROJECTS TO CONGRESS.—The Commandant shall submit to the Committee on Transportation and Infrastructure of the House of Representatives and the Committee on Commerce, Science, and Transportation of the Senate a prioritized list of projects eligible for environmental compliance and restoration funding for each fiscal year concurrent with the President's budget submission for that fiscal year.

(Added Pub. L. 115–282, title I, §104(c)(1)(B), Dec. 4, 2018, 132 Stat. 4198.)

§319. Unmanned System Program and Autonomous Control and Computer Vision Technology Project

(a) UNMANNED SYSTEM PROGRAM.—Not later than 2 years after the date of enactment of this section, the Secretary shall establish, under the control of the Commandant, an unmanned system program for the use by the Coast Guard of land-based, cutter-based, and aircraft-based unmanned systems for the purpose of increasing effectiveness and efficiency of mission execution.

(b) AUTONOMOUS CONTROL AND COMPUTER VISION TECHNOLOGY PROJECT.—

(1) IN GENERAL.—The Commandant shall conduct a project to retrofit 2 or more existing Coast Guard small boats deployed at operational units with—

(A) commercially available autonomous control and computer vision technology; and

(B) such sensors and methods of communication as are necessary to control, and technology to assist in conducting, search and rescue, surveillance, and interdiction missions.

(2) DATA COLLECTION.—As part of the project required under paragraph (1), the Commandant shall collect and evaluate field-collected operational data from the retrofit described in such paragraph to inform future requirements.

(3) BRIEFING.—Not later than 180 days after the date on which the project required under paragraph (1) is completed, the Commandant shall provide to the Committee on Commerce, Science, and Transportation of the Senate and the Committee on Transportation and Infrastructure of the House of Representatives a briefing on the project that includes an evaluation of the data collected from the project.

(c) UNMANNED SYSTEM DEFINED.—In this section, the term "unmanned system" means—

(1) an unmanned aircraft system (as such term is defined in section 44801 of title 49);

(2) an unmanned marine surface system; and

(3) an unmanned marine subsurface system.

(Added Pub. L. 115–282, title III, §304(a), Dec. 4, 2018, 132 Stat. 4244; amended Pub. L. 116–283, div. G, title LVXXXIV [LXXXIV], §8413(a), Jan. 1, 2021, 134 Stat. 4725; Pub. L. 117–263, div. K, title CXII, §11225(a), title CXVIII, §11803(a), Dec. 23, 2022, 136 Stat. 4024, 4163.)

§320. COAST GUARD JUNIOR RESERVE OFFICERS' TRAINING CORPS

(a) ESTABLISHMENT.—The Secretary of the department in which the Coast Guard is operating may establish and maintain a Junior Reserve Officers' Training Corps, organized into units, at public and private secondary educational institutions.

(b) APPLICABILITY.—Except as provided in subsection (d), the provisions of chapter 102 of title 10 shall apply to a Junior Reserve Officers' Training Corps established and maintained under this section in the same manner that such provisions apply to the Junior Reserve Officers' Training Corps of each military department. For purposes of the application of such provisions to this section—

(1) any reference in such provisions to a "military department" shall be treated as a reference to the department in which the Coast Guard is operating; and

(2) any reference in such provisions to a "Secretary of a military department", a "Secretary concerned", or the "Secretary of Defense" shall be treated as a reference to the Secretary of the department in which the Coast Guard is operating.

(c) SCOPE.—Beginning on December 31, 2025, the Secretary of the department in which the Coast Guard is operating shall maintain at all times a Junior Reserve Officers' Training Corps program with not fewer than 1 such program established in each Coast Guard district.

(d) EXCEPTION.—The requirements of chapter 102 of title 10 shall not apply to a unit of the Junior Reserve Officers' Training Corps established by the Secretary of the department in which the Coast Guard is operating before the date of the enactment of this section unless the Secretary determines it is appropriate to apply such requirements to such unit.

(Added Pub. L. 116–92, div. A, title V, §519(a), Dec. 20, 2019, 133 Stat. 1350; amended Pub. L. 117–263, div. K, title CXII, §11247(a), Dec. 23, 2022, 136 Stat. 4047.)

§321. CONGRESSIONAL AFFAIRS; DIRECTOR

The Commandant shall appoint a Director of Congressional Affairs from among officers of the Coast Guard who are in a grade above captain. The Director of Congressional Affairs is separate and distinct from the Director of Governmental and Public Affairs for the Coast Guard and is the principal advisor to the Commandant on all congressional and legislative matters for the Coast Guard and may have such additional functions as the Commandant may direct.

(Added Pub. L. 116–283, div. G, title LVXXXII [LXXXII], §8211(a), Jan. 1, 2021, 134 Stat. 4649.)

§322. REDISTRICTING NOTIFICATION REQUIREMENT

The Commandant shall notify the Committee on Transportation and Infrastructure of the House of Representatives and the Committee on Commerce, Science, and Transportation of the Senate at least 180 days before—

(1) implementing any plan to reduce the number of, change the location of, or change the geographic area covered by any existing Coast Guard Districts; or

(2) permanently transferring more than 10 percent of the personnel or equipment from a district office where such personnel or equipment is based.

(Added and amended Pub. L. 116–283, div. G, title LVXXXV [LXXXV], §8501(a)(1), Jan. 1, 2021, 134 Stat. 4745.)

§323. WESTERN ALASKA OIL SPILL PLANNING CRITERIA PROGRAM

(a) ESTABLISHMENT.—There is established within the Coast Guard a Western Alaska Oil Spill Planning Criteria Program (referred to in this section as the "Program") to develop and administer the Western Alaska oil spill planning criteria.

(b) PROGRAM MANAGER.—

(1) IN GENERAL.—Not later than 1 year after the date of enactment of this section, the Commandant shall select a permanent civilian career employee through a competitive

search process for a term of not less than 5 years to serve as the Western Alaska Oil Spill Criteria Program Manager (referred to in this section as the "Program Manager")—

    (A) the primary duty of whom shall be to administer the Program; and

    (B) who shall not be subject to frequent or routine reassignment.

(2) CONFLICTS OF INTEREST.—The individual selected to serve as the Program Manager shall not have conflicts of interest relating to entities regulated by the Coast Guard.

    (3) DUTIES.—

    (A) DEVELOPMENT OF GUIDANCE.—The Program Manager shall develop guidance for—

        (i) approval, drills, and testing relating to the Western Alaska oil spill planning criteria; and

        (ii) gathering input concerning such planning criteria from Federal agencies, State and local governments, Tribes, and relevant industry and nongovernmental entities.

    (B) ASSESSMENTS.—Not less frequently than once every 5 years, the Program Manager shall—

        (i) assess whether such existing planning criteria adequately meet the needs of vessels operating in the geographic area; and

        (ii) identify methods for advancing response capability so as to achieve, with respect to a vessel, compliance with national planning criteria.

    (C) ONSITE VERIFICATIONS.—The Program Manager shall address the relatively small number and limited nature of verifications of response capabilities for vessel response plans by increasing, within the Seventeenth Coast Guard District, the quantity and frequency of onsite verifications of the providers identified in vessel response plans.

(c) TRAINING.—The Commandant shall enhance the knowledge and proficiency of Coast Guard personnel with respect to the Program by—

    (1) developing formalized training on the Program that, at a minimum—

    (A) provides in-depth analysis of—

        (i) the national planning criteria described in part 155 of title 33, Code of Federal Regulations (as in effect on the date of enactment of this section);

        (ii) alternative planning criteria;

        (iii) Western Alaska oil spill planning criteria;

        (iv) Captain of the Port and Federal On-Scene Coordinator authorities related to activation of a vessel response plan;

        (v) the responsibilities of vessel owners and operators in preparing a vessel response plan for submission; and

        (vi) responsibilities of the Area Committee, including risk analysis, response capability, and development of alternative planning criteria;

(B) explains the approval processes of vessel response plans that involve alternative planning criteria or Western Alaska oil spill planning criteria; and

(C) provides instruction on the processes involved in carrying out the actions described in paragraphs (9)(D) and (9)(F) of section 311(j) of the Federal Water Pollution Control Act (33 U.S.C. 1321(j)), including instruction on carrying out such actions—

(i) in any geographic area in the United States; and

(ii) specifically in the Seventeenth Coast Guard District; and

(2) providing such training to all Coast Guard personnel involved in the Program.

(d) DEFINITIONS.—In this section:

(1) ALTERNATIVE PLANNING CRITERIA.—The term "alternative planning criteria" means criteria submitted under section 155.1065 or 155.5067 of title 33, Code of Federal Regulations (as in effect on the date of enactment of this section), for vessel response plans.

(2) TRIBE.—The term "Tribe" has the meaning given the term "Indian Tribe" in section 4 of the Indian Self-Determination and Education Assistance Act (25 U.S.C. 5304).

(3) VESSEL RESPONSE PLAN.—The term "vessel response plan" means a plan required to be submitted by the owner or operator of a tank vessel or a nontank vessel under regulations issued by the President under section 311(j)(5) of the Federal Water Pollution Control Act (33 U.S.C. 1321(j)(5)).

(4) WESTERN ALASKA OIL SPILL PLANNING CRITERIA.—The term "Western Alaska oil spill planning criteria" means the criteria required to be established under paragraph (9) of section 311(j) of the Federal Water Pollution Control Act (33 U.S.C. 1321(j)).

(Added Pub. L. 117–263, div. K, title CXIII, §11309(a)(1), Dec. 23, 2022, 136 Stat. 4079.)

CHAPTER 5—FUNCTIONS AND POWERS

SUBCHAPTER I—GENERAL POWERS

SUBCHAPTER II—LIFE SAVING AND LAW ENFORCEMENT AUTHORITIES

SUBCHAPTER III—AIDS TO NAVIGATION

SUBCHAPTER IV—MISCELLANEOUS

¹ Editorially supplied. Section added by Pub. L. 117–263 at the end of subchapter III without corresponding amendment of chapter analysis.

SUBCHAPTER I—GENERAL POWERS

§501. Secretary; General Powers

For the purpose of executing the duties and functions of the Coast Guard the Secretary may within the limits of appropriations made therefor:

(a) establish, change the limits of, consolidate, discontinue, and re-establish Coast Guard districts;

(b) arrange with the Secretaries of the Army, Navy and Air Force to assign members of the Coast Guard to any school maintained by the Army, Navy, and Air Force, for instruction and training, including aviation schools;

(c) construct, or cause to be constructed, Coast Guard shore establishments;

(d) design or cause to be designed, cause to be constructed, accept as gift, or otherwise acquire vessels, aircraft, and systems, and subject to applicable regulations under subtitle I of title 40 and division C (except sections 3302, 3501(b), 3509, 3906, 4710, and 4711) of subtitle I of title 41 dispose of them;

(e) acquire land or interests in land, including acceptance of gifts thereof, where required for the purpose of carrying out any project or purpose for which an appropriation has been made;

(f) exchange land or interests in land in part or in full payment for such other land or interests in land as may be necessary or desirable, the balance of such part payment to be defrayable in accordance with other provisions of this section;

(g) exercise any of the powers vested by this title in the Commandant in any case in which the Secretary deems it appropriate; and

(h) do any and all things necessary to carry out the purposes of this title.

(Aug. 4, 1949, ch. 393, 63 Stat. 503, §92; Oct. 31, 1951, ch. 654, §§1(32), 2(9), 3(3), 65 Stat. 702, 707, 708; Pub. L. 97–295, §2(4), Oct. 12, 1982, 96 Stat. 1301; Pub. L. 98–557, §15(a)(3)(D), Oct. 30, 1984, 98 Stat. 2865; Pub. L. 107–217, §3(c)(1), Aug. 21, 2002, 116 Stat. 1298; Pub. L. 111–350, §5(c)(1), Jan. 4, 2011, 124 Stat. 3847; Pub. L. 115–232, div. C, title XXXV, §3533(a), Aug. 13, 2018, 132 Stat. 2321; renumbered §501 and amended Pub. L. 115–282, title I, §105(b), title III, §311(a), Dec. 4, 2018, 132 Stat. 4200, 4248.)

§502. Delegation of Powers by the Secretary

The Secretary is authorized to confer or impose upon the Commandant any of the rights, privileges, powers, or duties, in respect to the administration of the Coast Guard, vested in or imposed upon the Secretary by this title or other provisions of law.

(Aug. 4, 1949, ch. 393, 63 Stat. 544, §631; Pub. L. 94–546, §1(33), Oct. 18, 1976, 90 Stat. 2521; renumbered §502, Pub. L. 115–282, title I, §105(b), Dec. 4, 2018, 132 Stat. 4200.)

§503. Regulations

In addition to the authority conferred by other provisions of this title the Secretary may promulgate such regulations and orders as he deems appropriate to carry out the provisions of this title or any other law applicable to the Coast Guard.

(Aug. 4, 1949, ch. 393, 63 Stat. 545, §633; renumbered §503, Pub. L. 115–282, title I, §105(b), Dec. 4, 2018, 132 Stat. 4200.)

§504. Commandant; general powers

(a) For the purpose of executing the duties and functions of the Coast Guard the Commandant may:

(1) maintain water, land, and air patrols, and ice-breaking facilities;

(2) establish and prescribe the purpose of, change the location of, consolidate, discontinue, re-establish, maintain, operate, and repair Coast Guard shore establishments;

(3) assign vessels, aircraft, vehicles, aids to navigation, equipment, appliances, and supplies to Coast Guard districts and shore establishments, and transfer any of the foregoing from one district or shore establishment to another;

(4) conduct experiments and investigate, or cause to be investigated, plans, devices, and inventions relating to the performance of any Coast Guard function, including research, development, test, or evaluation related to intelligence systems and capabilities;

(5) conduct any investigations or studies that may be of assistance to the Coast Guard in the performance of any of its powers, duties, or functions;

(6) collect, publish, and distribute information concerning Coast Guard operations;

(7) conduct or make available to personnel of the Coast Guard, and to eligible spouses as defined under section 2904, such specialized training and courses of instruction, including correspondence courses and the textbooks, manuals, and other materials required as part of such training or course of instruction, as may be necessary or desirable for the good of the service;

(8) design or cause to be designed, cause to be constructed, accept as gift, or otherwise acquire patrol boats and other small craft, equip, operate, maintain, supply, and repair such patrol boats, other small craft, aircraft, and vehicles, and subject to applicable regulations under subtitle I of title 40 and division C (except sections 3302, 3501(b), 3509, 3906, 4710, and 4711) of subtitle I of title 41 dispose of them;

(9) acquire, accept as gift, maintain, repair, and discontinue aids to navigation, appliances, equipment, and supplies;

(10) equip, operate, maintain, supply, and repair Coast Guard districts and shore establishments;

(11) establish, equip, operate, and maintain shops, depots, and yards for the manufacture and construction of aids to navigation, equipment, apparatus, vessels, vehicles, and aircraft not normally or economically obtainable from private contractors, and for the maintenance and repair of any property used by the Coast Guard;

(12) accept and utilize, in times of emergency in order to save life or protect property, such voluntary services as may be offered to the Coast Guard;

(13) rent or lease, under such terms and conditions as are deemed advisable, for a period not exceeding five years, such real property under the control of the Coast Guard as may not be required for immediate use by the Coast Guard, the monies received from any such rental or lease, less amount of expenses incurred (exclusive of governmental personal services), to be deposited in the fund established under section 2946;

(14) grant, under such terms and conditions as are deemed advisable, permits, licenses, easements, and rights-of-way over, across, in, and upon lands under the control of the Coast Guard when in the public interest and without substantially injuring the interests of the United States in the property thereby affected;

(15) establish, install, abandon, re-establish, reroute, operate, maintain, repair, purchase, or lease such telephone and telegraph lines and cables, together with all facilities, apparatus, equipment, structures, appurtenances, accessories, and supplies used or useful in connection with the installation, operation, maintenance, or repair of such lines and cables, including telephones in residences leased or owned by the Government of the United States when appropriate to assure efficient response to extraordinary operational contingencies of a limited duration, and acquire such real property rights of way, easements, or attachment privileges as may be required for the installation, operation, and maintenance of such lines, cables, and equipment;

(16) establish, install, abandon, reestablish, change the location of, operate, maintain, and repair radio transmitting and receiving stations;

(17) provide medical and dental care for personnel entitled thereto by law or regulation, including care in private facilities;

(18) accept, under terms and conditions the Commandant establishes, the service of an individual ordered to perform community service under the order of a Federal, State, or municipal court;

(19) notwithstanding any other law, enter into cooperative agreements with States, local governments, non-governmental organizations, and individuals, to accept and utilize voluntary services for the maintenance and improvement of natural and historic resources on, or to benefit natural and historic research on, Coast Guard facilities, subject to the requirement that—

(A) the cooperative agreements shall each provide for the parties to contribute funds or services on a matching basis to defray the costs of such programs, projects, and activities under the agreement; and

(B) an individual providing voluntary services under this subsection shall not be considered a Federal employee except for purposes of chapter 81 of title 5, United States Code, with respect to compensation for work-related injuries, and chapter 171 of title 28, United States Code, with respect to tort claims;

(20) enter into cooperative agreements with other Government agencies and the National Academy of Sciences;

(21) require that any member of the Coast Guard or Coast Guard Reserve (including a cadet or an applicant for appointment or enlistment to any of the foregoing and any member of a uniformed service who is assigned to the Coast Guard) request that all information contained in the National Driver Register pertaining to the individual, as described in section 30304(a) of title 49, be made available to the Commandant under section 30305(b)(7) of title 49, may receive that information, and upon receipt, shall make the information available to the individual;

(22) provide for the honorary recognition of individuals and organizations that significantly contribute to Coast Guard programs, missions, or operations, including State and local governments and commercial and nonprofit organizations, and pay

for, using any appropriations or funds available to the Coast Guard, plaques, medals, trophies, badges, and similar items to acknowledge such contribution (including reasonable expenses of ceremony and presentation);

(23) rent or lease, under such terms and conditions as are considered by the Secretary to be advisable, commercial vehicles to transport the next of kin of eligible retired Coast Guard military personnel to attend funeral services of the service member at a national cemetery;

(24) after informing the Secretary, make such recommendations to the Congress relating to the Coast Guard as the Commandant considers appropriate;

(25) enter into cooperative agreements, contracts, and other agreements with Federal entities and other public or private entities, including academic entities, to develop a positioning, navigation, and timing system to provide redundant capability in the event Global Positioning System signals are disrupted, which may consist of an enhanced LORAN system; and

(26) develop data workflows and processes for the leveraging of mission-relevant data by the Coast Guard to enhance operational effectiveness and efficiency.

(b)(1) Notwithstanding subsection (a)(13), a lease described in paragraph (2) of this subsection may be for a term of up to 20 years.

(2) A lease referred to in paragraph (1) is a lease—

(A) to the United States Coast Guard Academy Alumni Association for the construction of an Alumni Center on the grounds of the United States Coast Guard Academy; or

(B) to an entity with which the Commandant has a cooperative agreement under section 4(e) [1] of the Ports and Waterways Safety Act, and for which a term longer than 5 years is necessary to carry out the agreement.

(c) MARINE SAFETY RESPONSIBILITIES.—In exercising the Commandant's duties and responsibilities with regard to marine safety, the individual with the highest rank who meets the experience qualifications set forth in section 305(a)(3) shall serve as the principal advisor to the Commandant regarding—

(1) the operation, regulation, inspection, identification, manning, and measurement of vessels, including plan approval and the application of load lines;

(2) approval of materials, equipment, appliances, and associated equipment;

(3) the reporting and investigation of marine casualties and accidents;

(4) the licensing, certification, documentation, protection and relief of merchant mariners;

(5) suspension and revocation of licenses and certificates;

(6) enforcement of manning requirements, citizenship requirements, control of log books;

(7) documentation and numbering of vessels;

(8) State boating safety programs;

(9) commercial instruments and maritime liens;

(10) the administration of bridge safety;

(11) administration of the navigation rules;

(12) the prevention of pollution from vessels;

(13) ports and waterways safety;

(14) waterways management; including regulation for regattas and marine parades;

(15) aids to navigation; and

(16) other duties and powers of the Secretary related to marine safety and stewardship.

(d) OTHER AUTHORITY NOT AFFECTED.—Nothing in subsection (c) affects—

(1) the authority of Coast Guard officers and members to enforce marine safety regulations using authority under section 522 of this title; or

(2) the exercise of authority under section 527 of this title and the provisions of law codified at sections 191 through 195 of title 50 on the date of enactment of this paragraph.

(e) OPERATION AND MAINTENANCE OF COAST GUARD ASSETS AND FACILITIES.—All authority, including programmatic budget authority, for the operation and maintenance of Coast Guard vessels, aircraft, systems, aids to navigation, infrastructure, and other assets or facilities shall be allocated to and vested in the Coast Guard and the department in which the Coast Guard is operating.

(f) LEASING OF TIDELANDS AND SUBMERGED LANDS.—

(1) AUTHORITY.—The Commandant may lease under subsection (a)(13) submerged lands and tidelands under the control of the Coast Guard without regard to the limitation under that subsection with respect to lease duration.

(2) LIMITATION.—The Commandant may lease submerged lands and tidelands under paragraph (1) only if—

(A) the lease is for cash exclusively;

(B) the lease amount is equal to the fair market value of the use of the leased submerged lands or tidelands for the period during which such lands are leased, as determined by the Commandant;

(C) the lease does not provide authority to or commit the Coast Guard to use or support any improvements to such submerged lands and tidelands, or obtain goods and services from the lessee; and

(D) proceeds from the lease are deposited in the Coast Guard Housing Fund established under section 2946.

(Aug. 4, 1949, ch. 393, 63 Stat. 504, §93; Aug. 3, 1950, ch. 536, §2, 64 Stat. 406; Oct. 31, 1951, ch. 654, §§1(33), 2(10), 4(1), 65 Stat. 702, 707, 709; Pub. L. 94–546, §1(9), Oct. 18, 1976, 90 Stat. 2519; Pub. L. 97–136, §6(d), Dec. 29, 1981, 95 Stat. 1706; Pub. L. 97–276, §143, Oct. 2, 1982, 96 Stat. 1199; Pub. L. 97–295, §2(4), Oct. 12, 1982, 96 Stat. 1301; Pub. L. 97–322, title I, §115(c), Oct. 15, 1982, 96 Stat. 1586; Pub. L. 102–241, §7, Dec. 19, 1991, 105 Stat. 2212; Pub. L. 103–206, title II, §202, title III, §316, Dec. 20, 1993, 107 Stat. 2420, 2426; Pub. L. 104–324, title II, §207(a), Oct. 19, 1996, 110 Stat. 3908; Pub. L. 105–383, title II, §§202, 203, Nov. 13, 1998, 112 Stat. 3414, 3415; Pub. L. 107–217, §3(c)(2), Aug. 21, 2002, 116 Stat. 1298; Pub. L. 108–293, title II, §§201, 217, Aug. 9, 2004, 118 Stat. 1031, 1038; Pub. L. 109–241, title IX, §901(a), (c), July 11, 2006, 120 Stat. 564; Pub. L. 111–259, title IV, §442(1), Oct. 7, 2010, 124 Stat. 2733; Pub. L. 111–281, title V, §523, Oct. 15, 2010, 124 Stat. 2958; Pub. L. 111–350, §5(c)(2), Jan. 4, 2011, 124 Stat. 3847; Pub. L. 112–213, title II, §202, Dec. 20, 2012, 126 Stat. 1543; Pub. L. 113–281, title II, §§206(a), 207, 208(a), 209, 214(c), 222(1), Dec. 18, 2014, 128 Stat. 3025, 3026, 3034, 3038; Pub. L. 114–120, title II, §209(4), title VI, §610(b), Feb. 8, 2016, 130 Stat. 40, 85; Pub. L. 115–232, div. C, title XXXV, §3533(b), Aug. 13, 2018, 132 Stat. 2321; renumbered §504 and amended Pub. L. 115–282, title I,

§§105(b), 123(b)(2), Dec. 4, 2018, 132 Stat. 4200, 4240; Pub. L. 116–283, div. G, title LVXXXV [LXXXV], §8505(a)(3), Jan. 1, 2021, 134 Stat. 4747; Pub. L. 117–263, div. K, title CXII, §11229, Dec. 23, 2022, 136 Stat. 4029.)

[1] *See References in Text note below.*

§505. FUNCTIONS AND POWERS VESTED IN THE COMMANDANT

All powers and functions conferred upon the Coast Guard, or the Commandant, by or pursuant to this title or any other law shall, unless otherwise specifically stated, be executed by the Commandant subject to the general supervision of the Secretary. In order to execute the powers and functions vested in him, the Commandant may assign personnel of the Coast Guard to duty in the District of Columbia, elsewhere in the United States, in any territory of the United States, and in any foreign country, but such personnel shall not be assigned to duties in any foreign country without the consent of the government of that country; assign to such personnel such duties and authority as he deems necessary; and issue rules, orders, and instructions, not inconsistent with law, relating to the organization, internal administration, and personnel of the Coast Guard.

(Aug. 4, 1949, ch. 393, 63 Stat. 545, §632; renumbered §505, Pub. L. 115–282, title I, §105(b), Dec. 4, 2018, 132 Stat. 4200.)

§506. PROSPECTIVE PAYMENT OF FUNDS NECESSARY TO PROVIDE MEDICAL CARE

(a) PROSPECTIVE PAYMENT REQUIRED.—In lieu of the reimbursement required under section 1085 of title 10, the Secretary of Homeland Security shall make a prospective payment to the Secretary of Defense of an amount that represents the actuarial valuation of treatment or care—

(1) that the Department of Defense shall provide to members of the Coast Guard, former members of the Coast Guard, and dependents of such members and former members (other than former members and dependents of former members who are a Medicare-eligible beneficiary or for whom the payment for treatment or care is made from the Medicare-Eligible Retiree Health Care Fund as established under chapter 56 of title 10) at facilities under the jurisdiction of the Department of Defense or a military department; and

(2) for which a reimbursement would otherwise be made under section 1085.

(b) AMOUNT.—The amount of the prospective payment under subsection (a) shall be—

(1) in the case of treatment or care to be provided to members of the Coast Guard and their dependents, derived from amounts appropriated for the operations and support of the Coast Guard;

(2) in the case of treatment or care to be provided former members of the Coast Guard and their dependents, derived from amounts appropriated for retired pay;

(3) determined under procedures established by the Secretary of Defense;

(4) paid during the fiscal year in which treatment or care is provided; and

(5) subject to adjustment or reconciliation as the Secretaries determine appropriate during or promptly after such fiscal year in cases in which the prospective payment is

determined excessive or insufficient based on the services actually provided.

(c) No Prospective Payment When Service in Navy.—No prospective payment shall be made under this section for any period during which the Coast Guard operates as a service in the Navy.

(d) Relationship to TRICARE.—This section shall not be construed to require a payment for, or the prospective payment of an amount that represents the value of, treatment or care provided under any TRICARE program.

(Added Pub. L. 114–328, div. A, title VII, §722(a), Dec. 23, 2016, 130 Stat. 2228, §520; renumbered §506, Pub. L. 115–282, title I, §105(b), Dec. 4, 2018, 132 Stat. 4200; amended Pub. L. 116–283, div. G, title LVXXXV [LXXXV], §8513(a)(1), Jan. 1, 2021, 134 Stat. 4760.)

§507. Appointment of judges

The Secretary may appoint civilian employees of the department in which the Coast Guard is operating as appellate military judges, available for assignment to the Coast Guard Court of Criminal Appeals as provided for in section 866(a) of title 10.

(Added Pub. L. 111–281, title II, §201(a), Oct. 15, 2010, 124 Stat. 2909, §153; renumbered §507, Pub. L. 115–282, title I, §105(b), Dec. 4, 2018, 132 Stat. 4200.)

§508. Coast Guard health-care professionals; licensure portability

(a) In General.—Notwithstanding any other provision of law regarding the licensure of health-care providers, a health-care professional described in subsection (b) may practice the health profession or professions of the health-care professional at any location in any State, the District of Columbia, or a Commonwealth, territory, or possession of the United States, regardless of where such health-care professional or the patient is located, if the practice is within the scope of the authorized Federal duties of such health-care professional.

(b) Described Individuals.—A health-care professional described in this subsection is an individual—

(1) who is—

(A) a member of the Coast Guard;

(B) a civilian employee of the Coast Guard;

(C) a member of the Public Health Service who is assigned to the Coast Guard; or

(D) any other health-care professional credentialed and privileged at a Federal health-care institution or location specially designated by the Secretary; and

(2) who—

(A) has a current license to practice medicine, osteopathic medicine, dentistry, or another health profession; and

(B) is performing authorized duties for the Coast Guard.

(c) Definitions.—In this section, the terms "license" and "health-care professional" have the meanings given those terms in section 1094(e) of title 10.

(Added Pub. L. 115–282, title III, §305(a), Dec. 4, 2018, 132 Stat. 4245.)

§509. SPACE-AVAILABLE TRAVEL ON COAST GUARD AIRCRAFT

(a) ESTABLISHMENT.—

(1) IN GENERAL.—The Commandant may establish a program to provide transportation on Coast Guard aircraft on a space-available basis to the categories of eligible individuals described in subsection (c) (in this section referred to as the "program").

(2) POLICY DEVELOPMENT.—Not later than 1 year after the date on which the program is established, the Commandant shall develop a policy for the operation of the program.

(b) OPERATION OF PROGRAM.—

(1) IN GENERAL.—The Commandant shall operate the program in a budget-neutral manner.

(2) LIMITATIONS.—

(A) IN GENERAL.—Except as provided in subparagraph (B), no additional funds may be used, or flight hours performed, for the purpose of providing transportation under the program.

(B) DE MINIMIS EXPENDITURES.—The Commandant may make de minimis expenditures of resources required for the administrative aspects of the program.

(3) REIMBURSEMENT NOT REQUIRED.—Eligible individuals described in subsection (c) shall not be required to reimburse the Coast Guard for travel provided under this section.

(c) CATEGORIES OF ELIGIBLE INDIVIDUALS.—Subject to subsection (d), the categories of eligible individuals described in this subsection are the following:

(1) Members of the armed forces on active duty.

(2) Members of the Selected Reserve who hold a valid Uniformed Services Identification and Privilege Card.

(3) Retired members of a regular or reserve component of the armed forces, including retired members of reserve components who, but for being under the eligibility age applicable under section 12731 of title 10, would be eligible for retired pay under chapter 1223 of title 10.

(4) Subject to subsection (f), veterans with a permanent service-connected disability rated as total.

(5) Such categories of dependents of individuals described in paragraphs (1) through (3) as the Commandant shall specify in the policy under subsection (a)(2), under such conditions and circumstances as the Commandant shall specify in such policy.

(6) Such other categories of individuals as the Commandant considers appropriate.

(d) REQUIREMENTS.—In operating the program, the Commandant shall—

(1) in the sole discretion of the Commandant, establish an order of priority for transportation for categories of eligible individuals that is based on considerations of military necessity, humanitarian concerns, and enhancement of morale;

(2) give priority in consideration of transportation to the demands of members of the armed forces in the regular components and in the reserve components on active duty and to the need to provide such members, and their dependents, a means of respite from such demands; and

(3) implement policies aimed at ensuring cost control (as required under subsection (b)) and the safety, security, and efficient processing of travelers, including limiting the benefit under the program to 1 or more categories of otherwise eligible individuals, as the Commandant considers necessary.

(e) TRANSPORTATION.—

(1) IN GENERAL.—Notwithstanding subsection (d)(1), in establishing space-available transportation priorities under the program, the Commandant shall provide transportation for an individual described in paragraph (2), and a single dependent of the individual if needed to accompany the individual, at a priority level in the same category as the priority level for an unaccompanied dependent over the age of 18 years traveling on environmental and morale leave.

(2) INDIVIDUALS COVERED.—Subject to paragraph (3), paragraph (1) applies with respect to an individual described in subsection (c)(3) who—

(A) resides in or is located in a Commonwealth or possession of the United States; and

(B) is referred by a military or civilian primary care provider located in that Commonwealth or possession to a specialty care provider for services to be provided outside of such Commonwealth or possession.

(3) APPLICATION TO CERTAIN RETIRED INDIVIDUALS.—If an individual described in subsection (c)(3) is a retired member of a reserve component who is ineligible for retired pay under chapter 1223 of title 10 by reason of being under the eligibility age applicable under section 12731 of title 10, paragraph (1) applies to the individual only if the individual is also enrolled in the TRICARE program for certain members of the Retired Reserve authorized under section 1076e of title 10.

(4) PRIORITY.—The priority for space-available transportation required by this subsection applies with respect to—

(A) the travel from the Commonwealth or possession of the United States to receive the specialty care services; and

(B) the return travel.

(5) PRIMARY CARE PROVIDER AND SPECIALTY CARE PROVIDER DEFINED.—In this subsection, the terms "primary care provider" and "specialty care provider" refer to a medical or dental professional who provides health care services under chapter 55 of title 10.

(f) LIMITATIONS ON TRAVEL.—

(1) IN GENERAL.—Travel may not be provided under this section to a veteran eligible for travel pursuant to paragraph (4) of subsection (c) in priority over any member eligible for travel under paragraph (1) of that subsection or any dependent of such a member

eligible for travel under this section.

(2) RULE OF CONSTRUCTION.—Subsection (c)(4) may not be construed as—

(A) affecting or in any way imposing on the Coast Guard, any armed force, or any commercial entity with which the Coast Guard or an armed force contracts, an obligation or expectation that the Coast Guard or such armed force will retrofit or alter, in any way, military aircraft or commercial aircraft, or related equipment or facilities, used or leased by the Coast Guard or such armed force to accommodate passengers provided travel under such authority on account of disability; or

(B) preempting the authority of an aircraft commander to determine who boards the aircraft and any other matters in connection with safe operation of the aircraft.

(g) APPLICATION OF SECTION.—The authority to provide transportation under the program is in addition to any other authority under law to provide transportation on Coast Guard aircraft on a space-available basis.

(Added Pub. L. 117–263, div. K, title CXII, §11231(a), Dec. 23, 2022, 136 Stat. 4030.)

§510. CONVEYANCE OF COAST GUARD VESSELS FOR PUBLIC PURPOSES

(a) IN GENERAL.—On request by the Commandant, the Administrator of the General Services Administration may transfer ownership of a Coast Guard vessel or aircraft to an eligible entity for educational, cultural, historical, charitable, recreational, or other public purposes if such transfer is authorized by law.

(b) CONDITIONS OF CONVEYANCE.—The General Services Administration may not convey a vessel or aircraft to an eligible entity as authorized by law unless the eligible entity agrees—

(1) to provide the documentation needed by the General Services Administration to process a request for aircraft or vessels as if the request were being processed under section 102.37.225 of title 41, Code of Federal Regulations, as in effect on the date of the enactment of the Don Young Coast Guard Authorization Act of 2022;

(2) to comply with the special terms, conditions, and restrictions imposed on aircraft and vessels under section 102.37.460 of such title, as in effect on the date of the enactment of the Don Young Coast Guard Authorization Act of 2022;

(3) to make the vessel available to the United States Government if it is needed for use by the Commandant in time of war or a national emergency; and

(4) to hold the United States Government harmless for any claims arising from exposure to hazardous materials, including asbestos and polychlorinated biphenyls, that occurs after conveyance of the vessel, except for claims arising from use of the vessel by the United States Government under paragraph (3).

(c) OTHER OBLIGATIONS UNAFFECTED.—Nothing in this section amends or affects any obligation of the Coast Guard or any other person under the Toxic Substances Control Act (15 U.S.C. 2601 et seq.) or any other law regarding use or disposal of hazardous materials including asbestos and polychlorinated biphenyls.

(d) ELIGIBLE ENTITY DEFINED.—In this section, the term "eligible entity" means a State or local government, nonprofit corporation, educational agency, community development organization, or other entity that agrees to comply with the conditions established under this section.

(Added and amended Pub. L. 117–263, div. K, title CXII, §11258(a), (c), Dec. 23, 2022, 136 Stat. 4057.)

SUBCHAPTER II—LIFE SAVING AND LAW ENFORCEMENT AUTHORITIES

§521. SAVING LIFE AND PROPERTY

(a) In order to render aid to distressed individuals, vessels, and aircraft on and under the high seas and on and under the waters over which the United States has jurisdiction and in order to render aid to individuals and property imperiled by flood, the Coast Guard may:

(1) perform any and all acts necessary to rescue and aid individuals and protect and save property;

(2) take charge of and protect all property saved from marine or aircraft disasters, or floods, at which the Coast Guard is present, until such property is claimed by individuals legally authorized to receive it or until otherwise disposed of in accordance with law or applicable regulations, and care for bodies of those who may have perished in such catastrophes;

(3) furnish clothing, food, lodging, medicines, and other necessary supplies and services to individuals succored by the Coast Guard; and

(4) destroy or tow into port sunken or floating dangers to navigation.

(b)(1) Subject to paragraph (2), the Coast Guard may render aid to individuals and protect and save property at any time and at any place at which Coast Guard facilities and personnel are available and can be effectively utilized.

(2) The Commandant shall make full use of all available and qualified resources, including the Coast Guard Auxiliary and individuals licensed by the Secretary pursuant to section 8904(b) of title 46, United States Code, in rendering aid under this subsection in nonemergency cases.

(c) An individual who knowingly and willfully communicates a false distress message to the Coast Guard or causes the Coast Guard to attempt to save lives and property when no help is needed is

(1) guilty of a class D felony;

(2) subject to a civil penalty of not more than $10,000; and

(3) liable for all costs the Coast Guard incurs as a result of the individual's action.

(d) The Secretary shall establish a helicopter rescue swimming program for the purpose of training selected Coast Guard personnel in rescue swimming skills, which may include rescue diver training.

(e) An individual who knowingly and willfully operates a device with the intention of interfering with the broadcast or reception of a radio, microwave, or other signal (including a signal from a global positioning system) transmitted, retransmitted, or augmented by the Coast Guard for the purpose of maritime safety is—

(1) guilty of a class E felony; and

(2) subject to a civil penalty of not more than $1,000 per day for each violation.

(Aug. 4, 1949, ch. 393, 63 Stat. 501, §88; Pub. L. 91–278, §1(3), June 12, 1970, 84 Stat. 304; Pub. L. 100–448, §30(a), Sept. 28, 1988, 102 Stat. 1849; Pub. L. 101–595, title IV, §401, Nov. 16, 1990, 104 Stat.

2989; Pub. L. 104–324, title II, §213(a), Oct. 19, 1996, 110 Stat. 3915; Pub. L. 112–213, title II, §201, Dec. 20, 2012, 126 Stat. 1543; Pub. L. 113–281, title II, §205(a)(4), Dec. 18, 2014, 128 Stat. 3025; renumbered §521, Pub. L. 115–282, title I, §105(b), Dec. 4, 2018, 132 Stat. 4200; Pub. L. 116–283, div. G, title LVXXXV [LXXXV], §8505(a)(4), Jan. 1, 2021, 134 Stat. 4748.)

§522. LAW ENFORCEMENT

(a) The Coast Guard may make inquiries, examinations, inspections, searches, seizures, and arrests upon the high seas and waters over which the United States has jurisdiction, for the prevention, detection, and suppression of violations of laws of the United States. For such purposes, commissioned, warrant, and petty officers may at any time go on board of any vessel subject to the jurisdiction, or to the operation of any law, of the United States, address inquiries to those on board, examine the ship's documents and papers, and examine, inspect, and search the vessel and use all necessary force to compel compliance. When from such inquiries, examination, inspection, or search it appears that a breach of the laws of the United States rendering an individual liable to arrest is being, or has been committed, by any individual, such individual shall be arrested or, if escaping to shore, shall be immediately pursued and arrested on shore, or other lawful and appropriate action shall be taken; or, if it shall appear that a breach of the laws of the United States has been committed so as to render such vessel, or the merchandise, or any part thereof, on board of, or brought into the United States by, such vessel, liable to forfeiture, or so as to render such vessel liable to a fine or penalty and if necessary to secure such fine or penalty, such vessel or such merchandise, or both, shall be seized.

(b) The officers of the Coast Guard insofar as they are engaged, pursuant to the authority contained in this section, in enforcing any law of the United States shall:

(1) be deemed to be acting as agents of the particular executive department or independent establishment charged with the administration of the particular law; and

(2) be subject to all the rules and regulations promulgated by such department or independent establishment with respect to the enforcement of that law.

(c) The provisions of this section are in addition to any powers conferred by law upon such officers, and not in limitation of any powers conferred by law upon such officers, or any other officers of the United States.

(Aug. 4, 1949, ch. 393, 63 Stat. 502, §89; Aug. 3, 1950, ch. 536, §1, 64 Stat. 406; renumbered §522, Pub. L. 115–282, title I, §105(b), Dec. 4, 2018, 132 Stat. 4200; Pub. L. 116–283, div. G, title LVXXXV [LXXXV], §8505(a)(5), Jan. 1, 2021, 134 Stat. 4748.)

§523. ENFORCEMENT AUTHORITY

Subject to guidelines approved by the Secretary, members of the Coast Guard, in the performance of official duties, may—

(1) carry a firearm; and

(2) while at a facility (as defined in section 70101 of title 46)—

(A) make an arrest without warrant for any offense against the United States committed in their presence; and

(B) seize property as otherwise provided by law.

(Added Pub. L. 111–281, title II, §208(a), Oct. 15, 2010, 124 Stat. 2912, §99; renumbered §523, Pub. L. 115–282, title I, §105(b), Dec. 4, 2018, 132 Stat. 4200.)

§524. ENFORCEMENT OF COASTWISE TRADE LAWS

Officers and members of the Coast Guard are authorized to enforce chapter 551 of title 46. The Secretary shall establish a program for these officers and members to enforce that chapter.

(Added Pub. L. 111–281, title II, §216(a), Oct. 15, 2010, 124 Stat. 2917, §100; renumbered §524, Pub. L. 115–282, title I, §105(b), Dec. 4, 2018, 132 Stat. 4200.)

§525. SPECIAL AGENTS OF THE COAST GUARD INVESTIGATIVE SERVICE LAW ENFORCEMENT AUTHORITY

(a)(1) A special agent of the Coast Guard Investigative Service designated under subsection (b) has the following authority:

(A) To carry firearms.

(B) To execute and serve any warrant or other process issued under the authority of the United States.

(C) To make arrests without warrant for—

(i) any offense against the United States committed in the agent's presence; or

(ii) any felony cognizable under the laws of the United States if the agent has probable cause to believe that the individual to be arrested has committed or is committing the felony.

(2) The authorities provided in paragraph (1) shall be exercised only in the enforcement of statutes for which the Coast Guard has law enforcement authority, or in exigent circumstances.

(b) The Commandant may designate to have the authority provided under subsection (a) any special agent of the Coast Guard Investigative Service whose duties include conducting, supervising, or coordinating investigation of criminal activity in programs and operations of the United States Coast Guard.

(c) The authority provided under subsection (a) shall be exercised in accordance with guidelines prescribed by the Commandant and approved by the Attorney General and any other applicable guidelines prescribed by the Secretary or the Attorney General.

(Added Pub. L. 100–448, §10(a), Sept. 28, 1988, 102 Stat. 1842, §95; amended Pub. L. 105–383, title II, §205(a), Nov. 13, 1998, 112 Stat. 3415; Pub. L. 107–296, title XVII, §1704(a), Nov. 25, 2002, 116 Stat. 2314; Pub. L. 112–213, title II, §217(2), Dec. 20, 2012, 126 Stat. 1557; renumbered §525, Pub. L. 115–282, title I, §105(b), Dec. 4, 2018, 132 Stat. 4200; Pub. L. 116–283, div. G, title LVXXXV [LXXXV], §8505(a)(6), Jan. 1, 2021, 134 Stat. 4748.)

§526. STOPPING VESSELS; INDEMNITY FOR FIRING AT OR INTO VESSEL

(a)(1) Whenever any vessel liable to seizure or examination does not stop on being ordered to do so or on being pursued by an authorized vessel or authorized aircraft which has displayed the ensign, pennant, or other identifying insignia prescribed for an authorized vessel or authorized aircraft, the individual in command or in charge of the authorized vessel or authorized aircraft may, subject to paragraph (2), fire at or into the vessel which does not stop.

(2) Before firing at or into a vessel as authorized in paragraph (1), the individual in command or in charge of the authorized vessel or authorized aircraft shall fire a gun as a warning signal, except that the prior firing of a gun as a warning signal is not required if that individual determines that the firing of a warning signal would unreasonably endanger individuals or property in the vicinity of the vessel to be stopped.

(b) The individual in command of an authorized vessel or authorized aircraft and all individuals acting under that individual's direction shall be indemnified from any penalties or actions for damages for firing at or into a vessel pursuant to subsection (a). If any individual is killed or wounded by the firing, and the individual in command of the authorized vessel or authorized aircraft or any individual acting pursuant to their orders is prosecuted or arrested therefor, they shall be forthwith admitted to bail.

(c) A vessel or aircraft is an authorized vessel or authorized aircraft for purposes of this section if—

(1) it is a Coast Guard vessel or aircraft;

(2) it is a surface naval vessel or military aircraft on which one or more members of the Coast Guard are assigned pursuant to section 379 of title 10; [1] or

(3) it is any other vessel or aircraft on government noncommercial service when—

(A) the vessel or aircraft is under the tactical control of the Coast Guard; and

(B) at least one member of the Coast Guard is assigned and conducting a Coast Guard mission on the vessel or aircraft.

(Aug. 4, 1949, ch. 393, 63 Stat. 546, §637; Pub. L. 100–690, title VII, §7401(a), Nov. 18, 1988, 102 Stat. 4483; Pub. L. 106–65, div. A, title X, §1022, Oct. 5, 1999, 113 Stat. 746; Pub. L. 108–293, title II, §205(a)–(c), (e)(1), Aug. 9, 2004, 118 Stat. 1032, 1033; Pub. L. 111–281, title II, §213(a), Oct. 15, 2010, 124 Stat. 2915; Pub. L. 114–120, title II, §209(9), Feb. 8, 2016, 130 Stat. 41; renumbered §526, Pub. L. 115–282, title I, §105(b), Dec. 4, 2018, 132 Stat. 4200; Pub. L. 116–283, div. G, title LVXXXV [LXXXV], §8505(a)(7), Jan. 1, 2021, 134 Stat. 4748.)

[1] See References in Text note below.

§527. SAFETY OF VESSELS OF THE ARMED FORCES

(a) The Secretary may control the anchorage and movement of any vessel in the navigable waters of the United States to ensure the safety or security of any vessel of the Armed Forces in those waters.

(b) If the Secretary does not exercise the authority in subsection (a) of this section and immediate action is required, the senior officer present in command may control the anchorage or movement of any vessel in the navigable waters of the United States to ensure the safety and security of any vessel of the Armed Forces under the officer's command.

(c) If a person violates, or a vessel is operated in violation of, this section or a regulation or order issued under this section, the person or vessel is subject to the enforcement provisions in section 13 [1] of the Ports and Waterways Safety Act (33 U.S.C. 1232).

(d) As used in this section "navigable waters of the United States" includes all waters of the territorial sea of the United States as described in Presidential Proclamation No. 5928 of December 27, 1988.

(e) For purposes of this title, the term "vessel of the Armed Forces" means—

(1) any vessel owned or operated by the Department of Defense or the Coast Guard, other than a time- or voyage-chartered vessel; and

(2) any vessel owned and operated by the Department of Transportation that is designated by the Secretary of the department in which the Coast Guard is operating as a vessel equivalent to a vessel described in paragraph (1).

(Aug. 4, 1949, ch. 393, 63 Stat. 503, §91; Pub. L. 99–640, §10(a)(4), Nov. 10, 1986, 100 Stat. 3549; Pub. L. 109–241, title II, §201, July 11, 2006, 120 Stat. 519; renumbered §527 and amended Pub. L. 115–282, title I, §105(b), title III, §318(a), Dec. 4, 2018, 132 Stat. 4200, 4251.)

[1] *See References in Text note below.*

§528. PROTECTING AGAINST UNMANNED AIRCRAFT

For the purposes of section 210G(k)(3)(C)(iv) of the Homeland Security Act of 2002, the missions authorized to be performed by the United States Coast Guard shall be those related to—

(1) functions of the U.S. Coast Guard relating to security or protection of facilities and assets assessed to be high-risk and a potential target for unlawful unmanned aircraft activity, including the security and protection of—

(A) a facility, including a facility that is under the administrative control of the Commandant; and

(B) a vessel (whether moored or underway) or an aircraft, including a vessel or aircraft—

(i) that is operated by the Coast Guard, or that the Coast Guard is assisting or escorting; and

(ii) that is directly involved in a mission of the Coast Guard pertaining to—

(I) assisting or escorting a vessel of the Department of Defense;

(II) assisting or escorting a vessel of national security significance, a high interest vessel, a high capacity passenger vessel, or a high value unit, as those terms are defined by the Secretary;

(III) section 527(a) of this title;

(IV) assistance in protecting the President or the Vice President (or other officer next in order of succession to the Office of the President) pursuant to the Presidential Protection Assistance Act of 1976 (18 U.S.C. 3056 note);

(V) protection of a National Special Security Event and Special Event Assessment Rating events;

(VI) air defense of the United States, including air sovereignty, ground-based air defense, and the National Capital Region integrated air defense system; or

(VII) a search and rescue operation; and

(2) missions directed by the Secretary pursuant to 210G(k)(3)(C)(iii) [1] of the Homeland Security Act of 2002.

(Added Pub. L. 115–254, div. H, §1603(a), Oct. 5, 2018, 132 Stat. 3529, §104; renumbered §528 and amended Pub. L. 115–282, title I, §§105(b), 123(b)(2), Dec. 4, 2018, 132 Stat. 4200, 4240.)

[1] *So in original. Probably should be preceded by "section".*

SUBCHAPTER III—AIDS TO NAVIGATION

§541. AIDS TO NAVIGATION AUTHORIZED

(a) In order to aid navigation and to prevent disasters, collisions, and wrecks of vessels and aircraft, the Coast Guard may establish, maintain, and operate:

(1) aids to maritime navigation required to serve the needs of the armed forces or of the commerce of the United States;

(2) aids to air navigation required to serve the needs of the armed forces of the United States peculiar to warfare and primarily of military concern as determined by the Secretary of Defense or the Secretary of any department within the Department of Defense and as required by any of those officials; and

(3) electronic aids to navigation systems (a) required to serve the needs of the armed forces of the United States peculiar to warfare and primarily of military concern as determined by the Secretary of Defense or any department within the Department of Defense; or (b) required to serve the needs of the maritime commerce of the United States; or (c) required to serve the needs of the air commerce of the United States as requested by the Administrator of the Federal Aviation Administration.

These aids to navigation other than electronic aids to navigation systems shall be established and operated only within the United States, the waters above the Continental Shelf, the territories and possessions of the United States, the Trust Territory of the Pacific Islands, and beyond the territorial jurisdiction of the United States at places where naval or military bases of the United States are or may be located. The Coast Guard may establish, maintain, and operate aids to maritime navigation under paragraph (1) of this section by contract with any person, public body, or instrumentality.

(b) In the case of pierhead beacons, the Commandant may—

(1) acquire, by donation or purchase in behalf of the United States, the right to use and occupy sites for pierhead beacons; and

(2) properly mark all pierheads belonging to the United States situated on the northern and northwestern lakes, whenever the Commandant is duly notified by the department charged with the construction or repair of pierheads that the construction or repair of any such pierheads has been completed.

(Aug. 4, 1949, ch. 393, 63 Stat. 500, §81; June 22, 1951, ch. 150, 65 Stat. 89; Sept. 3, 1954, ch. 1263, §30, 68 Stat. 1237; Pub. L. 85–726, title XIV, §1404, Aug. 23, 1958, 72 Stat. 808; Pub. L. 89–662, §1, Oct. 14, 1966, 80 Stat. 912; Pub. L. 94–546, §1(3), Oct. 18, 1976, 90 Stat. 2519; Pub. L. 97–322, title I, §105(a), Oct. 15, 1982, 96 Stat. 1582; renumbered §541, Pub. L. 115–282, title I, §105(b), Dec. 4, 2018, 132 Stat. 4200; Pub. L. 116–283, div. G, title LVXXXV [LXXXV], §8509(a), Jan. 1, 2021, 134 Stat. 4755.)

§542. UNAUTHORIZED AIDS TO MARITIME NAVIGATION; PENALTY

No person, or public body, or instrumentality, excluding the armed services, shall establish, erect, or maintain any aid to maritime navigation in or adjacent to the waters subject to the jurisdiction of the United States, its territories or possessions, or the Trust Territory of the Pacific Islands, or on the high seas if that person, or public body, or instrumentality is subject to the jurisdiction of the United States, without first obtaining authority to do so from the Coast Guard in accordance with applicable regulations. Whoever violates the provisions of this section or any of the regulations issued by the Secretary in accordance herewith shall be guilty of a misdemeanor and shall be fined not more than $1,500 for each offense. Each day during which such violation continues shall be considered as a new offense.

(Aug. 4, 1949, ch. 393, 63 Stat. 500, §83; Pub. L. 93–283, §1(1), May 14, 1974, 88 Stat. 139; Pub. L. 113–281, title II, §205(a)(1), Dec. 18, 2014, 128 Stat. 3025; renumbered §542, Pub. L. 115–282, title I, §105(b), Dec. 4, 2018, 132 Stat. 4200.)

§543. INTERFERENCE WITH AIDS TO NAVIGATION; PENALTY

It shall be unlawful for any person, or public body, or instrumentality, excluding the armed forces, to remove, change the location of, obstruct, wilfully damage, make fast to, or interfere with any aid to navigation established, installed, operated, or maintained by the Coast Guard pursuant to section 541 of this title, or with any aid to navigation lawfully maintained under authority granted by the Coast Guard pursuant to section 542 of this title, or to anchor any vessel in any of the navigable waters of the United States so as to obstruct or interfere with range lights maintained therein. Whoever violates the provisions of this section shall be guilty of a misdemeanor and shall be fined not more than $1,500 for each offense. Each day during which such violation shall continue shall be considered as a new offense.

(Aug. 4, 1949, ch. 393, 63 Stat. 500, §84; Pub. L. 113–281, title II, §205(a)(2), Dec. 18, 2014, 128 Stat. 3025; renumbered §543 and amended Pub. L. 115–282, title I, §§105(b), 123(b)(2), Dec. 4, 2018, 132 Stat. 4200, 4240.)

§544. AIDS TO MARITIME NAVIGATION; PENALTY

The Secretary shall prescribe and enforce necessary and reasonable rules and regulations, for the protection of maritime navigation, relative to the establishment, maintenance, and operation of lights and other signals on fixed and floating structures in or over waters subject to the jurisdiction of the United States and in the high seas for structures owned or operated by persons subject to the jurisdiction of the United States. Any owner or operator of such a structure, excluding an agency of the United States, who violates any of the rules or regulations prescribed hereunder, commits a misdemeanor and shall be punished, upon conviction thereof, by a fine of not exceeding $1,500 for each day which such violation continues.

(Aug. 4, 1949, ch. 393, 63 Stat. 501, §85; June 4, 1956, ch. 351, §1, 70 Stat. 226; Pub. L. 93–283, §1(2), May 14, 1974, 88 Stat. 139; Pub. L. 113–281, title II, §205(a)(3), Dec. 18, 2014, 128 Stat. 3025; renumbered §544, Pub. L. 115–282, title I, §105(b), Dec. 4, 2018, 132 Stat. 4200.)

§545. MARKING OF OBSTRUCTIONS

The Secretary may mark for the protection of navigation any sunken vessel or other obstruction existing on the navigable waters or waters above the continental shelf of the United States in such manner and for so long as, in his judgment, the needs of maritime navigation require. The owner of such an obstruction shall be liable to the United States for the cost of such marking until such time as the obstruction is removed or its abandonment legally established or until such earlier time as the Secretary may determine. All moneys received by the United States from the owners of obstructions, in accordance with this section, shall be covered into the Treasury of the United States as miscellaneous receipts. This section shall not be construed so as to relieve the owner of any such obstruction from the duty and responsibility suitably to mark the same and remove it as required by law.

(Aug. 4, 1949, ch. 393, 63 Stat. 501, §86; Pub. L. 89–191, Sept. 17, 1965, 79 Stat. 822; Pub. L. 93–283, §1(3), May 14, 1974, 88 Stat. 139; renumbered §545, Pub. L. 115–282, title I, §105(b), Dec. 4, 2018, 132 Stat. 4200.)

§546. Deposit of Damage Payments

Whenever an aid to navigation or other property belonging to the Coast Guard is damaged or destroyed by a private person, and such private person or his agent shall pay to the satisfaction of the proper official of the Coast Guard for the cost of repair or replacement of such property, the Commandant may accept and deposit such payments, through proper officers of the Fiscal Service, Treasury Department, in special deposit accounts in the Treasury, for payment therefrom to the person or persons repairing or replacing the damaged property and refundment of amounts collected in excess of the cost of the repairs or replacements concerned. In the event that repair or replacement of the damaged property is effected by the Coast Guard, the appropriations bearing the cost thereof and current at the time collection is made shall be reimbursed from the special deposit account.

(Aug. 4, 1949, ch. 393, 63 Stat. 547, §642; renumbered §546, Pub. L. 115–282, title I, §105(b), Dec. 4, 2018, 132 Stat. 4200.)

§547. Rewards for Apprehension of Persons Interfering with Aids to Navigation

The Coast Guard may offer and pay rewards for the apprehension and conviction, or for information helpful therein, of persons found interfering in violation of law with aids to navigation maintained by the Coast Guard; or for information leading to the discovery of missing Coast Guard property or to recovery thereof.

(Aug. 4, 1949, ch. 393, 63 Stat. 547, §643; renumbered §547, Pub. L. 115–282, title I, §105(b), Dec. 4, 2018, 132 Stat. 4200.)

§548.[1] Prohibition Against Officers and Employees Being Interested in Contracts for Materials

No officer, enlisted member, or civilian member of the Coast Guard in any manner connected with the construction, operation, or maintenance of lighthouses, shall be interested, either directly or indirectly, in any contract for labor, materials, or supplies for the construction, operation, or maintenance of lighthouses, or in any patent, plan, or mode of construction or illumination, or in any article of supply for the construction, operation, or maintenance of lighthouses.

(Added Pub. L. 116–283, div. G, title LVXXXV [LXXXV], §8509(b), Jan. 1, 2021, 134 Stat. 4756.)

---

[1] Another section 548 is set out after section 550 of this title.

§549. Lighthouse and other sites; necessity and sufficiency of cession by State of jurisdiction

(a) No lighthouse, beacon, public pier, or landmark, shall be built or erected on any site until cession of jurisdiction over the same has been made to the United States.

(b) For the purposes of subsection (a), a cession by a State of jurisdiction over a place selected as the site of a lighthouse, or other structure or work referred to in subsection (a), shall be deemed sufficient if the cession contains a reservation that process issued under authority of such State may continue to be served within such place.

(c) If no reservation of service described in subsection (b) is contained in a cession, all process may be served and executed within the place ceded, in the same manner as if no cession had been made.

(Added Pub. L. 116–283, div. G, title LVXXXV [LXXXV], §8509(b), Jan. 1, 2021, 134 Stat. 4756.)

§550. Marking pierheads in certain lakes

The Commandant of the Coast Guard shall properly mark all pierheads belonging to the United States situated on the northern and northwestern lakes, whenever he is duly notified by the department charged with the construction or repair of pierheads that the construction or repair of any such pierhead has been completed.

(Added Pub. L. 116–283, div. G, title LVXXXV [LXXXV], §8509(b), Jan. 1, 2021, 134 Stat. 4756.)

§548.[1] Marking anchorage grounds by Commandant of the Coast Guard

The Commandant of the Coast Guard shall provide, establish, and maintain, out of the annual appropriations for the Coast Guard, buoys or other suitable marks for marking anchorage grounds for vessels in waters of the United States, when such anchorage grounds have been defined and established by proper authority in accordance with the laws of the United States.

(Added and amended Pub. L. 117–263, div. K, title CXVIII, §11808(c), Dec. 23, 2022, 136 Stat. 4166.)

[1] Another section 548 is set out after section 547 of this title.

SUBCHAPTER IV—MISCELLANEOUS

§561. ICEBREAKING IN POLAR REGIONS

(a) PROCUREMENT AUTHORITY.—

(1) IN GENERAL.—The Secretary may enter into one or more contracts for the procurement of—

(A) the Polar Security Cutters approved as part of a major acquisition program as of November 1, 2019; and

(B) 3 additional Polar Security Cutters.

(2) CONDITION FOR OUT-YEAR CONTRACT PAYMENTS.—A contract entered into under paragraph (1) shall provide that any obligation of the United States to make a payment under the contract during a fiscal year after fiscal year 2019 is subject to the availability of appropriations or funds for that purpose for such later fiscal year.

(b) PLANNING.—The Secretary shall facilitate planning for the design, procurement, maintenance, deployment, and operation of icebreakers as needed to support the statutory missions of the Coast Guard in the polar regions by allocating all funds to support icebreaking operations in such regions, except for recurring incremental costs associated with specific projects, to the Coast Guard.

(c) REIMBURSEMENT.—Nothing in this section shall preclude the Secretary from seeking reimbursement for operation and maintenance costs of the *Polar Star*, *Healy*, or any other Polar Security Cutter from other Federal agencies and entities, including foreign countries, that benefit from the use of those vessels.

(d) RESTRICTION.—

(1) IN GENERAL.—The Commandant may not—

(A) transfer, relinquish ownership of, dismantle, or recycle the *Polar Sea* or *Polar Star*;

(B) change the current homeport of the *Polar Sea* or *Polar Star*; or

(C) expend any funds—

(i) for any expenses directly or indirectly associated with the decommissioning of the *Polar Sea* or *Polar Star*, including expenses for dock use or other goods and services;

(ii) for any personnel expenses directly or indirectly associated with the decommissioning of the *Polar Sea* or *Polar Star*, including expenses for a decommissioning officer;

(iii) for any expenses associated with a decommissioning ceremony for the *Polar Sea* or *Polar Star*;

(iv) to appoint a decommissioning officer to be affiliated with the *Polar Sea* or *Polar Star*; or

(v) to place the *Polar Sea* or *Polar Star* in inactive status.

(2) SUNSET.—This subsection shall cease to have effect on September 30, 2022.

(e) LIMITATION.—

(1) IN GENERAL.—The Secretary may not expend amounts appropriated for the Coast Guard for any of fiscal years 2015 through 2024, for—

(A) design activities related to a capability of a Polar Security Cutter that is based solely on an operational requirement of a Federal department or agency other than the Coast Guard, except for amounts appropriated for design activities for a fiscal year before fiscal year 2016; or

(B) long-lead-time materials, production, or postdelivery activities related to such a capability.

(2) OTHER AMOUNTS.—Amounts made available to the Secretary under an agreement with a Federal department or agency other than the Coast Guard and expended on a capability of a Polar Security Cutter that is based solely on an operational requirement of such Federal department or agency shall not be treated as amounts expended by the Secretary for purposes of the limitation under paragraph (1).

(f) ENHANCED MAINTENANCE PROGRAM FOR THE POLAR STAR.—

(1) IN GENERAL.—Subject to the availability of appropriations, the Commandant shall conduct an enhanced maintenance program on the Polar Star [1] to extend the service life of such vessel until at least December 31, 2025.

(2) AUTHORIZATION OF APPROPRIATIONS.—The Commandant may use funds made available pursuant to section 4902(1)(A), to carry out this subsection.

(g) DEFINITIONS.—In this section:

(1) POLAR SEA.—The term "*Polar Sea*" means Coast Guard Cutter *Polar Sea* (WAGB 11).

(2) POLAR STAR.—The term "*Polar Star*" means Coast Guard Cutter *Polar Star* (WAGB 10).

(3) HEALY.—The term "*Healy*" means Coast Guard Cutter *Healy* (WAGB 20).

(Added Pub. L. 113–281, title V, §506(a), Dec. 18, 2014, 128 Stat. 3060, §87; renumbered §561, Pub. L. 115–282, title I, §105(b), Dec. 4, 2018, 132 Stat. 4200; amended Pub. L. 116–283, div. G, title LVXXXI [LXXXI], §8111(a), Jan. 1, 2021, 134 Stat. 4637.)

---

[1] *So in original. "Polar Star" probably should be italicized.*

§562. APPEALS AND WAIVERS

Except for the Commandant, any individual adjudicating an appeal or waiver of a decision regarding marine safety, including inspection or manning and threats to the environment, shall—

(1) be a qualified specialist with the training, experience, and qualifications in marine safety to effectively judge the facts and circumstances involved in the appeal and make a judgment regarding the merits of the appeal; or

(2) have a senior staff member who—

(A) meets the requirements of paragraph (1);

(B) actively advises the individual adjudicating the appeal; and

(C) concurs in writing on the decision on appeal.

(Added Pub. L. 111–281, title V, §524(a), Oct. 15, 2010, 124 Stat. 2958, §102; renumbered §101, Pub. L. 111–330, §1(6)(A), Dec. 22, 2010, 124 Stat. 3569; amended Pub. L. 115–232, div. C, title XXXV, §3531(c)(2), Aug. 13, 2018, 132 Stat. 2320; renumbered §562, Pub. L. 115–282, title I, §105(b), Dec. 4, 2018, 132 Stat. 4200.)

§563. NOTIFICATION OF CERTAIN DETERMINATIONS

(a) IN GENERAL.—At least 90 days prior to making a final determination that a waterway, or a portion thereof, is navigable for purposes of the jurisdiction of the Coast Guard, the Commandant shall provide notification regarding the proposed determination to—

(1) the Governor of each State in which such waterway, or portion thereof, is located;

(2) the public; and

(3) the Committee on Commerce, Science, and Transportation of the Senate and the Committee on Transportation and Infrastructure of the House of Representatives.

(b) CONTENT REQUIREMENT.—Each notification provided under subsection (a) to an entity specified in paragraph (3) of that subsection shall include—

(1) an analysis of whether vessels operating on the waterway, or portion thereof, subject to the proposed determination are subject to inspection or similar regulation by State or local officials;

(2) an analysis of whether operators of commercial vessels on such waterway, or portion thereof, are subject to licensing or similar regulation by State or local officials; and

(3) an estimate of the annual costs that the Coast Guard may incur in conducting operations on such waterway, or portion thereof.

(Added Pub. L. 113–281, title II, §210(a), Dec. 18, 2014, 128 Stat. 3027, §103; renumbered §563, Pub. L. 115–282, title I, §105(b), Dec. 4, 2018, 132 Stat. 4200.)

§564. ADMINISTRATION OF SEXUAL ASSAULT FORENSIC EXAMINATION KITS

(a) SEXUAL ASSAULT FORENSIC EXAM PROCEDURE.—

(1) IN GENERAL.—Before embarking on any prescheduled voyage, a Coast Guard vessel shall have in place a written operating procedure that ensures that an embarked victim of sexual assault shall have access to a sexual assault forensic examination—

(A) as soon as possible after the victim requests an examination; and

(B) that is treated with the same level of urgency as emergency medical care.

(2) REQUIREMENTS.—The written operating procedure required by paragraph (1),[1] shall, at a minimum, account for—

(A) the health, safety, and privacy of a victim of sexual assault;

(B) the proximity of ashore or afloat medical facilities, including coordination as necessary with the Department of Defense, including other military departments (as defined in section 101 of title 10);

(C) the availability of aeromedical evacuation;

(D) the operational capabilities of the vessel concerned;

(E) the qualifications of medical personnel onboard;

(F) coordination with law enforcement and the preservation of evidence;

(G) the means of accessing a sexual assault forensic examination and medical care with a restricted report of sexual assault;

(H) the availability of nonprescription pregnancy prophylactics; and

(I) other unique military considerations.

(Added Pub. L. 117–263, div. K, title CXII, §11272(a), Dec. 23, 2022, 136 Stat. 4066.)

---

[1] So in original. The comma probably should not appear.

CHAPTER 7—COOPERATION

[1] So in original. Does not conform to section catchline.

§701. COOPERATION WITH OTHER AGENCIES, STATES, TERRITORIES, AND POLITICAL SUBDIVISIONS

(a) The Coast Guard may, when so requested by proper authority, utilize its personnel and facilities (including members of the Auxiliary and facilities governed under chapter 39) to assist any Federal agency, State, Territory, possession, or political subdivision thereof, or the District of Columbia, to perform any activity for which such personnel and facilities are especially qualified. The Commandant may prescribe conditions, including reimbursement, under which personnel and facilities may be provided under this subsection.

(b) The Coast Guard, with the consent of the head of the agency concerned, may avail itself of such officers and employees, advice, information, and facilities of any Federal agency, State, Territory, possession, or political subdivision thereof, or the District of Columbia as may be helpful in the performance of its duties. In connection with the utilization of personal services of employees of state or local governments, the Coast Guard may make payments for necessary traveling and per diem expenses as prescribed for Federal employees by the standardized Government travel regulations.

(Aug. 4, 1949, ch. 393, 63 Stat. 505, §141; Pub. L. 104–324, title IV, §405(a), Oct. 19, 1996, 110 Stat. 3924; renumbered §701 and amended Pub. L. 115–282, title I, §§106(b), 123(c)(6), Dec. 4, 2018, 132 Stat. 4203, 4241.)

§702. STATE DEPARTMENT

The Coast Guard, through the Secretary, may exchange information, through the Secretary of State, with foreign governments and suggest to the Secretary of State international collaboration and conferences on all matters dealing with the safety of life and property at sea, other than radio communication.

(Aug. 4, 1949, ch. 393, 63 Stat. 505, §142; renumbered §702, Pub. L. 115–282, title I, §106(b), Dec. 4, 2018, 132 Stat. 4203.)

§703. TREASURY DEPARTMENT

Commissioned, warrant, and petty officers of the Coast Guard are deemed to be officers of the customs and when so acting shall, insofar as performance of the duties relating to customs laws are concerned, be subject to regulations issued by the Secretary of the Treasury governing officers of the customs.

(Aug. 4, 1949, ch. 393, 63 Stat. 506, §143; renumbered §703, Pub. L. 115–282, title I, §106(b), Dec. 4, 2018, 132 Stat. 4203.)

§704. DEPARTMENT OF THE ARMY AND DEPARTMENT OF THE AIR FORCE

(a) The Secretary of the Army or the Secretary of the Air Force at the request of the Secretary may, with or without reimbursement for the cost thereof, as agreed, receive members of the Coast Guard for instruction in any school, including any aviation school, maintained by the Army or the Air Force, and such members shall be subject to the regulations governing such schools.

(b) Officers and enlisted members of the Coast Guard shall be permitted to purchase quartermaster supplies from the Army at the same price as is charged the officers and enlisted members of the Army.

(c) Articles of ordnance property may be sold by the Secretary of the Army to officers of the Coast Guard for their use in the public service in the same manner as these articles are sold to officers of the Army.

(Aug. 4, 1949, ch. 393, 63 Stat. 506, §144; Pub. L. 94–546, §1(10), Oct. 18, 1976, 90 Stat. 2519; Pub. L. 98–557, §15(a)(3)(D), Oct. 30, 1984, 98 Stat. 2865; Pub. L. 115–232, div. C, title XXXV, §3533(c)(1), Aug. 13, 2018, 132 Stat. 2321; renumbered §704, Pub. L. 115–282, title I, §106(b), Dec. 4, 2018, 132 Stat. 4203.)

§705. NAVY DEPARTMENT

(a) The Secretary of the Navy, at the request of the Secretary may, with or without reimbursement for the cost thereof, as agreed:

(1) build any vessel for the Coast Guard at such Navy yards as the Secretary of the Navy may designate;

(2) receive members of the Coast Guard for instruction in any school, including any aviation school maintained by the Navy, and such members shall be subject to the regulations governing such schools;

(3) permit personnel of the Coast Guard and their dependents to occupy any public

quarters maintained by the Navy and available for the purpose; and

(4) detail personnel from the Chaplain Corps to provide services, pursuant to section 1789 of title 10, to the Coast Guard.

(b) Officers and enlisted members of the Coast Guard shall be permitted to purchase quartermaster supplies from the Navy and the Marine Corps at the same price as is charged the officers and enlisted members of the Navy and Marine Corps.

(c) When the Coast Guard is operating in the Department of Homeland Security, the Secretary shall provide for such peacetime training and planning of reserve strength and facilities as is necessary to insure an organized, manned, and equipped Coast Guard when it is required for wartime operation in the Navy. To this end, the Secretary of the Navy for the Navy, and the Secretary of Homeland Security, for the Coast Guard, may from time to time exchange such information, make available to each other such personnel, vessels, facilities, and equipment, and agree to undertake such assignments and functions for each other as they may agree are necessary and advisable.

(d)(1) As part of the services provided by the Secretary of the Navy pursuant to subsection (a)(4), the Secretary may provide support services to chaplain-led programs to assist members of the Coast Guard on active duty and their dependents, and members of the reserve component in an active status and their dependents, in building and maintaining a strong family structure.

(2) In this subsection, the term "support services" include transportation, food, lodging, child care, supplies, fees, and training materials for members of the Coast Guard on active duty and their dependents, and members of the reserve component in an active status and their dependents, while participating in programs referred to in paragraph (1), including participation at retreats and conferences.

(3) In this subsection, the term "dependents" has the same meaning as defined in section 1072(2) of title 10.

(Aug. 4, 1949, ch. 393, 63 Stat. 506, §145; Aug. 3, 1950, ch. 536, §3, 64 Stat. 406; Pub. L. 94–546, §1(11), Oct. 18, 1976, 90 Stat. 2519; Pub. L. 98–557, §15(a)(3)(D), Oct. 30, 1984, 98 Stat. 2865; Pub. L. 107–296, title XVII, §1704(a), Nov. 25, 2002, 116 Stat. 2314; Pub. L. 111–281, title II, §223, Oct. 15, 2010, 124 Stat. 2921; Pub. L. 115–232, div. C, title XXXV, §3533(c)(2), Aug. 13, 2018, 132 Stat. 2321; renumbered §705, Pub. L. 115–282, title I, §106(b), Dec. 4, 2018, 132 Stat. 4203.)

§706. United States Postal Service

Coast Guard facilities and personnel may be utilized for the transportation and delivery of mail matter during emergency conditions or at isolated locations under such arrangements as may be satisfactory to the Secretary and the United States Postal Service.

(Aug. 4, 1949, ch. 393, 63 Stat. 506, §146; Pub. L. 94–546, §1(12), Oct. 18, 1976, 90 Stat. 2519; Pub. L. 99–640, §10(a)(5), Nov. 10, 1986, 100 Stat. 3549; renumbered §706, Pub. L. 115–282, title I, §106(b), Dec. 4, 2018, 132 Stat. 4203.)

§707. Department of Commerce

In order to promote the safety of life and property on and over the high seas and waters over which the United States has jurisdiction, and to facilitate the preparation and dissemination by the National Oceanic and Atmospheric Administration of the weather reports, forecasts, and warnings essential to the safe and efficient conduct of domestic and international commerce on and over such seas and waters, the Commandant may cooperate with the Administrator, National Oceanic and Atmospheric Administration by procuring, maintaining, and making available, facilities and assistance for observing, investigating, and communicating weather phenomena and for disseminating weather data, forecasts and warnings, the mutually satisfactory terms of such cooperation in weather service to be agreed upon and arranged between the Commandant and the Administrator, National Oceanic and Atmospheric Administration.

(Aug. 4, 1949, ch. 393, 63 Stat. 507, §147; Pub. L. 94–546, §1(13), Oct. 18, 1976, 90 Stat. 2520; Pub. L. 97–295, §2(5), Oct. 12, 1982, 96 Stat. 1301; renumbered §707, Pub. L. 115–282, title I, §106(b), Dec. 4, 2018, 132 Stat. 4203.)

§708. DEPARTMENT OF HEALTH AND HUMAN SERVICES

(a) The Commandant may assist the Secretary of Health and Human Services in providing medical emergency helicopter transportation services to civilians. The Commandant may prescribe conditions, including reimbursement, under which resources may be provided under this section. The following specific limitations apply to assistance provided under this section:

(1) Assistance may be provided only in areas where Coast Guard units able to provide the assistance are regularly assigned. Coast Guard units may not be transferred from one area to another to provide the assistance.

(2) Assistance may be provided only to the extent it does not interfere with the performance of the Coast Guard mission.

(3) Providing assistance may not cause an increase in amounts required for the operation of the Coast Guard.

(b) An individual (or the estate of that individual) who is authorized by the Coast Guard to provide a service under a program established under subsection (a) and who is acting within the scope of that individual's duties is not liable for injury to, or loss of, property or personal injury or death that may be caused incident to providing the service.

(Added Pub. L. 97–295, §2(6)(A), Oct. 12, 1982, 96 Stat. 1301, §147a; renumbered §708, Pub. L. 115–282, title I, §106(b), Dec. 4, 2018, 132 Stat. 4203.)

§709. MARITIME INSTRUCTION

The Coast Guard may, when so requested by proper authority, detail members for duty in connection with maritime instruction and training by the several States, Territories, the District of Columbia, and Puerto Rico, and when requested by the Maritime Administrator, detail individuals in the Coast Guard for duty in connection with maritime instruction and training by the United States. The service rendered by any individual so detailed shall be considered Coast Guard duty.

(Aug. 4, 1949, ch. 393, 63 Stat. 507, §148; Pub. L. 97–31, §12(4), Aug. 6, 1981, 95 Stat. 154; Pub. L. 98–557, §15(a)(3)(D), Oct. 30, 1984, 98 Stat. 2865; renumbered §709, Pub. L. 115–282, title I, §106(b), Dec. 4, 2018, 132 Stat. 4203; Pub. L. 116–283, div. G, title LVXXXV [LXXXV], §8505(a)(8), Jan. 1, 2021, 134 Stat. 4748.)

§710. Assistance to Foreign Governments and Maritime Authorities

(a) Detail of Members to Assist Foreign Governments.—The President may upon application from the foreign governments concerned, and whenever in his discretion the public interests render such a course advisable, detail members of the Coast Guard to assist foreign governments in matters concerning which the Coast Guard may be of assistance.

(b) Technical Assistance to Foreign Maritime Authorities.—The Commandant, in coordination with the Secretary of State, may provide, in conjunction with regular Coast Guard operations, technical assistance (including law enforcement and maritime safety and security training) to foreign navies, coast guards, and other maritime authorities.

(c) Grants to International Maritime Organizations.—After consultation with the Secretary of State, the Commandant may make grants to, or enter into cooperative agreements, contracts, or other agreements with, international maritime organizations for the purpose of acquiring information or data about merchant vessel inspections, security, safety, environmental protection, classification, and port state or flag state law enforcement or oversight.

(d) Authorized Activities.—

(1) The Commandant may use funds for—

(A) the activities of traveling contact teams, including any transportation expense, translation services expense, or administrative expense that is related to such activities;

(B) the activities of maritime authority liaison teams of foreign governments making reciprocal visits to Coast Guard units, including any transportation expense, translation services expense, or administrative expense that is related to such activities;

(C) seminars and conferences involving members of maritime authorities of foreign governments;

(D) distribution of publications pertinent to engagement with maritime authorities of foreign governments; and

(E) personnel expenses for Coast Guard civilian and military personnel to the extent that those expenses relate to participation in an activity described in subparagraph (C) or (D).

(2) An activity may not be conducted under this subsection with a foreign country unless the Secretary of State approves the conduct of such activity in that foreign country.

(3) The amount of funds used under this subsection may not exceed $100,000 in any fiscal year.

(Aug. 4, 1949, ch. 393, 63 Stat. 507, §149; Pub. L. 98–557, §15(a)(3)(D), (E), (4)(A)(i), Oct. 30, 1984, 98 Stat. 2865; Pub. L. 109–241, title II, §202(a), July 11, 2006, 120 Stat. 520; Pub. L. 111–281, title II, §§206, 220, Oct. 15, 2010, 124 Stat. 2911, 2918; Pub. L. 112–213, title II, §§203, 216(d), Dec. 20, 2012, 126 Stat. 1543, 1555; renumbered §710, Pub. L. 115–282, title I, §106(b), Dec. 4, 2018, 132 Stat. 4203.)

§711. Coast Guard officers as attachés to missions

Commissioned officers may, with the consent of the Secretary of State, be regularly and officially attached to the diplomatic missions of the United States in those nations with which the United States is extensively engaged in maritime commerce. Expenses for the maintenance of such Coast Guard attachés abroad, including office rental and pay of employees and allowances for living quarters, including heat, fuel, and light, may be defrayed by the Coast Guard.

(Aug. 4, 1949, ch. 393, 63 Stat. 507, §150; renumbered §711, Pub. L. 115–282, title I, §106(b), Dec. 4, 2018, 132 Stat. 4203.)

§712. CONTRACTS WITH GOVERNMENT-OWNED ESTABLISHMENTS FOR WORK AND MATERIAL

(a) IN GENERAL.—All orders or contracts for work or material, under authorization of law, placed with Government-owned establishments by the Coast Guard, shall be considered as obligations in the same manner as provided for similar orders or contracts placed with private contractors, and appropriations for such work or material shall remain available for payment therefor as in the case of orders or contracts placed with private contractors.

(b) ORDERS AND AGREEMENTS FOR INDUSTRIAL ACTIVITIES.—Under this section, the Coast Guard industrial activities may accept orders from and enter into reimbursable agreements with establishments, agencies, and departments of the Department of Defense and the Department of Homeland Security.

(Aug. 4, 1949, ch. 393, 63 Stat. 507, §151; Pub. L. 111–281, title II, §202, Oct. 15, 2010, 124 Stat. 2909; renumbered §712, Pub. L. 115–282, title I, §106(b), Dec. 4, 2018, 132 Stat. 4203.)

§713. NONAPPROPRIATED FUND INSTRUMENTALITIES: CONTRACTS WITH OTHER AGENCIES AND INSTRUMENTALITIES TO PROVIDE OR OBTAIN GOODS AND SERVICES

The Coast Guard Exchange System, or a morale, welfare, and recreation system of the Coast Guard, may enter into a contract or other agreement with any element or instrumentality of the Coast Guard or with another Federal department, agency, or instrumentality to provide or obtain goods and services beneficial to the efficient management and operation of the Coast Guard Exchange System or that morale, welfare, and recreation system.

(Added Pub. L. 108–293, title II, §202(a), Aug. 9, 2004, 118 Stat. 1031, §152; renumbered §713, Pub. L. 115–282, title I, §106(b), Dec. 4, 2018, 132 Stat. 4203.)

§714. ARCTIC MARITIME DOMAIN AWARENESS

(a) IN GENERAL.—The Commandant shall improve maritime domain awareness in the Arctic—

(1) by promoting interagency cooperation and coordination;

(2) by employing joint, interagency, and international capabilities; and

(3) by facilitating the sharing of information, intelligence, and data related to the Arctic maritime domain between the Coast Guard and departments and agencies listed in subsection (b).

(b) COORDINATION.—The Commandant shall seek to coordinate the collection, sharing, and use of information, intelligence, and data related to the Arctic maritime domain between the Coast Guard and the following:

(1) The Department of Homeland Security.

(2) The Department of Defense.

(3) The Department of Transportation.

(4) The Department of State.

(5) The Department of the Interior.

(6) The National Aeronautics and Space Administration.

(7) The National Oceanic and Atmospheric Administration.

(8) The Environmental Protection Agency.

(9) The National Science Foundation.

(10) The Arctic Research Commission.

(11) Any Federal agency or commission or State the Commandant determines is appropriate.

(c) COOPERATION.—The Commandant and the head of a department or agency listed in subsection (b) may by agreement, on a reimbursable basis or otherwise, share personnel, services, equipment, and facilities to carry out the requirements of this section.

(d) 5-YEAR STRATEGIC PLAN.—Not later than January 1, 2016 and every 5 years thereafter, the Commandant shall submit to the Committee on Commerce, Science, and Transportation of the Senate and the Committee on Transportation and Infrastructure of the House of Representatives a 5-year strategic plan to guide interagency and international intergovernmental cooperation and coordination for the purpose of improving maritime domain awareness in the Arctic.

(e) DEFINITIONS.—In this section the term "Arctic" has the meaning given that term in section 112 of the Arctic Research and Policy Act of 1984 (15 U.S.C. 4111).

(Added Pub. L. 113–281, title V, §502(a), Dec. 18, 2014, 128 Stat. 3057, §154; renumbered §714, Pub. L. 115–282, title I, §106(b), Dec. 4, 2018, 132 Stat. 4203.)

§715. OCEANOGRAPHIC RESEARCH

The Coast Guard shall conduct such oceanographic research, use such equipment or instruments, and collect and analyze such oceanographic data, in cooperation with other agencies of the Government, or not, as may be in the national interest.

(Added Pub. L. 87–396, §1, Oct. 5, 1961, 75 Stat. 827, §94; renumbered §715, Pub. L. 115–282, title I, §106(b), Dec. 4, 2018, 132 Stat. 4203.)

§716. ARCTIC MARITIME TRANSPORTATION

(a) PURPOSE.—The purpose of this section is to ensure safe and secure maritime shipping in the Arctic including the availability of aids to navigation, vessel escorts, spill response capability, and maritime search and rescue in the Arctic.

(b) INTERNATIONAL MARITIME ORGANIZATION AGREEMENTS.—To carry out the purpose of this section, the Secretary is encouraged to enter into negotiations through the International Maritime Organization to conclude and execute agreements to promote

coordinated action among the United States, Russia, Canada, Iceland, Norway, and Denmark and other seafaring and Arctic nations to ensure, in the Arctic—
    (1) placement and maintenance of aids to navigation;
    (2) appropriate marine safety, tug, and salvage capabilities;
    (3) oil spill prevention and response capability;
    (4) maritime domain awareness, including long-range vessel tracking; and
    (5) search and rescue.

    (c) COORDINATION BY COMMITTEE ON THE MARITIME TRANSPORTATION SYSTEM.—The Committee on the Maritime Transportation System established under section 55501 [1] of title 46, United States Code, shall coordinate the establishment of domestic transportation policies in the Arctic necessary to carry out the purpose of this section.
    (d) AGREEMENTS AND CONTRACTS.—The Secretary may, subject to the availability of appropriations, enter into cooperative agreements, contracts, or other agreements with, or make grants to, individuals and governments to carry out the purpose of this section or any agreements established under subsection (b).
    (e) ICEBREAKING.—The Secretary shall promote safe maritime navigation by means of icebreaking where necessary, feasible, and effective to carry out the purposes of this section.
    (f) ARCTIC DEFINITION.—In this section, the term "Arctic" has the meaning given such term in section 112 of the Arctic Research and Policy Act of 1984 (15 U.S.C. 4111).

(Added Pub. L. 113–281, title V, §501(a), Dec. 18, 2014, 128 Stat. 3056, §90; amended Pub. L. 115–232, div. C, title XXXV, §3533(d), Aug. 13, 2018, 132 Stat. 2321; renumbered §716, Pub. L. 115–282, title I, §106(b), Dec. 4, 2018, 132 Stat. 4203.)

    [1] See References in Text note below.

§717. AGREEMENTS

    (a) IN GENERAL.—In carrying out section 504(a)(4), the Commandant may—
    (1) enter into cooperative agreements, contracts, and other agreements with—
      (A) Federal entities;
      (B) other public or private entities in the United States, including academic entities; and
      (C) foreign governments with the concurrence of the Secretary of State; and

    (2) impose on and collect from an entity subject to an agreement or contract under paragraph (1) a fee to assist with expenses incurred in carrying out such section.

    (b) DEPOSIT AND USE OF FEES.—Fees collected under this section shall be deposited in the general fund of the Treasury as offsetting receipts. The fees may be used, to the extent provided in advance in an appropriation law, only to carry out activities under section 504(a)(4).

(Added Pub. L. 113–281, title II, §206(b), Dec. 18, 2014, 128 Stat. 3025, §102; renumbered §717 and amended Pub. L. 115–282, title I, §§106(b), 123(b)(2), Dec. 4, 2018, 132 Stat. 4203, 4240.)

§718. Training; emergency response providers

(a) In General.—The Commandant may, on a reimbursable or a non-reimbursable basis, make a training available to emergency response providers whenever the Commandant determines that—

(1) a member of the Coast Guard, who is scheduled to participate in such training, is unable or unavailable to participate in such training;

(2) no other member of the Coast Guard, who is assigned to the unit to which the member of the Coast Guard who is unable or unavailable to participate in such training is assigned, is able or available to participate in such training; and

(3) such training, if made available to such emergency response providers, would further the goal of interoperability among Federal agencies, non-Federal governmental agencies, or both.

(b) Emergency Response Providers Defined.—In this section, the term "emergency response providers" has the meaning given that term in section 2 of the Homeland Security Act of 2002 (6 U.S.C. 101).

(c) Treatment of Reimbursement.—Any reimbursements for a training that the Coast Guard receives under this section shall be credited to the appropriation used to pay the costs for such training.

(d) Status; Limitation on Liability.—

(1) Status.—Any individual to whom, as an emergency response provider, training is made available under this section, who is not otherwise a Federal employee, shall not, because of that training, be considered a Federal employee for any purpose (including the purposes of chapter 81 of title 5 (relating to compensation for injury) and sections 2671 through 2680 of title 28 (relating to tort claims)).

(2) Limitation on liability.—The United States shall not be liable for actions taken by an individual in the course of training made available under this section.

(Added Pub. L. 115–282, title III, §306(a), Dec. 4, 2018, 132 Stat. 4247.)

§719. Research projects; transactions other than contracts and grants

(a) Additional Forms of Transactions Authorized.—

(1) In general.—The Commandant may enter into—

(A) transactions (other than contracts, cooperative agreements, and grants) in carrying out basic, applied, and advanced research projects; and

(B) agreements with the Director of the Defense Advanced Research Projects Agency, the Secretary of a military department, or any other official designated by the Secretary of Defense under section 2371b [1] of title 10 to participate in prototype projects and follow-on production contracts or transactions that are being carried out by such official and are directly relevant to the Coast Guard's cyber capability and Command, Control, Communications, Computers, and intelligence initiatives.

(2) ADDITIONAL AUTHORITY.—The authority under this subsection is in addition to the authority provided in section 717 to use contracts, cooperative agreements, and grants in carrying out such projects.

(3) FUNDING.—In carrying out paragraph (1)(B), the Commandant may use funds made available to the extent provided in advance in appropriations Acts for—

(A) operations and support;

(B) research, development, test, and evaluation; and

(C) procurement, construction, and improvement.

(b) RECOVERY OF FUNDS.—

(1) IN GENERAL.—Subject to subsection (d), a cooperative agreement for performance of basic, applied, or advanced research authorized by section 717, and a transaction authorized by subsection (a), may include a clause that requires a person or other entity to make payments to the Coast Guard or any other department or agency of the Federal Government as a condition for receiving support under the agreement or transaction, respectively.

(2) AVAILABILITY OF FUNDS.—The amount of any payment received by the Federal Government pursuant to a requirement imposed under paragraph (1) shall be deposited in the general fund of the Treasury. Amounts so deposited shall be available for the purposes of carrying out this section, to the extent provided in advance in appropriations Acts.

(c) CONDITIONS.—

(1) IN GENERAL.—The Commandant shall ensure that to the extent that the Commandant determines practicable, no cooperative agreement containing a clause described in subsection (c)(1),[2] and no transaction entered into under subsection (a), provides for research that duplicates research being conducted under existing programs carried out by the Coast Guard.

(2) OTHER AGREEMENTS NOT FEASIBLE.—A cooperative agreement containing a clause described in subsection (c)(1),[2] or under a transaction authorized by subsection (a), may be used for a research project only if the use of a standard contract, grant, or cooperative agreement for such project is not feasible or appropriate.

(d) EDUCATION AND TRAINING.—The Commandant shall—

(1) ensure that management, technical, and contracting personnel of the Coast Guard involved in the award or administration of transactions under this section or other innovative forms of contracting are afforded opportunities for adequate education and training; and

(2) establish minimum levels and requirements for continuous and experiential learning for such personnel, including levels and requirements for acquisition certification programs.

(e) PROTECTION OF CERTAIN INFORMATION FROM DISCLOSURE.—

(1) IN GENERAL.—Disclosure of information described in paragraph (2) is not required, and may not be compelled, under section 552 of title 5 for 5 years after the date on which

the information is received by the Coast Guard.

(2) LIMITATION.—

(A) IN GENERAL.—Paragraph (1) applies to information described in subparagraph (B) that is in the records of the Coast Guard only if the information was submitted to the Coast Guard in a competitive or noncompetitive process having the potential for resulting in an award, to the party submitting the information, of a cooperative agreement for performance of basic, applied, or advanced research authorized by section 717 or another transaction authorized by subsection (a).

(B) INFORMATION DESCRIBED.—The information referred to in subparagraph (A) is the following:

(i) A proposal, proposal abstract, and supporting documents.

(ii) A business plan submitted on a confidential basis.

(iii) Technical information submitted on a confidential basis.

(f) REGULATIONS.—The Commandant shall prescribe regulations, as necessary, to carry out this section.

(g) ANNUAL REPORT.—On the date on which the President submits to Congress a budget pursuant to section 1105 of title 31, the Commandant shall submit to the Committees on Appropriations and Transportation and Infrastructure of the House of Representatives and the Committees on Appropriations and Commerce, Science, and Transportation of the Senate a report describing each use of the authority provided under this section during the most recently completed fiscal year, including details of each use consisting of—

(1) the amount of each transaction;

(2) the entities or organizations involved;

(3) the product or service received;

(4) the research project for which the product or service was required; and

(5) the extent of the cost sharing among Federal Government and non-Federal sources.

(Added Pub. L. 116–283, div. G, title LVXXXII [LXXXII], §8218(a), Jan. 1, 2021, 134 Stat. 4653.)

[1] See References in Text note below.

[2] So in original. Probably should be "subsection (b)(1)".

§720. VHF COMMUNICATIONS SERVICES

(a) The Secretary of the department in which the Coast Guard is operating may authorize a person providing commercial VHF communications services to place commercial VHF communications equipment on real property under the administrative control of the Coast Guard (including towers) subject to any terms agreed to by the parties. The Secretary and that commercial VHF communications service provider also may enter into an agreement providing for VHF communications services to the Coast Guard (including digital selective calling and radio direction finding services) at a discounted rate or price based on providing such access to real property under the administrative control of the Coast Guard.

(b) Commercial VHF communication equipment placed on real property under the administrative control of the Coast Guard under this section shall not interfere in any manner with any current or future Coast Guard communication equipment.

(c) Nothing in this section shall affect the rights or obligations of the United States under section 704(c) of the Telecommunications Act of 1996 (47 U.S.C. 332 note) with respect to the availability of property or under section 359(d) of the Communications Act of 1934 (47 U.S.C. 357(d)) with respect to charges for transmission of distress messages.

(Added and amended Pub. L. 116–283, div. G, title LVXXXV [LXXXV], §8501(a)(2), Jan. 1, 2021, 134 Stat. 4745.)

§721. RESPONSES TO SAFETY RECOMMENDATIONS

(a) IN GENERAL.—Not later than 90 days after the National Transportation Safety Board submits to the Commandant a recommendation, and supporting justification for such recommendation, relating to transportation safety, the Commandant shall submit to the National Transportation Safety Board a written response to the recommendation, including whether the Commandant—

(1) concurs with the recommendation;

(2) partially concurs with the recommendation; or

(3) does not concur with the recommendation.

(b) EXPLANATION OF CONCURRENCE.—The Commandant shall include in a response submitted under subsection (a)—

(1) with respect to a recommendation with which the Commandant concurs or partially concurs, an explanation of the actions the Commandant intends to take to implement such recommendation or part of such recommendation; and

(2) with respect to a recommendation with which the Commandant does not concur, the reasons the Commandant does not concur.

(c) FAILURE TO RESPOND.—If the National Transportation Safety Board has not received the written response required under subsection (a) by the end of the time period described in such subsection, the National Transportation Safety Board shall notify the Committee on Commerce, Science, and Transportation of the Senate and the Committee on Transportation and Infrastructure of the House of Representatives that such response has not been received.

(Added Pub. L. 117–263, div. K, title CXV, §11501(a), Dec. 23, 2022, 136 Stat. 4127.)

CHAPTER 9—ADMINISTRATION
SUBCHAPTER I—REAL AND PERSONAL PROPERTY

SUBCHAPTER II—MISCELLANEOUS

SUBCHAPTER I—REAL AND PERSONAL PROPERTY

§901. Disposal of certain material

(a) The Commandant subject to applicable regulations under subtitle I of title 40 and division C (except sections 3302, 3501(b), 3509, 3906, 4710, and 4711) of subtitle I of title 41 may dispose of, with or without charge, to the Coast Guard Auxiliary, including any incorporated unit thereof, to the sea-scout service of the Boy Scouts of America, and to any public body or private organization not organized for profit having an interest therein for historical or other special reasons, such obsolete or other material as may not be needed for the Coast Guard.

(b) The Commandant may, under regulations prescribed by the Secretary, sell apparatus or equipment manufactured by or in use in the Coast Guard, which is not readily procurable in the open market. The money received from such sale shall be deposited in the Treasury to the credit of the current appropriation from which purchase of similar apparatus or equipment is authorized.

(c)(1) The Commandant may—

(A) provide for the sale of recyclable materials that the Coast Guard holds;

(B) provide for the operation of recycling programs at Coast Guard installations; and

(C) designate Coast Guard installations that have qualified recycling programs for the purposes of subsection (d)(2).

(2) Recyclable materials shall be sold in accordance with sections 541–555 of title 40, except that the Commandant may conduct sales of materials for which the proceeds of sale will not exceed $5,000 under regulations prescribed by the Commandant.

(d)(1) Proceeds from the sale of recyclable materials at a Coast Guard installation shall be credited to funds available for operations and maintenance at that installation in amounts sufficient to cover operations, maintenance, recycling equipment, and overhead costs for processing recyclable materials at the installation.

(2) If, after funds are credited, a balance remains available to a Coast Guard installation and the installation has a qualified recycling program, not more than 50 percent of that balance may be used at the installation for projects for pollution abatement, energy conservation, and occupational safety and health activities. The cost of the project may not be greater than 50 percent of the amount permissible for a minor construction project.

(3) The remaining balance available to a Coast Guard installation may be transferred to the Coast Guard Morale, Welfare, and Recreation Program.

(e) If the balance available to the Coast Guard installation under this section at the end of a fiscal year is in excess of $200,000, the amount of that excess shall be deposited in the general fund of the Treasury as offsetting receipts of the Department in which the Coast Guard is operating and ascribed to Coast Guard activities.

(Aug. 4, 1949, ch. 393, 63 Stat. 547, §641; Oct. 31, 1951, ch. 654, §2(11), 65 Stat. 707; Pub. L. 97–295, §2(4), Oct. 12, 1982, 96 Stat. 1301; Pub. L. 102–587, title V, §5202, Nov. 4, 1992, 106 Stat. 5071; Pub. L. 104–324, title IV, §408, title XI, §1119, Oct. 19, 1996, 110 Stat. 3925, 3973; Pub. L. 107–217, §3(c)(3), Aug. 21, 2002, 116 Stat. 1298; Pub. L. 111–350, §5(c)(3), Jan. 4, 2011, 124 Stat. 3847; Pub. L. 114–120, title II,

§209(10), Feb. 8, 2016, 130 Stat. 41; renumbered §901, Pub. L. 115–282, title I, §107(b), Dec. 4, 2018, 132 Stat. 4205.)

§902. EMPLOYMENT OF DRAFTSMEN AND ENGINEERS

The Coast Guard may employ temporarily, at the seat of government, draftsmen and engineers for the preparation of plans and specifications for vessels, lighthouses, aids to navigation, and other projects for the Coast Guard that may be authorized or appropriated for by Congress, to be paid from the appropriations applicable to such projects.

(Aug. 4, 1949, ch. 393, 63 Stat. 550, §653; renumbered §902, Pub. L. 115–282, title I, §107(b), Dec. 4, 2018, 132 Stat. 4205.)

§903. USE OF CERTAIN APPROPRIATED FUNDS

(a) Funds appropriated to or for the use of the Coast Guard for procurement, construction, and improvement of facilities and for research and development shall remain available until expended.

(b) The Secretary may use any funds appropriated to or for the use of the Coast Guard for other construction purposes to restore, repair, or replace facilities that have been damaged or destroyed, including acquisition of sites.

(c) The Secretary may use any funds appropriated to or for the use of the Coast Guard for other construction purposes to acquire, construct, convert, extend, and install at Coast Guard installations and facilities, needed permanent or temporary public works, including the preparation of sites and the furnishing of appurtenances, utilities, and equipment, but excluding the construction of family quarters, costing not more than $200,000 for any one project.

(d) MINOR CONSTRUCTION AND IMPROVEMENT.—

(1) IN GENERAL.—Subject to the reporting requirements set forth in paragraph (2), each fiscal year the Secretary may expend from amounts made available for the operations and support of the Coast Guard not more than $1,500,000 for minor construction and improvement projects at any location.

(2) REPORT.—Not later than the date on which the President submits to Congress a budget under section 1105 of title 31 each year, the Secretary shall submit to the Committee on Transportation and Infrastructure of the House of Representatives and the Committee on Commerce, Science, and Transportation of the Senate a report describing each project carried out under paragraph (1), in the most recently concluded fiscal year, for which the amount expended under such paragraph for such project was more than $1,000,000. If no such project was carried out during a fiscal year, no report under this paragraph shall be required with respect to that fiscal year.

(Added Pub. L. 88–45, §2, June 21, 1963, 77 Stat. 68, §656; amended Pub. L. 93–283, §1(9), May 14, 1974, 88 Stat. 140; Pub. L. 112–213, title II, §212(a), (b)(1), Dec. 20, 2012, 126 Stat. 1552; Pub. L. 113–281, title II, §221(b)(2), Dec. 18, 2014, 128 Stat. 3038; renumbered §903, Pub. L. 115–282, title I, §107(b), Dec. 4, 2018, 132 Stat. 4205; Pub. L. 116–283, div. G, title LVXXXV [LXXXV], §8513(a)(2), Jan. 1, 2021, 134 Stat. 4760.)

§904. LOCAL HIRE

(a) Notwithstanding any other law, each contract awarded by the Coast Guard for construction or services to be performed in whole or in part in a State that has an unemployment rate in excess of the national average rate of unemployment (as determined by the Secretary of Labor) shall include a provision requiring the contractor to employ, for the purpose of performing that portion of the contract in that State, individuals who are local residents and who, in the case of any craft or trade, possess or would be able to acquire promptly the necessary skills. The Secretary of the department in which the Coast Guard is operating may waive the requirements of this subsection in the interest of national security or economic efficiency.

(b) LOCAL RESIDENT DEFINED.—As used in this section, "local resident" means a resident of, or an individual who commutes daily to, a State described in subsection (a).

(Added Pub. L. 101–225, title II, §206(a), Dec. 12, 1989, 103 Stat. 1912, §666; amended Pub. L. 107–296, title XVII, §1704(a), Nov. 25, 2002, 116 Stat. 2314; Pub. L. 112–213, title II, §217(10), Dec. 20, 2012, 126 Stat. 1558; renumbered §904, Pub. L. 115–282, title I, §107(b), Dec. 4, 2018, 132 Stat. 4205.)

§905. PROCUREMENT AUTHORITY FOR FAMILY HOUSING

(a) The Secretary is authorized—

(1) to acquire, subject to the availability of appropriations sufficient to cover its full obligations, real property or interests therein by purchase, lease for a term not to exceed 5 years, or otherwise, for use as Coast Guard family housing units, including the acquisition of condominium units, which may include the obligation to pay maintenance, repair, and other condominium-related fees; and

(2) to dispose of by sale, lease, or otherwise, any real property or interest therein used for Coast Guard family housing units for adequate consideration.

(b)(1) For the purposes of this section, a multiyear contract is a contract to lease Coast Guard family housing units for at least one, but not more than 5, fiscal years.

(2) The Secretary may enter into multiyear contracts under subsection (a) of this section whenever the Coast Guard finds that—

(A) the use of a contract will promote the efficiency of the Coast Guard family housing program and will result in reduced total costs under the contract; and

(B) there are realistic estimates of both the cost of the contract and the anticipated cost avoidance through the use of a multiyear contract.

(3) A multiyear contract authorized under subsection (a) of this section shall contain cancellation and termination provisions to the extent necessary to protect the best interests of the United States, and may include consideration of both recurring and nonrecurring costs. The contract may provide for a cancellation payment to be made. Amounts that were originally obligated for the cost of the contract may be used for cancellation or termination costs.

(Added Pub. L. 103–206, title III, §302(a), Dec. 20, 1993, 107 Stat. 2423, §670; renumbered §905, Pub. L. 115–282, title I, §107(b), Dec. 4, 2018, 132 Stat. 4205.)

§906. AIR STATION CAPE COD IMPROVEMENTS

The Secretary may expend funds for the repair, improvement, restoration, or replacement of those federally or nonfederally owned support buildings, including appurtenances, which are on leased or permitted real property constituting Coast Guard Air Station Cape Cod, located on Massachusetts Military Reservation, Cape Cod, Massachusetts.

(Added Pub. L. 103–206, title III, §303(a), Dec. 20, 1993, 107 Stat. 2423, §671; renumbered §906, Pub. L. 115–282, title I, §107(b), Dec. 4, 2018, 132 Stat. 4205.)

§907. LONG-TERM LEASE OF SPECIAL PURPOSE FACILITIES

(a) The Secretary is authorized, subject to the availability of appropriations, to enter into lease agreements to acquire real property or interests therein for a term not to exceed 20 years, inclusive of any automatic renewal clauses, for special purpose facilities, including, aids to navigation (hereafter in this section referred to as "ATON") sites, vessel traffic service (hereafter in this section referred to as "VTS") sensor sites, or National Distress System (hereafter in this section referred to as "NDS") high level antenna sites. These lease agreements shall include cancellation and termination provisions to the extent necessary to protect the best interests of the United States. Cancellation payment provisions may include consideration of both recurring and nonrecurring costs associated with the real property interests under the contract. These lease agreements may provide for a cancellation payment to be made. Amounts that were originally obligated for the cost of the contract may be used for cancellation or termination costs.

(b) For purposes of this section, the term "special purpose facilities" means any facilities used to carry out Coast Guard aviation, maritime, or navigation missions other than general purpose office and storage space facilities.

(c) In the case of ATON, VTS, or NDS sites, the Secretary may enter into multiyear lease agreements under subsection (a) of this section whenever the Secretary finds that—

(1) the use of such a lease agreement will promote the efficiency of the ATON, VTS, or NDS programs and will result in reduced total costs under the agreement;

(2) the minimum need for the real property or interest therein to be leased is expected to remain substantially unchanged during the contemplated lease period; and

(3) the estimates of both the cost of the lease and the anticipated cost avoidance through the use of a multiyear lease are realistic.

(Added Pub. L. 103–206, title III, §304(a), Dec. 20, 1993, 107 Stat. 2424, §672; amended Pub. L. 104–324, title VII, §746(d), Oct. 19, 1996, 110 Stat. 3943; Pub. L. 108–293, title II, §212(a), Aug. 9, 2004, 118 Stat. 1036; renumbered §907, Pub. L. 115–282, title I, §107(b), Dec. 4, 2018, 132 Stat. 4205.)

§908. LONG-TERM LEASE AUTHORITY FOR LIGHTHOUSE PROPERTY

(a) The Commandant may lease to non-Federal entities, including private individuals, lighthouse property under the administrative control of the Coast Guard for terms not to exceed 30 years. Consideration for the use and occupancy of lighthouse property leased under this section, and for the value of any utilities and services furnished to a lessee of such property by the Commandant, may consist, in whole or in part, of non-pecuniary remuneration including the improvement, alteration, restoration, rehabilitation, repair, and maintenance of the leased premises by the lessee. Section 1302 of title 40 shall not apply to leases issued by the Commandant under this section.

(b) Amounts received from leases made under this section, less expenses incurred, shall be deposited in the fund established under section 2946.

(Added Pub. L. 107–295, title IV, §417(a), Nov. 25, 2002, 116 Stat. 2122, §672a; amended Pub. L. 113–281, title II, §208(b), Dec. 18, 2014, 128 Stat. 3026; Pub. L. 115–232, div. C, title XXXV, §§3531(c)(4), 3533(e), Aug. 13, 2018, 132 Stat. 2320, 2321; renumbered §908 and amended Pub. L. 115–282, title I, §§107(b), 123(b)(2), Dec. 4, 2018, 132 Stat. 4205, 4240.)

§909. SMALL BOAT STATION RESCUE CAPABILITY

The Secretary shall ensure that each Coast Guard small boat station (including a seasonally operated station) maintains, within the area of responsibility for the station, at least 1 vessel that is fully capable of performing offshore rescue operations, taking into consideration prevailing weather, marine conditions, and depositional geologic features such as sand bars.

(Added Pub. L. 104–324, title III, §309(a), Oct. 19, 1996, 110 Stat. 3919, §673; renumbered §674, Pub. L. 107–295, title IV, §405(a)(1), Nov. 25, 2002, 116 Stat. 2115; amended Pub. L. 107–296, title XVII, §1704(a), (f)(1), Nov. 25, 2002, 116 Stat. 2314, 2316; Pub. L. 112–213, title II, §217(12), Dec. 20, 2012, 126 Stat. 1558; renumbered §909, Pub. L. 115–282, title I, §107(b), Dec. 4, 2018, 132 Stat. 4205.)

§910. SMALL BOAT STATION CLOSURES

(a) CLOSURES.—The Secretary may not close a Coast Guard multimission small boat station or subunit unless the Secretary—

(1) determines that—

(A) remaining search and rescue capabilities maintain the safety of the maritime public in the area of the station or subunit;

(B) regional or local prevailing weather and marine conditions, including water temperature or unusual tide and current conditions, do not require continued operation of the station or subunit; and

(C) Coast Guard search and rescue standards related to search and rescue response times are met; and

(2) provides an opportunity for public comment and for public meetings in the area of the station or subunit with regard to the decision to close the station or subunit.

(b) OPERATIONAL FLEXIBILITY.—The Secretary may implement any management efficiencies within the small boat station system, such as modifying the operational posture of units or reallocating resources as necessary to ensure the safety of the maritime public nationwide. No stations or subunits may be closed under this subsection except in accordance with subsection (a).

(Added Pub. L. 104–324, title III, §309(a), Oct. 19, 1996, 110 Stat. 3919, §674; renumbered §675, Pub. L. 107–295, title IV, §405(a)(1), Nov. 25, 2002, 116 Stat. 2115; amended Pub. L. 107–296, title XVII, §1704(a), Nov. 25, 2002, 116 Stat. 2314; Pub. L. 112–213, title II, §217(13), Dec. 20, 2012, 126 Stat. 1558; renumbered §910, Pub. L. 115–282, title I, §107(b), Dec. 4, 2018, 132 Stat. 4205.)

§911. SEARCH AND RESCUE CENTER STANDARDS

(a) The Secretary shall establish, implement, and maintain the minimum standards necessary for the safe operation of all Coast Guard search and rescue center facilities, including with respect to the following:

(1) The lighting, acoustics, and temperature in the facilities.

(2) The number of individuals on a shift in the facility assigned search and rescue responsibilities (including communications), which may be adjusted based on seasonal workload.

(3) The length of time an individual may serve on watch to minimize fatigue, based on the best scientific information available.

(4) The scheduling of individuals having search and rescue responsibilities to minimize fatigue of the individual when on duty in the facility.

(5) The workload of each individual engaged in search and rescue responsibilities in the facility.

(6) Stress management for the individuals assigned search and rescue responsibilities in the facilities.

(7) The design of equipment and facilities to minimize fatigue and enhance search and rescue operations.

(8) The acquisition and maintenance of interim search and rescue command center communications equipment.

(9) Any other requirements that the Secretary believes will increase the safe operation of the search and rescue centers.

(b) SENSE OF CONGRESS.—It is the sense of the Congress that the Secretary should establish, implement, and maintain minimum standards necessary to ensure that an individual on duty or watch in a Coast Guard search and rescue command center facility does not work more than 12 hours in a 24-hour period, except in an emergency or unforeseen circumstances.

(c) DEFINITION.—For the purposes of this section, the term "search and rescue center facility" means a Coast Guard shore facility that maintains a search and rescue mission coordination and communications watch.

(Added Pub. L. 107–295, title IV, §405(a)(2), Nov. 25, 2002, 116 Stat. 2115, §676; amended Pub. L. 111–207, §4(a)(3), July 27, 2010, 124 Stat. 2251; renumbered §911, Pub. L. 115–282, title I, §107(b), Dec. 4, 2018, 132 Stat. 4205.)

§912. AIR FACILITY CLOSURES

(a) CLOSURES.—

(1) IN GENERAL.—Beginning on January 1, 2018, the Secretary may not close a Coast Guard air facility, except as specified by this section.

(2) DETERMINATIONS.—The Secretary may not propose closing or terminating operations at a Coast Guard air facility unless the Secretary determines that—

(A) remaining search and rescue capabilities maintain the safety of the maritime public in the area of the air facility;

(B) regional or local prevailing weather and marine conditions, including water temperatures or unusual tide and current conditions, do not require continued operation of the air facility; and

(C) Coast Guard search and rescue standards related to search and response times are met.

(3) PUBLIC NOTICE AND COMMENT.—

(A) IN GENERAL.—Prior to closing an air facility, the Secretary shall provide opportunities for public comment, including the convening of public meetings in communities in the area of responsibility of the air facility with regard to the proposed closure or cessation of operations at the air facility.

(B) PUBLIC MEETINGS.—Prior to convening a public meeting under subparagraph (A), the Secretary shall notify each congressional office representing any portion of the area of responsibility of the air station that is the subject to such public meeting of the schedule and location of such public meeting.

(4) NOTICE TO CONGRESS.—Prior to closure, cessation of operations, or any significant reduction in personnel and use of a Coast Guard air facility that is in operation on or after December 31, 2017, the Secretary shall—

(A) submit to the Congress a proposal for such closure, cessation, or reduction in operations along with the budget of the President submitted to Congress under section 1105(a) of title 31 that includes—

(i) a discussion of the determination made by the Secretary pursuant to paragraph (2); and

(ii) a report summarizing the public comments received by the Secretary under paragraph (3) [1]

(B) not later than 7 days after the date a proposal for an air facility is submitted pursuant to subparagraph (A), provide written notice of such proposal to each of the following:

(i) Each member of the House of Representatives who represents a district in which the air facility is located.

(ii) Each member of the Senate who represents a State in which the air facility is located.

(iii) Each member of the House of Representatives who represents a district in which assets of the air facility conduct search and rescue operations.

(iv) Each member of the Senate who represents a State in which assets of the air facility conduct search and rescue operations.

(v) The Committee on Appropriations of the House of Representatives.

(vi) The Committee on Transportation and Infrastructure of the House of Representatives.

(vii) The Committee on Appropriations of the Senate.

(viii) The Committee on Commerce, Science, and Transportation of the Senate.

(5) CONGRESSIONAL REVIEW.—The Secretary may not close, cease operations, or significantly reduce personnel and use of a Coast Guard air facility for which a written notice is provided under paragraph (4)(A) until a period of 18 months beginning on the date on which such notice is provided has elapsed.

(b) OPERATIONAL FLEXIBILITY.—The Secretary may implement any reasonable management efficiencies within the air station and air facility network, such as modifying the operational posture of units or reallocating resources as necessary to ensure the safety of the maritime public nationwide.

(Added Pub. L. 114–120, title II, §208(a), Feb. 8, 2016, 130 Stat. 38, §676a; amended Pub. L. 114–328, div. C, title XXXV, §3503(a), Dec. 23, 2016, 130 Stat. 2775; renumbered §912 and amended Pub. L. 115–282, title I, §107(b), title III, §319, Dec. 4, 2018, 132 Stat. 4205, 4252.)

---

[1] So in original. Probably should be followed by "; and".

§913. TURNKEY SELECTION PROCEDURES

(a) AUTHORITY TO USE.—The Secretary may use one-step turnkey selection procedures for the purpose of entering into contracts for construction projects.

(b) DEFINITIONS.—In this section, the following definitions apply:

(1) The term "one-step turnkey selection procedures" means procedures used for the selection of a contractor on the basis of price and other evaluation criteria to perform, in accordance with the provisions of a firm fixed-price contract, both the design and construction of a facility using performance specifications supplied by the Secretary.

(2) The term "construction" includes the construction, procurement, development, conversion, or extension of any facility.

(3) The term "facility" means a building, structure, or other improvement to real property.

(Added Pub. L. 109–241, title II, §205(a), July 11, 2006, 120 Stat. 521, §677; renumbered §913, Pub. L. 115–282, title I, §107(b), Dec. 4, 2018, 132 Stat. 4205.)

---

§914. DISPOSITION OF INFRASTRUCTURE RELATED TO E–LORAN

(a) IN GENERAL.—Notwithstanding any other provision of law, the Commandant may dismantle or dispose of any real or personal property under the administrative control of the Coast Guard and used for the LORAN–C system.

(b) RESTRICTION.—No action described in subsection (a) may be taken unless and until—

(1) the Commandant notifies the Secretary of Transportation and the Secretary of Defense in writing of the proposed dismantling or disposal of a LORAN–C system; and

(2) a period of 90 calendar days expires following the day on which the notice has been submitted.

(c) RECEIPT OF NOTIFICATION.—If, not later than 90 calendar days of receipt of the written notification under subsection (b), the Secretary of Transportation or the Secretary of Defense notifies the Commandant, in writing, of a determination under section 312(d) of title 49 that the property is required to provide a positioning, navigation, and timing system to provide redundant capability in the event the Global Positioning System signals are disrupted, the Commandant shall transfer the property to the Department of Transportation without any consideration.

(d) NOTIFICATION EXPIRATION.—If, at the end of the 90 calendar day period no notification under subsection (b) has been received, the Commandant shall notify the Committee on Transportation and Infrastructure and the Committee on Appropriations in the House of Representatives and the Committee on Commerce, Science, and Transportation and the Committee on Appropriations of the Senate that the period in subsection (b)(2) has expired, and may proceed with the dismantling and disposal of the personal property, and disposing of the real property in accordance with section 2945 of this title.

(e) EXCEPTION.—The prohibition on actions in subsection (b) does not apply to actions necessary for the safety of human life.

(Added Pub. L. 114–120, title VI, §610(a)(1), Feb. 8, 2016, 130 Stat. 83, §681; renumbered §914, Pub. L. 115–282, title I, §107(b), Dec. 4, 2018, 132 Stat. 4205; amended Pub. L. 116–283, div. G, title LVXXXII [LXXXII], §8216, Jan. 1, 2021, 134 Stat. 4653; Pub. L. 117–263, div. K, title CXII, §11211, Dec. 23, 2022, 136 Stat. 4012.)

SUBCHAPTER II—MISCELLANEOUS

§931. OATHS REQUIRED FOR BOARDS

The members of a retiring board, selection board, examining board, and any other board authorized to be assembled pursuant to this title shall be sworn to discharge their duties honestly and impartially, the oath to be administered to the members by the President or other presiding officer of the board, and to him by the junior member or recorder.

(Aug. 4, 1949, ch. 393, 63 Stat. 545, §635; renumbered §931, Pub. L. 115–282, title I, §107(b), Dec. 4, 2018, 132 Stat. 4205.)

§932. ADMINISTRATION OF OATHS

(a) Such commissioned and warrant officers of the Coast Guard as may be designated by the Commandant may, pursuant to rules prescribed by the Commandant, exercise the general powers of a notary public in the administration of oaths for the following purposes:

(1) execution, acknowledgment, and attestation of instruments and papers, oaths of allegiance in connection with recruiting, oaths in connection with courts and boards, and all other notarial acts in connection with the proper execution of Coast Guard functions;

(2) execution, acknowledgment, and attestation of instruments and papers, and all other notarial acts in time of war or national emergency; and

(3) execution, acknowledgment, and attestation of instruments and papers, and all other notarial acts in Alaska and places beyond the continental limits of the United States where the Coast Guard is serving.

(b) No fee of any character shall be charged by any commissioned or warrant officer for performing notarial acts. The signature and indication of grade of any commissioned or warrant officer performing any notarial act shall be prima facie evidence of his authority.

(Aug. 4, 1949, ch. 393, 63 Stat. 545, §636; renumbered §932, Pub. L. 115–282, title I, §107(b), Dec. 4, 2018, 132 Stat. 4205.)

§933. COAST GUARD ENSIGNS AND PENNANTS

(a) Vessels and aircraft authorized by the Secretary shall be distinguished from other vessels and aircraft by an ensign, pennant, or other identifying insignia of such design as prescribed by the Secretary. Such ensign, pennant, or other identifying insignia shall be displayed in accordance with regulations prescribed by the Secretary.

(b) No vessel or aircraft without authority shall carry, hoist, or display any ensign, pennant, or other identifying insignia prescribed for, or intended to resemble, any ensign, pennant, or other identifying insignia prescribed for Coast Guard vessels or aircraft. An individual violating this subsection shall be fined not more than $5,000, or imprisoned for not more than two years, or both.

(Aug. 4, 1949, ch. 393, 63 Stat. 546, §638; Pub. L. 111–281, title II, §213(b), Oct. 15, 2010, 124 Stat. 2915; renumbered §933, Pub. L. 115–282, title I, §107(b), Dec. 4, 2018, 132 Stat. 4205; Pub. L. 116–283, div. G, title LVXXXV [LXXXV], §8505(a)(9), Jan. 1, 2021, 134 Stat. 4748.)

§934. PENALTY FOR UNAUTHORIZED USE OF WORDS "COAST GUARD"

No individual, association, partnership, or corporation shall, without authority of the Commandant, use the combination of letters "USCG" or "USCGR", the words "Coast Guard," "United States Coast Guard," "Coast Guard Reserve," "United States Coast Guard Reserve," "Coast Guard Auxiliary," "United States Coast Guard Auxiliary," "Lighthouse Service," "Life Saving Service," or any combination or variation of such letters or words alone or with other letters or words, as the name under which he or it shall do business, for the purpose of trade, or by way of advertisement to induce the effect of leading the public to believe that any such individual, association, partnership, or corporation has any connection with the Coast Guard. No individual, association, partnership, or corporation shall falsely advertise, or otherwise represent falsely by any device whatsoever, that any project or business in which he or it is engaged, or product which he or it manufactures, deals in, or sells, has been in any way endorsed, authorized, or approved by the Coast Guard. Every person violating this section shall be fined not more than $10,000, or imprisoned not more than one year, or both.

(Aug. 4, 1949, ch. 393, 63 Stat. 546, §639; Aug. 3, 1950, ch. 536, §30, 64 Stat. 408; Pub. L. 113–281, title II, §205(b), Dec. 18, 2014, 128 Stat. 3025; renumbered §934, Pub. L. 115–282, title I, §107(b), Dec. 4, 2018, 132 Stat. 4205.)

§935. COAST GUARD BAND RECORDINGS FOR COMMERCIAL SALE

(a) The Coast Guard band may produce recordings for commercial sale.

(b) Amounts received as proceeds from the sale of any such recordings may be credited to applicable appropriations of the Coast Guard for expenses of the Coast Guard band.

(c) The Secretary shall prescribe regulations governing the accounting of such proceeds.

(Added Pub. L. 101–510, div. A, title III, §327(d)(1), Nov. 5, 1990, 104 Stat. 1532, §640; renumbered §935, Pub. L. 115–282, title I, §107(b), Dec. 4, 2018, 132 Stat. 4205.)

§936. CONFIDENTIALITY OF MEDICAL QUALITY ASSURANCE RECORDS; QUALIFIED IMMUNITY FOR PARTICIPANTS

(a) In this section—

(1) "medical quality assurance program" means any activity carried out by or for the Coast Guard to assess the quality of medical care, including activities conducted by individuals, military medical or dental treatment facility committees, or other review bodies responsible for quality assurance, credentials, infection control, patient care assessment (including treatment procedures, blood, drugs, and therapeutics) medical records, health resources management review and identification and prevention of medical or dental incidents and risks.

(2) "medical quality assurance record" means the proceedings, records, minutes, and reports that emanate from quality assurance program activities described in paragraph (1) and are produced or compiled by the Coast Guard as part of a medical quality assurance program.

(3) "health care provider" means any military or civilian health care professional who, under regulations prescribed by the Secretary, is granted clinical practice privileges to

provide health care services in a military medical or dental treatment facility or who is licensed or certified to perform health care services by a governmental board or agency or professional health care society or organization.

(b) Medical quality assurance records created by or for the Coast Guard as part of a medical quality assurance program are confidential and privileged. The records may not be disclosed to any person or entity except as provided in subsection (d).

(c)(1) Medical quality assurance records are not subject to discovery and may not be admitted into evidence in any judicial or administrative proceeding, except as provided in subsection (d).

(2) Except as provided in this section, an individual who reviews or creates medical quality assurance records for the Coast Guard or who participates in any proceeding that reviews or creates the records may not testify in any judicial or administrative proceeding with respect to the records or with respect to any finding, recommendation, evaluation, opinion, or action taken by that person in connection with the records.

(d)(1) Subject to paragraph (2), a medical quality assurance record may be disclosed, and an individual referred to in subsection (c) may testify in connection with a record only as follows:

(A) To a Federal executive agency or private organization, if necessary to license, accredit, or monitor Coast Guard health care facilities.

(B) To an administrative or judicial proceeding commenced by a present or former Coast Guard or Coast Guard assigned Public Health Service health care provider concerning the termination, suspension, or limitation of clinical privileges of the health care provider.

(C) To a governmental board or agency or to a professional health care society or organization, if necessary to perform licensing, or privileging, or to monitor professional standards for a health care provider who is or was a member or an employee of the Coast Guard or the Public Health Service assigned to the Coast Guard.

(D) To a hospital, medical center, or other institution that provides health care services, if necessary to assess the professional qualifications of any health care provider who is or was a member or employee of the Coast Guard or the Public Health Service assigned to the Coast Guard and who has applied for or been granted authority or employment to provide health care services in or on behalf of the institution.

(E) To an officer, member, employee, or contractor of the Coast Guard or the Public Health Service assigned to the Coast Guard if for official purposes.

(F) To a criminal or civil law enforcement agency or instrumentality charged under applicable law with the protection of the public health or safety, if a qualified representative of the agency or instrumentality makes a written request that the record or testimony be provided for a purpose authorized by law.

(G) In an administrative or judicial proceeding commenced by a criminal or civil law enforcement agency or instrumentality referred to in subparagraph (F), but only with respect to the subject of the proceeding.

(2) Except in a quality assurance action, the identity of any individual receiving health care services from the Coast Guard or the identity of any other individual associated with

the agency for the purposes of a medical quality assurance program that is disclosed in a medical quality assurance record shall be deleted from that record or document before any disclosure of the record is made outside the Coast Guard. This requirement does not apply to the release of information under section 552a of title 5.

(e) Except as provided in this section, a person having possession of or access to a record or testimony described by this section may not disclose the contents of the record or testimony.

(f) Medical quality assurance records may not be made available to any person under section 552 of title 5.

(g) An individual who participates in or provides information to an individual that reviews or creates medical quality assurance records is not civilly liable for participating or providing the information if the participation or provision of information was in good faith based on prevailing professional standards at the time the medical quality assurance program activity took place.

(h) Nothing in this section shall be construed as—

(1) authority to withhold from any person aggregate statistical information regarding the results of Coast Guard medical quality assurance programs;

(2) authority to withhold any medical quality assurance record from a committee of either House of Congress, any joint committee of Congress, or the Government Accountability Office if the record pertains to any matter within their respective jurisdictions;

(3) limiting access to the information in a record created and maintained outside a medical quality assurance program, including a patient's medical records, on the grounds that the information was presented during meetings of a review body that are part of a medical quality assurance program.

(i) Except as otherwise provided in this section, an individual who willfully discloses a medical quality assurance record knowing that the record is a medical quality assurance record, is liable to the United States Government for a civil penalty of not more than $3,000 in the case of a first offense and not more than $20,000 in the case of a subsequent offense.

(Added Pub. L. 102–587, title V, §5203(a), Nov. 4, 1992, 106 Stat. 5072, §645; amended Pub. L. 104–324, title VII, §746(b), Oct. 19, 1996, 110 Stat. 3943; Pub. L. 108–271, §8(b), July 7, 2004, 118 Stat. 814; renumbered §936, Pub. L. 115–282, title I, §107(b), Dec. 4, 2018, 132 Stat. 4205.)

§937. ADMIRALTY CLAIMS AGAINST THE UNITED STATES

(a) The Secretary may consider, ascertain, adjust, determine, compromise, or settle, and pay in an amount not more than $425,000, an admiralty claim against the United States for—

(1) damage caused by a vessel in the Coast Guard service or by other property under the jurisdiction of the Department in which the Coast Guard is operating;

(2) compensation for towage and salvage services, including contract salvage, rendered to a vessel in the Coast Guard service or to other property under the jurisdiction of the Department in which the Coast Guard is operating; or

(3) damage caused by a maritime tort committed by an agent or employee of the

Department in which the Coast Guard is operating or by property under the jurisdiction of that Department.

(b) Upon acceptance of payment by the claimant, the settlement or compromise of a claim under this section is final and conclusive notwithstanding any other law.

(c) If a claim under this section is settled or compromised for more than $100,000, the Secretary shall certify it to Congress.

(Aug. 4, 1949, ch. 393, 63 Stat. 548, §646; Pub. L. 86–533, §1(3)(A), June 29, 1960, 74 Stat. 245; Pub. L. 92–417, §2(a), Aug. 29, 1972, 86 Stat. 655; renumbered §937, Pub. L. 115–282, title I, §107(b), Dec. 4, 2018, 132 Stat. 4205; Pub. L. 116–283, div. G, title LVXXXII [LXXXII], §8212(a), Jan. 1, 2021, 134 Stat. 4649.)

§938. CLAIMS FOR DAMAGE TO PROPERTY OF THE UNITED STATES

The Secretary may consider, ascertain, adjust, determine, compromise, or settle claims for damage cognizable in admiralty in a district court of the United States and all claims for damage caused by a vessel or floating object, to property of the United States under the jurisdiction of the Coast Guard or property for which the Coast Guard may have assumed, by contract or otherwise, any obligation to respond for damage thereto. The Secretary is further authorized to receive in payment of any such claim the amount due the United States pursuant to determination, compromise, or settlement as herein authorized and, upon acceptance of such payment but not until then, such determination, settlement, or compromise of such claim shall be final and conclusive for all purposes, any law to the contrary notwithstanding. All such payments shall be deposited in the Treasury of the United States as miscellaneous receipts. The Secretary is further authorized to execute on behalf of the United States and to deliver in exchange for such payment a full release of such claim. This section, as respects the determination, compromise, settlement, and payment of claims, shall be supplementary to, and not in lieu of, all other provisions of law authorizing the determination, compromise, or settlement of claims for damage to property hereinabove described. No settlement or compromise where there is involved a payment in the net amount of over $425,000 is authorized by this section.

(Aug. 4, 1949, ch. 393, 63 Stat. 549, §647, Pub. L. 86–533, §1(3)(B), June 29, 1960, 74 Stat. 245; Pub. L. 94–546, §1(34), Oct. 18, 1976, 90 Stat. 2521; Pub. L. 98–557, §17(b)(3)(A), Oct. 30, 1984, 98 Stat. 2868; renumbered §938, Pub. L. 115–282, title I, §107(b), Dec. 4, 2018, 132 Stat. 4205; Pub. L. 116–283, div. G, title LVXXXII [LXXXII], §8212(b), Jan. 1, 2021, 134 Stat. 4650.)

§939. ACCOUNTING FOR INDUSTRIAL WORK

(a) IN GENERAL.—The Secretary may prescribe regulations governing accounting for industrial work, including charges for overhead for civilian labor and for maintenance of industrial plant and equipment, performed at the Coast Guard Yard or such similar Coast Guard industrial establishments as he may designate. Any orders placed for such industrial work shall be covered by a transfer or advance of funds to cover the estimated cost thereof, and shall be credited to such accounts as may be necessary and established by the Secretary to carry out the provisions of this section. Accounts so established shall be available for materials, supplies, or equipment, and civilian labor, including overhead and maintenance, required in performing the work ordered. Upon completion of an order an adjustment will be made to make the amount transferred or advanced equal to the actual cost as computed in accordance with the accounting regulations prescribed by the Secretary or in accordance with subsection (b).

(b) INCENTIVE CONTRACTS.—

(1) The parties to an order for industrial work to be performed by the Coast Guard Yard or a Coast Guard industrial establishment designated under subsection (a) may enter into an order or a cost-plus-incentive-fee order in accordance with this subsection.

(2) If such parties enter into such an order or a cost-plus-incentive-fee order, an agreed-upon amount of any adjustment described in subsection (a) may be distributed as an incentive to the wage-grade industrial employees who complete the order.

(3) Before entering into such an order or cost-plus-incentive-fee order such parties must agree that the wage-grade employees of the Coast Guard Yard or Coast Guard industrial establishment will take action to improve the delivery schedule or technical performance agreed to in the order for industrial work to which such parties initially agreed.

(4) Notwithstanding any other provision of law, if the industrial workforce of the Coast Guard Yard or Coast Guard industrial establishment satisfies the performance target established in such an order or cost-plus-incentive-fee order—

(A) the adjustment to be made pursuant to subsection (a) shall be reduced by an agreed-upon amount and distributed to such wage-grade industrial employees; and

(B) the remainder of the adjustment shall be credited to the appropriation for such order current at that time.

(Aug. 4, 1949, ch. 393, 63 Stat. 549, §648; renumbered §939 and amended Pub. L. 115–282, title I, §107(b), title III, §307, Dec. 4, 2018, 132 Stat. 4205, 4247.)

§940. SUPPLIES AND EQUIPMENT FROM STOCK

Supplies and equipment for special work of the Coast Guard may be furnished from general stock and the applicable appropriation reimbursed therefor from the respective appropriations for such special work.

(Aug. 4, 1949, ch. 393, 63 Stat. 550, §649; renumbered §940, Pub. L. 115–282, title I, §107(b), Dec. 4, 2018, 132 Stat. 4205.)

§941. COAST GUARD SUPPLY FUND

(a) A Coast Guard Supply Fund is authorized. The Secretary may prescribe regulations for designating the classification of materials to be stocked. In these regulations, whenever the fund is extended to include items not previously stocked, or spare parts obtained as part of a procurement under a different account of major items such as vessels or aircraft, whether or not such parts were previously stocked, the Secretary may authorize an increase in the existing capital of the fund by the value of such usable materials transferred thereto from Coast Guard inventories carried in other accounts. Except for the materials so transferred, the fund shall be charged with the cost of materials purchased or otherwise acquired. The fund shall be credited with the value of materials consumed, issued for use, sold, or otherwise disposed of, such values to be determined on a basis that will approximately cover the cost thereof.

(b) Obligations may, without regard to fiscal year limitations, be incurred against anticipated reimbursement to the Coast Guard Supply Fund in such amount and for such period, as the Secretary, with approval of the Director of the Office of Management and Budget, may determine to be necessary to maintain stock levels consistently with planned operations for the next year.

(Aug. 4, 1949, ch. 393, 63 Stat. 550, §650; Aug. 7, 1956, ch. 1023, §1(a), 70 Stat. 1077; Pub. L. 91–278, §1(13), June 12, 1970, 84 Stat. 306; Pub. L. 94–546, §1(35), Oct. 18, 1976, 90 Stat. 2521; Pub. L. 96–376, §5, Oct. 3, 1980, 94 Stat. 1509; renumbered §941, Pub. L. 115–282, title I, §107(b), Dec. 4, 2018, 132 Stat. 4205.)

§942. PUBLIC AND COMMERCIAL VESSELS AND OTHER WATERCRAFT; SALE OF FUEL, SUPPLIES, AND SERVICES

The Secretary under such regulations as he may prescribe, may sell to public and commercial vessels and other watercraft, such fuel, supplies and furnish such services as may be required to meet the necessities of the vessel or watercraft if such vessel or watercraft is unable—

(1) to procure the fuel, supplies, or services from other sources at its present location; and

(2) to proceed to the nearest port where they may be obtained without endangering the safety of the ship, the health and comfort of its personnel, or the safe condition of the property carried aboard.

Sales under this section shall be at such prices as the Secretary considers reasonable. Payment will be made on a cash basis or on such other basis as will reasonably assure prompt payment. Amounts received from such a sale shall, unless otherwise directed by another provision of law, be credited to the current appropriation concerned and are available for the same purposes as that appropriation.

(Added Pub. L. 86–159, §1, Aug. 14, 1959, 73 Stat. 357, §654; amended Pub. L. 89–444, §1(22), June 9, 1966, 80 Stat. 197; renumbered §942, Pub. L. 115–282, title I, §107(b), Dec. 4, 2018, 132 Stat. 4205.)

§943. ARMS AND AMMUNITION; IMMUNITY FROM TAXATION

No tax on the sale or transfer of firearms, pistols, revolvers, shells, or cartridges may be imposed on such articles when bought with funds appropriated for the Coast Guard.

(Added Pub. L. 87–526, §1(6), July 10, 1962, 76 Stat. 142, §655; amended Pub. L. 94–546, §1(37), Oct. 18, 1976, 90 Stat. 2522; renumbered §943, Pub. L. 115–282, title I, §107(b), Dec. 4, 2018, 132 Stat. 4205.)

§944. CONFIDENTIAL INVESTIGATIVE EXPENSES

Not more than $250,000 each fiscal year appropriated for the operations and support of the Coast Guard shall be available for investigative expenses of a confidential character, to be expended on the approval or authority of the Commandant and payment to be made on the Commandant's certificate of necessity for confidential purposes, and the Commandant's determination shall be final and conclusive upon the accounting officers of the Government.

(Added Pub. L. 93–283, §1(10), May 14, 1974, 88 Stat. 140, §658; amended Pub. L. 108–293, title II, §221,

Aug. 9, 2004, 118 Stat. 1040; renumbered §944 and amended Pub. L. 115–282, title I, §107(b), title III, §308, Dec. 4, 2018, 132 Stat. 4205, 4248; Pub. L. 116–283, div. G, title LVXXXV [LXXXV], §8513(a)(3), Jan. 1, 2021, 134 Stat. 4760.)

§945. Assistance to film producers

(a) Notwithstanding any other provision of law, when the Secretary determines that it is appropriate, and that it will not interfere with Coast Guard missions, the Secretary may conduct operations with Coast Guard vessels, aircraft, facilities, or personnel, in such a way as to give assistance to film producers. As used in this section, "film producers" includes commercial or noncommercial producers of material for cinema, television, or videotape.

(b) The Secretary shall keep account of costs incurred as a result of providing assistance to film producers, not including costs which would otherwise be incurred in Coast Guard operations or training, or shall estimate such costs in advance, and such costs shall be paid to the Secretary by the film producers who request such assistance, on terms determined by the Secretary. The Secretary may waive costs not exceeding $200 for one production, and may waive other costs related to noncommercial productions which the Secretary determines to be in the public interest. The Secretary shall reimburse the amounts collected under this section to the Coast Guard appropriation account under which the costs were incurred.

(Added Pub. L. 100–448, §29(a), Sept. 28, 1988, 102 Stat. 1849, §659; renumbered §945, Pub. L. 115–282, title I, §107(b), Dec. 4, 2018, 132 Stat. 4205.)

§946. User fees

(a) A fee or charge for a service or thing of value provided by the Coast Guard shall be prescribed as provided in section 9701 of title 31.

(b) Amounts collected by the Secretary for a service or thing of value provided by the Coast Guard shall be deposited in the general fund of the Treasury as proprietary receipts of the department in which the Coast Guard is operating and ascribed to Coast Guard activities.

(c) In addition to the collection of fees and charges established under this section, the Secretary may recover from the person liable for the fee or charge the costs of collecting delinquent payments of the fee or charge, and enforcement costs associated with delinquent payments of the fees and charges.

(d)(1) The Secretary may employ any Federal, State, or local agency or instrumentality, or any private enterprise or business, to collect a fee or charge established under this section.

(2) A private enterprise or business employed by the Secretary to collect fees or charges—

(A) shall be subject to reasonable terms and conditions agreed to by the Secretary and the enterprise or business;

(B) shall provide appropriate accounting to the Secretary; and

(C) may not institute litigation as part of that collection.

(e)(1) In addition to the collection of fees and charges established under this section, in the provision of a service or thing of value by the Coast Guard the Secretary may accept in-kind transportation, travel, and subsistence.

(2) The value of in-kind transportation, travel, and subsistence accepted under this paragraph may not exceed applicable per diem rates set forth in regulations prescribed under section 464 of title 37.

(f) The Secretary shall account for the agency's costs of collecting a fee or charge as a reimbursable expense, subject to the availability of appropriations, and the costs shall be credited to the account from which expended.

(g) Before January 1 of each year, the Secretary shall submit a report to the Committee on Transportation and Infrastructure of the House of Representatives and the Committee on Commerce, Science, and Transportation of the Senate that includes—

(1) a verification of each activity for which a fee or charge is collected under any law stating—

(A) the amount collected in the prior fiscal year; and

(B) that the amount spent on that activity in that fiscal year is not less than the amount collected; and

(2) the amount expected to be collected under any law in the current fiscal year for each activity for which a fee or charge is expected to be collected.

(h) In this section the term "costs of collecting a fee or charge" includes the reasonable administrative, accounting, personnel, contract, equipment, supply, training, and travel expenses of calculating, assessing, collecting, enforcing, reviewing, adjusting, and reporting on a fee or charge.

(Added Pub. L. 99–509, title V, §5102(a)(3), Oct. 21, 1986, 100 Stat. 1926, §664; amended Pub. L. 101–225, title II, §211, Dec. 12, 1989, 103 Stat. 1914; Pub. L. 107–295, title IV, §408(a)(3), Nov. 25, 2002, 116 Stat. 2117; Pub. L. 108–293, title II, §206, Aug. 9, 2004, 118 Stat. 1033; Pub. L. 113–281, title III, §311(b), Dec. 18, 2014, 128 Stat. 3048; renumbered §946, Pub. L. 115–282, title I, §107(b), Dec. 4, 2018, 132 Stat. 4205.)

§947. Vessel construction bonding requirements

The Secretary or the Commandant may require bid, payment, performance, payment and performance, or completion bonds or other financial instruments from contractors for construction, alteration, repair, or maintenance of Coast Guard vessels if—

(1) the bond is required by law; or

(2) the Secretary or Commandant determines after investigation that the amount of the bond in excess of 20 percent of the value of the base contract quantity excluding options, would not prevent a responsible bidder or offeror from competing for award of the contract.

(Added Pub. L. 101–595, title III, §306(a), Nov. 16, 1990, 104 Stat. 2985, §667; renumbered §947, Pub. L. 115–282, title I, §107(b), Dec. 4, 2018, 132 Stat. 4205.)

§948. Contracts for medical care for retirees, dependents, and

SURVIVORS: ALTERNATIVE DELIVERY OF HEALTH CARE

(a) The Secretary may contract for the delivery of health care to which covered beneficiaries are entitled under chapter 55 of title 10. The Secretary may enter into a contract under this section with any of the following:

    (1) Health maintenance organizations.

    (2) Preferred provider organizations.

    (3) Individual providers, individual medical facilities, or insurers.

    (4) Consortiums of these providers, facilities, or insurers.

(b) A contract entered into under this section may provide for the delivery of—

    (1) selected health care services;

    (2) total health care services for selected covered beneficiaries; or

    (3) total health care services for all covered beneficiaries who reside in a geographic area designated by the Secretary.

(c) The Secretary may prescribe a premium, deductible, copayment, or other change for health care provided under this section.

(Added Pub. L. 101–595, title III, §319(a), Nov. 16, 1990, 104 Stat. 2989, §668; renumbered §948, Pub. L. 115–282, title I, §107(b), Dec. 4, 2018, 132 Stat. 4205.)

§949. TELEPHONE INSTALLATION AND CHARGES

Under regulations prescribed by the Secretary, amounts appropriated to the Department of Homeland Security are available to install, repair, and maintain telephone wiring in residences owned or leased by the United States Government and, if necessary for national defense purposes in other private residences.

(Added Pub. L. 102–587, title V, §5204(a), Nov. 4, 1992, 106 Stat. 5074, §669; amended Pub. L. 107–296, title XVII, §1704(a), Nov. 25, 2002, 116 Stat. 2314; renumbered §949, Pub. L. 115–282, title I, §107(b), Dec. 4, 2018, 132 Stat. 4205.)

§950. DESIGNATION, POWERS, AND ACCOUNTABILITY OF DEPUTY DISBURSING OFFICIALS

(a)(1) Subject to paragraph (3), a disbursing official of the Coast Guard may designate a deputy disbursing official—

    (A) to make payments as the agent of the disbursing official;

    (B) to sign checks drawn on disbursing accounts of the Secretary of the Treasury; and

    (C) to carry out other duties required under law.

(2) The penalties for misconduct that apply to a disbursing official apply to a deputy disbursing official designated under this subsection.

(3) A disbursing official may make a designation under paragraph (1) only with the approval of the Secretary.

(b)(1) If a disbursing official of the Coast Guard dies, becomes disabled, or is separated from office, a deputy disbursing official may continue the accounts and payments in the name of the former disbursing official until the last day of the second month after the month in which the death, disability, or separation occurs. The accounts and payments shall be allowed, audited, and settled as provided by law. The Secretary of the Treasury shall honor checks signed in the name of the former disbursing official in the same way as if the former disbursing official had continued in office.

(2) The deputy disbursing official, and not the former disbursing official or the estate of the former disbursing official, is liable for the actions of the deputy disbursing official under this subsection.

(c)(1) Except as provided in paragraph (2), this section does not apply to the Coast Guard when section 2773 of title 10 applies to the Coast Guard by reason of the operation of the Coast Guard as a service in the Navy.

(2) A designation of a deputy disbursing official under subsection (a) that is made while the Coast Guard is not operating as a service in the Navy continues in effect for purposes of section 2773 of title 10 while the Coast Guard operates as a service in the Navy unless and until the designation is terminated by the disbursing official who made the designation or an official authorized to approve such a designation under subsection (a)(3) of such section.

(Added Pub. L. 104–201, div. A, title X, §1009(a)(2)(A), Sept. 23, 1996, 110 Stat. 2634, §673; amended Pub. L. 107–296, title XVII, §1704(a), Nov. 25, 2002, 116 Stat. 2314; Pub. L. 112–213, title II, §217(11), Dec. 20, 2012, 126 Stat. 1558; renumbered §950, Pub. L. 115–282, title I, §107(b), Dec. 4, 2018, 132 Stat. 4205.)

§951. AIRCRAFT ACCIDENT INVESTIGATIONS

(a) IN GENERAL.—Whenever the Commandant conducts an accident investigation of an accident involving an aircraft under the jurisdiction of the Commandant, the records and report of the investigation shall be treated in accordance with this section.

(b) PUBLIC DISCLOSURE OF CERTAIN ACCIDENT INVESTIGATION INFORMATION.—

(1) IN GENERAL.—Subject to paragraph (2), the Commandant, upon request, shall publicly disclose unclassified tapes, scientific reports, and other factual information pertinent to an aircraft accident investigation.

(2) CONDITIONS.—The Commandant shall only disclose information requested pursuant to paragraph (1) if the Commandant determines—

(A) that such tapes, reports, or other information would be included within and releasable with the final accident investigation report; and

(B) that release of such tapes, reports, or other information—

(i) would not undermine the ability of accident or safety investigators to continue to conduct the investigation; and

(ii) would not compromise national security.

(3) RESTRICTION.—A disclosure under paragraph (1) may not be made by or through officials with responsibility for, or who are conducting, a safety investigation with respect to the accident.

(c) OPINIONS REGARDING CAUSATION OF ACCIDENT.—Following an aircraft accident referred to in subsection (a)—

(1) if the evidence surrounding the accident is sufficient for the investigators who conduct the accident investigation to come to an opinion as to the cause or causes of the accident, the final report of the accident investigation shall set forth the opinion of the investigators as to the cause or causes of the accident; and

(2) if the evidence surrounding the accident is not sufficient for the investigators to come to an opinion as to the cause or causes of the accident, the final report of the accident investigation shall include a description of those factors, if any, that, in the opinion of the investigators, substantially contributed to or caused the accident.

(d) USE OF INFORMATION IN CIVIL OR CRIMINAL PROCEEDINGS.—For purposes of any civil or criminal proceeding arising from an aircraft accident referred to in subsection (a), any opinion of the accident investigators as to the cause of, or the factors contributing to, the accident set forth in the accident investigation report may not be considered as evidence in such proceeding, nor may such report be considered an admission of liability by the United States or by any person referred to in such report.

(e) DEFINITIONS.—For purposes of this section—

(1) the term "accident investigation" means any form of investigation by Coast Guard personnel of an aircraft accident referred to in subsection (a), other than a safety investigation; and

(2) the term "safety investigation" means an investigation by Coast Guard personnel of an aircraft accident referred to in subsection (a) that is conducted solely to determine the cause of the accident and to obtain information that may prevent the occurrence of similar accidents.

(Added Pub. L. 112–213, title II, §214(a), Dec. 20, 2012, 126 Stat. 1553, §678; amended Pub. L. 115–232, div. C, title XXXV, §3531(c)(5), Aug. 13, 2018, 132 Stat. 2320; renumbered §951, Pub. L. 115–282, title I, §107(b), Dec. 4, 2018, 132 Stat. 4205.)

§952. CONSTRUCTION OF COAST GUARD VESSELS AND ASSIGNMENT OF VESSEL PROJECTS

The assignment of Coast Guard vessel conversion, alteration, and repair projects shall be based on economic and military considerations and may not be restricted by a requirement that certain parts of Coast Guard shipwork be assigned to a particular type of shipyard or geographical area or by a similar requirement.

(Added Pub. L. 115–282, title III, §310(a), Dec. 4, 2018, 132 Stat. 4248.)

§953. SUPPORT FOR COAST GUARD ACADEMY

(a) AUTHORITY.—

(1) CONTRACTS AND COOPERATIVE AGREEMENTS.—

(A) IN GENERAL.—The Commandant may enter contract and cooperative agreements with 1 or more qualified organizations for the purpose of supporting the athletic programs of the Coast Guard Academy.

(B) AUTHORITY.—Notwithstanding section 3201(e) of title 10, the Commandant may enter into such contracts and cooperative agreements on a sole source basis pursuant to section 3204(a) of title 10.

(C) ACQUISITIONS.—Notwithstanding chapter 63 of title 31, a cooperative agreement under this section may be used to acquire property or services for the direct benefit or use of the Coast Guard Academy.

(2) FINANCIAL CONTROLS.—

(A) IN GENERAL.—Before entering into a contract or cooperative agreement under paragraph (1), the Commandant shall ensure that the contract or agreement includes appropriate financial controls to account for the resources of the Coast Guard Academy and the qualified organization concerned in accordance with accepted accounting principles.

(B) CONTENTS.—Any such contract or cooperative agreement shall contain a provision that allows the Commandant to review, as the Commandant considers necessary, the financial accounts of the qualified organization to determine whether the operations of the qualified organization—

(i) are consistent with the terms of the contract or cooperative agreement; and

(ii) would compromise the integrity or appearance of integrity of any program of the Department of Homeland Security.

(3) LEASES.—For the purpose of supporting the athletic programs of the Coast Guard Academy, the Commandant may, consistent with section 504(a)(13), rent or lease real property located at the Coast Guard Academy to a qualified organization, except that proceeds from such a lease shall be retained and expended in accordance with subsection (f).

(b) SUPPORT SERVICES.—

(1) AUTHORITY.—To the extent required by a contract or cooperative agreement under subsection (a), the Commandant may provide support services to a qualified organization while the qualified organization conducts support activities at the Coast Guard Academy only if the Commandant determines that the provision of such services is essential for the support of the athletic programs of the Coast Guard Academy.

(2) NO LIABILITY OF THE UNITED STATES.—Support services may only be provided without any liability of the United States to a qualified organization.

(3) SUPPORT SERVICES DEFINED.—In this subsection, the term "support services" includes utilities, office furnishings and equipment, communications services, records staging and archiving, audio and video support, and security systems, in conjunction with the leasing or licensing of property.

(c) TRANSFERS FROM NONAPPROPRIATED FUND OPERATION.—

(1) IN GENERAL.—Except as provided in paragraph (2), the Commandant may, subject to the acceptance of the qualified organization concerned, transfer to the qualified organization all title to and ownership of the assets and liabilities of the Coast Guard nonappropriated fund instrumentality, the function of which includes providing support for the athletic programs of the Coast Guard Academy, including bank accounts and financial reserves in the accounts of such fund instrumentality, equipment, supplies, and

other personal property.

(2) LIMITATION.—The Commandant may not transfer under paragraph (1) any interest in real property.

(d) ACCEPTANCE OF SUPPORT FROM QUALIFIED ORGANIZATION.—

(1) IN GENERAL.—Notwithstanding section 1342 of title 31, the Commandant may accept from a qualified organization funds, supplies, and services for the support of the athletic programs of the Coast Guard Academy.

(2) EMPLOYEES OF QUALIFIED ORGANIZATION.—For purposes of this section, employees or personnel of the qualified organization may not be considered to be employees of the United States.

(3) FUNDS RECEIVED FROM NCAA.—The Commandant may accept funds from the National Collegiate Athletic Association to support the athletic programs of the Coast Guard Academy.

(4) LIMITATION.—The Commandant shall ensure that contributions under this subsection and expenditure of funds pursuant to subsection (f) do not—

(A) reflect unfavorably on the ability of the Coast Guard, any employee of the Coast Guard, or any member of the armed forces (as such term is defined in section 101(a) of title 10) to carry out any responsibility or duty in a fair and objective manner; or

(B) compromise the integrity or appearance of integrity of any program of the Coast Guard, or any individual involved in such a program.

(e) TRADEMARKS AND SERVICE MARKS.—

(1) LICENSING, MARKETING, AND SPONSORSHIP AGREEMENTS.—An agreement under subsection (a) may, consistent with section 2260 of title 10 (other than subsection (d) of such section), authorize a qualified organization to enter into licensing, marketing, and sponsorship agreements relating to trademarks and service marks identifying the Coast Guard Academy, subject to the approval of the Commandant.

(2) LIMITATIONS.—A licensing, marketing, or sponsorship agreement may not be entered into under paragraph (1) if—

(A) such agreement would reflect unfavorably on the ability of the Coast Guard, any employee of the Coast Guard, or any member of the armed forces to carry out any responsibility or duty in a fair and objective manner; or

(B) the Commandant determines that the use of the trademark or service mark would compromise the integrity or appearance of integrity of any program of the Coast Guard or any individual involved in such a program.

(f) RETENTION AND USE OF FUNDS.—Funds received by the Commandant under this section may be retained for use to support the athletic programs of the Coast Guard Academy and shall remain available until expended.

(g) CONDITIONS.—The authority provided in this section with respect to a qualified organization is available only so long as the qualified organization continues—

(1) to operate in accordance with this section, the law of the State of Connecticut, and the constitution and bylaws of the qualified organization; and

(2) to operate exclusively to support the athletic programs of the Coast Guard

Academy.

(h) QUALIFIED ORGANIZATION DEFINED.—In this section, the term "qualified organization" means an organization—
(1) that operates as an organization under subsection (c)(3) of section 501 of the Internal Revenue Code of 1986 and exempt from taxation under subsection (a) of that section;
(2) for which authorization under sections 1033(a) and 1589(a) of title 10 may be provided; and
(3) established by the Coast Guard Academy Alumni Association solely for the purpose of supporting Coast Guard athletics.

(Added Pub. L. 117–263, div. K, title CXII, §11250(a), Dec. 23, 2022, 136 Stat. 4049.)

§954. MIXED-FUNDED ATHLETIC AND RECREATIONAL EXTRACURRICULAR PROGRAMS

(a) AUTHORITY.—In the case of a Coast Guard Academy mixed-funded athletic or recreational extracurricular program, the Commandant may designate funds appropriated to the Coast Guard and available for that program to be treated as nonappropriated funds and expended for that program in accordance with laws applicable to the expenditure of nonappropriated funds. Appropriated funds so designated shall be considered to be nonappropriated funds for all purposes and shall remain available until expended.

(b) COVERED PROGRAMS.—In this section, the term "Coast Guard Academy mixed-funded athletic or recreational extracurricular program" means an athletic or recreational extracurricular program of the Coast Guard Academy to which each of the following applies:
(1) The program is not considered a morale, welfare, or recreation program.
(2) The program is supported through appropriated funds.
(3) The program is supported by a nonappropriated fund instrumentality.
(4) The program is not a private organization and is not operated by a private organization.

(Added Pub. L. 117–263, div. K, title CXII, §11250(a), Dec. 23, 2022, 136 Stat. 4051.)

CHAPTER 11—ACQUISITIONS

SUBCHAPTER I—GENERAL PROVISIONS

SUBCHAPTER II—IMPROVED ACQUISITION PROCESS AND PROCEDURES

SUBCHAPTER III—PROCUREMENT

SUBCHAPTER IV—DEFINITIONS

SUBCHAPTER I—GENERAL PROVISIONS

§1101. ACQUISITION DIRECTORATE

(a) ESTABLISHMENT.—The Commandant shall establish an acquisition directorate to provide guidance and oversight for the implementation and management of all Coast Guard acquisition processes, programs, and projects.

(b) MISSION.—The mission of the acquisition directorate is—

(1) to acquire and deliver assets and systems that increase operational readiness, enhance mission performance, and create a safe working environment;

(2) to assist in the development of a workforce that is trained and qualified to further the Coast Guard's missions and deliver the best-value products and services to the Nation; and

(3) to meet the needs of customers of major acquisition programs in the most cost-effective manner practicable.

(Added Pub. L. 111–281, title IV, §402(a), Oct. 15, 2010, 124 Stat. 2931, §561; amended Pub. L. 114–328, div. A, title VIII, §899(b)(1)(A), Dec. 23, 2016, 130 Stat. 2333; Pub. L. 115–232, div. C, title XXXV, §3531(c)(6), Aug. 13, 2018, 132 Stat. 2320; renumbered §1101, Pub. L. 115–282, title I, §108(b), Dec. 4, 2018, 132 Stat. 4208.)

§1102. IMPROVEMENTS IN COAST GUARD ACQUISITION MANAGEMENT

(a) PROJECT OR PROGRAM MANAGERS.—

(1) LEVEL 1 PROJECTS.—An individual may not be assigned as the project or program manager for a Level 1 acquisition unless the individual holds a Level III acquisition certification as a program manager.

(2) LEVEL 2 PROJECTS.—An individual may not be assigned as the project or program manager for a Level 2 acquisition unless the individual holds a Level II acquisition certification as a program manager.

(b) ACQUISITION WORKFORCE.—

(1) IN GENERAL.—The Commandant shall designate a sufficient number of positions to be in the Coast Guard's acquisition workforce to perform acquisition-related functions at Coast Guard headquarters and field activities.

(2) REQUIRED POSITIONS.—In designating positions under subsection (a), the Commandant shall include, at a minimum, positions encompassing the following competencies and functions:

(A) Program management.

(B) Systems planning, research, development, engineering, and testing.

(C) Procurement, including contracting.

(D) Industrial and contract property management.

(E) Life-cycle logistics.

(F) Quality control and assurance.

(G) Manufacturing and production.

(H) Business, cost estimating, financial management, and auditing.

(I) Acquisition education, training, and career development.

(J) Construction and facilities engineering.

(K) Testing and evaluation.

(3) ACQUISITION MANAGEMENT HEADQUARTER ACTIVITIES.—The Commandant shall also designate as positions in the acquisition workforce under paragraph (1) those acquisition-related positions located at Coast Guard headquarters units.

(4) APPROPRIATE EXPERTISE REQUIRED.—The Commandant shall ensure that each individual assigned to a position in the acquisition workforce has the appropriate expertise to carry out the responsibilities of that position.

(c) MANAGEMENT INFORMATION SYSTEM.—

(1) IN GENERAL.—The Commandant shall establish a management information system capability to improve acquisition workforce management and reporting.

(2) INFORMATION MAINTAINED.—Information maintained with such capability shall include the following standardized information on individuals assigned to positions in the workforce:

(A) Qualifications, assignment history, and tenure of those individuals assigned to positions in the acquisition workforce or holding acquisition-related certifications.

(B) Promotion rates for officers and members of the Coast Guard in the acquisition workforce.

(d) APPOINTMENTS TO ACQUISITION POSITIONS.—The Commandant shall ensure that no requirement or preference for officers or members of the Coast Guard is used in the consideration of individuals for positions in the acquisition workforce.

(e) CAREER PATHS.—

(1) IDENTIFICATION OF CAREER PATHS.—To establish acquisition management as a core competency of the Coast Guard, the Commandant shall—

(A) ensure that career paths for officers, members, and employees of the Coast Guard who wish to pursue careers in acquisition are identified in terms of the education, training, experience, and assignments necessary for career progression of those officers, members, and employees to the most senior positions in the acquisition workforce; and

(B) publish information on such career paths.

(2) PROMOTION PARITY.—The Commandant shall ensure that promotion parity is established for officers and members of the Coast Guard who have been assigned to the acquisition workforce relative to officers and members who have not been assigned to the acquisition workforce.

(Added Pub. L. 111–281, title IV, §402(a), Oct. 15, 2010, 124 Stat. 2931, §562; amended Pub. L. 111–330, §1(4), Dec. 22, 2010, 124 Stat. 3569; Pub. L. 112–213, title II, §210(c)(2)(A), Dec. 20, 2012, 126 Stat. 1551; Pub. L. 114–328, div. A, title VIII, §899(b)(1)(B), Dec. 23, 2016, 130 Stat. 2333; renumbered §1102, Pub. L. 115–282, title I, §108(b), Dec. 4, 2018, 132 Stat. 4208; Pub. L. 116–283, div. G, title LVXXXV [LXXXV], §8505(a)(10), Jan. 1, 2021, 134 Stat. 4748.)

§1103. ROLE OF VICE COMMANDANT IN MAJOR ACQUISITION PROGRAMS

The Vice Commandant—

(1) shall represent the customer of a major acquisition program with regard to trade-offs made among cost, schedule, technical feasibility, and performance with respect to such program; and

(2) shall advise the Commandant in decisions regarding the balancing of resources against priorities, and associated trade-offs referred to in paragraph (1), on behalf of the customer of a major acquisition program.

(Added Pub. L. 114–328, div. A, title VIII, §899(b)(1)(E), Dec. 23, 2016, 130 Stat. 2334, §578; renumbered §1103, Pub. L. 115–282, title I, §108(b), Dec. 4, 2018, 132 Stat. 4208.)

§1104. RECOGNITION OF COAST GUARD PERSONNEL FOR EXCELLENCE IN ACQUISITION

(a) IN GENERAL.—The Commandant shall maintain a program to recognize excellent performance by individuals and teams comprised of officers, members, and employees of the Coast Guard that contributed to the long-term success of a Coast Guard acquisition project or program.

(b) ELEMENTS.—The program shall include—

(1) specific award categories, criteria, and eligibility and manners of recognition;

(2) procedures for the nomination by personnel of the Coast Guard of individuals and teams comprised of officers, members, and employees of the Coast Guard for recognition under the program; and

(3) procedures for the evaluation of nominations for recognition under the program by one or more panels of individuals from the Government, academia, and the private sector who have such expertise and are appointed in such manner as the Commandant shall establish for the purposes of this program.

(c) AWARD OF CASH BONUSES.—As part of the program required by subsection (a), the Commandant, subject to the availability of appropriations, may award to any civilian employee recognized pursuant to the program a cash bonus to the extent that the performance of such individual so recognized warrants the award of such bonus.

(Added Pub. L. 111–281, title IV, §402(a), Oct. 15, 2010, 124 Stat. 2934, §563; amended Pub. L. 111–330, §1(4), Dec. 22, 2010, 124 Stat. 3569; Pub. L. 114–328, div. A, title VIII, §899(b)(1)(C), Dec. 23, 2016, 130 Stat. 2333; renumbered §1104, Pub. L. 115–282, title I, §108(b), Dec. 4, 2018, 132 Stat. 4208.)

§1105. PROHIBITION ON USE OF LEAD SYSTEMS INTEGRATORS

(a) IN GENERAL.—

(1) USE OF LEAD SYSTEMS INTEGRATOR.—The Commandant may not use a private sector entity as a lead systems integrator.

(2) FULL AND OPEN COMPETITION.—The Commandant shall use full and open competition for any acquisition contract unless otherwise excepted in accordance with Federal acquisition laws and regulations promulgated under those laws, including the

Federal Acquisition Regulation.

(3) No EFFECT ON SMALL BUSINESS ACT.—Nothing in this subsection shall be construed to supersede or otherwise affect the authorities provided by and under the Small Business Act (15 U.S.C. 631 et seq.).

(b) LIMITATION ON FINANCIAL INTEREST IN SUBCONTRACTORS.—Neither an entity performing lead systems integrator functions for a Coast Guard acquisition nor a Tier 1 subcontractor for any acquisition may have a financial interest in a subcontractor below the Tier 1 subcontractor level unless—

(1) the subcontractor was selected by the prime contractor through full and open competition for such procurement;

(2) the procurement was awarded by an entity performing lead systems integrator functions or a subcontractor through full and open competition;

(3) the procurement was awarded by a subcontractor through a process over which the entity performing lead systems integrator functions or a Tier 1 subcontractor exercised no control; or

(4) the Commandant has determined that the procurement was awarded in a manner consistent with Federal acquisition laws and regulations promulgated under those laws, including the Federal Acquisition Regulation.

(Added Pub. L. 111–281, title IV, §402(a), Oct. 15, 2010, 124 Stat. 2935, §564; amended Pub. L. 111–330, §1(4), Dec. 22, 2010, 124 Stat. 3569; Pub. L. 112–213, title II, §217(7), Dec. 20, 2012, 126 Stat. 1557; Pub. L. 114–328, div. A, title VIII, §899(b)(1)(D), Dec. 23, 2016, 130 Stat. 2333; renumbered §1105 and amended Pub. L. 115–282, title I, §108(b), title III, §304(d), Dec. 4, 2018, 132 Stat. 4208, 4245.)

§1106. REQUIRED CONTRACT TERMS

(a) IN GENERAL.—The Commandant shall ensure that a contract awarded or a delivery order or task order issued for an acquisition of a capability or an asset with an expected service life of 10 or more years and with a total acquisition cost that is equal to or exceeds $10,000,000—

(1) provides that all certifications for an end-state capability or asset under such contract, delivery order, or task order, respectively, will be conducted by the Commandant or an independent third party, and that self-certification by a contractor or subcontractor is not allowed;

(2) provides that the Commandant shall maintain the authority to establish, approve, and maintain technical requirements;

(3) requires that any measurement of contractor and subcontractor performance be based on the status of all work performed, including the extent to which the work performed met all performance, cost, and schedule requirements;

(4) specifies that, for the acquisition or upgrade of air, surface, or shore capabilities and assets for which compliance with TEMPEST certification is a requirement, the standard for determining such compliance will be the air, surface, or shore standard then used by the Department of the Navy for that type of capability or asset; and

(5) for any contract awarded to acquire an Offshore Patrol Cutter, includes provisions specifying the service life, fatigue life, and days underway in general Atlantic and North

Pacific Sea conditions, maximum range, and maximum speed the cutter will be built to achieve.

(b) PROHIBITED PROVISIONS.—

(1) IN GENERAL.—The Commandant shall ensure that any contract awarded or delivery order or task order issued by the Coast Guard does not include any provision allowing for equitable adjustment that is not consistent with the Federal Acquisition Regulations.

(2) EXTENSION OF PROGRAM.—A contract, contract modification, or award term extending a contract with a lead systems integrator—

(A) may not include any minimum requirements for the purchase of a given or determinable number of specific capabilities or assets; and

(B) shall be reviewed by an independent third party with expertise in acquisition management, and the results of that review shall be submitted to the appropriate congressional committees at least 60 days prior to the award of the contract, contract modification, or award term.

(c) INTEGRATED PRODUCT TEAMS.—Integrated product teams, and all teams that oversee integrated product teams, shall be chaired by officers, members, or employees of the Coast Guard.

(d) TECHNICAL AUTHORITY.—The Commandant shall maintain or designate the technical authority to establish, approve, and maintain technical requirements. Any such designation shall be made in writing and may not be delegated to the authority of the Chief Acquisition Officer established by section 308 of this title.

(Added Pub. L. 111–281, title IV, §402(a), Oct. 15, 2010, 124 Stat. 2936, §565; amended Pub. L. 111–330, §1(4), Dec. 22, 2010, 124 Stat. 3569; Pub. L. 115–232, div. C, title XXXV, §3533(f), Aug. 13, 2018, 132 Stat. 2321; renumbered §1106 and amended Pub. L. 115–282, title I, §§108(b), 123(b)(2), Dec. 4, 2018, 132 Stat. 4208, 4240.)

§1107. EXTENSION OF MAJOR ACQUISITION PROGRAM CONTRACTS

(a) IN GENERAL.—Notwithstanding section 1105(a)(2) of this title and section 2304 [1] of title 10, and subject to subsections (b) and (c) of this section, the Secretary may acquire additional units procured under a Coast Guard major acquisition program contract, by extension of such contract without competition, if the Director of the Cost Analysis Division of the Department of Homeland Security determines that the costs that would be saved through award of a new contract in accordance with such sections would not exceed the costs of such an award.

(b) LIMITATION ON NUMBER OF ADDITIONAL UNITS.—The number of additional units acquired under a contract extension under this section may not exceed the number of additional units for which such determination is made.

(c) DETERMINATION OF COSTS UPON REQUEST.—The Director of the Cost Analysis Division of the Department of Homeland Security shall, at the request of the Secretary, determine for purposes of this section—

(1) the costs that would be saved through award of a new major acquisition program contract in accordance with section 1105(a)(2) for the acquisition of a number of

additional units specified by the Secretary; and

(2) the costs of such award, including the costs that would be incurred due to acquisition schedule delays and asset design changes associated with such award.

(d) NUMBER OF EXTENSIONS.—A contract may be extended under this section more than once.

(Added Pub. L. 114–328, div. A, title VIII, §899(b)(1)(E), Dec. 23, 2016, 130 Stat. 2334, §579; renumbered §1107 and amended Pub. L. 115–282, title I, §§108(b), 123(b)(2), Dec. 4, 2018, 132 Stat. 4208, 4240.)

¹ See References in Text note below.

§1108. DEPARTMENT OF DEFENSE CONSULTATION

(a) IN GENERAL.—The Commandant shall make arrangements as appropriate with the Secretary of Defense for support in contracting and management of Coast Guard acquisition programs. The Commandant shall also seek opportunities to make use of Department of Defense contracts, and contracts of other appropriate agencies, to obtain the best possible price for assets acquired for the Coast Guard.

(b) INTERSERVICE TECHNICAL ASSISTANCE.—The Commandant shall seek to maintain a memorandum of understanding or a memorandum of agreement with the Secretary of the Navy to obtain the assistance of the Office of the Assistant Secretary of the Navy for Research, Development, and Acquisition, including the Navy Systems Command, with the oversight of Coast Guard major acquisition programs. The memorandum of understanding or memorandum of agreement shall, at a minimum, provide for—

(1) the exchange of technical assistance and support that the Assistant Commandants for Acquisition, Human Resources, Engineering, and Information technology may identify;

(2) the use, as appropriate, of Navy technical expertise; and

(3) the temporary assignment or exchange of personnel between the Coast Guard and the Office of the Assistant Secretary of the Navy for Research, Development, and Acquisition, including Naval Systems Command, to facilitate the development of organic capabilities in the Coast Guard.

(c) TECHNICAL REQUIREMENT APPROVAL PROCEDURES.—The Chief Acquisition Officer shall adopt, to the extent practicable, procedures modeled after those used by the Navy Senior Acquisition Official to approve all technical requirements.

(Added Pub. L. 111–281, title IV, §402(a), Oct. 15, 2010, 124 Stat. 2937, §566; amended Pub. L. 111–330, §1(4), Dec. 22, 2010, 124 Stat. 3569; Pub. L. 115–232, div. C, title XXXV, §3534, Aug. 13, 2018, 132 Stat. 2322; renumbered §1108, Pub. L. 115–282, title I, §108(b), Dec. 4, 2018, 132 Stat. 4208.)

§1109. UNDEFINITIZED CONTRACTUAL ACTIONS

(a) IN GENERAL.—The Coast Guard may not enter into an undefinitized contractual action unless such action is directly approved by the Head of Contracting Activity of the Coast Guard.

(b) REQUESTS FOR UNDEFINITIZED CONTRACTUAL ACTIONS.—Any request to the Head of Contracting Activity for approval of an undefinitized contractual action shall include a description of the anticipated effect on requirements of the Coast Guard if a delay is incurred for the purposes of determining contractual terms, specifications, and price before performance is begun under the contractual action.

(c) REQUIREMENTS FOR UNDEFINITIZED CONTRACTUAL ACTIONS.—

(1) DEADLINE FOR AGREEMENT ON TERMS, SPECIFICATIONS, AND PRICE.—A contracting officer of the Coast Guard may not enter into an undefinitized contractual action unless the contractual action provides for agreement upon contractual terms, specification, and price by the earlier of—

(A) the end of the 180-day period beginning on the date on which the contractor submits a qualifying proposal to definitize the contractual terms, specifications, and price; or

(B) the date on which the amount of funds obligated under the contractual action is equal to more than 50 percent of the negotiated overall ceiling price for the contractual action.

(2) LIMITATION ON OBLIGATIONS.—

(A) IN GENERAL.—Except as provided in subparagraph (B), the contracting officer for an undefinitized contractual action may not obligate under such contractual action an amount that exceeds 50 percent of the negotiated overall ceiling price until the contractual terms, specifications, and price are definitized for such contractual action.

(B) EXCEPTION.—Notwithstanding subparagraph (A), if a contractor submits a qualifying proposal to definitize an undefinitized contractual action before an amount that exceeds 50 percent of the negotiated overall ceiling price is obligated on such action, the contracting officer for such action may not obligate with respect to such contractual action an amount that exceeds 75 percent of the negotiated overall ceiling price until the contractual terms, specifications, and price are definitized for such contractual action.

(3) WAIVER.—The Commandant may waive the application of this subsection with respect to a contract if the Commandant determines that the waiver is necessary to support—

(A) a contingency operation (as that term is defined in section 101(a)(13) of title 10);

(B) operations to prevent or respond to a transportation security incident (as defined in section 70101(6) [1] of title 46);

(C) an operation in response to an emergency that poses an unacceptable threat to human health or safety or to the marine environment; or

(D) an operation in response to a natural disaster or major disaster or emergency designated by the President under the Robert T. Stafford Disaster Relief and Emergency Assistance Act (42 U.S.C. 5121 et seq.).

(4) LIMITATION ON APPLICATION.—This subsection does not apply to an undefinitized contractual action for the purchase of initial spares.

(d) INCLUSION OF NONURGENT REQUIREMENTS.—Requirements for spare parts and support equipment that are not needed on an urgent basis may not be included in an undefinitized contractual action by the Coast Guard for spare parts and support equipment that are needed on an urgent basis unless the Commandant approves such inclusion as being—

(1) good business practice; and

(2) in the best interests of the United States.

(e) MODIFICATION OF SCOPE.—The scope of an undefinitized contractual action under which performance has begun may not be modified unless the Commandant approves such modification as being—

(1) good business practice; and

(2) in the best interests of the United States.

(f) ALLOWABLE PROFIT.—The Commandant shall ensure that the profit allowed on an undefinitized contractual action for which the final price is negotiated after a substantial portion of the performance required is completed reflects—

(1) the possible reduced cost risk of the contractor with respect to costs incurred during performance of the contract before the final price is negotiated; and

(2) the reduced cost risk of the contractor with respect to costs incurred during performance of the remaining portion of the contract.

(g) DEFINITIONS.—In this section:

(1) UNDEFINITIZED CONTRACTUAL ACTION.—

(A) IN GENERAL.—Except as provided in subparagraph (B), the term "undefinitized contractual action" means a new procurement action entered into by the Coast Guard for which the contractual terms, specifications, or price are not agreed upon before performance is begun under the action.

(B) EXCLUSION.—The term "undefinitized contractual action" does not include contractual actions with respect to—

(i) foreign military sales;

(ii) purchases in an amount not in excess of the amount of the simplified acquisition threshold; or

(iii) special access programs.

(2) QUALIFYING PROPOSAL.—The term "qualifying proposal" means a proposal that contains sufficient information to enable complete and meaningful audits of the information contained in the proposal as determined by the contracting officer.

(Added Pub. L. 111–281, title IV, §402(a), Oct. 15, 2010, 124 Stat. 2938, §567; renumbered §1109, Pub. L. 115–282, title I, §108(b), Dec. 4, 2018, 132 Stat. 4208.)

[1] *See References in Text note below.*

§1110. ELEVATION OF DISPUTES TO THE CHIEF ACQUISITION OFFICER

If, after 90 days following the elevation to the Chief Acquisition Officer of any design or other dispute regarding level 1 or level 2 acquisition, the dispute remains unresolved, the Commandant shall provide to the appropriate congressional committees a detailed description of the issue and the rationale underlying the decision taken by the Chief Acquisition Officer to resolve the issue.

(Added Pub. L. 116–283, div. G, title LVXXXV [LXXXV], §8501(a)(5), Jan. 1, 2021, 134 Stat. 4745.)

§1111. ACQUISITION WORKFORCE AUTHORITIES

(a) EXPEDITED HIRING AUTHORITY.—

(1) IN GENERAL.—For the purposes of section 3304 of title 5, the Commandant may—

(A) designate any category of acquisition positions within the Coast Guard as shortage category positions; and

(B) use the authorities in such section to recruit and appoint highly qualified persons directly to positions so designated.

(2) REPORTS.—The Commandant shall include in reports under section 1102 information described in such section regarding positions designated under this subsection.

(b) REEMPLOYMENT AUTHORITY.—

(1) IN GENERAL.—Except as provided in paragraph (2), if an annuitant receiving an annuity from the Civil Service Retirement and Disability Fund becomes employed in any category of acquisition positions designated by the Commandant under subsection (a), the annuity of the annuitant so employed shall continue. The annuitant so reemployed shall not be considered an employee for purposes of subchapter III of chapter 83 or chapter 84 of title 5.

(2)(A) ELECTION.—An annuitant retired under section 8336(d)(1) or 8414(b)(1)(A) of title 5, receiving an annuity from the Civil Service Retirement and Disability Fund, who becomes employed in any category of acquisition positions designated by the Commandant under subsection (a) after the date of the enactment of the Elijah E. Cummings Coast Guard Authorization Act of 2020, may elect to be subject to section 8344 or 8468 of such title (as the case may be).

(i) DEADLINE.—An election for coverage under this subsection shall be filed not later than 90 days after the Commandant takes reasonable actions to notify an employee who may file an election.

(ii) COVERAGE.—If an employee files an election under this subsection, coverage shall be effective beginning on the first day of the first applicable pay period beginning on or after the date of the filing of the election.

(B) APPLICATION.—Paragraph (1) shall apply to an individual who is eligible to file an election under subparagraph (A) and does not file a timely election under clause (i) of such subparagraph.

(Added Pub. L. 116–283, div. G, title LVXXXII [LXXXII], §8219(a), Jan. 1, 2021, 134 Stat. 4655.)

SUBCHAPTER II—IMPROVED ACQUISITION PROCESS AND PROCEDURES

§1131. IDENTIFICATION OF MAJOR SYSTEM ACQUISITIONS

(a) IN GENERAL.—

(1) SUPPORT MECHANISMS.—The Commandant shall develop and implement mechanisms to support the establishment of mature and stable operational requirements for all acquisitions.

(2) MISSION ANALYSIS; AFFORDABILITY ASSESSMENT.—The Commandant may not initiate a Level 1 or Level 2 acquisition project or program until the Commandant—

(A) completes a mission analysis that—

(i) identifies the specific capability gaps to be addressed by the project or program; and

(ii) develops a clear mission need to be addressed by the project or program; and

(B) prepares a preliminary affordability assessment for the project or program.

(b) ELEMENTS.—

(1) REQUIREMENTS.—The mechanisms required by subsection (a) shall ensure the implementation of a formal process for the development of a mission-needs statement, concept-of-operations document, capability development plan, and resource proposal for the initial project or program funding, and shall ensure the project or program is included in the Coast Guard Capital Investment Plan.

(2) ASSESSMENT OF TRADE-OFFS.—In conducting an affordability assessment under subsection (a)(2)(B), the Commandant shall develop and implement mechanisms to ensure that trade-offs among cost, schedule, and performance are considered in the establishment of preliminary operational requirements for development and production of new assets and capabilities for Level 1 and Level 2 acquisitions projects and programs.

(c) HUMAN RESOURCE CAPITAL PLANNING.—The Commandant shall develop staffing predictions, define human capital performance initiatives, and identify preliminary training needs required to implement each Level 1 and Level 2 acquisition project and program.

(Added Pub. L. 111–281, title IV, §402(a), Oct. 15, 2010, 124 Stat. 2941, §571; renumbered §1131, Pub. L. 115–282, title I, §108(b), Dec. 4, 2018, 132 Stat. 4208.)

§1132. ACQUISITION

(a) IN GENERAL.—The Commandant may not establish a Level 1 or Level 2 acquisition project or program until the Commandant—

(1) clearly defines the operational requirements for the project or program;

(2) establishes the feasibility of alternatives;

(3) develops an acquisition project or program baseline;

(4) produces a life-cycle cost estimate; and

(5) assesses the relative merits of alternatives to determine a preferred solution in accordance with the requirements of this section.

(b) SUBMISSION REQUIRED BEFORE PROCEEDING.—Any Coast Guard Level 1 or Level 2 acquisition project or program may not begin to obtain any capability or asset or proceed beyond that phase of its development that entails approving the supporting acquisition until the Commandant submits to the appropriate congressional committees the following:

(1) The key performance parameters, the key system attributes, and the operational performance attributes of the capability or asset to be acquired under the proposed acquisition project or program.

(2) A detailed list of the systems or other capabilities with which the capability or asset to be acquired is intended to be interoperable, including an explanation of the attributes of interoperability.

(3) The anticipated acquisition project or program baseline and acquisition unit cost for the capability or asset to be acquired under the project or program.

(4) A detailed schedule for the acquisition process showing when all capability and asset acquisitions are to be completed and when all acquired capabilities and assets are to be initially and fully deployed.

(c) ANALYSIS OF ALTERNATIVES.—

(1) IN GENERAL.—The Coast Guard may not acquire an experimental or technically immature capability or asset or implement a Level 1 or Level 2 acquisition project or program, unless it has prepared an analysis of alternatives for the capability or asset to be acquired in the concept and technology development phase of the acquisition process for the capability or asset.

(2) REQUIREMENTS.—The analysis of alternatives shall be prepared by a federally funded research and development center, a qualified entity of the Department of Defense, or a similar independent third-party entity that has appropriate acquisition expertise and has no financial interest in any part of the acquisition project or program that is the subject of the analysis. At a minimum, the analysis of alternatives shall include—

(A) an assessment of the technical maturity of the capability or asset, and technical and other risks;

(B) an examination of capability, interoperability, and other advantages and disadvantages;

(C) an evaluation of whether different combinations or quantities of specific assets or capabilities could meet the Coast Guard's overall performance needs;

(D) a discussion of key assumptions and variables, and sensitivity to change in such assumptions and variables;

(E) when an alternative is an existing capability, asset, or prototype, an evaluation of relevant safety and performance records and costs;

(F) a calculation of life-cycle costs including—

(i) an examination of likely research and development costs and the levels of uncertainty associated with such estimated costs;

(ii) an examination of likely production and deployment costs and the levels of uncertainty associated with such estimated costs;

(iii) an examination of likely operating and support costs and the levels of uncertainty associated with such estimated costs;

(iv) if they are likely to be significant, an examination of likely disposal costs and the levels of uncertainty associated with such estimated costs; and

(v) such additional measures as the Commandant or the Secretary of the department in which the Coast Guard is operating determines to be necessary for appropriate evaluation of the capability or asset; and

(G) the business case for each viable alternative.

(d) TEST AND EVALUATION MASTER PLAN.—

(1) IN GENERAL.—For any Level 1 or Level 2 acquisition project or program the Chief Acquisition Officer must approve a test and evaluation master plan specific to the acquisition project or program for the capability, asset, or subsystems of the capability or asset and intended to minimize technical, cost, and schedule risk as early as practicable in the development of the project or program.

(2) TEST AND EVALUATION STRATEGY.—The master plan shall—

(A) set forth an integrated test and evaluation strategy that will verify that capability-level or asset-level and subsystem-level design and development, including performance and supportability, have been sufficiently proven before the capability, asset, or subsystem of the capability or asset is approved for production; and

(B) require that adequate developmental tests and evaluations and operational tests and evaluations established under subparagraph (A) are performed to inform production decisions.

(3) OTHER COMPONENTS OF THE MASTER PLAN.—At a minimum, the master plan shall identify—

(A) the key performance parameters to be resolved through the integrated test and evaluation strategy;

(B) the performance data to be used to determine whether the key performance parameters have been resolved;

(C) critical operational issues to be assessed in addition to the key performance parameters;

(D) the results during test and evaluation that will be required to demonstrate that a capability, asset, or subsystem meets performance requirements;

(E) specific development test and evaluation phases and the scope of each phase;

(F) modeling and simulation activities to be performed, if any, and the scope of such activities;

(G) early operational assessments to be performed, if any, and the scope of such assessments;

(H) operational test and evaluation phases;

(I) an estimate of the resources, including funds, that will be required for all test, evaluation, assessment, modeling, and simulation activities; and

(J) the Government entity or independent entity that will perform the test, evaluation, assessment, modeling, and simulation activities.

(4) UPDATE.—The Chief Acquisition Officer must approve an updated master plan whenever there is a revision to project or program test and evaluation strategy, scope, or phasing.

(5) LIMITATION.—The Coast Guard may not—

(A) proceed beyond that phase of the acquisition process that entails approving the supporting acquisition of a capability or asset before the master plan is approved by the Chief Acquisition Officer; or

(B) award any production contract for a capability, asset, or subsystem for which a master plan is required under this subsection before the master plan is approved by the Chief Acquisition Officer.

(e) LIFE-CYCLE COST ESTIMATES.—

(1) IN GENERAL.—The Commandant shall implement mechanisms to ensure the development and regular updating of life-cycle cost estimates for each acquisition with a total acquisition cost that equals or exceeds $10,000,000 and an expected service life of 10 or more years, and to ensure that these estimates are considered in decisions to develop or produce new or enhanced capabilities and assets.

(2) TYPES OF ESTIMATES.—For each Level 1 or Level 2 acquisition project or program, in addition to life-cycle cost estimates developed under paragraph (1), the Commandant shall require that—

(A) life-cycle cost estimates developed under paragraph (1) be updated before—

(i) each milestone decision is concluded; and

(ii) the project or program enters a new acquisition phase; and

(B) an independent cost estimate or independent cost assessment, as appropriate, be developed to validate life-cycle cost estimates developed under paragraph (1).

(Added Pub. L. 111–281, title IV, §402(a), Oct. 15, 2010, 124 Stat. 2942, §572; amended Pub. L. 114–120, title II, §204(a), Feb. 8, 2016, 130 Stat. 34; renumbered §1132, Pub. L. 115–282, title I, §108(b), Dec. 4, 2018, 132 Stat. 4208; Pub. L. 117–263, div. K, title CXII, §11210, Dec. 23, 2022, 136 Stat. 4012.)

§1133. PRELIMINARY DEVELOPMENT AND DEMONSTRATION

(a) IN GENERAL.—The Commandant shall ensure that developmental test and evaluation, operational test and evaluation, life-cycle cost estimates, and the development and demonstration requirements applied by this chapter to acquisition projects and programs are met to confirm that the projects or programs meet the requirements identified in the mission-analysis and affordability assessment prepared under section 1131(a)(2), the operational requirements developed under section 1132(a)(1) and the following development and demonstration objectives:

(1) To demonstrate that the design, manufacturing, and production solution is based upon a stable, producible, and cost-effective product design.

(2) To ensure that the product capabilities meet contract specifications, acceptable operational performance requirements, and system security requirements.

(3) To ensure that the product design is mature enough to commit to full production and deployment.

(b) TESTS AND EVALUATIONS.—

(1) IN GENERAL.—The Commandant shall ensure that the Coast Guard conducts developmental tests and evaluations and operational tests and evaluations of a capability or asset and the subsystems of the capability or asset in accordance with the master plan prepared for the capability or asset under section 1132(d)(1).[1]

(2) USE OF THIRD PARTIES.—The Commandant shall ensure that the Coast Guard uses independent third parties with expertise in testing and evaluating the capabilities or assets and the subsystems of the capabilities or assets being acquired to conduct developmental tests and evaluations and operational tests and evaluations whenever the Coast Guard lacks the capability to conduct the tests and evaluations required by a master plan.

(3) COMMUNICATION OF SAFETY CONCERNS.—The Commandant shall ensure that independent third parties and Government employees that identify safety concerns during developmental or operational tests and evaluations or through independent or Government-conducted design assessments of capabilities or assets and subsystems of capabilities or assets to be acquired by the Coast Guard communicate such concerns as soon as practicable, but not later than 30 days after the completion of the test or assessment event or activity that identified the safety concern, to the program manager for the capability or asset and the subsystems concerned and to the Chief Acquisition Officer.

(4) REPORTING OF SAFETY CONCERNS.—The Commandant shall ensure that any safety concerns that have been communicated under paragraph (3) for an acquisition program or project are reported to the appropriate congressional committees at least 90 days before the award of any contract or issuance of any delivery order or task order for low, initial, or full-rate production of the capability or asset concerned if they will remain uncorrected or unmitigated at the time such a contract is awarded or delivery order or task order is issued. The report shall include a justification for the approval of that level of production of the capability or asset before the safety concerns are corrected or mitigated. The report shall also include an explanation of the actions that will be taken to correct or mitigate the safety concerns, the date by which those actions will be taken, and the adequacy of current funding to correct or mitigate the safety concerns.

(5) ASSET ALREADY IN LOW, INITIAL, OR FULL-RATE PRODUCTION.—The Commandant shall ensure that if an independent third party or a Government employee identifies a safety concern with a capability or asset or any subsystems of a capability or asset not previously identified during operational test and evaluation of a capability or asset already in low, initial, or full-rate production—

(A) the Commandant, through the Assistant Commandant for Capability, shall notify the program manager and the Chief Acquisition Officer of the safety concern as soon as practicable, but not later than 30 days after the completion of the test and evaluation event or activity that identified the safety concern; and

(B) the Deputy Commandant for Mission Support shall notify the Commandant and the Deputy Commandant for Operations of the safety concern within 50 days after the notification required under subparagraph (A), and include in such notification—

(i) an explanation of the actions that will be taken to correct or mitigate the safety concern in all capabilities or assets and subsystems of the capabilities or assets yet to be produced, and the date by which those actions will be taken;

(ii) an explanation of the actions that will be taken to correct or mitigate the safety concern in previously produced capabilities or assets and subsystems of the capabilities or assets, and the date by which those actions will be taken; and

(iii) an assessment of the adequacy of current funding to correct or mitigate the safety concern in capabilities or assets and subsystems of the capabilities or assets and in previously produced capabilities or assets and subsystems.

(c) TECHNICAL CERTIFICATION.—

(1) IN GENERAL.—The Commandant shall ensure that any Level 1 or Level 2 acquisition project or program is certified by the technical authority of the Coast Guard after review by an independent third party with capabilities in the mission area, asset, or particular asset component.

(2) TEMPEST TESTING.—The Commandant shall—

(A) cause all electronics on all aircraft, surface, and shore capabilities and assets that require TEMPEST certification to be tested in accordance with TEMPEST standards and communications security (comsec) standards by an independent third party that is authorized by the Federal Government to perform such testing; and

(B) certify that the assets meet all applicable TEMPEST requirements.

(3) CUTTER CLASSIFICATION.—

(A) IN GENERAL.—The Commandant shall cause each cutter, other than a National Security Cutter, acquired by the Coast Guard and delivered after the date of enactment of the Coast Guard Authorization Act of 2010 to be classed by the American Bureau of Shipping before final acceptance.

[(B) Repealed. Pub. L. 112–213, title II, §210(c)(2)(B), Dec. 20, 2012, 126 Stat. 1551.]

(4) OTHER VESSELS.—The Commandant shall cause the design and construction of each National Security Cutter, other than National Security Cutters 1, 2, and 3, to be assessed by an independent third party with expertise in vessel design and construction certification.

(5) AIRCRAFT AIRWORTHINESS.—The Commandant shall cause all aircraft and aircraft engines acquired by the Coast Guard to be assessed for airworthiness by an independent third party with expertise in aircraft and aircraft engine certification before final acceptance.

(Added Pub. L. 111–281, title IV, §402(a), Oct. 15, 2010, 124 Stat. 2944, §573; amended Pub. L. 112–213, title II, §210(c)(2)(B), Dec. 20, 2012, 126 Stat. 1551; Pub. L. 115–232, div. C, title XXXV, §3522, Aug. 13, 2018, 132 Stat. 2314; renumbered §1133 and amended Pub. L. 115–282, title I, §§108(b), 123(b)(2), Dec. 4, 2018, 132 Stat. 4208, 4240.)

[1] *See References in Text note below.*

§1134. ACQUISITION, PRODUCTION, DEPLOYMENT, AND SUPPORT

(a) IN GENERAL.—The Commandant shall—

(1) ensure there is a stable and efficient production and support capability to develop an asset or capability for the Coast Guard;

(2) conduct follow-on testing to confirm and monitor performance and correct deficiencies; and

(3) conduct acceptance tests and trials prior to the delivery of each asset or system to ensure the delivered asset or system achieves full operational capability.

(b) ELEMENTS.—The Commandant shall—

(1) execute production contracts;

(2) ensure that delivered assets and capabilities meet operational cost and schedules requirements established in the acquisition program baseline;

(3) validate manpower and training requirements to meet system needs to operate, maintain, support, and instruct the assets or capabilities; and

(4) prepare an acquisition project or program transition plan to enter into programmatic sustainment, operations, and support.

(Added Pub. L. 111–281, title IV, §402(a), Oct. 15, 2010, 124 Stat. 2947, §574; renumbered §1134, Pub. L. 115–282, title I, §108(b), Dec. 4, 2018, 132 Stat. 4208.)

§1135. ACQUISITION PROGRAM BASELINE BREACH

(a) IN GENERAL.—The Commandant shall submit a report to the appropriate congressional committees and the Committee on Homeland Security of the House of Representatives as soon as possible, but not later than 30 days, after the Chief Acquisition Officer of the Coast Guard becomes aware of the breach of an acquisition program baseline for any Level 1 or Level 2 acquisition program, by—

(1) a likely cost overrun greater than 15 percent of the acquisition program baseline for that individual capability or asset or a class of capabilities or assets;

(2) a likely delay of more than 180 days in the delivery schedule for any individual capability or asset or class of capabilities or assets; or

(3) an anticipated failure for any individual capability or asset or class of capabilities or assets to satisfy any key performance threshold or parameter under the acquisition program baseline.

(b) CONTENT.—The report submitted under subsection (a) shall include—

(1) a detailed description of the breach and an explanation of its cause;

(2) the projected impact to performance, cost, and schedule;

(3) an updated acquisition program baseline and the complete history of changes to the original acquisition program baseline;

(4) the updated acquisition schedule and the complete history of changes to the original schedule;

(5) a full life-cycle cost analysis for the capability or asset or class of capabilities or assets;

(6) a remediation plan identifying corrective actions and any resulting issues or risks;

and

(7) a description of how progress in the remediation plan will be measured and monitored.

(c) Substantial Variances in Costs or Schedule.—If a likely cost overrun is greater than 20 percent or a likely delay is greater than 12 months from the costs and schedule described in the acquisition program baseline for any Level 1 or Level 2 acquisition project or program of the Coast Guard, the Commandant shall include in the report a written determination, with a supporting explanation, of whether—

(1) the capability or asset or capability or asset class to be acquired under the project or program is essential to the accomplishment of Coast Guard missions;

(2) there are no alternatives to such capability or asset or capability or asset class that will provide equal or greater capability in both a more cost-effective and timely manner;

(3) the new acquisition schedule and estimates for total acquisition cost are reasonable; and

(4) the management structure for the acquisition program is adequate to manage and control performance, cost, and schedule.

(d) Notice to Congress With Respect to Breach of Contract.—Not later than 48 hours after the Commandant becomes aware that a major acquisition contract cannot be carried out under the terms specified in the contract, the Commandant shall provide a written notification to the Committee on Commerce, Science, and Transportation of the Senate and the Committee on Transportation and Infrastructure of the House of Representatives that includes—

(1) a description of the terms of the contract that cannot be met; and

(2) an assessment of whether the applicable contract officer has issued a cease and desist order to the contractor based on the breach of such terms of the contract.

(Added Pub. L. 111–281, title IV, §402(a), Oct. 15, 2010, 124 Stat. 2947, §575; amended Pub. L. 115–232, div. C, title XXXV, §3533(g), Aug. 13, 2018, 132 Stat. 2321; renumbered §1135, Pub. L. 115–282, title I, §108(b), Dec. 4, 2018, 132 Stat. 4208; Pub. L. 116–283, div. G, title LVXXXII [LXXXII], §8221(b), Jan. 1, 2021, 134 Stat. 4657.)

§1136. Acquisition approval authority

Nothing in this subchapter shall be construed as altering or diminishing in any way the statutory authority and responsibility of the Secretary of the department in which the Coast Guard is operating, or the Secretary's designee, to—

(1) manage and administer department procurements, including procurements by department components, as required by section 701 of the Homeland Security Act of 2002 (6 U.S.C. 341); or

(2) manage department acquisition activities and act as the Acquisition Decision Authority with regard to the review or approval of a Coast Guard Level 1 or Level 2 acquisition project or program, as required by section 16 [1] of the Office of Federal Procurement Policy Act (41 U.S.C. 414) and related implementing regulations and directives.

(Added Pub. L. 111–281, title IV, §402(a), Oct. 15, 2010, 124 Stat. 2948, §576; renumbered §1136, Pub. L. 115–282, title I, §108(b), Dec. 4, 2018, 132 Stat. 4208.)

¹ *See References in Text note below.*

§1137. CONTRACTING FOR MAJOR ACQUISITIONS PROGRAMS

(a) IN GENERAL.—In carrying out authorities provided to the Secretary to design, construct, accept, or otherwise acquire assets and systems under section 501(d), the Secretary, acting through the Commandant or the head of an integrated program office established for a major acquisition program, may enter into contracts for a major acquisition program and 3 Polar Security Cutters in addition to those approved as part of a major acquisition program on November 1, 2019.

(b) AUTHORIZED METHODS.—Contracts entered into under subsection (a)—

(1) may be block buy contracts;

(2) may be incrementally funded;

(3) may include combined purchases, also known as economic order quantity purchases, of—

(A) materials and components; and

(B) long lead time materials; and

(4) as provided in section 3501 of title 10, may be multiyear contracts.

(c) SUBJECT TO APPROPRIATIONS.—Any contract entered into under subsection (a) shall provide that any obligation of the United States to make a payment under the contract is subject to the availability of amounts specifically provided in advance for that purpose in subsequent appropriations Acts.

(Added Pub. L. 115–282, title III, §311(b), Dec. 4, 2018, 132 Stat. 4249; amended Pub. L. 116–283, div. G, title LVXXXI [LXXXI], §8111(b), Jan. 1, 2021, 134 Stat. 4639; Pub. L. 117–81, div. A, title XVII, §1702(d)(2), Dec. 27, 2021, 135 Stat. 2156.)

SUBCHAPTER III—PROCUREMENT

§1151. RESTRICTION ON CONSTRUCTION OF VESSELS IN FOREIGN SHIPYARDS

(a) Except as provided in subsection (b), no Coast Guard vessel, and no major component of the hull or superstructure of a Coast Guard vessel, may be constructed in a foreign shipyard.

(b) The President may authorize exceptions to the prohibition in subsection (a) when the President determines that it is in the national security interest of the United States to do so. The President shall transmit notice to Congress of any such determination, and no contract may be made pursuant to the exception authorized until the end of the 30-day period beginning on the date the notice of such determination is received by Congress.

(Added Pub. L. 100–448, §26(a), Sept. 28, 1988, 102 Stat. 1847, §665; renumbered §1151, Pub. L. 115–282, title I, §108(b), Dec. 4, 2018, 132 Stat. 4208.)

§1152. ADVANCE PROCUREMENT FUNDING

(a) IN GENERAL.—With respect to any Coast Guard vessel for which amounts are appropriated and any amounts otherwise made available for vessels for the Coast Guard in any fiscal year, the Commandant may enter into a contract or place an order, in advance of a contract or order for construction of a vessel, for—

(1) materials, parts, components, and labor for the vessel;

(2) the advance construction of parts or components for the vessel;

(3) protection and storage of materials, parts, or components for the vessel; and

(4) production planning, design, and other related support services that reduce the overall procurement lead time of the vessel.

(b) USE OF MATERIALS, PARTS, AND COMPONENTS MANUFACTURED IN THE UNITED STATES. In entering into contracts and placing orders under subsection (a), the Commandant may give priority to persons that manufacture materials, parts, and components in the United States.

(Added Pub. L. 112–213, title II, §211(a), Dec. 20, 2012, 126 Stat. 1551, §577; amended Pub. L. 115–232, div. C, title XXXV, §3531(c)(7), Aug. 13, 2018, 132 Stat. 2320; renumbered §1152, Pub. L. 115–282, title I, §108(b), Dec. 4, 2018, 132 Stat. 4208.)

§1153. PROHIBITION ON OVERHAUL, REPAIR, AND MAINTENANCE OF COAST GUARD VESSELS IN FOREIGN SHIPYARDS

A Coast Guard vessel the home port of which is in the United States or Guam may not be overhauled, repaired, or maintained in a shipyard outside the United States or Guam, other than in the case of voyage repairs.

(Added Pub. L. 104–324, title III, §311(a), Oct. 19, 1996, 110 Stat. 3920, §96; amended Pub. L. 111–281, title II, §218, Oct. 15, 2010, 124 Stat. 2918; renumbered §1153, Pub. L. 115–282, title I, §108(b), Dec. 4, 2018, 132 Stat. 4208.)

§1154. Procurement of Buoy Chain

(a) Except as provided in subsection (b), the Coast Guard may not procure buoy chain—

    (1) that is not manufactured in the United States; or

    (2) substantially all of the components of which are not produced or manufactured in the United States.

(b) The Coast Guard may procure buoy chain that is not manufactured in the United States if the Secretary determines that—

    (1) the price of buoy chain manufactured in the United States is unreasonable; or

    (2) emergency circumstances exist.

(Added Pub. L. 104–324, title XI, §1128(a), Oct. 19, 1996, 110 Stat. 3984, §97; renumbered §1154, Pub. L. 115–282, title I, §108(b), Dec. 4, 2018, 132 Stat. 4208.)

§1155. Contract Termination

(a) In General.—

    (1) Notification.—Before terminating a procurement or acquisition contract with a total value of more than $1,000,000, the Commandant of the Coast Guard shall notify each vendor under such contract and require the vendor to maintain all work product related to the contract until the earlier of—

        (A) not less than 1 year after the date of the notification; or

        (B) the date the Commandant notifies the vendor that maintenance of such work product is no longer required.

(b) Work Product Defined.—In this section the term "work product"—

    (1) means tangible and intangible items and information produced or possessed as a result of a contract referred to in subsection (a); and

    (2) includes—

        (A) any completed end items;

        (B) any uncompleted end items; and

        (C) any property in the contractor's possession in which the United States Government has an interest.

(c) Penalty.—A vendor that fails to maintain work product as required under subsection (a) is liable to the United States for a civil penalty of not more than $25,000 for each day on which such work product is unavailable.

(d) Report.—

    (1) In general.—Except as provided in paragraph (2), not later than 45 days after the end of each fiscal year the Commandant of the Coast Guard shall provide to the Committee on Transportation and Infrastructure of the House of Representatives and the Committee on Commerce, Science, and Transportation of the Senate a report detailing—

        (A) all Coast Guard contracts with a total value of more than $1,000,000 that were terminated in the fiscal year;

(B) all vendors who were notified under subsection (a)(1) in the fiscal year, and the date of such notification;

(C) all criminal, administrative, and other investigations regarding any contract with a total value of more than $1,000,000 that were initiated by the Coast Guard in the fiscal year;

(D) all criminal, administrative, and other investigations regarding contracts with a total value of more than $1,000,000 that were completed by the Coast Guard in the fiscal year; and

(E) an estimate of costs incurred by the Coast Guard, including contract line items and termination costs, as a result of the requirements of this section.

(2) LIMITATION.—The Commandant is not required to provide a report under paragraph (1) for any fiscal year for which there is no responsive information as described in subparagraphs (A) through (E) of paragraph (1).

(Added Pub. L. 115–232, div. C, title XXXV, §3523(a), Aug. 13, 2018, 132 Stat. 2315, §657; renumbered §1155, Pub. L. 115–282, title I, §108(b), Dec. 4, 2018, 132 Stat. 4208.)

§1156. LIMITATION ON UNMANNED AIRCRAFT SYSTEMS

(a) IN GENERAL.—During any fiscal year for which funds are appropriated for the design or construction of an Offshore Patrol Cutter, the Commandant—

(1) may not award a contract for design of an unmanned aircraft system for use by the Coast Guard; and

(2) may lease, acquire, or acquire the services of an unmanned aircraft system only if such system—

(A) has been part of a program of record of, procured by, or used by a Federal entity (or funds for research, development, test, and evaluation have been received from a Federal entity with regard to such system) before the date on which the Commandant leases, acquires, or acquires the services of the system; and

(B) is leased, acquired, or utilized by the Commandant through an agreement with a Federal entity, unless such an agreement is not practicable or would be less cost-effective than an independent contract action by the Coast Guard.

(b) SMALL UNMANNED AIRCRAFT EXEMPTION.—Subsection (a)(2) does not apply to small unmanned aircraft.

(c) DEFINITIONS.—In this section, the terms "small unmanned aircraft" and "unmanned aircraft system" have the meanings given those terms in section 44801 of title 49.

(Added Pub. L. 115–282, title III, §304(b), Dec. 4, 2018, 132 Stat. 4244; amended Pub. L. 117–263, div. K, title CXVIII, §11803(b), Dec. 23, 2022, 136 Stat. 4163.)

§1157. EXTRAORDINARY RELIEF

(a) IN GENERAL.—With respect to any prime contracting entity receiving extraordinary relief pursuant to the Act entitled "An Act to authorize the making, amendment, and modification of contracts to facilitate the national defense", approved August 28, 1958

(Public Law 85–804; 50 U.S.C. 1432 et seq.) for a major acquisition, the Secretary shall not consider any further request by the prime contracting entity for extraordinary relief under such Act for such major acquisition.

(b) INAPPLICABILITY TO SUBCONTRACTORS.—The limitation under subsection (a) shall not apply to subcontractors of a prime contracting entity.

(c) QUARTERLY REPORT.—Not less frequently than quarterly during each fiscal year in which extraordinary relief is approved or provided to an entity under the Act referred to in subsection (a) for the acquisition of Offshore Patrol Cutters, the Commandant shall provide to the Committee on Commerce, Science, and Transportation of the Senate and the Committee on Transportation and Infrastructure of the House of Representatives a report that describes in detail such relief and the compliance of the entity with the oversight measures required as a condition of receiving such relief.

(Added Pub. L. 116–283, div. G, title LVXXXII [LXXXII], §8221(a)(1), Jan. 1, 2021, 134 Stat. 4657.)

§1158. AUTHORITY TO ENTER INTO TRANSACTIONS OTHER THAN CONTRACTS AND GRANTS TO PROCURE COST-EFFECTIVE, ADVANCED TECHNOLOGY FOR MISSION-CRITICAL NEEDS

(a) IN GENERAL.—Subject to subsections (b) and (c), the Commandant may enter into transactions (other than contracts, cooperative agreements, and grants) to operate, test, and acquire cost-effective technology for the purpose of meeting the mission needs of the Coast Guard.

(b) OPERATION, TESTING, AND ACQUISITION.—Operation, testing, and acquisition of technologies under subsection (a) shall be—

(1) carried out in accordance with Coast Guard policies and guidance; and

(2) consistent with the operational requirements of the Coast Guard.

(c) LIMITATIONS.—The Commandant may not enter into a transaction under subsection (a) with respect to a technology that—

(1) does not comply with the cybersecurity standards of the Coast Guard; or

(2) is sourced from an entity domiciled in the People's Republic of China, unless the Commandant determines that the prototype or procurement of such a technology is for the purpose of—

(A) counter-UAS or surrogate testing; or

(B) intelligence, electronic warfare, and information warfare, testing, and analysis.

(d) EDUCATION AND TRAINING.—The Commandant shall ensure that management, technical, and contracting personnel of the Coast Guard involved in the award or administration of transactions under this section are provided adequate education and training with respect to the authority under this section.

(e) REGULATIONS.—The Commandant shall prescribe regulations as necessary to carry out this section.

(f) COUNTER-UAS DEFINED.—In this section, the term "counter-UAS" has the meaning given such term in section 44801 of title 49.

(Added Pub. L. 117–263, div. K, title CXII, §11205(a), Dec. 23, 2022, 136 Stat. 4009.)

SUBCHAPTER IV—DEFINITIONS

§1171. Definitions

In this chapter:

(1) APPROPRIATE CONGRESSIONAL COMMITTEES.—The term "appropriate congressional committees" means the Committee on Transportation and Infrastructure of the House of Representatives and the Committee on Commerce, Science, and Transportation of the Senate.

(2) CHIEF ACQUISITION OFFICER.—The term "Chief Acquisition Officer" means the officer appointed under section 308 of this title.

(3) CUSTOMER OF A MAJOR ACQUISITION PROGRAM.—The term "customer of a major acquisition program" means the operating field unit of the Coast Guard that will field the system or systems acquired under a major acquisition program.

(4) LEVEL 1 ACQUISITION.—The term "Level 1 acquisition" means—

    (A) an acquisition by the Coast Guard—

        (i) the estimated life-cycle costs of which exceed \$1,000,000,000; or

        (ii) the estimated total acquisition costs of which exceed \$300,000,000; or

    (B) any acquisition that the Chief Acquisition Officer of the Coast Guard determines to have a special interest—

        (i) due to—

            (I) the experimental or technically immature nature of the asset;

           (II) the technological complexity of the asset;

           (III) the commitment of resources; or

           (IV) the nature of the capability or set of capabilities to be achieved; or

        (ii) because such acquisition is a joint acquisition.

(5) LEVEL 2 ACQUISITION.—The term "Level 2 acquisition" means an acquisition by the Coast Guard—

    (A) the estimated life-cycle costs of which are equal to or less than \$1,000,000,000, but greater than \$300,000,000; or

    (B) the estimated total acquisition costs of which are equal to or less than \$300,000,000, but greater than \$100,000,000.

(6) LIFE-CYCLE COST.—The term "life-cycle cost" means all costs for development, procurement, construction, and operations and support for a particular capability or asset, without regard to funding source or management control.

(7) MAJOR ACQUISITION PROGRAM.—The term "major acquisition program" means an ongoing acquisition undertaken by the Coast Guard with a life-cycle cost estimate greater than or equal to \$300,000,000.

(8) PROJECT OR PROGRAM MANAGER DEFINED.—The term "project or program manager" means an individual designated—

(A) to develop, produce, and deploy a new asset to meet identified operational requirements; and

(B) to manage cost, schedule, and performance of the acquisition, project, or program.

(9) SAFETY CONCERN.—The term "safety concern" means any hazard associated with a capability or asset or a subsystem of a capability or asset that is likely to cause serious bodily injury or death to a typical Coast Guard user in testing, maintaining, repairing, or operating the capability, asset, or subsystem or any hazard associated with the capability, asset, or subsystem that is likely to cause major damage to the capability, asset, or subsystem during the course of its normal operation by a typical Coast Guard user.

(10) DEVELOPMENTAL TEST AND EVALUATION.—The term "developmental test and evaluation" means—

(A) the testing of a capability or asset and the subsystems of the capability or asset to determine whether they meet all contractual performance requirements, including technical performance requirements, supportability requirements, and interoperability requirements and related specifications; and

(B) the evaluation of the results of such testing.

(11) OPERATIONAL TEST AND EVALUATION.—The term "operational test and evaluation" means—

(A) the testing of a capability or asset and the subsystems of the capability or asset, under conditions similar to those in which the capability or asset and subsystems will actually be deployed, for the purpose of determining the effectiveness and suitability of the capability or asset and subsystems for use by typical Coast Guard users to conduct those missions for which the capability or asset and subsystems are intended to be used; and

(B) the evaluation of the results of such testing.

(Added Pub. L. 111–281, title IV, §402(a), Oct. 15, 2010, 124 Stat. 2948, §581; amended Pub. L. 114–120, title II, §209(8), Feb. 8, 2016, 130 Stat. 41; Pub. L. 114–328, div. A, title VIII, §899(b)(1)(F), Dec. 23, 2016, 130 Stat. 2334; Pub. L. 115–232, div. C, title XXXV, §3531(c)(8), Aug. 13, 2018, 132 Stat. 2320; renumbered §1171 and amended Pub. L. 115–282, title I, §§108(b), 123(b)(2), Dec. 4, 2018, 132 Stat. 4208, 4240.)

SUBTITLE II
PERSONNEL

SUBTITLE II—PERSONNEL

CHAPTER 19—COAST GUARD ACADEMY

SUBCHAPTER I—ADMINISTRATION

SUBCHAPTER II—CADETS

SUBCHAPTER III—FACULTY

SUBCHAPTER I—ADMINISTRATION

§1901. ADMINISTRATION OF ACADEMY

The immediate government and military command of the Coast Guard Academy shall be in the Superintendent of the Academy, subject to the direction of the Commandant under the general supervision of the Secretary. The Commandant may select a superintendent from the active list of the Coast Guard who shall serve in the pleasure of the Commandant.

(Aug. 4, 1949, ch. 393, 63 Stat. 508, §181; renumbered §1901, Pub. L. 115–282, title I, §110(b), Dec. 4, 2018, 132 Stat. 4212.)

§1902. POLICY ON SEXUAL HARASSMENT AND SEXUAL VIOLENCE

(a) REQUIRED POLICY.—The Commandant shall direct the Superintendent of the Coast Guard Academy to prescribe a policy on sexual harassment and sexual violence applicable to the cadets and other personnel of the Academy.

(b) MATTERS TO BE SPECIFIED IN POLICY.—The policy on sexual harassment and sexual violence under this section shall include specification of the following:

(1) Programs to promote awareness of the incidence of rape, acquaintance rape, and other sexual offenses of a criminal nature that involve cadets or other Academy personnel.

(2) Information about how the Coast Guard and the Academy will protect the confidentiality of victims of sexual harassment or sexual violence, including how any records, statistics, or reports intended for public release will be formatted such that the confidentiality of victims is not jeopardized.

(3) Procedures that cadets and other Academy personnel should follow in the case of an occurrence of sexual harassment or sexual violence, including—

(A) if the victim chooses to report an occurrence of sexual harassment or sexual violence, a specification of the individual or individuals to whom the alleged offense should be reported and options for confidential reporting, including written information to be given to victims that explains how the Coast Guard and the Academy will protect the confidentiality of victims;

(B) a specification of any other individual whom the victim should contact; and

(C) procedures on the preservation of evidence potentially necessary for proof of criminal sexual assault.

(4) Procedures for disciplinary action in cases of criminal sexual assault involving a cadet or other Academy personnel.

(5) Sanctions authorized to be imposed in a substantiated case of sexual harassment or sexual violence involving a cadet or other Academy personnel, including with respect to rape, acquaintance rape, or other criminal sexual offense, whether forcible or nonforcible.

(6) Required training on the policy for all cadets and other Academy personnel who process allegations of sexual harassment or sexual violence involving a cadet or other Academy personnel.

(c) ASSESSMENT.—

(1) IN GENERAL.—The Commandant shall direct the Superintendent to conduct at the Academy during each Academy program year an assessment to determine the effectiveness of the policies of the Academy with respect to sexual harassment and sexual violence involving cadets or other Academy personnel.

(2) BIENNIAL SURVEY.—For the assessment at the Academy under paragraph (1) with respect to an Academy program year that begins in an odd-numbered calendar year, the Superintendent shall conduct a survey of cadets and other Academy personnel—

(A) to measure—

(i) the incidence, during that program year, of sexual harassment and sexual violence events, on or off the Academy reservation, that have been reported to an official of the Academy; and

(ii) the incidence, during that program year, of sexual harassment and sexual violence events, on or off the Academy reservation, that have not been reported to an official of the Academy; and

(B) to assess the perceptions of the cadets and other Academy personnel with respect to—

(i) the Academy's policies, training, and procedures on sexual harassment and sexual violence involving cadets or other Academy personnel;

(ii) the enforcement of such policies;

(iii) the incidence of sexual harassment and sexual violence involving cadets or other Academy personnel; and

(iv) any other issues relating to sexual harassment and sexual violence involving cadets or other Academy personnel.

(d) REPORT.—

(1) IN GENERAL.—The Commandant shall direct the Superintendent to submit to the Commandant a report on sexual harassment and sexual violence involving cadets or other Academy personnel for each Academy program year.

(2) REPORT SPECIFICATIONS.—Each report under paragraph (1) shall include, for the Academy program year covered by the report, the following:

(A) The number of sexual assaults, rapes, and other sexual offenses involving cadets or other Academy personnel that have been reported to Academy officials during the Academy program year and, of those reported cases, the number that have been substantiated.

(B) A plan for the actions that are to be taken in the following Academy program year regarding prevention of and response to sexual harassment and sexual violence involving cadets or other Academy personnel.

(3) BIENNIAL SURVEY.—Each report under paragraph (1) for an Academy program year that begins in an odd-numbered calendar year shall include the results of the survey conducted in that Academy program year under subsection (c)(2).

(4) TRANSMISSION OF REPORT.—The Commandant shall transmit each report received

by the Commandant under this subsection, together with the Commandant's comments on the report, to—
    (A) the Committee on Commerce, Science, and Transportation of the Senate; and
    (B) the Committee on Transportation and Infrastructure of the House of Representatives.

(5) FOCUS GROUPS.—
    (A) IN GENERAL.—For each Academy program year with respect to which the Superintendent is not required to conduct a survey at the Academy under subsection (c)(2), the Commandant shall require focus groups to be conducted at the Academy for the purposes of ascertaining information relating to sexual assault and sexual harassment issues at the Academy.
    (B) INCLUSION IN REPORTS.—Information derived from a focus group under subparagraph (A) shall be included in the next transmitted Commandant's report under this subsection.

(e) VICTIM CONFIDENTIALITY.—To the extent that information collected under the authority of this section is reported or otherwise made available to the public, such information shall be provided in a form that is consistent with applicable privacy protections under Federal law and does not jeopardize the confidentiality of victims.

(Added Pub. L. 112–213, title II, §205(a), Dec. 20, 2012, 126 Stat. 1543, §200; amended Pub. L. 115–232, div. C, title XXXV, §3531(c)(9), Aug. 13, 2018, 132 Stat. 2320; renumbered §1902, Pub. L. 115–282, title I, §110(b), Dec. 4, 2018, 132 Stat. 4212; Pub. L. 116–283, div. G, title LVXXXV [LXXXV], §8505(a)(11), Jan. 1, 2021, 134 Stat. 4748.)

§1903. ANNUAL BOARD OF VISITORS

(a) IN GENERAL.—A Board of Visitors to the Coast Guard Academy is established to review and make recommendations on the operation of the Academy.
    (b) MEMBERSHIP.—
        (1) IN GENERAL.—The membership of the Board shall consist of the following:
        (A) The chairman of the Committee on Commerce, Science, and Transportation of the Senate, or the chairman's designee.
        (B) The chairman of the Committee on Transportation and Infrastructure of the House of Representatives, or the chairman's designee.
        (C) 3 Members of the Senate designated by the Vice President.
        (D) 4 Members of the House of Representatives designated by the Speaker of the House of Representatives.
        (E) 6 individuals designated by the President.

        (2) LENGTH OF SERVICE.—
        (A) MEMBERS OF CONGRESS.—A Member of Congress designated under subparagraph (C) or (D) of paragraph (1) as a member of the Board shall be designated as a member in the First Session of a Congress and serve for the duration of that Congress.

(B) INDIVIDUALS DESIGNATED BY THE PRESIDENT.—Each individual designated by the President under subparagraph (E) of paragraph (1) shall serve as a member of the Board for 3 years, except that any such member whose term of office has expired shall continue to serve until a successor is appointed by the President.

(3) DEATH OR RESIGNATION OF A MEMBER.—If a member of the Board dies or resigns, a successor shall be designated for any unexpired portion of the term of the member by the official who designated the member.

(c) ACADEMY VISITS.—
(1) ANNUAL VISIT.—The Board shall visit the Academy annually to review the operation of the Academy.
(2) ADDITIONAL VISITS.—With the approval of the Secretary, the Board or individual members of the Board may make other visits to the Academy in connection with the duties of the Board or to consult with the Superintendent of the Academy.

(d) SCOPE OF REVIEW.—The Board shall review, with respect to the Academy—
(1) the state of morale and discipline;
(2) recruitment and retention, including diversity, inclusion, and issues regarding women specifically;
(3) the curriculum;
(4) instruction;
(5) physical equipment;
(6) fiscal affairs; and
(7) other matters relating to the Academy that the Board determines appropriate.

(e) REPORT.—Not later than 60 days after the date of an annual visit of the Board under subsection (c)(1), the Board shall submit to the Secretary, the Committee on Commerce, Science, and Transportation of the Senate, and the Committee on Transportation and Infrastructure of the House of Representatives a report on the actions of the Board during such visit and the recommendations of the Board pertaining to the Academy.
(f) ADVISORS.—If approved by the Secretary, the Board may consult with advisors in carrying out this section.
(g) REIMBURSEMENT.—Each member of the Board and each adviser consulted by the Board under subsection (f) shall be reimbursed, to the extent permitted by law, by the Coast Guard for actual expenses incurred while engaged in duties as a member or adviser.

(Aug. 4, 1949, ch. 393, 63 Stat. 510, §194; Pub. L. 101–595, title III, §304, Nov. 16, 1990, 104 Stat. 2984; Pub. L. 107–295, title IV, §408(a)(1), Nov. 25, 2002, 116 Stat. 2117; Pub. L. 113–281, title II, §211, Dec. 18, 2014, 128 Stat. 3027; renumbered §1903, Pub. L. 115–282, title I, §110(b), Dec. 4, 2018, 132 Stat. 4212; Pub. L. 116–283, div. G, title LVXXXII [LXXXII], §8277, Jan. 1, 2021, 134 Stat. 4687; Pub. L. 117–81, div. A, title V, §554(d), Dec. 27, 2021, 135 Stat. 1738.)

§1904. ADVISORY BOARD ON WOMEN AT THE COAST GUARD ACADEMY

(a) IN GENERAL.—The Superintendent of the Academy shall establish at the Coast Guard Academy an advisory board to be known as the Advisory Board on Women at the Coast

Guard Academy (referred to in this section as the "Advisory Board").

(b) MEMBERSHIP.—The Advisory Board shall be composed of not fewer than 12 current cadets of the Coast Guard Academy, including not fewer than 3 cadets from each current class.

(c) APPOINTMENT; TERM.—Cadets shall serve on the Advisory Board pursuant to appointment by the Superintendent of the Academy. Appointments shall be made not later than 60 days after the date of the swearing in of a new class of cadets at the Academy. The term of membership of a cadet on the Advisory Board shall be 1 academic year.

(d) REAPPOINTMENT.—The Superintendent of the Academy may reappoint not more than 6 cadets from the previous term to serve on the Advisory Board for an additional academic year if the Superintendent of the Academy determines such reappointment to be in the best interests of the Coast Guard Academy.

(e) MEETINGS.—The Advisory Board shall meet with the Commandant at least once each academic year on the activities of the Advisory Board. The Advisory Board shall meet in person with the Superintendent of the Academy not less than twice each academic year on the duties of the Advisory Board.

(f) DUTIES.—The Advisory Board shall identify opportunities and challenges facing cadets at the Academy who are women, including an assessment of culture, leadership development, and access to health care of cadets at the Academy who are women.

(g) WORKING GROUPS.—The Advisory Board may establish one or more working groups to assist the Advisory Board in carrying out its duties, including working groups composed in part of cadets at the Academy who are not current members of the Advisory Board.

(h) REPORTS AND BRIEFINGS.—The Advisory Board shall regularly provide the Commandant and the Superintendent reports and briefings on the results of its duties, including recommendations for actions to be taken in light of such results. Such reports and briefings may be provided in writing, in person, or both.

(Added Pub. L. 116–283, div. G, title LVXXXII [LXXXII], §8215(b)(2), Jan. 1, 2021, 134 Stat. 4651.)

§1905. COAST GUARD ACADEMY MINORITY OUTREACH TEAM PROGRAM

(a) IN GENERAL.—There is established within the Coast Guard Academy a minority outreach team program (in this section referred to as the "Program") under which officers, including minority officers and officers from territories and other possessions of the United States, who are Academy graduates may volunteer their time to recruit minority students and strengthen cadet retention through mentorship of cadets.

(b) ADMINISTRATION.—Not later than January 1, 2021, the Commandant, in consultation with Program volunteers and Academy alumni that participated in prior programs at the Academy similar to the Program, shall appoint a permanent civilian position at the Academy to administer the Program by, among other things—

(1) overseeing administration of the Program;

(2) serving as a resource to volunteers and outside stakeholders;

(3) advising Academy leadership on recruitment and retention efforts based on recommendations from volunteers and outside stakeholders;

(4) establishing strategic goals and performance metrics for the Program with input from active volunteers and Academy leadership; and

(5) reporting annually to the Commandant on academic year and performance outcomes of the goals for the Program before the end of each academic year.

(Added Pub. L. 116–283, div. G, title LVXXXII [LXXXII], §8275(a), Jan. 1, 2021, 134 Stat. 4685.)

§1906. PARTICIPATION IN FEDERAL, STATE, OR OTHER EDUCATIONAL RESEARCH GRANTS

(a) IN GENERAL.—Notwithstanding any other provision of law, the United States Coast Guard Academy may compete for and accept Federal, State, or other educational research grants, subject to the following limitations:

(1) No award may be accepted for the acquisition or construction of facilities.

(2) No award may be accepted for the routine functions of the Academy.

(b) QUALIFIED ORGANIZATIONS.—

(1) IN GENERAL.—The Commandant may—

(A) enter into a contract, cooperative agreement, lease, or licensing agreement with a qualified organization;

(B) allow a qualified organization to use, at no cost, personal property of the Coast Guard; and

(C) notwithstanding section 504, accept funds, supplies, and services from a qualified organization.

(2) SOLE-SOURCE BASIS.—Notwithstanding chapter 65 of title 31 and sections 3201 through 3205 of title 10, the Commandant may enter into a contract or cooperative agreement under paragraph (1)(A) on a sole-source basis.

(3) MAINTAINING FAIRNESS, OBJECTIVITY, AND INTEGRITY.—The Commandant shall ensure that contributions under this subsection do not—

(A) reflect unfavorably on the ability of the Coast Guard, any of its employees, or any member of the armed forces to carry out any responsibility or duty in a fair and objective manner; or

(B) compromise the integrity or appearance of integrity of any program of the Coast Guard, or any individual involved in such a program.

(4) LIMITATION.—For purposes of this subsection, employees or personnel of a qualified organization shall not be employees of the United States.

(5) QUALIFIED ORGANIZATION DEFINED.—In this subsection the term "qualified organization" means an organization—

(A) described under section 501(c)(3) of the Internal Revenue Code of 1986 and exempt from taxation under section 501(a) of that Code; and

(B) established by the Coast Guard Academy Alumni Association solely for the purpose of supporting academic research and applying for and administering Federal, State, or other educational research grants on behalf of the Coast Guard Academy.

(Added Pub. L. 103–206, title III, §305(a), Dec. 20, 1993, 107 Stat. 2424, §196; amended Pub. L. 114–120, title II, §218, Feb. 8, 2016, 130 Stat. 47; Pub. L. 115–232, div. C, title XXXV, §3531(c)(10), Aug. 13, 2018, 132 Stat. 2320; renumbered §1904 and amended Pub. L. 115–282, title I, §§110(b), 123(b)(2), Dec. 4, 2018, 132 Stat. 4212, 4240; renumbered §1906, Pub. L. 116–283, div. G, title LVXXXII [LXXXII], §8215(b)(1),

Jan. 1, 2021, 134 Stat. 4650; Pub. L. 117–81, div. A, title XVII, §1702(d)(3), Dec. 27, 2021, 135 Stat. 2156.)

SUBCHAPTER II—CADETS

§1921. CORPS OF CADETS AUTHORIZED STRENGTH

The number of cadets appointed annually to the Academy shall be as determined by the Secretary but the number appointed in any one year shall not exceed six hundred.

(Added Pub. L. 115–282, title I, §110(c)(1)(B), Dec. 4, 2018, 132 Stat. 4213.)

§1922. APPOINTMENTS

Appointments to cadetships shall be made under regulations prescribed by the Secretary, who shall determine age limits, methods of selection of applicants, term of service as a cadet before graduation, and all other matters affecting such appointments. In the administration of this section, the Secretary shall take such action as may be necessary and appropriate to insure [1] that female individuals shall be eligible for appointment and admission to the Coast Guard Academy, and that the relevant standards required for appointment, admission, training, graduation, and commissioning of female individuals shall be the same as those required for male individuals, except for those minimum essential adjustments in such standards required because of physiological differences between male and female individuals.

(Added Pub. L. 115–282, title I, §110(c)(1)(B), Dec. 4, 2018, 132 Stat. 4213.)

[1] So in original. Probably should be "ensure".

§1923. ADMISSION OF FOREIGN NATIONALS FOR INSTRUCTION; RESTRICTIONS; CONDITIONS

(a) A foreign national may not receive instruction at the Academy except as authorized by this section.

(b) The President may designate not more than 36 foreign nationals whom the Secretary may permit to receive instruction at the Academy.

(c) A foreign national receiving instruction under this section is entitled to the same pay, allowances, and emoluments, to be paid from the same appropriations, as a cadet appointed pursuant to section 1922 of this title. A foreign national may receive instruction under this section only if his country agrees in advance to reimburse the United States, at a rate determined by the Secretary, for the cost of providing such instruction, including pay, allowances, and emoluments, unless a waiver therefrom has been granted to that country by the Secretary. Funds received by the Secretary for this purpose shall be credited to the appropriations bearing the cost thereof, and may be apportioned between fiscal years.

(d) A foreign national receiving instruction under this section is—

(1) not entitled to any appointment in the Coast Guard by reason of his graduation from the Academy; and

(2) subject to those regulations applicable to the Academy governing admission, attendance, discipline, resignation, discharge, dismissal, and graduation, except as may otherwise be prescribed by the Secretary.

(Added Pub. L. 91–278, §1(6), June 12, 1970, 84 Stat. 304, §195; amended Pub. L. 94–468, Oct. 11, 1976, 90 Stat. 2002; Pub. L. 112–213, title II, §204, Dec. 20, 2012, 126 Stat. 1543; renumbered §1923 and amended Pub. L. 115–282, title I, §§110(b), 123(c)(1), Dec. 4, 2018, 132 Stat. 4212, 4240.)

§1924. Conduct

The Secretary may summarily dismiss from the Coast Guard any cadet who, during his cadetship, is found unsatisfactory in either studies or conduct, or may be deemed not adapted for a career in the Coast Guard. Cadets shall be subject to rules governing discipline prescribed by the Commandant.

(Added Pub. L. 115–282, title I, §110(c)(1)(C), Dec. 4, 2018, 132 Stat. 4214.)

§1925. Agreement

(a) Each cadet shall sign an agreement with respect to the cadet's length of service in the Coast Guard. The agreement shall provide that the cadet agrees to the following:

(1) That the cadet will complete the course of instruction at the Coast Guard Academy.

(2) That upon graduation from the Coast Guard Academy the cadet—

(A) will accept an appointment, if tendered, as a commissioned officer of the Coast Guard; and

(B) will serve on active duty for at least five years immediately after such appointment.

(3) That if an appointment described in paragraph (2) is not tendered or if the cadet is permitted to resign as a regular officer before the completion of the commissioned service obligation of the cadet, the cadet—

(A) will accept an appointment as a commissioned officer in the Coast Guard Reserve; and

(B) will remain in that reserve component until completion of the commissioned service obligation of the cadet.

(b)(1) The Secretary may transfer to the Coast Guard Reserve, and may order to active duty for such period of time as the Secretary prescribes (but not to exceed four years), a cadet who breaches an agreement under subsection (a). The period of time for which a cadet is ordered to active duty under this paragraph may be determined without regard to section 651(a) of title 10.

(2) A cadet who is transferred to the Coast Guard Reserve under paragraph (1) shall be transferred in an appropriate enlisted grade or rating, as determined by the Secretary.

(3) For the purposes of paragraph (1), a cadet shall be considered to have breached an agreement under subsection (a) if the cadet is separated from the Coast Guard Academy under circumstances which the Secretary determines constitute a breach by the cadet of the cadet's agreement to complete the course of instruction at the Coast Guard Academy and accept an appointment as a commissioned officer upon graduation from the Coast Guard Academy.

(c) The Secretary shall prescribe regulations to carry out this section. Those regulations shall include—

(1) standards for determining what constitutes, for the purpose of subsection (b), a breach of an agreement under subsection (a);

(2) procedures for determining whether such a breach has occurred; and

(3) standards for determining the period of time for which a person may be ordered to serve on active duty under subsection (b).

(d) In this section, "commissioned service obligation", with respect to an officer who is a graduate of the Academy, means the period beginning on the date of the officer's appointment as a commissioned officer and ending on the sixth anniversary of such appointment or, at the discretion of the Secretary, any later date up to the eighth anniversary of such appointment.

(e)(1) This section does not apply to a cadet who is not a citizen or national of the United States.

(2) In the case of a cadet who is a minor and who has parents or a guardian, the cadet may sign the agreement required by subsection (a) only with the consent of the parent or guardian.

(f) A cadet or former cadet who does not fulfill the terms of the obligation to serve as specified under section (a), or the alternative obligation imposed under subsection (b), shall be subject to the repayment provisions of section 303a(e) of title 37.

(Added Pub. L. 115–282, title I, §110(c)(1)(C), Dec. 4, 2018, 132 Stat. 4214.)

§1926. Cadet applicants; preappointment travel to Academy

The Secretary is authorized to expend appropriated funds for selective preappointment travel to the Academy for orientation visits of cadet applicants.

(Added Pub. L. 98–557, §24(a), Oct. 30, 1984, 98 Stat. 2872, §181a; renumbered §1926, Pub. L. 115–282, title I, §110(b), Dec. 4, 2018, 132 Stat. 4212.)

§1927. Cadets; initial clothing allowance

The Secretary may prescribe a sum which shall be credited to each new cadet upon first admission to the Academy, to cover the cost of an initial clothing and equipment issue, which sum shall be deducted subsequently from the pay of such cadet. Each cadet discharged prior to graduation who is indebted to the United States on account of advances of pay to purchase required clothing and equipment shall be required to turn in to the Academy all clothing and equipment of a distinctively military nature to the extent required to discharge such indebtedness; and, if the value of such clothing and equipment so turned in does not cover the indebtedness incurred, then such indebtedness shall be canceled.

(Aug. 4, 1949, ch. 393, 63 Stat. 508, §183; Aug. 22, 1951, ch. 340, §3, 65 Stat. 196; renumbered §1927, Pub. L. 115–282, title I, §110(b), Dec. 4, 2018, 132 Stat. 4212; Pub. L. 116–283, div. G, title LVXXXV [LXXXV], §8506(a), Jan. 1, 2021, 134 Stat. 4752.)

§1928. Cadets; degree of bachelor of science

The Superintendent of the Academy may, under such rules and regulations as the Secretary shall prescribe, confer the degree of bachelor of science upon all graduates of the Academy and may, in addition, confer the degree of bachelor of science upon such other living graduates of the Academy as shall have met the requirements of the Academy for such degree.

(Aug. 4, 1949, ch. 393, 63 Stat. 508, §184; renumbered §1928, Pub. L. 115–282, title I, §110(b), Dec. 4, 2018, 132 Stat. 4212.)

§1929. CADETS; APPOINTMENT AS ENSIGN

The President may, by and with the advice and consent of the Senate, appoint as ensigns in the Coast Guard all cadets who shall graduate from the Academy. Ensigns so commissioned on the same date shall take rank according to their proficiency as shown by the order of their merit at date of graduation.

(Aug. 4, 1949, ch. 393, 63 Stat. 508, §185; renumbered §1929, Pub. L. 115–282, title I, §110(b), Dec. 4, 2018, 132 Stat. 4212.)

§1930. CADETS: CHARGES AND FEES FOR ATTENDANCE; LIMITATION

(a) PROHIBITION.—Except as provided in subsection (b), no charge or fee for tuition, room, or board for attendance at the Academy may be imposed unless the charge or fee is specifically authorized by a law enacted after October 5, 1994.

(b) EXCEPTION.—The prohibition specified in subsection (a) does not apply with respect to any item or service provided to cadets for which a charge or fee is imposed as of October 5, 1994. The Secretary shall notify Congress of any change made by the Academy in the amount of a charge or fee authorized under this subsection.

(Added Pub. L. 108–375, div. A, title V, §545(d)(1), Oct. 28, 2004, 118 Stat. 1909, §197; amended Pub. L. 113–281, title II, §222(2), Dec. 18, 2014, 128 Stat. 3038; renumbered §1930, Pub. L. 115–282, title I, §110(b), Dec. 4, 2018, 132 Stat. 4212.)

SUBCHAPTER III—FACULTY

§1941. CIVILIAN TEACHING STAFF

(a) The Secretary may appoint in the Coast Guard such number of civilian faculty members at the Academy as the needs of the Service may require. They shall have such titles and perform duties as prescribed by the Secretary. Leaves of absence and hours of work for civilian faculty members shall be governed by regulations promulgated by the Secretary, without regard to the provisions of title 5.

(b) The compensation of individuals employed under this section is as prescribed by the Secretary.

(Aug. 4, 1949, ch. 393, 63 Stat. 509, §186; Sept. 3, 1954, ch. 1263, §32, 68 Stat. 1238; Pub. L. 86–474, §1(9), May 14, 1960, 74 Stat. 145; Pub. L. 89–444, §1(9), June 9, 1966, 80 Stat. 195; Pub. L. 94–546, §1(14), Oct. 18, 1976, 90 Stat. 2520; renumbered §1941, Pub. L. 115–282, title I, §110(b), Dec. 4, 2018, 132 Stat. 4212; Pub. L. 116–283, div. G, title LVXXXV [LXXXV], §8505(a)(12), Jan. 1, 2021, 134 Stat. 4748.)

§1942. PERMANENT COMMISSIONED TEACHING STAFF; COMPOSITION

The permanent commissioned teaching staff at the Academy shall consist of professors, associate professors, assistant professors and instructors, in such numbers as the needs of the Service require. They shall perform duties as prescribed by the Commandant, and exercise command only in the academic department of the Academy.

(Aug. 4, 1949, ch. 393, 63 Stat. 509, §187; Pub. L. 86–474, §1(10), May 14, 1960, 74 Stat. 145; renumbered §1942, Pub. L. 115–282, title I, §110(b), Dec. 4, 2018, 132 Stat. 4212.)

§1943. APPOINTMENT OF PERMANENT COMMISSIONED TEACHING STAFF

The President may appoint in the Coast Guard, by and with the advice and consent of the Senate, the professors, associate professors, assistant professors, and instructors who are to serve on the permanent commissioned teaching staff of the Academy. An original appointment to the permanent commissioned teaching staff, unless the appointee has served as a civilian member of the teaching staff, regular commissioned officer, temporary commissioned officer, or reserve commissioned officer in the Coast Guard, shall be a temporary appointment until the appointee has satisfactorily completed a probationary term of four years of service; thereafter he may be regularly appointed and his rank shall date from the date of his temporary appointment in the grade in which permanently appointed.

(Aug. 4, 1949, ch. 393, 63 Stat. 509, §188; Pub. L. 86–474, §1(11), May 14, 1960, 74 Stat. 145; Pub. L. 94–546, §1(15), Oct. 18, 1976, 90 Stat. 2520; renumbered §1943, Pub. L. 115–282, title I, §110(b), Dec. 4, 2018, 132 Stat. 4212.)

§1944. GRADE OF PERMANENT COMMISSIONED TEACHING STAFF

Professors shall be commissioned officers with grade not above captain, associate and assistant professors with grade not above commander, and instructors with grade not above lieutenant commander. All officers of the permanent commissioned teaching staff shall receive the pay and allowances of other commissioned officers of the same grade and length of service. When any such professor, associate professor, assistant professor, or instructor is appointed or commissioned with grade less than the highest grade permitted, he shall be promoted under regulations prescribed by the Secretary.

(Aug. 4, 1949, ch. 393, 63 Stat. 509, §189; Pub. L. 86–474, §1(12), May 14, 1960, 74 Stat. 145; renumbered §1944, Pub. L. 115–282, title I, §110(b), Dec. 4, 2018, 132 Stat. 4212.)

§1945. Retirement of Permanent Commissioned Teaching Staff

Professors, associate professors, assistant professors, and instructors in the Coast Guard shall be subject to retirement or discharge from active service for any cause on the same basis as other commissioned officers of the Coast Guard, except that they shall not be required to retire from active service under the provisions of section 2149 of this title, nor shall they be subject to the provisions of section 2150 of this title, nor shall they be required to retire at age sixty-two but may be permitted to serve until age sixty-four at which time unless earlier retired or separated they shall be retired. The Secretary may retire any member of the permanent commissioned teaching staff who has completed thirty years' active service. Service as a civilian member of the teaching staff at the Academy in addition to creditable service authorized by any other law in any of the military services rendered prior to an appointment as a professor, associate professor, assistant professor, or instructor shall be credited in computing length of service for retirement purposes. The provisions of law relating to retirement for disability in line of duty shall not apply in the case of a professor, associate professor, assistant professor, or instructor serving under a temporary appointment.

(Aug. 4, 1949, ch. 393, 63 Stat. 509, §190; Pub. L. 86–474, §1(13), May 14, 1960, 74 Stat. 145; Pub. L. 88–130, §1(8), Sept. 24, 1963, 77 Stat. 175; Pub. L. 89–444, §1(10), June 9, 1966, 80 Stat. 196; Pub. L. 91–278, §1(5), June 12, 1970, 84 Stat. 304; renumbered §1945 and amended Pub. L. 115–282, title I, §§110(b), 123(b)(2), Dec. 4, 2018, 132 Stat. 4212, 4240.)

§1946. Credit for Service as Member of Civilian Teaching Staff

Service as a member of the civilian teaching staff at the Academy in addition to creditable services authorized by any other law in any of the military services rendered prior to an appointment as professor, associate professor, assistant professor, or instructor shall be credited in computing length of service as a professor, associate professor, assistant professor, or instructor for purposes of pay and allowances.

(Aug. 4, 1949, ch. 393, 63 Stat. 510, §191; Pub. L. 86–474, §1(14), May 14, 1960, 74 Stat. 146; renumbered §1946, Pub. L. 115–282, title I, §110(b), Dec. 4, 2018, 132 Stat. 4212.)

§1947. Assignment of Personnel as Instructors

The Commandant may assign any member to appropriate instruction duty at the Academy.

(Aug. 4, 1949, ch. 393, 63 Stat. 510, §192; Pub. L. 98–557, §15(a)(3)(H), Oct. 30, 1984, 98 Stat. 2865; renumbered §1947, Pub. L. 115–282, title I, §110(b), Dec. 4, 2018, 132 Stat. 4212.)

§1948. Marine Safety Curriculum

The Commandant shall ensure that professional courses of study in marine safety are provided at the Coast Guard Academy, and during other officer accession programs, to give Coast Guard cadets and other officer candidates a background and understanding of the marine safety program. These courses may include such topics as program history, vessel design and construction, vessel inspection, casualty investigation, and administrative law and regulations.

(Added Pub. L. 111–281, title V, §525(a), Oct. 15, 2010, 124 Stat. 2959, §200; renumbered §199 and amended Pub. L. 111–330, §1(7)(A), Dec. 22, 2010, 124 Stat. 3569; Pub. L. 115–232, div. C, title XXXV, §3531(c)(11), Aug. 13, 2018, 132 Stat. 2320; renumbered §1948, Pub. L. 115–282, title I, §110(b), Dec. 4, 2018, 132 Stat. 4212.)

CHAPTER 21—PERSONNEL; OFFICERS

SUBCHAPTER I—APPOINTMENT AND PROMOTION

SUBCHAPTER II—DISCHARGES; RETIREMENTS; REVOCATION OF COMMISSIONS; SEPARATION FOR CAUSE

SUBCHAPTER III—GENERAL PROVISIONS

SUBCHAPTER I—APPOINTMENT AND PROMOTION

§2101. ORIGINAL APPOINTMENT OF PERMANENT COMMISSIONED OFFICERS

(a)(1) The President may appoint permanent commissioned officers in the Regular Coast Guard in grades appropriate to their qualification, experience, and length of service, as the needs of the Coast Guard may require, from among the following categories:

(A) Graduates of the Coast Guard Academy.

(B) Commissioned warrant officers, warrant officers, and enlisted members of the Regular Coast Guard.

(C) Members of the Coast Guard Reserve who have served at least 2 years as such.

(D) Licensed officers of the United States merchant marine who have served 2 or more years aboard a vessel of the United States in the capacity of a licensed officer.

(2) Original appointments under this section in the grades of lieutenant commander and above shall be made by the President by and with the advice and consent of the Senate.

(3) Original appointments under this section in the grades of ensign through lieutenant shall be made by the President alone.

(b) No individual shall be appointed a commissioned officer under this section until his mental, moral, physical, and professional fitness to perform the duties of a commissioned officer has been established under such regulations as the Secretary shall prescribe.

(c) Appointees under this section shall take precedence in the grade to which appointed in accordance with the dates of their commissions as commissioned officers in such grade. Appointees whose dates of commission are the same shall take precedence with each other as the Secretary shall determine.

(d) For the purposes of this section, the term "original", with respect to the appointment of a member of the Coast Guard, refers to that member's most recent appointment in the Coast Guard that is neither a promotion nor a demotion.

(Added Pub. L. 88–130, §1(10)(C), Sept. 24, 1963, 77 Stat. 177, §211; amended Pub. L. 89–444, §1(11), June 30, 1966, 80 Stat. 196; Pub. L. 98–557, §15(a)(3)(B), Oct. 30, 1984, 98 Stat. 2865; Pub. L. 109–241, title II, §217(a), July 11, 2006, 120 Stat. 525; Pub. L. 112–213, title II, §206, Dec. 20, 2012, 126 Stat. 1546; renumbered §2101, Pub. L. 115–282, title I, §112(b), Dec. 4, 2018, 132 Stat. 4216; Pub. L. 116–283, div. G, title LVXXXV [LXXXV], §8505(a)(13), Jan. 1, 2021, 134 Stat. 4748.)

§2102. ACTIVE DUTY PROMOTION LIST

(a) The Secretary shall maintain a single active duty promotion list of officers of the Coast Guard on active duty in the grades of ensign and above. Reserve officers on active duty, other than pursuant to an active duty agreement executed under section 12311 of title 10, retired officers, and officers of the permanent commissioned teaching staff of the Coast Guard Academy shall not be included on the active duty promotion list.

(b) Officers shall be carried on the active duty promotion list in the order of seniority of the grades in which they are serving. Officers serving in the same grade shall be carried in the order of their seniority in that grade. The Secretary may correct any erroneous position

155

on the active duty promotion list that was caused by administrative error.

(c) An individual appointed in the grade of ensign or above in the Regular Coast Guard shall be placed on the active duty promotion list in the order of his date of rank and seniority.

(d) A Reserve officer, other than one excluded by subsection (a), shall, when he enters on active duty, be placed on the active duty promotion list in accordance with his grade and seniority. The position of such a Reserve officer among other officers of the Coast Guard on active duty who have the same date of rank shall be determined by the Secretary.

(Added Pub. L. 88–130, §1(1), Sept. 24, 1963, 77 Stat. 174, §41a; amended Pub. L. 91–278, §1(2), June 12, 1970, 84 Stat. 304; Pub. L. 93–174, §1(1), Dec. 5, 1973, 87 Stat. 692; Pub. L. 97–136, §6(a), Dec. 29, 1981, 95 Stat. 1706; Pub. L. 103–206, title II, §205(a), Dec. 20, 1993, 107 Stat. 2422; Pub. L. 103–337, div. A, title XVI, §1677(b)(1), Oct. 5, 1994, 108 Stat. 3019; renumbered §2102, Pub. L. 115–282, title I, §112(b), Dec. 4, 2018, 132 Stat. 4216; Pub. L. 116–283, div. G, title LVXXXV [LXXXV], §8505(a)(14), Jan. 1, 2021, 134 Stat. 4748.)

§2103. Number and distribution of commissioned officers on active duty promotion list

(a) Maximum Total Number.—

(1) In general.—The total number of Coast Guard commissioned officers on the active duty promotion list, excluding warrant officers, shall not exceed—

(A) 7,100 in fiscal year 2022;

(B) 7,200 in fiscal year 2023;

(C) 7,300 in fiscal year 2024; and

(D) 7,400 in fiscal year 2025 and each subsequent fiscal year.

(2) Temporary increase.—Notwithstanding paragraph (1), the Commandant may temporarily increase the total number of commissioned officers permitted under such paragraph by up to 4 percent for not more than 60 days after the date of the commissioning of a Coast Guard Academy class.

(3) Notification.—Not later than 30 days after exceeding the total number of commissioned officers permitted under paragraphs (1) and (2), and each 30 days thereafter until the total number of commissioned officers no longer exceeds the number of such officers permitted under paragraphs (1) and (2), the Commandant shall notify the Committee on Transportation and Infrastructure of the House of Representatives and the Committee on Commerce, Science, and Transportation of the Senate of the number of officers on the active duty promotion list on the last day of the preceding 30-day period.

(b) Distribution Percentages by Grade.—

(1) Required.—The total number of commissioned officers authorized by this section shall be distributed in grade in the following percentages: 0.375 percent for rear admiral; 0.375 percent for rear admiral (lower half); 6.0 percent for captain; 15.0 percent for commander; and 22.0 percent for lieutenant commander.

(2) Discretionary.—The Secretary shall prescribe the percentages applicable to the grades of lieutenant, lieutenant (junior grade), and ensign.

(3) AUTHORITY OF SECRETARY TO REDUCE PERCENTAGE.—The Secretary—

    (A) may reduce, as the needs of the Coast Guard require, any of the percentages set forth in paragraph (1); and

    (B) shall apply that total percentage reduction to any other lower grade or combination of lower grades.

(c) COMPUTATIONS.—

    (1) IN GENERAL.—The Secretary shall compute, at least once each year, the total number of commissioned officers authorized to serve in each grade by applying the grade distribution percentages established by or under this section to the total number of commissioned officers listed on the current active duty promotion list.

    (2) ROUNDING FRACTIONS.—Subject to subsection (a), in making the computations under paragraph (1), any fraction shall be rounded to the nearest whole number.

    (3) TREATMENT OF OFFICERS SERVING OUTSIDE COAST GUARD.—The number of commissioned officers on the active duty promotion list below the rank of vice admiral serving with other Federal departments or agencies on a reimbursable basis or excluded under section 324(d) of title 49 shall not be counted against the total number of commissioned officers authorized to serve in each grade.

(d) USE OF NUMBERS; TEMPORARY INCREASES.—The numbers resulting from computations under subsection (c) shall be, for all purposes, the authorized number in each grade; except that the authorized number for a grade is temporarily increased during the period between one computation and the next by the number of officers originally appointed in that grade during that period and the number of officers of that grade for whom vacancies exist in the next higher grade but whose promotion has been delayed for any reason.

(e) OFFICERS SERVING COAST GUARD ACADEMY AND RESERVE.—The number of officers authorized to be serving on active duty in each grade of the permanent commissioned teaching staff of the Coast Guard Academy and of the Reserve serving in connection with organizing, administering, recruiting, instructing, or training the reserve components shall be prescribed by the Secretary.

(Aug. 4, 1949, ch. 393, 63 Stat. 497, §42; July 20, 1956, ch. 647, §2, 70 Stat. 588; Pub. L. 86–474, §1(2), May 14, 1960, 74 Stat. 144; Pub. L. 88–130, §1(2), Sept. 24, 1963, 77 Stat. 174; Pub. L. 89–444, §1(2), June 9, 1966, 80 Stat. 195; Pub. L. 90–385, July 5, 1968, 82 Stat. 293; Pub. L. 92–451, §1(2), Oct. 2, 1972, 86 Stat. 755; Pub. L. 93–174, §1(2), Dec. 5, 1973, 87 Stat. 692; Pub. L. 96–23, §4, June 13, 1979, 93 Stat. 68; Pub. L. 97–417, §2(2), Jan. 4, 1983, 96 Stat. 2085; Pub. L. 97–449, §5(b), Jan. 12, 1983, 96 Stat. 2442; Pub. L. 98–557, §25(a)(1), Oct. 30, 1984, 98 Stat. 2872; Pub. L. 99–145, title V, §514(c)(1), Nov. 8, 1985, 99 Stat. 629; Pub. L. 103–206, title II, §201, Dec. 20, 1993, 107 Stat. 2420; Pub. L. 108–293, title II, §214, Aug. 9, 2004, 118 Stat. 1037; Pub. L. 111–281, title II, §204(a), Oct. 15, 2010, 124 Stat. 2910; Pub. L. 113–281, title II, §201, Dec. 18, 2014, 128 Stat. 3024; renumbered §2103, Pub. L. 115–282, title I, §112(b), Dec. 4, 2018, 132 Stat. 4216; Pub. L. 116–283, div. G, title LVXXXII [LXXXII], §8217, Jan. 1, 2021, 134 Stat. 4653; Pub. L. 117–263, div. K, title CXII, §11236(a), Dec. 23, 2022, 136 Stat. 4035.)

§2104. APPOINTMENT OF TEMPORARY OFFICERS

    (a) The president may appoint temporary commissioned officers—

      (1) in the Regular Coast Guard in a grade, not above lieutenant, appropriate to their

qualifications, experience, and length of service, as the needs of the Coast Guard may require, from among the commissioned warrant officers, warrant officers, and enlisted members of the Coast Guard, and from holders of licenses issued under chapter 71 of title 46; and

(2) in the Coast Guard Reserve in a grade, not above lieutenant, appropriate to their qualifications, experience, and length of service, as the needs of the Coast Guard may require, from among the commissioned warrant officers of the Coast Guard Reserve.

(b) Temporary appointments under this section do not change the permanent, probationary, or acting status of individuals so appointed, prejudice them in regard to promotion or appointment, or abridge their rights or benefits. An individual who is appointed under this section may not suffer any reduction in the rate of pay and allowances to which he would have been entitled had he remained in his former grade and continued to receive the increases in pay and allowances authorized for that grade.

(c) An appointment under this section, or a subsequent promotion appointment of a temporary officer, may be vacated by the appointing officer at any time. Each officer whose appointment is so vacated shall revert to his permanent status.

(d) Appointees under this section shall take precedence in the grade to which appointed in accordance with the dates of their appointments as officers in such grade. Appointees whose dates of appointment are the same shall take precedence with each other as the Secretary shall determine.

(Added Pub. L. 88–130, §1(10)(C), Sept. 24, 1963, 77 Stat. 178, §214; amended Pub. L. 89–444, §1(12)–(14), June 9, 1966, 80 Stat. 196; Pub. L. 93–283, §1(5), May 14, 1974, 88 Stat. 140; Pub. L. 96–376, §6, Oct. 3, 1980, 94 Stat. 1509; Pub. L. 98–557, §15(a)(3)(B), Oct. 30, 1984, 98 Stat. 2865; Pub. L. 103–337, div. A, title V, §541(f)(6), Oct. 5, 1994, 108 Stat. 2767; Pub. L. 104–324, title II, §211(a), Oct. 19, 1996, 110 Stat. 3915; Pub. L. 111–281, title II, §211, Oct. 15, 2010, 124 Stat. 2914; renumbered §2104, Pub. L. 115–282, title I, §112(b), Dec. 4, 2018, 132 Stat. 4216; Pub. L. 116–283, div. G, title LVXXXV [LXXXV], §8505(a)(15), Jan. 1, 2021, 134 Stat. 4748.)

§2105. RANK OF WARRANT OFFICERS

(a) Among warrant officer grades, warrant officers of a higher numerical designation are senior to warrant officer grades of a lower numerical designation.

(b) Warrant officers shall take precedence in the grade to which appointed in accordance with the dates of their commissions as commissioned officers in the Coast Guard in such grade. Precedence among warrant officers of the same grade who have the same date of commission shall be determined by regulations prescribed by the Secretary.

(Added Pub. L. 103–337, div. A, title V, §541(e)(1), Oct. 5, 1994, 108 Stat. 2766, §215; renumbered §2105, Pub. L. 115–282, title I, §112(b), Dec. 4, 2018, 132 Stat. 4216.)

§2106. SELECTION BOARDS; CONVENING OF BOARDS

At least once a year and at such other times as the needs of the service require, the Secretary shall convene selection boards to recommend for promotion to the next higher grade officers on the active duty promotion list in each grade from lieutenant (junior grade) through captain, with separate boards for each grade. However, the Secretary is not required to convene a board to recommend officers for promotion to a grade when no vacancies exist in the grade concerned, and he estimates that none will occur in the next twelve months.

(Added Pub. L. 88–130, §1(10)(C), Sept. 24, 1963, 77 Stat. 178, §251; renumbered §2106, Pub. L. 115–282, title I, §112(b), Dec. 4, 2018, 132 Stat. 4216.)

§2107. SELECTION BOARDS; COMPOSITION OF BOARDS

A board convened under section 2106 of this title shall consist of five or more officers on the active duty promotion list who are serving in or above the grade to which the board may recommend officers for promotion. No officer may be a member of two successive boards convened to consider officers of the same grade for promotion.

(Added Pub. L. 88–130, §1(10)(C), Sept. 24, 1963, 77 Stat. 179, §252; renumbered §2107 and amended Pub. L. 115–282, title I, §§112(b), 123(b)(2), Dec. 4, 2018, 132 Stat. 4216, 4240.)

§2108. SELECTION BOARDS; NOTICE OF CONVENING; COMMUNICATION WITH BOARD

(a) Before a board is convened under section 2106 of this title, notice of the convening date, the promotion zone to be considered, and the officers eligible for consideration shall be given to the service at large.

(b) Each officer eligible for consideration by a selection board convened under section 2106 of this title may send a communication through official channels to the board, to arrive not later than the date the board convenes, inviting attention to any matter of record in the armed forces concerning such officer. A communication sent under this section may not criticize any officer or reflect upon the character, conduct, or motive of any officer.

(Added Pub. L. 88–130, §1(10)(C), Sept. 24, 1963, 77 Stat. 179, §253; amended Pub. L. 89–444, §1(15), June 9, 1966, 80 Stat. 196; Pub. L. 111–281, title II, §212(1), Oct. 15, 2010, 124 Stat. 2914; renumbered §2108 and amended Pub. L. 115–282, title I, §§112(b), 123(b)(2), Dec. 4, 2018, 132 Stat. 4216, 4240; Pub. L. 116–283, div. G, title LVXXXV [LXXXV], §8506(b), Jan. 1, 2021, 134 Stat. 4752.)

§2109. SELECTION BOARDS; OATH OF MEMBERS

Each member of a selection board shall swear—

(1) that the member will, without prejudice or partiality, and having in view both the special fitness of officers and the efficiency of the Coast Guard, perform the duties imposed upon the member; and

(2) an oath in accordance with section 931.

(Added Pub. L. 88–130, §1(10)(C), Sept. 24, 1963, 77 Stat. 179, §254; amended Pub. L. 112–213, title II, §207, Dec. 20, 2012, 126 Stat. 1546; renumbered §2109 and amended Pub. L. 115–282, title I, §§112(b), 123(b)(2), Dec. 4, 2018, 132 Stat. 4216, 4240.)

§2110. NUMBER OF OFFICERS TO BE SELECTED FOR PROMOTION

Before convening a board under section 2106 of this title to recommend officers for promotion to any grade, the Secretary shall determine the total number of officers to be selected for promotion to that grade. This number shall be equal to the number of vacancies existing in the grade, plus the number of additional vacancies estimated for the next twelve months, less the number of officers on the selection list for the grade.

(Added Pub. L. 88–130, §1(10)(C), Sept. 24, 1963, 77 Stat. 179, §255; renumbered §2110 and amended Pub. L. 115–282, title I, §§112(b), 123(b)(2), Dec. 4, 2018, 132 Stat. 4216, 4240.)

§2111. PROMOTION ZONES

(a) Before convening a selection board to recommend officers for promotion to any grade above lieutenant (junior grade) and below rear admiral (lower half), the Secretary shall establish a promotion zone for the grade to be considered. The promotion zone for each grade shall consist of the most senior officers of that grade on the active duty promotion list who are eligible for consideration for promotion to the next higher grade and who have not previously been placed in a promotion zone for selection for promotion to the next higher grade. The number of officers in each zone shall be determined after considering—

(1) the needs of the service;

(2) the estimated numbers of vacancies available in future years to provide comparable opportunity for promotion of officers in successive year groups; and

(3) the extent to which current terms of service in that grade conform to a desirable career promotion pattern.

However, such number of officers shall not exceed the number to be selected for promotion divided by one-half.

(b) Promotion zones from which officers will be selected for promotion to the grade of rear admiral (lower half) shall be established by the Secretary as the needs of the service require.

(Added Pub. L. 88–130, §1(10)(C), Sept. 24, 1963, 77 Stat. 179, §256; amended Pub. L. 89–444, §1(16), June 9, 1966, 80 Stat. 196; Pub. L. 97–417, §2(3), Jan. 4, 1983, 96 Stat. 2085; Pub. L. 99–145, title V, §514(c)(1), Nov. 8, 1985, 99 Stat. 629; Pub. L. 99–661, div. A, title XIII, §1343(c), Nov. 14, 1986, 100 Stat. 3995; renumbered §2111 and amended Pub. L. 115–282, title I, §112(b), title III, §312, Dec. 4, 2018, 132 Stat. 4216, 4249.)

§2112. PROMOTION YEAR; DEFINED

For the purposes of this chapter, "promotion year" means the period which commences on July 1 of each year and ends on June 30 of the following year.

(Added Pub. L. 94–546, §1(17), Oct. 18, 1976, 90 Stat. 2520, §256a; renumbered §2112, Pub. L. 115–282, title I, §112(b), Dec. 4, 2018, 132 Stat. 4216.)

§2113. ELIGIBILITY OF OFFICERS FOR CONSIDERATION FOR PROMOTION

(a) An officer on the active duty promotion list becomes eligible for consideration for promotion to the next higher grade at the beginning of the promotion year in which he completes the following amount of service computed from his date of rank in the grade in which he is serving:

(1) two years in the grade of lieutenant (junior grade);

(2) three years in the grade of lieutenant;

(3) four years in the grade of lieutenant commander;

(4) four years in the grade of commander; and

(5) three years in the grade of captain.

(b) For the purpose of this section, service in a grade includes all qualifying service in that grade or a higher grade, under either a temporary or permanent appointment. However, service in a grade under a temporary service appointment under section 2125 of this title is considered as service only in the grade that the officer concerned would have held had he not been so appointed.

(c) No officer may become eligible for consideration for promotion until all officers of his grade senior to him are so eligible.

(d) Except when his name is on a list of selectees, each officer who becomes eligible for consideration for promotion to the next higher grade remains eligible so long as he—

(1) continues on active duty; and

(2) is not promoted to that grade.

(e) An officer whose involuntary retirement or separation is deferred under section 2156 of this title is not eligible for consideration for promotion to the next higher grade during the period of that deferment.

(f) The Secretary may waive subsection (a) to the extent necessary to allow officers described therein to have at least two opportunities for consideration for promotion to the next higher grade as officers below the promotion zone.

(g)(1) Notwithstanding subsection (a), the Commandant may provide that an officer may, upon the officer's request and with the approval of the Commandant, be excluded from consideration by a selection board convened under section 2106.

(2) The Commandant shall approve a request under paragraph (1) only if—

(A) the basis for the request is to allow the officer to complete a broadening assignment, advanced education, another assignment of significant value to the Coast Guard, a career progression requirement delayed by the assignment or education, or a qualifying personal or professional circumstance, as determined by the Commandant;

(B) the Commandant determines the exclusion from consideration is in the best interest of the Coast Guard; and

(C) the officer has not previously failed of selection for promotion to the grade for which the officer requests the exclusion from consideration.

(Added Pub. L. 88–130, §1(10)(C), Sept. 24, 1963, 77 Stat. 179, §257; amended Pub. L. 94–546, §1(19), Oct. 18, 1976, 90 Stat. 2520; Pub. L. 98–557, §17(b)(1), Oct. 30, 1984, 98 Stat. 2867; Pub. L. 109–241, title II, §203, July 11, 2006, 120 Stat. 520; renumbered §2113 and amended Pub. L. 115–282, title I, §§112(b), 123(b)(2), Dec. 4, 2018, 132 Stat. 4216, 4240; Pub. L. 116–283, div. G, title LVXXXII [LXXXII], §8202(a), Jan. 1, 2021, 134 Stat. 4642.)

§2114. United States Deputy Marshals in Alaska

Commissioned officers may be appointed as United States Deputy Marshals in Alaska.

(Added Pub. L. 115–282, title I, §112(c)(3), Dec. 4, 2018, 132 Stat. 4221.)

§2115. SELECTION BOARDS; INFORMATION TO BE FURNISHED BOARDS

(a) IN GENERAL.—The Secretary shall furnish the appropriate selection board convened under section 2106 of this title with—

(1) the number of officers that the board may recommend for promotion to the next higher grade;

(2) the names and records of all officers who are eligible for consideration for promotion to the grade to which the board will recommend officers for promotion; and

(3) in the case of an eligible officer considered for promotion to a rank above lieutenant, any credible information of an adverse nature, including any substantiated adverse finding or conclusion from an officially documented investigation or inquiry and any information placed in the personnel service record of the officer under section 1745(a) of the National Defense Authorization Act for Fiscal Year 2014 (Public Law 113–66; 10 U.S.C. 1561 note), shall be furnished to the selection board in accordance with standards and procedures set out in the regulations prescribed by the Secretary.

(b) PROVISION OF DIRECTION AND GUIDANCE.—

(1) In addition to the information provided pursuant to subsection (a), the Secretary may furnish the selection board—

(A) specific direction relating to the needs of the Coast Guard for officers having particular skills, including direction relating to the need for a minimum number of officers with particular skills within a specialty; and

(B) any other guidance that the Secretary believes may be necessary to enable the board to properly perform its functions.

(2) Selections made based on the direction and guidance provided under this subsection shall not exceed the maximum percentage of officers who may be selected from below the announced promotion zone at any given selection board convened under section 2106 of this title.

(Added Pub. L. 88–130, §1(10)(C), Sept. 24, 1963, 77 Stat. 180, §258; amended Pub. L. 89–444, §1(17), June 9, 1966, 80 Stat. 196; Pub. L. 104–324, title II, §212, Oct. 19, 1996, 110 Stat. 3915; Pub. L. 111–281, title II, §212(2), Oct. 15, 2010, 124 Stat. 2914; renumbered §2115 and amended Pub. L. 115–282, title I, §§112(b), 123(b)(2), Dec. 4, 2018, 132 Stat. 4216, 4240; Pub. L. 117–263, div. K, title CXII, §11245(a), Dec. 23, 2022, 136 Stat. 4043.)

§2116. OFFICERS TO BE RECOMMENDED FOR PROMOTION

(a) A selection board convened to recommend officers for promotion shall recommend those eligible officers whom the board, giving due consideration to the needs of the Coast Guard for officers with particular skills so noted in specific direction furnished to the board by the Secretary under section 2115 of this title, considers best qualified of the officers under consideration for promotion. No officer may be recommended for promotion unless he receives the recommendation of at least a majority of the members of a board composed of five members, or at least two-thirds of the members of a board composed of more than five members.

(b) The number of officers that a board convened under section 2106 of this title may recommend for promotion to a grade below rear admiral (lower half) from among eligible officers junior in rank to the junior officer in the appropriate promotion zone may not exceed—

(1) 5 percent of the total number of officers that the board is authorized to recommend for promotion to the grade of lieutenant or lieutenant commander;

(2) 7½ percent of the total number of officers that the board is authorized to recommend for promotion to the grade of commander; and

(3) 10 percent of the total number of officers that the board is authorized to recommend for promotion to the grade of captain;

unless such percentage is a number less than one, in which case the board may recommend one such officer for promotion.

(c)(1) In selecting the officers to be recommended for promotion, a selection board may recommend officers of particular merit, from among those officers chosen for promotion, to be placed at the top of the list of selectees promulgated by the Secretary under section 2121(a) of this title. The number of officers that a board may recommend to be placed at the top of the list of selectees may not exceed three times the percentages set forth in subsection (b) unless such a percentage is a number less than one, in which case the board may recommend one officer for such placement. No officer may be recommended to be placed at the top of the list of selectees unless he or she receives the recommendation of at least a majority of the members of a board composed of five members, or at least two-thirds of the members of a board composed of more than five members.

(2) The Secretary shall conduct a survey of the Coast Guard officer corps to determine if implementation of this subsection will improve Coast Guard officer retention. A selection board may not make any recommendation under this subsection before the date on which the Secretary publishes a finding, based upon the results of the survey, that implementation of this subsection will improve Coast Guard officer retention.

(3) The Secretary shall submit any finding made by the Secretary pursuant to paragraph (2) to the Committee on Transportation and Infrastructure of the House of Representatives and the Committee on Commerce, Science, and Transportation of the Senate.

(Added Pub. L. 88–130, §1(10)(C), Sept. 24, 1963, 77 Stat. 180, §259; amended Pub. L. 97–417, §2(4), Jan. 4, 1983, 96 Stat. 2085; Pub. L. 99–145, title V, §514(c)(1), Nov. 8, 1985, 99 Stat. 629; Pub. L. 107–295, title III, §313(1), Nov. 25, 2002, 116 Stat. 2102; Pub. L. 111–281, title II, §212(3), Oct. 15, 2010, 124 Stat. 2915; Pub. L. 112–213, title II, §217(3), Dec. 20, 2012, 126 Stat. 1557; renumbered §2116 and amended Pub. L. 115–282, title I, §§112(b), 123(b)(2), Dec. 4, 2018, 132 Stat. 4216, 4240; Pub. L. 117–263, div. K, title CXII, §11238, Dec. 23, 2022, 136 Stat. 4037.)

§2117. SELECTION BOARDS; REPORTS

(a) Each board convened under section 2106 of this title shall submit a report in writing, signed by all the members thereof, containing the names of the officers recommended for promotion and the names of those officers recommended to be advanced to the top of the list of selectees established by the Secretary under section 2121(a) of this title.

(b) A board convened under section 2106 of this title shall certify that, in the opinion of at least a majority of the members if the board has five members, or in the opinion of at least two-thirds of the members if the board has more than five members, the officers recommended for promotion are the best qualified for promotion to meet the needs of the service (as noted in specific direction furnished the board by the Secretary under section 2115 of this title) of those officers whose names have been furnished to the board.

(Added Pub. L. 88–130, §1(10)(C), Sept. 24, 1963, 77 Stat. 180, §260; amended Pub. L. 107–295, title III, §313(2), Nov. 25, 2002, 116 Stat. 2103; Pub. L. 111–281, title II, §212(4), Oct. 15, 2010, 124 Stat. 2915; renumbered §2117 and amended Pub. L. 115–282, title I, §§112(b), 123(b)(2), Dec. 4, 2018, 132 Stat. 4216, 4240.)

§2118. SELECTION BOARDS; SUBMISSION OF REPORTS

(a) A board convened under section 2106 of this title shall submit its report to the Secretary. If the board has acted contrary to law or regulation, the Secretary may return the report for proceedings in revision and resubmission to the Secretary. After his final review, the Secretary shall submit the report of the board to the President for his approval, modification, or disapproval.

(b) If any officer recommended for promotion is not acceptable to the President, the President may remove the name of that officer from the report of the board.

(c) Upon approval by the President the names of officers selected for promotion by a board convened under section 2106 of this title shall be promptly disseminated to the service at large.

(d) Except as required by this section, the proceedings of a selection board, including a special selection board convened under section 2120, shall not be disclosed to any individual who is not a member of the board.

(e) If the Secretary makes a recommendation under this section that the name of an officer be removed from a report of a selection board and the recommendation is accompanied by information that was not presented to that selection board, that information shall be made available to that officer. The officer shall then be afforded a reasonable opportunity to submit comments on that information to the officials making the recommendation and the officials reviewing the recommendation. If an eligible officer cannot be given access to such information because of its classification status, the officer shall, to the maximum extent practicable, be provided with an appropriate summary of the information.

(Added Pub. L. 88–130, §1(10)(C), Sept. 24, 1963, 77 Stat. 181, §261; amended Pub. L. 112–213, title II, §208(b), Dec. 20, 2012, 126 Stat. 1549; renumbered §2118 and amended Pub. L. 115–282, title I, §§112(b), 123(b)(2), Dec. 4, 2018, 132 Stat. 4216, 4240; Pub. L. 116–283, div. G, title LVXXXV [LXXXV], §8505(a)(16), Jan. 1, 2021, 134 Stat. 4748; Pub. L. 117–263, div. K, title CXII, §11245(c), Dec. 23, 2022, 136 Stat. 4045.)

§2119. FAILURE OF SELECTION FOR PROMOTION

An officer, other than an officer serving in the grade of captain, who is, or is senior to, the junior officer in the promotion zone established for his grade under section 2111 of this title, fails of selection if he is not selected for promotion by the selection board which considered him, or if having been recommended for promotion by the board, his name is thereafter removed from the report of the board by the President.

(Added Pub. L. 88–130, §1(10)(C), Sept. 24, 1963, 77 Stat. 181, §262; amended Pub. L. 112–213, title II, §208(c), Dec. 20, 2012, 126 Stat. 1549; renumbered §2119 and amended Pub. L. 115–282, title I, §§112(b), 123(b)(2), Dec. 4, 2018, 132 Stat. 4216, 4240.)

§2120. SPECIAL SELECTION BOARDS; CORRECTION OF ERRORS

(a) OFFICERS NOT CONSIDERED DUE TO ADMINISTRATIVE ERROR.—

(1) IN GENERAL.—If the Secretary determines that as the result of an administrative error—

(A) an officer or former officer was not considered for selection for promotion by a selection board convened under section 2106; or

(B) the name of an officer or former officer was not placed on an all-fully-qualified-officers list;

the Secretary shall convene a special selection board to determine whether such officer or former officer should be recommended for promotion and such officer or former officer shall not be considered to have failed of selection for promotion prior to the consideration of the special selection board.

(2) EFFECT OF FAILURE TO RECOMMEND FOR PROMOTION.—If a special selection board convened under paragraph (1) does not recommend for promotion an officer or former officer, whose grade is below the grade of captain and whose name was referred to that board for consideration, the officer or former officer shall be considered to have failed of selection for promotion.

(b) OFFICERS CONSIDERED BUT NOT SELECTED; MATERIAL ERROR.—

(1) IN GENERAL.—In the case of an officer or former officer who was eligible for promotion, was considered for selection for promotion by a selection board convened under section 2106, and was not selected for promotion by that board, the Secretary may convene a special selection board to determine whether the officer or former officer should be recommended for promotion, if the Secretary determines that—

(A) an action of the selection board that considered the officer or former officer—

(i) was contrary to law in a matter material to the decision of the board; or

(ii) involved material error of fact or material administrative error; or

(B) the selection board that considered the officer or former officer did not have before it for consideration material information.

(2) EFFECT OF FAILURE TO RECOMMEND FOR PROMOTION.—If a special selection board convened under paragraph (1) does not recommend for promotion an officer or former officer, whose grade is that of commander or below and whose name was referred to that board for consideration, the officer or former officer shall be considered—

(A) to have failed of selection for promotion with respect to the board that considered the officer or former officer prior to the consideration of the special selection board; and

(B) to incur no additional failure of selection for promotion as a result of the action of the special selection board.

(c) REQUIREMENTS FOR SPECIAL SELECTION BOARDS.—Each special selection board convened under this section shall—

(1) be composed in accordance with section 2107 and the members of the board shall be required to swear the oaths described in section 2109;

(2) consider the record of an applicable officer or former officer as that record, if corrected, would have appeared to the selection board that should have considered or did consider the officer or former officer prior to the consideration of the special selection board and that record shall be compared with a sampling of the records of—

(A) those officers of the same grade who were recommended for promotion by such prior selection board; and

(B) those officers of the same grade who were not recommended for promotion by such prior selection board; and

(3) submit to the Secretary a written report in a manner consistent with sections 2117 and 2118.

(d) APPOINTMENT OF OFFICERS RECOMMENDED FOR PROMOTION.—

(1) IN GENERAL.—An officer or former officer whose name is placed on a promotion list as a result of the recommendation of a special selection board convened under this section shall be appointed, as soon as practicable, to the next higher grade in accordance with the law and policies that would have been applicable to the officer or former officer had the officer or former officer been recommended for promotion by the selection board that should have considered or did consider the officer or former officer prior to the consideration of the special selection board.

(2) EFFECT.—An officer or former officer who is promoted to the next higher grade as a result of the recommendation of a special selection board convened under this section shall have, upon such promotion, the same date of rank, the same effective date for the pay and allowances of that grade, and the same position on the active duty promotion list as the officer or former officer would have had if the officer or former officer had been recommended for promotion to that grade by the selection board that should have considered or did consider the officer or former officer prior to the consideration of the special selection board.

(3) RECORD CORRECTION.—If the report of a special selection board convened under this section, as approved by the President, recommends for promotion to the next higher grade an officer not eligible for promotion or a former officer whose name was referred to the board for consideration, the Secretary may act under section 1552 of title 10 to correct the military record of the officer or former officer to correct an error or remove an injustice resulting from the officer or former officer not being selected for promotion by the selection board that should have considered or did consider the officer or former officer prior to the consideration of the special selection board.

(e) APPLICATION PROCESS AND TIME LIMITS.—The Secretary shall issue regulations regarding the process by which an officer or former officer may apply to have a matter considered by a special selection board convened under this section, including time limits related to such applications.

(f) LIMITATION OF OTHER JURISDICTION.—No official or court of the United States shall have authority or jurisdiction over any claim based in any way on the failure of an officer or former officer to be selected for promotion by a selection board convened under section 2106, until—

(1) the claim has been referred to a special selection board convened under this section and acted upon by that board; or

(2) the claim has been rejected by the Secretary without consideration by a special selection board convened under this section.

(g) JUDICIAL REVIEW.—

(1) IN GENERAL.—A court of the United States may review—

(A) a decision of the Secretary not to convene a special selection board under this section to determine if the court finds that the decision of the Secretary was arbitrary or capricious, not based on substantial evidence, or otherwise contrary to law; and

(B) an action of a special selection board under this section to determine if the court finds that the action of the special selection board was contrary to law or involved material error of fact or material administrative error.

(2) REMAND AND RECONSIDERATION.—If, with respect to a review under paragraph (1), a court makes a finding described in subparagraph (A) or (B) of that paragraph, the court shall remand the case to the Secretary and the Secretary shall provide the applicable officer or former officer consideration by a new special selection board convened under this section.

(h) DESIGNATION OF BOARDS.—The Secretary may designate a selection board convened under section 2106 as a special selection board convened under this section. A selection board so designated may function in the capacity of a selection board convened under section 2106 and a special selection board convened under this section.

(Added Pub. L. 112–213, title II, §208(a), Dec. 20, 2012, 126 Stat. 1546, §263; renumbered §2120 and amended Pub. L. 115–282, title I, §§112(b), 123(b)(2), Dec. 4, 2018, 132 Stat. 4216, 4240.)

§2120A. SPECIAL SELECTION REVIEW BOARDS

(a) IN GENERAL.—(1) If the Secretary determines that a person recommended by a promotion board for promotion to a grade at or below the grade of rear admiral is the subject of credible information of an adverse nature, including any substantiated adverse finding or conclusion described in section 2115(a)(3) of this title that was not furnished to the promotion board during its consideration of the person for promotion as otherwise required by such section, the Secretary shall convene a special selection review board under this section to review the person and recommend whether the recommendation for promotion of the person should be sustained.

(2) If a person and the recommendation for promotion of the person is subject to review

under this section by a special selection review board convened under this section, the name of the person—

    (A) shall not be disseminated or publicly released on the list of officers recommended for promotion by the promotion board recommending the promotion of the person; and

    (B) shall not be forwarded to the President or the Senate, as applicable, or included on a promotion list under section 2121 of this title.

    (b) CONVENING.—(1) Any special selection review board convened under this section shall be convened in accordance with the provisions of section 2120(c) of this title.

    (2) Any special selection review board convened under this section may review such number of persons, and recommendations for promotion of such persons, as the Secretary shall specify in convening such special selection review board.

    (c) INFORMATION CONSIDERED.—(1) In reviewing a person and recommending whether the recommendation for promotion of the person should be sustained under this section, a special selection review board convened under this section shall be furnished and consider the following:

    (A) The record and information concerning the person furnished in accordance with section 2115 of this title to the promotion board that recommended the person for promotion.

    (B) Any credible information of an adverse nature on the person, including any substantiated adverse finding or conclusion from an officially documented investigation or inquiry described in section 2115(a)(3) of this title.

    (2) The furnishing of information to a special selection review board under paragraph (1)(B) shall be governed by the standards and procedures referred to in section 2115 of this title.

    (3)(A) Before information on a person described in paragraph (1)(B) is furnished to a special selection review board for purposes of this section, the Secretary shall ensure that—

    (i) such information is made available to the person; and

    (ii) subject to subparagraphs (C) and (D), the person is afforded a reasonable opportunity to submit comments on such information to the special selection review board before its review of the person and the recommendation for promotion of the person under this section.

    (B) If information on a person described in paragraph (1)(B) is not made available to the person as otherwise required by subparagraph (A)(i) due to the classification status of such information, the person shall, to the maximum extent practicable, be furnished a summary of such information appropriate to the person's authorization for access to classified information.

    (C)(i) An opportunity to submit comments on information is not required for a person under subparagraph (A)(ii) if—

    (I) such information was made available to the person in connection with the furnishing of such information under section 2115(a) of this title to the promotion board that recommended the promotion of the person subject to review under this section; and

    (II) the person submitted comments on such information to that promotion board.

(ii) The comments on information of a person described in clause (i)(II) shall be furnished to the special selection review board.

(D) A person may waive either or both of the following:

(i) The right to submit comments to a special selection review board under subparagraph (A)(ii).

(ii) The furnishing of comments to a special selection review board under subparagraph (C)(ii).

(d) CONSIDERATION.—(1) In considering the record and information on a person under this section, the special selection review board shall compare such record and information with an appropriate sampling of the records of those officers who were recommended for promotion by the promotion board that recommended the person for promotion, and an appropriate sampling of the records of those officers who were considered by and not recommended for promotion by that promotion board.

(2) Records and information shall be presented to a special selection review board for purposes of paragraph (1) in a manner that does not indicate or disclose the person or persons for whom the special selection review board was convened.

(3) In considering whether the recommendation for promotion of a person should be sustained under this section, a special selection review board shall, to the greatest extent practicable, apply standards used by the promotion board that recommended the person for promotion.

(4) The recommendation for promotion of a person may be sustained under this section only if the special selection review board determines that the person—

(A) ranks on an order of merit created by the special selection review board as better qualified for promotion than the sample officer highest on the order of merit list who was considered by and not recommended for promotion by the promotion board concerned; and

(B) is comparable in qualification for promotion to those sample officers who were recommended for promotion by that promotion board.

(5) A recommendation for promotion of a person may be sustained under this section only by a vote of a majority of the members of the special selection review board.

(6) If a special selection review board does not sustain a recommendation for promotion of a person under this section, the person shall be considered to have failed of selection for promotion.

(e) REPORTS.—(1) Each special selection review board convened under this section shall submit to the Secretary a written report, signed by each member of the board, containing the name of each person whose recommendation for promotion it recommends for sustainment and certifying that the board has carefully considered the record and information of each person whose name was referred to it.

(2) The provisions of sections 2117(a) of this title apply to the report and proceedings of a special selection review board convened under this section in the same manner as they apply to the report and proceedings of a promotion board convened under section 2106 of this title.

(f) APPOINTMENT OF PERSONS.—(1) If the report of a special selection review board convened under this section recommends the sustainment of the recommendation for promotion to the next higher grade of a person whose name was referred to it for review under this section, and the President approves the report, the person shall, as soon as practicable, be appointed to that grade in accordance with section 2121 of this title.

(2) A person who is appointed to the next higher grade as described in paragraph (1) shall, upon that appointment, have the same date of rank, the same effective date for the pay and allowances of that grade, and the same position on the active-duty list as the person would have had pursuant to the original recommendation for promotion of the promotion board concerned.

(g) REGULATIONS.—The Secretary shall prescribe regulations to carry out this section.

(h) PROMOTION BOARD DEFINED.—In this section, the term "promotion board" means a selection board convened by the Secretary under section 2106 of this title.

(Added Pub. L. 117–263, div. K, title CXII, §11245(b)(1), Dec. 23, 2022, 136 Stat. 4043.)

§2121. PROMOTIONS; APPOINTMENTS

(a) When the report of a board convened to recommend officers for promotion has been approved by the President, the Secretary shall place the names of all officers selected and approved on a list of selectees in the order of their seniority on the active duty promotion list. The names of all officers approved by the President and recommended by the board to be placed at the top of the list of selectees shall be placed at the top of the list of selectees in the order of seniority on the active duty promotion list.

(b) Officers on the list of selectees may be promoted by appointment in the next higher grade to fill vacancies in the authorized active duty strength of the grade as determined under section 2103 of this title after officers on any previous list of selectees for that grade have been promoted. Officers shall be promoted in the order that their names appear on the list of selectees. The date of rank of an officer promoted under this subsection shall be the date of his appointment in that grade.

(c) An officer serving on active duty in the grade of ensign may, if found fully qualified for promotion in accordance with regulations prescribed by the Secretary, be promoted to the grade of lieutenant (junior grade) by appointment after he has completed twelve months' active service in grade. The date of rank of an officer promoted under this subsection shall be the date of his appointment in the grade of lieutenant (junior grade) as specified by the Secretary.

(d) When a vacancy in the grade of rear admiral occurs, the senior rear admiral (lower half) serving on the active duty promotion list shall be appointed by the President, by and with the advice and consent of the Senate, to fill the vacancy. The appointment shall be effective on the date the vacancy occurred.

(e) Appointments of regular officers under this section shall be made by the President, by and with the advice and consent of the Senate except that advice and consent is not required for appointments under this section in the grade of lieutenant (junior grade) or lieutenant. Appointments of Reserve officers shall be made as prescribed in section 12203 of title 10.

(f)(1) The promotion of an officer may be delayed without prejudice if any of the following applies:

(A) The officer is under investigation or proceedings of a court-martial or a board of officers are pending against the officer.

(B) A criminal proceeding in a Federal or State court is pending against the officer.

(C) The Secretary determines that credible information of an adverse nature, including a substantiated adverse finding or conclusion described in section 2115(a)(3), with respect to the officer will result in the convening of a special selection review board under section 2120a of this title to review the officer and recommend whether the recommendation for promotion of the officer should be sustained.

(2)(A) Subject to subparagraph (B), a promotion may be delayed under this subsection until, as applicable—

(i) the completion of the investigation or proceedings described in subparagraph (A);

(ii) a final decision in the proceeding described in subparagraph (B) is issued; or

(iii) the special selection review board convened under section 2120a of this title issues recommendations with respect to the officer.

(B) Unless the Secretary determines that a further delay is necessary in the public interest, a promotion may not be delayed under this subsection for more than one year after the date the officer would otherwise have been promoted.

(3) An officer whose promotion is delayed under this subsection and who is subsequently promoted shall be given the date of rank and position on the active duty promotion list in the grade to which promoted that he would have held had his promotion not been so delayed.

(Added Pub. L. 88–130, §1(10)(C), Sept. 24, 1963, 77 Stat. 181, §271; amended Pub. L. 91–278, §1(8), June 12, 1970, 84 Stat. 305; Pub. L. 97–417, §2(5), Jan. 4, 1983, 96 Stat. 2085; Pub. L. 99–145, title V, §514(c)(1), Nov. 8, 1985, 99 Stat. 629; Pub. L. 101–225, title II, §203(2), Dec. 12, 1989, 103 Stat. 1911; Pub. L. 103–337, div. A, title XVI, §1677(b)(2), Oct. 5, 1994, 108 Stat. 3020; Pub. L. 107–295, title III, §313(3), Nov. 25, 2002, 116 Stat. 2103; renumbered §2121 and amended Pub. L. 115–282, title I, §§112(b), 123(b)(2), Dec. 4, 2018, 132 Stat. 4216, 4240; Pub. L. 117–263, div. K, title CXII, §11245(d), Dec. 23, 2022, 136 Stat. 4046.)

§2122. REMOVAL OF OFFICER FROM LIST OF SELECTEES FOR PROMOTION

(a) The President may remove the name of any officer from a list of selectees established under section 2121 of this title.

(b) If the Senate does not consent to the appointment of an officer whose name is on a list of selectees established under section 2121 of this title, that officer's name shall be removed from this list.

(c) An officer whose name is removed from a list under subsection (a) or (b) continues to be eligible for consideration for promotion. If he is selected for promotion by the next selection board and promoted, he shall be given the date of rank and position on the active duty promotion list in the grade to which promoted that he would have held if his name had not been removed. However, if the officer is not selected by the next selection board or if his name is again removed from the list of selectees, he shall be considered for all purposes as having twice failed of selection for promotion.

(Added Pub. L. 88–130, §1(10)(C), Sept. 24, 1963, 77 Stat. 182, §272; renumbered §2122 and amended Pub. L. 115–282, title I, §§112(b), 123(b)(2), Dec. 4, 2018, 132 Stat. 4216, 4240.)

§2123. PROMOTIONS; ACCEPTANCE; OATH OF OFFICE

(a) An officer who receives an appointment under section 2121 of this title is considered to have accepted his appointment on its effective date, unless he expressly declines the appointment.

(b) An officer who has served continuously since he subscribed to the oath of office prescribed in section 3331 of title 5 is not required to take a new oath upon his appointment in a higher grade.

(Added Pub. L. 88–130, §1(10)(C), Sept. 24, 1963, 77 Stat. 182, §273; amended Pub. L. 94–546, §1(20), Oct. 18, 1976, 90 Stat. 2520; renumbered §2123 and amended Pub. L. 115–282, title I, §§112(b), 123(b)(2), Dec. 4, 2018, 132 Stat. 4216, 4240.)

§2124. PROMOTIONS; PAY AND ALLOWANCES

An officer who is promoted under section 2121 of this title shall be entitled to the pay and allowances of the grade to which promoted from his date of rank in such grade.

(Added Pub. L. 88–130, §1(10)(C), Sept. 24, 1963, 77 Stat. 182, §274; renumbered §2124 and amended Pub. L. 115–282, title I, §§112(b), 123(b)(2), Dec. 4, 2018, 132 Stat. 4216, 4240.)

§2125. WARTIME TEMPORARY SERVICE PROMOTIONS

(a) In time of war, or of national emergency declared by the President or Congress, the President may suspend any section of this chapter relating to the selection, promotion, or involuntary separation of officers. Such a suspension may not continue beyond six months after the termination of the war or national emergency.

(b) When the preceding sections of this chapter relating to selection and promotion of officers are suspended in accordance with subsection (a), and the needs of the service require, the President may, under regulations prescribed by him, promote to a higher grade any officer serving on active duty in the grade of ensign or above in the Coast Guard.

(c) In time of war, or of national emergency declared by the President or Congress, the President may, under regulations to be prescribed by him, promote to the next higher warrant officer grade any warrant officer serving on active duty in a grade below chief warrant officer, W–4.

[(d) Repealed. Pub. L. 97–417, §2(6), Jan. 4, 1983, 96 Stat. 2085.]

(e) A promotion under this section to a grade above lieutenant may be made only upon the recommendation of a board of officers convened for that purpose.

(f) A promotion under this section shall be made by an appointment for temporary service. Original appointments under this section in the grades of lieutenant commander and above shall be made by the President by and with the advice and consent of the Senate. Original appointments under this section in the grades of ensign through lieutenant shall be made by the President alone. Any other appointments under this section shall be made by the President alone.

(g) An appointment under this section, unless expressly declined, is regarded as accepted on the date specified by the Secretary as the date of the appointment, and the officer so promoted is entitled to pay and allowances of the grade to which appointed from that date.

(h) An appointment under this section does not terminate any appointments held by an officer concerned under any other provisions of this title. The President may terminate temporary appointments made under this section at any time. An appointment under this section is effective for such period as the President determines. However, an appointment may not be effective later than six months after the end of the war or national emergency. When his temporary appointment under this section is terminated or expires, the officer shall revert to his former grade.

(i) Not later than six months after the end of the war or national emergency the President shall, under such regulations as he may prescribe, reestablish the active duty promotion list with adjustments and additions appropriate to the conditions of original appointment and wartime service of all officers to be included thereon. The President may, by and with the advice and consent of the Senate, appoint officers on the reestablished active duty promotion list to fill vacancies in the authorized active duty strength of each grade. Such appointments shall be considered to have been made under section 2121 of this title.

(Added Pub. L. 88–130, §1(10)(C), Sept. 24, 1963, 77 Stat. 182, §275; amended Pub. L. 92–129, title VI, §605, Sept. 28, 1971, 85 Stat. 362; Pub. L. 97–417, §2(6), Jan. 4, 1983, 96 Stat. 2085; Pub. L. 109–241, title II, §217(b), July 11, 2006, 120 Stat. 526; renumbered §2125 and amended Pub. L. 115–282, title I, §§112(b), 123(b)(2), Dec. 4, 2018, 132 Stat. 4216, 4240.)

§2126. PROMOTION OF OFFICERS NOT INCLUDED ON ACTIVE DUTY PROMOTION LIST

Officers who are not included on the active duty promotion list may be promoted under regulations to be prescribed by the Secretary. These regulations shall, as to officers serving in connection with organizing, administering, recruiting, instructing, or training the reserve components, provide as nearly as practicable, that such officers will be selected and promoted in the same manner and will be afforded equal opportunity for promotion as officers of the corresponding grade on the active duty promotion list.

(Added Pub. L. 88–130, §1(10)(C), Sept. 24, 1963, 77 Stat. 183, §276; renumbered §2126, Pub. L. 115–282, title I, §112(b), Dec. 4, 2018, 132 Stat. 4216.)

§2127. RECALL TO ACTIVE DUTY DURING WAR OR NATIONAL EMERGENCY

In time of war or national emergency, the Secretary may order any regular officer on the retired list to active duty.

(Added Pub. L. 88–130, §1(10)(C), Sept. 24, 1963, 77 Stat. 189, §331; renumbered §2127, Pub. L. 115–282, title I, §112(b), Dec. 4, 2018, 132 Stat. 4216.)

§2128. RECALL TO ACTIVE DUTY WITH CONSENT OF OFFICER

(a) Any regular officer on the retired list may, with that officer's consent, be assigned to such duties as that officer may be able to perform.

(b) The number of retired officers on active duty in the grade of lieutenant commander, commander, or captain shall not exceed 2 percent of the authorized number of officers on active duty in each such grade. However, this limitation does not apply to retired officers of these grades recalled to serve as members of courts, boards, panels, surveys, or special projects for periods not to exceed one year.

(Added Pub. L. 88–130, §1(10)(C), Sept. 24, 1963, 77 Stat. 189, §332; amended Pub. L. 89–444, §1(18), June 9, 1966, 80 Stat. 196; Pub. L. 91–278, §1(9), June 12, 1970, 84 Stat. 305; Pub. L. 102–241, §14, Dec. 19, 1991, 105 Stat. 2213; renumbered §2128, Pub. L. 115–282, title I, §112(b), Dec. 4, 2018, 132 Stat. 4216.)

§2129. AVIATION CADETS; APPOINTMENT AS RESERVE OFFICERS

(a) An aviation cadet designated under section 2317 who fulfills the eligibility requirements of section 2003 of title 10 for designation as a naval aviator may be appointed an ensign in the Coast Guard Reserve and designated a Coast Guard aviator.

(b) Aviation cadets who complete their training at approximately the same time are considered for all purposes to have begun their commissioned service on the same date, and the decision of the Secretary in this regard is conclusive.

(Added Pub. L. 89–444, §1(20), June 9, 1966, 80 Stat. 197, §373; amended Pub. L. 94–546, §1(28), Oct. 18, 1976, 90 Stat. 2521; renumbered §2129 and amended Pub. L. 115–282, title I, §112(b), title III, §313, Dec. 4, 2018, 132 Stat. 4216, 4249.)

§2130. PROMOTION TO CERTAIN GRADES FOR OFFICERS WITH CRITICAL SKILLS: CAPTAIN, COMMANDER, LIEUTENANT COMMANDER, LIEUTENANT

(a) IN GENERAL.—An officer in the grade of lieutenant (junior grade), lieutenant, lieutenant commander, or commander who is described in subsection (b) may be temporarily promoted to the grade of lieutenant, lieutenant commander, commander, or captain under regulations prescribed by the Secretary. Appointments under this section shall be made by the President, by and with the advice and consent of the Senate.

(b) COVERED OFFICERS.—An officer described in this subsection is any officer in a grade specified in subsection (a) who—

(1) has a skill in which the Coast Guard has a critical shortage of personnel (as determined by the Secretary); and

(2) is serving in a position (as determined by the Secretary) that—

(A) is designated to be held by a lieutenant, lieutenant commander, commander, or captain; and

(B) requires that an officer serving in such position have the skill possessed by such officer.

(c) PRESERVATION OF POSITION AND STATUS OF OFFICERS APPOINTED.—

(1) The temporary positions authorized under this section shall not be counted among or included in the list of positions on the active duty promotion list.

(2) An appointment under this section does not change the position on the active duty list or the permanent, probationary, or acting status of the officer so appointed, prejudice the officer in regard to other promotions or appointments, or abridge the rights or benefits of the officer.

(d) BOARD RECOMMENDATION REQUIRED.—A temporary promotion under this section may be made only upon the recommendation of a board of officers convened by the Secretary for the purpose of recommending officers for such promotions.

(e) ACCEPTANCE AND EFFECTIVE DATE OF APPOINTMENT.—Each appointment under this section, unless expressly declined, is, without formal acceptance, regarded as accepted on the date such appointment is made, and a member so appointed is entitled to the pay and allowances of the grade of the temporary promotion under this section beginning on the date the appointment is made.

(f) TERMINATION OF APPOINTMENT.—Unless sooner terminated, an appointment under this section terminates—

(1) on the date the officer who received the appointment is promoted to the permanent grade of lieutenant, lieutenant commander, commander, or captain;

(2) on the date the officer is detached from a position described in subsection (b)(2), unless the officer is on a promotion list to the permanent grade of lieutenant, lieutenant commander, commander, or captain, in which case the appointment terminates on the date the officer is promoted to that grade;

(3) when the appointment officer determines that the officer who received the appointment has engaged in misconduct or has displayed substandard performance; or

(4) when otherwise determined by the Commandant to be in the best interests of the Coast Guard.

(g) LIMITATION ON NUMBER OF ELIGIBLE POSITIONS.—An appointment under this section may only be made for service in a position designated by the Secretary for the purposes of this section. The number of positions so designated may not exceed the following percentages of the respective grades:

(1) As lieutenant, 0.5 percent.

(2) As lieutenant commander, 3.0 percent.

(3) As commander, 2.6 percent.

(4) As captain, 2.6 percent.

(Added Pub. L. 116–283, div. G, title LVXXXII [LXXXII], §8203(a), Jan. 1, 2021, 134 Stat. 4643.)

§2131. COLLEGE STUDENT PRE-COMMISSIONING INITIATIVE

(a) IN GENERAL.—There is authorized within the Coast Guard a college student pre-commissioning initiative program (in this section referred to as the "Program") for eligible undergraduate students to enlist and receive a guaranteed commission as an officer in the Coast Guard.

(b) CRITERIA FOR SELECTION.—To be eligible for the Program a student must meet the following requirements upon submitting an application:

(1) AGE.—A student must be not less than 19 years old and not more than 27 years old as of September 30 of the fiscal year in which the Program selection panel selecting such student convenes.

(2) CHARACTER.—

(A) ALL APPLICANTS.—All applicants must be of outstanding moral character and meet other character requirements as set forth by the Commandant.

(B) COAST GUARD APPLICANTS.—An applicant serving in the Coast Guard may not be commissioned if in the 36 months prior to the first Officer Candidate School class convening date in the selection cycle, such applicant was convicted by a court-martial or awarded nonjudicial punishment, or did not meet performance or character requirements set forth by the Commandant.

(3) CITIZENSHIP.—A student must be a United States citizen.

(4) CLEARANCE.—A student must be eligible for a secret clearance.

(5) DEPENDENCY.—

(A) IN GENERAL.—A student may not have more than 2 dependents.

(B) SOLE CUSTODY.—A student who is single may not have sole or primary custody of dependents.

(6) EDUCATION.—

(A) INSTITUTION.—A student must be an undergraduate sophomore or junior—

(i) at a historically Black college or university described in section 322(2) of the Higher Education Act of 1965 (20 U.S.C. 1061(2)) or an institution of higher education described in section 371(a) of the Higher Education Act of 1965 (20 U.S.C. 1067q(a)); or

(ii) an undergraduate sophomore or junior enrolled at an institution of higher education (as defined in section 101 of the Higher Education Act of 1965 (20 U.S.C. 1001)) that, at the time of application of the sophomore or junior, has had for 3 consecutive years an enrollment of undergraduate full-time equivalent students (as defined in section 312(e) of such Act (20 U.S.C. 1058(e))) that is a total of at least 50 percent Black American, Hispanic, Asian American (as defined in section 371(c) of such Act (20 U.S.C. 1067q(c))), Native American Pacific Islander (as defined in such section), or Native American (as defined in such section), among other criteria, as determined by the Commandant.

(B) LOCATION.—The institution at which such student is an undergraduate must be within 100 miles of a Coast guard [1] unit or Coast Guard Recruiting Office unless otherwise approved by the Commandant.

(C) RECORDS.—A student must meet credit and grade point average requirements set forth by the Commandant.

(7) MEDICAL AND ADMINISTRATIVE.—A student must meet other medical and administrative requirements as set forth by the Commandant.

(c) ENLISTMENT AND OBLIGATION.—Individuals selected and accept to participate in the Program shall enlist in the Coast Guard in pay grade E–3 with a 4-year duty obligation and 4-year inactive Reserve obligation.

(d) MILITARY ACTIVITIES PRIOR TO OFFICER CANDIDATE SCHOOL.—Individuals enrolled in the Program shall participate in military activities each month, as required by the Commandant, prior to attending Officer Candidate School.

(e) PARTICIPATION IN OFFICER CANDIDATE SCHOOL.—Each graduate of the Program shall attend the first enrollment of Officer Candidate School that commences after the date of such graduate's graduation.

(f) COMMISSIONING.—Upon graduation from Officer Candidate School, Program graduates shall be discharged from enlisted status and commissioned as an O–1 with an initial 3-year duty obligation.

(g) BRIEFING.—

(1) IN GENERAL.—Not later than August 15 of each year, the Commandant shall provide a briefing to the Committee on Transportation and Infrastructure of the House of Representatives and the Committee on Commerce, Science, and Transportation of the Senate on the Program.

(2) CONTENTS.—The briefing required under paragraph (1) shall describe—

(A) outreach and recruitment efforts over the previous year; and

(B) demographic information of enrollees including—

(i) race;

(ii) ethnicity;

(iii) gender;

(iv) geographic origin; and

(v) educational institution.

(Added Pub. L. 116–283, div. G, title LVXXXII [LXXXII], §8276(a), Jan. 1, 2021, 134 Stat. 4685.)

1 So in original. Probably should be "Guard".

SUBCHAPTER II—DISCHARGES; RETIREMENTS; REVOCATION OF COMMISSIONS; SEPARATION FOR CAUSE

§2141. REVOCATION OF COMMISSIONS DURING FIRST FIVE YEARS OF COMMISSIONED SERVICE

The Secretary, under such regulations as he may prescribe, may revoke the commission of any regular officer on active duty who, at the date of such revocation, has had less than five years of continuous service as a commissioned officer in the Regular Coast Guard.

(Added Pub. L. 88–130, §1(10)(C), Sept. 24, 1963, 77 Stat. 183, §281; amended Pub. L. 107–295, title IV, §416(a)(1), Nov. 25, 2002, 116 Stat. 2121; renumbered §2141, Pub. L. 115–282, title I, §112(b), Dec. 4, 2018, 132 Stat. 4216.)

§2142. REGULAR LIEUTENANTS (JUNIOR GRADE); SEPARATION FOR FAILURE OF SELECTION FOR PROMOTION

Each officer of the Regular Coast Guard appointed under section 2101 of this title who is serving in the grade of lieutenant (junior grade) and who has failed of selection for promotion to the grade of lieutenant for the second time, shall:

(1) be honorably discharged on June 30 of the promotion year in which his second failure of selection occurs; or

(2) if he so requests, be honorably discharged at an earlier date without loss of benefits that would accrue if he were discharged on that date under clause (1); or

(3) if, on the date specified for his discharge in this section, he is eligible for retirement under any law, be retired on that date.

(Added Pub. L. 88–130, §1(10)(C), Sept. 24, 1963, 77 Stat. 184, §282; amended Pub. L. 94–546, §1(21), Oct. 18, 1976, 90 Stat. 2520; renumbered §2142 and amended Pub. L. 115–282, title I, §§112(b), 123(b)(2), Dec. 4, 2018, 132 Stat. 4216, 4240.)

§2143. REGULAR LIEUTENANTS; SEPARATION FOR FAILURE OF SELECTION FOR PROMOTION; CONTINUATION

(a) Each officer of the Regular Coast Guard appointed under section 2101 of this title who is serving in the grade of lieutenant and who has failed of selection for promotion to the grade of lieutenant commander for the second time shall:

(1) be honorably discharged on June 30 of the promotion year in which his second failure of selection occurs; or

(2) if he so requests, be honorably discharged at an earlier date without loss of benefits that would accrue if he were discharged on that date under clause (1); or

(3) if, on the date specified for his discharge in this section, he has completed at least 20 years of active service or is eligible for retirement under any law, be retired on that date; or

(4) if, on the date specified for his discharge in clause (1), he has completed at least eighteen years of active service, be retained on active duty and retired on the last day of the month in which he completes twenty years of active service, unless earlier removed under another provision of law.

(b)(1) When the needs of the service require, the Secretary may direct a selection board, which has been convened under section 2106 of this title, to recommend for continuation on active duty for terms of not less than two nor more than four years a designated number of officers of the grade of lieutenant who would otherwise be discharged or retired under this section. When so directed, the board shall recommend for continuation on active duty those officers under consideration who are, in the opinion of the board, best qualified for continuation. Each officer so recommended may, with the approval of the Secretary, and notwithstanding subsection (a), be continued on active duty for the term recommended.

(2) Upon the completion of a term under paragraph (1), an officer shall, unless selected for further continuation—

(A) except as provided in subparagraph (B), be honorably discharged with separation pay computed under section 2146 of this title;

(B) in the case of an officer who has completed at least 18 years of active service on the date of discharge under subparagraph (A), be retained on active duty and retired on the last day of the month in which the officer completes 20 years of active service, unless earlier removed under another provision of law; or

(C) if, on the date specified for the officer's discharge under this section, the officer has completed at least 20 years of active service or is eligible for retirement under any law, be retired on that date.

(c) Each officer who has been continued on active duty under subsection (b) shall, unless earlier removed from active duty, be retired on the last day of the month in which he completes twenty years of active service.

(Added Pub. L. 88–130, §1(10)(C), Sept. 24, 1963, 77 Stat. 184, §283; amended Pub. L. 93–283, §1(6), May 14, 1974, 88 Stat. 140; Pub. L. 94–546, §1(22), Oct. 18, 1976, 90 Stat. 2520; Pub. L. 97–295, §2(9), Oct. 12, 1982, 96 Stat. 1302; Pub. L. 104–324, title II, §205, Oct. 19, 1996, 110 Stat. 3907; Pub. L. 107–295, title IV, §416(a)(2), Nov. 25, 2002, 116 Stat. 2121; renumbered §2143 and amended Pub. L. 115–282, title I, §§112(b), 123(b)(2), Dec. 4, 2018, 132 Stat. 4216, 4240.)

§2144. REGULAR COAST GUARD; OFFICERS SERVING UNDER TEMPORARY APPOINTMENTS

(a) Each officer of the Regular Coast Guard appointed under section 2104 of this title who is serving in the grade of lieutenant (junior grade) or lieutenant and who has failed of selection for promotion to the grade of lieutenant or lieutenant commander, respectively, for the second time shall:

(1) be honorably discharged on June 30 of the promotion year in which his second failure of selection occurs; or

(2) if he so requests, be honorably discharged at an earlier date without loss of benefits that would accrue if he were discharged on that date under clause (1); or

(3) if on the date specified for his discharge in this section he is eligible for retirement under any law, be retired under that law on that date.

(b) Each officer subject to discharge or retirement under subsection (a) may elect to revert to his permanent grade.

(Added Pub. L. 88–130, §1(10)(C), Sept. 24, 1963, 77 Stat. 184, §284; amended Pub. L. 94–546, §1(23), Oct. 18, 1976, 90 Stat. 2520; renumbered §2144 and amended Pub. L. 115–282, title I, §§112(b), 123(b)(2), Dec. 4, 2018, 132 Stat. 4216, 4240.)

§2145. REGULAR LIEUTENANT COMMANDERS AND COMMANDERS; RETIREMENT FOR FAILURE OF SELECTION FOR PROMOTION

(a) Each officer of the Regular Coast Guard serving in the grade of lieutenant commander or commander, who has failed of selection for promotion to the grade of commander or captain, respectively, for the second time shall:

(1) if he has completed at least 20 years of active service or is eligible for retirement under any law on June 30 of the promotion year in which his second failure of selection occurs, be retired on that date; or

(2) if ineligible for retirement on the date specified in clause (1) be retained on active duty and retired on the last day of the month in which he completes twenty years of active service, unless earlier removed under another provision of law.

(b) A lieutenant commander or commander of the Regular Coast Guard subject to discharge or retirement under subsection (a) may be continued on active duty when the Secretary directs a selection board convened under section 2106 of this title to continue up to a specified number of lieutenant commanders or commanders on active duty. When so directed, the selection board shall recommend those officers who in the opinion of the board are best qualified to advance the needs and efficiency of the Coast Guard. When the recommendations of the board are approved by the Secretary, the officers recommended for continuation shall be notified that they have been recommended for continuation and offered an additional term of service that fulfills the needs of the Coast Guard.

(c)(1) An officer who holds the grade of lieutenant commander of the Regular Coast Guard may not be continued on active duty under subsection (b) for a period that extends beyond 24 years of active commissioned service unless promoted to the grade of commander of the Regular Coast Guard. An officer who holds the grade of commander of the Regular Coast Guard may not be continued on active duty under subsection (b) for a period that extends beyond 26 years of active commissioned service unless promoted to the grade of captain of the Regular Coast Guard.

(2) Unless retired or discharged under another provision of law, each officer who is continued on active duty under subsection (b) but is not subsequently promoted or continued on active duty, and is not on a list of officers recommended for continuation or for promotion to the next higher grade, shall, if eligible for retirement under any provision of law, be retired under that law on the first day of the first month following the month in which the period of continued service is completed.

(Added Pub. L. 88–130, §1(10)(C), Sept. 24, 1963, 77 Stat. 185, §285; amended Pub. L. 93–283, §1(7),

May 14, 1974, 88 Stat. 140; Pub. L. 94–546, §1(24), Oct. 18, 1976, 90 Stat. 2521; Pub. L. 107–295, title IV, §412, Nov. 25, 2002, 116 Stat. 2118; renumbered §2145 and amended Pub. L. 115–282, title I, §§112(b), 123(b)(2), Dec. 4, 2018, 132 Stat. 4216, 4240.)

§2146. DISCHARGE IN LIEU OF RETIREMENT; SEPARATION PAY

(a) Each officer who is retained on active duty under section 2143(a)(4), 2143(b), or 2145 of this title may, if he so requests, with the approval of the Secretary, be honorably discharged at any time prior to the date otherwise specified for his retirement or discharge.

(b) An officer of the Regular Coast Guard who is discharged under this section or section 2142, 2143, or 2144 of this title and has completed 6 or more, but less than 20, continuous years of active service immediately before that discharge or release is entitled to separation pay computed under subsection (d)(1) of section 1174 of title 10.

(c) An officer of the Regular Coast Guard who is discharged under section 2164 of this title and has completed 6 or more, but less than 20, continuous years of active service immediately before that discharge or release is entitled to separation pay computed under subsection (d)(1) or (d)(2) of section 1174 of title 10 as determined under regulations promulgated by the Secretary.

(d) Notwithstanding subsections (a) and (b), an officer discharged under this chapter for twice failing of selection for promotion to the next higher grade is not entitled to separation pay under this section if the officer requested in writing or otherwise sought not to be selected for promotion, or requested removal from the list of selectees.

(Added Pub. L. 88–130, §1(10)(C), Sept. 24, 1963, 77 Stat. 185, §286; amended Pub. L. 107–295, title IV, §416(a)(3), Nov. 25, 2002, 116 Stat. 2121; renumbered §2146 and amended Pub. L. 115–282, title I, §§112(b), 123(b)(2), (c)(2)(A), Dec. 4, 2018, 132 Stat. 4216, 4240.)

§2147. REGULAR WARRANT OFFICERS: SEPARATION PAY

(a) A regular warrant officer of the Coast Guard who is discharged under section 580 of title 10, and has completed 6 or more, but less than 20, continuous years of active service immediately before that discharge is entitled to separation pay computed under subsection (d)(1) of section 1174 of title 10.

(b) A regular warrant officer of the Coast Guard who is discharged under section 1165 or 1166 of title 10, and has completed 6 or more, but less than 20, continuous years of active service immediately before that discharge is entitled to separation pay computed under subsection (d)(1) or (d)(2) of section 1174 of title 10, as determined under regulations promulgated by the Secretary.

(c) In determining a member's years of active service for the purpose of computing separation pay under this section, each full month of service that is in addition to the number of full years of service creditable to the member is counted as one-twelfth of a year and any remaining fractional part of a month is disregarded.

(d) The acceptance of separation pay under this section does not deprive an individual of any retirement benefits from the United States. However, there shall be deducted from each of his retirement payments so much thereof as is based on the service for which he has received separation pay under this section, until the total deductions equal the amount of such separation pay.

(Added Pub. L. 96–513, title V, §505(a)(1), Dec. 12, 1980, 94 Stat. 2918, §286a; amended Pub. L. 102–190, div. A, title XI, §1125(b)(1), Dec. 5, 1991, 105 Stat. 1505; Pub. L. 103–337, div. A, title V, §541(f)(2), Oct. 5, 1994, 108 Stat. 2766; Pub. L. 105–383, title II, §201(a), (b), Nov. 13, 1998, 112 Stat. 3414; Pub. L. 107–295, title IV, §416(a)(4), Nov. 25, 2002, 116 Stat. 2121; Pub. L. 112–213, title II, §217(4), Dec. 20, 2012, 126 Stat. 1557; renumbered §2147, Pub. L. 115–282, title I, §112(b), Dec. 4, 2018, 132 Stat. 4216; Pub. L. 116–283, div. G, title LVXXXV [LXXXV], §8505(a)(17), Jan. 1, 2021, 134 Stat. 4748.)

§2148. SEPARATION FOR FAILURE OF SELECTION FOR PROMOTION OR CONTINUATION; TIME OF

If, under section 2142, 2143, 2144, 2145, 2150, or 2151 of this title, the discharge or retirement of any officer would be required less than six months following approval of the report of the board which considered but did not select him for promotion or continuation, the discharge or retirement of such officer shall be deferred until the last day of the sixth calendar month after such approval.

(Added Pub. L. 88–130, §1(10)(C), Sept. 24, 1963, 77 Stat. 185, §287; amended Pub. L. 92–451, §1(6), Oct. 2, 1972, 86 Stat. 755; renumbered §2148 and amended Pub. L. 115–282, title I, §§112(b), 123(b)(2), Dec. 4, 2018, 132 Stat. 4216, 4240.)

§2149. REGULAR CAPTAINS; RETIREMENT

(a) Each officer of the Regular Coast Guard serving in the grade of captain whose name is not carried on an approved list of officers selected for promotion to the grade of rear admiral (lower half) shall, unless retired under some other provision of law, be retired on June 30 of the promotion year in which he, or any captain junior to him on the active duty promotion list who has not lost numbers or precedence, completes thirty years of active commissioned service in the Coast Guard. An officer advanced in precedence on the active duty promotion list because of his promotion resulting from selection for promotion from below the zone, or from being placed at the top of the list of selectees promulgated by the Secretary under section 2121(a) of this title, is not subject to involuntary retirement under this section earlier than if he had not been selected from below the zone or placed at the top of the list of selectees, as applicable.

(b) Retired pay computed under section 2504(a) of this title of an officer retired under this section shall not be less than 50 percent of the basic pay upon which the computation of his retired pay is based.

(Added Pub. L. 88–130, §1(10)(C), Sept. 24, 1963, 77 Stat. 185, §288; amended Pub. L. 93–283, §1(8), May 14, 1974, 88 Stat. 140; Pub. L. 94–546, §1(25), Oct. 18, 1976, 90 Stat. 2521; Pub. L. 96–342, title VIII, §813(f)(1), Sept. 8, 1980, 94 Stat. 1109; Pub. L. 97–417, §2(7), Jan. 4, 1983, 96 Stat. 2085; Pub. L. 99–348, title II, §205(b)(4), July 1, 1986, 100 Stat. 700; Pub. L. 99–661, div. A, title XIII, §1343(c), Nov. 14, 1986, 100 Stat. 3995; renumbered §2149 and amended Pub. L. 115–282, title I, §§112(b), 123(b)(2), title III, §309, Dec. 4, 2018, 132 Stat. 4216, 4240, 4248.)

§2150. CAPTAINS; CONTINUATION ON ACTIVE DUTY; INVOLUNTARY RETIREMENT

(a) The Secretary may, whenever the needs of the service require, but not more often than annually, convene a board consisting of not less than six officers of the grade of rear admiral (lower half) or rear admiral to recommend for continuation on active duty officers on the active duty promotion list serving in the grade of captain, who during the promotion year in which the board meets will complete at least three years' service in that grade and who have not been selected for promotion to the grade of rear admiral (lower half). Officers who are subject to retirement under section 2149 of this title during the promotion year in which the board meets shall not be considered by this board.

(b) Whenever he convenes a board under this section, the Secretary shall establish a continuation zone. The zone shall consist of the most senior captains eligible for consideration for continuation on active duty who have not previously been placed in a continuation zone under this section. The Secretary shall, based upon the needs of the service, prescribe the number of captains to be included in the zone.

(c) Based on the needs of the service the Secretary shall furnish the board with the number of officers that may be recommended for continuation on active duty. This number shall be no less than 50 percent of the number considered. The board shall select from the designated continuation zone, in the number directed by the Secretary, those officers who are, in the opinion of the board, best qualified for continuation on active duty.

(d) The provisions of sections 2108, 2109, 2115, and 2117 of this title relating to selection for promotion shall, to the extent that they are not inconsistent with the provisions of this section, apply to boards convened under this section.

(e) The Secretary shall prescribe by regulation the detailed procedures whereby officers in a continuation zone will be selected for continuation on active duty.

(f) A board convened under this section shall submit its report to the Secretary. If the board has acted contrary to law or regulation, the Secretary may return the report for proceedings in revision and resubmission to the Secretary. After his final review the Secretary shall submit the report of the board to the President for his approval. Except as required by the procedures of this section, the proceedings of the board shall not be disclosed to any individual who is not a member of the board.

(g) Each officer who is considered but not recommended for continuation on active duty under the provisions of this section shall, unless retired under some other provision of law, be retired on June 30 of the promotion year in which the report of the continuation board convened under this section is approved, or the last day of the month in which he completes twenty years of active service, whichever is later.

(h) Notwithstanding subsection (g) and section 2149 of this title, the Commandant may by annual action retain on active duty from promotion year to promotion year any officer who would otherwise be retired under subsection (g) or section 2149 of this title. An officer so retained, unless retired under some other provision of law, shall be retired on June 30 of that promotion year in which no action is taken to further retain the officer under this subsection.

(Added Pub. L. 88–130, §1(10)(C), Sept. 24, 1963, 77 Stat. 186, §289; amended Pub. L. 94–546, §1(26), Oct. 18, 1976, 90 Stat. 2521; Pub. L. 97–417, §2(8), Jan. 4, 1983, 96 Stat. 2085; Pub. L. 99–145, title V, §514(c)(1), Nov. 8, 1985, 99 Stat. 629; Pub. L. 101–225, title II, §203(3), Dec. 12, 1989, 103 Stat. 1911;

Pub. L. 104–324, title II, §203, Oct. 19, 1996, 110 Stat. 3907; Pub. L. 107–295, title IV, §414, Nov. 25, 2002, 116 Stat. 2120; renumbered §2150 and amended Pub. L. 115–282, title I, §§112(b), 123(b)(2), Dec. 4, 2018, 132 Stat. 4216, 4240; Pub. L. 116–283, div. G, title LVXXXV [LXXXV], §8505(a)(18), Jan. 1, 2021, 134 Stat. 4748.)

§2151. REAR ADMIRALS AND REAR ADMIRALS (LOWER HALF); CONTINUATION ON ACTIVE DUTY; INVOLUNTARY RETIREMENT

(a) The Secretary shall from time to time convene boards to recommend for continuation on active duty the most senior officers on the active duty promotion list serving in the grade of rear admiral (lower half) or rear admiral who have not previously been considered for continuation in that grade. Officers serving for the time being or who have served in or above the grade of vice admiral are not subject to consideration for continuation under this subsection, and as to all other provisions of this section shall be considered as having been continued at the grade of rear admiral. A board shall consist of at least 5 officers (other than the Commandant) serving in the grade of admiral or vice admiral or as rear admirals previously continued. Boards shall be convened frequently enough to assure that each officer serving in the grade of rear admiral (lower half) or rear admiral is subject to consideration for continuation during a promotion year in which that officer completes not less than four or more than five years combined service in the grades of rear admiral (lower half) and rear admiral.

(b) The Secretary shall, based upon the needs of the service, furnish each board convened under this section with the number of officers to be considered for continuation on active duty. The number that may be recommended for continuation shall be not less than 50 per centum or more than 75 per centum of the number of officers being considered for continuation.

(c) The provisions of sections 2108, 2109, 2115, and 2117 of this title relating to selection and continuation boards shall to the extent they are not inconsistent with the provisions of this section, apply to boards convened under this section.

(d) A board convened under this section shall submit its report to the Secretary. If the board has acted contrary to law or regulation, the Secretary may return the report for proceedings in revision and resubmission to the Secretary. After final review the Secretary shall submit the report of the board to the President for approval.

(e) Each officer who is considered but not continued on active duty under the provisions of this section shall, unless retired under some other provision of law, be retired on July 1 of the promotion year immediately following the promotion year in which the report of the continuation board convened under this section is approved.

(f)(1) Unless retired under another provision of law, each officer who is continued on active duty under this section shall, except as provided in paragraph (2), be retired on July 1 of the promotion year immediately following the promotion year in which that officer completes seven years of combined service in the grades of rear admiral (lower half) and rear admiral, unless that officer is selected for or serving in the grade of admiral or vice admiral or the position of Superintendent of the Coast Guard Academy.

(2) The Commandant, with the approval of the Secretary, may by annual action retain on active duty from promotion year to promotion year any officer who would otherwise be

185

retired under paragraph (1). Unless selected for or serving in the grade of admiral or vice admiral or the position of Superintendent of the Coast Guard Academy, or retired under another provision of law, an officer so retained shall be retired on July 1 of the promotion year immediately following the promotion year in which no action is taken to further retain that officer under this paragraph.

(g)(1) Unless retired under another provision of law, an officer subject to this section shall, except as provided in paragraph (2), be retired on July 1 of the promotion year immediately following the promotion year in which that officer completes a total of thirty-six years of active commissioned service unless selected for or serving in the grade of admiral.

(2) The Commandant, with the approval of the Secretary, may by annual action retain on active duty from promotion year to promotion year any officer who would otherwise be retired under paragraph (1). Unless selected for or serving in the grade of admiral or retired under another provision of law, an officer so retained shall be retired on July 1 of the promotion year immediately following the promotion year in which no action is taken to further retain that officer under this paragraph.

(Added Pub. L. 88–130, §1(10)(C), Sept. 24, 1963, 77 Stat. 187, §290; amended Pub. L. 92–451, §1(7), Oct. 2, 1972, 86 Stat. 756; Pub. L. 94–546, §1(27), Oct. 18, 1976, 90 Stat. 2521; Pub. L. 97–136, §6(b), Dec. 29, 1981, 95 Stat. 1706; Pub. L. 97–417, §2(9)(A), Jan. 4, 1983, 96 Stat. 2086; Pub. L. 98–557, §25(a)(2), Oct. 30, 1984, 98 Stat. 2872; Pub. L. 99–145, title V, §514(c)(1), (2)(A), Nov. 8, 1985, 99 Stat. 629; Pub. L. 102–241, §5, Dec. 19, 1991, 105 Stat. 2210; Pub. L. 103–206, title II, §205(d), Dec. 20, 1993, 107 Stat. 2422; Pub. L. 111–281, title V, §511(e), Oct. 15, 2010, 124 Stat. 2952; Pub. L. 112–213, title II, §217(5), Dec. 20, 2012, 126 Stat. 1557; Pub. L. 114–328, div. C, title XXXV, §3522, Dec. 23, 2016, 130 Stat. 2793; Pub. L. 115–232, div. C, title XXXV, §3537, Aug. 13, 2018, 132 Stat. 2322; renumbered §2151 and amended Pub. L. 115–282, title I, §§112(b), 123(b)(2), Dec. 4, 2018, 132 Stat. 4216, 4240.)

§2152. Voluntary Retirement After Twenty Years' Service

Any regular commissioned officer who has completed twenty years' active service in the Coast Guard, Navy, Army, Air Force, Marine Corps, or Space Force, or the Reserve components thereof, including active duty for training, at least ten years of which shall have been active commissioned service, may, upon his own application, in the discretion of the President, be retired from active service.

(Added Pub. L. 88–130, §1(10)(C), Sept. 24, 1963, 77 Stat. 187, §291; amended Pub. L. 99–348, title II, §205(b)(5), July 1, 1986, 100 Stat. 700; renumbered §2152, Pub. L. 115–282, title I, §112(b), Dec. 4, 2018, 132 Stat. 4216; Pub. L. 116–283, div. A, title IX, §927(b)(1), Jan. 1, 2021, 134 Stat. 3831.)

§2153. Voluntary Retirement After Thirty Years' Service

Any regular commissioned officer who has completed thirty years' service may, upon his own application, in the discretion of the Secretary, be retired from active service.[1]

(Added Pub. L. 88–130, §1(10)(C), Sept. 24, 1963, 77 Stat. 187, §292; amended Pub. L. 99–348, title II, §205(b)(5), July 1, 1986, 100 Stat. 700; renumbered §2153, Pub. L. 115–282, title I, §112(b), Dec. 4, 2018, 132 Stat. 4216.)

¹ *See 1986 Amendment note below.*

§2154. Compulsory retirement

(a) Regular Commissioned Officers.—Any regular commissioned officer, except a commissioned warrant officer, serving in a grade below rear admiral (lower half) shall be retired on the first day of the month following the month in which the officer becomes 62 years of age.

(b) Flag-Officer Grades.—(1) Except as provided in paragraph (2), any regular commissioned officer serving in a grade of rear admiral (lower half) or above shall be retired on the first day of the month following the month in which the officer becomes 64 years of age.

(2) The retirement of an officer under paragraph (1) may be deferred—

(A) by the President, but such a deferment may not extend beyond the first day of the month following the month in which the officer becomes 68 years of age; or

(B) by the Secretary of the department in which the Coast Guard is operating, but such a deferment may not extend beyond the first day of the month following the month in which the officer becomes 66 years of age.

(Added Pub. L. 111–281, title II, §215(a), Oct. 15, 2010, 124 Stat. 2916, §293; renumbered §2154, Pub. L. 115–282, title I, §112(b), Dec. 4, 2018, 132 Stat. 4216.)

§2155. Retirement for physical disability after selection for promotion; grade in which retired

An officer whose name appears on an approved list of officers selected for promotion to the next higher grade and who is retired for physical disability under the provisions of chapter 61 of title 10 prior to being promoted shall be retired in the grade to which he was selected for promotion.

(Added Pub. L. 88–130, §1(10)(C), Sept. 24, 1963, 77 Stat. 187, §294; renumbered §2155, Pub. L. 115–282, title I, §112(b), Dec. 4, 2018, 132 Stat. 4216.)

§2156. Deferment of retirement or separation for medical reasons

(a) Subject to subsection (b), the Secretary may defer the retirement or separation of a commissioned officer, other than a commissioned warrant officer, if the evaluation of the physical condition of the officer and determination of the officer's entitlement to retirement or separation for physical disability require hospitalization, medical observation, or other physical disability processing that cannot be completed before the date on which the officer would otherwise be retired or separated.

(b) A deferment under subsection (a)—

(1) may only be made with the consent of the officer involved; and

(2) if the Secretary receives written notice from the officer withdrawing that consent, shall end not later than the end of the sixty-day period beginning on the date the Secretary receives that notice.

(Added Pub. L. 98–557, §17(b)(2)(A), Oct. 30, 1984, 98 Stat. 2867, §295; renumbered §2156, Pub. L.

115–282, title I, §112(b), Dec. 4, 2018, 132 Stat. 4216.)

§2157. FLAG OFFICERS

During any period in which the Coast Guard is not operating as a service in the Navy, section 1216(d) of title 10 does not apply with respect to flag officers of the Coast Guard.

(Added Pub. L. 113–281, title II, §212(a), Dec. 18, 2014, 128 Stat. 3029, §296; renumbered §2157, Pub. L. 115–282, title I, §112(b), Dec. 4, 2018, 132 Stat. 4216.)

§2158. REVIEW OF RECORDS OF OFFICERS

The Secretary may at any time convene a board of officers to review the record of any officer of the Regular Coast Guard to determine whether he shall be required to show cause for his retention on active duty—

(1) because his performance of duty has fallen below the standards prescribed by the Secretary, or

(2) because of moral dereliction, professional dereliction, or because his retention is not clearly consistent with the interests of national security.

(Added Pub. L. 88–130, §1(10)(C), Sept. 24, 1963, 77 Stat. 187, §321; renumbered §2158, Pub. L. 115–282, title I, §112(b), Dec. 4, 2018, 132 Stat. 4216.)

§2159. BOARDS OF INQUIRY

(a) Boards of inquiry shall be convened at such places as the Secretary may prescribe to receive evidence and make findings and recommendations whether an officer who is required to show cause for retention under section 2158 of this title should be retained on active duty.

(b) A fair and impartial hearing before a board of inquiry shall be given to each officer so required to show cause for retention.

(c) If a board of inquiry determines that the officer has failed to establish that he should be retained, it shall send the record of its proceedings to a board of review.

(d) If a board of inquiry determines that the officer has established that he should be retained, his case is closed. However, at any time after one year from the date of the determination in a case arising under clause (1) of section 2158 of this title, and at any time after the date of the determination in a case arising under clause (2) of that section, an officer may again be required to show cause for retention.

(Added Pub. L. 88–130, §1(10)(C), Sept. 24, 1963, 77 Stat. 188, §322; amended Pub. L. 97–295, §2(10), Oct. 12, 1982, 96 Stat. 1302; renumbered §2159 and amended Pub. L. 115–282, title I, §§112(b), 123(b)(2), Dec. 4, 2018, 132 Stat. 4216, 4240.)

§2160. BOARDS OF REVIEW

(a) Boards of review shall be convened at such times as the Secretary may prescribe, to review the records of cases of officers recommended by boards of inquiry for removal.

(b) If, after reviewing the record of the case, a board of review determines that the officer

188

has failed to establish that he should be retained, it shall send its recommendation to the Secretary for his action.

(c) If, after reviewing the record of the case, a board of review determines that the officer has established that he should be retained on active duty, his case is closed. However, at any time after one year from the date of the determination in a case arising under clause (1) of section 2158 of this title and at any time after the date of the determination in a case arising under clause (2) of that section, an officer may again be required to show cause for retention.

(Added Pub. L. 88–130, §1(10)(C), Sept. 24, 1963, 77 Stat. 188, §323; amended Pub. L. 97–295, §2(10), Oct. 12, 1982, 96 Stat. 1302; renumbered §2160 and amended Pub. L. 115–282, title I, §§112(b), 123(b)(2), Dec. 4, 2018, 132 Stat. 4216, 4240.)

§2161. COMPOSITION OF BOARDS

(a) A board convened under section 2158, 2159, or 2160 of this title shall consist of at least three officers of the grade of commander or above, all of whom are serving in a grade senior to the grade of any officer considered by the board.

(b) No individual may be a member of more than one board convened under section 2158, 2159, or 2160 of this title to consider the same officer.

(Added Pub. L. 88–130, §1(10)(C), Sept. 24, 1963, 77 Stat. 188, §324; renumbered §2161 and amended Pub. L. 115–282, title I, §§112(b), 123(b)(2), Dec. 4, 2018, 132 Stat. 4216, 4240; Pub. L. 116–283, div. G, title LVXXXV [LXXXV], §8505(a)(19), Jan. 1, 2021, 134 Stat. 4748.)

§2162. RIGHTS AND PROCEDURES

Each officer under consideration for removal under section 2159 of this title shall be—

(1) notified in writing at least thirty days before the hearing of the case by a board of inquiry of the reasons for which the officer is being required to show cause for retention;

(2) allowed reasonable time, as determined by the board of inquiry under regulations of the Secretary, to prepare his defense;

(3) allowed to appear in person and by counsel at proceedings before a board of inquiry; and

(4) allowed full access to, and furnished copies of, records relevant to the case at all stages of the proceeding, except that a board shall withhold any records that the Secretary determines should be withheld in the interests of national security. In any case where any records are withheld under this clause, the officer whose case is under consideration shall, to the extent that the national security permits, be furnished a summary of the records so withheld.

(Added Pub. L. 88–130, §1(10)(C), Sept. 24, 1963, 77 Stat. 188, §325; renumbered §2162 and amended Pub. L. 115–282, title I, §§112(b), 123(b)(2), Dec. 4, 2018, 132 Stat. 4216, 4240.)

§2163. REMOVAL OF OFFICER FROM ACTIVE DUTY; ACTION BY SECRETARY

The Secretary may remove an officer from active duty if his removal is recommended by a board of review under section 2160 of this title. The Secretary's action in such as case is final and conclusive.

(Added Pub. L. 88–130, §1(10)(C), Sept. 24, 1963, 77 Stat. 189, §326; renumbered §2163 and amended Pub. L. 115–282, title I, §§112(b), 123(b)(2), Dec. 4, 2018, 132 Stat. 4216, 4240.)

§2164. Officers considered for removal; retirement or discharge; separation benefits

(a) At any time during proceedings under section 2159 or 2160 of this title, and before the removal of an officer, the Secretary may grant a request—
  (1) for voluntary retirement, if the officer is otherwise qualified therefor; or
  (2) for discharge with separation benefits under section 2146(c) of this title.

(b) Each officer removed from active duty under section 2163 of this title shall—
  (1) if on the date of removal the officer is eligible for voluntary retirement under any law, be retired in the grade for which he would be eligible if retired at his request; or
  (2) if on that date the officer is ineligible for voluntary retirement under any law, be honorably discharged with separation benefits under section 2146(c) of this title, unless under regulations promulgated by the Secretary the condition under which the officer is discharged does not warrant an honorable discharge.

(Added Pub. L. 88–130, §1(10)(C), Sept. 24, 1963, 77 Stat. 189, §327; amended Pub. L. 97–295, §2(10), Oct. 12, 1982, 96 Stat. 1302; Pub. L. 99–348, title II, §205(b)(6), July 1, 1986, 100 Stat. 700; Pub. L. 105–383, title II, §201(c), Nov. 13, 1998, 112 Stat. 3414; Pub. L. 107–295, title IV, §416(a)(5), Nov. 25, 2002, 116 Stat. 2122; renumbered §2164 and amended Pub. L. 115–282, title I, §§112(b), 123(b)(2), Dec. 4, 2018, 132 Stat. 4216, 4240.)

§2165. Relief of retired officer promoted while on active duty

Any regular officer on the retired list recalled to active duty who during such active duty is advanced to a higher grade under an appointment shall, upon relief from active duty, if his performance of duty under such appointment has been satisfactory, be advanced on the retired list to the highest grade held while on such active duty.

(Added Pub. L. 88–130, §1(10)(C), Sept. 24, 1963, 77 Stat. 189, §333; renumbered §2165, Pub. L. 115–282, title I, §112(b), Dec. 4, 2018, 132 Stat. 4216.)

§2166. Continuation on active duty; Coast Guard officers with certain critical skills

(a) In General.—The Commandant may authorize an officer in a grade above grade O–2 to remain on active duty after the date otherwise provided for the retirement of such officer in section 2154 of this title, if the officer possesses a critical skill, or specialty, or is in a career field designated pursuant to subsection (b).

(b) Critical Skills, Specialty, or Career Field.—The Commandant shall designate any critical skill, specialty, or career field eligible for continuation on active duty as provided in subsection (a).

(c) Duration of Continuation.—An officer continued on active duty pursuant to this section shall, if not earlier retired, be retired on the first day of the month after the month in which the officer completes 40 years of active service.

(d) POLICY.—The Commandant shall carry out this section by prescribing policy which shall specify the criteria to be used in designating any critical skill, specialty, or career field for purposes of subsection (b).

(Added Pub. L. 117–263, div. K, title CXII, §11235(a), Dec. 23, 2022, 136 Stat. 4035.)

SUBCHAPTER III—GENERAL PROVISIONS

§2181. PHYSICAL FITNESS OF OFFICERS

The Secretary shall prescribe regulations under which the physical fitness of officers to perform their duties shall be periodically determined.

(Added Pub. L. 88–130, §1(10)(C), Sept. 24, 1963, 77 Stat. 190, §335; renumbered §2181, Pub. L. 115–282, title I, §112(b), Dec. 4, 2018, 132 Stat. 4216.)

§2182. MULTIRATER ASSESSMENT OF CERTAIN PERSONNEL

(a) MULTIRATER ASSESSMENT OF CERTAIN PERSONNEL.—

(1) IN GENERAL.—Commencing not later than one year after the date of the enactment of the Coast Guard Authorization Act of 2016, the Commandant shall develop and implement a plan to conduct every two years a multirater assessment for each of the following:

(A) Each flag officer of the Coast Guard.

(B) Each member of the Senior Executive Service of the Coast Guard.

(C) Each officer of the Coast Guard nominated for promotion to the grade of flag officer.

(2) OFFICERS.—Each officer of the Coast Guard shall undergo a multirater assessment before promotion to—

(A) the grade of O–4;

(B) the grade of O–5; and

(C) the grade of O–6.

(3) ENLISTED MEMBERS.—Each enlisted member of the Coast Guard shall undergo a multirater assessment before advancement to—

(A) the grade of E–7;

(B) the grade of E–8;

(C) the grade of E–9; and

(D) the grade of E–10.

(4) SELECTION.—An individual assessed shall not be permitted to select the peers and subordinates who provide opinions for the multirater assessment of such individual.

(5) POST-ASSESSMENT ELEMENTS.—

(A) IN GENERAL.—Following an assessment of an individual pursuant to paragraphs (1) through (3), the individual shall be provided appropriate post-assessment counseling and leadership coaching.

(B) AVAILABILITY OF RESULTS.—The supervisor of the individual assessed shall be provided with the results of the multirater assessment.

(b) MULTIRATER ASSESSMENT DEFINED.—In this section, the term "multirater assessment" means a review that seeks opinion from members senior to the reviewee and the peers and subordinates of the reviewee.

(Added Pub. L. 114–120, title II, §214(a)(1), Feb. 8, 2016, 130 Stat. 43, §429; amended Pub. L. 114–328, div. C, title XXXV, §3503(a), Dec. 23, 2016, 130 Stat. 2775; Pub. L. 115–232, div. C, title XXXV, §3531(c)(12), Aug. 13, 2018, 132 Stat. 2320; renumbered §2182, Pub. L. 115–282, title I, §112(b), Dec. 4, 2018, 132 Stat. 4216; Pub. L. 117–263, div. K, title CXII, §11244(a), Dec. 23, 2022, 136 Stat. 4042.)

CHAPTER 23—PERSONNEL; ENLISTED

Sec.

§2301. RECRUITING CAMPAIGNS

The Secretary shall initiate and carry forward an intensified voluntary enlistment campaign to obtain the required personnel strengths.

(Added Aug. 10, 1956, ch. 1041, §7(a), 70A Stat. 620, §350; renumbered §2301, Pub. L. 115–282, title I, §113(b), Dec. 4, 2018, 132 Stat. 4221.)

§2302. ENLISTMENTS; TERM, GRADE

(a) Under regulations prescribed by the Secretary, the Commandant may enlist persons for the duration of their minority or a period of at least two years but not more than six years.

(b) The Secretary shall prescribe the grades or ratings for persons enlisting in the Regular Coast Guard.

(Aug. 4, 1949, ch. 393, 63 Stat. 520, §351; Aug. 3, 1950, ch. 536, §16, 64 Stat. 407; Aug. 10, 1956, ch. 1041, §§8(a), 53, 70A Stat. 620, 679; Pub. L. 98–557, §15(a)(3)(F), Oct. 30, 1984, 98 Stat. 2865; Pub. L. 108–293, title II, §203, Aug. 9, 2004, 118 Stat. 1032; Pub. L. 115–232, div. C, title XXXV, §3533(h), Aug. 13, 2018, 132 Stat. 2321; renumbered §2302, Pub. L. 115–282, title I, §113(b), Dec. 4, 2018, 132 Stat. 4221.)

§2303. PROMOTION

Enlisted members shall be advanced in rating by the Commandant under regulations prescribed by the Secretary.

(Aug. 4, 1949, ch. 393, 63 Stat. 520, §352; Pub. L. 98–557, §15(a)(3)(C), Oct. 30, 1984, 98 Stat. 2865;

renumbered §2303, Pub. L. 115–282, title I, §113(b), Dec. 4, 2018, 132 Stat. 4221.)

§2304. COMPULSORY RETIREMENT AT AGE OF SIXTY-TWO

Any enlisted member who has reached the age of sixty-two shall be retired from active service.

(Aug. 4, 1949, ch. 393, 63 Stat. 520, §353; Pub. L. 98–557, §15(a)(3)(A), Oct. 30, 1984, 98 Stat. 2865; Pub. L. 99–348, title II, §205(b)(8), July 1, 1986, 100 Stat. 700; renumbered §2304, Pub. L. 115–282, title I, §113(b), Dec. 4, 2018, 132 Stat. 4221.)

§2305. VOLUNTARY RETIREMENT AFTER THIRTY YEARS' SERVICE

Any enlisted member who has completed thirty years' service may, upon his own application, in the discretion of the Commandant, be retired from active service.

(Aug. 4, 1949, ch. 393, 63 Stat. 521, §354; Pub. L. 98–557, §15(a)(3)(A), Oct. 30, 1984, 98 Stat. 2865; Pub. L. 99–348, title II, §205(b)(8), July 1, 1986, 100 Stat. 700; renumbered §2305, Pub. L. 115–282, title I, §113(b), Dec. 4, 2018, 132 Stat. 4221.)

§2306. VOLUNTARY RETIREMENT AFTER TWENTY YEARS' SERVICE

Any enlisted member who has completed twenty years' service may, upon his own application, in the discretion of the Commandant, be retired from active service.

(Aug. 4, 1949, ch. 393, 63 Stat. 521, §355; Pub. L. 98–557, §15(a)(3)(A), Oct. 30, 1984, 98 Stat. 2865; Pub. L. 99–348, title II, §205(b)(8), July 1, 1986, 100 Stat. 700; renumbered §2306, Pub. L. 115–282, title I, §113(b), Dec. 4, 2018, 132 Stat. 4221.)

§2307. RETIREMENT OF ENLISTED MEMBERS: INCREASE IN RETIRED PAY

An enlisted member voluntarily or involuntarily retired after twenty years of service who was cited for extraordinary heroism in the line of duty shall be entitled to an increase in retired pay. The retired pay shall be increased by 10 percent of—

(1) the active-duty pay and permanent additions thereto of the grade or rating with which retired when the member's retired pay is computed under section 2504(a) of this title; or

(2) the member's retired pay base under section 1407 of title 10, when a member's retired pay is computed under section 2504(b) of this title.

(Aug. 4, 1949, ch. 393, 63 Stat. 521, §357; Aug. 3, 1950, ch. 536, §17, 64 Stat. 407; Pub. L. 88–114, §1(1), Sept. 6, 1963, 77 Stat. 144; Pub. L. 98–557, §15(a)(3)(A), (B), Oct. 30, 1984, 98 Stat. 2865; Pub. L. 99–348, title II, §205(b)(9), July 1, 1986, 100 Stat. 700; Pub. L. 102–241, §6, Dec. 19, 1991, 105 Stat. 2210; Pub. L. 114–120, title II, §215(a), (b)(1), Feb. 8, 2016, 130 Stat. 45, 46; renumbered §2307 and amended Pub. L. 115–282, title I, §§113(b), 123(b)(2), Dec. 4, 2018, 132 Stat. 4221, 4240.)

§2308. RECALL TO ACTIVE DUTY DURING WAR OR NATIONAL EMERGENCY

In times of war or national emergency, the Commandant may order any enlisted member on the retired list to active duty.

(Aug. 4, 1949, ch. 393, 63 Stat. 522, §359; Aug. 3, 1950, ch. 536, §18, 64 Stat. 407; Pub. L. 98–557, §15(a)(3)(A), Oct. 30, 1984, 98 Stat. 2865; renumbered §2308, Pub. L. 115–282, title I, §113(b), Dec. 4, 2018, 132 Stat. 4221.)

§2309. RECALL TO ACTIVE DUTY WITH CONSENT OF MEMBER

Any enlisted member on the retired list may, with his consent, be assigned to such duties as he may be able to perform, except that no enlisted member on the retired list who has reached the age of sixty-two years shall be recalled in time of peace.

(Aug. 4, 1949, ch. 393, 63 Stat. 522, §360; Aug. 3, 1950, ch. 536, §19, 64 Stat. 407; Pub. L. 98–557, §15(a)(3)(A), (4)(B)(i), Oct. 30, 1984, 98 Stat. 2865; renumbered §2309, Pub. L. 115–282, title I, §113(b), Dec. 4, 2018, 132 Stat. 4221.)

§2310. RELIEF OF RETIRED ENLISTED MEMBER PROMOTED WHILE ON ACTIVE DUTY

Any enlisted member on the retired list recalled to active duty who during such active duty is advanced to a higher grade or rating under a permanent or temporary appointment or promotion shall, upon relief from active duty be advanced on the retired list to the highest grade or rating held while on active duty. In case the appointment or promotion was temporary the advancement on the retired list shall be made only to such grade or rating in which the member served satisfactorily on active duty.

(Aug. 4, 1949, ch. 393, 63 Stat. 522, §361; Aug. 3, 1950, ch. 536, §20, 64 Stat. 407; Pub. L. 98–557, §15(a)(3)(A), (G), (4)(C)(i), Oct. 30, 1984, 98 Stat. 2865; renumbered §2310, Pub. L. 115–282, title I, §113(b), Dec. 4, 2018, 132 Stat. 4221.)

§2311. RETIREMENT IN CASES WHERE HIGHER GRADE OR RATING HAS BEEN HELD

Any enlisted member who is retired under any provision of section 2304, 2305, 2306, or 2307 of this title shall be retired from active service with the highest grade or rating held by him while on active duty in which, as determined by the Secretary, his performance of duty was satisfactory, but not lower than his permanent grade or rating.

(Aug. 4, 1949, ch. 393, 63 Stat. 522, §362; Aug. 3, 1950, ch. 536, §21, 64 Stat. 407; Pub. L. 97–295, §2(9), Oct. 12, 1982, 96 Stat. 1302; Pub. L. 98–557, §15(a)(3)(A), Oct. 30, 1984, 98 Stat. 2865; Pub. L. 99–348, title II, §205(b)(8), July 1, 1986, 100 Stat. 700; renumbered §2311 and amended Pub. L. 115–282, title I, §§113(b), 123(b)(?), Dec. 4, 2018, 132 Stat. 4221, 4240.)

§2312. EXTENSION OF ENLISTMENTS

Under regulations prescribed by the Secretary, the term of enlistment of any enlisted member may, by voluntary written agreement, be extended and re-extended for a period not exceeding six full years from the date of expiration of the then-existing term of enlistment, and subsequent to such date an enlisted member who so extends his term of enlistment shall receive the same pay and allowances in all respects as though regularly discharged and reenlisted immediately upon expiration of his term of enlistment. However, the total of all such extensions of an enlistment may not exceed six years. No such extension shall operate to deprive the enlisted member concerned, upon discharge at the termination thereof, of any right, privilege, or benefit to which he would have been entitled if his term of enlistment had not been so extended.

(Aug. 4, 1949, ch. 393, 63 Stat. 523, §365; Pub. L. 86–474, §1(18), May 14, 1960, 74 Stat. 146; Pub. L. 98–557, §15(a)(3)(A), Oct. 30, 1984, 98 Stat. 2865; renumbered §2312, Pub. L. 115–282, title I, §113(b), Dec. 4, 2018, 132 Stat. 4221.)

§2313. Retention beyond term of enlistment in case of disability

Any enlisted member of the Coast Guard in the active service whose term of enlistment expires while he is suffering disease or injury incident to service and not due to misconduct, and who is in need of medical care or hospitalization, may, with his consent, be retained in such service beyond the expiration of his term of enlistment. Any such enlisted member shall be entitled to receive at Government expense medical care or hospitalization and his pay and allowances, including credit for longevity, until he shall have recovered to such extent as would enable him to meet the physical requirements for reenlistment, or until it shall have been ascertained by competent authority of the Coast Guard that the disease or injury is of a character that recovery to such an extent would be impossible. Any enlisted member whose enlistment is so extended shall be subject to forfeitures in the same manner and to the same extent as if his term of enlistment had not expired. Nothing contained in this section shall prevent any enlisted member from being held in the service without his consent under section 2314 of this title.

(Aug. 4, 1949, ch. 393, 63 Stat. 523, §366; Pub. L. 98–557, §15(a)(3)(A), Oct. 30, 1984, 98 Stat. 2865; renumbered §2313 and amended Pub. L. 115–282, title I, §§113(b), 123(b)(2), Dec. 4, 2018, 132 Stat. 4221, 4240.)

§2314. Detention beyond term of enlistment

Under regulations prescribed by the Secretary, an enlisted member may be detained in the Coast Guard beyond the term of his enlistment:

(1) until the first arrival of the vessel on which he is serving at its permanent station, or at a port in a State of the United States or in the District of Columbia; or

(2) if attached to a shore station beyond the continental limits of the United States or in Alaska, until his first arrival at a port in any State of the United States or in the District of Columbia where his reenlistment or discharge may be effected, or until he can be discharged or reenlisted at his station beyond the continental limits of the United States or in Alaska, whichever is earlier, but in no event to exceed three months; or

(3) during a period of war or national emergency as proclaimed by the President, and, in the interest of national defense, for a period not to exceed six months after the end of the war or the termination of the emergency; or

(4) for a period of not exceeding thirty days in other cases whether or not specifically covered by this section, when essential to the public interests, and the determination that such detention is essential to the public interests, made in accordance with regulations prescribed by the Secretary, shall be final and conclusive.

Any member detained in the Coast Guard as provided in this section shall be entitled to receive pay and allowances and benefits under the same conditions as though his enlistment period had not expired, and shall be subject in all respects to the laws and regulations for the government of the Coast Guard until his discharge therefrom. Enlisted members detained under the provisions of clause (1) shall be entitled to the pay and allowances provided for enlisted personnel of the Navy detained under similar circumstances.

(Aug. 4, 1949, ch. 393, 63 Stat. 523, §367; Aug. 3, 1950, ch. 536, §22, 64 Stat. 407; July 24, 1956, ch. 692, §§2(4), 3, 70 Stat. 631; Pub. L. 98–557, §§15(a)(3)(A), (C), 17(b)(4), Oct. 30, 1984, 98 Stat. 2865, 2868; renumbered §2314, Pub. L. 115–282, title I, §113(b), Dec. 4, 2018, 132 Stat. 4221.)

§2315. INCLUSION OF CERTAIN CONDITIONS IN ENLISTMENT CONTRACT

The enlistment contract shall contain the substance of sections 2312 to 2314,[1] inclusive, of this title.

(Aug. 4, 1949, ch. 393, 63 Stat. 524, §369; renumbered §2315 and amended Pub. L. 115–282, title I, §§113(b), 123(b)(2), Dec. 4, 2018, 132 Stat. 4221, 4240.)

[1] *See 2018 Amendment note below.*

§2316. DISCHARGE WITHIN THREE MONTHS BEFORE EXPIRATION OF ENLISTMENT

Under regulations prescribed by the Secretary, any enlisted member may be discharged at any time within three months before the expiration of his term of enlistment or extended enlistment without prejudice to any right, privilege, or benefit that he would have received, except pay and allowances for the unexpired period not served, or to which he would thereafter become entitled, had he served his full term of enlistment or extended enlistment.

(Added June 8, 1955, ch. 136, §2, 69 Stat. 88, §370; amended Pub. L. 98–557, §15(a)(3)(A), Oct. 30, 1984, 98 Stat. 2865; renumbered §2316, Pub. L. 115–282, title I, §113(b), Dec. 4, 2018, 132 Stat. 4221.)

§2317. AVIATION CADETS; PROCUREMENT; TRANSFER

(a) The grade of aviation cadet is established as a special enlisted grade in the Coast Guard. Under such regulations as the Secretary prescribes, citizens in civil life may be enlisted as, and enlisted members of the Coast Guard with their consent may be designated as, aviation cadets.

(b) Except in time of war or national emergency declared by Congress, not less than 20 percent of the aviation cadets procured in each fiscal year shall be procured from qualified enlisted members of the Coast Guard.

(c) No individuals may be enlisted or designated as an aviation cadet unless—

(1) the individual agrees in writing that, upon successful completion of the course of training as an aviation cadet, the individual will accept a commission as an ensign in the Coast Guard Reserve and will serve on active duty as such for at least three years, unless sooner released; and

(2) if under twenty-one years of age, the individual has the consent of the individual's parent or guardian to the agreement.

(d) Under such regulations as the Secretary prescribes, an aviation cadet may be transferred to another enlisted grade or rating in the Coast Guard, released from active duty, or discharged.

(Added Pub. L. 89–444, §1(20), June 9, 1966, 80 Stat. 196, §371; amended Pub. L. 97–295, §2(11), Oct. 12, 1982, 96 Stat. 1302; Pub. L. 98–557, §15(a)(1), Oct. 30, 1984, 98 Stat. 2864; renumbered §2317, Pub. L. 115–282, title I, §113(b), Dec. 4, 2018, 132 Stat. 4221; Pub. L. 116–283, div. G, title LVXXXV [LXXXV], §8505(a)(20), Jan. 1, 2021, 134 Stat. 4748.)

§2318. AVIATION CADETS; BENEFITS

Except as provided in section 402(c) of title 37, aviation cadets or their beneficiaries are entitled to the same allowances, pensions, gratuities, and other benefits as are provided for enlisted members in pay grade E–4. While on active duty, an aviation cadet is entitled to uniforms, clothing, and equipment at the expense of the United States.

(Added Pub. L. 89–444, §1(20), June 9, 1966, 80 Stat. 197, §372; renumbered §2318, Pub. L. 115–282, title I, §113(b), Dec. 4, 2018, 132 Stat. 4221.)

§2319. CRITICAL SKILL TRAINING BONUS

(a) The Secretary may provide a bonus, not to exceed $20,000, to an enlisted member who completes training in a skill designated as critical, if at least four years of obligated active service remain on the member's enlistment at the time the training is completed. A bonus under this section may be paid in a single lump sum or in periodic installments.

(b) If an enlisted member voluntarily or because of misconduct does not complete the member's term of obligated active service, the Secretary may require the member to repay the United States, on a pro rata basis, all sums paid under this section. The Secretary may charge interest on the amount repaid at a rate, to be determined quarterly, equal to 150 percent of the average of the yields on the 91-day Treasury bills auctioned during the calendar quarter preceding the date on which the amount to be repaid is determined.

(Added Pub. L. 108–293, title II, §204(a), Aug. 9, 2004, 118 Stat. 1032, §374; renumbered §2319, Pub. L. 115–282, title I, §113(b), Dec. 4, 2018, 132 Stat. 4221.)

CHAPTER 25—PERSONNEL; GENERAL PROVISIONS

SUBCHAPTER I—GENERAL PROVISIONS

SUBCHAPTER II—ADVISORY BOARD ON WOMEN IN THE COAST GUARD

[SUBCHAPTER III—REPEALED]

SUBCHAPTER I—GENERAL PROVISIONS

§2501. GRADE ON RETIREMENT

(a) COMMISSIONED OFFICERS.—

(1) IN GENERAL.—A commissioned officer who is retired under any provision of this title, shall be retired from active service with the highest grade held by the commissioned officer for not less than six months while on active duty in which, as determined by the Secretary, the commissioned officer's performance of duty was satisfactory.

(2) CONDITIONAL DETERMINATION.—When a commissioned officer is under investigation for alleged misconduct at the time of retirement—

(A) the Secretary may conditionally determine the highest grade of satisfactory service of the commissioned officer pending completion of the investigation; and

(B) the grade under subparagraph (A) is subject to resolution under subsection (c)(2).

(b) WARRANT OFFICERS.—Any warrant officer who is retired under any provision of section 580, 1263, 1293, or 1305 of title 10, shall be retired from active service with the highest commissioned grade above chief warrant officer, W–4, held by the warrant officer for not less than six months on active duty in which, as determined by the Secretary, the warrant officer's performance of duty was satisfactory.

(c) RETIREMENT IN LOWER GRADE.—

(1) MISCONDUCT IN LOWER GRADE.—In the case of a commissioned officer whom the Secretary determines committed misconduct in a lower grade, the Secretary may determine the commissioned officer has not served satisfactorily in any grade equal to or higher than that lower grade.

(2) ADVERSE FINDINGS.—A determination of the retired grade of a commissioned officer shall be resolved following a conditional determination under subsection (a)(2) if the investigation of or personnel action against the commissioned officer results in adverse findings.

(3) RECALCULATION OF RETIRED PAY.—If the retired grade of a commissioned officer is reduced pursuant to this subsection, the retired pay of the commissioned officer shall be recalculated under chapter 71 of title 10, and any modification of the retired pay of the commissioned officer shall go into effect on the effective date of the reduction in retired grade.

(d) FINALITY OF RETIRED GRADE DETERMINATIONS.—

(1) IN GENERAL.—Except as provided in paragraph (2), a determination of the retired grade of a commissioned officer under this section is administratively final on the day the commissioned officer is retired, and may not be reopened.

(2) REOPENING DETERMINATIONS.—A determination of the retired grade of a commissioned officer may be reopened if—

(A) the retirement or retired grade of the commissioned officer was procured by fraud;

(B) substantial evidence comes to light after the retirement that could have led to a lower retired grade under this section and such evidence was not known by competent authority at the time of retirement;

(C) a mistake of law or calculation was made in the determination of the retired grade;

(D) in the case of a retired grade following a conditional determination under subsection (a)(2), the investigation of or personnel action against the commissioned officer results in adverse findings; or

(E) the Secretary determines, under regulations prescribed by the Secretary, that good cause exists to reopen the determination.

(3) REQUIREMENTS.—If a determination of the retired grade of a commissioned officer is reopened under paragraph (2), the Secretary—

(A) shall notify the commissioned officer of the reopening; and

(B) may not make an adverse determination on the retired grade of the commissioned officer until the commissioned officer has had a reasonable opportunity to respond regarding the basis of the reopening.

(4) RECALCULATION OF RETIRED PAY.—If the retired grade of a commissioned officer is reduced through the reopening of the commissioned officer's retired grade under paragraph (2), the retired pay of the commissioned officer shall be recalculated under chapter 71 of title 10, and any modification of the retired pay of the commissioned officer shall go into effect on the effective date of the reduction in retired grade.

(e) INAPPLICABILITY TO COMMISSIONED WARRANT OFFICERS.—This section, including subsection (b), shall not apply to commissioned warrant officers.

(Added Pub. L. 88–130, §1(10)(C), Sept. 24, 1963, 77 Stat. 190, §334; amended Pub. L. 89–444, §1(19), June 9, 1966, 80 Stat. 196; Pub. L. 99–348, title II, §205(b)(7), July 1, 1986, 100 Stat. 700; Pub. L. 102–190, div. A, title XI, §1125(b)(2), Dec. 5, 1991, 105 Stat. 1505; Pub. L. 103–337, div. A, title V, §541(f)(3), Oct. 5, 1994, 108 Stat. 2766; renumbered §2501, Pub. L. 115–282, title I, §114(b), Dec. 4, 2018, 132 Stat. 4223; Pub. L. 116–283, div. G, title LVXXXII [LXXXII], §8201(c), Jan. 1, 2021, 134 Stat. 4641.)

§2502. RETIREMENT

(a) Every commissioned officer, warrant officer, or enlisted member who is retired under any provisions of this title shall be retired with the permanent grade or rate held at the time of retirement, unless entitled to retire with a higher grade or rate under any provision of this title or any other law.

(b) Where an officer is entitled, under any provision of law, to retire with one grade higher than the grade in which serving at the time of retirement, the next higher grade in the case of captain shall be rear admiral (lower half), and the next higher grade in the case of commissioned warrant officer shall be lieutenant (junior grade).

(Aug. 4, 1949, ch. 393, 63 Stat. 524, §421; Pub. L. 97–417, §2(10), Jan. 4, 1983, 96 Stat. 2086; Pub. L. 98–557, §15(a)(3)(A), Oct. 30, 1984, 98 Stat. 2865; Pub. L. 99–145, title V, §514(c)(1), Nov. 8, 1985, 99 Stat. 629; Pub. L. 99–348, title II, §205(b)(10), July 1, 1986, 100 Stat. 700; renumbered §2502, Pub. L. 115–282, title I, §114(b), Dec. 4, 2018, 132 Stat. 4223.)

§2503. STATUS OF RECALLED PERSONNEL

All retired personnel when recalled to active duty shall serve in the grade or rate in which they were serving at the time of retirement.

(Aug. 4, 1949, ch. 393, 63 Stat. 524, §422; Pub. L. 99–348, title II, §205(b)(10), July 1, 1986, 100 Stat. 700; renumbered §2503, Pub. L. 115–282, title I, §114(b), Dec. 4, 2018, 132 Stat. 4223.)

§2504. COMPUTATION OF RETIRED PAY

(a)(1) The retired pay of a member who first became a member of a uniformed service (as defined in section 101 of title 10) before September 8, 1980, is determined by multiplying—

(A) the sum of—

(i) the basic pay of the member's retired grade or rate, and

(ii) all permanent additions thereto including longevity credit to which the member was entitled at the time of retirement; by

(B) the retired pay multiplier determined under section 1409 of title 10 for the number of years of service that may be credited to the member under section 1405 of such title.

(2) In the case of an officer who served as Commandant, retired pay under paragraph (1) shall be computed at the highest rate of basic pay applicable to the officer while so serving.

(3) In the case of an enlisted member who served as the master chief petty officer of the Coast Guard, retired pay under paragraph (1) shall be computed at the highest rate of basic pay to which the member was entitled while so serving, if that basic pay is greater than the basic pay of the grade or rate to which the member is otherwise entitled at the time of retirement.

(4) In the case of an officer whose retired pay is computed on the pay of a grade for which basic pay is not based upon years of service, retired pay under paragraph (1) shall be computed on the basis of the number of years of service for which the officer would be entitled to credit in the computation of pay on the active list had the officer been serving in the grade of captain at the time of retirement.

(b) The retired pay of a member who first became a member of a uniformed service (as defined in section 101 of title 10) on or after September 8, 1980, is determined by multiplying—

(1) the retired pay base determined under section 1407 of title 10; by

(2) the retired pay multiplier determined under section 1409 of title 10 for the number of years of service that may be credited to the member under section 1405 of such title.

(c)(1) In computing for the purpose of subsection (a) or (b) the number of years of service that may be credited to a member under section 1405 of title 10—

(A) each full month of service that is in addition to the number of full years of service creditable to the member shall be counted as 1/12 of a year; and

(B) any remaining fractional part of a month shall be disregarded.

(2) Retired pay computed under this section, if not a multiple of $1, shall be rounded to the next lower multiple of $1.

(d) In addition to amounts computed pursuant to subsections (a) through (c) of this section, a full TSP member (as defined in section 8440e(a) of title 5) of the Coast Guard is entitled to continuation pay pursuant to section 356 of title 37.

(Aug. 4, 1949, ch. 393, 63 Stat. 525, §423; Aug. 3, 1950, ch. 536, §23, 64 Stat. 407; Pub. L. 85–422, §11(b), May 20, 1958, 72 Stat. 132; Pub. L. 88–132, §5(i), Oct. 2, 1963, 77 Stat. 214; Pub. L. 92–455, §2, Oct. 2, 1972, 86 Stat. 761; Pub. L. 96–342, title VIII, §813(f)(2), Sept. 8, 1980, 94 Stat. 1109; Pub. L. 97–295, §2(12), Oct. 12, 1982, 96 Stat. 1302; Pub. L. 98–94, title IX, §§922(b), 923(d), Sept. 24, 1983, 97 Stat. 642, 643; Pub. L. 98–557, §15(a)(3)(A), Oct. 30, 1984, 98 Stat. 2865; Pub. L. 99–348, title II, §205(a), July 1, 1986, 100 Stat. 699; Pub. L. 115–141, div. F, title II, §225, Mar. 23, 2018, 132 Stat. 616; Pub. L. 115–232, div. C, title XXXV, §3531(c)(13), Aug. 13, 2018, 132 Stat. 2320; renumbered §2504, Pub. L. 115–282, title I, §114(b), Dec. 4, 2018, 132 Stat. 4223.)

§2505. LIMITATIONS ON RETIREMENT AND RETIRED PAY

(a) The provisions of any section of this title shall not be construed so as to prevent any member from being placed on the retired list with the highest grade or rate and the highest retired pay to which the member may be entitled under the provisions of any other section of this title or under any other law.

(b) In no case may the retired pay of a member exceed 75 percent of (1) the sum of the active-duty pay and all permanent additions thereto (including longevity credit to which the member is entitled) of the grade or rate on which the member's pay is computed, or (2) the retired pay base determined under section 1407 of title 10, as appropriate.

(Aug. 4, 1949, ch. 393, 63 Stat. 525, §424; Pub. L. 98–557, §15(a)(3)(A), Oct. 30, 1984, 98 Stat. 2865; Pub. L. 99–348, title II, §205(b)(11), July 1, 1986, 100 Stat. 700; renumbered §2505, Pub. L. 115–282, title I, §114(b), Dec. 4, 2018, 132 Stat. 4223.)

§2506. SUSPENSION OF PAYMENT OF RETIRED PAY OF MEMBERS WHO ARE ABSENT FROM THE UNITED STATES TO AVOID PROSECUTION

Under procedures prescribed by the Secretary, the Secretary may suspend the payment of the retired pay of a member or former member during periods in which the member willfully remains outside the United States to avoid criminal prosecution or civil liability. The procedures shall address the types of criminal offenses and civil proceedings for which the procedures may be used, including the offenses specified in section 8312 of title 5, and the manner by which a member, upon the return of the member to the United States, may obtain retired pay withheld during the member's absence.

(Added Pub. L. 107–295, title IV, §444(a), Nov. 25, 2002, 116 Stat. 2132, §424a; renumbered §2506, Pub. L. 115–282, title I, §114(b), Dec. 4, 2018, 132 Stat. 4223.)

§2507. BOARD FOR CORRECTION OF MILITARY RECORDS DEADLINE

(a) DEADLINE FOR COMPLETION OF ACTION.—The Secretary shall complete processing of an application for correction of military records under section 1552 of title 10 by not later than 10 months after the date the Secretary receives the completed application.

(b) REMEDIES DEEMED EXHAUSTED.—Ten months after a complete application for correction of military records is received by the Board for Correction of Military Records of the Coast Guard, administrative remedies are deemed to have been exhausted, and—

(1) if the Board has rendered a recommended decision, its recommendation shall be

final agency action and not subject to further review or approval within the department in which the Coast Guard is operating; or

(2) if the Board has not rendered a recommended decision, agency action is deemed to have been unreasonably delayed or withheld and the applicant is entitled to—

(A) an order under section 706(1) of title 5, directing final action be taken within 30 days from the date the order is entered; and

(B) from amounts appropriated to the department in which the Coast Guard is operating, the costs of obtaining the order, including a reasonable attorney's fee.

(Added Pub. L. 104–324, title II, §209(a), Oct. 19, 1996, 110 Stat. 3914, §425; renumbered §2507, Pub. L. 115–282, title I, §114(b), Dec. 4, 2018, 132 Stat. 4223.)

§2508. EMERGENCY LEAVE RETENTION AUTHORITY

(a) IN GENERAL.—A duty assignment for an active duty member of the Coast Guard in support of a declaration of a major disaster or emergency by the President under the Robert T. Stafford Disaster Relief and Emergency Assistance Act (42 U.S.C. 5121 et seq.) or in response to a spill of national significance shall be treated, for the purpose of section 701(e) of title 10, as a duty assignment in support of a contingency operation.

(b) DEFINITIONS.—In this section:

(1) SPILL OF NATIONAL SIGNIFICANCE.—The term "spill of national significance" means a discharge of oil or a hazardous substance that is declared by the Commandant to be a spill of national significance.

(2) DISCHARGE.—The term "discharge" has the meaning given that term in section 1001 of the Oil Pollution Act of 1990 (33 U.S.C. 2701).

(Added Pub. L. 111–281, title II, §207(a), Oct. 15, 2010, 124 Stat. 2912, §426; renumbered §2508, Pub. L. 115–282, title I, §114(b), Dec. 4, 2018, 132 Stat. 4223; amended Pub. L. 117–263, div. A, title VI, §631(c)(1), Dec. 23, 2022, 136 Stat. 2631.)

§2509. PROHIBITION OF CERTAIN INVOLUNTARY ADMINISTRATIVE SEPARATIONS

(a) IN GENERAL.—Except as provided in subsection (b), the Secretary may not authorize the involuntary administrative separation of a covered individual based on a determination that the covered individual is unsuitable for deployment or other assignment due to a medical condition of the covered individual considered by a Physical Evaluation Board during an evaluation of the covered individual that resulted in the covered individual being determined to be fit for duty.

(b) REEVALUATION.—

(1) IN GENERAL.—The Secretary may require a Physical Evaluation Board to reevaluate any covered individual if the Secretary determines there is reason to believe that a medical condition of the covered individual considered by a Physical Evaluation Board during an evaluation of the covered individual renders the covered individual unsuitable for continued duty.

(2) RETIREMENTS AND SEPARATIONS.—A covered individual who is determined, based on a reevaluation under paragraph (1), to be unfit to perform the duties of the covered

individual's office, grade, rank, or rating may be retired or separated for physical disability under chapter 61 of title 10.

(c) COVERED INDIVIDUAL DEFINED.—In this section, the term "covered individual" means any member of the Coast Guard who has been determined by a Physical Evaluation Board, pursuant to a physical evaluation by that board, to be fit for duty.

(Added Pub. L. 112–213, title II, §209(a), Dec. 20, 2012, 126 Stat. 1549, §427; amended Pub. L. 114–120, title II, §209(6), Feb. 8, 2016, 130 Stat. 41; renumbered §2509, Pub. L. 115–282, title I, §114(b), Dec. 4, 2018, 132 Stat. 4223.)

§2510. SEA SERVICE LETTERS

(a) IN GENERAL.—The Secretary shall provide a sea service letter to a member or former member of the Coast Guard who—

(1) accumulated sea service on a vessel of the Armed Forces (as such term is defined in section 527(e)); and

(2) requests such letter.

(b) DEADLINE.—Not later than 30 days after receiving a request for a sea service letter from a member or former member of the Coast Guard under subsection (a), the Secretary shall provide such letter to such member or former member if such member or former member satisfies the requirement under subsection (a)(1).

(Added Pub. L. 113–281, title III, §305(b)(1), Dec. 18, 2014, 128 Stat. 3044, §428; renumbered §2510 and amended Pub. L. 115–282, title I, §114(b), title III, §318(c), Dec. 4, 2018, 132 Stat. 4223, 4252.)

§2511. INVESTIGATIONS OF FLAG OFFICERS AND SENIOR EXECUTIVE SERVICE EMPLOYEES

In conducting an investigation into an allegation of misconduct by a flag officer or member of the Senior Executive Service serving in the Coast Guard, the Inspector General of the Department of Homeland Security shall—

(1) conduct the investigation in a manner consistent with Department of Defense policies for such an investigation; and

(2) consult with the Inspector General of the Department of Defense.

(Added Pub. L. 114–120, title II, §220(a), Feb. 8, 2016, 130 Stat. 48, §430; renumbered §2511, Pub. L. 115–282, title I, §114(b), Dec. 4, 2018, 132 Stat. 4223.)

§2512. LEAVE POLICIES FOR THE COAST GUARD

(a) IN GENERAL.—Except as provided in subsection (b), not later than 1 year after the date on which the Secretary of the Navy promulgates a new rule, policy, or memorandum pursuant to section 704 of title 10, United States Code, with respect to leave associated with the birth or adoption of a child, the Secretary of the department in which the Coast Guard is operating shall promulgate a similar rule, policy, or memorandum that provides leave to officers and enlisted members of the Coast Guard that is equal in duration and compensation to that provided by the Secretary of the Navy.

(b) LEAVE ASSOCIATED WITH BIRTH OR ADOPTION OF CHILD.—Notwithstanding subsection (a), sections 701 and 704 of title 10, or any other provision of law, all officers and enlisted members of the Coast Guard shall be authorized leave associated with the birth or adoption of a child during the 1-year period immediately following such birth or adoption and, at the discretion of the Commanding Officer, such officer or enlisted member shall be permitted—

(1) to take such leave in increments; and

(2) to use flexible work schedules (pursuant to a program established by the Secretary in accordance with chapter 61 of title 5).

(Added Pub. L. 114–120, title II, §222(a), Feb. 8, 2016, 130 Stat. 49, §431; renumbered §2512 and amended Pub. L. 115–282, title I, §114(b), title III, §315(a), Dec. 4, 2018, 132 Stat. 4223, 4250.)

§2513. COMPUTATION OF LENGTH OF SERVICE

In computing length of service of officers and enlisted personnel for any purpose all creditable service in the Army, Navy, Marine Corps, Air Force, Space Force, Coast Guard, Revenue Cutter Service, and Life Saving Service shall be included in addition to any other creditable service authorized by any other law.

(Aug. 4, 1949, ch. 393, 63 Stat. 531, §467; renumbered §2513, Pub. L. 115–282, title I, §114(b), Dec. 4, 2018, 132 Stat. 4223; Pub. L. 116–283, div. A, title IX, §927(b)(2), Jan. 1, 2021, 134 Stat. 3831.)

§2514. CAREER FLEXIBILITY TO ENHANCE RETENTION OF MEMBERS

(a) PROGRAMS AUTHORIZED.—The Commandant may carry out a program under which members of the Coast Guard may be inactivated from active duty in order to meet personal or professional needs and returned to active duty at the end of such period of inactivation from active duty.

(b) PERIOD OF INACTIVATION FROM ACTIVE DUTY; EFFECT OF INACTIVATION.—

(1) IN GENERAL.—The period of inactivation from active duty under a program under this section of a member participating in the program shall be such period as the Commandant shall specify in the agreement of the member under subsection (c), except that such period may not exceed 3 years.

(2) EXCLUSION FROM YEARS OF SERVICE.—Any service by a Reserve officer while participating in a program under this section shall be excluded from computation of the total years of service of that officer pursuant to section 14706(a) of title 10.

(3) EXCLUSION FROM RETIREMENT.—Any period of participation of a member in a program under this section shall not count toward—

(A) eligibility for retirement or transfer to the Ready Reserve under either chapter 841 or 1223 of title 10; or

(B) computation of retired or retainer pay under chapter 71 or 1223 of title 10.

(c) AGREEMENT.—Each member of the Coast Guard who participates in a program under this section shall enter into a written agreement with the Commandant under which that member shall agree as follows:

(1) To accept an appointment or enlist, as applicable, and serve in the Coast Guard

Ready Reserve during the period of the inactivation of the member from active duty under the program.

(2) To undergo during the period of the inactivation of the member from active duty under the program such inactive service training as the Commandant shall require in order to ensure that the member retains proficiency, at a level determined by the Commandant to be sufficient, in the military skills, professional qualifications, and physical readiness of the member during the inactivation of the member from active duty.

(3) Following completion of the period of the inactivation of the member from active duty under the program, to serve 2 months as a member of the Coast Guard on active duty for each month of the period of the inactivation of the member from active duty under the program.

(d) CONDITIONS OF RELEASE.—The Commandant shall prescribe regulations specifying the guidelines regarding the conditions of release that must be considered and addressed in the agreement required by subsection (c). At a minimum, the Commandant shall prescribe the procedures and standards to be used to instruct a member on the obligations to be assumed by the member under paragraph (2) of such subsection while the member is released from active duty.

(e) ORDER TO ACTIVE DUTY.—Under regulations prescribed by the Commandant, a member of the Coast Guard participating in a program under this section may, in the discretion of the Commandant, be required to terminate participation in the program and be ordered to active duty.

(f) PAY AND ALLOWANCES.—

(1) BASIC PAY.—During each month of participation in a program under this section, a member who participates in the program shall be paid basic pay in an amount equal to two-thirtieths of the amount of monthly basic pay to which the member would otherwise be entitled under section 204 of title 37 as a member of the uniformed services on active duty in the grade and years of service of the member when the member commences participation in the program.

(2) SPECIAL OR INCENTIVE PAY OR BONUS.—

(A) PROHIBITION.—A member who participates in such a program shall not, while participating in the program, be paid any special or incentive pay or bonus to which the member is otherwise entitled under an agreement under chapter 5 of title 37 that is in force when the member commences participation in the program.

(B) NOT TREATED AS FAILURE TO PERFORM SERVICES.—The inactivation from active duty of a member participating in a program shall not be treated as a failure of the member to perform any period of service required of the member in connection with an agreement for a special or incentive pay or bonus under chapter 5 of title 37 that is in force when the member commences participation in the program.

(3) RETURN TO ACTIVE DUTY.—

(A) SPECIAL OR INCENTIVE PAY OR BONUS.—Subject to subparagraph (B), upon the return of a member to active duty after completion by the member of participation in a program—

(i) any agreement entered into by the member under chapter 5 of title 37 for the payment of a special or incentive pay or bonus that was in force when the member commenced participation in the program shall be revived, with the term of such agreement after revival being the period of the agreement remaining to run when the member commenced participation in the program; and

(ii) any special or incentive pay or bonus shall be payable to the member in accordance with the terms of the agreement concerned for the term specified in clause (i).

(B) LIMITATION.—

(i) IN GENERAL.—Subparagraph (A) shall not apply to any special or incentive pay or bonus otherwise covered by such subparagraph with respect to a member if, at the time of the return of the member to active duty as described in that subparagraph—

(I) such pay or bonus is no longer authorized by law; or

(II) the member does not satisfy eligibility criteria for such pay or bonus as in effect at the time of the return of the member to active duty.

(ii) PAY OR BONUS CEASES BEING AUTHORIZED.—Subparagraph (A) shall cease to apply to any special or incentive pay or bonus otherwise covered by such subparagraph with respect to a member if, during the term of the revived agreement of the member under subparagraph (A)(i), such pay or bonus ceases being authorized by law.

(C) REPAYMENT.—A member who is ineligible for payment of a special or incentive pay or bonus otherwise covered by this paragraph by reason of subparagraph (B)(i)(II) shall be subject to the requirements for repayment of such pay or bonus in accordance with the terms of the applicable agreement of the member under chapter 5 of title 37.

(D) REQUIRED SERVICE IS ADDITIONAL.—Any service required of a member under an agreement covered by this paragraph after the member returns to active duty as described in subparagraph (A) shall be in addition to any service required of the member under an agreement under subsection (c).

(4) TRAVEL AND TRANSPORTATION ALLOWANCE.—

(A) IN GENERAL.—Subject to subparagraph (B), a member who participates in a program is entitled, while participating in the program, to the travel and transportation allowances authorized by section 474 [1] of title 37 for—

(i) travel performed from the residence of the member, at the time of release from active duty to participate in the program, to the location in the United States designated by the member as the member's residence during the period of participation in the program; and

(ii) travel performed to the residence of the member upon return to active duty at the end of the participation of the member in the program.

(B) SINGLE RESIDENCE.—An allowance is payable under this paragraph only with respect to travel of a member to and from a single residence.

(5) LEAVE BALANCE.—A member who participates in a program is entitled to carry forward the leave balance existing as of the day on which the member begins participation and accumulated in accordance with section 701 of title 10, but not to exceed 60 days.

(g) PROMOTION.—

(1) OFFICERS.—

(A) IN GENERAL.—An officer participating in a program under this section shall not, while participating in the program, be eligible for consideration for promotion under chapter 21 or 37 of this title.

(B) RETURN TO DUTY.—Upon the return of an officer to active duty after completion by the officer of participation in a program—

(i) the Commandant may adjust the date of rank of the officer in such manner as the Commandant may prescribe in regulations for purposes of this section; and

(ii) the officer shall be eligible for consideration for promotion when officers of the same grade and seniority are eligible for consideration for promotion.

(2) ENLISTED MEMBERS.—An enlisted member participating in a program under this section shall not be eligible for consideration for advancement during the period that—

(A) begins on the date of the inactivation of the member from active duty under the program; and

(B) ends at such time after the return of the member to active duty under the program that the member is treatable as eligible for promotion by reason of time in grade and such other requirements as the Commandant shall prescribe in regulations for purposes of the program.

(h) CONTINUED ENTITLEMENTS.—A member participating in a program under this section shall, while participating in the program, be treated as a member of the Armed Forces on active duty for a period of more than 30 days for purposes of—

(1) the entitlement of the member and of the dependents of the member to medical and dental care under the provisions of chapter 55 of title 10; and

(2) retirement or separation for physical disability under the provisions of chapter 61 of title 10 and chapters 21 and 23 of this title.

(Added Pub. L. 116–283, div. G, title LVXXXII [LXXXII], §8204(a), Jan. 1, 2021, 134 Stat. 4645.)

[1] See References in Text note below.

§2515. CALCULATION OF ACTIVE SERVICE

Any service described, including service described prior to the date of enactment of the Don Young Coast Guard Authorization Act of 2022, in writing, including by electronic communication, by a representative of the Coast Guard Personnel Service Center as service that counts toward total active service for regular retirement under section 2152 or section 2306 shall be considered by the President as active service for purposes of applying section

2152 or section 2306 with respect to the determination of the retirement qualification for any officer or enlisted member to whom a description was provided.

(Added Pub. L. 117–263, div. K, title CXII, §11242(a), Dec. 23, 2022, 136 Stat. 4040.)

§2516. MEMBERS ASSERTING POST-TRAUMATIC STRESS DISORDER OR TRAUMATIC BRAIN INJURY

(a) MEDICAL EXAMINATION REQUIRED.—

(1) IN GENERAL.—The Secretary shall ensure that a member of the Coast Guard who has performed Coast Guard operations or has been sexually assaulted during the preceding 2-year period, and who is diagnosed by an appropriate licensed or certified healthcare professional as experiencing post-traumatic stress disorder or traumatic brain injury or who otherwise alleges, based on the service of the member or based on such sexual assault, the influence of such a condition, receives a medical examination to evaluate a diagnosis of post-traumatic stress disorder or traumatic brain injury.

(2) RESTRICTION ON ADMINISTRATIVE SEPARATION.—A member described in paragraph (1) shall not be administratively separated under conditions other than honorable, including an administrative separation in lieu of a court-martial, until the results of the medical examination have been reviewed by appropriate authorities responsible for evaluating, reviewing, and approving the separation case, as determined by the Secretary.

(3) POST-TRAUMATIC STRESS DISORDER.—In a case involving post-traumatic stress disorder under this subsection, a medical examination shall be—

(A) performed by—

(i) a board-certified or board-eligible psychiatrist; or

(ii) a licensed doctorate-level psychologist; or

(B) performed under the close supervision of—

(i) a board-certified or board-eligible psychiatrist; or

(ii) a licensed doctorate-level psychologist, a doctorate-level mental health provider, a psychiatry resident, or a clinical or counseling psychologist who has completed a 1-year internship or residency.

(4) TRAUMATIC BRAIN INJURY.—In a case involving traumatic brain injury under this subsection, a medical examination shall be performed by a physiatrist, psychiatrist, neurosurgeon, or neurologist.

(b) PURPOSE OF MEDICAL EXAMINATION.—The medical examination required under subsection (a) shall assess whether the effects of mental or neurocognitive disorders, including post-traumatic stress disorder and traumatic brain injury, constitute matters in extenuation that relate to the basis for administrative separation under conditions other than honorable or the overall characterization of the service of the member as other than honorable.

(c) INAPPLICABILITY TO PROCEEDINGS UNDER UNIFORM CODE OF MILITARY JUSTICE.—The medical examination and procedures required by this section do not apply to courts-martial or other proceedings conducted pursuant to the Uniform Code of Military

213

Justice.

(d) COAST GUARD OPERATIONS DEFINED.—In this section, the term "Coast Guard operations" has the meaning given that term in section 888(a) of the Homeland Security Act of 2002 (6 U.S.C. 468(a)).

(Added Pub. L. 117–263, div. K, title CXIV, §11410(a), Dec. 23, 2022, 136 Stat. 4116.)

SUBCHAPTER II—ADVISORY BOARD ON WOMEN IN THE COAST GUARD

§2521. ADVISORY BOARD ON WOMEN IN THE COAST GUARD

(a) IN GENERAL.—The Commandant shall establish within the Coast Guard an Advisory Board on Women in the Coast Guard.

(b) MEMBERSHIP.—The Advisory Board established under subsection (a) shall be composed of such number of members as the Commandant considers appropriate, selected by the Commandant through a public selection process from among applicants for membership on the Board. The members of the Board shall, to the extent practicable, represent the diversity of the Coast Guard. The members of the Committee shall include an equal number of each of the following:

(1) Active duty officers of the Coast Guard.

(2) Active duty enlisted members of the Coast Guard.

(3) Members of the Coast Guard Reserve.

(4) Retired members of the Coast Guard.

(c) DUTIES.—The Advisory Board established under subsection (a)—

(1) shall advise the Commandant on improvements to the recruitment, retention, wellbeing, and success of women serving in the Coast Guard and attending the Coast Guard Academy, including recommendations for the report on gender diversity in the Coast Guard required by section 5109 of chapter 51 of title 14;

(2) may submit to the Commandant recommendations in connection with its duties under this subsection, including recommendations to implement the advice described in paragraph (1); and

(3) may brief Congress on its duties under this subsection, including the advice described in paragraph (1) and any recommendations described in paragraph (2).

(Added Pub. L. 116–283, div. G, title LVXXXII [LXXXII], §8215(c)(2), Jan. 1, 2021, 134 Stat. 4651.)

SUBCHAPTER H—ADVISORY BOARD ON PROVISIONS IN THE COAST GUARD

§2.25 ... BOARD ...

§2.25 ... The ... shall establish within the Coast Guard an Advisory Board to Report to the Coast Guard.

(a) Membership. The Advisory Board established under this subpart (a) shall be composed of such number of members as are appointed ... routinely appointed, selected by the Commandant through a public selection process from among applicants for membership in the Board. The members of the Board shall, to the extent practicable, represent the interest of the Coast Guard ... the members. This Committee shall be established in equal measure from each of the following:

(1) Navigation and Preservation area Guard ...
(2) Navy related members of the Coast Guard.
(3) Officers of the Coast Guard Reserve.
(4) ... Coast Guard ...

(b) Appointment. The appointment of Members ...

216

§2531 to 2534. Repealed. Pub. L. 117–263, div.
., title CXVIII, §11808(a)(18), Dec. 23, 2022,

CHAPTER 25—PERSONNEL; GENERAL
PROVISIONS

[SUBCHAPTER III—REPEALED]

[§§2531 TO 2534. REPEALED. PUB. L. 117–263, DIV. K, TITLE CXVIII, §11808(A)(18), DEC. 23, 2022, 136 STAT. 4166]

Section 2531, act Aug. 4, 1949, ch. 393, 63 Stat. 526, §432; Aug. 9, 1955, ch. 650, §§1, 2, 69 Stat. 577; Pub. L. 86–309, Sept. 21, 1959, 73 Stat. 585; Pub. L. 91–278, §1(10), June 12, 1970, 84 Stat. 305; Pub. L. 96–23, §5(a), June 13, 1979, 93 Stat. 68; Pub. L. 97–295, §2(11), (13), Oct. 12, 1982, 96 Stat. 1302; Pub. L. 98–557, §15(a)(3)(B), Oct. 30, 1984, 98 Stat. 2865; Pub. L. 99–640, §10(a)(7), Nov. 10, 1986, 100 Stat. 3549; renumbered §2531, Pub. L. 115–282, title I, §114(b), Dec. 4, 2018, 132 Stat. 4223; Pub. L. 116–283, div. G, title LVXXXV [LXXXV], §8505(a)(21), Jan. 1, 2021, 134 Stat. 4748, related to personnel of former Lighthouse Service.

Section 2532, added Pub. L. 116–283, div. G, title LVXXXV [LXXXV], §8510(b), Jan. 1, 2021, 134 Stat. 4757, related to retirement of certain employees of former Lighthouse Service.

Section 2533, added Pub. L. 116–283, div. G, title LVXXXV [LXXXV], §8511(a), Jan. 1, 2021, 134 Stat. 4758, related to surviving spouses of current or former employees of Lighthouse Service.

Section 2534, added and amended Pub. L. 116–283, div. G, title LVXXXV [LXXXV], §8511(b), Jan. 1, 2021, 134 Stat. 4758, related to application for section 2533 benefits.

§§2531 to 2534. Repealed. Pub. L. 117–263, div.
X, title CXVIII, §11808(a)(18), Dec. 23, 2022,

CHAPTER 27—PAY, ALLOWANCES,
AWARDS, AND OTHER RIGHTS AND

CHAPTER 27—PAY, ALLOWANCES, AWARDS, AND OTHER RIGHTS AND BENEFITS

SUBCHAPTER I—PERSONNEL RIGHTS AND BENEFITS

SUBCHAPTER II—AWARDS

SUBCHAPTER III—PAYMENTS

[§§2531 to 2534. Repealed. Pub. L. 117–263, div.
K, title CXVIII, §11808(a)(18), Dec. 23, 2022,

CHAPTER 27—PAY, ALLOWANCE:
AWARDS, AND OTHER RIGHTS AN]

SUBCHAPTER I—PERSONNEL RIGHTS AND BENEFITS

§2701. PROCUREMENT OF PERSONNEL

The Coast Guard may expend operations and support funds for recruiting activities, including advertising and entertainment, to—
(1) obtain recruits for the Service and cadet applicants; and
(2) gain support of recruiting objectives from those who may assist in the recruiting effort.

(Aug. 4, 1949, ch. 393, 63 Stat. 531, §468; Pub. L. 104–324, title II, §206(b), Oct. 19, 1996, 110 Stat. 3908; renumbered §2701, Pub. L. 115–282, title I, §116(b), Dec. 4, 2018, 132 Stat. 4226; Pub. L. 116–283, div. G, title LVXXXV [LXXXV], §8513(a)(4), Jan. 1, 2021, 134 Stat. 4760.)

§2702. TRAINING

The Coast Guard may make expenditures for the training of personnel, including books, school supplies, correspondence courses, motion picture equipment, and other equipment for instructional purposes.

(Aug. 4, 1949, ch. 393, 63 Stat. 531, §469; renumbered §2702, Pub. L. 115–282, title I, §116(b), Dec. 4, 2018, 132 Stat. 4226.)

§2703. CONTINGENT EXPENSES

The Commandant may expend for contingencies of the Coast Guard a sum not to exceed $50,000 in any one fiscal year.

(Aug. 4, 1949, ch. 393, 63 Stat. 532, §476; Pub. L. 108–293, title II, §219, Aug. 9, 2004, 118 Stat. 1039; renumbered §2703, Pub. L. 115–282, title I, §116(b), Dec. 4, 2018, 132 Stat. 4226.)

§2704. EQUIPMENT TO PREVENT ACCIDENTS

The Coast Guard may make such expenditures as are deemed appropriate for promotion and maintenance of the safety and occupational health of, and the prevention of accidents affecting, personnel of the Coast Guard, including the purchase of clothing, equipment, and other materials necessary thereto.

(Aug. 4, 1949, ch. 393, 63 Stat. 532, §477; renumbered §2704, Pub. L. 115–282, title I, §116(b), Dec. 4, 2018, 132 Stat. 4226.)

[§2705. REPEALED. PUB. L. 115–282, TITLE III, §316, DEC. 4, 2018, 132 STAT. 4250]

Section, Aug. 4, 1949, ch. 393, 63 Stat. 533, §482; Pub. L. 98–557, §15(a)(3)(C), Oct. 30, 1984, 98 Stat. 2865; renumbered §2705, Pub. L. 115–282, title I, §116(b), Dec. 4, 2018, 132 Stat. 4226, related to clothing at time of discharge for good of service.

§2706. RIGHT TO WEAR UNIFORM

When authorized by and in accordance with applicable regulations:
(a) any member who has served honorably in the Coast Guard during war shall when

221

not in active service, whether or not on the retired list, be entitled to bear the official title and upon occasions of ceremony to wear the uniform of the highest rank or rating held by him during his war service, and

(b) any member on the retired list shall be entitled to wear the uniform of his rank or rating.

(Aug. 4, 1949, ch. 393, 63 Stat. 533, §483; Pub. L. 98–557, §15(a)(3)(H), Oct. 30, 1984, 98 Stat. 2865; renumbered §2706, Pub. L. 115–282, title I, §116(b), Dec. 4, 2018, 132 Stat. 4226.)

§2707. PROTECTION OF UNIFORM

The provisions of law relating to the protection of the uniform of the United States Army, Navy, or Marine Corps shall apply to the protection of the uniform of the Coast Guard, in the same manner, to the same extent, and under the same conditions.

(Aug. 4, 1949, ch. 393, 63 Stat. 533, §484; renumbered §2707, Pub. L. 115–282, title I, §116(b), Dec. 4, 2018, 132 Stat. 4226.)

§2708. CLOTHING FOR OFFICERS AND ENLISTED PERSONNEL

(a) The Coast Guard may purchase uniforms, accouterments, and related equipment for sale to officer personnel and cadets of the Coast Guard.

(b) The Coast Guard may purchase uniform clothing for sale to enlisted personnel of the Coast Guard. The actual cost of the clothing thus sold to enlisted personnel may be withheld from their pay.

(Aug. 4, 1949, ch. 393, 63 Stat. 534, §485; Aug. 3, 1950, ch. 536, §33, 64 Stat. 408; Pub. L. 87–649, §14d(4), Sept. 7, 1962, 76 Stat. 502; renumbered §2708, Pub. L. 115–282, title I, §116(b), Dec. 4, 2018, 132 Stat. 4226.)

§2709. PROCUREMENT AND SALE OF STORES TO MEMBERS AND CIVILIAN EMPLOYEES

Such stores as the Secretary may designate may be procured and sold to members of the Coast Guard, and to the surviving spouses of such members. Such designated stores may also be procured and sold to civilian officers and employees of the United States, and to such other individuals as may be specifically authorized by the Secretary, at Coast Guard stations and other units beyond the continental limits of the United States or in Alaska.

(Aug. 4, 1949, ch. 393, 63 Stat. 534, §487; Pub. L. 98–557, §15(a)(2), (3)(D), (4)(D)(i), Oct. 30, 1984, 98 Stat. 2865, 2866; renumbered §2709, Pub. L. 115–282, title I, §116(b), Dec. 4, 2018, 132 Stat. 4226; Pub. L. 116–283, div. G, title LVXXXV [LXXXV], §8505(a)(22), Jan. 1, 2021, 134 Stat. 4749.)

§2710. DISPOSITION OF EFFECTS OF DECEDENTS

All moneys, articles of value, papers, keepsakes, and other similar effects belonging to the deceased individuals in the Coast Guard, not claimed by their legal heirs or next of kin, shall be deposited in safe custody, and if any such moneys, articles of value, papers, keepsakes, or other similar effects so deposited have been, or shall hereafter be, unclaimed for a period of two years from the date of the death of such individual, such articles and effects shall be sold and the proceeds thereof, together with the moneys above mentioned, shall be deposited in the Treasury as miscellaneous receipts. The Secretary shall make diligent inquiry in every instance after the death of such individual to ascertain the whereabouts of his heirs or next of kin, and prescribe necessary regulations to carry out the foregoing provisions. Claims may be presented hereunder at any time within five years after such moneys or proceeds have been so deposited in the Treasury, and, when supported by competent proof in any case after such deposit in the Treasury, shall be certified to Congress for consideration.

(Aug. 4, 1949, ch. 393, 63 Stat. 538, §507; renumbered §2710, Pub. L. 115–282, title I, §116(b), Dec. 4, 2018, 132 Stat. 4226; Pub. L. 116–283, div. G, title LVXXXV [LXXXV], §8505(a)(23), Jan. 1, 2021, 134 Stat. 4749.)

§2711. Deserters; payment of expenses incident to apprehension and delivery; penalties

(a) The Coast Guard may, pursuant to regulations prescribed by the Secretary, make such expenditures as are deemed necessary for the apprehension and delivery of deserters, stragglers, and prisoners.

(b) No individual who is convicted by court martial for desertion from the Coast Guard in time of war, and as the result of such conviction is dismissed or dishonorably discharged from the Coast Guard shall afterwards be enlisted, appointed, or commissioned in any military or naval service under the United States, unless the disability resulting from desertion, as established by this section is removed by a board of commissioned officers of the Coast Guard convened for consideration of the case, and the action of the Board is approved by the Secretary; or unless he is restored to duty in time of war.

(Added May 5, 1950, ch. 169, §16(a), 64 Stat. 148, §508; amended July 10, 1952, ch. 631, §2, 66 Stat. 540; renumbered §2711, Pub. L. 115–282, title I, §116(b), Dec. 4, 2018, 132 Stat. 4226; Pub. L. 116–283, div. G, title LVXXXV [LXXXV], §8505(a)(24), Jan. 1, 2021, 134 Stat. 4749.)

§2712. Payment for the apprehension of stragglers

The Coast Guard may offer and pay rewards for the apprehension and delivery of deserters, stragglers, and prisoners.

(Aug. 4, 1949, ch. 393, 63 Stat. 547, §644; renumbered §2712, Pub. L. 115–282, title I, §116(b), Dec. 4, 2018, 132 Stat. 4226.)

§2713. Employment assistance

(a) In General.—In order to improve the accuracy and completeness of a certification or verification of job skills and experience required by section 1143(a)(1) of title 10, the Secretary shall—

(1) establish a database to record all training performed by members of the Coast Guard that may have application to employment in the civilian sector; and

(2) make unclassified information regarding such information available to States and other potential employers referred to in section 1143(c) of title 10 so that States and other potential employers may allow military training to satisfy licensing or certification requirements to engage in a civilian profession.

(b) Form of Certification or Verification.—The Secretary shall ensure that a certification or verification of job skills and experience required by section 1143(a)(1) of title 10 is rendered in such a way that States and other potential employers can confirm the accuracy and authenticity of the certification or verification.

(c) REQUESTS BY STATES.—A State may request that the Secretary confirm the accuracy and authenticity of a certification or verification of job skills and experience provided under section 1143(c) of title 10.

(Added Pub. L. 116–283, div. G, title LVXXXII [LXXXII], §8206(a), Jan. 1, 2021, 134 Stat. 4649.)

SUBCHAPTER II—AWARDS

§2731. DELEGATION OF POWERS TO MAKE AWARDS; RULES AND REGULATIONS

The President may delegate to the Secretary, under such conditions, regulations, and limitations as he prescribes, the powers conferred upon him to make the awards designated in this chapter, and the President may make any and all rules, regulations, and orders which he deems necessary in the conferring of such awards.

(Aug. 4, 1949, ch. 393, 63 Stat. 536, §499; renumbered §2731, Pub. L. 115–282, title I, §116(b), Dec. 4, 2018, 132 Stat. 4226.)

§2732. MEDAL OF HONOR

The President may award, and present in the name of Congress, a medal of honor of appropriate design, with ribbons and appurtenances, to an individual who, while a member of the Coast Guard, displays conspicuous gallantry and intrepidity at the risk of such individual's life above and beyond the call of duty—

(1) while engaged in an action against an enemy of the United States;

(2) while engaged in military operations involving conflict with an opposing foreign force;

(3) while serving with friendly foreign forces engaged in an armed conflict against an opposing armed force in which the United States is not a belligerent party.

(Aug. 4, 1949, ch. 393, 63 Stat. 535, §491; Pub. L. 88–77, §4, July 25, 1963, 77 Stat. 95; renumbered §2732, Pub. L. 115–282, title I, §116(b), Dec. 4, 2018, 132 Stat. 4226; Pub. L. 116–283, div. G, title LVXXXV [LXXXV], §§8505(a)(25), 8506(c), Jan. 1, 2021, 134 Stat. 4749, 4752.)

§2733. MEDAL OF HONOR: DUPLICATE MEDAL

An individual awarded a medal of honor shall, upon written application of that individual, be issued, without charge, one duplicate medal of honor with ribbons and appurtenances. Such duplicate medal of honor shall be marked, in such manner as the Secretary may determine, as a duplicate or for display purposes only.

(Added Pub. L. 107–107, div. A, title V, §553(d)(1)(A), Dec. 28, 2001, 115 Stat. 1116, §504; renumbered §2733, Pub. L. 115–282, title I, §116(b), Dec. 4, 2018, 132 Stat. 4226; amended Pub. L. 116–283, div. G, title LVXXXV [LXXXV], §8505(a)(26), Jan. 1, 2021, 134 Stat. 4749.)

§2734. MEDAL OF HONOR: PRESENTATION OF MEDAL OF HONOR FLAG

The President shall provide for the presentation of the Medal of Honor Flag designated under section 903 of title 36 to each individual to whom a medal of honor is awarded under section 2732 of this title. Presentation of the flag shall be made at the same time as the presentation of the medal under section 2732 or 2743 of this title. In the case of a posthumous presentation of the medal, the flag shall be presented to the individual to whom the medal is presented.

(Added Pub. L. 107–248, title VIII, §8143(c)(4)(A), Oct. 23, 2002, 116 Stat. 1571, §505; amended Pub. L. 107–314, div. A, title X, §1062(b)(1), Dec. 2, 2002, 116 Stat. 2650; Pub. L. 109–364, div. A, title V, §555(a),

Oct. 17, 2006, 120 Stat. 2217; renumbered §2734 and amended Pub. L. 115–282, title I, §§116(b), 123(b)(2), Dec. 4, 2018, 132 Stat. 4226, 4240; Pub. L. 116–283, div. G, title LVXXXV [LXXXV], §8505(a)(27), Jan. 1, 2021, 134 Stat. 4749.)

§2735. COAST GUARD CROSS

The President may award a Coast Guard cross of appropriate design, with ribbons and appurtenances, to an individual who, while serving in any capacity with the Coast Guard, when the Coast Guard is not operating under the Department of the Navy, distinguishes himself or herself by extraordinary heroism not justifying the award of a medal of honor—

(1) while engaged in an action against an enemy of the United States;

(2) while engaged in military operations involving conflict with an opposing foreign force or international terrorist organization; or

(3) while serving with friendly foreign forces engaged in an armed conflict against an opposing armed force in which the United States is not a belligerent party.

(Added Pub. L. 111–281, title II, §224(a), Oct. 15, 2010, 124 Stat. 2921, §491a; renumbered §2735, Pub. L. 115–282, title I, §116(b), Dec. 4, 2018, 132 Stat. 4226; amended Pub. L. 116–283, div. G, title LVXXXV [LXXXV], §8505(a)(28), Jan. 1, 2021, 134 Stat. 4749.)

§2736. DISTINGUISHED SERVICE MEDAL

The President may present, but not in the name of Congress, a distinguished service medal of appropriate design, with accompanying ribbon, together with a rosette or other device, to be worn in lieu thereof, to any individual who, while serving in any capacity with the Coast Guard, performs exceptionally meritorious service to the Government in a duty of great responsibility.

(Aug. 4, 1949, ch. 393, 63 Stat. 535, §492; renumbered §2736, Pub. L. 115–282, title I, §116(b), Dec. 4, 2018, 132 Stat. 4226; Pub. L. 116–283, div. G, title LVXXXV [LXXXV], §§8505(a)(29), 8506(d), Jan. 1, 2021, 134 Stat. 4749, 4752.)

§2737. SILVER STAR MEDAL

The President may award a silver star medal of appropriate design, with ribbons and appurtenances, to an individual who, while serving in any capacity with the Coast Guard, when the Coast Guard is not operating under the Department of the Navy, is cited for gallantry in action that does not warrant a medal of honor or Coast Guard cross—

(1) while engaged in an action against an enemy of the United States;

(2) while engaged in military operations involving conflict with an opposing foreign force or international terrorist organization; or

(3) while serving with friendly foreign forces engaged in an armed conflict against an opposing armed force in which the United States is not a belligerent party.

(Added Pub. L. 111–281, title II, §224(b)(2), Oct. 15, 2010, 124 Stat. 2922, §492a; renumbered §2737, Pub. L. 115–282, title I, §116(b), Dec. 4, 2018, 132 Stat. 4226; amended Pub. L. 116–283, div. G, title LVXXXV [LXXXV], §8505(a)(30), Jan. 1, 2021, 134 Stat. 4749.)

§2738. DISTINGUISHED FLYING CROSS

The President may present, but not in the name of Congress, a distinguished flying cross of appropriate design, with accompanying ribbon, to any individual who, while serving in any capacity with the Coast Guard, displays heroism or extraordinary achievement while participating in an aerial flight.

(Added Aug. 10, 1956, ch. 1041, §12(a), 70A Stat. 624, §492a; renumbered §492b, Pub. L. 111–281, title II, §224(b)(1), Oct. 15, 2010, 124 Stat. 2922; renumbered §2738, Pub. L. 115–282, title I, §116(b), Dec. 4, 2018, 132 Stat. 4226; amended Pub. L. 116–283, div. G, title LVXXXV [LXXXV], §§8505(a)(31), 8506(e), Jan. 1, 2021, 134 Stat. 4749, 4752.)

§2739. COAST GUARD MEDAL

The President may present, but not in the name of Congress, a medal to be known as the Coast Guard medal, of appropriate design, with accompanying ribbon, together with a rosette or other device to be worn in lieu thereof, to any individual who, while serving in any capacity with the Coast Guard, displays heroism not involving actual conflict with an enemy.

(Aug. 4, 1949, ch. 393, 63 Stat. 535, §493; renumbered §2739, Pub. L. 115–282, title I, §116(b), Dec. 4, 2018, 132 Stat. 4226; Pub. L. 116–283, div. G, title LVXXXV [LXXXV], §§8505(a)(32), 8506(f), Jan. 1, 2021, 134 Stat. 4749, 4752.)

§2740. INSIGNIA FOR ADDITIONAL AWARDS

No more than one Coast Guard cross, distinguished service medal, silver star medal, distinguished flying cross, or Coast Guard medal shall be issued to any one individual; but for each succeeding deed or service sufficient to justify the awarding of a Coast Guard cross, distinguished service medal, silver star medal, distinguished flying cross, or Coast Guard medal, the President may award a suitable emblem or insignia to be worn with the decoration and a corresponding rosette or other device.

(Aug. 4, 1949, ch. 393, 63 Stat. 535, §494; Aug. 10, 1956, ch. 1041, §13, 70A Stat. 624; Pub. L. 111–281, title II, §224(c)(1), Oct. 15, 2010, 124 Stat. 2922; Pub. L. 113–281, title II, §213, Dec. 18, 2014, 128 Stat. 3029; renumbered §2740, Pub. L. 115–282, title I, §116(b), Dec. 4, 2018, 132 Stat. 4226; Pub. L. 116–283, div. G, title LVXXXV [LXXXV], §8505(a)(33), Jan. 1, 2021, 134 Stat. 4749.)

§2741. TIME LIMIT ON AWARD; REPORT CONCERNING DEED

(a) No medal of honor, Coast Guard cross, distinguished service medal, silver star medal, distinguished flying cross, Coast Guard medal, or bar, emblem, or insignia in lieu thereof may be awarded to an individual unless—

(1) the award is made within five years after the date of the deed or service justifying the award;

(2) a statement setting forth the deed or distinguished service and recommending official recognition of it was made by his superior through official channels within three years from the date of that deed or termination of the service.

(b) If the Secretary determines that—

(1) a statement setting forth the deed or distinguished service and recommending

official recognition of it was made by the individual's superior through official channels within three years from the date of that deed or termination of the service and was supported by sufficient evidence within that time; and

(2) no award was made, because the statement was lost or through inadvertence the recommendation was not acted upon; a medal of honor, Coast Guard cross, distinguished service medal, silver star medal, distinguished flying cross, Coast Guard medal, or bar, emblem, or insignia in lieu thereof, as the case may be, may be awarded to the individual within two years after the date of that determination.

(Aug. 4, 1949, ch. 393, 63 Stat. 536, §496; Pub. L. 87–526, §1(5), July 10, 1962, 76 Stat. 141; Pub. L. 111–281, title II, §224(c)(2), Oct. 15, 2010, 124 Stat. 2922; renumbered §2741, Pub. L. 115–282, title I, §116(b), Dec. 4, 2018, 132 Stat. 4226; Pub. L. 116–283, div. G, title LVXXXV [LXXXV], §8505(a)(34), Jan. 1, 2021, 134 Stat. 4749.)

§2742. Honorable subsequent service as condition to award

No medal of honor, Coast Guard cross, distinguished service medal, silver star medal, distinguished flying cross, Coast Guard medal, or emblem, or insignia in lieu thereof shall be awarded or presented to any individual, or to the representative of any individual, whose entire service subsequent to the time of the acts resulting in the consideration of such award shall not in the opinion of the Commandant have been honorable.

(Aug. 4, 1949, ch. 393, 63 Stat. 536, §497; Aug. 10, 1956, ch. 1041, §13, 70A Stat. 624; Pub. L. 111–281, title II, §224(c)(3), Oct. 15, 2010, 124 Stat. 2922; renumbered §2742, Pub. L. 115–282, title I, §116(b), Dec. 4, 2018, 132 Stat. 4226; Pub. L. 116–283, div. G, title LVXXXV [LXXXV], §8506(g), Jan. 1, 2021, 134 Stat. 4752.)

§2743. Posthumous awards

In case an individual who dies before the making of any award to which such individual may be entitled, as authorized in this chapter, the award may be made and presented within five years from the date of the act or service justifying the award to such next of kin as may have been designated by the individual, or in the absence of such designation, or if the designated individual is not alive at the time of the award, or the relationship between such individual and the serviceman shall have been terminated before his death, then to such representative as the President designates. In the event of a posthumous award when the award will be made to the parents of the deceased and the parents have been divorced or separated, a duplicate award may be made to each parent.

(Aug. 4, 1949, ch. 393, 63 Stat. 536, §498; renumbered §2743, Pub. L. 115–282, title I, §116(b), Dec. 4, 2018, 132 Stat. 4226; Pub. L. 116–283, div. G, title LVXXXV [LXXXV], §§8505(a)(35), 8506(h), Jan. 1, 2021, 134 Stat. 4749, 4752.)

§2744. Life-saving medals

(a) The Secretary may, under regulations prescribed by him, award a Life-saving medal of gold or silver to any individual, including personnel of the Coast Guard, who rescues or endeavors to rescue any other individual from drowning, shipwreck, or other peril of the water in accordance with the following provisions:

(1) if such rescue or attempted rescue is made at the risk of one's own life and evidences extreme and heroic daring, the medal shall be of gold;

(2) if such rescue or attempted rescue is not sufficiently distinguished to deserve the medal of gold, but evidences the exercise of such signal exertion as to merit recognition, the medal shall be of silver.

(b) In order for an individual to be eligible for the Life-saving Medals the rescue or attempted rescue must take place in waters within the United States or subject to the jurisdiction thereof, or if the rescue or attempted rescue takes place outside such waters, one or the other of the parties must be a citizen of the United States or from a vessel or aircraft owned or operated by citizens of the United States.

(c) No individual shall receive more than one gold medal and one silver medal; but any individual who has received or may hereafter receive a gold or silver medal and who again performs an act which would entitle him to receive another medal of the same class may be awarded, in lieu of a second medal of the same class, a gold or silver bar, as the case may be, to be worn with the medal already bestowed, and for every such additional act, an additional bar may be awarded. Medals and bars in lieu thereof, authorized by this subsection, may be awarded posthumously.

(Aug. 4, 1949, ch. 393, 63 Stat. 536, §500; Pub. L. 94–546, §1(31), Oct. 18, 1976, 90 Stat. 2521; renumbered §2744, Pub. L. 115–282, title I, §116(b), Dec. 4, 2018, 132 Stat. 4226; Pub. L. 116–283, div. G, title LVXXXV [LXXXV], §8505(a)(36), Jan. 1, 2021, 134 Stat. 4749.)

§2745. REPLACEMENT OF MEDALS

In those cases where a medal, or a bar, emblem, or insignia in lieu thereof, awarded pursuant to this chapter has been stolen, lost, destroyed, or rendered unfit for use without fault or neglect on the part of the individual to whom it was awarded, such medal, or bar, emblem, or insignia in lieu thereof, shall be replaced without charge, or, in the discretion of the Secretary, upon condition that the Government is reimbursed for the cost thereof.

(Aug. 4, 1949, ch. 393, 63 Stat. 537, §501; Pub. L. 107–107, div. A, title V, §553(d)(2), Dec. 28, 2001, 115 Stat. 1117; renumbered §2745, Pub. L. 115–282, title I, §116(b), Dec. 4, 2018, 132 Stat. 4226; Pub. L. 116–283, div. G, title LVXXXV [LXXXV], §8505(a)(37), Jan. 1, 2021, 134 Stat. 4749.)

§2746. AWARD OF OTHER MEDALS

Coast Guard personnel, notwithstanding the provisions of this chapter, may be awarded medals, bars, emblems, or insignia to which such personnel may be entitled under other provisions of law.

(Aug. 4, 1949, ch. 393, 63 Stat. 537, §502; renumbered §2746, Pub. L. 115–282, title I, §116(b), Dec. 4, 2018, 132 Stat. 4226.)

§2747. AWARDS AND INSIGNIA FOR EXCELLENCE IN SERVICE OR CONDUCT

The Coast Guard may award trophies, badges, and cash prizes to Coast Guard personnel or groups thereof, including personnel of the reserve components thereof whether or not on active duty, for excellence in accomplishments related to Coast Guard service, to incur such expenses as may be necessary to enter such personnel in competitions, and to provide badges or buttons in recognition of special service, good conduct, and discharge under conditions other than dishonorable.

(Aug. 4, 1949, ch. 393, 63 Stat. 537, §503; renumbered §2747, Pub. L. 115–282, title I, §116(b), Dec. 4,

2018, 132 Stat. 4226.)

§2748. PRESENTATION OF UNITED STATES FLAG UPON RETIREMENT

(a) PRESENTATION OF FLAG.—Upon the release of a member of the Coast Guard from active duty for retirement, the Secretary shall present a United States flag to the member.

(b) MULTIPLE PRESENTATIONS NOT AUTHORIZED.—A member is not eligible for a presentation of a flag under subsection (a) if the member has previously been presented a flag under this section or any other provision of law providing for the presentation of a United States flag incident to release from active service for retirement.

(c) NO COST TO RECIPIENT.—The presentation of a flag under this section shall be at no cost to the recipient.

(Added Pub. L. 105–261, div. A, title VI, §644(d)(1), Oct. 17, 1998, 112 Stat. 2049, §516; amended Pub. L. 106–65, div. A, title VI, §652(e), Oct. 5, 1999, 113 Stat. 666; Pub. L. 107–296, title XVII, §1704(a), Nov. 25, 2002, 116 Stat. 2314; Pub. L. 107–314, div. A, title X, §1062(b)(2), Dec. 2, 2002, 116 Stat. 2650; Pub. L. 112–213, title II, §217(6), Dec. 20, 2012, 126 Stat. 1557; renumbered §2748, Pub. L. 115–282, title I, §116(b), Dec. 4, 2018, 132 Stat. 4226.)

SUBCHAPTER III—PAYMENTS

§2761. INDIVIDUALS DISCHARGED AS RESULT OF COURT-MARTIAL; ALLOWANCES TO

The Secretary may furnish individuals discharged pursuant to the sentence of a Coast Guard court-martial suitable civilian clothing and a monetary allowance not to exceed $25 if the individual discharged would not otherwise have suitable clothing or funds to meet immediate needs.

(Added May 5, 1950, ch. 169, §16(a), 64 Stat. 148, §509; amended Pub. L. 90–377, §8, July 5, 1968, 82 Stat. 288; renumbered §2761, Pub. L. 115–282, title I, §116(b), Dec. 4, 2018, 132 Stat. 4226; Pub. L. 116–283, div. G, title LVXXXV [LXXXV], §8505(a)(38)(A), Jan. 1, 2021, 134 Stat. 4749.)

§2762. SHORE PATROL DUTY; PAYMENT OF EXPENSES

An officer or cadet of the Coast Guard who is assigned shore patrol duty away from his vessel or other duty station may be paid his actual expenses.

(Added Aug. 10, 1956, ch. 1041, §14(a), 70A Stat. 624, §510; renumbered §2762, Pub. L. 115–282, title I, §116(b), Dec. 4, 2018, 132 Stat. 4226.)

§2763. COMPENSATORY ABSENCE FROM DUTY FOR MILITARY PERSONNEL AT ISOLATED DUTY STATIONS

The Secretary may grant compensatory absence from duty to military personnel of the Coast Guard serving at isolated duty stations of the Coast Guard when conditions of duty result in confinement because of isolation or in long periods of continuous duty.

(Added Aug. 9, 1955, ch. 650, §4, 69 Stat. 577, §511; amended Pub. L. 94–546, §1(32), Oct. 18, 1976, 90 Stat. 2521; Pub. L. 107–295, title III, §312(a), Nov. 25, 2002, 116 Stat. 2102; renumbered §2763, Pub. L. 115–282, title I, §116(b), Dec. 4, 2018, 132 Stat. 4226.)

§2764. MONETARY ALLOWANCE FOR TRANSPORTATION OF HOUSEHOLD EFFECTS

The transportation and reimbursement authorized by section 453(c) of title 37 shall be available hereafter to pay a monetary allowance in place of such transportation to a member who, under regulations prescribed by the Secretary, participates in a program designated by the Secretary in which his baggage and household effects are moved by a privately owned or rental vehicle. This allowance shall not be limited to reimbursement for actual expenses and may be paid in advance of the transportation of the baggage and household effects. The allowance shall, however, be in an amount that will result in savings to the Government when the total cost of the movement of baggage and household effects is compared with the cost that otherwise would have been incurred under section 453(c) of title 37.

(Added Pub. L. 96–376, §7(a), Oct. 3, 1980, 94 Stat. 1510, §512; amended Pub. L. 97–295, §2(16), Oct. 12,

1982, 96 Stat. 1302; Pub. L. 112–81, div. A, title VI, §631(f)(4)(B), Dec. 31, 2011, 125 Stat. 1465; Pub. L. 112–239, div. A, title X, §1076(a)(9), Jan. 2, 2013, 126 Stat. 1948; renumbered §2764, Pub. L. 115–282, title I, §116(b), Dec. 4, 2018, 132 Stat. 4226; Pub. L. 117–263, div. A, title VI, §626(d), Dec. 23, 2022, 136 Stat. 2629.)

§2765. RETROACTIVE PAYMENT OF PAY AND ALLOWANCES DELAYED BY ADMINISTRATIVE ERROR OR OVERSIGHT

Under regulations prescribed by the Secretary, the Coast Guard may authorize retroactive payment of pay and allowances, including selective reenlistment bonuses, to enlisted members if entitlement to the pay and allowances was delayed in vesting solely because of an administrative error or oversight.

(Added Pub. L. 100–448, §13(a), Sept. 28, 1988, 102 Stat. 1844, §513; renumbered §2765, Pub. L. 115–282, title I, §116(b), Dec. 4, 2018, 132 Stat. 4226.)

§2766. TRAVEL CARD MANAGEMENT

(a) IN GENERAL.—The Secretary may require that travel or transportation allowances due a civilian employee or military member of the Coast Guard be disbursed directly to the issuer of a Federal contractor-issued travel charge card, but only in an amount not to exceed the authorized travel expenses charged by that Coast Guard member to that travel charge card issued to that employee or member.

(b) WITHHOLDING OF NONDISPUTED OBLIGATIONS.—The Secretary may also establish requirements similar to those established by the Secretary of Defense pursuant to section 2784a of title 10 for deduction or withholding of pay or retired pay from a Coast Guard employee, member, or retired member who is delinquent in payment under the terms of the contract under which the card was issued and does not dispute the amount of the delinquency.

(Added Pub. L. 108–293, title II, §210(a), Aug. 9, 2004, 118 Stat. 1036, §517; renumbered §2766, Pub. L. 115–282, title I, §116(b), Dec. 4, 2018, 132 Stat. 4226.)

§2767. REIMBURSEMENT FOR MEDICAL-RELATED TRAVEL EXPENSES FOR CERTAIN INDIVIDUALS RESIDING ON ISLANDS IN THE CONTINENTAL UNITED STATES

In any case in which a covered beneficiary (as defined in section 1072(5) of title 10) resides on an island that is located in the 48 contiguous States and the District of Columbia and that lacks public access roads to the mainland, the Secretary shall reimburse the reasonable travel expenses of the covered beneficiary and, when accompaniment by an adult is necessary, for a parent or guardian of the covered beneficiary or another member of the covered beneficiary's family who is at least 21 years of age, if—

(1) the covered beneficiary is referred by a primary care physician to a specialty care provider (as defined in section 1074i(b) of title 10) on the mainland who provides services less than 100 miles from the location where the beneficiary resides; or

(2) the Coast Guard medical regional manager for the area in which such island is

located determines that the covered beneficiary requires services of a primary care, specialty care, or dental provider and such a provider who is part of the network of providers of a TRICARE program (as that term is defined in section 1072(7) of title 10) does not practice on such island.

(Added Pub. L. 111–281, title II, §203(a), Oct. 15, 2010, 124 Stat. 2909, §518; amended Pub. L. 115–232, div. C, title XXXV, §3524, Aug. 13, 2018, 132 Stat. 2316; renumbered §2767, Pub. L. 115–282, title I, §116(b), Dec. 4, 2018, 132 Stat. 4226; Pub. L. 116–283, div. G, title LVXXXV [LXXXV], §8505(a)(39)(A), Jan. 1, 2021, 134 Stat. 4750.)

§2768. Annual audit of pay and allowances of members undergoing permanent change of station

The Commandant shall conduct each calendar year an audit of member pay and allowances for the members who transferred to new units during such calendar year. The audit for a calendar year shall be completed by the end of the calendar year.

(Added Pub. L. 114–120, title II, §216(a)(1), Feb. 8, 2016, 130 Stat. 46, §519; renumbered §2768, Pub. L. 115–282, title I, §116(b), Dec. 4, 2018, 132 Stat. 4226.)

§2769. Remission of indebtedness

The Secretary may have remitted or cancelled any part of an individual's indebtedness to the United States or any instrumentality of the United States if—

(1) the indebtedness was incurred while the individual served as a member of the Coast Guard, whether as a regular or a reserve in active status; and

(2) the Secretary determines that remitting or cancelling the indebtedness is in the best interest of the United States.

(Aug. 4, 1949, ch. 393, 63 Stat. 530, §461; Sept. 3, 1954, ch. 1263, §33(b), 68 Stat. 1238; Pub. L. 87–526, §1(1), July 10, 1962, 76 Stat. 141; Pub. L. 87–649, §14d(7), Sept. 7, 1962, as added Pub. L. 89–718, §73(a)(3), Nov. 2, 1966, 80 Stat. 1124; Pub. L. 89–718, §73(c)(1), Nov. 2, 1966, 80 Stat. 1124; Pub. L. 90–83, §2, Sept. 11, 1967, 81 Stat. 220; Pub. L. 94–546, §1(29), Oct. 18, 1976, 90 Stat. 2521; Pub. L. 114–120, title II, §203(a), Feb. 8, 2016, 130 Stat. 34; Pub. L. 114–328, div. A, title VI, §671(b)(4), Dec. 23, 2016, 130 Stat. 2173; renumbered §2769, Pub. L. 115–282, title I, §116(b), Dec. 4, 2018, 132 Stat. 4226; Pub. L. 116–283, div. G, title LVXXXV [LXXXV], §8505(a)(40), Jan. 1, 2021, 134 Stat. 4750.)

§2770. Special instruction at universities

Coast Guard personnel may be assigned for special instruction at private or state colleges or universities, and their expenses, including tuition, books, laboratory equipment and fees, and school supplies, may be defrayed by the Coast Guard.

(Aug. 4, 1949, ch. 393, 63 Stat. 531, §470; renumbered §2770, Pub. L. 115–282, title I, §116(b), Dec. 4, 2018, 132 Stat. 4226.)

§2771. Attendance at professional meetings

Coast Guard personnel may be directed to attend meetings of technical, professional, scientific, and other similar organizations and may be reimbursed for expenses thereby incurred at the rates authorized by law.

(Aug. 4, 1949, ch. 393, 63 Stat. 532, §471; renumbered §2771, Pub. L. 115–282, title I, §116(b), Dec. 4, 2018, 132 Stat. 4226.)

§2772. EDUCATION LOAN REPAYMENT PROGRAM FOR MEMBERS ON ACTIVE DUTY IN SPECIFIED MILITARY SPECIALTIES

(a) IN GENERAL.—

(1) REPAYMENT.—Subject to the provisions of this section, the Secretary may repay—

(A) any loan made, insured, or guaranteed under part B of title IV of the Higher Education Act of 1965 (20 U.S.C. 1071 et seq.);

(B) any loan made under part D of such title (the William D. Ford Federal Direct Loan Program, 20 U.S.C. 1087a et seq.);

(C) any loan made under part E of such title (20 U.S.C. 1087aa et seq.); or

(D) any loan incurred for educational purposes made by a lender that is—

(i) an agency or instrumentality of a State;

(ii) a financial or credit institution (including an insurance company) that is subject to examination and supervision by an agency of the United States or any State;

(iii) a pension fund approved by the Secretary for purposes of this section; or

(iv) a nonprofit private entity designated by a State, regulated by such State, and approved by the Secretary for purposes of this section.

(2) REQUIREMENT.—Repayment of any such loan shall be made on the basis of each complete year of service performed by the borrower.

(3) ELIGIBILITY.—The Secretary may repay loans described in paragraph (1) in the case of any person for service performed on active duty as a member in an officer program or military specialty specified by the Secretary.

(b) AMOUNT.—The portion or amount of a loan that may be repaid under subsection (a) is 33 1/3 percent or $1,500, whichever is greater, for each year of service.

(c) INTEREST ACCRUAL.—If a portion of a loan is repaid under this section for any year, interest on the remainder of such loan shall accrue and be paid in the same manner as is otherwise required.

(d) RULE OF CONSTRUCTION.—Nothing in this section shall be construed to authorize refunding any repayment of a loan.

(e) FRACTIONAL CREDIT FOR TRANSFER.—An individual who transfers from service making the individual eligible for repayment of loans under this section (as described in subsection (a)(3)) to service making the individual eligible for repayment of loans under section 16301 of title 10 (as described in subsection (a)(2) or (g) of that section) during a year shall be eligible to have repaid a portion of such loan determined by giving appropriate fractional credit for each portion of the year so served, in accordance with regulations of the Secretary concerned.

(f) SCHEDULE FOR ALLOCATION.—The Secretary shall prescribe a schedule for the allocation of funds made available to carry out the provisions of this section and section 16301 of title 10 during any year for which funds are not sufficient to pay the sum of the amounts eligible for repayment under subsection (a) and section 16301(a) of title 10.

(g) FAILURE TO COMPLETE PERIOD OF SERVICE.—Except an individual described in subsection (e) who transfers to service making the individual eligible for repayment of loans under section 16301 of title 10, a member of the Coast Guard who fails to complete the period of service required to qualify for loan repayment under this section shall be subject to the repayment provisions of section 303a(e) or 373 of title 37.

(h) AUTHORITY TO ISSUE REGULATIONS.—The Secretary may prescribe procedures for implementing this section, including standards for qualified loans and authorized payees and other terms and conditions for making loan repayments. Such regulations may include exceptions that would allow for the payment as a lump sum of any loan repayment due to a member under a written agreement that existed at the time of a member's death or disability.

(Added Pub. L. 108–293, title II, §218(a), Aug. 9, 2004, 118 Stat. 1038, §472; renumbered §2772, Pub. L. 115–282, title I, §116(b), Dec. 4, 2018, 132 Stat. 4226; amended Pub. L. 116–283, div. G, title LVXXXV [LXXXV], §8505(a)(41), Jan. 1, 2021, 134 Stat. 4750; Pub. L. 117–263, div. K, title CXII, §11239(a), Dec. 23, 2022, 136 Stat. 4037.)

§2773. RATIONS OR COMMUTATION THEREFOR IN MONEY

(a) Enlisted members of the Coast Guard, civilian officers and civilian crews of vessels, and working parties in the field shall be allowed a ration or commutation thereof in money, in such amount and under limitations and regulations prescribed by the Secretary.

(b) Money for commuted rations shall be paid, under such regulations as the Secretary shall prescribe, on proper vouchers, or pay rolls, to individuals entitled to receive it, or to the officers designated by the Commandant to administer the financial affairs of the messes in which such individuals may be subsisted.

(c) Money paid for commuted rations to the designated officer may be deposited in general or limited depositories of public money or in any bank in which deposits are insured. Such funds shall be expended and accounted for under such regulations as the Secretary shall prescribe.

(d) Nothing contained in this section shall be construed as modifying or changing in any manner the provisions of law pertaining to subsistence allowances for enlisted members, but no ration or commutation thereof shall be allowed an individual receiving a subsistence allowance.

(Aug. 4, 1949, ch. 393, 63 Stat. 532, §478; Pub. L. 98–557, §15(a)(3)(B), (C), Oct. 30, 1984, 98 Stat. 2865; renumbered §2773, Pub. L. 115–282, title I, §116(b), Dec. 4, 2018, 132 Stat. 4226; Pub. L. 116–283, div. G, title LVXXXV [LXXXV], §8505(a)(42), Jan. 1, 2021, 134 Stat. 4750.)

§2774. SALES OF RATION SUPPLIES TO MESSES

Ration supplies may be purchased by the cabin, wardroom, warrant officers', and other authorized messes and payment therefor made in cash to the commissary officer. The prices to be charged for such supplies shall not be less than the invoice prices, and the cash received from such sales shall be accounted for on the ration return and may be expended for the general mess.

(Aug. 4, 1949, ch. 393, 63 Stat. 533, §479; renumbered §2774, Pub. L. 115–282, title I, §116(b), Dec. 4, 2018, 132 Stat. 4226.)

§2775. FLIGHT RATIONS

There may be furnished to officers, enlisted members, and civilian employees, while actually engaged in flight operations, an aircraft flight ration in kind, chargeable to the proper Coast Guard appropriation, which flight ration shall be supplementary to any ration or subsistence allowance now granted to such personnel. No part of an aircraft flight ration shall be furnished without cost to any individual in a travel status or to any individual to whom a per diem allowance is granted in lieu of actual subsistence.

(Aug. 4, 1949, ch. 393, 63 Stat. 533, §480; Pub. L. 98–557, §15(a)(3)(B), Oct. 30, 1984, 98 Stat. 2865; renumbered §2775, Pub. L. 115–282, title I, §116(b), Dec. 4, 2018, 132 Stat. 4226; Pub. L. 116–283, div. G, title LVXXXV [LXXXV], §8505(a)(43), Jan. 1, 2021, 134 Stat. 4750.)

§2776. PAYMENTS AT TIME OF DISCHARGE FOR GOOD OF SERVICE

Enlisted members discharged by dishonorable discharge, bad-conduct discharge, or any other discharge for the good of the service, may, upon discharge, be paid a sum not to exceed $25. The sum paid shall be fixed by and in the discretion of the Commandant, and shall be paid only in cases where the individual so discharged would otherwise be without funds to meet his immediate needs.

(Aug. 4, 1949, ch. 393, 63 Stat. 533, §481; Pub. L. 98–557, §15(a)(3)(C), Oct. 30, 1984, 98 Stat. 2865; renumbered §2776, Pub. L. 115–282, title I, §116(b), Dec. 4, 2018, 132 Stat. 4226; Pub. L. 116–283, div. G, title LVXXXV [LXXXV], §8505(a)(44), Jan. 1, 2021, 134 Stat. 4750.)

§2777. CLOTHING FOR DESTITUTE SHIPWRECKED INDIVIDUALS

The Coast Guard may furnish clothing and subsistence to destitute shipwrecked individuals, and the Coast Guard may reimburse, in cash or in kind, Coast Guard personnel who furnish clothing and subsistence to destitute shipwrecked individuals.

(Aug. 4, 1949, ch. 393, 63 Stat. 534, §486; renumbered §2777, Pub. L. 115–282, title I, §116(b), Dec. 4, 2018, 132 Stat. 4226; Pub. L. 116–283, div. G, title LVXXXV [LXXXV], §8505(a)(45)(A), Jan. 1, 2021, 134 Stat. 4750.)

§2778. ADVANCEMENT OF PUBLIC FUNDS TO PERSONNEL

The Commandant, under regulations prescribed by the Secretary, may advance public funds to personnel when required to meet expenses of members detailed on emergency shore duty. Funds so advanced shall not exceed a reasonable estimate of the actual expenditures to be made and for which reimbursement is authorized by law.

(Aug. 4, 1949, ch. 393, 63 Stat. 534, §488; Pub. L. 98–557, §15(a)(3)(I), Oct. 30, 1984, 98 Stat. 2865; renumbered §2778, Pub. L. 115–282, title I, §116(b), Dec. 4, 2018, 132 Stat. 4226.)

§2779. TRANSPORTATION TO AND FROM CERTAIN PLACES OF EMPLOYMENT

(a) Whenever the Secretary determines that it is necessary for the effective conduct of the affairs of the Coast Guard, he may, at reasonable rates of fare fixed under regulations to be prescribed by him, provide assured and adequate transportation by motor vehicle or water carrier to and from their places of employment for individuals attached to, or employed by, the Coast Guard; and during a war or during a national emergency declared by Congress or the President, for individuals attached to, or employed in, a private plant that is manufacturing material for the Coast Guard.

(b) Transportation may not be provided under subsection (a) unless the Secretary or an officer designated by the Secretary, determines that—

(1) other transportation facilities are inadequate and cannot be made adequate;

(2) a reasonable effort has been made to induce operators of private facilities to provide the necessary transportation; and

(3) the service to be furnished will make proper use of transportation facilities and will supply the most efficient transportation to the individuals concerned.

(c) To provide transportation under subsection (a), the Secretary may—

(1) buy, lease, or charter motor vehicles or water carriers having a seating capacity of 12 or more passengers;

(2) maintain and operate that equipment by enlisted members or employees of the Coast Guard, or by private individuals under contract; and

(3) lease or charter the equipment to private or public carriers for operation under terms that are considered necessary by the Secretary or by an officer designated by the Secretary, and that may provide for the pooling of government-owned and privately owned equipment and facilities and for the reciprocal use of that equipment.

(d) Fares received under subsection (a), and proceeds of the leasing or chartering of equipment under subsection (c)(3), shall be covered into the Treasury as miscellaneous receipts.

(Added Pub. L. 96–376, §10(a), Oct. 3, 1980, 94 Stat. 1510, §660; amended Pub. L. 99–145, title XVI, §1623, Nov. 8, 1985, 99 Stat. 778; Pub. L. 99–550, §2(e), Oct. 27, 1986, 100 Stat. 3070; renumbered §2779, Pub. L. 115–282, title I, §116(b), Dec. 4, 2018, 132 Stat. 4226; Pub. L. 116–283, div. G, title LVXXXV [LXXXV], §8505(a)(46), Jan. 1, 2021, 134 Stat. 4750.)

CHAPTER 29—COAST GUARD FAMILY SUPPORT, CHILD CARE, AND HOUSING

SUBCHAPTER I—COAST GUARD FAMILIES

SUBCHAPTER II—COAST GUARD CHILD CARE

SUBCHAPTER III—HOUSING

SUBCHAPTER I—COAST GUARD FAMILIES

§2901. WORK-LIFE POLICIES AND PROGRAMS

The Commandant is authorized—

(1) to establish an office for the purpose of developing, promulgating, and coordinating policies, programs, and activities related to the families of Coast Guard members;

(2) to implement and oversee policies, programs, and activities described in paragraph (1) as the Commandant considers necessary; and

(3) to perform such other duties as the Commandant considers necessary.

(Added Pub. L. 113–281, title II, §214(a), Dec. 18, 2014, 128 Stat. 3029, §531; renumbered §2901, Pub. L. 115–282, title I, §117(b), Dec. 4, 2018, 132 Stat. 4230.)

§2902. SURVEYS OF COAST GUARD FAMILIES

(a) AUTHORITY.—The Commandant, in order to determine the effectiveness of Federal policies, programs, and activities related to the families of Coast Guard members, may survey—

(1) any Coast Guard member;

(2) any retired Coast Guard member;

(3) the immediate family of any Coast Guard member or retired Coast Guard member; and

(4) any survivor of a deceased Coast Guard member.

(b) VOLUNTARY PARTICIPATION.—Participation in any survey conducted under subsection (a) shall be voluntary.

(c) FEDERAL RECORDKEEPING.—Each individual surveyed under subsection (a) shall be considered an employee of the United States for purposes of section 3502(3)(A)(i) of title 44.

(Added Pub. L. 113–281, title II, §214(a), Dec. 18, 2014, 128 Stat. 3029, §532; renumbered §2902, Pub. L. 115–282, title I, §117(b), Dec. 4, 2018, 132 Stat. 4230; amended Pub. L. 116–283, div. G, title LVXXXV [LXXXV], §8505(a)(47), Jan. 1, 2021, 134 Stat. 4750.)

§2903. REIMBURSEMENT FOR ADOPTION EXPENSES

(a) AUTHORIZATION TO REIMBURSE.—The Secretary shall carry out a program under which a member of the Coast Guard may be reimbursed, as provided in this section, for qualifying adoption expenses incurred by the member in the adoption of a child under 18 years of age.

(b) ADOPTIONS COVERED.—An adoption for which expenses may be reimbursed under this section includes an adoption by a single individual, an infant adoption, an intercountry adoption, and an adoption of a child with special needs (as defined in section 473(c) of the Social Security Act (42 U.S.C. 673(c))).

(c) BENEFITS PAID AFTER ADOPTION IS FINAL.—Benefits paid under this section in the case of an adoption may be paid only after the adoption is final.

(d) TREATMENT OF OTHER BENEFITS.—A benefit may not be paid under this section for any expense paid to or for a member of the Coast Guard under any other adoption benefits program administered by the Federal Government or under any such program administered by a State or local government.

(e) LIMITATIONS.—(1) Not more than $2,000 may be paid under this section to a member of the Coast Guard, or to two such members who are spouses of each other, for expenses incurred in the adoption of a child.

(2) Not more than $5,000 may be paid under this section to a member of the Coast Guard, or to two such members who are spouses of each other, for adoptions by such member (or members) in any calendar year.

(f) REGULATIONS.—The Secretary shall prescribe regulations to carry out this section.

(g) DEFINITIONS.—In this section:

(1) The term "qualifying adoption expenses" means reasonable and necessary expenses that are directly related to the legal adoption of a child under 18 years of age, but only if such adoption is arranged by a qualified adoption agency. Such term does not include any expense incurred—

(A) by an adopting parent for travel; or

(B) in connection with an adoption arranged in violation of Federal, State, or local law.

(2) The term "reasonable and necessary expenses" includes—

(A) public and private agency fees, including adoption fees charged by an agency in a foreign country;

(B) placement fees, including fees charged adoptive parents for counseling;

(C) legal fees (including court costs) in connection with services that are unavailable to a member of the Coast Guard under section 1044 or 1044a of title 10; and

(D) medical expenses, including hospital expenses of the biological mother of the child to be adopted and of a newborn infant to be adopted.

(3) The term "qualified adoption agency" means any of the following:

(A) A State or local government agency which has responsibility under State or local law for child placement through adoption.

(B) A nonprofit, voluntary adoption agency which is authorized by State or local law to place children for adoption.

(C) Any other source authorized by a State to provide adoption placement if the adoption is supervised by a court under State or local law.

(Added Pub. L. 102–190, div. A, title VI, §651(b)(1), Dec. 5, 1991, 105 Stat. 1386, §514; amended Pub. L. 102–484, div. A, title X, §1054(g), Oct. 23, 1992, 106 Stat. 2503; Pub. L. 104–201, div. A, title VI, §652(b), Sept. 23, 1996, 110 Stat. 2582; renumbered §541, Pub. L. 113–281, title II, §214(b)(1)(A), Dec. 18, 2014, 128 Stat. 3033; renumbered §2903, Pub. L. 115–282, title I, §117(b), Dec. 4, 2018, 132 Stat. 4230; Pub. L. 116–283, div. G, title LVXXXV [LXXXV], §8505(a)(48), Jan. 1, 2021, 134 Stat. 4750.)

§2904. EDUCATION AND TRAINING OPPORTUNITIES FOR COAST GUARD SPOUSES

(a) TUITION ASSISTANCE.—The Commandant may provide, subject to the availability of appropriations, tuition assistance to an eligible spouse to facilitate the acquisition of—

(1) education and training required for a degree or credential at an accredited college, university, or technical school in the United States that expands employment and portable career opportunities for the spouse; or

(2) education prerequisites and a professional license or credential required, by a government or government-sanctioned licensing body, for an occupation that expands employment and portable career opportunities for the spouse.

(b) DEFINITIONS.—In this section, the following definitions apply:

(1) ELIGIBLE SPOUSE.—

(A) IN GENERAL.—The term "eligible spouse" means the spouse of a member of the Coast Guard who is serving on active duty and includes a spouse who receives transitional compensation under section 1059 of title 10.

(B) EXCLUSION.—The term "eligible spouse" does not include an individual who—

(i) is married to, but legally separated from, a member of the Coast Guard under a court order or statute of any State or territorial possession of the United States; or

(ii) is eligible for tuition assistance as a member of the Armed Forces.

(2) PORTABLE CAREER.—The term "portable career" includes an occupation that requires education, training, or both that results in a credential that is recognized by an industry, profession, or specific type of business.

(Added Pub. L. 113–281, title II, §214(a), Dec. 18, 2014, 128 Stat. 3030, §542; renumbered §2904, Pub. L. 115–282, title I, §117(b), Dec. 4, 2018, 132 Stat. 4230; amended Pub. L. 116–283, div. G, title LVXXXV [LXXXV], §8505(a)(49), Jan. 1, 2021, 134 Stat. 4750.)

§2905. YOUTH SPONSORSHIP INITIATIVES

(a) IN GENERAL.—The Commandant is authorized to establish, within any Coast Guard unit, an initiative to help integrate into new surroundings the dependent children of members of the Coast Guard who received permanent change of station orders.

(b) DESCRIPTION OF INITIATIVE.—An initiative established under subsection (a) shall—

(1) provide for the involvement of a dependent child of a member of the Coast Guard in the dependent child's new Coast Guard community; and

(2) primarily focus on preteen and teenaged children.

(c) AUTHORITY.—In carrying out an initiative under subsection (a), the Commandant may—

(1) provide to a dependent child of a member of the Coast Guard information on youth programs and activities available in the dependent child's new Coast Guard community; and

(2) enter into agreements with nonprofit entities to provide youth programs and activities to such child.

(Added Pub. L. 113–281, title II, §214(a), Dec. 18, 2014, 128 Stat. 3030, §543; renumbered §2905, Pub. L. 115–282, title I, §117(b), Dec. 4, 2018, 132 Stat. 4230.)

§2906. DEPENDENT SCHOOL CHILDREN

(a) The Secretary may provide, out of funds appropriated to or for the use of the Coast Guard, for the primary and secondary schooling of dependents of Coast Guard personnel stationed outside the continental United States at costs for any given area not in excess of those of the Department of Defense for the same area, when it is determined by the Secretary that the schools, if any, available in the locality are unable to provide adequately for the education of those dependents.

(b) Whenever the Secretary, under such regulations as he may prescribe, determines that schools located in the same area in which a Coast Guard facility is located are not accessible by public means of transportation on a regular basis, he may provide, out of funds appropriated to or for the use of the Coast Guard, for the transportation of dependents of Coast Guard personnel between the schools serving the area and the Coast Guard facility.

(Added Pub. L. 91–278, §1(14), June 12, 1970, 84 Stat. 306, §657; amended Pub. L. 93–430, §5, Oct. 1, 1974, 88 Stat. 1182; renumbered §544 and amended Pub. L. 113–281, title II, §214(b)(1)(C), Dec. 18, 2014, 128 Stat. 3033; renumbered §2906, Pub. L. 115–282, title I, §117(b), Dec. 4, 2018, 132 Stat. 4230.)

SUBCHAPTER II—COAST GUARD CHILD CARE

§2921. DEFINITIONS

In this subchapter, the following definitions apply:

(1) CHILD ABUSE AND NEGLECT.—The term "child abuse and neglect" has the meaning given that term in section 3 of the Child Abuse Prevention and Treatment Act (42 U.S.C. 5101 note).

(2) CHILD DEVELOPMENT CENTER EMPLOYEE.—The term "child development center employee" means a civilian employee of the Coast Guard who is employed to work in a Coast Guard child development center without regard to whether the employee is paid from appropriated or nonappropriated funds.

(3) COAST GUARD CHILD DEVELOPMENT CENTER.—The term "Coast Guard child development center" means a facility on Coast Guard property or on property under the jurisdiction of the commander of a Coast Guard unit at which child care services are provided for members of the Coast Guard.

(4) COMPETITIVE SERVICE POSITION.—The term "competitive service position" means a position in the competitive service (as defined in section 2102 of title 5).

(5) FAMILY HOME DAYCARE.—The term "family home daycare" means home-based child care services provided for a member of the Coast Guard by an individual who—

(A) is certified by the Commandant as qualified to provide home-based child care services; and

(B) provides home-based child care services on a regular basis in exchange for monetary compensation.

(Added Pub. L. 113–281, title II, §214(a), Dec. 18, 2014, 128 Stat. 3031, §551; renumbered §2921, Pub. L. 115–282, title I, §117(b), Dec. 4, 2018, 132 Stat. 4230.)

§2922. CHILD DEVELOPMENT SERVICES

(a)(1) The Commandant may make child development services available, in such priority as the Commandant considers to be appropriate and consistent with readiness and resources and in the best interests of dependents of members and civilian employees of the Coast Guard, for—

(A) members and civilian employees of the Coast Guard;

(B) surviving dependents of service members who have died on active duty, if such dependents were beneficiaries of a Coast Guard child development service at the time of the death of such members;

(C) members of the armed forces (as defined in section 101(a) of title 10); and

(D) Federal civilian employees.

(2) Child development service benefits provided under the authority of this section shall be in addition to benefits provided under other laws.

(b)(1) The Commandant is authorized to use appropriated funds available to the Coast Guard to provide child development services.

(2)(A) The Commandant is authorized to establish, by regulations, fees to be charged parents for the attendance of children at Coast Guard child development centers.

(B) Fees to be charged, pursuant to subparagraph (A), shall be based on family income and whether a family is participating in an initiative established under section 2925(b), except that the Commandant may, on a case-by-base basis, establish fees at lower rates if such rates would not be competitive with rates at local child development centers.

(C) The Commandant is authorized to collect and expend fees, established pursuant to this subparagraph, and such fees shall, without further appropriation, remain available until expended for the purpose of providing services, including the compensation of employees and the purchase of consumable and disposable items, at Coast Guard child development centers.

(D) In the case of an active duty member with two or more children attending a Coast Guard child development center, the Commandant may modify the fees to be charged for attendance for the second and any subsequent child of such member by an amount that is 15 percent less than the amount of the fee otherwise chargeable for the attendance of the first such child enrolled at the center, or another fee as the Commandant determines appropriate, consistent with multiple children.

(3) The Commandant is authorized to use appropriated funds available to the Coast Guard to provide assistance to family home daycare providers so that family home daycare services can be provided to uniformed service members and civilian employees of the Coast Guard at a cost comparable to the cost of services provided by Coast Guard child development centers.

(4) To the maximum extent practicable, the Commandant shall ensure that, in a location in which Coast Guard family child care centers (as such term is defined in section 8239 of the Elijah E. Cummings Coast Guard Authorization Act of 2020) are necessary to meet the demand for child care for qualified families (as such term is defined in such section), not fewer than two housing units are maintained in accordance with safety inspection standards so as to accommodate family child care providers.

(c) The Secretary shall promulgate regulations to implement this section. The regulations shall establish fees to be charged for child development services provided under this section which take into consideration total family income.

(Added Pub. L. 104–324, title II, §201(a), Oct. 19, 1996, 110 Stat. 3906, §515; amended Pub. L. 111–281, title II, §222, Oct. 15, 2010, 124 Stat. 2920; renumbered §552 and amended Pub. L. 113–281, title II, §214(b)(1)(B), Dec. 18, 2014, 128 Stat. 3033; renumbered §2922 and amended Pub. L. 115–282, title I, §§117(b), 123(b)(2), Dec. 4, 2018, 132 Stat. 4230, 4240; Pub. L. 116–283, div. G, title LVXXXII [LXXXII], §8235, Jan. 1, 2021, 134 Stat. 4664; Pub. L. 117–263, div. K, title CXIV, §§11401(a), 11402, Dec. 23, 2022, 136 Stat. 4106, 4109.)

§2923. CHILD DEVELOPMENT CENTER STANDARDS AND INSPECTIONS

(a) STANDARDS.—The Commandant shall require each Coast Guard child development center to meet standards of operation—

(1) that the Commandant considers appropriate to ensure the health, safety, and welfare of the children and employees at the center; and

(2) necessary for accreditation by an appropriate national early childhood programs accrediting entity.

(b) INSPECTIONS.—

(1) IN GENERAL.—Not less than twice annually, the Commandant shall ensure that each Coast Guard child development center is subject to an unannounced inspection.

(2) RESPONSIBILITY FOR INSPECTIONS.—Of the biannual inspections under paragraph (1)—

(A) 1 shall be carried out by a representative of the Coast Guard installation served by the Coast Guard child development center concerned; and

(B) 1 shall be carried out by a representative of the Coast Guard child development services work-life programs.

(c) NATIONAL REPORTING.—

(1) IN GENERAL.—The Commandant shall maintain and publicize a means by which an individual can report, with respect to a Coast Guard child development center or a family home daycare—

(A) any suspected violation of—

(i) standards established under subsection (a); or

(ii) any other applicable law or standard;

(B) suspected child abuse or neglect; or

(C) any other deficiency.

(2) ANONYMOUS REPORTING.—The Commandant shall ensure that an individual making a report pursuant to paragraph (1) may do so anonymously if so desired by the individual.

(3) PROCEDURES.—The Commandant shall establish procedures for investigating reports made pursuant to paragraph (1).

(Added Pub. L. 113–281, title II, §214(a), Dec. 18, 2014, 128 Stat. 3031, §553; renumbered §2923, Pub. L. 115–282, title I, §117(b), Dec. 4, 2018, 132 Stat. 4230; amended Pub. L. 116–283, div. G, title LVXXXII [LXXXII], §8237(a), Jan. 1, 2021, 134 Stat. 4664; Pub. L. 117–263, div. K, title CXIV, §11401(b), Dec. 23, 2022, 136 Stat. 4106.)

§2924. CHILD DEVELOPMENT CENTER EMPLOYEES

(a) TRAINING.—

(1) IN GENERAL.—The Commandant shall establish a training program for Coast Guard child development center employees and satisfactory completion of the training program shall be a condition of employment for each employee of a Coast Guard child development center.

(2) TIMING FOR NEW HIRES.—The Commandant shall require each employee of a Coast Guard child development center to complete the training program established under paragraph (1) not later than 6 months after the date on which the employee is hired.

(3) MINIMUM REQUIREMENTS.—The training program established under paragraph (1) shall include, at a minimum, instruction with respect to—

(A) early childhood development;

(B) activities and disciplinary techniques appropriate to children of different ages;

(C) child abuse and neglect prevention and detection; and

(D) cardiopulmonary resuscitation and other emergency medical procedures.

(4) USE OF DEPARTMENT OF DEFENSE PROGRAMS.—The Commandant may use Department of Defense training programs, on a reimbursable or nonreimbursable basis, for purposes of this subsection.

(b) TRAINING AND CURRICULUM SPECIALISTS.—

(1) SPECIALIST REQUIRED.—The Commandant shall require that at least 1 employee at each Coast Guard child development center be a specialist in training and curriculum development with appropriate credentials and experience.

(2) DUTIES.—The duties of the specialist described in paragraph (1) shall include—

(A) special teaching activities;

(B) daily oversight and instruction of other child care employees;

(C) daily assistance in the preparation of lesson plans;

(D) assisting with child abuse and neglect prevention and detection; and

(E) advising the director of the center on the performance of the other child care employees.

(3) COMPETITIVE SERVICE.—Each specialist described in paragraph (1) shall be an employee in a competitive service position.

(Added Pub. L. 113–281, title II, §214(a), Dec. 18, 2014, 128 Stat. 3032, §554; renumbered §2924, Pub. L. 115–282, title I, §117(b), Dec. 4, 2018, 132 Stat. 4230.)

§2925. PARENT PARTNERSHIPS WITH CHILD DEVELOPMENT CENTERS

(a) PARENT BOARDS.—

(1) FORMATION.—The Commandant shall require that there be formed at each Coast Guard child development center a board of parents, to be composed of parents of children attending the center.

(2) FUNCTIONS.—Each board of parents formed under paragraph (1) shall—

(A) meet periodically with the staff of the center at which the board is formed and the commander of the unit served by the center, for the purpose of discussing problems and concerns; and

(B) be responsible, together with the staff of the center, for coordinating any parent participation initiative established under subsection (b).

(3) CHAPTER 10 OF TITLE 5.—Chapter 10 of title 5 does not apply to a board of parents formed under paragraph (1).

(b) PARENT PARTICIPATION INITIATIVE.—The Commandant is authorized to establish a parent participation initiative at each Coast Guard child development center to encourage and facilitate parent participation in educational and related activities at the center.

(Added Pub. L. 113–281, title II, §214(a), Dec. 18, 2014, 128 Stat. 3032, §555; renumbered §2925, Pub. L.

115–282, title I, §117(b), Dec. 4, 2018, 132 Stat. 4230; amended Pub. L. 117–286, §4(a)(60), Dec. 27, 2022, 136 Stat. 4312.)

§2926. FAMILY CHILD CARE PROVIDERS

(a) IN GENERAL.—Not less frequently than quarterly, the Commandant shall ensure that each family child care provider is subject to inspection.

(b) RESPONSIBILITY FOR INSPECTIONS.—Of the quarterly inspections under subsection (a) each year—

(1) 3 inspections shall be carried out by a representative of the Coast Guard installation served by the family child care provider concerned; and

(2) 1 inspection shall be carried out by a representative of the Coast Guard child development services work-life programs.

(Added Pub. L. 116–283, div. G, title LVXXXII [LXXXII], §8237(b)(1), Jan. 1, 2021, 134 Stat. 4665.)

§2927. CHILD CARE SUBSIDY PROGRAM

(a) IN GENERAL.—

(1) AUTHORITY.—The Commandant may operate a child care subsidy program to provide financial assistance to eligible providers that provide child care services or youth program services to members of the Coast Guard, members of the Coast Guard with dependents who are participating in the child care subsidy program, and any other individual the Commandant considers appropriate, if—

(A) providing such financial assistance—

(i) is in the best interests of the Coast Guard; and

(ii) enables supplementation or expansion of the provision of Coast Guard child care services, while not supplanting or replacing Coast Guard child care services; and

(B) the Commandant ensures, to the extent practicable, that the eligible provider is able to comply, and does comply, with the regulations, policies, and standards applicable to Coast Guard child care services.

(2) ELIGIBLE PROVIDERS.—A provider of child care services or youth program services is eligible for financial assistance under this section if the provider—

(A) is licensed to provide such services under applicable State and local law or meets all applicable State and local health and safety requirements if licensure is not required;

(B) is either—

(i) is [1] a family home daycare; or

(ii) is [1] a provider of family child care services that—

(I) otherwise provides federally funded or federally sponsored child development services;

(II) provides such services in a child development center owned and operated by a private, not-for-profit organization;

(III) provides a before-school or after-school child care program in a public school facility;

(IV) conducts an otherwise federally funded or federally sponsored school-age child care or youth services program; or

(V) conducts a school-age child care or youth services program operated by a not-for-profit organization; or

(C) is a provider of another category of child care services or youth program services the Commandant considers appropriate for meeting the needs of members or civilian employees of the Coast Guard.

(3) FINANCIAL ASSISTANCE FOR IN-HOME CHILD CARE.—

(A) IN GENERAL.—The Commandant may provide financial assistance to members of the Coast Guard who pay for services provided by in-home child care providers.

(B) REQUIREMENTS.—In carrying out such program, the Commandant shall establish a policy and procedures to—

(i) support the needs of families who request services provided by in-home childcare providers;

(ii) provide the appropriate amount of financial assistance to provide to families described in paragraph, that is at minimum consistent with the program authorized in subsection (a)(1); and

(iii) ensure the appropriate qualifications for such in-home child care provider, which shall at minimum—

(I) take into consideration qualifications for available in-home child care providers in the private sector; and

(II) ensure that the qualifications the Commandant determines appropriate under this paragraph are comparable to the qualifications for a provider of child care services in a Coast Guard child development center or family home day care.

(b) DIRECT PAYMENT.—

(1) IN GENERAL.—In carrying out a child care subsidy program under subsection (a)(1), subject to paragraph (3), the Commandant shall provide financial assistance under the program to an eligible member or individual the Commandant considers appropriate by direct payment to such eligible member or individual through monthly pay, direct deposit, or other direct form of payment.

(2) POLICY.—Not later than 180 days after the date of the enactment of this section, the Commandant shall establish a policy to provide direct payment as described in paragraph (1).

(3) ELIGIBLE PROVIDER FUNDING CONTINUATION.—With the approval of an eligible member or an individual the Commandant considers appropriate, which shall include the written consent of such member or individual, the Commandant may continue to provide financial assistance under the child care subsidy program directly to an eligible provider on behalf of such member or individual.

(4) RULE OF CONSTRUCTION.—Nothing in this subsection may be construed to affect any preexisting reimbursement arrangement between the Coast Guard and a qualified

provider.

(Added Pub. L. 117–263, div. K, title CXIV, §11401(c)(1)(A), Dec. 23, 2022, 136 Stat. 4106.)

---

[1] *So in original. The word "is" probably should not appear.*

SUBCHAPTER III—HOUSING

§2941. DEFINITIONS

In this chapter:

(1) The term "construct" means to build, renovate, or improve military family housing and military unaccompanied housing.

(2) The term "construction" means building, renovating, or improving military family housing and military unaccompanied housing.

(3) The term "military unaccompanied housing" means military housing intended to be occupied by members of the armed forces serving a tour of duty unaccompanied by dependents.

(4) The term "United States" includes the Commonwealth of Puerto Rico, Guam, the United States Virgin Islands, and the District of Columbia.

(Added Pub. L. 104–324, title II, §208(a), Oct. 19, 1996, 110 Stat. 3909, §680; amended Pub. L. 108–293, title II, §207(a), Aug. 9, 2004, 118 Stat. 1034; Pub. L. 111–281, title II, §221(a)(1), Oct. 15, 2010, 124 Stat. 2919; renumbered §2941, Pub. L. 115–282, title I, §117(b), Dec. 4, 2018, 132 Stat. 4230.)

§2942. GENERAL AUTHORITY

(a) AUTHORITY.—In addition to any other authority providing for the acquisition or construction of military family housing or military unaccompanied housing, the Secretary may acquire or construct the following:

(1) Military family housing on or near Coast Guard installations within the United States and its territories and possessions.

(2) Military unaccompanied housing on or near such Coast Guard installations.

(b) LIMITATION ON APPROPRIATIONS.—No appropriation shall be made to acquire or construct military family housing or military unaccompanied housing under this chapter if that acquisition or construction has not been approved by resolutions adopted by the Committee on Transportation and Infrastructure of the House of Representatives and the Committee on Commerce, Science, and Transportation of the Senate.

(Added Pub. L. 104–324, title II, §208(a), Oct. 19, 1996, 110 Stat. 3909, §681; amended Pub. L. 107–295, title IV, §402(a), Nov. 25, 2002, 116 Stat. 2113; Pub. L. 111–281, title II, §221(a)(2), Oct. 15, 2010, 124 Stat. 2919; renumbered §2942, Pub. L. 115–282, title I, §117(b), Dec. 4, 2018, 132 Stat. 4230.)

§2943. LEASING AND HIRING OF QUARTERS; RENTAL OF INADEQUATE HOUSING

(a) The Secretary is authorized to lease housing facilities at or near Coast Guard installations, wherever located, for assignment as public quarters to military personnel and their dependents, if any, without rental charge upon a determination by the Secretary, or his designee, that there is a lack of adequate housing facilities at or near such Coast Guard installations. The Secretary is also authorized to lease housing facilities for assignment as public quarters, without rental charge, to military personnel who are on sea duty or duty at remote offshore Coast Guard stations and who do not have dependents. Such authority shall be effective in any fiscal year only to such extent or in such amounts as are provided in appropriation Acts. When any such lease involves housing facilities in a foreign country, the lease may be made on a multiyear basis for a period not to exceed five years, and, in accordance with local custom and practice, advance payment may be made for the lease. Such public housing facilities may be leased on an individual or multiple-unit basis. Expenditures for the rental of such housing facilities may not exceed the average authorized for the Department of Defense in any year except where the Secretary finds that the average is so low as to prevent rental of necessary housing facilities in some areas, in which event he is authorized to reallocate existing funds to high-cost areas so that rental expenditures in such areas exceed the average authorized for the Department of Defense.

(b) The Secretary is authorized, subject to regulations approved by the President—

(1) to designate as rental housing such housing as he may determine to be inadequate as public quarters; and

(2) to lease inadequate housing to members of the Coast Guard for occupancy by them and their dependents.

(c) Where sufficient quarters are not possessed by the United States, the Commandant may hire quarters for personnel, including personnel on sea duty at such times as they may be deprived of their quarters on board ship due to repairs or other conditions which may render them uninhabitable. Such accommodations shall not be available for occupancy by the dependents of such personnel.

(Aug. 4, 1949, ch. 393, 63 Stat. 532, §475; Pub. L. 91–278, §1(11), June 12, 1970, 84 Stat. 305; Pub. L. 92–343, §4, July 10, 1972, 86 Stat. 450; Pub. L. 93–65, §5, July 9, 1973, 87 Stat. 151; Pub. L. 94–406, §4, Sept. 10, 1976, 90 Stat. 1236; Pub. L. 94–478, Oct. 11, 1976, 90 Stat. 2077; Pub. L. 94–546, §1(30), Oct. 18, 1976, 90 Stat. 2521; Pub. L. 96–376, §4, Oct. 3, 1980, 94 Stat. 1509; Pub. L. 96–470, title I, §112(d), Oct. 19, 1980, 94 Stat. 2240; Pub. L. 97–136, §7, Dec. 29, 1981, 95 Stat. 1706; Pub. L. 97–295, §2(11), Oct. 12, 1982, 96 Stat. 1302; Pub. L. 97–322, title I, §106, Oct. 15, 1982, 96 Stat. 1582; Pub. L. 100–180, div. A, title VI, §632(b)(2), Dec. 4, 1987, 101 Stat. 1105; renumbered §2943, Pub. L. 115–282, title I, §117(b), Dec. 4, 2018, 132 Stat. 4230.)

§2944. Retired service members and dependents serving on advisory committees

A committee that—

(1) advises or assists the Coast Guard with respect to a function that affects a member of the Coast Guard or a dependent of such a member; and

(2) includes in its membership a retired Coast Guard member or a dependent of such a retired member;

shall not be considered an advisory committee under chapter 10 of title 5 solely because of such membership.

(Added Pub. L. 113–281, title II, §218(a), Dec. 18, 2014, 128 Stat. 3036, §680; renumbered §2944, Pub. L. 115–282, title I, §117(b), Dec. 4, 2018, 132 Stat. 4230; amended Pub. L. 117–286, §4(a)(61), Dec. 27, 2022, 136 Stat. 4312.)

§2945. CONVEYANCE OF REAL PROPERTY

(a) CONVEYANCE AUTHORIZED.—Notwithstanding any other provision of law, the Secretary may convey, at fair market value, real property, owned or under the administrative control of the Coast Guard, for the purpose of expending the proceeds from such conveyance to acquire and construct military family housing and military unaccompanied housing.

(b) TERMS AND CONDITIONS.—

(1) The conveyance of real property under this section shall be by sale, for cash. The Secretary shall deposit the proceeds from the sale in the Coast Guard Housing Fund established under section 2946 of this title, for the purpose of expending such proceeds to acquire and construct military family housing and military unaccompanied housing.

(2) The conveyance of real property under this section shall not diminish the mission capacity of the Coast Guard, but further the mission support capability of the Coast Guard with regard to military family housing or military unaccompanied housing.

(c) RELATIONSHIP TO ENVIRONMENTAL LAW.—This section does not affect or limit the application of or obligation to comply with any environmental law, including section 120(h) of the Comprehensive Environmental Response, Compensation, and Liability Act of 1980 (42 U.S.C. 9620(h)).

(Added Pub. L. 104–324, title II, §208(a), Oct. 19, 1996, 110 Stat. 3911, §685; amended Pub. L. 106–400, §2, Oct. 30, 2000, 114 Stat. 1675; Pub. L. 107–217, §3(c)(4), Aug. 21, 2002, 116 Stat. 1299; Pub. L. 111–281, title II, §221(a)(4), Oct. 15, 2010, 124 Stat. 2919; Pub. L. 111–350, §5(c)(4), Jan. 4, 2011, 124 Stat. 3847; renumbered §2945 and amended Pub. L. 115–282, title I, §§117(b), 123(b)(2), Dec. 4, 2018, 132 Stat. 4230, 4240.)

§2946. COAST GUARD HOUSING FUND

(a) ESTABLISHMENT.—There is hereby established on the books of the Treasury an account to be known as the Coast Guard Housing Fund (in this section referred to as the "Fund").

(b) CREDITS TO FUND.—There shall be credited to the Fund the following:

(1) Amounts authorized for and appropriated to that Fund.

(2) Subject to subsection (e), any amounts that the Secretary transfers, in such amounts as provided in appropriation Acts, to that Fund from amounts authorized and appropriated to the Department of Homeland Security or Coast Guard for the acquisition or construction of military family housing or military unaccompanied housing.

(3) Proceeds from the conveyance of property under section 2945 of this title for the purpose of carrying out activities under this chapter with respect to military family housing and military unaccompanied housing.

(4) Monies received under section 504(a)(13).

(5) Amounts received under section 908(b).

(c) USE OF AMOUNTS IN FUND.—(1) In such amounts as provided in appropriations Acts, and except as provided in subsection (d), the Secretary may use amounts in the Coast Guard Housing Fund to carry out activities under this chapter with respect to military family housing and military unaccompanied housing, including—

(A) the planning, execution, and administration of the conveyance of real property;

(B) all necessary expenses, including expenses for environmental compliance and restoration, to prepare real property for conveyance; and

(C) the conveyance of real property.

(2) Amounts made available under this subsection shall remain available until expended.

(d) LIMITATION ON OBLIGATIONS.—The Secretary may not incur an obligation under a contract or other agreements entered into under this chapter in excess of the unobligated balance, at the time the contract is entered into, of the Fund required to be used to satisfy the obligation.

(e) NOTIFICATION REQUIRED FOR TRANSFERS.—A transfer of appropriated amounts to the Fund under subsection (b)(2) of this section may be made only after the end of a 30-day period beginning on the date the Secretary submits written notice of, and justification for, the transfer to the appropriate committees of Congress.

(Added Pub. L. 104–324, title II, §208(a), Oct. 19, 1996, 110 Stat. 3912, §687; amended Pub. L. 107–295, title IV, §402(b), (c), Nov. 25, 2002, 116 Stat. 2114; Pub. L. 107–296, title XVII, §1704(a), Nov. 25, 2002, 116 Stat. 2314; Pub. L. 108–293, title II, §207(d), Aug. 9, 2004, 118 Stat. 1034; Pub. L. 111–281, title II, §221(a)(6), Oct. 15, 2010, 124 Stat. 2919; Pub. L. 111–330, §1(2), Dec. 22, 2010, 124 Stat. 3569; Pub. L. 113–281, title II, §208(c), Dec. 18, 2014, 128 Stat. 3026; renumbered §2946 and amended Pub. L. 115–282, title I, §§117(b), 123(b)(2), Dec. 4, 2018, 132 Stat. 4230, 4240.)

§2947. REPORTS

The Secretary shall prepare and submit to Congress, concurrent with the budget submitted pursuant to section 1105 of title 31, a report identifying the contracts or agreements for the conveyance of properties pursuant to this chapter executed during the prior calendar year.

(Added Pub. L. 104–324, title II, §208(a), Oct. 19, 1996, 110 Stat. 3913, §688; amended Pub. L. 107–296, title XVII, §1704(a), Nov. 25, 2002, 116 Stat. 2314; Pub. L. 111–281, title II, §221(a)(8), Oct. 15, 2010, 124 Stat. 2920; renumbered §2947, Pub. L. 115–282, title I, §117(b), Dec. 4, 2018, 132 Stat. 4230.)

SUBTITLE III
COAST GUARD RESERVE AND AUXILIARY

SUBTITLE III—COAST GUARD RESERVE AND AUXILIARY

CHAPTER 37—COAST GUARD RESERVE

SUBCHAPTER I—ADMINISTRATION

SUBCHAPTER II—PERSONNEL

SUBCHAPTER I—ADMINISTRATION

§3701. ORGANIZATION

The Coast Guard Reserve is a component of the Coast Guard. It shall be organized, administered, trained, and supplied under the direction of the Commandant.

(Added Pub. L. 96–322, §1, Aug. 4, 1980, 94 Stat. 1003, §701; renumbered §3701, Pub. L. 115–282, title I, §118(b), Dec. 4, 2018, 132 Stat. 4233.)

§3702. AUTHORIZED STRENGTH

(a) The President shall prescribe the authorized strength of the Coast Guard Reserve if not otherwise prescribed by law.

(b) Subject to the authorized strength of the Coast Guard Reserve, the Secretary shall determine, at least annually, the authorized strength in numbers in each grade necessary to provide for mobilization requirements. Without the consent of the member concerned, a member of the Reserve may not be reduced in grade because of the Secretary's determination.

(c) The Secretary may vary the authorized end strength of the Coast Guard Selected Reserves for a fiscal year by a number equal to not more than 3 percent of such end strength upon a determination by the Secretary that varying such authorized end strength is in the national interest.

(d) The Commandant may increase the authorized end strength of the Coast Guard Selected Reserves by a number equal to not more than 2 percent of such authorized end strength upon a determination by the Commandant that such increase would enhance manning and readiness in essential units or in critical specialties or ratings.

(Added Pub. L. 96–322, §1, Aug. 4, 1980, 94 Stat. 1003, §702; renumbered §3702, Pub. L. 115–282, title I, §118(b), Dec. 4, 2018, 132 Stat. 4233; amended Pub. L. 117–263, div. K, title CXII, §11234, Dec. 23, 2022, 136 Stat. 4034.)

§3703. COAST GUARD RESERVE BOARDS

(a) The Secretary shall convene a Coast Guard Reserve Policy Board at least annually to consider, recommend, and report to the Secretary on Reserve policy matters. At least one-half of the members of the Board shall be Reserve officers.

(b) The Secretary may convene any other Reserve Board the Secretary considers necessary.

(Added Pub. L. 96–322, §1, Aug. 4, 1980, 94 Stat. 1003, §703; renumbered §3703, Pub. L. 115–282, title I, §118(b), Dec. 4, 2018, 132 Stat. 4233.)

§3704. GRADES AND RATINGS; MILITARY AUTHORITY

The grades and ratings in the Reserve, including cadets but not grades above rear admiral, are those prescribed by law or regulation for the Coast Guard. A member of the Reserve on active duty or inactive-duty training has the same authority, rights, and privileges in the performance of that duty as a member of the Regular Coast Guard of corresponding grade or rating.

(Added Pub. L. 96–322, §1, Aug. 4, 1980, 94 Stat. 1003, §704; renumbered §3704, Pub. L. 115–282, title I, §118(b), Dec. 4, 2018, 132 Stat. 4233.)

§3705. BENEFITS

(a) A member of the Reserve on active duty, on inactive-duty training, or engaged in authorized travel to or from that duty, is entitled to the same benefits as a member of the Navy Reserve of corresponding grade, rating, and length of service. In determining length of service for the purpose of this section, there shall be included all service for which credit is given by law to members of the Regular Coast Guard.

(b) Chapter 27 of this title applies to a member of the Reserve under the same conditions and limitations as it applies to a member of the Regular Coast Guard.

(c) A member of the Reserve who suffers sickness, disease, disability, or death is entitled to the same benefits as prescribed by law for a member of the Navy Reserve who suffers sickness, disease, disability, or death under similar conditions.

(d) A member of the Reserve on active duty or when retired for disability is entitled to the benefits of section 253(a) of title 42. A member of the Reserve when on active duty (other than for training) or when retired for disability is entitled to the benefits of chapter 55 of title 10.

(e) A member of the Reserve, except an enlisted member retiring on the basis of years of active service, is entitled to the same retirement rights, benefits, and privileges as prescribed by law for a member of the Navy Reserve, and wherever a law confers authority upon the Secretary of the Navy, similar authority is given to the Secretary to be exercised with respect to the Coast Guard when the Coast Guard is not operating as a service in the Navy. An enlisted member of the Reserve who retires on the basis of years of active service is entitled to the same retirement rights, benefits, and privileges as prescribed by law for an enlisted member of the Regular Coast Guard.

(f) A member of the Coast Guard Reserve not on active duty who is enrolled in an officer candidate program authorized by section 12209 of title 10 leading to a commission in the Coast Guard Reserve, and is a full-time student in an accredited college curriculum leading to a bachelor's degree may be paid a subsistence allowance for each month of the member's academic year at the same rate as that prescribed by section 209(a) of title 37.

(Added Pub. L. 96–322, §1, Aug. 4, 1980, 94 Stat. 1003, §705; amended Pub. L. 97–417, §1, Jan. 4, 1983, 96 Stat. 2085; Pub. L. 104–106, div. A, title XV, §1501(e)(1)(A), Feb. 10, 1996, 110 Stat. 501; Pub. L. 109–163, div. A, title V, §515(c), Jan. 6, 2006, 119 Stat. 3235; renumbered §3705 and amended Pub. L. 115–282, title I, §§118(b), 123(c)(3), Dec. 4, 2018, 132 Stat. 4233, 4241.)

§3706. TEMPORARY MEMBERS OF THE RESERVE; ELIGIBILITY AND COMPENSATION

A citizen of the United States, its territories, or possessions who is a member of the

Auxiliary, an officer or member of the crew of a motorboat or yacht placed at the disposal of the Coast Guard, or an individual (including a Government employee without pay other than the compensation of that individual's civilian position) who by reason of special training and experience is considered by the Commandant to be qualified for duty, may be enrolled by the Commandant as a temporary member of the Reserve, for duty under conditions the Commandant may prescribe, including part-time and intermittent active duty with or without pay, without regard to age. The Commandant is authorized to define the powers and duties of temporary members of the Reserve, and to confer upon them, appropriate to their qualifications and experience, the same grades and ratings as provided for members of the Reserve. When performing active duty with pay as authorized by this section, temporary members of the Reserve are entitled to receive the pay and allowances of their rank, grade, or rating.

(Added Pub. L. 96–322, §1, Aug. 4, 1980, 94 Stat. 1004, §706; renumbered §3706, Pub. L. 115–282, title I, §118(b), Dec. 4, 2018, 132 Stat. 4233; amended Pub. L. 116–283, div. G, title LVXXXV [LXXXV], §8505(a)(50), Jan. 1, 2021, 134 Stat. 4750.)

§3707. Temporary members of the Reserve; disability or death benefits

(a) If a temporary member of the Reserve is physically injured, or dies as a result of physical injury, and the injury is incurred incident to service while performing active duty, or engaged in authorized travel to or from that duty, the law authorizing compensation for employees of the United States suffering injuries while in the performance of their duties, applies, subject to this section. That law shall be administered by the Secretary of Labor to the same extent as if the member was a civil employee of the United States and was injured in the performance of that duty. For benefit computation, regardless of pay or pay status, the member is considered to have had monthly pay of the monthly equivalent of the minimum rate of basic pay in effect for grade GS–9 of the General Schedule on the date the injury is incurred.

(b) This section does not apply if the workmen's compensation law of a State, a territory, or another jurisdiction provides coverage because of a concurrent employment status of the temporary member. When the temporary member or a dependent is entitled to a benefit under this section and also to a concurrent benefit from the United States on account of the same disability or death, the temporary member or dependent, as appropriate, shall elect which benefit to receive.

(c) If a claim is filed under this section with the Secretary of Labor for benefits because of an alleged injury or death, the Secretary of Labor shall notify the Commandant who shall direct an investigation into the facts surrounding the alleged injury or death. The Commandant shall then certify to the Secretary of Labor whether or not the injured or deceased individual was a temporary member of the Reserve, the individual's military status, and whether or not the injury or death was incurred incident to military service.

(d) A temporary member of the Reserve, who incurs a physical disability or contracts sickness or disease while performing a duty to which the member has been assigned by competent authority, is entitled to the same hospital treatment afforded a member of the Regular Coast Guard.

(e) In administering section 8133 of title 5, for an individual covered by this section—

(1) the percentages applicable to payments under that section are—

(A) 45 percent under subsection (a)(2) of that section, where the member died fully or currently insured under title II of the Social Security Act (42 U.S.C. 401 et seq.), with no additional payments for a child or children so long as the widow or widower remains eligible for payments under that subsection;

(B) 20 percent under subsection (a)(3) of that section, for one child, and 10 percent additional for each additional child, not to exceed a total of 75 percent, where the member died fully or currently insured under title II of the Social Security Act; and

(C) 25 percent under subsection (a)(4) of that section, if one parent was wholly dependent for support upon the deceased member at the time of the member's death and the other was not dependent to any extent; 16 percent to each if both were wholly dependent; and if one was, or both were, partly dependent, a proportionate amount in the discretion of the Secretary of Labor;

(2) payments may not be made under subsection (a)(5) of that section; and

(3) the Secretary of Labor shall inform the Commissioner of Social Security whenever a claim is filed and eligibility for compensation is established under subsection (a)(2) or (a)(3) of section 8133 of title 5. The Commissioner of Social Security shall then certify to the Secretary of Labor whether or not the member concerned was fully or currently insured under title II of the Social Security Act at the time of the member's death.

(Added Pub. L. 96–322, §1, Aug. 4, 1980, 94 Stat. 1004, §707; amended Pub. L. 97–136, §8(a), Dec. 29, 1981, 95 Stat. 1706; Pub. L. 97–295, §2(21), Oct. 12, 1982, 96 Stat. 1303; Pub. L. 103–296, title I, §108(g), Aug. 15, 1994, 108 Stat. 1487; renumbered §3707, Pub. L. 115–282, title I, §118(b), Dec. 4, 2018, 132 Stat. 4233; Pub. L. 116–283, div. G, title LVXXXV [LXXXV], §8505(a)(51), Jan. 1, 2021, 134 Stat. 4750.)

§3708. TEMPORARY MEMBERS OF THE RESERVE; CERTIFICATE OF HONORABLE SERVICE

In recognition of the service of temporary members of the Reserve, the Secretary may upon request issue an appropriate certificate of honorable service in lieu of a certificate of disenrollment issued to any individual following disenrollment under honorable conditions from service as a temporary member. Issuance of a certificate of honorable service to any individual under this section does not entitle that individual to any rights, privileges, or benefits under any law of the United States.

(Added Pub. L. 96–322, §1, Aug. 4, 1980, 94 Stat. 1005, §708; renumbered §3708, Pub. L. 115–282, title I, §118(b), Dec. 4, 2018, 132 Stat. 4233; amended Pub. L. 116–283, div. G, title LVXXXV [LXXXV], §8505(a)(52), Jan. 1, 2021, 134 Stat. 4750.)

§3709. RESERVE STUDENT AVIATION PILOTS; RESERVE AVIATION PILOTS; APPOINTMENTS IN COMMISSIONED GRADE

(a) Under regulations prescribed by the Secretary an enlisted member of the Reserve may be designated as a student aviation pilot.

(b) A member who is not a qualified aviator may not be designated as a student aviation pilot unless the member agrees in writing to serve on active duty for a period of two years after successful completion of flight training, unless sooner released. A student aviation pilot may be released from active duty or discharged at any time as provided for in the regulations prescribed by the Secretary.

(c) A student aviation pilot who is a qualified civilian aviator may be given a brief refresher course in flight training.

(d) A student aviation pilot undergoing flight training is entitled to have uniforms and equipment provided at Government expense.

(e) Under regulations prescribed by the Secretary, a student aviation pilot may be designated an aviation pilot upon the successful completion of flight training.

(f) In time of peace, an aviation pilot obligated under subsection (b) to serve on active duty for two years may serve for an additional period of not more than two years.

(g) An aviation pilot may be released from active duty or discharged at any time as provided for in the regulations prescribed by the Secretary.

(h) If qualified under regulations prescribed by the Secretary, an aviation pilot may be appointed as an ensign in the Reserve.

(Added Pub. L. 96–322, §1, Aug. 4, 1980, 94 Stat. 1005, §709; renumbered §3709, Pub. L. 115–282, title I, §118(b), Dec. 4, 2018, 132 Stat. 4233.)

§3710. Reserve student pre-commissioning assistance program

(a) The Secretary may provide financial assistance to an eligible enlisted member of the Coast Guard Reserve, not on active duty, for expenses of the member while the member is pursuing on a full-time basis at an institution of higher education a program of education approved by the Secretary that leads to—

(1) a baccalaureate degree in not more than 5 academic years; or

(2) a post-baccalaureate degree.

(b)(1) To be eligible for financial assistance under this section, an enlisted member of the Coast Guard Reserve shall—

(A) be enrolled on a full-time basis in a program of education referred to in subsection (a) at any institution of higher education; and

(B) enter into a written agreement with the Coast Guard described in paragraph (2).

(2) A written agreement referred to in paragraph (1)(B) is an agreement between the member and the Secretary in which the member agrees—

(A) to accept an appointment as a commissioned officer in the Coast Guard Reserve, if tendered;

(B) to serve on active duty for up to five years; and

(C) under such terms and conditions as shall be prescribed by the Secretary, to serve in the Coast Guard Reserve until the eighth anniversary of the date of the appointment.

(c) Expenses for which financial assistance may be provided under this section are the following:

(1) Tuition and fees charged by the institution of higher education involved.

(2) The cost of books.

(3) In the case of a program of education leading to a baccalaureate degree, laboratory expenses.

(4) Such other expenses as are deemed appropriate by the Secretary.

(d) The amount of financial assistance provided to a member under this section shall be prescribed by the Secretary, but may not exceed $25,000 for any academic year.

(e) Financial assistance may be provided to a member under this section for up to 5 consecutive academic years.

(f) A member who receives financial assistance under this section may be ordered to active duty in the Coast Guard Reserve by the Secretary to serve in a designated enlisted grade for such period as the Secretary prescribes, but not more than 4 years, if the member—

(1) completes the academic requirements of the program and refuses to accept an appointment as a commissioned officer in the Coast Guard Reserve when offered;

(2) fails to complete the academic requirements of the institution of higher education involved; or

(3) fails to maintain eligibility for an original appointment as a commissioned officer.

(g)(1) If a member requests to be released from the program and the request is accepted by the Secretary, or if the member fails because of misconduct to complete the period of active duty specified, or if the member fails to fulfill any term or condition of the written agreement required to be eligible for financial assistance under this section, the financial assistance shall be terminated. The Secretary may request the member to reimburse the United States in an amount that bears the same ratio to the total costs of the education provided to that member as the unserved portion of active duty bears to the total period of active duty the member agreed to serve. The Secretary shall have the option to order such reimbursement without first ordering the member to active duty. An obligation to reimburse the United States imposed under this paragraph is a debt owed to the United States.

(2) The Secretary may waive the service obligated under subsection (f) of a member who becomes unqualified to serve on active duty due to a circumstance not within the control of that member or who is not physically qualified for appointment and who is determined to be unqualified for service as an enlisted member of the Coast Guard Reserve due to a physical or medical condition that was not the result of the member's own misconduct or grossly negligent conduct.

(3) A discharge in bankruptcy under title 11 that is entered less than 5 years after the termination of a written agreement entered into under subsection (b) does not discharge the individual signing the agreement from a debt arising under such agreement or under paragraph (1).

(h) As used in this section, the term "institution of higher education" has the meaning given that term in section 101 of the Higher Education Act of 1965 (20 U.S.C. 1001).

(Added Pub. L. 107–295, title IV, §413(a), Nov. 25, 2002, 116 Stat. 2119, §709a; renumbered §3710, Pub. L. 115–282, title I, §118(b), Dec. 4, 2018, 132 Stat. 4233.)

§3711. APPOINTMENT OR WARTIME PROMOTION; RETENTION OF GRADE UPON RELEASE FROM ACTIVE DUTY

(a) A member of the Reserve on active duty, who is appointed or promoted under section 2104 or 2125 of this title, is entitled upon release from that duty to the highest grade satisfactorily held by reason of that appointment or promotion. The Secretary shall determine the highest grade satisfactorily held.

(b) Unless otherwise entitled to a higher grade, a member recalled to active duty shall be recalled in the grade in which released under subsection (a).

(Added Pub. L. 96–322, §1, Aug. 4, 1980, 94 Stat. 1006, §710; renumbered §3711 and amended Pub. L. 115–282, title I, §§118(b), 123(b)(2), Dec. 4, 2018, 132 Stat. 4233, 4240.)

§3712. EXCLUSIVENESS OF SERVICE

No member of the Reserve, other than a temporary member, may be a member of another military organization. A temporary member of the Reserve who is a member of another military component shall, if ordered to active duty therein, be disenrolled as a temporary member of the Reserve.

(Added Pub. L. 96–322, §1, Aug. 4, 1980, 94 Stat. 1006, §711; amended Pub. L. 97–136, §6(c)(1), (2), Dec. 29, 1981, 95 Stat. 1706; renumbered §3712, Pub. L. 115–282, title I, §118(b), Dec. 4, 2018, 132 Stat. 4233.)

§3713. ACTIVE DUTY FOR EMERGENCY AUGMENTATION OF REGULAR FORCES

(a) Notwithstanding another law, and for the emergency augmentation of the Regular Coast Guard forces during a, or to aid in prevention of an imminent, serious natural or manmade disaster, accident, catastrophe, act of terrorism (as defined in section 2 of the Homeland Security Act of 2002 (6 U.S.C. 101)), or transportation security incident as defined in section 70101 of title 46, the Secretary may, without the consent of the member affected, order to active duty of not more than 120 days in any 2-year period an organized training unit of the Coast Guard Ready Reserve, a member thereof, or a member not assigned to a unit organized to serve as a unit.

(b) Under the circumstances of the domestic emergency involved, a reasonable time shall be allowed between the date when a Reserve member ordered to active duty under this section is alerted for that duty and the date when the member is required to enter upon that duty. Unless the Secretary determines that the nature of the domestic emergency does not allow it, this period shall be at least two days.

(c) Active duty served under this section—

(1) satisfies on a day-for-day basis all or a part of the annual active duty for training requirement of section 10147 of title 10;

(2) does not satisfy any part of the active duty obligation of a member whose statutory Reserve obligation is not already terminated; and

(3) entitles a member while engaged therein, or while engaged in authorized travel to or from that duty, to all rights and benefits, including pay and allowances and time creditable for pay and retirement purposes, to which the member would be entitled while performing other active duty.

(d) Reserve members ordered to active duty under this section shall not be counted in computing authorized strength of members on active duty or members in grade under this title or under any other law.

(e) For purposes of calculating the duration of active duty allowed pursuant to subsection (a), each period of active duty shall begin on the first day that a member reports to active duty, including for purposes of training.

(Added Pub. L. 96–322, §1, Aug. 4, 1980, 94 Stat. 1006, §712; amended Pub. L. 102–241, §13, Dec. 19, 1991, 105 Stat. 2213; Pub. L. 103–337, div. A, title XVI, §1677(b)(3), Oct. 5, 1994, 108 Stat. 3020; Pub. L. 104–324, title II, §204, Oct. 19, 1996, 110 Stat. 3907; Pub. L. 109–241, title II, §206, July 11, 2006, 120 Stat. 521; Pub. L. 110–53, title V, §502(c)(2), Aug. 3, 2007, 121 Stat. 311; Pub. L. 113–281, title II, §219, Dec. 18, 2014, 128 Stat. 3037; Pub. L. 114–328, div. A, title XIX, §1913(b)(3), Dec. 23, 2016, 130 Stat. 2687; renumbered §3713, Pub. L. 115–282, title I, §118(b), Dec. 4, 2018, 132 Stat. 4233.)

§3714. Enlistment of members engaged in schooling

The initial period of active duty for training required by section 12103(d) of title 10, may be divided into two successive annual periods of not less than six weeks each, to permit the enlistment of a Reserve member without interrupting any full-time schooling in which the member is engaged.

(Added Pub. L. 96–322, §1, Aug. 4, 1980, 94 Stat. 1007, §713; amended Pub. L. 103–337, div. A, title XVI, §1677(b)(4), Oct. 5, 1994, 108 Stat. 3020; renumbered §3714, Pub. L. 115–282, title I, §118(b), Dec. 4, 2018, 132 Stat. 4233.)

SUBCHAPTER II—PERSONNEL

§3731. Definitions

As used in this subchapter—

(1) "Reserve officer" means a commissioned officer in the Reserve, except an officer excluded by section 3732 of this title or a commissioned warrant officer; and

(2) "discharged" means released from an appointment as a Reserve officer.

(Added Pub. L. 96–322, §1, Aug. 4, 1980, 94 Stat. 1007, §720; renumbered §3731 and amended Pub. L. 115–282, title I, §§118(b), 123(b)(2), Dec. 4, 2018, 132 Stat. 4233, 4240.)

§3732. Applicability of this subchapter

This subchapter applies only to the Reserve; except that it does not apply to a temporary member of the Reserve.

(Added Pub. L. 96–322, §1, Aug. 4, 1980, 94 Stat. 1007, §721; renumbered §3732, Pub. L. 115–282, title I, §118(b), Dec. 4, 2018, 132 Stat. 4233.)

§3733. Suspension of this subchapter in time of war or national emergency

In time of war or national emergency declared by Congress, the President may suspend the operation of this subchapter or any part hereof. If this subchapter or any part hereof is suspended by the President, prior to placing the suspended provision in operation, the President shall by regulation, in so far as practicable, adjust the grades of Reserve officers in the same manner as adjustments in grade are made for Regular officers.

(Added Pub. L. 96–322, §1, Aug. 4, 1980, 94 Stat. 1007, §722; renumbered §3733, Pub. L. 115–282, title I, §118(b), Dec. 4, 2018, 132 Stat. 4233.)

§3734. Effect of this subchapter on retirement and retired pay

Except as provided in subsection 3757(b) [1] of this title, nothing in this subchapter authorizes the retirement of a Reserve officer or the payment of retired, retainer, or severance pay to a Reserve officer; or affects in any manner the law relating to the retirement of, or the granting of retired or retainer pay or other benefits to a Reserve officer.

(Added Pub. L. 96–322, §1, Aug. 4, 1980, 94 Stat. 1007, §723; renumbered §3734 and amended Pub. L. 115–282, title I, §§118(b), 123(b)(2), Dec. 4, 2018, 132 Stat. 4233, 4240.)

[1] So in original. Probably should be "section 3757(b)".

§3735. Authorized number of officers

(a) The authorized number of officers in the Reserve in an active status is 5,000. Reserve officers on an active-duty list shall not be counted as part of the authorized number of officers in the Reserve. The actual number of Reserve officers in an active status at any time shall not exceed the authorized number unless the Secretary determines that a greater number is necessary for planned mobilization requirements, or unless the excess results directly from the operation of law.

(b)(1) The Secretary shall make, at least once each year, a computation to determine the number of Reserve officers in an active status authorized to be serving in each grade. The number in each grade shall be computed by applying the applicable percentage to the total number of such officers serving in an active status on the date the computation is made. The number of Reserve officers in an active status below the grade of rear admiral (lower half) shall be distributed by pay grade so as not to exceed percentages of commissioned officers authorized by section 2103(b) of this title. When the actual number of Reserve officers in an active status in a particular pay grade is less than the maximum percentage authorized, the difference may be applied to the number in the next lower grade. A Reserve officer may not be reduced in rank or grade solely because of a reduction in an authorized number as provided for in this subsection, or because an excess results directly from the operation of law.

(2) The authorized number of Reserve Officers in an active status not on active duty in the grades of rear admiral (lower half) and rear admiral is a total of two. However, the Secretary of the department in which the Coast Guard is operating may authorize an additional number of Reserve officers not on active duty in the grades of rear admiral (lower half) and rear admiral as necessary in order to meet planned mobilization requirements.

(c) DEFERRAL OF LIMITATION.—If at the end of any fiscal year there is in effect a declaration of war or national emergency, the President may defer the effectiveness of any end-strength limitation with respect to that fiscal year prescribed by law for any military or civilian component of the Coast Guard Reserve, for a period not to exceed 6 months after the end of the war or termination of the national emergency.

(Added Pub. L. 96–322, §1, Aug. 4, 1980, 94 Stat. 1007, §724; amended Pub. L. 97–417, §2(12), Jan. 4, 1983, 96 Stat. 2086; Pub. L. 98–557, §25(a)(4), Oct. 30, 1984, 98 Stat. 2872; Pub. L. 99–145, title V, §514(c)(1), Nov. 8, 1985, 99 Stat. 629; Pub. L. 107–295, title I, §105(b), Nov. 25, 2002, 116 Stat. 2085; Pub. L. 109–241, title II, §207, July 11, 2006, 120 Stat. 521; renumbered §3735 and amended Pub. L. 115–282, title I, §§118(b), 123(b)(2), Dec. 4, 2018, 132 Stat. 4233, 4240.)

§3736. PRECEDENCE

(a) Reserve officers rank and take precedence in their respective grades among themselves and with officers of the same grade on the active duty promotion list and the permanent commissioned teaching staff in accordance with their dates of rank. When Reserve officers and officers on the active duty promotion list or the permanent commissioned teaching staff have the same date of rank in a grade, they take precedence as determined by the Secretary.

(b) Notwithstanding any other law, a Reserve officer shall not lose precedence when transferred to or from the active duty promotion list, nor shall that officer's date of rank be changed due to the transfer.

(c) A Reserve officer shall, when on the active duty promotion list, be promoted in the same manner as any other officer on the active duty promotion list regardless of the length of active duty service of the Reserve officer.

(d) Notwithstanding any other law, a Reserve officer shall not lose precedence by reason of promotion to the grade of rear admiral or rear admiral (lower half), if the promotion is determined in accordance with a running mate system.

(e) The Secretary shall adjust the date of rank of a Reserve officer so that no changes of precedence occur.

(Added Pub. L. 96–322, §1, Aug. 4, 1980, 94 Stat. 1008, §725; amended Pub. L. 108–293, title II, §220(a), Aug. 9, 2004, 118 Stat. 1039; renumbered §3736, Pub. L. 115–282, title I, §118(b), Dec. 4, 2018, 132 Stat. 4233.)

§3737. Running mates

(a) The Secretary shall assign a running mate to each Reserve officer in an active status not on the active duty promotion list. The officer initially assigned as a running mate under this section shall be that officer on the active duty promotion list of the same grade who is next senior in precedence to the Reserve officer concerned. An officer who has twice failed of selection or who has been considered but has not been recommended for continuation under section 2150 of this title shall not be assigned as a running mate under this section.

(b) A Reserve officer in an active status not on the active duty promotion list shall be assigned a new running mate as follows:

(1) If a previously assigned running mate is promoted from below the promotion zone, is removed from the active duty promotion list, suffers a loss of numbers, fails of selection, fails to qualify for promotion, or declines an appointment after being selected for promotion, the new running mate shall be that officer on the active duty promotion list, of the same grade, who is next senior to the previous running mate and who is, or may become, eligible for consideration for promotion. If the previous running mate was on a list of selectees for promotion, the new running mate shall be that officer on the active duty promotion list, of the same grade, who is on a list of selectees for promotion and who is next senior to the previous running mate.

(2) If a Reserve officer suffers a loss of numbers, the new running mate shall be that officer on the active duty promotion list who, after the loss of numbers has been effected, is the running mate of the Reserve officer next senior to the Reserve officer concerned.

(3) If a Reserve officer is considered for promotion and fails of selection, fails to qualify for promotion, declines an appointment after being selected for promotion, or has his or her name removed from a list of selectees for promotion, and that officer's running mate is promoted, the new running mate shall be that officer on the active duty promotion list, of the same grade, who, at the time the previous running mate was considered for promotion, was next senior to the previous running mate, was eligible for consideration for promotion, and whose name was not included on a list of selectees for promotion.

(4) In a situation not expressly covered by this subsection, the Secretary may assign a new running mate as necessary to effect the intent of this section that inequitable changes of precedence do not occur.

(c) A Reserve officer on the active duty promotion list shall, to the extent practicable and consistent with the limitations imposed by this section, be assigned as the running mate of all Reserve officers junior to the officer, who are in an active status not on the active duty promotion list, and who had a running mate in common with the officer just prior to the time the officer was placed on the active duty promotion list.

(d) The Secretary may adjust, as necessary, the date of rank of a Reserve officer not on active duty so that the date will correspond with that of the running mate assigned to the officer in accordance with this section. If an overpayment of pay or allowances results from adjusting the date of rank, the overpayment is not subject to recoupment.

(Added Pub. L. 96–322, §1, Aug. 4, 1980, 94 Stat. 1008, §726; renumbered §3737 and amended Pub. L. 115–282, title I, §§118(b), 123(b)(2), Dec. 4, 2018, 132 Stat. 4233, 4240.)

§3738. CONSTRUCTIVE CREDIT UPON INITIAL APPOINTMENT

Under regulations prescribed by the Secretary, an individual, appointed as a Reserve officer, may be assigned a date of rank and precedence which reflects that individual's experience, education, or other qualifications. For the purpose of this subchapter only, an individual appointed for the purpose of assignment or designation as a judge advocate in the Reserve shall be credited with a minimum of one year service in an active status. An individual holding a doctor of philosophy, or a comparable degree, in medicine or in a science allied to medicine as determined by the Secretary, may be credited with a minimum of three years service in an active status if appointed for an assignment comparable to that of an officer in the Navy Medical Department.

(Added Pub. L. 96–322, §1, Aug. 4, 1980, 94 Stat. 1009, §727; amended Pub. L. 108–293, title II, §208, Aug. 9, 2004, 118 Stat. 1035; Pub. L. 109–241, title II, §218(b)(1), July 11, 2006, 120 Stat. 526; renumbered §3738, Pub. L. 115–282, title I, §118(b), Dec. 4, 2018, 132 Stat. 4233; Pub. L. 116–283, div. G, title LVXXXV [LXXXV], §8505(a)(53), Jan. 1, 2021, 134 Stat. 4750.)

§3738A. DIRECT COMMISSIONING AUTHORITY FOR INDIVIDUALS WITH CRITICAL SKILLS

An individual with critical skills that the Commandant considers necessary for the Coast Guard to complete its missions who is not currently serving as an officer in the Coast Guard may be commissioned into the Coast Guard at a grade up to and including commander.

(Added Pub. L. 116–283, div. G, title LVXXXII [LXXXII], §8205(a), Jan. 1, 2021, 134 Stat. 4648.)

§3739. PROMOTION OF RESERVE OFFICERS ON ACTIVE DUTY

(a) A Reserve officer on active duty, other than for training, duty on a board, or duty of a limited or temporary nature if assigned to active duty from an inactive duty status, shall not be eligible for consideration for promotion under this subchapter; but shall be considered for promotion under chapter 21 of this title. If promoted while serving on active duty the officer shall be considered as having been promoted under this subchapter and shall be an extra number in the grade to which promoted for the purpose of grade distribution as prescribed in this subchapter. Upon release from active duty the officer shall be included in the grade distribution authorized by this subchapter.

(b) Notwithstanding subsection (a) of this section, a Reserve officer who has been selected for promotion to the next higher grade under this subchapter at the time the officer reports for active duty, shall be promoted to that grade under chapter 21 of this title.

(c) A Reserve officer who, at the time the officer is released from active duty, has been selected for promotion to the next higher grade under chapter 21 of this title, shall be promoted to that grade as though selected under this subchapter.

(d) A failure of selection for promotion to the next higher grade occurring under this subchapter or under chapter 21 of this title shall count for all purposes.

(Added Pub. L. 96–322, §1, Aug. 4, 1980, 94 Stat. 1009, §728; renumbered §3739 and amended Pub. L. 115–282, title I, §§118(b), 123(c)(2)(B), Dec. 4, 2018, 132 Stat. 4233, 4241.)

§3740. PROMOTION; RECOMMENDATIONS OF SELECTION BOARDS

(a) Except as otherwise provided by law, a Reserve officer shall only be promoted pursuant to the recommendation of a selection board.

(b) The Secretary shall convene selection boards from time to time to recommend Reserve officers for promotion to the next higher grade. A board may be convened to consider officers in one or more grades.

(c) A selection board shall, from among the names of those eligible Reserve officers submitted to it, recommend for promotion to the next higher grade:

(1) those officers serving in the grade of lieutenant (junior grade) or above whom it considers to be best qualified; and

(2) those officers serving in the grade of ensign whom it considers to be fully qualified.

(d)(1) Before convening a selection board to recommend Reserve officers for promotion, the Secretary shall establish a promotion zone for officers serving in each grade to be considered by the board. The Secretary shall determine the number of officers in the promotion zone for officers serving in any grade from among officers who are eligible for promotion in that grade.

(2)(A) Before convening a selection board to recommend Reserve officers for promotion to a grade (other than the grade of lieutenant (junior grade)), the Secretary shall determine the maximum number of officers in that grade that the board may recommend for promotion.

(B) The Secretary shall make the determination under subparagraph (A) of the maximum number that may be recommended with a view to having in an active status a sufficient number of Reserve officers in each grade to meet the needs of the Coast Guard for Reserve officers in an active status.

(C) In order to make the determination under subparagraph (B), the Secretary shall determine the following:

(i) The number of positions needed to accomplish mission objectives that require officers in the grade to which the board will recommend officers for promotion.

(ii) The estimated number of officers needed to fill vacancies in such positions during the period in which it is anticipated that officers selected for promotion will be promoted.

(iii) The number of officers authorized by the Secretary to serve in an active status in the grade under consideration.

(iv) Any statutory limitation on the number of officers in any grade authorized to be in an active status.

(3)(A) The Secretary may, when the needs of the Coast Guard require, authorize the consideration of officers in a grade above lieutenant (junior grade) for promotion to the next higher grade from below the promotion zone.

(B) When selection from below the promotion zone is authorized, the Secretary shall establish the number of officers that may be recommended for promotion from below the promotion zone. That number may not exceed the number equal to 10 percent of the maximum number of officers that the board is authorized to recommend for promotion, except that the Secretary may authorize a greater number, not to exceed 15 percent of the total number of officers that the board is authorized to recommend for promotion, if the Secretary determines that the needs of the Coast Guard so require. If the maximum number determined under this subparagraph is less than one, the board may recommend one officer for promotion from below the promotion zone.

(C) The number of officers recommended for promotion from below the promotion zone does not increase the maximum number of officers that the board is authorized to recommend for promotion under paragraph (2).

(e) The law and regulations relating to the selection for promotion of a commissioned officer of the Regular Coast Guard to the grades of rear admiral (lower half) and rear admiral apply to a Reserve officer, except that to be eligible for consideration for promotion to the grade of rear admiral (lower half) an officer shall have completed at least ten years commissioned service, of which the last five years shall have been served in the Coast Guard Reserve.

(f) The provisions of section 2117 of this title apply to boards convened under this section. The Secretary shall determine the procedure to be used by a selection board.

(g) The report of a selection board shall be submitted to the Secretary for review and transmission to the President for approval. When an officer recommended by a board for promotion is not acceptable to the President, the President may remove the name of that officer from the report of the board.

(h) The recommendations of a selection board, as approved by the President, constitute a list of selectees from which the promotions of Reserve officers shall be made. An officer on a list of selectees remains thereon until promoted unless removed by the President under section 3749 of this title. If an existing list of selectees has not been exhausted by the time a later list has been approved, all officers remaining on the older list shall be tendered appointments prior to those on the later list.

(i) A Reserve officer whose name is on a list of selectees for promotion shall, unless that officer's promotion is lawfully withheld, be tendered an appointment in the next higher grade on the date a vacancy occurs, or as soon thereafter as practicable in the grade to which the officer was selected for promotion or, if promotion was determined in accordance with a running mate system, at the same time, or as soon thereafter as practicable, as that officer's running mate is tendered a similar appointment.

(Added Pub. L. 96–322, §1, Aug. 4, 1980, 94 Stat. 1010, §729; amended Pub. L. 97–417, §2(13), Jan. 4, 1983, 96 Stat. 2086; Pub. L. 99–145, title V, §514(c)(1), Nov. 8, 1985, 99 Stat. 629; Pub. L. 106–398, §1 [[div. A], title V, §502(a)], Oct. 30, 2000, 114 Stat. 1654, 1654A–99; Pub. L. 107–295, title IV, §411(a), Nov.

25, 2002, 116 Stat. 2118; renumbered §3740 and amended Pub. L. 115–282, title I, §§118(b), 123(b)(2), Dec. 4, 2018, 132 Stat. 4233, 4240.)

§3741. SELECTION BOARDS; APPOINTMENT

(a) A selection board shall (1) be appointed and convened by the Secretary; (2) consist of at least 50 per centum Reserve officer membership, except in the case of a flag officer selection board where, to the extent practicable, it shall consist of at least 50 per centum Reserve officer membership; (3) consist only of members, Reserve or Regular, senior in grade to any officer being considered by that board; and (4) be composed of not less than five members, which number constitutes a quorum.

(b) A selection board serves for the length of time prescribed by the Secretary, but no board may serve longer than one year. No officer may serve on two consecutive selection boards for the same grade when the second of those boards considers an officer who was considered, but not recommended for promotion, by the first selection board.

(c) Each member of a selection board shall swear that he will, without prejudice or partiality, and having in view both the special fitness required of officers and the efficiency of the Coast Guard, perform the duties imposed upon him. Not less than a majority of the total membership of a selection board shall concur in each recommendation made by the board.

(d) An officer eligible for consideration for promotion by a selection board may forward, through official channels, a written communication inviting the attention of the board to any matter in the officer's record in the armed forces that, in the opinion of the officer concerned, is important to the board's consideration. A communication forwarded under this subsection shall arrive in time to allow delivery to the board prior to its convening, and may not criticize or reflect upon the character, conduct, or motive of any officer.

(Added Pub. L. 96–322, §1, Aug. 4, 1980, 94 Stat. 1011, §730; renumbered §3741, Pub. L. 115–282, title I, §118(b), Dec. 4, 2018, 132 Stat. 4233.)

§3742. ESTABLISHMENT OF PROMOTION ZONES UNDER RUNNING MATE SYSTEM

(a) AUTHORITY TO USE RUNNING MATE SYSTEM.—The Secretary may by regulation implement section 3740(d)(1) of this title by requiring that the promotion zone for consideration of Reserve officers in an active status for promotion to the next higher grade be determined in accordance with a running mate system as provided in subsection (b).

(b) CONSIDERATION FOR PROMOTION.—If promotion zones are determined as authorized under subsection (a), a Reserve officer shall, subject to the eligibility requirements of this subchapter, be placed in a promotion zone when that officer's running mate is placed in a promotion zone and shall, in accordance with the provisions of this subchapter, be considered for promotion at approximately the same time as that officer's running mate or as soon thereafter as practicable, or in the event that promotion is not determined in accordance with a running mate system, then a Reserve officer becomes eligible for consideration for promotion to the next higher grade at the beginning of the promotion year in which he or she completes the following amount of service computed from the date of rank in the grade in which he or she is serving:

(1) two years in the grade of lieutenant (junior grade);

(2) three years in the grade of lieutenant;

(3) four years in the grade of lieutenant commander;

(4) four years in the grade of commander; and

(5) three years in the grade of captain.

(c) CONSIDERATION OF OFFICERS BELOW THE ZONE.—If the Secretary authorizes the selection of officers for promotion from below the promotion zone in accordance with section 3740(d)(3) of this title, the number of officers to be considered from below the zone may be established through the application of the running mate system under this subchapter or otherwise as the Secretary determines to be appropriate to meet the needs of the Coast Guard.

(Added Pub. L. 96–322, §1, Aug. 4, 1980, 94 Stat. 1011, §731; amended Pub. L. 106–398, §1 [[div. A], title V, §502(b)(1), (2)(A)], Oct. 30, 2000, 114 Stat. 1654, 1654A–100; Pub. L. 107–295, title IV, §411(b), Nov. 25, 2002, 116 Stat. 2118; renumbered §3742 and amended Pub. L. 115–282, title I, §§118(b), 123(b)(2), Dec. 4, 2018, 132 Stat. 4233, 4240.)

§3743. ELIGIBILITY FOR PROMOTION

(a) IN GENERAL.—Except as provided in subsection (b), a Reserve officer is eligible for consideration for promotion and for promotion under this subchapter if that officer is in an active status.

(b) EXCEPTION.—A Reserve officer who has been considered but not recommended for retention in an active status by a board convened under subsection 3752(a) [1] of this title is not eligible for consideration for promotion.

(c) REQUEST FOR EXCLUSION.—

(1) IN GENERAL.—The Commandant may provide that an officer may, upon the officer's request and with the approval of the Commandant, be excluded from consideration by a selection board convened under section 3740(b) of this title to consider officers for promotion to the next higher grade.

(2) APPROVAL OF REQUEST.—The Commandant shall approve a request under paragraph (1) only if—

(A) the basis for the request is to allow an officer to complete a broadening assignment, advanced education, another assignment of significant value to the Coast Guard, a career progression requirement delayed by the assignment or education, or a qualifying personal or professional circumstance, as determined by the Commandant;

(B) the Commandant determines the exclusion from consideration is in the best interest of the Coast Guard; and

(C) the officer has not previously failed of selection for promotion to the grade for which the officer requests the exclusion from consideration.

(Added Pub. L. 96–322, §1, Aug. 4, 1980, 94 Stat. 1011, §732; renumbered §3743 and amended Pub. L. 115–282, title I, §§118(b), 123(b)(2), Dec. 4, 2018, 132 Stat. 4233, 4240; Pub. L. 116–283, div. G, title LVXXXII [LXXXII], §8202(b), Jan. 1, 2021, 134 Stat. 4643.)

§3744. RECOMMENDATION FOR PROMOTION OF AN OFFICER PREVIOUSLY REMOVED FROM AN ACTIVE STATUS

A Reserve officer recommended for promotion by a selection board but not promoted because of removal from an active status shall be reconsidered by a selection board after returning to an active status and if selected shall be placed on a recommended list of selectees for promotion. A Reserve officer to whom this section applies is not considered to have failed of selection when eliminated from a list of selectees for promotion solely as a result of being removed from an active status.

(Added Pub. L. 96–322, §1, Aug. 4, 1980, 94 Stat. 1012, §733; renumbered §3744, Pub. L. 115–282, title I, §118(b), Dec. 4, 2018, 132 Stat. 4233.)

§3745. QUALIFICATIONS FOR PROMOTION

(a) A Reserve officer shall not be promoted to a higher grade unless the officer has been found to be physically qualified and the character of the officer's service subsequent to the convening of the selection board which recommended the officer for promotion has been verified as satisfactory.

(b) Subsection (a) of this section does not exclude from promotion a Reserve officer physically disqualified by a medical board for duty at sea or in the field, if the disqualification results from wounds received in the line of duty, and those wounds do not incapacitate the officer for other duties in the grade to which the officer is to be promoted.

(Added Pub. L. 96–322, §1, Aug. 4, 1980, 94 Stat. 1012, §734; renumbered §3745, Pub. L. 115–282, title I, §118(b), Dec. 4, 2018, 132 Stat. 4233.)

§3746. PROMOTION; ACCEPTANCE; OATH OF OFFICE

(a) A Reserve officer who has been appointed under this subchapter is considered to have accepted the appointment unless delivery thereof cannot be effected.

(b) A Reserve officer who has served continuously since taking the oath of office prescribed in section 3331 of title 5, is not required to take a new oath of office upon appointment in a higher grade.

(Added Pub. L. 96–322, §1, Aug. 4, 1980, 94 Stat. 1012, §735; renumbered §3746, Pub. L. 115–282, title I, §118(b), Dec. 4, 2018, 132 Stat. 4233.)

§3747. DATE OF RANK UPON PROMOTION; ENTITLEMENT TO PAY

(a) When a Reserve officer is promoted to the next higher grade under this subchapter, the date of rank shall be the date of appointment in that grade, unless the promotion was determined in accordance with a running mate system, in which event the same date of rank shall be assigned as that assigned to the officer's running mate. A Reserve officer so promoted shall be allowed the pay and allowances of the higher grade for duty performed from the date of the officer's appointment thereto.

(b) Notwithstanding any other provision of law and subject to subsection (c), if promotion of an inactive duty promotion list officer to the grade of rear admiral or rear admiral (lower half) is determined in accordance with a running mate system, a reserve officer, if acceptable to the President and the Senate, shall be promoted to the next higher grade no later than the date the officer's running mate is promoted.

(c) For the purposes of this section, the date of appointment shall be that date when promotion authority is exercised by the Secretary. However, the Secretary may adjust the date of appointment—

(1) if a delay in the finding required under section 3745(a) of this title is beyond the control of the officer and the officer is otherwise qualified for promotion; or

(2) for any other reason that equity requires.

(Added Pub. L. 96–322, §1, Aug. 4, 1980, 94 Stat. 1012, §736; amended Pub. L. 97–417, §2(14), Jan. 4, 1983, 96 Stat. 2086; Pub. L. 99–145, title V, §514(c)(1), Nov. 8, 1985, 99 Stat. 629; Pub. L. 101–225, title II, §203(4), Dec. 12, 1989, 103 Stat. 1911; Pub. L. 107–295, title IV, §411(c), Nov. 25, 2002, 116 Stat. 2118; Pub. L. 108–293, title II, §220(b), (c), Aug. 9, 2004, 118 Stat. 1039; renumbered §3747 and amended Pub. L. 115–282, title I, §§118(b), 123(b)(2), Dec. 4, 2018, 132 Stat. 4233, 4240.)

§3748. TYPE OF PROMOTION; TEMPORARY

Notwithstanding any other law, if a Reserve officer is promoted when the officer's running mate is promoted and the promotion of the running mate is on a temporary basis, the promotion of the Reserve officer is also on a temporary basis. If subsequently the running mate is reverted to a lower grade, other than for reasons of discipline, incompetence, or at the running mate's request, the Reserve officer shall likewise revert to the same lower grade with corresponding precedence.

(Added Pub. L. 96–322, §1, Aug. 4, 1980, 94 Stat. 1012, §737; renumbered §3748, Pub. L. 115–282, title I, §118(b), Dec. 4, 2018, 132 Stat. 4233.)

§3749. EFFECT OF REMOVAL BY THE PRESIDENT OR FAILURE OF CONSENT OF THE SENATE

(a) The President may, for cause, remove the name of any officer from a list of selectees established under section 3740 of this title.

(b) If the Senate, where required, does not consent to the appointment of an officer whose name is on a list of selectees established under section 3740 of this title, that officer's name shall be removed from the list.

(c) An officer whose name is removed from a list of selectees under subsection (a) or (b) continues to be eligible for consideration for promotion. If selected for promotion by the next selection board and promoted, that officer shall be assigned the date of rank and precedence that would have been assigned if the officer's name had not been previously removed. However, if the officer is not selected by the next selection board, or if the officer's name is again removed from the list of selectees, the officer shall be considered for all purposes as having twice failed of selection for promotion.

(Added Pub. L. 96–322, §1, Aug. 4, 1980, 94 Stat. 1013, §738; renumbered §3749 and amended Pub. L. 115–282, title I, §§118(b), 123(b)(2), Dec. 4, 2018, 132 Stat. 4233, 4240.)

§3750. FAILURE OF SELECTION FOR PROMOTION

(a) A Reserve officer, other than one serving in the grade of captain, who is, or is senior to, the junior officer in the promotion zone established for the officer's grade, fails of selection if not selected for promotion by the selection board that considered the officer, or if having been selected for promotion by the board, the officer's name is thereafter removed from the report of the board by the President.

(b) A Reserve officer is not considered to have failed of selection if the officer was not considered by a selection board because of administrative error. If that officer is selected by the next appropriate selection board after the error is discovered, and is promoted, the same date of rank and precedence shall be assigned that would have been assigned if the officer had been recommended for promotion by the selection board that originally would have considered the officer but for the error.

(Added Pub. L. 96–322, §1, Aug. 4, 1980, 94 Stat. 1013, §739; renumbered §3750, Pub. L. 115–282, title I, §118(b), Dec. 4, 2018, 132 Stat. 4233.)

§3751. FAILURE OF SELECTION AND REMOVAL FROM AN ACTIVE STATUS

(a) The Secretary—

(1) may remove from an active status a Reserve officer who has twice failed of selection to the next higher grade; and

(2) shall remove from an active status a Reserve officer serving in the grade of captain who has completed thirty years of total commissioned service and whose name is not carried on an approved list of selectees for promotion to the grade of rear admiral (lower half).

(b) A Reserve officer who has twice failed of selection to the next higher grade and who is not removed from an active status under subsection (a)(1) of this section shall be retained for the period prescribed by the Secretary.

(c) Subject to section 12646 of title 10, a Reserve officer who is removed from an active status under subsection (a) of this section shall be given an opportunity to transfer to the Retired Reserve, if qualified, but unless so transferred shall, in the discretion of the Secretary, be transferred to the inactive status list or discharged as follows:

(1) if removed from an active status under subsection (a)(1) of this section, on June 30 next following the approval date of the board report by virtue of which the officer's second failure of selection occurs; or

(2) if removed from an active status under subsection (a)(2) of this section, on June 30 next following the date on which the officer completes thirty years of total commissioned service as computed under this section.

(d) For the purpose of this section, the total commissioned service of an officer who has served continuously in the Reserve following appointment in the grade of ensign shall be computed from the date on which that appointment to the Reserve was accepted. A Reserve officer initially appointed in a grade above ensign is considered to have the actual total commissioned service performed in a grade above commissioned warrant officer or the same total commissioned service as an officer of the Regular Coast Guard who has served continuously from an original appointment as ensign, who has not lost numbers or precedence, and who is, or was, junior to the Reserve officer, whichever is greater.

(Added Pub. L. 96–322, §1, Aug. 4, 1980, 94 Stat. 1013, §740; amended Pub. L. 97–417, §2(15), Jan. 4, 1983, 96 Stat. 2086; Pub. L. 99–145, title V, §514(c)(1), Nov. 8, 1985, 99 Stat. 629; Pub. L. 103–337, div. A, title XVI, §1677(b)(5), Oct. 5, 1994, 108 Stat. 3020; Pub. L. 112–213, title II, §217(14), Dec. 20, 2012, 126 Stat. 1558; renumbered §3751, Pub. L. 115–282, title I, §118(b), Dec. 4, 2018, 132 Stat. 4233.)

§3752. RETENTION BOARDS; REMOVAL FROM AN ACTIVE STATUS TO PROVIDE A FLOW OF PROMOTION

(a) Notwithstanding any other provision of this title, whenever the Secretary determines that it is necessary to reduce the number of Reserve officers in an active status in any grade to provide a steady flow of promotion, or that there is an excessive number of Reserve officers in an active status in any grade, the Secretary may appoint and convene a retention board to consider all of the Reserve officers in that grade in an active status who have 18 years or more of service for retirement, except those officers who—

(1) are on extended active duty;

(2) are on a list of selectees for promotion;

(3) will complete 30 years total commissioned service by June 30th following the date that the retention board is convened; or

(4) have reached age 59 by the date on which the retention board is convened.

The retention board shall select and recommend a specified number of the officers under consideration for retention in an active status.

(b) This board shall—

(1) to the extent practicable, consist of at least 50 per centum Reserve officers;

(2) consist only of officers who are senior in rank to any officers being considered by that board; and

(3) to the extent practicable, consist of officers who have not served on the last previous retention board which considered officers of the same grade.

(c) Subject to section 12646 of title 10, a Reserve officer who is not recommended for retention in an active status under this section shall be given an opportunity to transfer to the Retired Reserve, if qualified, but unless so transferred shall, in the discretion of the Secretary, be transferred to the inactive status list or discharged on June 30 next following the date on which the report of the retention board is approved.

(d) The provisions of section 2117 of this title shall, to the extent that they are not inconsistent with this subchapter, apply to boards convened under this section.

(Added Pub. L. 96–322, §1, Aug. 4, 1980, 94 Stat. 1014, §741; amended Pub. L. 101–225, title II, §203(5), Dec. 12, 1989, 103 Stat. 1911; Pub. L. 103–206, title II, §203, Dec. 20, 1993, 107 Stat. 2420; Pub. L. 103–337, div. A, title XVI, §1677(b)(5), Oct. 5, 1994, 108 Stat. 3020; Pub. L. 104–106, div. A, title XV, §1501(e)(1)(B), Feb. 10, 1996, 110 Stat. 501; renumbered §3752 and amended Pub. L. 115–282, title I, §§118(b), 123(b)(2), Dec. 4, 2018, 132 Stat. 4233, 4240.)

§3753. MAXIMUM AGES FOR RETENTION IN AN ACTIVE STATUS

(a) A Reserve officer, if qualified, shall be transferred to the Retired Reserve on the day the officer becomes 60 years of age unless on active duty. If not qualified for retirement, a Reserve officer shall be discharged effective upon the day the officer becomes 60 years of age unless on active duty.

(b) A Reserve officer on active duty shall, if qualified, be retired effective upon the day the officer become 62 years of age. If not qualified for retirement, a Reserve officer on active duty shall be discharged effective upon the day the officer becomes 62 years of age.

(c) Notwithstanding subsections (a) and (b), the Secretary may authorize the retention of a Reserve rear admiral or rear admiral (lower half) in an active status not longer than the day on which the officer concerned becomes 64 years of age.

(d) For purposes of this section, "active duty" does not include active duty for training, duty on a board, or duty of a limited or temporary nature if assigned to active duty from an inactive duty status.

(Added Pub. L. 96–322, §1, Aug. 4, 1980, 94 Stat. 1014, §742; amended Pub. L. 97–417, §2(16), Jan. 4, 1983, 96 Stat. 2086; Pub. L. 99–145, title V, §514(c)(1), Nov. 8, 1985, 99 Stat. 629; Pub. L. 108–293, title II, §209, Aug. 9, 2004, 118 Stat. 1035; Pub. L. 114–120, title II, §209(13), Feb. 8, 2016, 130 Stat. 41; renumbered §3753, Pub. L. 115–282, title I, §118(b), Dec. 4, 2018, 132 Stat. 4233.)

§3754. REAR ADMIRAL AND REAR ADMIRAL (LOWER HALF); MAXIMUM SERVICE IN GRADE

(a) Unless retained in or removed from an active status under any other law, a reserve rear admiral or rear admiral (lower half) shall be retired on July 1 of the promotion year immediately following the promotion year in which that officer completes 4 years of service after the appointment of the officer to rear admiral (lower half).

(b) Notwithstanding any other provision of law, if promotion of inactive duty promotion list officers to the grade of rear admiral is not determined in accordance with a running mate system, a Reserve officer serving in an active status in the grade of rear admiral (lower half) shall be promoted to the grade of rear admiral, if acceptable to the President and the Senate, on the date the officer has served 2 years in an active status in grade of rear admiral (lower half), or in the case of a vacancy occurring prior to having served 2 years in an active status, on the date the vacancy occurs, if the officer served at least 1 year in an active status in the grade of rear admiral (lower half).

(Added Pub. L. 96–322, §1, Aug. 4, 1980, 94 Stat. 1015, §743; amended Pub. L. 97–417, §2(17)(A), Jan. 4, 1983, 96 Stat. 2086; Pub. L. 99–145, title V, §514(c)(1), (3)(A), Nov. 8, 1985, 99 Stat. 629; Pub. L. 108–293, title II, §220(d), Aug. 9, 2004, 118 Stat. 1039; renumbered §3754, Pub. L. 115–282, title I, §118(b), Dec. 4, 2018, 132 Stat. 4233.)

§3755. APPOINTMENT OF A FORMER NAVY OR COAST GUARD OFFICER

A former officer of the Regular Navy or Coast Guard who applies for a Reserve commission within one year of resigning the officer's Regular commission, and who is appointed in the same grade previously held in the Regular Navy or Coast Guard, shall be given the same date of rank in that grade as that previously assigned to the officer while a member of the Regular Navy or Coast Guard.

(Added Pub. L. 96–322, §1, Aug. 4, 1980, 94 Stat. 1015, §744; renumbered §3755, Pub. L. 115–282, title I, §118(b), Dec. 4, 2018, 132 Stat. 4233.)

§3756. GRADE ON ENTRY UPON ACTIVE DUTY

A Reserve officer ordered to active duty or active duty for training shall be ordered in the grade held; except that the Secretary may authorize a higher grade.

(Added Pub. L. 96–322, §1, Aug. 4, 1980, 94 Stat. 1015, §745; renumbered §3756, Pub. L. 115–282, title I, §118(b), Dec. 4, 2018, 132 Stat. 4233.)

§3757. RECALL OF A RETIRED OFFICER; GRADE UPON RELEASE

(a) When an officer in the Retired Reserve or an officer on a Reserve retired list is recalled to active duty, that officer shall be recalled in a manner similar to the recall of a Regular retired officer.

(b) An officer in the Retired Reserve or an officer on a Reserve retired list recalled to active duty shall upon release therefrom be advanced in the Retired Reserve or on the Reserve retired list to the highest grade held on active duty, if: (1) appointed to a higher grade while on that duty, and (2) the officer's performance has been satisfactory in the higher grade.

(Added Pub. L. 96–322, §1, Aug. 4, 1980, 94 Stat. 1015, §746; renumbered §3757, Pub. L. 115–282, title I, §118(b), Dec. 4, 2018, 132 Stat. 4233.)

CHAPTER 39—COAST GUARD AUXILIARY

§3901. ADMINISTRATION OF THE COAST GUARD AUXILIARY

(a) The Coast Guard Auxiliary is a nonmilitary organization administered by the Commandant under the direction of the Secretary. For command, control, and administrative purposes, the Auxiliary shall include such organizational elements and units as are approved by the Commandant, including but not limited to, a national board and staff (to be known as the "Auxiliary headquarters unit"), districts, regions, divisions, flotillas, and other organizational elements and units. The Auxiliary organization and its officers shall have such rights, privileges, powers, and duties as may be granted to them by the Commandant, consistent with this title and other applicable provisions of law. The Commandant may delegate to officers of the Auxiliary the authority vested in the Commandant by this section, in the manner and to the extent the Commandant considers necessary or appropriate for the functioning, organization, and internal administration of the Auxiliary.

(b) Each organizational element or unit of the Coast Guard Auxiliary organization (but excluding any corporation formed by an organizational element or unit of the Auxiliary under subsection (c) of this section), shall, except when acting outside the scope of section 3902, at all times be deemed to be an instrumentality of the United States, for purposes of the following:

(1) Chapter 171 of title 28 (popularly known as the Federal Tort Claims Act).
(2) Section 2733 of title 10 (popularly known as the Military Claims Act).
(3) Section 30101 of title 46 (popularly known as the Admiralty Extension Act).
(4) Chapter 309 of title 46 (known as the Suits in Admiralty Act).
(5) Chapter 311 of title 46 (known as the Public Vessels Act).
(6) Other matters related to noncontractual civil liability.

(c) The national board of the Auxiliary, and any Auxiliary district or region, may form a corporation under State law in accordance with policies established by the Commandant.

(d)(1) Except as provided in paragraph (2), personal property of the auxiliary shall not be considered property of the United States.

(2) The Secretary may treat personal property of the auxiliary as property of the United States—

(A) for the purposes of—

(i) the statutes and matters referred to in paragraphs (1) through (6) of subsection (b); and

(ii) section 901 of this title; and

(B) as otherwise provided in this chapter.

(3) The Secretary may reimburse the Auxiliary, and each organizational element and unit of the Auxiliary, for necessary expenses of operation, maintenance, and repair or replacement of personal property of the Auxiliary.

(4) In this subsection, the term "personal property of the Auxiliary" means motor boats, yachts, aircraft, radio stations, motorized vehicles, trailers, or other equipment that is under the administrative jurisdiction of the Coast Guard Auxiliary or an organizational element or unit of the Auxiliary and that is used solely for the purposes described in this subsection.

(Aug. 4, 1949, ch. 393, 63 Stat. 555, §821; Pub. L. 104–324, title IV, §401(a), Oct. 19, 1996, 110 Stat. 3922; Pub. L. 108–293, title II, §226, Aug. 9, 2004, 118 Stat. 1041; Pub. L. 109–304, §17(c), Oct. 6, 2006, 120 Stat. 1707; Pub. L. 114–120, title II, §209(14), Feb. 8, 2016, 130 Stat. 41; renumbered §3901 and amended Pub. L. 115–282, title I, §§119(b), 123(b)(2), Dec. 4, 2018, 132 Stat. 4236, 4240.)

§3902. PURPOSE OF THE COAST GUARD AUXILIARY

(a) IN GENERAL.—The purpose of the Auxiliary is to assist the Coast Guard as authorized by the Commandant, in performing any Coast Guard function, power, duty, role, mission, or operation authorized by law.

(b) LIMITATION.—The Auxiliary may conduct a patrol of a waterway, or a portion thereof, only if—

(1) the Commandant has determined such waterway, or portion thereof, is navigable for purposes of the jurisdiction of the Coast Guard; or

(2) a State or other proper authority has requested such patrol pursuant to section 701 of this title or section 13109 of title 46.

(Aug. 4, 1949, ch. 393, 63 Stat. 555, §822; Pub. L. 104–324, title IV, §402(a), Oct. 19, 1996, 110 Stat. 3923; Pub. L. 114–120, title II, §205(a), Feb. 8, 2016, 130 Stat. 36; renumbered §3902 and amended Pub. L. 115–282, title I, §§119(b), 123(b)(2), Dec. 4, 2018, 132 Stat. 4236, 4240.)

§3903. ELIGIBILITY; ENROLLMENTS

The Auxiliary shall be composed of nationals of the United States, as defined in section 101(a)(22) of the Immigration and Nationality Act (8 U.S.C. 1101(a)(22)), and aliens lawfully admitted for permanent residence, as defined in section 101(a)(20) of the Immigration and Nationality Act (8 U.S.C. 1101(a)(20))—

(1) who—

(A) are owners, sole or part, of motorboats, yachts, aircraft, or radio stations; or

(B) by reason of their special training or experience are deemed by the Commandant to be qualified for duty in the Auxiliary; and

(2) who may be enrolled therein pursuant to applicable regulations.

(Aug. 4, 1949, ch. 393, 63 Stat. 555, §823; Pub. L. 112–213, title II, §215(a), Dec. 20, 2012, 126 Stat. 1555; renumbered §3903, Pub. L. 115–282, title I, §119(b), Dec. 4, 2018, 132 Stat. 4236.)

§3904. Members of the Auxiliary; status

(a) Except as otherwise provided in this chapter, a member of the Coast Guard Auxiliary shall not be considered to be a Federal employee and shall not be subject to the provisions of law relating to Federal employment, including those relating to hours of work, rates of compensation, leave, unemployment compensation, Federal employee benefits, ethics, conflicts of interest, and other similar criminal or civil statutes and regulations governing the conduct of Federal employees. However, nothing in this subsection shall constrain the Commandant from prescribing standards for the conduct and behavior of members of the Auxiliary.

(b) A member of the Auxiliary while assigned to duty shall be deemed to be a Federal employee only for the purposes of the following:

(1) Chapter 171 of title 28 (popularly known as the Federal Tort Claims Act).

(2) Section 2733 of title 10 (popularly known as the Military Claims Act).

(3) Section 30101 of title 46 (popularly known as the Admiralty Extension Act).

(4) Chapter 309 of title 46 (known as the Suits in Admiralty Act).

(5) Chapter 311 of title 46 (known as the Public Vessels Act).

(6) Other matters related to noncontractual civil liability.

(7) Compensation for work injuries under chapter 81 of title 5.

(8) The resolution of claims relating to damage to or loss of personal property of the member incident to service under the Military Personnel and Civilian Employees' Claims Act of 1964 (31 U.S.C. 3721).[1]

(9) Section 651 of Public Law 104–208.

(c) A member of the Auxiliary, while assigned to duty, shall be deemed to be a person acting under an officer of the United States or an agency thereof for purposes of section 1442(a)(1) of title 28.

(Added Pub. L. 104–324, title IV, §403(a), Oct. 19, 1996, 110 Stat. 3923, §823a; amended Pub. L. 107–295, title IV, §415, Nov. 25, 2002, 116 Stat. 2121; Pub. L. 109–304, §17(c), Oct. 6, 2006, 120 Stat. 1707; Pub. L. 114–120, title II, §209(15), Feb. 8, 2016, 130 Stat. 41; Pub. L. 115–232, div. C, title XXXV, §3533(i), Aug. 13, 2018, 132 Stat. 2321; renumbered §3904, Pub. L. 115–282, title I, §119(b), Dec. 4, 2018, 132 Stat. 4236.)

[1] *See References in Text note below.*

§3905. Disenrollment

Members of the Auxiliary may be disenrolled pursuant to applicable regulations.

(Aug. 4, 1949, ch. 393, 63 Stat. 555, §824; renumbered §3905, Pub. L. 115–282, title I, §119(b), Dec. 4, 2018, 132 Stat. 4236.)

§3906. Membership in other organizations

Members of the Auxiliary may be appointed or enlisted in the Reserve, pursuant to applicable regulations, and membership in the Auxiliary shall not be a bar to membership in any other naval or military organization.

(Aug. 4, 1949, ch. 393, 63 Stat. 555, §825; renumbered §3906, Pub. L. 115–282, title I, §119(b), Dec. 4, 2018, 132 Stat. 4236.)

§3907. Use of member's facilities

(a) Motor Boats, Yachts, Aircraft, and Radio Stations.—The Coast Guard may utilize for any purpose incident to carrying out its functions and duties as authorized by the Secretary any motorboat, yacht, aircraft, or radio station placed at its disposition for any of such purposes by any member of the Auxiliary, by any corporation, partnership, or association, or by any State or political subdivision thereof.

(b) Motor Vehicles.—The Coast Guard may utilize to carry out its functions and duties as authorized by the Secretary any motor vehicle (as defined in section 30102 of title 49) placed at its disposition by any member of the Auxiliary, by any corporation, partnership, or association, or by any State or political subdivision thereof, to tow Federal Government property.

(Aug. 4, 1949, ch. 393, 63 Stat. 555, §826; Aug. 3, 1950, ch. 536, §35, 64 Stat. 408; Pub. L. 109–241, title II, §208(a), July 11, 2006, 120 Stat. 522; Pub. L. 115–232, div. C, title XXXV, §3533(j), Aug. 13, 2018, 132 Stat. 2321; renumbered §3907, Pub. L. 115–282, title I, §119(b), Dec. 4, 2018, 132 Stat. 4236.)

§3908. Vessel deemed public vessel

While assigned to authorized Coast Guard duty, any motorboat or yacht shall be deemed to be a public vessel of the United States and a vessel of the Coast Guard within the meaning of sections 937 and 938 of this title and other applicable provisions of law.

(Aug. 4, 1949, ch. 393, 63 Stat. 555, §827; Pub. L. 104–324, title IV, §406, Oct. 19, 1996, 110 Stat. 3924; renumbered §3908 and amended Pub. L. 115–282, title I, §§119(b), 123(b)(2), Dec. 4, 2018, 132 Stat. 4236, 4240.)

§3909. Aircraft deemed public aircraft

While assigned to authorized Coast Guard duty, any aircraft shall be deemed to be a Coast Guard aircraft, a public vessel of the United States, and a vessel of the Coast Guard within the meaning of sections 937 and 938 of this title and other applicable provisions of law. Subject to the provisions of sections 3904 and 3912 of this title, while assigned to duty, qualified Auxiliary pilots shall be deemed to be Coast Guard pilots.

(Aug. 4, 1949, ch. 393, 63 Stat. 556, §828; Pub. L. 104–324, title IV, §407, Oct. 19, 1996, 110 Stat. 3925; renumbered §3909 and amended Pub. L. 115–282, title I, §§119(b), 123(b)(2), Dec. 4, 2018, 132 Stat. 4236, 4240.)

§3910. Radio station deemed government station

Any radio station, while assigned to authorized Coast Guard duty shall be deemed to be a radio station of the Coast Guard and a "government station" within the meaning of section 305 of the Communications Act of 1934 (47 U.S.C. 305).

(Aug. 4, 1949, ch. 393, 63 Stat. 556, §829; Pub. L. 94–546, §1(38), Oct. 18, 1976, 90 Stat. 2522; Pub. L. 99–640, §10(a)(8), Nov. 10, 1986, 100 Stat. 3549; renumbered §3910, Pub. L. 115–282, title I, §119(b), Dec. 4, 2018, 132 Stat. 4236.)

§3911. Availability of appropriations

(a) Appropriations of the Coast Guard shall be available for the payment of actual necessary traveling expense and subsistence, or commutation of ration allowance in lieu of subsistence, of members of the Auxiliary assigned to authorized duties and for actual necessary expenses of operation of any motorboat, yacht, aircraft, radio station, or motorized vehicle utilized under section 3907(b) when assigned to Coast Guard duty, but shall not be available for the payment of compensation for personal services, incident to such operation, other than to personnel of the Coast Guard or the Reserve. The term "actual necessary expenses of operation," as used in this section, shall include payment for fuel, oil, power, water, supplies, provisions, replacement or repair of equipment, repair of any damaged motorboat, yacht, aircraft, radio station, or motorized vehicle utilized under section 3907(b) and for the constructive or actual loss of any motorboat, yacht, aircraft, radio station, or motorized vehicle utilized under section 3907(b) where it is determined, under applicable regulations, that responsibility for the loss or damage necessitating such replacement or repair of equipment, or for the damage or loss, constructive or actual, of such motorboat, yacht, aircraft, radio station, or motorized vehicle utilized under section 3907(b) rests with the Coast Guard.

(b) The Secretary may pay interest on a claim under this section in any case in which a payment authorized under this section is not made within 60 days after the submission of the claim in a manner prescribed by the Secretary. The rate of interest for purposes of this section shall be the annual rate established under section 6621 of the Internal Revenue Code of 1986.

(Aug. 4, 1949, ch. 393, 63 Stat. 556, §830; Pub. L. 99–640, §8, Nov. 10, 1986, 100 Stat. 3548; Pub. L. 104–324, title IV, §404(a), Oct. 19, 1996, 110 Stat. 3924; Pub. L. 109–241, title II, §208(b), July 11, 2006, 120 Stat. 522; Pub. L. 115–232, div. C, title XXXV, §3533(k), Aug. 13, 2018, 132 Stat. 2321; renumbered §3911 and amended Pub. L. 115–282, title I, §§119(b), 123(b)(2), Dec. 4, 2018, 132 Stat. 4236, 4240.)

§3912. Assignment and performance of duties

No member of the Auxiliary, solely by reason of such membership, shall be vested with, or exercise, any right, privilege, power, or duty vested in or imposed upon the personnel of the Coast Guard or the Reserve, except that any such member may, under applicable regulations, be assigned duties, which, after appropriate training and examination, he has been found competent to perform, to effectuate the purposes of the Auxiliary. No member of the Auxiliary shall be placed in charge of a motorboat, yacht, aircraft, or radio station assigned to Coast Guard duty unless he has been specifically designated by authority of the Commandant to perform such duty. Members of the Auxiliary, when assigned to duties as herein authorized shall, unless otherwise limited by the Commandant, be vested with the same power and authority, in the execution of such duties, as members of the regular Coast Guard assigned to similar duty. When any member of the Auxiliary is assigned to such duty he may, pursuant to regulations issued by the Secretary, be paid actual necessary traveling expenses, including a per diem allowance in conformity with standardized Government travel regulations in lieu of subsistence, while traveling and while on duty away from his home. No per diem shall be paid for any period during which quarters and subsistence in kind are furnished by the Government, and no per diem shall be paid for any period while such member is performing duty on a vessel.

(Aug. 4, 1949, ch. 393, 63 Stat. 556, §831; Pub. L. 104–324, title IV, §404(b), Oct. 19, 1996, 110 Stat. 3924; renumbered §3912, Pub. L. 115–282, title I, §119(b), Dec. 4, 2018, 132 Stat. 4236.)

§3913. INJURY OR DEATH IN LINE OF DUTY

When any member of the Auxiliary is physically injured or dies as a result of physical injury incurred while performing any duty to which he has been assigned by competent Coast Guard authority, such member or his beneficiary shall be entitled to the same benefits provided for temporary members of the Reserve who suffer physical injury or death resulting from physical injury incurred incident to service. Members of the Auxiliary who incur physical injury or contract sickness or disease while performing any duty to which they have been assigned by competent Coast Guard authority shall be entitled to the same hospital treatment afforded members of the Coast Guard. The performance of a duty as the term is used in this section includes time engaged in traveling back and forth between the place of assigned duty and the permanent residence of a member of the Auxiliary.

(Aug. 4, 1949, ch. 393, 63 Stat. 556, §832; Pub. L. 93–283, §1(15), May 14, 1974, 88 Stat. 141; Pub. L. 98–557, §15(a)(3)(D), Oct. 30, 1984, 98 Stat. 2865; Pub. L. 104–324, title IV, §404(c), Oct. 19, 1996, 110 Stat. 3924; renumbered §3913, Pub. L. 115–282, title I, §119(b), Dec. 4, 2018, 132 Stat. 4236.)

CHAPTER 41—GENERAL PROVISIONS FOR COAST GUARD RESERVE AND AUXILIARY

Sec.
4101.   Flags; pennants; uniforms and insignia.
4102.   Penalty.
4103.   Limitation on rights of members of the Auxiliary and temporary members of the Reserve.
4104.   Availability of facilities and appropriations.

§4101. FLAGS; PENNANTS; UNIFORMS AND INSIGNIA

The Secretary may prescribe one or more suitable distinguishing flags, pennants, or other identifying insignia to be displayed by the motorboats, yachts, aircraft, and radio stations owned by members of the Auxiliary and one or more suitable insignia which may be worn by members of the Reserve or the Auxiliary, and may prescribe one or more suitable uniforms which may be worn by members of the Auxiliary. Such flags, pennants, uniforms, and insignia may be furnished by the Coast Guard at actual cost, and the proceeds received therefor shall be credited to current appropriations from which purchase of these articles is authorized.

(Aug. 4, 1949, ch. 393, 63 Stat. 557, §891; renumbered §4101, Pub. L. 115–282, title I, §120(b), Dec. 4, 2018, 132 Stat. 4237.)

§4102. PENALTY

Whoever, without proper authority, flies from any building, aircraft, motorboat, yacht, or other vessel, any flag or pennant or displays any identifying insignia or wears any uniform or insignia of the Reserve or the Auxiliary shall be fined not more than $500.

(Aug. 4, 1949, ch. 393, 63 Stat. 557, §892; renumbered §4102, Pub. L. 115–282, title I, §120(b), Dec. 4, 2018, 132 Stat. 4237.)

§4103. LIMITATION ON RIGHTS OF MEMBERS OF THE AUXILIARY AND TEMPORARY MEMBERS OF THE RESERVE

Members of the Auxiliary and temporary members of the Reserve shall be entitled only to such rights, privileges, and benefits as are specifically set forth for them in this title or as may be specifically provided for them in any other Act of Congress. Any Act of Congress which grants rights, privileges, or benefits generally to military personnel, or among others, to personnel of the Coast Guard and the Coast Guard Reserve, without specifically granting such rights, privileges, or benefits to members of the Auxiliary or temporary members of the Reserve, shall not be deemed applicable to members of the Auxiliary or to temporary members of the Reserve.

(Aug. 4, 1949, ch. 393, 63 Stat. 557, §893; renumbered §4103, Pub. L. 115–282, title I, §120(b), Dec. 4, 2018, 132 Stat. 4237.)

§4104. Availability of facilities and appropriations

The services and facilities of and appropriations for the Coast Guard shall be available to effectuate the purposes of the Reserve and the Auxiliary.

(Aug. 4, 1949, ch. 393, 63 Stat. 557, §894; renumbered §4104, Pub. L. 115–282, title I, §120(b), Dec. 4, 2018, 132 Stat. 4237.)

SUBTITLE IV
COAST GUARD AUTHORIZATIONS AND REPORTS TO CONGRESS

SUBTITLE IV—COAST GUARD AUTHORIZATIONS AND REPORTS TO CONGRESS

CHAPTER 49—AUTHORIZATIONS

§4901. REQUIREMENT FOR PRIOR AUTHORIZATION OF APPROPRIATIONS

Amounts may be appropriated to or for the use of the Coast Guard for the following matters only if the amounts have been authorized by law after December 31, 1976:

(1) For the operation and support of the Coast Guard, not otherwise provided for.

(2) For the procurement, construction, renovation, and improvement of aids to navigation, shore facilities, vessels, aircraft, and systems, including equipment related thereto, and for maintenance, rehabilitation, lease, and operation of facilities and equipment.

(3) For research and development.[1] of technologies, materials, and human factors directly related to improving the performance of the Coast Guard.

(Added Pub. L. 97–295, §2(20)(A), Oct. 12, 1982, 96 Stat. 1303, §662; amended Pub. L. 101–225, title II, §222(c), Dec. 12, 1989, 103 Stat. 1919; Pub. L. 111–259, title IV, §442(2), Oct. 7, 2010, 124 Stat. 2733; renumbered §2701 and amended Pub. L. 114–120, title I, §101(b), Feb. 8, 2016, 130 Stat. 30; Pub. L. 115–232, div. C, title XXXV, §3538(a), Aug. 13, 2018, 132 Stat. 2322; renumbered §4901 and amended Pub. L. 115–282, title I, §§121(b), 123(c)(5)(A), Dec. 4, 2018, 132 Stat. 4238, 4241; Pub. L. 116–283, div. G, title LVXXXV [LXXXV], §8513(a)(5), Jan. 1, 2021, 134 Stat. 4760.)

[1] *So in original. The period probably should not appear.*

§4902. AUTHORIZATIONS OF APPROPRIATIONS

Funds are authorized to be appropriated for fiscal years 2022 and 2023 for necessary expenses of the Coast Guard as follows:

(1)(A) For the operation and maintenance of the Coast Guard, not otherwise provided for—

(i) $10,000,000,000 for fiscal year 2022; and

(ii) $10,750,000,000 for fiscal year 2023.

(B) Of the amount authorized under subparagraph (A)(i), $23,456,000 shall be for environmental compliance and restoration.

(C) Of the amount authorized under subparagraph (A)(ii), $24,353,000 shall be for environmental compliance and restoration.

(2)(A) For the procurement, construction, renovation, and improvement of aids to navigation, shore facilities, vessels, aircraft, and systems, including equipment related thereto, and for maintenance, rehabilitation, lease, and operation of facilities and equipment—

(i) $3,312,114,000 for fiscal year 2022; and

    (ii) $3,477,600,000 for fiscal year 2023.

  (B) Of the amounts authorized under subparagraph (A), the following amounts shall be for the alteration of bridges:
    (i) $20,400,000 for fiscal year 2022; and
    (ii) $20,808,000 for fiscal year 2023.

  (3) To the Commandant for research, development, test, and evaluation of technologies, materials, and human factors directly related to improving the performance of the Coast Guard's mission with respect to search and rescue, aids to navigation, marine safety, marine environmental protection, enforcement of laws and treaties, ice operations, oceanographic research, and defense readiness, and for maintenance, rehabilitation, lease, and operation of facilities and equipment—
    (A) $7,476,000 for fiscal year 2022; and
    (B) $14,681,084 for fiscal year 2023.

  (4) For the Coast Guard's Medicare-eligible retiree health care fund contribution to the Department of Defense—
    (A) $240,577,000 for fiscal year 2022; and
    (B) $252,887,000 for fiscal year 2023.

(Added Pub. L. 114–120, title I, §101(a), Feb. 8, 2016, 130 Stat. 29, §2702; amended Pub. L. 114–328, div. C, title XXXV, §3503(d)(1), Dec. 23, 2016, 130 Stat. 2775; Pub. L. 115–232, div. C, title XXXV, §§3531(c)(14), 3538(b), Aug. 13, 2018, 132 Stat. 2320, 2322; renumbered §4902 and amended Pub. L. 115–282, title I, §§121(b), 123(c)(5)(B), title II, §202, Dec. 4, 2018, 132 Stat. 4238, 4241; Pub. L. 116–283, div. G, title LVXXXI [LXXXI], §8101, Jan. 1, 2021, 134 Stat. 4634; Pub. L. 117–263, div. K, title CXI, §11101, Dec. 23, 2022, 136 Stat. 4003.)

§4903. AUTHORIZATION OF PERSONNEL END STRENGTHS

  (a) For each fiscal year, Congress shall authorize the strength for active duty personnel of the Coast Guard as of the end of that fiscal year. Amounts may be appropriated for a fiscal year to or for the use of active duty personnel of the Coast Guard only if the end strength for active duty personnel for that fiscal year has been authorized by law. If at the end of any fiscal year there is in effect a declaration of war or national emergency, the President may defer the effectiveness of any end-strength limitation with respect to that fiscal year prescribed by law for any military or civilian component of the Coast Guard, for a period not to exceed 6 months after the end of the war or termination of the national emergency.
  (b)(1) Congress shall authorize the average military training student loads for the Coast Guard for each fiscal year. That authorization is required for student loads for the following individual training categories:
    (A) Recruit and specialized training.
    (B) Flight training.
    (C) Professional training in military and civilian institutions.
    (D) Officer acquisition training.

  (2) Amounts may be appropriated for a fiscal year for use in training military personnel

of the Coast Guard in the categories referred to in paragraph (1) only if the average student loads for the Coast Guard for that fiscal year have been authorized by law.

(Added Pub. L. 97–295, §2(20)(A), Oct. 12, 1982, 96 Stat. 1302, §661; amended Pub. L. 107–295, title I, §105(a), Nov. 25, 2002, 116 Stat. 2085; renumbered §2703, Pub. L. 114–120, title I, §101(c), Feb. 8, 2016, 130 Stat. 31; renumbered §4903, Pub. L. 115–282, title I, §121(b), Dec. 4, 2018, 132 Stat. 4238.)

§4904. AUTHORIZED LEVELS OF MILITARY STRENGTH AND TRAINING

(a) ACTIVE DUTY STRENGTH.—The Coast Guard is authorized an end-of-year strength for active duty personnel of 44,500 for each of fiscal years 2022 and 2023.

(b) MILITARY TRAINING STUDENT LOADS.—The Coast Guard is authorized average military training student loads for each of fiscal years 2022 and 2023 as follows:

(1) For recruit and special training, 2,500 student years.

(2) For flight training, 165 student years.

(3) For professional training in military and civilian institutions, 385 student years.

(4) For officer acquisition, 1,200 student years.

(Added Pub. L. 114–120, title I, §101(a), Feb. 8, 2016, 130 Stat. 29, §2704; renumbered §4904 and amended Pub. L. 115–282, title I, §121(b), title II, §203, Dec. 4, 2018, 132 Stat. 4238, 4242; Pub. L. 116–283, div. G, title LVXXXI [LXXXI], §8102, Jan. 1, 2021, 134 Stat. 4634; Pub. L. 117–263, div. K, title CXI, §11102, title CXIV, §11413(c), Dec. 23, 2022, 136 Stat. 4004, 4120.)

CHAPTER 51—REPORTS

Sec.

§5101. TRANSMISSION OF ANNUAL COAST GUARD AUTHORIZATION REQUEST

(a) IN GENERAL.—Not later than 30 days after the date on which the President submits to Congress a budget for a fiscal year pursuant to section 1105 of title 31, the Secretary shall submit to the Committee on Transportation and Infrastructure of the House of Representatives and the Committee on Commerce, Science, and Transportation of the Senate a Coast Guard authorization request with respect to such fiscal year.

(b) COAST GUARD AUTHORIZATION REQUEST DEFINED.—In this section, the term "Coast Guard authorization request" means a proposal for legislation that, with respect to the Coast Guard for the relevant fiscal year—

(1) recommends end strengths for personnel for that fiscal year, as described in section 4903;

(2) recommends authorizations of appropriations for that fiscal year, including with respect to matters described in section 4901; and

(3) addresses any other matter that the Secretary determines is appropriate for inclusion in a Coast Guard authorization bill.

(Added Pub. L. 113–281, title II, §216(a), Dec. 18, 2014, 128 Stat. 3035, §662a; renumbered §2901 and amended Pub. L. 114–120, title I, §101(d)(1), Feb. 8, 2016, 130 Stat. 31; renumbered §5101 and amended Pub. L. 115–282, title I, §§122(b), 123(b)(2), Dec. 4, 2018, 132 Stat. 4239, 4240.)

§5102. CAPITAL INVESTMENT PLAN

(a) IN GENERAL.—Not later than 60 days after the date on which the President submits to Congress a budget pursuant to section 1105 of title 31, the Commandant shall submit to the Committee on Transportation and Infrastructure of the House of Representatives and the Committee on Commerce, Science, and Transportation of the Senate a capital investment plan for the Coast Guard that identifies for each capital asset for which appropriations are proposed in that budget—

(1) the proposed appropriations included in the budget;

(2) the total estimated cost of completion based on the proposed appropriations included in the budget;

(3) projected funding levels for each fiscal year for the next 5 fiscal years or until project completion, whichever is earlier;

(4) an estimated completion date based on the proposed appropriations included in the budget;

(5) an acquisition program baseline, as applicable; and

(6) projected commissioning and decommissioning dates for each asset.

(b) NEW CAPITAL ASSETS.—In the fiscal year following each fiscal year for which appropriations are enacted for a new capital asset, the report submitted under subsection (a) shall include—

(1) an estimated life-cycle cost estimate for the new capital asset;

(2) an assessment of the impact the new capital asset will have on—

    (A) delivery dates for each capital asset;

    (B) estimated completion dates for each capital asset;

    (C) the total estimated cost to complete each capital asset; and

    (D) other planned construction or improvement projects; and

(3) recommended funding levels for each capital asset necessary to meet the estimated completion dates and total estimated costs included in the such [1] asset's approved acquisition program baseline.

(c) DEFINITIONS.—In this section, the term "new capital asset" means—

(1) an acquisition program that does not have an approved acquisition program baseline; or

(2) the acquisition of a capital asset in excess of the number included in the approved acquisition program baseline.

(Added Pub. L. 97–295, §2(20)(A), Oct. 12, 1982, 96 Stat. 1303, §663; amended Pub. L. 100–448, §25, Sept. 28, 1988, 102 Stat. 1847; Pub. L. 101–595, title III, §311(c), Nov. 16, 1990, 104 Stat. 2987; Pub. L. 107–295, title IV, §408(a)(2), Nov. 25, 2002, 116 Stat. 2117; Pub. L. 112–213, title II, §213(a), Dec. 20, 2012, 126 Stat. 1552; renumbered §2902 and amended Pub. L. 114–120, title I, §101(d)(2), title II, §204(b), Feb. 8, 2016, 130 Stat. 31, 34; Pub. L. 115–232, div. C, title XXXV, §§3525, 3531(c)(15), Aug. 13, 2018, 132 Stat. 2316, 2320; renumbered §5102 and amended Pub. L. 115–282, title I, §122(b), title III, §317(a), Dec. 4, 2018, 132 Stat. 4239, 4250.)

[1] So in original.

§5103. MAJOR ACQUISITIONS

(a) IN GENERAL.—In conjunction with the transmittal by the President to Congress of the budget of the United States for fiscal year 2014 and biennially thereafter, the Secretary shall submit to the Committee on Commerce, Science, and Transportation of the Senate and the Committee on Transportation and Infrastructure of the House of Representatives a report on the status of all major acquisition programs.

(b) INFORMATION TO BE INCLUDED.—Each report under subsection (a) shall include for each major acquisition program—

(1) a statement of the Coast Guard's mission needs and performance goals relating to such program, including a justification for any change to those needs and goals subsequent to a report previously submitted under this section;

(2) a justification explaining how the projected number and capabilities of assets acquired under such program meet applicable mission needs and performance goals;

(3) an identification of any and all mission hour gaps, accompanied by an explanation of how and when the Coast Guard will close those gaps;

(4) an identification of any changes with respect to such program, including—

(A) any changes to the timeline for the acquisition of each new asset and the phaseout of legacy assets; and

(B) any changes to—

(i) the costs of new assets or legacy assets for that fiscal year or future fiscal years; or

(ii) the total acquisition cost;

(5) a justification explaining how any change to such program fulfills the mission needs and performance goals of the Coast Guard;

(6) a description of how the Coast Guard is planning for the integration of each new asset acquired under such program into the Coast Guard, including needs related to shore-based infrastructure and human resources;

(7) an identification of how funds in the applicable fiscal year's budget request will be allocated, including information on the purchase of specific assets;

(8) a projection of the remaining operational lifespan and life-cycle cost of each legacy asset that also identifies any anticipated resource gaps;

(9) a detailed explanation of how the costs of legacy assets are being accounted for within such program; and

(10) an annual performance comparison of new assets to legacy assets.

(c) ADEQUACY OF ACQUISITION WORKFORCE.—Each report under subsection (a) shall—

(1) include information on the scope of the acquisition activities to be performed in the next fiscal year and on the adequacy of the current acquisition workforce to meet that anticipated workload;

(2) specify the number of officers, members, and employees of the Coast Guard currently and planned to be assigned to each position designated under section 1102(c); [1] and

(3) identify positions that are or will be understaffed and actions that will be taken to correct such understaffing.

(d) CUTTERS NOT MAINTAINED IN CLASS.—Each report under subsection (a) shall identify which, if any, Coast Guard cutters that have been issued a certificate of classification by the American Bureau of Shipping have not been maintained in class, with an explanation detailing the reasons why the cutters have not been maintained in class.

(e) LONG-TERM MAJOR ACQUISITIONS PLAN.—Each report under subsection (a) shall include a plan that describes for the upcoming fiscal year, and for each of the 20 fiscal years thereafter—

(1) the numbers and types of cutters and aircraft to be decommissioned;

(2) the numbers and types of cutters and aircraft to be acquired to—

(A) replace the cutters and aircraft identified under paragraph (1); or

(B) address an identified capability gap; and

(3) the estimated level of funding in each fiscal year required to—

(A) acquire the cutters and aircraft identified under paragraph (2);

(B) operate and sustain the cutters and aircraft described in paragraph (2);

(C) acquire related command, control, communications, computer, intelligence, surveillance, and reconnaissance systems; and

(D) acquire, construct, or renovate shoreside infrastructure.

(f) MAJOR ACQUISITION PROGRAM DEFINED.—In this section, the term "major acquisition program" means an ongoing acquisition undertaken by the Coast Guard with a life-cycle cost estimate greater than or equal to $300,000,000.

(Added Pub. L. 112–213, title II, §210(a), Dec. 20, 2012, 126 Stat. 1550, §569a; renumbered §2903 and amended Pub. L. 114–120, title I, §101(d)(3), title II, §204(e), Feb. 8, 2016, 130 Stat. 31, 35; Pub. L. 115–232, div. C, title XXXV, §3526(c), Aug. 13, 2018, 132 Stat. 2317; renumbered §5103 and amended Pub. L. 115–282, title I, §§122(b), 123(b)(2), Dec. 4, 2018, 132 Stat. 4239, 4240; Pub. L. 116–283, div. G, title LVXXXII [LXXXII], §8214, Jan. 1, 2021, 134 Stat. 4650.)

[1] *See References in Text note below.*

§5104. MANPOWER REQUIREMENTS PLAN

(a) IN GENERAL.—On the date on which the President submits to the Congress a budget for fiscal year 2017 under section 1105 of title 31, on the date on which the President submits to the Congress a budget for fiscal year 2019 under such section, and every 4 years thereafter, the Commandant shall submit to the Committee on Transportation and Infrastructure of the House of Representatives and the Committee on Commerce, Science, and Transportation of the Senate a manpower requirements plan.

(b) SCOPE.—A manpower requirements plan submitted under subsection (a) shall include for each mission of the Coast Guard—

(1) an assessment of all projected mission requirements for the upcoming fiscal year and for each of the 3 fiscal years thereafter;

(2) the number of active duty, reserve, and civilian personnel assigned or available to fulfill such mission requirements—

(A) currently; and

(B) as projected for the upcoming fiscal year and each of the 3 fiscal years thereafter;

(3) the number of active duty, reserve, and civilian personnel required to fulfill such mission requirements—

(A) currently; and

(B) as projected for the upcoming fiscal year and each of the 3 fiscal years thereafter;

(4) an identification of any capability gaps between mission requirements and mission performance caused by deficiencies in the numbers of personnel available—

(A) currently; and

(B) as projected for the upcoming fiscal year and each of the 3 fiscal years thereafter; and

(5) an identification of the actions the Commandant will take to address capability gaps identified under paragraph (4).

(c) CONSIDERATION.—In composing a manpower requirements plan for submission under subsection (a), the Commandant shall consider—

(1) the marine safety strategy required under section 2116 of title 46;

(2) information on the adequacy of the acquisition workforce included in the most recent report under section 5103 of this title; and

(3) any other Federal strategic planning effort the Commandant considers appropriate.

(Added Pub. L. 114–120, title I, §101(a), Feb. 8, 2016, 130 Stat. 30, §2904; renumbered §5104 and amended Pub. L. 115–282, title I, §§122(b), 123(b)(2), Dec. 4, 2018, 132 Stat. 4239, 4240.)

§5105. INVENTORY OF REAL PROPERTY

(a) IN GENERAL.—The Commandant shall maintain an inventory of all real property, including submerged lands, under the control of the Coast Guard, which shall include—

(1) the size, the location, and any other appropriate description of each unit of such property;

(2) an assessment of the physical condition of each unit of such property, excluding lands;

(3) a determination of whether each unit of such property should be—

(A) retained to fulfill a current or projected Coast Guard mission requirement; or

(B) subject to divestiture; and

(4) other information the Commandant considers appropriate.

(b) UPDATES.—The Commandant shall update information on each unit of real property included in the inventory required under subsection (a) not later than 30 days after any change relating to the control of such property.

(c) RECOMMENDATIONS TO CONGRESS.—Not later than March 30, 2016, and every 5 years thereafter, the Commandant shall submit to the Committee on Transportation and Infrastructure of the House of Representatives and the Committee on Commerce, Science, and Transportation of the Senate a report that includes—

(1) a list of all real property under the control of the Coast Guard and the location of such property by property type;

(2) recommendations for divestiture with respect to any units of such property; and

(3) recommendations for consolidating any units of such property, including—

(A) an estimate of the costs or savings associated with each recommended consolidation; and

(B) a discussion of the impact that such consolidation would have on Coast Guard mission effectiveness.

(Added Pub. L. 113–281, title II, §217(a), Dec. 18, 2014, 128 Stat. 3035, §679; amended Pub. L. 115–232, div. C, title XXXV, §3539, Aug. 13, 2018, 132 Stat. 2322; renumbered §5105, Pub. L. 115–282, title I, §122(b), Dec. 4, 2018, 132 Stat. 4239.)

§5106. ANNUAL PERFORMANCE REPORT

Not later than the date on which the President submits to Congress a budget pursuant to section 1105 of title 31, the Commandant of the Coast Guard shall make available on a public website and submit to the Committee on Transportation and Infrastructure of the House of Representatives and the Committee on Commerce, Science, and Transportation of the Senate an update on Coast Guard mission performance during the previous fiscal year.

(Added Pub. L. 115–232, div. C, title XXXV, §3521(b)(1), Aug. 13, 2018, 132 Stat. 2314, §2905; renumbered §5106, Pub. L. 115–282, title I, §122(b), Dec. 4, 2018, 132 Stat. 4239.)

§5107. MAJOR ACQUISITION PROGRAM RISK ASSESSMENT

(a) IN GENERAL.—Not later than October 15 of each year, the Commandant of the Coast Guard shall provide to the Committee on Transportation and Infrastructure of the House of Representatives and the Committee on Commerce, Science, and Transportation of the Senate a briefing regarding a current assessment of the risks associated with all current major acquisition programs, as that term is defined in section 5103(f).

(b) ELEMENTS.—Each assessment under this subsection shall include, for each current major acquisition program, discussion of the following:

(1) The top five current risks to such program.

(2) Any failure of such program to demonstrate a key performance parameter or threshold during operational test and evaluation conducted during the previous fiscal year.

(3) Whether there has been any decision in such fiscal year to order full-rate production before all key performance parameters or thresholds are met.

(4) Whether there has been any breach of major acquisition program cost (as defined by the Major Systems Acquisition Manual) in such fiscal year.

(5) Whether there has been any breach of major acquisition program schedule (as so defined) during such fiscal year.

(Added Pub. L. 115–232, div. C, title XXXV, §3526(a), Aug. 13, 2018, 132 Stat. 2317, §2906; renumbered §5107 and amended Pub. L. 115–282, title I, §§122(b), 123(b)(2), Dec. 4, 2018, 132 Stat. 4239, 4240; Pub. L. 116–283, div. G, title LVXXXII [LXXXII], §8240(e), Jan. 1, 2021, 134 Stat. 4667.)

§5108. UNFUNDED PRIORITIES LIST

(a) IN GENERAL.—Not later than 60 days after the date on which the President submits to Congress a budget pursuant to section 1105 of title 31, the Commandant shall submit to the Committee on Transportation and Infrastructure of the House of Representatives and the Committee on Commerce, Science, and Transportation of the Senate a list of each unfunded priority for the Coast Guard.

(b) PRIORITIZATION.—The list required under subsection (a) shall present the unfunded priorities in order from the highest priority to the lowest, as determined by the Commandant.

(c) UNFUNDED PRIORITY DEFINED.—In this section, the term "unfunded priority" means a program or mission requirement that—

(1) has not been selected for funding in the applicable proposed budget;

(2) is necessary to fulfill a requirement associated with an operational need; and

(3) the Commandant would have recommended for inclusion in the applicable proposed budget had additional resources been available or had the requirement emerged before the budget was submitted.

(Added Pub. L. 115–282, title III, §317(b), Dec. 4, 2018, 132 Stat. 4251.)

§5109. REPORT ON GENDER DIVERSITY IN THE COAST GUARD

(a) IN GENERAL.—Not later than January 15, 2022, and biennially thereafter, the Commandant shall submit to the Committee on Transportation and Infrastructure of the House of Representatives and the Committee on Commerce, Science, and Transportation of the Senate a report on gender diversity in the Coast Guard.

(b) CONTENTS.—The report required under subsection (a) shall contain the following:

(1) GENDER DIVERSITY OVERVIEW.—An overview of Coast Guard active duty and reserve members, including the number of officers and enlisted members and the percentages of men and women in each.

(2) RECRUITMENT AND RETENTION.—

(A) An analysis of the changes in the recruitment and retention of women over the previous 2 years.

(B) A discussion of any changes to Coast Guard recruitment and retention over the previous 2 years that were aimed at increasing the recruitment and retention of female members.

(3) PARENTAL LEAVE.—

(A) The number of men and women who took parental leave during each year covered by the report, including the average length of such leave periods.

(B) A discussion of the ways in which the Coast Guard worked to mitigate the impacts of parental leave on Coast Guard operations and on the careers of the members taking such leave.

(4) LIMITATIONS.—An analysis of current gender-based limitations on Coast Guard career opportunities, including discussion of—

(A) shipboard opportunities;

(B) opportunities to serve at remote units; and

(C) any other limitations on the opportunities of female members.

(5) PROGRESS UPDATE.—An update on the Coast Guard's progress on the implementation of the action plan required under subsection (a) of section 8215 of the Elijah E. Cummings Coast Guard Authorization Act of 2020.

(Added Pub. L. 116–283, div. G, title LVXXXII [LXXXII], §8215(d)(1), Jan. 1, 2021, 134 Stat. 4652.)

§5110. MISSION NEED STATEMENT

(a) IN GENERAL.—On the date on which the President submits to Congress a budget for fiscal year 2019 under section 1105 of title 31 and every 4 years thereafter, the Commandant shall submit to the Committee on Transportation and Infrastructure of the House of Representatives and the Committee on Commerce, Science, and Transportation of the Senate an integrated major acquisition mission need statement.

(b) DEFINITIONS.—In this section, the following definitions apply:

(1) INTEGRATED MAJOR ACQUISITION MISSION NEED STATEMENT.—The term "integrated major acquisition mission need statement" means a document that—

(A) identifies current and projected gaps in Coast Guard mission capabilities using mission hour targets;

(B) explains how each major acquisition program addresses gaps identified under subparagraph (A) if funded at the levels provided for such program in the most recently submitted capital investment plan; and

(C) describes the missions the Coast Guard will not be able to achieve, by fiscal year, for each gap identified under subparagraph (A).

(2) MAJOR ACQUISITION PROGRAM.—The term "major acquisition program" has the meaning given that term in section 5103.

(3) CAPITAL INVESTMENT PLAN.—The term "capital investment plan" means the plan required under section 5102(a)(1).

(Added Pub. L. 111–281, title IV, §402(a), Oct. 15, 2010, 124 Stat. 2940, §569; amended Pub. L. 112–213, title II, §217(8), Dec. 20, 2012, 126 Stat. 1558; Pub. L. 113–281, title II, §215(a), Dec. 18, 2014, 128 Stat. 3034; Pub. L. 114–120, title I, §102(f), Feb. 8, 2016, 130 Stat. 33; Pub. L. 115–232, div. C, title XXXV, §3536, Aug. 13, 2018, 132 Stat. 2322; renumbered §1110 and amended Pub. L. 115–282, title I, §§108(b), 123(b)(2), Dec. 4, 2018, 132 Stat. 4208, 4240; renumbered §5110, Pub. L. 116–283, div. G, title LVXXXV [LXXXV], §8501(a)(3), Jan. 1, 2021, 134 Stat. 4745.)

§5111. REPORT ON DIVERSITY AT COAST GUARD ACADEMY

(a) IN GENERAL.—Not later than January 15, 2021, and annually thereafter, the Commandant shall submit a report on diversity at the Coast Guard Academy to the Committee on Transportation and Infrastructure of the House of Representatives and the Committee on Commerce, Science, and Transportation of the Senate.

(b) CONTENTS.—The report required under subsection (a) shall include—

(1) the status of the implementation of the plan required under section 8272 of the

Elijah E. Cummings Coast Guard Authorization Act of 2020;

(2) specific information on outreach and recruitment activities for the preceding year, including the effectiveness of the Coast Guard Academy minority outreach team program described under section 1905 and of outreach and recruitment activities in the territories and other possessions of the United States;

(3) enrollment information about the incoming class, including the gender, race, ethnicity, religion, socioeconomic background, and State of residence of Coast Guard Academy cadets;

(4) information on class retention, outcomes, and graduation rates, including the race, gender, ethnicity, religion, socioeconomic background, and State of residence of Coast Guard Academy cadets;

(5) information on efforts to retain diverse cadets, including through professional development and professional advancement programs for staff and faculty; and

(6) a summary of reported allegations of discrimination on the basis of race, color, national origin, sex, gender, or religion for the preceding 5 years.

(Added Pub. L. 116–283, div. G, title LVXXXII [LXXXII], §8273, Jan. 1, 2021, 134 Stat. 4683.)

§5112. SEXUAL ASSAULT AND SEXUAL HARASSMENT IN THE COAST GUARD

(a) IN GENERAL.—Not later than January 15 of each year, the Commandant of the Coast Guard shall submit a report on the sexual assaults and incidents of sexual harassment involving members of the Coast Guard to the Committee on Transportation and Infrastructure and the Committee on Homeland Security of the House of Representatives and the Committee on Commerce, Science, and Transportation of the Senate.

(b) CONTENTS.—The report required under subsection (a) shall contain the following:

(1) The number of sexual assaults and incidents of sexual harassment against members of the Coast Guard, and the number of sexual assaults and incidents of sexual harassment by members of the Coast Guard, that were reported to military officials during the year covered by such report, and the number of the cases so reported that were substantiated.

(2) A synopsis of, and the disciplinary action taken in, each substantiated case.

(3) The policies, procedures, and processes implemented by the Secretary concerned during the year covered by such report in response to incidents of sexual assault and sexual harassment involving members of the Coast Guard concerned.

(4) A plan for the actions that are to be taken in the year following the year covered by such report on the prevention of and response to sexual assault and sexual harassment involving members of the Coast Guard concerned.

(5)(A) The number of instances in which a covered individual was accused of misconduct or crimes considered collateral to the investigation of a sexual assault committed against the individual.

(B) The number of instances in which adverse action was taken against a covered individual who was accused of collateral misconduct or crimes as described in subparagraph (A).

(C) The percentage of investigations of sexual assaults that involved an accusation or adverse action against a covered individual as described in subparagraphs (A) and (B).

(D) In this paragraph, the term "covered individual" means an individual who is identified as a victim of a sexual assault in the case files of a military criminal investigative organization.

(Added and amended Pub. L. 116–283, div. G, title LVXXXV [LXXXV], §8501(a)(7), Jan. 1, 2021, 134 Stat. 4745.)

§5113. Officers not on active duty promotion list

Not later than 60 days after the date on which the President submits to Congress a budget pursuant to section 1105 of title 31, the Commandant shall submit to the Committee on Transportation and Infrastructure of the House of Representatives and the Committee on Commerce, Science, and Transportation of the Senate the number of Coast Guard officers serving at other Federal entities on a reimbursable basis, and the number of Coast Guard officers who are serving at other Federal agencies on a non-reimbursable basis, but not on the active duty promotion list.

(Added Pub. L. 117–263, div. K, title CXII, §11236(b)(1), Dec. 23, 2022, 136 Stat. 4036.)

§5114. Expenses of performing and executing defense readiness missions

Not later than 1 year after the date of enactment of this section, and every February 1 thereafter, the Commandant shall submit to the Committee on Commerce, Science, and Transportation of the Senate and the Committee on Transportation and Infrastructure of the House of Representatives a report that adequately represents a calculation of the annual costs and expenditures of performing and executing all defense readiness mission activities, including—

(1) all expenses related to the Coast Guard's coordination, training, and execution of defense readiness mission activities in the Coast Guard's capacity as an armed force (as such term is defined in section 101 of title 10) in support of Department of Defense national security operations and activities or for any other military department or Defense Agency (as such terms are defined in such section);

(2) costs associated with Coast Guard detachments assigned in support of the defense readiness mission of the Coast Guard; and

(3) any other related expenses, costs, or matters the Commandant considers appropriate or otherwise of interest to Congress.

(Added Pub. L. 117–263, div. K, title CXII, §11256(a), Dec. 23, 2022, 136 Stat. 4056.)

§5115. Major grants, contracts, or other transactions

(a) Notification.—

(1) In general.—Subject to subsection (b), the Commandant shall notify the appropriate committees of Congress and the Coast Guard Office of Congressional and Governmental Affairs not later than 3 full business days in advance of the Coast Guard—

(A) making or awarding a grant allocation or grant in excess of $1,000,000;

(B) making or awarding a contract, other transaction agreement, or task or delivery order for the Coast Guard on the multiple award contract, or issuing a letter of intent totaling more than $4,000,000;

    (C) awarding a task or delivery order requiring an obligation of funds in an amount greater than $10,000,000 from multi-year Coast Guard funds;

    (D) making a sole-source grant award; or

    (E) announcing publicly the intention to make or award an item described in subparagraph (A), (B), (C), or (D), including a contract covered by the Federal Acquisition Regulation.

    (2) ELEMENT.—A notification under this subsection shall include—

    (A) the amount of the award;

    (B) the fiscal year for which the funds for the award were appropriated;

    (C) the type of contract;

    (D) an identification of the entity awarded the contract, such as the name and location of the entity; and

    (E) the account from which the funds are to be drawn.

(b) EXCEPTION.—If the Commandant determines that compliance with subsection (a) would pose a substantial risk to human life, health, or safety, the Commandant—

    (1) may make an award or issue a letter described in such subsection without the notification required under such subsection; and

    (2) shall notify the appropriate committees of Congress not later than 5 full business days after such an award is made or letter issued.

(c) APPLICABILITY.—Subsection (a) shall not apply to funds that are not available for obligation.

(d) APPROPRIATE COMMITTEES OF CONGRESS DEFINED.—In this section, the term "appropriate committees of Congress" means—

    (1) the Committee on Commerce, Science, and Transportation and the Committee on Appropriations of the Senate; and

    (2) the Committee on Transportation and Infrastructure and the Committee on Appropriations of the House of Representatives.

(Added Pub. L. 117–263, div. K, title CXII, §11262(a), Dec. 23, 2022, 136 Stat. 4060.)

SELECTED PROVISIONS OF
TITLE 46 U.S.C. — SHIPPING

CURRENT THROUGH PUBLIC LAW 118-233, EXCEPT FOR
PUBLIC LAW 118-159

SUBTITLE I
GENERAL

TITLE 46—SHIPPING

This title was enacted by Pub. L. 98–89, §1, Aug. 26, 1983, 97 Stat. 500; Pub. L. 99–509, title V, subtitle B, §5101, Oct. 21, 1986, 100 Stat. 1913; Pub. L. 100–424, §6, Sept. 9, 1988, 102 Stat. 1591; Pub. L. 100–710, title I, §102, Nov. 23, 1988, 102 Stat. 4738; Pub. L. 109–304, Oct. 6, 2006, 120 Stat. 1485

Subtitle I—General

CHAPTER 1—DEFINITIONS

§101. AGENCY

In this title, the term "agency" means a department, agency, or instrumentality of the United States Government.

(Pub. L. 109–304, §4, Oct. 6, 2006, 120 Stat. 1486.)

§102. BARGE

In this title, the term "barge" means a non-self-propelled vessel.

(Pub. L. 109–304, §4, Oct. 6, 2006, 120 Stat. 1486.)

§103. BOUNDARY LINE

In this title, the term "Boundary Line" means a line established under section 2(b) of the Act of February 19, 1895 (33 U.S.C. 151(b)).

(Pub. L. 109–304, §4, Oct. 6, 2006, 120 Stat. 1486; Pub. L. 114–120, title III, §306(a)(1), Feb. 8, 2016, 130 Stat. 54.)

§104. CITIZEN OF THE UNITED STATES

In this title, the term "citizen of the United States", when used in reference to a natural person, means an individual who is a national of the United States as defined in section 101(a)(22) of the Immigration and Nationality Act (8 U.S.C. 1101(a)(22)).

(Pub. L. 109–304, §4, Oct. 6, 2006, 120 Stat. 1486.)

§105. CONSULAR OFFICER

In this title, the term "consular officer" means an officer or employee of the United States Government designated under regulations to issue visas.

(Pub. L. 109–304, §4, Oct. 6, 2006, 120 Stat. 1486.)

§106. DOCUMENTED VESSEL

In this title, the term "documented vessel" means a vessel for which a certificate of documentation has been issued under chapter 121 of this title.

(Pub. L. 109–304, §4, Oct. 6, 2006, 120 Stat. 1486.)

§107. EXCLUSIVE ECONOMIC ZONE

In this title, the term "exclusive economic zone" means the zone established by Presidential Proclamation 5030 of March 10, 1983 (16 U.S.C. 1453 note).

(Pub. L. 109–304, §4, Oct. 6, 2006, 120 Stat. 1487.)

§108. FISHERIES

In this title, the term "fisheries" includes processing, storing, transporting (except in foreign commerce), planting, cultivating, catching, taking, or harvesting fish, shellfish, marine animals, pearls, shells, or marine vegetation in the navigable waters of the United States or in the exclusive economic zone.

(Pub. L. 109–304, §4, Oct. 6, 2006, 120 Stat. 1487.)

§109. FOREIGN COMMERCE OR TRADE

(a) IN GENERAL.—In this title, the terms "foreign commerce" and "foreign trade" mean commerce or trade between a place in the United States and a place in a foreign country.

(b) CAPITAL CONSTRUCTION FUNDS AND CONSTRUCTION-DIFFERENTIAL SUBSIDIES.—In the context of capital construction funds under chapter 535 of this title, and in the context of construction-differential subsidies under title V of the Merchant Marine Act, 1936, the terms "foreign commerce" and "foreign trade" also include, in the case of liquid and dry bulk cargo carrying services, trading between foreign ports in accordance with normal commercial bulk shipping practices in a manner that will permit bulk vessels of the United States to compete freely with foreign bulk vessels in their operation or competition for charters, subject to regulations prescribed by the Secretary of Transportation.

(Pub. L. 109–304, §4, Oct. 6, 2006, 120 Stat. 1487.)

§110. FOREIGN VESSEL

In this title, the term "foreign vessel" means a vessel of foreign registry or operated under the authority of a foreign country.

(Pub. L. 109–304, §4, Oct. 6, 2006, 120 Stat. 1487.)

§111. NUMBERED VESSEL

In this title, the term "numbered vessel" means a vessel for which a number has been issued under chapter 123 of this title.

(Pub. L. 109–304, §4, Oct. 6, 2006, 120 Stat. 1487.)

§112. State

In this title, the term "State" means a State of the United States, the District of Columbia, Guam, Puerto Rico, the Virgin Islands, American Samoa, the Northern Mariana Islands, and any other territory or possession of the United States.

(Pub. L. 109–304, §4, Oct. 6, 2006, 120 Stat. 1487.)

§113. Undocumented

In this title, the term "undocumented" means not having and not required to have a certificate of documentation issued under chapter 121 of this title.

(Pub. L. 109–304, §4, Oct. 6, 2006, 120 Stat. 1487.)

§114. United States

In this title, the term "United States", when used in a geographic sense, means the States of the United States, the District of Columbia, Guam, Puerto Rico, the Virgin Islands, American Samoa, the Northern Mariana Islands, and any other territory or possession of the United States.

(Pub. L. 109–304, §4, Oct. 6, 2006, 120 Stat. 1487.)

§115. Vessel

In this title, the term "vessel" has the meaning given that term in section 3 of title 1.

(Pub. L. 109–304, §4, Oct. 6, 2006, 120 Stat. 1487.)

§116. Vessel of the United States

In this title, the term "vessel of the United States" means a vessel documented under chapter 121 of this title (or exempt from documentation under section 12102(c) of this title), numbered under chapter 123 of this title, or titled under the law of a State.

(Pub. L. 109–304, §4, Oct. 6, 2006, 120 Stat. 1488.)

[CHAPTER 3—TRANSFERRED]

[§§301 TO 308. RENUMBERED §§46101 TO 46108]

CHAPTER 5—OTHER GENERAL PROVISIONS

§501. Waiver of navigation and vessel-inspection laws

(a) On Request of Secretary of Defense.—

(1) In general.—On request of the Secretary of Defense, the head of an agency responsible for the administration of the navigation or vessel-inspection laws shall waive compliance with those laws to the extent the Secretary considers necessary in the interest of national defense to address an immediate adverse effect on military operations.

(2) Submittal of explanation to congress.—Not later than 24 hours after making a request under paragraph (1), the Secretary of Defense shall submit to the Committee on Transportation and Infrastructure and the Committee on Armed Services of the House of Representatives and the Committee on Commerce, Science, and Transportation and the Committee on Armed Services of the Senate a written explanation of the circumstances requiring such a waiver in the interest of national defense, including a confirmation that there are insufficient qualified vessels to meet the needs of national defense without such a waiver.

(b) By Head of Agency.—

(1) In general.—Upon a determination by the President that a waiver of the navigation or vessel-inspection laws is necessary in the interest of national defense, the head of an agency responsible for the administration of such laws,[1] may waive compliance with such laws—

(A) following a determination in accordance with the requirements of paragraph (3) by the Maritime Administrator, acting in the Administrator's capacity as Director, National Shipping Authority, of the non-availability of qualified United States flag capacity to meet national defense requirements;

(B) not earlier than 48 hours after a waiver request is published under paragraph (6)(A); and

(C) on a vessel specific basis to the extent, in the manner, and on the terms the head of such agency, in consultation with the Administrator, acting in such capacity, prescribes.

(2) Duration of waiver.—

(A) In general.—Subject to subparagraphs (B) and (C), a waiver issued under this subsection shall be for a period of not more than 10 days.

(B) Waiver extension.—Upon the termination of the period of a waiver issued under this subsection, the head of an agency may extend the waiver for an additional period of not more than 10 days, if the Maritime Administrator makes the determination referred to in paragraph (1)(A).

(C) AGGREGATE DURATION.—The aggregate duration of the period of all waivers and extensions of waivers under this subsection with respect to any one set of events shall not exceed 45 days.

(3) DETERMINATIONS.—The Maritime Administrator shall—

(A) for each determination referred to in paragraph (1)(A)—

(i) identify any actions that could be taken to enable qualified United States flag capacity to meet national defense requirements prior to the issuance of a waiver; and

(ii) not assess the non-availability of qualified United States flag capacity to meet national defense requirements retrospectively after the date on which a waiver is requested;

(B) provide notice of each such determination to the Secretary of Transportation and the head of the agency referred to in paragraph (1) for which the determination is made; and

(C) publish each such determination on the Internet Web site of the Department of Transportation not later than 48 hours after notice of the determination is provided to the Secretary of Transportation.

(4) NOTICE TO CONGRESS.—

(A) IN GENERAL.—The head of an agency referred to in paragraph (1) shall notify the Committee on Transportation and Infrastructure and the Committee on Armed Services of the House of Representatives and the Committee on Commerce, Science, and Transportation and the Committee on Armed Services of the Senate—

(i) of any request for a waiver of the navigation or vessel-inspection laws under this section not later than 48 hours after receiving such a request; and

(ii) of the issuance of any such waiver not later than 48 hours after such issuance.

(B) CONTENTS.—Such head of an agency shall include in each notification under subparagraph (A)(ii) an explanation of—

(i) the reasons the waiver is necessary; and

(ii) the reasons actions referred to in paragraph (3)(A) are not feasible.

(C) NOTIFICATION REQUIRED FOR EXTENSIONS.—For purposes of this paragraph, an extension requested or issued under paragraph (2)(B) shall be treated in the same manner as a waiver requested or issued under this subsection.

(5) PROSPECTIVE APPLICATION.—No waiver shall be issued for a vessel if, at the time of the waiver request under this section, such vessel is laden with merchandise that, pursuant to the requested waiver, could be unladen at points or places to which the coastwise laws apply.

(6) PUBLICATION REQUIREMENTS.—

(A) PUBLICATION OF WAIVER REQUESTS.—Upon receiving a request for a waiver under this subsection, the head of an agency referred to in paragraph (1) shall publish such request on the website of such agency.

(B) PUBLICATION OF WAIVER DENIAL.—Not later than 48 hours after denying a waiver requested under this subsection, the head of an agency referred to in paragraph (1) shall publish on the website of such agency an explanation for denying such waiver, including applicable findings to support the denial.

(c) REPORT.—

(1) IN GENERAL.—Not later than 10 days after the date of the conclusion of the voyage of a vessel that, during such voyage, operated under a waiver issued under this section, the owner or operator of the vessel and the individual requesting such waiver (if not the owner or operator of the vessel) shall submit to the Maritime Administrator a report that includes—

(A) the name and flag of the vessel;

(B) the name of the owner and operator of the vessel;

(C) the dates of the voyage;

(D) any relevant ports of call;

(E) a description of the cargo carried;

(F) an explanation as to why the waiver was in the interest of national defense; and

(G) any other information the Maritime Administrator determines necessary.

(2) PUBLICATION.—Not later than 48 hours after receiving a report under paragraph (1), the Maritime Administrator shall publish such report on an appropriate website of the Department of Transportation.

(d) TERMINATION OF AUTHORITY.—The authority granted by this section shall terminate at such time as the Congress by concurrent resolution or the President may designate.

(Pub. L. 109–304, §4, Oct. 6, 2006, 120 Stat. 1490; Pub. L. 110–417, div. C, title XXXV, §3510, Oct. 14, 2008, 122 Stat. 4769; Pub. L. 112–213, title III, §301, Dec. 20, 2012, 126 Stat. 1562; Pub. L. 112–239, div. C, title XXXV, §3517(a)(2), Jan. 2, 2013, 126 Stat. 2229; Pub. L. 116–283, div. C, title XXXV, §3502(a)(1), Jan. 1, 2021, 134 Stat. 4397, Pub. L. 117 263, div. C, title XXXV, §3541, Dec. 23, 2022, 136 Stat. 3093.)

¹ So in original. The comma probably should not appear.

§502. CARGO EXEMPT FROM FORFEITURE

Cargo on a vessel is exempt from forfeiture under this title if—

(1) the cargo is owned in good faith by a person not the owner, master, or crewmember of the vessel; and

(2) the customs duties on the cargo have been paid or secured for payment as provided by law.

(Pub. L. 109–304, §4, Oct. 6, 2006, 120 Stat. 1490.)

§503. NOTICE OF SEIZURE

When a forfeiture of a vessel or cargo accrues, the official of the United States Government required to give notice of the seizure of the vessel or cargo shall include in the notice, if they are known to that official, the name and the place of residence of the owner or consignee at the time of the seizure.

(Pub. L. 109–304, §4, Oct. 6, 2006, 120 Stat. 1490.)

§504. REMISSION OF FEES AND PENALTIES

Any part of a fee, tax, or penalty paid or a forfeiture incurred under a law or regulation relating to vessels or seamen may be remitted if—

(1) application for the remission is made within one year after the date of the payment or forfeiture; and

(2) it is found that the fee, tax, penalty, or forfeiture was improperly or excessively imposed.

(Pub. L. 109–304, §4, Oct. 6, 2006, 120 Stat. 1491.)

§505. PENALTY FOR VIOLATING REGULATION OR ORDER

A person convicted of knowingly and willfully violating a regulation or order of the Federal Maritime Commission or the Secretary of Transportation under subtitle IV or V of this title, for which no penalty is expressly provided, shall be fined not more than $500. Each day of a continuing violation is a separate offense.

(Pub. L. 109–304, §4, Oct. 6, 2006, 120 Stat. 1491.)

SUBTITLE II
VESSELS AND SEAMEN

Subtitle II—Vessels and Seamen

PART A—GENERAL PROVISIONS

CHAPTER 21—GENERAL

§2101. GENERAL DEFINITIONS

In this subtitle—

(1) "associated equipment"—

(A) means—

(i) a system, accessory, component, or appurtenance of a recreational vessel; or

(ii) a marine safety article intended for use on board a recreational vessel; but

(B) with the exception of emergency locator beacons for recreational vessels operating beyond 3 nautical miles from the baselines from which the territorial sea of the United States is measured or beyond 3 nautical miles from the coastline of the Great Lakes, does not include radio equipment.

(2) "Coast Guard" means the organization established and continued under section 1 [1] of title 14.

(3) "Commandant" means the Commandant of the Coast Guard.

(4) "commercial service" includes any type of trade or business involving the transportation of goods or individuals, except service performed by a combatant vessel.

(5) "consideration" means an economic benefit, inducement, right, or profit including pecuniary payment accruing to an individual, person, or entity, but not including a voluntary sharing of the actual expenses of the voyage, by monetary contribution or

donation of fuel, food, beverage, or other supplies.

(6) "crude oil" means a liquid hydrocarbon mixture occurring naturally in the earth, whether or not treated to render it suitable for transportation, and includes crude oil from which certain distillate fractions may have been removed, and crude oil to which certain distillate fractions may have been added.

(7) "crude oil tanker" means a tanker engaged in the trade of carrying crude oil.

(8) "dangerous drug" means a narcotic drug, a controlled substance, or a controlled substance analog (as defined in section 102 of the Comprehensive Drug Abuse Prevention and Control Act of 1970 (21 U.S.C. 802)).

(9) "discharge", when referring to a substance discharged from a vessel, includes spilling, leaking, pumping, pouring, emitting, emptying, or dumping, however caused.

(10) "ferry" means a vessel that is used on a regular schedule—

(A) to provide transportation only between places that are not more than 300 miles apart; and

(B) to transport only—

(i) passengers; or

(ii) vehicles, or railroad cars, that are being used, or have been used, in transporting passengers or goods.

(11) "fish" means finfish, mollusks, crustaceans, and all other forms of marine animal and plant life, except marine mammals and birds.

(12) "fishing vessel" means a vessel that commercially engages in the catching, taking, or harvesting of fish or an activity that can reasonably be expected to result in the catching, taking, or harvesting of fish.

(13) "fish processing vessel" means a vessel that commercially prepares fish or fish products other than by gutting, decapitating, gilling, skinning, shucking, icing, freezing, or brine chilling.

(14) "fish tender vessel" means a vessel that commercially supplies, stores, refrigerates, or transports fish, fish products, or materials directly related to fishing or the preparation of fish to or from a fishing, fish processing, or fish tender vessel or a fish processing facility.

(15) "freight vessel" means a motor vessel of more than 15 gross tons as measured under section 14502 of this title, or an alternate tonnage measured under section 14302 of this title as prescribed by the Secretary under section 14104 of this title that carries freight for hire, except an oceanographic research vessel or an offshore supply vessel.

(16) "Great Lakes barge" means a non-self-propelled vessel of at least 3,500 gross tons as measured under section 14502 of this title, or an alternate tonnage measured under section 14302 of this title as prescribed by the Secretary under section 14104 of this title operating on the Great Lakes.

(17) "hazardous material" means a liquid material or substance that is—

(A) flammable or combustible;

(B) designated a hazardous substance under section 311(b) of the Federal Water Pollution Control Act (33 U.S.C. 1321); or

(C) designated a hazardous material under section 5103(a) of title 49.

(18) "major conversion" means a conversion of a vessel that—
(A) substantially changes the dimensions or carrying capacity of the vessel;
(B) changes the type of the vessel;
(C) substantially prolongs the life of the vessel; or
(D) otherwise so changes the vessel that it is essentially a new vessel, as decided by the Secretary.

(19) "marine environment" means—
(A) the navigable waters of the United States and the land and resources in and under those waters;
(B) the waters and fishery resources of an area over which the United States asserts exclusive fishery management authority;
(C) the seabed and subsoil of the outer Continental Shelf of the United States, the resources of the Shelf, and the waters superjacent to the Shelf; and
(D) the recreational, economic, and scenic values of the waters and resources referred to in subclauses (A)–(C) of this clause.

(20) "mobile offshore drilling unit" means a vessel capable of engaging in drilling operations for the exploration or exploitation of subsea resources.
(21) "motor vessel" means a vessel propelled by machinery other than steam.
(22) "nautical school vessel" means a vessel operated by or in connection with a nautical school or an educational institution under section 558 of title 40.
(23) "navigable waters of the United States" includes all waters of the territorial sea of the United States as described in Presidential Proclamation No. 5928 of December 27, 1988.
(24) "oceanographic research vessel" means a vessel that the Secretary finds is being employed only in instruction in oceanography or limnology, or both, or only in oceanographic or limnological research, including studies about the sea such as seismic, gravity meter, and magnetic exploration and other marine geophysical or geological surveys, atmospheric research, and biological research.
(25) "offshore supply vessel" means a motor vessel that regularly carries goods, supplies, individuals in addition to the crew, or equipment in support of exploration, exploitation, or production of offshore mineral or energy resources.
(26) "oil" includes oil of any type or in any form, including petroleum, fuel oil, sludge, oil refuse, and oil mixed with wastes except dredged spoil.
(27) "oil spill response vessel" means a vessel that is designated in its certificate of inspection as such a vessel, or that is adapted to respond to a discharge of oil or a hazardous material.
(28) "overall in length" means—
(A) for a foreign vessel or a vessel engaged on a foreign voyage, the greater of—
(i) 96 percent of the length on a waterline at 85 percent of the least molded depth measured from the top of the keel (or on a vessel designed with a rake of keel, on a waterline parallel to the designed waterline); or
(ii) the length from the fore side of the stem to the axis of the rudder stock on that waterline; and

(B) for any other vessel, the horizontal distance of the hull between the foremost part of the stem and the aftermost part of the stern, excluding fittings and attachments.

(29) "passenger"—
(A) means an individual carried on the vessel except—
(i) the owner or an individual representative of the owner or, in the case of a vessel under charter, an individual charterer or individual representative of the charterer;
(ii) the master; or
(iii) a member of the crew engaged in the business of the vessel who has not contributed consideration for carriage and who is paid for on board services;

(B) on an offshore supply vessel, means an individual carried on the vessel except—
(i) an individual included in clause (i), (ii), or (iii) of subparagraph (A) of this paragraph;
(ii) an employee of the owner, or of a subcontractor to the owner, engaged in the business of the owner;
(iii) an employee of the charterer, or of a subcontractor to the charterer, engaged in the business of the charterer; or
(iv) an individual employed in a phase of exploration, exploitation, or production of offshore mineral or energy resources served by the vessel;

(C) on a fishing vessel, fish processing vessel, or fish tender vessel, means an individual carried on the vessel except—
(i) an individual included in clause (i), (ii), or (iii) of subparagraph (A) of this paragraph;
(ii) a managing operator;
(iii) an employee of the owner, or of a subcontractor to the owner, engaged in the business of the owner;
(iv) an employee of the charterer, or of a subcontractor to the charterer, engaged in the business of the charterer; or
(v) an observer or sea sampler on board the vessel pursuant to a requirement of State or Federal law; or

(D) on a sailing school vessel, means an individual carried on the vessel except—
(i) an individual included in clause (i), (ii), or (iii) of subparagraph (A) of this paragraph;
(ii) an employee of the owner of the vessel engaged in the business of the owner, except when the vessel is operating under a demise charter;
(iii) an employee of the demise charterer of the vessel engaged in the business of the demise charterer; or
(iv) a sailing school instructor or sailing school student.

(30) "passenger for hire" means a passenger for whom consideration is contributed as

a condition of carriage on the vessel, whether directly or indirectly flowing to the owner, charterer, operator, agent, or any other person having an interest in the vessel.

(31) "passenger vessel" means a vessel of at least 100 gross tons as measured under section 14502 of this title, or an alternate tonnage measured under section 14302 of this title as prescribed by the Secretary under section 14104 of this title—

    (A) carrying more than 12 passengers, including at least one passenger for hire;

    (B) that is chartered and carrying more than 12 passengers;

    (C) that is a submersible vessel carrying at least one passenger for hire; or

    (D) that is a ferry carrying a passenger.

(32) "product carrier" means a tanker engaged in the trade of carrying oil except crude oil.

(33) "public vessel" means a vessel that—

    (A) is owned, or demise chartered, and operated by the United States Government or a government of a foreign country; and

    (B) is not engaged in commercial service.

(34) "recreational vessel" means a vessel—

    (A) being manufactured or operated primarily for pleasure; or

    (B) leased, rented, or chartered to another for the latter's pleasure.

(35) "recreational vessel manufacturer" means a person engaged in the manufacturing, construction, assembly, or importation of recreational vessels, components, or associated equipment.

(36) "riding gang member" means an individual who—

    (A) has not been issued a merchant mariner document under chapter 73;

    (B) does not perform—

        (i) watchstanding, automated engine room duty watch, or personnel safety functions; or

        (ii) cargo handling functions, including any activity relating to the loading or unloading of cargo, the operation of cargo-related equipment (whether or not integral to the vessel), and the handling of mooring lines on the dock when the vessel is made fast or let go;

    (C) does not serve as part of the crew complement required under section 8101;

    (D) is not a member of the steward's department; and

    (E) is not a citizen or temporary or permanent resident of a country designated by the United States as a sponsor of terrorism or any other country that the Secretary, in consultation with the Secretary of State and the heads of other appropriate United States agencies, determines to be a security threat to the United States.

(37) "sailing instruction" means teaching, research, and practical experience in operating vessels propelled primarily by sail and may include—

    (A) any subject related to that operation and to the sea, including seamanship, navigation, oceanography, other nautical and marine sciences, and maritime history and literature; and

(B) only when in conjunction with a subject referred to in subclause (A) of this clause, instruction in mathematics and language arts skills to sailing school students having learning disabilities.

(38) "sailing school instructor" means an individual who is on board a sailing school vessel to provide sailing instruction, but does not include an operator or crewmember who is among those required to be on board the vessel to meet a requirement established under part F of this subtitle.

(39) "sailing school student" means an individual who is on board a sailing school vessel to receive sailing instruction.

(40) "sailing school vessel" means a vessel—

(A) that is less than 500 gross tons as measured under section 14502 of this title, or an alternate tonnage measured under section 14302 of this title as prescribed by the Secretary under section 14104 of this title;

(B) carrying more than 6 individuals who are sailing school instructors or sailing school students;

(C) principally equipped for propulsion by sail, even if the vessel has an auxiliary means of propulsion; and

(D) owned or demise chartered, and operated by an organization described in section 501(c)(3) of the Internal Revenue Code of 1986 (26 U.S.C. 501(c)(3)) and exempt from tax under section 501(a) of that Code, or by a State or political subdivision of a State, during times that the vessel is operated by the organization, State, or political subdivision only for sailing instruction.

(41)(A) Subject to subparagraph (B), "scientific personnel" means individuals on board an oceanographic research vessel only to engage in scientific research, or to instruct or receive instruction in oceanography or limnology.

(B)(i) Such term includes an individual who is on board an oceanographic research vessel only to—

(I) engage in scientific research;

(II) instruct in oceanography or limnology; or

(III) receive instruction in oceanography or limnology.

(ii) For purposes of clause (i), the age of an individual may not be considered in determining whether the individual is described in such clause.

(42) "seagoing barge" means a non-self-propelled vessel of at least 100 gross tons as measured under section 14502 of this title, or an alternate tonnage measured under section 14302 of this title as prescribed by the Secretary under section 14104 of this title making voyages beyond the Boundary Line.

(43) "seagoing motor vessel" means a motor vessel of at least 300 gross tons as measured under section 14502 of this title, or an alternate tonnage measured under section 14302 of this title as prescribed by the Secretary under section 14104 of this title making voyages beyond the Boundary Line.

(44) "Secretary" means the Secretary of the department in which the Coast Guard is

operating.

(45) "sexual assault" means any form of abuse or contact as defined in chapter 109A of title 18, or a substantially similar offense under State, local, or Tribal law.

(46) "sexual harassment" means—

(A) conduct that—

(i) involves unwelcome sexual advances, requests for sexual favors, or deliberate or repeated offensive comments or gestures of a sexual nature if any—

(I) submission to such conduct is made either explicitly or implicitly a term or condition of employment, pay, career, benefits, or entitlements of the individual;

(II) submission to, or rejection, of such conduct by an individual is used as a basis for decisions affecting that individual's job, pay, career, benefits, or entitlements;

(III) such conduct has the purpose or effect of unreasonably interfering with an individual's work performance or creates an intimidating, hostile, or offensive work environment; or

(IV) conduct may have been by an individual's supervisor, a supervisor in another area, a co-worker, or another credentialed mariner; and

(ii) is so severe or pervasive that a reasonable person would perceive, and the victim does perceive, the environment as hostile or offensive;

(B) any use or condonation associated with first-hand or personal knowledge, by any individual in a supervisory or command position, of any form of sexual behavior to control, influence, or affect the career, pay, benefits, entitlements, or employment of a subordinate; and

(C) any intentional or repeated unwelcome verbal comment or gesture of a sexual nature towards or about an individual by the individual's supervisor, a supervisor in another area, a coworker, or another credentialed mariner.

(47) "small passenger vessel" means a wing-in-ground craft, regardless of tonnage, carrying at least one passenger for hire, and a vessel of less than 100 gross tons as measured under section 14502 of this title, or an alternate tonnage measured under section 14302 of this title as prescribed by the Secretary under section 14104 of this title—

(A) carrying more than 6 passengers, including at least one passenger for hire;

(B) that is chartered with the crew provided or specified by the owner or the owner's representative and carrying more than 6 passengers;

(C) that is chartered with no crew provided or specified by the owner or the owner's representative and carrying more than 12 passengers;

(D) that is a submersible vessel carrying at least one passenger for hire; or

(E) that is a ferry carrying more than 6 passengers.

(48) "steam vessel" means a vessel propelled in whole or in part by steam, except a recreational vessel of not more than 40 feet in length.

(49) "submersible vessel" means a vessel that is capable of operating below the surface

of the water.

(50) "tanker" means a self-propelled tank vessel constructed or adapted primarily to carry oil or hazardous material in bulk in the cargo spaces.

(51) "tank vessel" means a vessel that is constructed or adapted to carry, or that carries, oil or hazardous material in bulk as cargo or cargo residue, and that—

(A) is a vessel of the United States;

(B) operates on the navigable waters of the United States; or

(C) transfers oil or hazardous material in a port or place subject to the jurisdiction of the United States.

(52) "towing vessel" means a commercial vessel engaged in or intending to engage in the service of pulling, pushing, or hauling along side, or any combination of pulling, pushing, or hauling along side.

(53) "uninspected passenger vessel" means an uninspected vessel—

(A) of at least 100 gross tons as measured under section 14502 of this title, or an alternate tonnage measured under section 14302 of this title as prescribed by the Secretary under section 14104 of this title—

(i) carrying not more than 12 passengers, including at least one passenger for hire; or

(ii) that is chartered with the crew provided or specified by the owner or the owner's representative and carrying not more than 12 passengers; and

(B) of less than 100 gross tons as measured under section 14502 of this title, or an alternate tonnage measured under section 14302 of this title as prescribed by the Secretary under section 14104 of this title—

(i) carrying not more than 6 passengers, including at least one passenger for hire; or

(ii) that is chartered with the crew provided or specified by the owner or the owner's representative and carrying not more than 6 passengers.

(54) "uninspected vessel" means a vessel not subject to inspection under section 3301 of this title that is not a recreational vessel.

(55) "vessel of war" means a vessel—

(A) belonging to the armed forces of a country;

(B) bearing the external marks distinguishing vessels of war of that country;

(C) under the command of an officer commissioned by the government of that country and whose name appears in the appropriate service list or its equivalent; and

(D) staffed by a crew under regular armed forces discipline.

(56) "wing-in-ground craft" means a vessel that is capable of operating completely above the surface of the water on a dynamic air cushion created by aerodynamic lift due to the ground effect between the vessel and the water's surface.

(Pub. L. 98–89, Aug. 26, 1983, 97 Stat. 501; Pub. L. 98–364, title IV, §402(1), July 17, 1984, 98 Stat. 445; Pub. L. 98–454, title III, §301(a), Oct. 5, 1984, 98 Stat. 1734; Pub. L. 98–557, §34(a), Oct. 30, 1984, 98 Stat. 2876; Pub. L. 99–307, §1(1), (2), May 19, 1986, 100 Stat. 444; Pub. L. 99–509, title V, §5102(b)(1), Oct.

21, 1986, 100 Stat. 1926; Pub. L. 99–514, §2, Oct. 22, 1986, 100 Stat. 2095; Pub. L. 99–640, §§10(b)(1), 11(a), 13(d), Nov. 10, 1986, 100 Stat. 3549–3551; Pub. L. 100–239, §6(a)(1), Jan. 11, 1988, 101 Stat. 1781; Pub. L. 100–424, §8(c)(1), Sept. 9, 1988, 102 Stat. 1593; Pub. L. 100–710, title I, §104(a)(1), (2), Nov. 23, 1988, 102 Stat. 4749; Pub. L. 101–225, title II, §209, Dec. 12, 1989, 103 Stat. 1913; Pub. L. 101–380, title IV, §4103(a)(2)(A), Aug. 18, 1990, 104 Stat. 511; Pub. L. 101–595, title VI, §603(1), Nov. 16, 1990, 104 Stat. 2993; Pub. L. 102–587, title V, §5208(a), Nov. 4, 1992, 106 Stat. 5075; Pub. L. 103–206, title V, §§502–510, Dec. 20, 1993, 107 Stat. 2439–2441; Pub. L. 103–272, §5(l), July 5, 1994, 108 Stat. 1375; Pub. L. 104–324, title VII, §709, title XI, §1104(a), Oct. 19, 1996, 110 Stat. 3934, 3966; Pub. L. 105–383, title III, §301(b)(1), Nov. 13, 1998, 112 Stat. 3417; Pub. L. 107–217, §3(m)(1), Aug. 21, 2002, 116 Stat. 1302; Pub. L. 107–295, title IV, §419, Nov. 25, 2002, 116 Stat. 2124; Pub. L. 109–241, title III, §§301, 312(b), July 11, 2006, 120 Stat. 526, 533; Pub. L. 109–304, §15(2), Oct. 6, 2006, 120 Stat. 1702; Pub. L. 111–281, title VI, §§617(a)(1)(A), 618, Oct. 15, 2010, 124 Stat. 2972, 2975; Pub. L. 111–330, §1(9), Dec. 22, 2010, 124 Stat. 3570; Pub. L. 115–232, div. C, title XXXV, §3541(a)(1), Aug. 13, 2018, 132 Stat. 2322; Pub. L. 115–282, title V, §515, Dec. 4, 2018, 132 Stat. 4279; Pub. L. 117–263, div. K, title CXVI, §11601(a), Dec. 23, 2022, 136 Stat. 4145.)

[1] *See References in Text note below.*

§2102. LIMITED DEFINITIONS

In chapters 33, 45, 51, 81, and 87 of this title, "Aleutian trade" means the transportation of cargo (including fishery related products) for hire on board a fish tender vessel to or from a place in Alaska west of 153 degrees west longitude and east of 172 degrees east longitude, if that place receives weekly common carrier service by water, to or from a place in the United States (except a place in Alaska).

(Pub. L. 98–89, Aug. 26, 1983, 97 Stat. 505; Pub. L. 98–369, div. A, title X, §1011(a), July 18, 1984, 98 Stat. 1013; Pub. L. 99–509, title V, §5102(b)(2), Oct. 21, 1986, 100 Stat. 1926; Pub. L. 101–595, title VI, §602(a), Nov. 16, 1990, 104 Stat. 2990; Pub. L. 109–304, §§15(3), 16(a), Oct. 6, 2006, 120 Stat. 1702, 1705.)

§2103. SUPERINTENDENCE OF THE MERCHANT MARINE

The Secretary has general superintendence over the merchant marine of the United States and of merchant marine personnel insofar as the enforcement of this subtitle is concerned and insofar as those vessels and personnel are not subject, under other law, to the supervision of another official of the United States Government. In the interests of marine safety and seamen's welfare, the Secretary shall enforce this subtitle and shall carry out correctly and uniformly administer this subtitle. The Secretary may prescribe regulations to carry out the provisions of this subtitle.

(Pub. L. 98–89, Aug. 26, 1983, 97 Stat. 506; Pub. L. 99–307, §9, May 19, 1986, 100 Stat. 447.)

§2104. DELEGATION

(a) The Secretary may delegate the duties and powers conferred by this subtitle to any officer, employee, or member of the Coast Guard, and may provide for the subdelegation of those duties and powers.

(b) When this subtitle authorizes an officer or employee of the Customs Service to act in place of a Coast Guard official, the Secretary may designate that officer or employee subject to the approval of the Secretary of the Treasury.

(Pub. L. 98–89, Aug. 26, 1983, 97 Stat. 506.)

§2105. REPORT

The Secretary shall provide for the investigation of the operation of this subtitle and of all laws related to marine safety, and shall require that a report be made to the Secretary annually about those matters that may require improvement or amendment.

(Pub. L. 98–89, Aug. 26, 1983, 97 Stat. 506.)

§2106. LIABILITY IN REM

When a vessel is made liable in rem under this subtitle, the vessel may be libeled and proceeded against in the district court of the United States for any district in which the vessel is found.

(Pub. L. 98–89, Aug. 26, 1983, 97 Stat. 506; Pub. L. 109–304, §15(4), Oct. 6, 2006, 120 Stat. 1702.)

§2107. CIVIL PENALTY PROCEDURES

(a) After notice and an opportunity for a hearing, a person found by the Secretary to have violated this subtitle or subtitle VII or a regulation prescribed under this subtitle or subtitle VII for which a civil penalty is provided, is liable to the United States Government for the civil penalty provided. The amount of the civil penalty shall be assessed by the Secretary by written notice. In determining the amount of the penalty, the Secretary shall consider the nature, circumstances, extent, and gravity of the prohibited acts committed and, with respect to the violator, the degree of culpability, any history of prior offenses, ability to pay, and other matters that justice requires.

(b) The Secretary may compromise, modify, or remit, with or without consideration, a civil penalty under this subtitle or subtitle VII until the assessment is referred to the Attorney General.

(c) If a person fails to pay an assessment of a civil penalty after it has become final, the Secretary may refer the matter to the Attorney General for collection in an appropriate district court of the United States.

(Pub. L. 98–89, Aug. 26, 1983, 97 Stat. 506; Pub. L. 109–241, title III, §306(b), July 11, 2006, 120 Stat. 528.)

[§2108. REPEALED. PUB. L. 109–304, §15(5), OCT. 6, 2006, 120 STAT. 1702]

Section, Pub. L. 98–89, Aug. 26, 1983, 97 Stat. 507, related to refund of penalties unlawfully, improperly, or excessively imposed. See section 504 of this title.

§2109. PUBLIC VESSELS

Except as otherwise provided, this subtitle does not apply to a public vessel of the United States. However, this subtitle does apply to a vessel (except a Great Lakes St. Lawrence Seaway Development Corporation vessel) owned or operated by the Department of Transportation or by any corporation organized or controlled by the Department.

(Pub. L. 98–89, Aug. 26, 1983, 97 Stat. 507; Pub. L. 99–509, title V, §5102(b)(3), Oct. 21, 1986, 100 Stat. 1927; Pub. L. 109–241, title IX, §902(e)(1), July 11, 2006, 120 Stat. 567; Pub. L. 111–281, title IX, §903(a)(5)(A), Oct. 15, 2010, 124 Stat. 3010; Pub. L. 116–260, div. AA, title V, §512(c)(6)(A), Dec. 27, 2020, 134 Stat. 2756.)

§2110. FEES

(a)(1) Except as otherwise provided in this title, the Secretary shall establish a fee or charge for a service or thing of value provided by the Secretary under this subtitle, in accordance with section 9701 of title 31.

(2) The Secretary may not establish a fee or charge under paragraph (1) for inspection or examination of a non-self-propelled tank vessel under part B of this subtitle that is more than $500 annually. The Secretary may not establish a fee or charge under paragraph (1) for inspection or examination of a small passenger vessel under this title that is more than $300 annually for such vessels under 65 feet in length, or more than $600 annually for such vessels 65 feet in length and greater. The Secretary may not establish a fee or charge under paragraph (1) for inspection or examination under this title for any publicly-owned ferry.

(3) The Secretary may, by regulation, adjust a fee or charge collected under this subsection to accommodate changes in the cost of providing a specific service or thing of value, but the adjusted fee or charge may not exceed the total cost of providing the service or thing of value for which the fee or charge is collected, including the cost of collecting the fee or charge.

(4) The Secretary may not collect a fee or charge under this subsection that is in conflict with the international obligations of the United States.

(5) The Secretary may not collect a fee or charge under this subsection for any search or rescue service.

(b)(1) In addition to the collection of fees and charges established under subsection (a), in providing a service or thing of value under this subtitle the Secretary may accept in-kind transportation, travel, and subsistence.

(2) The value of in-kind transportation, travel, and subsistence accepted under this paragraph may not exceed applicable per diem rates set forth in regulations prescribed under section 464 of title 37.

(c) In addition to the collection of fees and charges established under subsection (a), the Secretary may recover appropriate collection and enforcement costs associated with delinquent payments of the fees and charges.

(d)(1) The Secretary may employ any Federal, State, or local agency or instrumentality, or any private enterprise or business, to collect a fee or charge established under this section. A private enterprise or business selected by the Secretary to collect fees or charges—

(A) shall be subject to reasonable terms and conditions agreed to by the Secretary and the enterprise or business;

(B) shall provide appropriate accounting to the Secretary; and

(C) may not institute litigation as part of that collection.

(2) A Federal agency shall account for the agency's costs of collecting the fee or charge under this subsection as a reimbursable expense, and the costs shall be credited to the account from which expended.

(e) A person that violates this section by failing to pay a fee or charge established under this section is liable to the United States Government for a civil penalty of not more than $5,000 for each violation.

(f) When requested by the Secretary, the Secretary of Homeland Security shall deny the clearance required by section 60105 of this title to a vessel for which a fee or charge established under this section has not been paid until the fee or charge is paid or until a bond is posted for the payment.

(g) The Secretary may exempt a person from paying a fee or charge established under this section if the Secretary determines that it is in the public interest to do so.

(h) Fees and charges collected by the Secretary under this section shall be deposited in the general fund of the Treasury as offsetting receipts of the department in which the Coast Guard is operating and ascribed to Coast Guard activities.

(i) The collection of a fee or charge under this section does not alter or expand the functions, powers, responsibilities, or liability of the United States under any law for the performance of services or the provision of a thing of value for which a fee or charge is collected under this section.

(j) The Secretary may not establish or collect a fee or charge for the inspection under part B of this subtitle of training vessels operated by State maritime academies.

(Pub. L. 98–89, Aug. 26, 1983, 97 Stat. 507; Pub. L. 99–509, title V, §5102(b)(4), Oct. 21, 1986, 100 Stat. 1927; Pub. L. 100–710, title I, §104(a)(3), Nov. 23, 1988, 102 Stat. 4749; Pub. L. 101–508, title X, §10401(a), Nov. 5, 1990, 104 Stat. 1388–397; Pub. L. 102–241, §53, Dec. 19, 1991, 105 Stat. 2232; Pub. L. 102–582, title V, §501(a), Nov. 2, 1992, 106 Stat. 4909; Pub. L. 102–587, title V, §5207, Nov. 4, 1992, 106 Stat. 5075; Pub. L. 104–324, title XI, §1112, Oct. 19, 1996, 110 Stat. 3970; Pub. L. 105–383, title II, §207, Nov. 13, 1998, 112 Stat. 3416; Pub. L. 107–295, title III, §344, Nov. 25, 2002, 116 Stat. 2106; Pub. L. 109–304, §15(6), Oct. 6, 2006, 120 Stat. 1702; Pub. L. 113–281, title III, §311(a), Dec. 18, 2014, 128 Stat. 3047; Pub. L. 115–232, div. C, title XXXV, §3546(a), Aug. 13, 2018, 132 Stat. 2326.)

§2111. PAY FOR OVERTIME SERVICES

(a) The Secretary may prescribe a reasonable rate of extra pay for overtime services of civilian officers and employees of the Coast Guard required to remain on duty between 5 p.m. and 8 a.m., or on Sundays or holidays, to perform services related to—

(1) the inspection of vessels or their equipment;

(2) the engagement and discharge of crews of vessels;

(3) the measurement of vessels; and

(4) the documentation of vessels.

(b) Except for Sundays and holidays, the overtime rate provided under subsection (a) of this section is one-half day's additional pay for each 2 hours of overtime (or part of 2 hours of at least one hour). The total extra pay may be not more than 2 and one-half days' pay for any one period from 5 p.m. to 8 a.m.

(c) The overtime rate provided under subsection (a) of this section for Sundays and holidays is 2 additional days' pay.

(d) The owner, charterer, managing operator, agent, master, or individual in charge of the vessel shall pay the amount of the overtime pay provided under this section to the official designated by regulation. The official shall deposit the amount paid to the Treasury as miscellaneous receipts. Payment to the officer or employee entitled to the pay shall be made from the annual appropriations for salaries and expenses of the Coast Guard.

(e) The overtime pay provided under this section shall be paid if the authorized officers and employees have been ordered to report for duty and have reported, even if services requested were not performed.

(Pub. L. 98–89, Aug. 26, 1983, 97 Stat. 507.)

§2112. AUTHORITY TO CHANGE WORKING HOURS

In a port at which the customary working hours begin before 8 a.m. or end after 5 p.m., the Secretary may regulate the working hours of the officers and employees referred to in section 2111 of this title so that those hours conform to the prevailing working hours of the port. However—

(1) the total period for which overtime pay may be required under section 2111 of this title may not be more than 15 hours between any 2 periods of ordinary working hours on other than Sundays and holidays;

(2) the length of the working day for the officers and employees involved may not be changed; and

(3) the rate of overtime pay may not be changed.

(Pub. L. 98–89, Aug. 26, 1983, 97 Stat. 508.)

§2113. AUTHORITY TO EXEMPT CERTAIN VESSELS

If the Secretary decides that the application of a provision of part B, C, F, or G of this subtitle is not necessary in performing the mission of the vessel engaged in excursions or an oceanographic research vessel, or not necessary for the safe operation of certain vessels carrying passengers, the Secretary by regulation may—

(1) for a vessel, issue a special permit specifying the conditions of operation and equipment;

(2) exempt an oceanographic research vessel from that provision under conditions the Secretary may specify;

(3) establish different operating and equipment requirements for vessels defined in section 2101(53)(A) of this title; and

(4) maintain different structural fire protection, manning, operating, and equipment requirements for vessels that satisfied requirements set forth in the Passenger Vessel Safety Act of 1993 (Public Law 103–206) before June 21, 1994.

(Pub. L. 98 89, Aug. 26, 1983, 97 Stat. 508; Pub. L. 103–206, title V, §511(a), Dec. 20, 1993, 107 Stat. 2441; Pub. L. 104–324, title VII, §710, Oct. 19, 1996, 110 Stat. 3935; Pub. L. 115–232, div. C, title XXXV, §§3541(b)(6), 3542(a), Aug. 13, 2018, 132 Stat. 2323, 2324; Pub. L. 117–263, div. K, title CXVI, §11601(c)(1), Dec. 23, 2022, 136 Stat. 4146.)

§2114. PROTECTION OF SEAMEN AGAINST DISCRIMINATION

(a)(1) A person may not discharge or in any manner discriminate against a seaman because—

(A) the seaman in good faith has reported or is about to report to the Coast Guard or other appropriate Federal agency or department that the seaman believes that a violation of a maritime safety law or regulation prescribed under that law or regulation has occurred;

(B) the seaman in good faith has reported or is about to report to the vessel owner, Coast Guard or other appropriate Federal agency or department sexual harassment or sexual assault against the seaman or knowledge of sexual harassment or sexual assault against another seaman;

(C) the seaman has refused to perform duties ordered by the seaman's employer because the seaman has a reasonable apprehension or expectation that performing such duties would result in serious injury to the seaman, other seamen, or the public;

(D) the seaman testified in a proceeding brought to enforce a maritime safety law or regulation prescribed under that law;

(E) the seaman notified, or attempted to notify, the vessel owner or the Secretary of a work-related personal injury or work-related illness of a seaman;

(F) the seaman cooperated with a safety investigation by the Secretary or the National Transportation Safety Board;

(G) the seaman furnished information to the Secretary, the National Transportation Safety Board, or any other public official as to the facts relating to any marine casualty resulting in injury or death to an individual or damage to property occurring in connection with vessel transportation; or

(H) the seaman accurately reported hours of duty under this part.

(2) The circumstances causing a seaman's apprehension of serious injury under paragraph (1)(C) must be of such a nature that a reasonable person, under similar circumstances, would conclude that there is a real danger of an injury or serious impairment of health resulting from the performance of duties as ordered by the seaman's employer.

(3) To qualify for protection against the seaman's employer under paragraph (1)(C), the employee must have sought from the employer, and been unable to obtain, correction of the unsafe condition.

(b) A seaman alleging discharge or discrimination in violation of subsection (a) of this section, or another person at the seaman's request, may file a complaint with respect to such allegation in the same manner as a complaint may be filed under subsection (b) of section 31105 of title 49. Such complaint shall be subject to the procedures, requirements, and rights described in that section, including with respect to the right to file an objection, the right of a person to file for a petition for review under subsection (c) of that section, and the requirement to bring a civil action under subsection (d) of that section.

(Added Pub. L. 98–557, §13(a), Oct. 30, 1984, 98 Stat. 2863; amended Pub. L. 107–295, title IV, §428, Nov. 25, 2002, 116 Stat. 2127; Pub. L. 111–281, title VI, §611(a), Oct. 15, 2010, 124 Stat. 2969; Pub. L. 117–263, div. K, title CXVI, §11605, Dec. 23, 2022, 136 Stat. 4148.)

§2115. CIVIL PENALTY TO ENFORCE ALCOHOL AND DANGEROUS DRUG TESTING

Any person who fails to implement or conduct, or who otherwise fails to comply with the requirements prescribed by the Secretary for, chemical testing for dangerous drugs or for evidence of alcohol use, as prescribed under this subtitle or a regulation prescribed by the Secretary to carry out the provisions of this subtitle, is liable to the United States Government for a civil penalty of not more than $5,000 for each violation. Each day of a continuing violation shall constitute a separate violation.

(Added Pub. L. 104–324, title III, §303(a), Oct. 19, 1996, 110 Stat. 3917; amended Pub. L. 105–383, title III, §304(b), Nov. 13, 1998, 112 Stat. 3419.)

§2116. MARINE SAFETY STRATEGY, GOALS, AND PERFORMANCE ASSESSMENTS

(a) LONG-TERM STRATEGY AND GOALS.—In conjunction with existing federally required strategic planning efforts, the Secretary shall develop a long-term strategy for improving vessel safety and the safety of individuals on vessels. The 5-year strategy shall include the issuance of a plan and schedule for achieving the following goals:

(1) Reducing the number and rates of marine casualties.

(2) Improving the consistency and effectiveness of vessel and operator enforcement and compliance programs.

(3) Identifying and targeting enforcement efforts at high-risk vessels and operators.

(4) Improving research efforts to enhance and promote vessel and operator safety and performance.

(b) 5-YEAR STRATEGY AND PLAN.—

(1) MEASURABLE GOALS.—The 5-year strategy and plan shall include specific numeric or measurable goals designed to achieve the goals set forth in subsection (a). The purposes of the numeric or measurable goals are the following:

(A) To increase the number of safety examinations on all high-risk vessels.

(B) To eliminate the backlog of marine safety-related rulemakings.

(C) To improve the quality and effectiveness of marine safety information databases by ensuring that all Coast Guard personnel accurately and effectively report all safety, casualty, and injury information.

(D) To provide for a sufficient number of Coast Guard marine safety personnel, and provide adequate facilities and equipment to carry out the functions referred to in section 93(c) [1] of title 14.

(2) RESOURCE NEEDS.—The 5-year strategy and plan shall include estimates of—

(A) the funds and staff resources needed to accomplish each activity included in the strategy and plan; and

(B) the staff skills and training needed for timely and effective accomplishment of each goal.

(c) SUBMISSION WITH THE PRESIDENT'S BUDGET.—Not later than 5 years after the date of the enactment of the Elijah E. Cummings Coast Guard Authorization Act of 2020, and every 5 years thereafter, the Secretary shall submit to Congress the strategy and plan not later than 60 days following the transmission of the President's budget submission under section 1105 of title 31.

(d) ACHIEVEMENT OF GOALS.—

(1) PROGRESS ASSESSMENT.—In conjunction with the submission of the 5-year strategy and plan, the Commandant shall assess the progress of the Coast Guard toward achieving the goals set forth in subsection (b). The Commandant shall convey the Commandant's assessment to the employees of the marine safety workforce and shall identify any deficiencies that should be remedied before the next progress assessment.

(2) PERIODIC BRIEFINGS.—The Secretary shall periodically brief the Committee on Commerce, Science, and Transportation of the Senate and the Committee on Transportation and Infrastructure of the House of Representatives—

(A) on the performance of the marine safety program in achieving the goals of the marine safety strategy and plan under subsection (a) for the period covered by the briefing;

(B) on the program's mission performance in achieving numerical measurable goals established under subsection (b), including—

(i) the number of civilian and military Coast Guard personnel assigned to marine safety positions; and

(ii) an identification of marine safety positions that are understaffed to meet the workload required to accomplish each activity included in the strategy and plan under subsection (a); and

(C) recommendations on how to improve performance of the program.

(Added Pub. L. 111–281, title V, §522(a), Oct. 15, 2010, 124 Stat. 2956; amended Pub. L. 113–281, title II, §221(b)(1)(A), title III, §307(a), Dec. 18, 2014, 128 Stat. 3037, 3045; Pub. L. 115–232, div. C, title XXXV, §§3541(b)(7), 3546(b), Aug. 13, 2018, 132 Stat. 2323, 2326; Pub. L. 115–265, title II, §214, Oct. 11, 2018, 132 Stat. 3751; Pub. L. 116–283, div. G, title LVXXXII [LXXXII], §8240(c), Jan. 1, 2021, 134 Stat. 4666.)

[1] See References in Text note below.

§2117. TERMINATION FOR UNSAFE OPERATION

An individual authorized to enforce this title—

(1) may remove a certificate required by this title from a vessel that is operating in a condition that does not comply with the provisions of the certificate;

(2) may order the individual in charge of a vessel that is operating that does not have on board the certificate required by this title to return the vessel to a mooring and to remain there until the vessel is in compliance with this title; and

(3) may direct the individual in charge of a vessel to which this title applies to immediately take reasonable steps necessary for the safety of individuals on board the vessel if the official observes the vessel being operated in an unsafe condition that the official believes creates an especially hazardous condition, including ordering the individual in charge to return the vessel to a mooring and to remain there until the situation creating the hazard is corrected or ended.

(Added Pub. L. 111–281, title VI, §608(a), Oct. 15, 2010, 124 Stat. 2967.)

§2118. ESTABLISHMENT OF EQUIPMENT STANDARDS

(a) In establishing standards for approved equipment required on vessels subject to part B of this subtitle, the Secretary shall establish standards that are—

(1) based on performance using the best available technology that is economically achievable; and

(2) operationally practical.

(b) Using the standards established under subsection (a), the Secretary may also certify lifesaving equipment that is not required to be carried on vessels subject to part B of this subtitle to ensure that such equipment is suitable for its intended purpose.

(c) At least once every 10 years the Secretary shall review and revise the standards established under subsection (a) to ensure that the standards meet the requirements of this section.

(Added Pub. L. 111–281, title VI, §608(a), Oct. 15, 2010, 124 Stat. 2968; amended Pub. L. 114–120, title III, §306(a)(2), Feb. 8, 2016, 130 Stat. 54.)

CHAPTER 23—OPERATION OF VESSELS GENERALLY

§2301. APPLICATION

Except as provided in sections 2304 and 2306 of this title, this chapter applies to a vessel operated on waters subject to the jurisdiction of the United States (including the territorial sea of the United States as described in Presidential Proclamation No. 5928 of December 27, 1988) and, for a vessel owned in the United States, on the high seas.

(Pub. L. 98–89, Aug. 26, 1983, 97 Stat. 508; Pub. L. 98–498, title II, §212(a)(2), Oct. 19, 1984, 98 Stat. 2305; Pub. L. 105–383, title III, §301(b)(2), Nov. 13, 1998, 112 Stat. 3417; Pub. L. 109–304, §15(7), Oct. 6, 2006, 120 Stat. 1702.)

§2302. PENALTIES FOR NEGLIGENT OPERATIONS AND INTERFERING WITH SAFE OPERATION

(a) A person operating a vessel in a negligent manner or interfering with the safe operation of a vessel, so as to endanger the life, limb, or property of a person is liable to the United States Government for a civil penalty of not more than $5,000 in the case of a recreational vessel, or $25,000 in the case of any other vessel.

(b) A person operating a vessel in a grossly negligent manner that endangers the life, limb, or property of a person commits a class A misdemeanor.

(c) An individual who is under the influence of alcohol, or a dangerous drug in violation of a law of the United States when operating a vessel, as determined under standards prescribed by the Secretary by regulation—

(1) is liable to the United States Government for a civil penalty of not more than $5,000; or

(2) commits a class A misdemeanor.

(d) For a penalty imposed under this section, the vessel also is liable in rem unless the vessel is—

(1) owned by a State or a political subdivision of a State;

(2) operated principally for governmental purposes; and

(3) identified clearly as a vessel of that State or subdivision.

(e)(1) A vessel may not transport Government-impelled cargoes if—

(A) the vessel has been detained and determined to be substandard by the Secretary for

349

violation of an international safety convention to which the United States is a party, and the Secretary has published notice of that detention and determination in an electronic form, including the name of the owner of the vessel; or

(B) the operator of the vessel has on more than one occasion had a vessel detained and determined to be substandard by the Secretary for violation of an international safety convention to which the United States is a party, and the Secretary has published notice of that detention and determination in an electronic form, including the name of the owner of the vessel.

(2) The prohibition in paragraph (1) expires for a vessel on the earlier of—

(A) 1 year after the date of the publication in electronic form on which the prohibition is based; or

(B) any date on which the owner or operator of the vessel prevails in an appeal of the violation of the relevant international convention on which the detention is based.

(3) As used in this subsection, the term "Government-impelled cargo" means cargo for which a Federal agency contracts directly for shipping by water or for which (or the freight of which) a Federal agency provides financing, including financing by grant, loan, or loan guarantee, resulting in shipment of the cargo by water.

(Pub. L. 98–89, Aug. 26, 1983, 97 Stat. 508; Pub. L. 98–557, §7(a), Oct. 30, 1984, 98 Stat. 2862; Pub. L. 101–380, title IV, §§4105(b)(2), 4302(a), Aug. 18, 1990, 104 Stat. 513, 537; Pub. L. 102–587, title V, §5102, Nov. 4, 1992, 106 Stat. 5071; Pub. L. 105–383, title III, §§302(a), 304(c), title IV, §408(a), Nov. 13, 1998, 112 Stat. 3417, 3419, 3430; Pub. L. 107–295, title III, §325, Nov. 25, 2002, 116 Stat. 2105.)

§2303. Duties related to marine casualty assistance and information

(a) The master or individual in charge of a vessel involved in a marine casualty shall—

(1) render necessary assistance to each individual affected to save that affected individual from danger caused by the marine casualty, so far as the master or individual in charge can do so without serious danger to the master's or individual's vessel or to individuals on board; and

(2) give the master's or individual's name and address and identification of the vessel to the master or individual in charge of any other vessel involved in the casualty, to any individual injured, and to the owner of any property damaged.

(b) An individual violating this section or a regulation prescribed under this section shall be fined not more than $1,000 or imprisoned for not more than 2 years. The vessel also is liable in rem to the United States Government for the fine.

(c) An individual complying with subsection (a) of this section or gratuitously and in good faith rendering assistance at the scene of a marine casualty without objection by an individual assisted, is not liable for damages as a result of rendering assistance or for an act or omission in providing or arranging salvage, towage, medical treatment, or other assistance when the individual acts as an ordinary, reasonable, and prudent individual would have acted under the circumstances.

(Pub. L. 98–89, Aug. 26, 1983, 97 Stat. 509.)

§2303A. POST SERIOUS MARINE CASUALTY ALCOHOL TESTING

(a) The Secretary shall establish procedures to ensure that after a serious marine casualty occurs, alcohol testing of crew members or other individuals responsible for the operation or other safety-sensitive functions of the vessel or vessels involved in such casualty is conducted no later than 2 hours after the casualty occurs, unless such testing cannot be completed within that time due to safety concerns directly related to the casualty.

(b) The procedures in subsection (a) shall require that if alcohol testing cannot be completed within 2 hours of the occurrence of the casualty, such testing shall be conducted as soon thereafter as the safety concerns in subsection (a) have been adequately addressed to permit such testing, except that such testing may not be required more than 8 hours after the casualty occurs.

(Added Pub. L. 105–383, title III, §304(d)(1), Nov. 13, 1998, 112 Stat. 3419; amended Pub. L. 116–283, div. G, title LVXXXV [LXXXV], §8505(b)(1), Jan. 1, 2021, 134 Stat. 4751.)

§2304. DUTY TO PROVIDE ASSISTANCE AT SEA

(a)(1) A master or individual in charge of a vessel shall render assistance to any individual found at sea in danger of being lost, so far as the master or individual in charge can do so without serious danger to the master's or individual's vessel or individuals on board.

(2) Paragraph (1) does not apply to a vessel of war or a vessel owned by the United States Government appropriated only to a public service.

(b) A master or individual violating this section shall be fined not more than $1,000, imprisoned for not more than 2 years, or both.

(Pub. L. 98–89, Aug. 26, 1983, 97 Stat. 509; Pub. L. 109–304, §15(8), Oct. 6, 2006, 120 Stat. 1703.)

§2305. INJUNCTIONS

(a) The district courts of the United States have jurisdiction to enjoin the negligent operation of vessels prohibited by this chapter on the petition of the Attorney General for the United States Government.

(b) When practicable, the Secretary shall—

(1) give notice to any person against whom an action for injunctive relief is considered under this section an opportunity to present that person's views; and

(2) except for a knowing and willful violation, give the person a reasonable opportunity to achieve compliance.

(c) The failure to give notice and opportunity to present views under subsection (b) of this section does not preclude the court from granting appropriate relief.

(Pub. L. 98–89, Aug. 26, 1983, 97 Stat. 509.)

§2306. VESSEL REPORTING REQUIREMENTS

(a)(1) An owner, charterer, managing operator, or agent of a vessel of the United States, having reason to believe (because of lack of communication with or nonappearance of a vessel or any other incident) that the vessel may have been lost or imperiled, immediately

[§2307. Repealed. Pub. L. 115–282, title IV, §402(d), Dec. 4, 2018, 132 Stat. 4264]

CHAPTER 23—OPERATION OF VESSEL GENERALL'

shall—
    (A) notify the Coast Guard; and
    (B) use all available means to determine the status of the vessel.

(2) When more than 48 hours have passed since the owner, charterer, managing operator, or agent of a vessel required to report to the United States Flag Merchant Vessel Location Filing System under authority of section 50113 of this title has received a communication from the vessel, the owner, charterer, managing operator, or agent immediately shall—
    (A) notify the Coast Guard; and
    (B) use all available means to determine the status of the vessel.

(3) An owner, charterer, managing operator, or agent of a vessel of the United States notifying the Coast Guard under paragraph (1) or (2) shall—
    (A) provide the name and identification number of the vessel, the names of individuals on board, and other information that may be requested by the Coast Guard; and
    (B) submit written confirmation to the Coast Guard within 24 hours after nonwritten notification to the Coast Guard under such paragraphs.

(4) An owner, charterer, managing operator, or agent violating this subsection is liable to the United States Government for a civil penalty of not more than $5,000 for each day during which the violation occurs.

(b)(1) The master of a vessel of the United States required to report to the System shall report to the owner, charterer, managing operator, or agent at least once every 48 hours.

(2) A master violating this subsection is liable to the Government for a civil penalty of not more than $1,000 for each day during which the violation occurs.

(c) The Secretary may prescribe regulations to carry out this section.

(Added Pub. L. 98–498, title II, §212(a)(3), Oct. 19, 1984, 98 Stat. 2305; amended Pub. L. 109–304, §15(9), Oct. 6, 2006, 120 Stat. 1703; Pub. L. 116–283, div. G, title LVXXXV [LXXXV], §8505(b)(2), Jan. 1, 2021, 134 Stat. 4751.)

[§2307. Repealed. Pub. L. 115–282, title IV, §402(d), Dec. 4, 2018, 132 Stat. 4264]

Section, added Pub. L. 107–295, title IV, §431(a), Nov. 25, 2002, 116 Stat. 2128; amended Pub. L. 112–213, title III, §302(a), Dec. 20, 2012, 126 Stat. 1562, related to limitation of liability for Coast Guard Vessel Traffic Service pilots and non-Federal vessel traffic service operators.

Part B—Inspection and Regulation of Vessels

CHAPTER 31—GENERAL

§3101. AUTHORITY TO SUSPEND INSPECTION

When the President decides that the needs of foreign commerce require, the President may suspend a provision of this part for a foreign-built vessel registered as a vessel of the United States on conditions the President may specify.

(Pub. L. 98–89, Aug. 26, 1983, 97 Stat. 510.)

§3102. IMMERSION SUITS

(a) The Secretary shall by regulation require immersion suits on vessels designated by the Secretary that operate in the Atlantic Ocean north of 32 degrees North latitude or south of 32 degrees South latitude and in all other waters north of 35 degrees North latitude or south of 35 degrees South latitude. The Secretary may not exclude a vessel from designation under this section only because that vessel carries other lifesaving equipment.

(b) The Secretary shall establish standards for an immersion suit required by this section, including standards to guarantee adequate thermal protection, buoyance, and flotation stability.

(c)(1) The owner, charterer, managing operator, agent, master, or individual in charge of a vessel violating this section or a regulation prescribed under this section is liable to the United States Government for a civil penalty of not more than $5,000. The vessel also is liable in rem for the penalty.

(2) The owner, charterer, managing operator, agent, master, or individual in charge of a vessel violating this section or a regulation prescribed under this section may be fined not more than $25,000, imprisoned for not more than 5 years, or both.

(Added Pub. L. 98–557, §22(a)(1), Oct. 30, 1984, 98 Stat. 2871; amended Pub. L. 98–623, title VII, §701(a)(1), Nov. 8, 1984, 98 Stat. 3413; Pub. L. 99–36, §2, May 15, 1985, 99 Stat. 68; Pub. L. 100–424, §8(a)(1), (2), Sept. 9, 1988, 102 Stat. 1592, 1593.)

§3103. USE OF REPORTS, DOCUMENTS, AND RECORDS

The Secretary may rely, as evidence of compliance with this subtitle, on—

(1) reports, documents, and records of other persons who have been determined by the Secretary to be reliable; and

(2) other methods the Secretary has determined to be reliable.

(Added Pub. L. 104–324, title VI, §603(a), Oct. 19, 1996, 110 Stat. 3930.)

§3104. SURVIVAL CRAFT

(a) REQUIREMENT TO EQUIP.—The Secretary shall require that a passenger vessel be equipped with survival craft that ensures that no part of an individual is immersed in water, if—

(1) such vessel is built or undergoes a major conversion after January 1, 2016; and

(2) operates in cold waters as determined by the Secretary.

(b) HIGHER STANDARD OF SAFETY.—The Secretary may revise part 117 or part 180 of title 46, Code of Federal Regulations, as in effect before January 1, 2016, if such revision provides a higher standard of safety than is provided by the regulations in effect on or before the date of the enactment of the Coast Guard Authorization Act of 2016.

(c) INNOVATIVE AND NOVEL DESIGNS.—The Secretary may, in lieu of the requirements set out in part 117 or part 180 of title 46, Code of Federal Regulations, as in effect on the date of the enactment of the Coast Guard Authorization Act of 2016, allow a passenger vessel to be equipped with a life-saving appliance or arrangement of an innovative or novel design that—

(1) ensures no part of an individual is immersed in water; and

(2) provides an equal or higher standard of safety than is provided by such requirements as in effect before such date of the enactment.

(d) BUILT DEFINED.—In this section, the term "built" has the meaning that term has under section 4503(d).

(Added Pub. L. 111–281, title VI, §609(a), Oct. 15, 2010, 124 Stat. 2968; amended Pub. L. 112–213, title III, §303, Dec. 20, 2012, 126 Stat. 1563; Pub. L. 114–120, title III, §301(a), Feb. 8, 2016, 130 Stat. 50; Pub. L. 114–328, div. C, title XXXV, §3503(a), Dec. 23, 2016, 130 Stat. 2775; Pub. L. 115–282, title V, §508(e), Dec. 4, 2018, 132 Stat. 4273.)

§3105. ELECTRONIC CHARTS

(a) SYSTEM REQUIREMENTS.—

(1) ELECTRONIC CHARTS IN LIEU OF MARINE CHARTS, CHARTS, AND MAPS.—Subject to paragraph (2), the following vessels, while operating on the navigable waters of the United States, equipped with and operating electronic navigational charts that are produced by a government hydrographic office or conform to a standard acceptable to the Secretary, shall be deemed in compliance with any requirement under title 33 or title 46, Code of Federal Regulations, to have a chart, marine chart, or map on board such vessel:

(A) A self-propelled commercial vessel of at least 65 feet in overall length.

(B) A vessel carrying more than a number of passengers for hire determined by the Secretary.

(C) A towing vessel of more than 26 feet in overall length and 600 horsepower.

(D) Any other vessel for which the Secretary decides that electronic charts are necessary for the safe navigation of the vessel.

(2) EXEMPTIONS AND WAIVERS.—The Secretary may—

(A) exempt a vessel from paragraph (1), if the Secretary finds that electronic charts are not necessary for the safe navigation of the vessel on the waters on which the vessel operates;

(B) waive the application of paragraph (1) with respect to operation of vessels on navigable waters of the United States specified by the Secretary, if the Secretary finds that electronic charts are not needed for safe navigation on those waters; and

(C) permit vessels described in subparagraphs (A) through (D) of paragraph (1) that operate solely landward of the baseline from which the territorial sea of the United States is measured to utilize software-based, platform-independent electronic chart systems that the Secretary determines are capable of displaying electronic navigational charts with necessary scale and detail to ensure safe navigation for the intended voyage.

(b) LIMITATION ON APPLICATION.—Except pursuant to an international treaty, convention, or agreement, to which the United States is a party, this section shall not apply to any foreign vessel that is not destined for, or departing from, a port or place subject to the jurisdiction of the United States and that is in—

(1) innocent passage through the territorial sea of the United States; or

(2) transit through the navigable waters of the United States that form a part of an international strait.

(Added and amended Pub. L. 115–282, title IV, §402(a)(1), Dec. 4, 2018, 132 Stat. 4263, 4264; Pub. L. 116–283, div. G, title LVXXXIII [LXXXIII], §8301, Jan. 1, 2021, 134 Stat. 4691.)

§3106. MASTER KEY CONTROL SYSTEM

(a) IN GENERAL.—The owner of a vessel subject to inspection under section 3301 shall—

(1) ensure that such vessel is equipped with a vessel master key control system, manual or electronic, which provides controlled access to all copies of the vessel's master key of which access shall only be available to the individuals described in paragraph (2);

(2) establish a list of all crew, identified by position, allowed to access and use the master key and maintain such list upon the vessel, within owner records and included in the vessel safety management system;

(3) record in a log book information on all access and use of the vessel's master key, including—

(A) dates and times of access;

(B) the room or location accessed; and

(C) the name and rank of the crew member that used the master key; and

(4) make the list under paragraph (2) and the log book under paragraph (3) available upon request to any agent of the Federal Bureau of Investigation, any member of the Coast Guard, and any law enforcement officer performing official duties in the course and scope of an investigation.

(b) PROHIBITED USE.—Crew not included on the list described in subsection (a)(2) shall not have access to or use the master key unless in an emergency and shall immediately notify the master and owner of the vessel following use of such key.

(c) REQUIREMENTS FOR LOG BOOK.—The log book described in subsection (a)(3) and required to be included in a safety management system under section 3203(a)(6)—

(1) may be electronic; and

(2) shall be located in a centralized location that is readily accessible to law enforcement personnel.

(d) PENALTY.—Any crew member who uses the master key without having been granted access pursuant to subsection (a)(2) shall be liable to the United States Government for a civil penalty of not more than $1,000 and may be subject to suspension or revocation under section 7703.

(e) EXEMPTION.—This section shall not apply to vessels subject to section 3507(f).

(Added Pub. L. 117–263, div. K, title CXVI, §11608(a), Dec. 23, 2022, 136 Stat. 4151.)

CHAPTER 32—MANAGEMENT OF VESSELS

§3201. DEFINITIONS

In this chapter—

(1) "International Safety Management Code" has the same meaning given that term in chapter IX of the Annex to the International Convention for the Safety of Life at Sea, 1974;

(2) "responsible person" means—

(A) the owner of a vessel to which this chapter applies; or

(B) any other person that has—

(i) assumed the responsibility for operation of a vessel to which this chapter applies from the owner; and

(ii) agreed to assume with respect to the vessel responsibility for complying with all the requirements of this chapter and the regulations prescribed under this chapter.

(3) "vessel engaged on a foreign voyage" means a vessel to which this chapter applies—

(A) arriving at a place under the jurisdiction of the United States from a place in a foreign country;

(B) making a voyage between places outside the United States; or

(C) departing from a place under the jurisdiction of the United States for a place in a foreign country.

(Added Pub. L. 104–324, title VI, §602(a), Oct. 19, 1996, 110 Stat. 3928.)

§3202. APPLICATION

(a) FOREIGN VOYAGES AND FOREIGN VESSELS.—This chapter applies to a vessel that—

(1)(A) is transporting more than 12 passengers described in section 2101(29)(A) of this title; or

(B) is of at least 500 gross tons as measured under section 14302 of this title and is a tanker, freight vessel, bulk freight vessel, high speed freight vessel, or self-propelled mobile offshore drilling unit; and

(2)(A) is engaged on a foreign voyage; or

(B) is a foreign vessel departing from a place under the jurisdiction of the United States on a voyage, any part of which is on the high seas.

(b) OTHER PASSENGER VESSELS.—

(1) IN GENERAL.—This chapter applies to a vessel that is—

(A) a passenger vessel or small passenger vessel; and

(B) is transporting more passengers than a number prescribed by the Secretary based on the number of individuals on the vessel that could be killed or injured in a marine casualty.

(2) SAFETY MANAGEMENT SYSTEM.—Notwithstanding any other provision in this chapter, including paragraph (1)(B), any regulations under section 3203, including the safety management system established by such regulations, issued on or after the date of enactment of the Elijah E. Cummings Coast Guard Authorization Act of 2020, shall apply to all covered small passenger vessels, as defined in section 3306(n)(5).

(c) VOLUNTARY APPLICATION.—This chapter applies to a vessel not described in subsection (a) of this section if the owner of the vessel requests the Secretary to apply this chapter to the vessel.

(d) EXCEPTION.—Except as provided in subsection (c) of this section, this chapter does not apply to—

(1) a barge;

(2) a recreational vessel not engaged in commercial service;

(3) a fishing vessel;

(4) a vessel operating on the Great Lakes or its tributary and connecting waters that is not described in subsection (b) of this section; or

(5) a public vessel.

(Added Pub. L. 104–324, title VI, §602(a), Oct. 19, 1996, 110 Stat. 3928; amended Pub. L. 108–293, title IV, §405(a), Aug. 9, 2004, 118 Stat. 1043; Pub. L. 111–281, title VI, §610(a), Oct. 15, 2010, 124 Stat. 2969; Pub. L. 115–232, div. C, title XXXV, §3541(b)(8), Aug. 13, 2018, 132 Stat. 2323; Pub. L. 116–283, div. G, title LVXXXIV [LXXXIV], §8441(b), Jan. 1, 2021, 134 Stat. 4744.)

§3203. SAFETY MANAGEMENT SYSTEM

(a) IN GENERAL.—The Secretary shall prescribe regulations which establish a safety management system for responsible persons and vessels to which this chapter applies (including, for purposes of this section, all covered small passenger vessels, as defined in section 3306(n)(5)), including—

(1) a safety and environmental protection policy;

(2) instructions and procedures to ensure safe operation of those vessels and protection of the environment in compliance with international and United States law;

(3) defined levels of authority and lines of communications between, and among, personnel on shore and on the vessel;

(4) procedures for reporting accidents and nonconformities with this chapter;

(5) with respect to sexual harassment and sexual assault, procedures for, and annual training requirements for all responsible persons and vessels to which this chapter applies on—

(A) prevention;

(B) bystander intervention;

(C) reporting;

(D) response; and

(E) investigation;

(6) the list required under section 3106(a)(2) and the log book required under section 3106(a)(3);

(7) procedures for preparing for and responding to emergency situations; and

(8) procedures for internal audits and management reviews of the system.

(b) PROCEDURES AND TRAINING REQUIREMENTS.—In prescribing regulations for the procedures and training requirements described in subsection (a)(5), such procedures and requirements shall be consistent with the requirements to report sexual harassment or sexual assault under section 10104.

(c) AUDITS.—

(1) CERTIFICATES.—

(A) SUSPENSION.—During an audit of a safety management system of a vessel required under section 10104(e), the Secretary may suspend the Safety Management Certificate issued for the vessel under section 3205 and issue a separate Safety Management Certificate for the vessel to be in effect for a 3-month period beginning on the date of the issuance of such separate certificate.

(B) REVOCATION.—At the conclusion of an audit of a safety management system required under section 10104(e), the Secretary shall revoke the Safety Management Certificate issued for the vessel under section 3205 if the Secretary determines—

(i) that the holder of the Safety Management Certificate knowingly, or repeatedly, failed to comply with section 10104; or

(ii) other failure of the safety management system resulted in the failure to comply with such section.

(2) DOCUMENTS OF COMPLIANCE.—

(A) IN GENERAL.—Following an audit of the safety management system of a vessel required under section 10104(e), the Secretary may audit the safety management system of the responsible person for the vessel.

(B) SUSPENSION.—During an audit under subparagraph (A), the Secretary may suspend the Document of Compliance issued to the responsible person under section 3205 and issue a separate Document of Compliance to such person to be in effect for a 3-month period beginning on the date of the issuance of such separate document.

(C) REVOCATION.—At the conclusion of an assessment or an audit of a safety management system under subparagraph (A), the Secretary shall revoke the Document of Compliance issued to the responsible person if the Secretary determines—

(i) that the holder of the Document of Compliance knowingly, or repeatedly, failed to comply with section 10104; or

(ii) that other failure of the safety management system resulted in the failure to comply with such section.

(d) COMPLIANCE WITH CODE.—Regulations prescribed under this section shall be consistent with the International Safety Management Code with respect to vessels to which this chapter applies under section 3202(a) of this title.

(e) In prescribing regulations for passenger vessels and small passenger vessels, the Secretary shall consider—

(1) the characteristics, methods of operation, and nature of the service of these vessels; and

(2) with respect to vessels that are ferries, the sizes of the ferry systems within which the vessels operate.

(Added Pub. L. 104–324, title VI, §602(a), Oct. 19, 1996, 110 Stat. 3928; amended Pub. L. 108–293, title IV, §405(b), Aug. 9, 2004, 118 Stat. 1043; Pub. L. 111–281, title VI, §610(b), Oct. 15, 2010, 124 Stat. 2969; Pub. L. 116–283, div. G, title LVXXXIV [LXXXIV], §8441(c), Jan. 1, 2021, 134 Stat. 4744; Pub. L. 117–263, div. K, title CXVI, §11610(a), Dec. 23, 2022, 136 Stat. 4154.)

§3204. IMPLEMENTATION OF SAFETY MANAGEMENT SYSTEM

(a) SAFETY MANAGEMENT PLAN.—Each responsible person shall establish and submit to the Secretary for approval a safety management plan describing how that person and vessels of the person to which this chapter applies will comply with the regulations prescribed under section 3203(a) of this title.

(b) APPROVAL.—Upon receipt of a safety management plan submitted under subsection (a), the Secretary shall review the plan and approve it if the Secretary determines that it is consistent with and will assist in implementing the safety management system established under section 3203.

(c) PROHIBITION ON VESSEL OPERATION.—A vessel to which this chapter applies under section 3202(a) may not be operated without having on board a Safety Management Certificate and a copy of a Document of Compliance issued for the vessel under section 3205 of this title.

(Added Pub. L. 104–324, title VI, §602(a), Oct. 19, 1996, 110 Stat. 3929.)

§3205. CERTIFICATION

(a) ISSUANCE OF CERTIFICATE AND DOCUMENT.—After verifying that the responsible person for a vessel to which this chapter applies and the vessel comply with the applicable requirements under this chapter, the Secretary shall issue for the vessel, on request of the responsible person, a Safety Management Certificate and a Document of Compliance.

(b) MAINTENANCE OF CERTIFICATE AND DOCUMENT.—A Safety Management Certificate and a Document of Compliance issued for a vessel under this section shall be maintained by the responsible person for the vessel as required by the Secretary.

(c) VERIFICATION OF COMPLIANCE.—The Secretary shall—

(1) periodically, or upon discovery from other sources of information acquired by the Coast Guard, including a discovery made during an audit or systematic review conducted under section 10104(e) of a failure of a responsible person or vessel to comply with a requirement of a safety management system for which a Safety Management Certificate and a Document of compliance [1] has been issued under this section, including a failure to comply with regulations prescribed under section 3203(a)(7) and (8), review whether

a responsible person having a safety management plan approved under section 3204(b) and each vessel to which the plan applies is complying with the plan; and

(2) revoke the Secretary's approval of the plan and each Safety Management Certificate and Document of Compliance issued to the person for a vessel to which the plan applies, if the Secretary determines that the person or a vessel to which the plan applies has not complied with the plan.

(d) ENFORCEMENT.—At the request of the Secretary, the Secretary of Homeland Security shall withhold or revoke the clearance required by section 60105 of this title of a vessel that is subject to this chapter under section 3202(a) of this title or to the International Safety Management Code, if the vessel does not have on board a Safety Management Certificate and a copy of a Document of Compliance for the vessel. Clearance may be granted on filing a bond or other surety satisfactory to the Secretary.

(Added Pub. L. 104–324, title VI, §602(a), Oct. 19, 1996, 110 Stat. 3929; amended Pub. L. 109–304, §15(10), Oct. 6, 2006, 120 Stat. 1703; Pub. L. 110–181, div. C, title XXXV, §3529(b)(1)(A), Jan. 28, 2008, 122 Stat. 603; Pub. L. 117–263, div. K, title CXVI, §11610(b), Dec. 23, 2022, 136 Stat. 4155.)

---

[1] *So in original. Probably should be "Compliance".*

CHAPTER 33—INSPECTION GENERALLY

§3301. Vessels subject to inspection

The following categories of vessels are subject to inspection under this part:
(1) freight vessels.
(2) nautical school vessels.
(3) offshore supply vessels.
(4) passenger vessels.
(5) sailing school vessels.
(6) seagoing barges.
(7) seagoing motor vessels.
(8) small passenger vessels.
(9) steam vessels.
(10) tank vessels.
(11) fish processing vessels.
(12) fish tender vessels.
(13) Great Lakes barges.
(14) oil spill response vessels.
(15) towing vessels.

(Pub. L. 98–89, Aug. 26, 1983, 97 Stat. 510; Pub. L. 98–364, title IV, §402(2), July 17, 1984, 98 Stat. 445; Pub. L. 102–587, title V, §5208(b), Nov. 4, 1992, 106 Stat. 5076; Pub. L. 104–324, title XI, §1104(g), Oct. 19, 1996, 110 Stat. 3967; Pub. L. 108–293, title IV, §415(a), Aug. 9, 2004, 118 Stat. 1047.)

§3302. EXEMPTIONS

(a) A vessel is not excluded from one category only because the vessel is—

(1) included in another category of section 3301 of this title; or

(2) excluded by this section from another category of section 3301 of this title.

(b) Except as provided in subsection (c)(3) of this section, a fishing vessel, including a vessel chartered part-time as a fish tender vessel, is exempt from section 3301(1), (7), (11), and (12) of this title.

(c)(1) Except as provided in paragraph (3) of this subsection, a fish processing vessel of not more than 5,000 gross tons as measured under section 14502 of this title, or an alternate tonnage measured under section 14302 of this title as prescribed by the Secretary under section 14104 of this title is exempt from section 3301(1), (6), (7), (11), and (12) of this title.

(2) Except as provided in paragraphs (3) and (4) of this subsection, the following fish tender vessels are exempt from section 3301(1), (6), (7), (11), and (12) of this title:

(A) A vessel of not more than 500 gross tons as measured under section 14502 of this title or an alternate tonnage measured under section 14302 of this title as prescribed by the Secretary under section 14104 of this title.

(B) A vessel engaged in the Aleutian trade that is not more than 2,500 gross tons as measured under section 14302 of this title.

(3)(A) A fishing vessel or fish processing vessel is exempt from section 3301(1), (6), and (7) of this title when transporting cargo (including fisheries-related cargo) to or from a place in Alaska if—

(i) that place does not receive weekly common carrier service by water from a place in the United States;

(ii) that place receives such common carrier service and the cargo is of a type not accepted by that common carrier service; or

(iii) the cargo is proprietary cargo owned by the owner of the vessel or any affiliated entity or subsidiary.

(B) A fish tender vessel of not more than 500 gross tons as measured under section 14502 of this title, or less than 500 gross tons as measured under section 14502 of this title, or is less than 2,500 gross tons as measured under section 14302 of this title, which is qualified to engage in the Aleutian trade is exempt from section 3301(1), (6), and (7) of this title when transporting cargo (including fisheries-related cargo) to or from a place in Alaska outside the Aleutian trade geographic area if—

(i) that place does not receive weekly common carrier service by water from a place in the United States;

(ii) that place receives such common carrier service and the cargo is of a type not accepted by that common carrier service; or

(iii) the cargo is proprietary cargo owned by the owner of the vessel or any affiliated entity or subsidiary.

(C) In this paragraph, the term "proprietary cargo" means cargo that—

(i) is used by the owner of the vessel or any affiliated entity or subsidiary in activities directly related to fishing or the processing of fish;

(ii) is consumed by employees of the owner of the vessel or any affiliated entity or subsidiary who are engaged in fishing or in the processing of fish; or

(iii) consists of fish or fish products harvested or processed by the owner of the vessel or any affiliated entity or subsidiary.

(D) Notwithstanding the restrictions in subparagraph (B) of this paragraph, vessels qualifying under subparagraph (B) may transport cargo (including fishery-related products) from a place in Alaska receiving weekly common carrier service by water to a final destination in Alaska not receiving weekly service by water from common carriers.

(4) A fish tender vessel is exempt from section 3301(1), (6), and (7) of this title when engaged in the Aleutian trade if the vessel—

(A) is not more than 500 gross tons as measured under section 14502 of this title, or less than 500 gross tons as measured under section 14502 of this title, or is less than 2,500 gross tons as measured under section 14302 of this title;

(B) has an incline test performed by a marine surveyor; and

(C) has written stability instructions posted on board the vessel.

(d)(1) A motor vessel of less than 150 gross tons as measured under section 14502 of this title, or an alternate tonnage measured under section 14302 of this title as prescribed by the Secretary under section 14104 of this title, constructed before August 23, 1958, is not subject to inspection under section 3301(1) of this title if the vessel is owned or demise chartered to a cooperative or association that only transports cargo owned by at least one of its members on a nonprofit basis between places within the waters of—

(A) southeastern Alaska shoreward of the Boundary Line; or

(B) southeastern Alaska shoreward of the Boundary Line and—

(i) Prince Rupert, British Columbia; or

(ii) waters of Washington shoreward of the Boundary Line, via sheltered waters, as defined in article I of the treaty dated December 9, 1933, between the United States and Canada defining certain waters as sheltered waters.

(2) The transportation authorized under this subsection is limited to and from places not receiving annual weekly transportation service from any part of the United States by an established water common carrier. However, the limitation does not apply to transporting cargo of a character not accepted for transportation by that carrier.

(e) A vessel laid up, dismantled, or out of commission is exempt from inspection.

(f) Section 3301(4) and (8) of this title does not apply to an oceanographic research vessel because it is carrying scientific personnel.

(g)(1) Except when compliance with major structural or major equipment requirements is necessary to remove an especially hazardous condition, an offshore supply vessel is not subject to regulations or standards for those requirements if the vessel—

(A) was operating as an offshore supply vessel before January 2, 1979; or

(B) was contracted for before January 2, 1979, and entered into service as an offshore supply vessel before October 6, 1980.

(2) This subsection does not apply to an offshore supply vessel that is at least 20 years of age.

(h) An offshore supply vessel operating on January 1, 1979, under a certificate of inspection issued by the Secretary, is subject to an inspection standard or requirement only if the standard or requirement could have been prescribed for the vessel under authority existing under law on October 5, 1980.

(i)(1) The Secretary may issue a permit exempting a vessel from any part of the requirements of this part for vessels transporting cargo, including bulk fuel, from one place in Alaska to another place in Alaska only if the vessel—

(A) is not more than 300 gross tons as measured under section 14502 of this title, or an alternate tonnage measured under section 14302 of this title as prescribed by the Secretary under section 14104 of this title;

(B) is in a condition that does not present an immediate threat to the safety of life or the environment; and

(C) was operating in the waters off Alaska as of June 1, 1976, or the vessel is a replacement for a vessel that was operating in the waters off Alaska as of June 1, 1976, if the vessel being replaced is no longer in service.

(2) Except in a situation declared to be an emergency by the Secretary, a vessel operating under a permit may not transport cargo to or from a place if the cargo could be transported by another commercial vessel that is reasonably available and that does not require exemptions to operate legally or if the cargo could be readily transported by overland routes.

(3) A permit may be issued for a specific voyage or for not more than one year. The permit may impose specific requirements about the amount or type of cargo to be carried, manning, the areas or specific routes over which the vessel may operate, or other similar matters. The duration of the permit and restrictions contained in the permit shall be at the sole discretion of the Secretary.

(4) A designated Coast Guard official who has reason to believe that a vessel issued a permit is in a condition or is operated in a manner that creates an immediate threat to the safety of life or the environment or is operated in a manner that is inconsistent with the terms of the permit, may direct the master or individual in charge to take immediate and reasonable steps to safeguard life and the environment, including directing the vessel to a port or other refuge.

(5) If a vessel issued a permit creates an immediate threat to the safety of life or the environment, or is operated in a manner inconsistent with the terms of the permit or the requirements of paragraph (2) of this subsection, the permit may be revoked. The owner, charterer, managing operator, agent, master, or individual in charge of a vessel issued a permit, that willfully permits the vessel to be operated, or operates, the vessel in a manner inconsistent with the terms of the permit, is liable to the United States Government for a civil penalty of not more than $1,000.

(j) Notwithstanding another provision of this chapter, the Secretary is not required to inspect or prescribe regulations for a nautical school vessel of not more than 15 gross tons as measured under section 14502 of this title, or an alternate tonnage measured under

section 14302 of this title as prescribed by the Secretary under section 14104 of this title—
　　(1) when used in connection with a course of instruction dealing with any aspect of maritime education or study; and
　　(2) operated by—
　　　　(A) the United States Merchant Marine Academy; or
　　　　(B) a State maritime academy assisted under chapter 515 of this title.

(k) Only the boiler, engine, and other operating machinery of a steam vessel that is a recreational vessel of not more than 65 feet overall in length are subject to inspection under section 3301(9) of this title.

(l)(1) The Secretary may issue a permit exempting the following vessels from the requirements of this part for passenger vessels so long as the vessels are owned by nonprofit organizations and operated as nonprofit memorials to merchant mariners:
　　(A) The steamship John W. Brown (United States official number 242209), owned by Project Liberty Ship Baltimore, Incorporated, located in Baltimore, Maryland.
　　(B) The steamship Lane Victory (United States official number 248094), owned by the United States Merchant Marine Veterans of World War II, located in San Pedro, California.
　　(C) The steamship Jeremiah O'Brien (United States official number 243622), owned by the National Liberty Ship Memorial, Inc.
　　(D) The SS Red Oak Victory (United States official number 249410), owned by the Richmond Museum Association, located in Richmond, California.
　　(E) The SS American Victory (United States official number 248005), owned by Victory Ship, Inc., of Tampa, Florida.
　　(F) The LST–325, owned by USS LST Ship Memorial, Incorporated, located in Mobile, Alabama.

(2) The Secretary may issue a permit for a specific voyage or for not more than one year. The Secretary may impose specific requirements about the number of passengers to be carried, manning, the areas or specific routes over which the vessel may operate, or other similar matters.

(3) A designated Coast Guard official who has reason to believe that a vessel operating under this subsection is in a condition or is operated in a manner that creates an immediate threat to life or the environment or is operated in a manner that is inconsistent with this section, may direct the master or individual in charge to take immediate and reasonable steps to safeguard life and the environment, including directing the vessel to a port or other refuge.

(m) A seagoing barge or a Great Lakes barge is not subject to inspection under paragraph (6) or (13) of section 3301 of this title if the vessel is unmanned and does not carry—
　　(1) a hazardous material as cargo; or
　　(2) a flammable or combustible liquid, including oil, in bulk.

(n)(1) A seagoing motor vessel is not subject to inspection under section 3301(7) of this title if the vessel—
　　(A) is a recreational vessel (as defined in section 2101 of this title) over 300 gross tons

367

as measured under section 14502, or an alternate tonnage measured under section 14302 of this title as prescribed by the Secretary under section 14104 of this title;

(B) does not carry any cargo or passengers for hire; and

(C) is found by the Secretary to comply with large recreational vessel regulations issued by the Secretary.

(2) This subsection shall apply only on and after the effective date of regulations referred to in paragraph (1)(C).

(Pub. L. 98–89, Aug. 26, 1983, 97 Stat. 510; Pub. L. 98–364, title IV, §402(3), July 17, 1984, 98 Stat. 445; Pub. L. 99–307, §1(3), (4), May 19, 1986, 100 Stat. 444; Pub. L. 101–595, title III, §303(a), title VI, §§602(b), 603(2), Nov. 16, 1990, 104 Stat. 2983, 2990, 2993; Pub. L. 103–206, title III, §311, Dec. 20, 1993, 107 Stat. 2426; Pub. L. 104–324, title VII, §711, title XI, §1110, Oct. 19, 1996, 110 Stat. 3935, 3969; Pub. L. 106–65, div. C, title XXXVI, §3604, Oct. 5, 1999, 113 Stat. 976; Pub. L. 107–295, title II, §208, Nov. 25, 2002, 116 Stat. 2098; Pub. L. 109–241, title III, §311, July 11, 2006, 120 Stat. 530; Pub. L. 109–304, §15(11), Oct. 6, 2006, 120 Stat. 1703; Pub. L. 115–232, div. C, title XXXV, §§3529(b), 3546(c), Aug. 13, 2018, 132 Stat. 2319, 2326; Pub. L. 117–263, div. K, title CXII, §11216, Dec. 23, 2022, 136 Stat. 4017.)

§3303. RECIPROCITY FOR FOREIGN VESSELS

Except as provided in chapter 37 and section 3505 of this title, a foreign vessel of a country having inspection laws and standards similar to those of the United States and that has an unexpired certificate of inspection issued by proper authority of its respective country, is subject to an inspection to ensure that the condition of the vessel is as stated in its current certificate of inspection. A foreign country is considered to have inspection laws and standards similar to those of the United States when it is a party to an International Convention for Safety of Life at Sea to which the United States Government is currently a party. A foreign certificate of inspection may be accepted as evidence of lawful inspection only when presented by a vessel of a country that has by its laws accorded to vessels of the United States visiting that country the same privileges accorded to vessels of that country visiting the United States.

(Pub. L. 98–89, Aug. 26, 1983, 97 Stat. 512; Pub. L. 102–587, title V, §5210(a), Nov. 4, 1992, 106 Stat. 5076; Pub. L. 104–324, title XI, §1111, Oct. 19, 1996, 110 Stat. 3970; Pub. L. 108–293, title IV, §411(b), Aug. 9, 2004, 118 Stat. 1046.)

§3304. TRANSPORTING INDIVIDUALS IN ADDITION TO CREW

(a) A documented vessel transporting cargo that transports not more than 12 individuals in addition to the crew on international voyages, or not more than 16 individuals in addition to the crew on other voyages, is not subject to inspection as a passenger vessel or a small passenger vessel if the vessel is otherwise subject to inspection under this chapter.

(b) Except when subsection (e) of this section applies, before an individual in addition to the crew is transported on a vessel as permitted by this section, the owner, charterer, managing operator, agent, master, or individual in charge of the vessel first shall notify the individual of the presence on board of dangerous articles as defined by law, and of other conditions or circumstances that would constitute a risk of safety to the individual on board.

(c) A privilege authorized by this section applies to a vessel of a foreign country that affords a similar privilege to vessels of the United States in trades not restricted to vessels under its own flag.

(d) A fishing, fish processing, or fish tender vessel that transports not more than 12 individuals employed in the fishing industry in addition to the crew is not subject to inspection as a passenger or small passenger vessel.

(e) The Secretary may by regulation allow individuals in addition to the crew to be transported in an emergency or under section 2304 of this title.

(Pub. L. 98–89, Aug. 26, 1983, 97 Stat. 513; Pub. L. 98–364, title IV, §402(4), July 17, 1984, 98 Stat. 446; Pub. L. 99–307, §1(5)(A), May 19, 1986, 100 Stat. 444.)

§3305. SCOPE AND STANDARDS OF INSPECTION

(a)(1) The inspection process shall ensure that a vessel subject to inspection—

    (A) is of a structure suitable for the service in which it is to be employed;

    (B) is equipped with proper appliances for lifesaving, fire prevention, and firefighting;

    (C) has suitable accommodations for the crew, sailing school instructors, and sailing school students, and for passengers on the vessel if authorized to carry passengers;

    (D) has an adequate supply of potable water for drinking and washing by passengers and crew;

    (E) is in a condition to be operated with safety to life and property; and

    (F) complies with applicable marine safety laws and regulations.

(2) In determining the adequacy of the supply of potable water under paragraph (1)(D), the Secretary shall consider—

    (A) the size and type of vessel;

    (B) the number of passengers or crew on board;

    (C) the duration and routing of voyages; and

    (D) guidelines for potable water recommended by the Centers for Disease Control and Prevention and the Public Health Service.

(b) If an inspection, or examination under section 3308 of this title, reveals that a life preserver, lifesaving device, or firehose is defective and incapable of being repaired, the owner or master shall destroy the life preserver, lifesaving device, or firehose in the presence of the official conducting the inspection or examination.

(c) A nautical school vessel operated by a civilian nautical school or by an educational institution under section 558 of title 40 shall be inspected like a small passenger vessel or a passenger vessel, depending on its tonnage.

(d)(1) The Commandant of the Coast Guard shall ensure that Officers in Charge, Marine Inspections consistently interpret regulations and standards under this subtitle and chapter 700 to avoid disruption and undue expense to industry.

(2)(A) Subject to subparagraph (B), in the event of a disagreement regarding the condition of a vessel or the interpretation of a regulation or standard referred to in subsection (a) between a local Officer in Charge, Marine Inspection conducting an inspection of the vessel and the Officer in Charge, Marine Inspection that issued the most recent certificate of inspection for the vessel, such Officers shall seek to resolve such disagreement.

(B) If a disagreement described in subparagraph (A) involves vessel design or plan review, the Coast Guard marine safety center shall be included in all efforts to resolve such disagreement.

(C) If a disagreement described in subparagraph (A) or (B) cannot be resolved, the local Officer in Charge, Marine Inspection shall submit to the Commandant of the Coast Guard, through the cognizant Coast Guard district commander, a request for a final agency determination of the matter in disagreement.

(3) The Commandant of the Coast Guard shall—

(A) provide to each person affected by a decision or action by an Officer in Charge, Marine Inspection or by the Coast Guard marine safety center all information necessary for such person to exercise any right to appeal such decision or action; and

(B) if such an appeal is filed, process such appeal under parts 1 through 4 of title 46, Code of Federal Regulations, as in effect on the date of enactment of the Frank LoBiondo Coast Guard Authorization Act of 2018.

(4) In this section, the term "Officer in Charge, Marine Inspection" means any person from the civilian or military branch of the Coast Guard who—

(A) is designated as such by the Commandant; and

(B) under the superintendence and direction of the cognizant Coast Guard district commander, is in charge of an inspection zone for the performance of duties with respect to the inspections under, and enforcement and administration of, subtitle II, chapter 700, and regulations under such laws.

(Pub. L. 98–89, Aug. 26, 1983, 97 Stat. 513; Pub. L. 99–36, §1(a)(1), May 15, 1985, 99 Stat. 67; Pub. L. 99–640, §13(e), Nov. 10, 1986, 100 Stat. 3551; Pub. L. 107–217, §3(m)(2), Aug. 21, 2002, 116 Stat. 1302; Pub. L. 108–293, title IV, §416, Aug. 9, 2004, 118 Stat. 1047; Pub. L. 109–241, title IX, §901(f), July 11, 2006, 120 Stat. 564; Pub. L. 115–282, title V, §501(a), Dec. 4, 2018, 132 Stat. 4268; Pub. L. 116–283, div. G, title LVXXXV [LXXXV], §8507(a)(1), Jan. 1, 2021, 134 Stat. 4752.)

§3306. Regulations

(a) To carry out this part and to secure the safety of individuals and property on board vessels subject to inspection, including covered small passenger vessels (as defined in subsection (n)(5)), the Secretary shall prescribe necessary regulations to ensure the proper execution of, and to carry out, this part in the most effective manner for—

(1) the design, construction, alteration, repair, and operation of those vessels, including superstructures, hulls, fittings, equipment, appliances, propulsion machinery, auxiliary machinery, boilers, unfired pressure vessels, piping, electric installations, and accommodations for passengers and crew, sailing school instructors, and sailing school students;

(2) lifesaving equipment and its use;

(3) firefighting equipment, its use, and precautionary measures to guard against fire;

(4) inspections and tests related to paragraphs (1), (2), and (3) of this subsection; and

(5) the use of vessel stores and other supplies of a dangerous nature, including rechargeable devices utilized for personal or commercial electronic equipment.

(b)(1) Equipment and material subject to regulation under this section may not be used on any vessel without prior approval of the Secretary.

(2) Except with respect to use on a public vessel, the Secretary may treat an approval of

equipment or materials by a foreign government as approval by the Secretary for purposes of paragraph (1) if the Secretary determines that—

(A) the design standards and testing procedures used by that government meet the requirements of the International Convention for the Safety of Life at Sea, 1974;

(B) the approval of the equipment or material by the foreign government will secure the safety of individuals and property on board vessels subject to inspection; and

(C) for lifesaving equipment, the foreign government—

(i) has given equivalent treatment to approvals of lifesaving equipment by the Secretary; and

(ii) otherwise ensures that lifesaving equipment approved by the Secretary may be used on vessels that are documented and subject to inspection under the laws of that country.

(c) In prescribing regulations for sailing school vessels, the Secretary shall consult with representatives of the private sector having experience in the operation of vessels likely to be certificated as sailing school vessels. The regulations shall—

(1) reflect the specialized nature of sailing school vessel operations, and the character, design, and construction of vessels operating as sailing school vessels; and

(2) include requirements for notice to sailing school instructors and sailing school students about the specialized nature of sailing school vessels and applicable safety regulations.

(d) In prescribing regulations for nautical school vessels operated by the United States Merchant Marine Academy or by a State maritime academy (as defined in section 51102 of this title), the Secretary shall consider the function, purpose, and operation of the vessels, their routes, and the number of individuals who may be carried on the vessels.

(e) When the Secretary finds it in the public interest, the Secretary may suspend or grant exemptions from the requirements of a regulation prescribed under this section related to lifesaving and firefighting equipment, muster lists, ground tackle and hawsers, and bilge systems.

(f) In prescribing regulations for offshore supply vessels, the Secretary shall consider the characteristics, methods of operation, and the nature of the service of offshore supply vessels.

(g) In prescribing regulations for fish processing or fish tender vessels, the Secretary shall consult with representatives of the private sector having experience in the operation of these vessels. The regulations shall reflect the specialized nature and economics of fish processing or fish tender vessel operations and the character, design, and construction of fish processing or fish tender vessels.

(h) The Secretary shall establish appropriate structural fire protection, manning, operating, and equipment requirements for vessels of at least 100 gross tons but less than 300 gross tons as measured under section 14502 of this title, or an alternate tonnage measured under section 14302 of this title as prescribed by the Secretary under section 14104 of this title carrying not more than 150 passengers on domestic voyages, which meet the eligibility criteria of section 2113(4) of this title.

(i) The Secretary shall establish appropriate structural fire protection, manning, operating, and equipment requirements for former public vessels of the United States of at least 100 gross tons but less that 500 gross tons as measured under section 14502 of this title, or an alternate tonnage measured under section 14302 of this title as prescribed by the Secretary under section 14104 of this title carrying not more than 150 passengers on domestic voyages, which meet the eligibility criteria of section 2113(4) of this title.

(j) The Secretary may establish by regulation a safety management system appropriate for the characteristics, methods of operation, and nature of service of towing vessels.

(k)(1) Each vessel of the United States that is constructed under a contract entered into after the date of enactment of the Maritime Safety Act of 2010, or that is delivered after January 1, 2011, with an aggregate capacity of 600 cubic meters or more of oil fuel, shall comply with the requirements of Regulation 12A under Annex I to the Protocol of 1978 relating to the International Convention for the Prevention of Pollution from Ships, 1973, entitled "Oil Fuel Tank Protection".

(2) The Secretary may prescribe regulations to apply the requirements described in Regulation 12A to vessels described in paragraph (1) that are not otherwise subject to that convention. Any such regulation shall be considered to be an interpretive rule for the purposes of section 553 of title 5.

(3) In this subsection the term "oil fuel" means any oil used as fuel in connection with the propulsion and auxiliary machinery of the vessel in which such oil is carried.

(l)(1) The Secretary shall require that a freight vessel inspected under this chapter be outfitted with distress signaling and location technology for the higher of—

(A) the minimum complement of officers and crew specified on the certificate of inspection for such vessel; or

(B) the number of persons onboard the vessel; and

(2) the requirement described in paragraph (1) shall not apply to vessels operating within the baseline from which the territorial sea of the United States is measured.

(m)(1) The Secretary shall promulgate regulations requiring companies to maintain records of all incremental weight changes made to freight vessels inspected under this chapter, and to track weight changes over time to facilitate rapid determination of the aggregate total.

(2) Records maintained under paragraph (1) shall be stored, in paper or electronic form, onboard such vessels for not less than 3 years and shoreside for the life of the vessel.

(n) COVERED SMALL PASSENGER VESSELS.—

(1) REGULATIONS.—The Secretary shall prescribe additional regulations to secure the safety of individuals and property on board covered small passenger vessels.

(2) COMPREHENSIVE REVIEW.—In order to prescribe the regulations under paragraph (1), the Secretary shall conduct a comprehensive review of all requirements (including calculations), in existence on the date of enactment of the Elijah E. Cummings Coast Guard Authorization Act of 2020, that apply to covered small passenger vessels, with respect to fire detection, protection, and suppression systems, and avenues of egress, on board such vessels.

(3) REQUIREMENTS.—

(A) IN GENERAL.—Subject to subparagraph (B), the regulations prescribed under paragraph (1) shall include, with respect to covered small passenger vessels, regulations for—

(i) marine firefighting training programs to improve crewmember training and proficiency, including emergency egress training for each member of the crew, to occur for all members on the crew—

(I) at least monthly while such members are employed on board the vessel; and

(II) each time a new crewmember joins the crew of such vessel;

(ii) in all areas on board the vessel where passengers and crew have access, including dining areas, sleeping quarters, and lounges—

(I) interconnected fire detection equipment, including audible and visual alarms; and

(II) additional fire extinguishers and other firefighting equipment;

(iii) the installation and use of monitoring devices to ensure the wakefulness of the required night watch;

(iv) increased fire detection and suppression systems (including additional fire extinguishers) on board such vessels in unmanned areas with machinery or areas with other potential heat sources;

(v) all general areas accessible to passengers to have no less than 2 independent avenues of escape that are—

(I) constructed and arranged to allow for free and unobstructed egress from such areas;

(II) located so that if one avenue of escape is not available, another avenue of escape is available; and

(III) not located directly above, or dependent on, a berth;

(vi) the handling, storage, and operation of flammable items, such as rechargeable batteries, including lithium ion batteries utilized for commercial purposes on board such vessels;

(vii) passenger emergency egress drills for all areas on the vessel to which passengers have access, which shall occur prior to the vessel beginning each excursion; and

(viii) all passengers to be provided a copy of the emergency egress plan for the vessel.

(B) APPLICABILITY TO CERTAIN COVERED SMALL PASSENGER VESSELS.—The requirements described in clauses (iii), (v), (vii), and (viii) of subparagraph (A) shall only apply to a covered small passenger vessel that has overnight passenger accommodations.

(4) INTERIM REQUIREMENTS.—

(A) INTERIM REQUIREMENTS.—The Secretary shall, prior to issuing final regulations under paragraph (1), implement interim requirements to enforce the requirements under paragraph (3).

(B) IMPLEMENTATION.—The Secretary shall implement the interim requirements under subparagraph (A) without regard to chapters 5 and 6 of title 5 and Executive Order Nos. 12866 and 13563 (5 U.S.C. 601 note; relating to regulatory planning and review and relating to improving regulation and regulatory review).

(5) DEFINITION OF COVERED SMALL PASSENGER VESSEL.—In this subsection, the term "covered small passenger vessel"—

(A) except as provided in subparagraph (B), means a small passenger vessel (as defined in section 2101) that—

(i) has overnight passenger accommodations; or

(ii) is operating on a coastwise or oceans route; and

(B) does not include a ferry (as defined in section 2101) or fishing vessel (as defined in section 2101).

(Pub. L. 98–89, Aug. 26, 1983, 97 Stat. 513; Pub. L. 98–364, title IV, §402(5), July 17, 1984, 98 Stat. 446; Pub. L. 103–206, title V, §512(a), Dec. 20, 1993, 107 Stat. 2442; Pub. L. 104–324, title VI, §604(a), (c), title VII, §712, Oct. 19, 1996, 110 Stat. 3930, 3931, 3936; Pub. L. 108–293, title IV, §415(b), Aug. 9, 2004, 118 Stat. 1047; Pub. L. 109–304, §15(12), Oct. 6, 2006, 120 Stat. 1703; Pub. L. 111–281, title VI, §612, Oct. 15, 2010, 124 Stat. 2970; Pub. L. 115–232, div. C, title XXXV, §3542(b), Aug. 13, 2018, 132 Stat. 2324; Pub. L. 115–265, title II, §206(a)(1), Oct. 11, 2018, 132 Stat. 3746; Pub. L. 116–283, div. G, title LVXXXIV [LXXXIV], §8441(a), Jan. 1, 2021, 134 Stat. 4742.)

§3307. FREQUENCY OF INSPECTION

Each vessel subject to inspection under this part shall undergo an initial inspection for certification before being put into service. After being put into service—

(1) each passenger vessel, nautical school vessel, and small passenger vessel allowed to carry more than 12 passengers on a foreign voyage shall be inspected at least once a year; and

(2) any other vessel shall be inspected at least once every 5 years.

(Pub. L. 98–89, Aug. 26, 1983, 97 Stat. 514; Pub. L. 104–324, title VI, §605(a), Oct. 19, 1996, 110 Stat. 3931.)

§3308. EXAMINATIONS

In addition to inspections required by section 3307 of this title, the Secretary shall examine or have examined—

(1) each vessel subject to inspection at proper times to ensure compliance with law and regulations; and

(2) crewmember accommodations on each vessel subject to inspection at least once a month or when the vessel enters United States ports to ensure that the accommodations are—

(A) of the size required by law and regulations;

(B) properly ventilated and in a clean and sanitary condition; and

(C) equipped with proper plumbing and mechanical appliances required by law and regulations, and the appliances are in good working condition.

(Pub. L. 98–89, Aug. 26, 1983, 97 Stat. 514; Pub. L. 104–324, title VI, §603(c), Oct. 19, 1996, 110 Stat. 3930.)

§3309. CERTIFICATE OF INSPECTION

(a) When an inspection under section 3307 of this title has been made and a vessel has been found to be in compliance with the requirements of law and regulations, a certificate of inspection, in a form prescribed by the Secretary, shall be issued to the vessel.

(b) The Secretary may issue a temporary certificate of inspection in place of a regular certificate of inspection issued under subsection (a) of this section.

(c) At least 30 days before the current certificate of inspection issued to a vessel under subsection (a) of this section expires, the owner, charterer, managing operator, agent, master, or individual in charge of the vessel shall submit to the Secretary in writing a notice that the vessel—

(1) will be required to be inspected; or

(2) will not be operated so as to require an inspection.

(d) A certificate of inspection issued under this section shall be signed by the senior Coast Guard member or civilian employee who inspected the vessel, in addition to the officer in charge of marine inspection.

(Pub. L. 98–89, Aug. 26, 1983, 97 Stat. 515; Pub. L. 98–498, title II, §211(a), Oct. 19, 1984, 98 Stat. 2303; Pub. L. 104–324, title VI, §606, Oct. 19, 1996, 110 Stat. 3931; Pub. L. 111–281, title V, §522(c), Oct. 15, 2010, 124 Stat. 2957.)

§3310. RECORDS OF CERTIFICATION

The Secretary shall keep records of certificates of inspection of vessels and of all acts in the examination and inspection of vessels, whether of approval or disapproval.

(Pub. L. 98–89, Aug. 26, 1983, 97 Stat. 515.)

§3311. CERTIFICATE OF INSPECTION REQUIRED

(a) Except as provided in subsection (b), a vessel subject to inspection under this part may not be operated without having on board a certificate of inspection issued under section 3309 of this title.

(b) The Secretary may direct the owner, charterer, managing operator, agent, master, or individual in charge of a vessel subject to inspection under this chapter and not having on board a certificate of inspection—

(1) to have the vessel proceed to mooring and remain there until a certificate of inspection is issued;

(2) to take immediate steps necessary for the safety of the vessel, individuals on board the vessel, or the environment; or

(3) to have the vessel proceed to a place to make repairs necessary to obtain a certificate of inspection.

(Pub. L. 98–89, Aug. 26, 1983, 97 Stat. 515; Pub. L. 98–498, title II, §211(b), Oct. 19, 1984, 98 Stat. 2304.)

§3312. DISPLAY OF CERTIFICATE OF INSPECTION

The certificate of inspection issued to a vessel under section 3309 of this title shall be displayed, suitably framed, in a conspicuous place on the vessel. When it is not practicable to so display the certificate, it shall be carried in the manner prescribed by regulation.

(Pub. L. 98–89, Aug. 26, 1983, 97 Stat. 515.)

§3313. COMPLIANCE WITH CERTIFICATE OF INSPECTION

(a) During the term of a vessel's certificate of inspection, the vessel must be in compliance with its conditions, unless relieved by a suspension or an exemption granted under section 3306(e) of this title.

(b) When a vessel is not in compliance with its certificate or fails to meet a standard prescribed by this part or a regulation prescribed under this part—

(1) the owner, charterer, managing operator, agent, master, or individual in charge shall be ordered in writing to correct the noted deficiencies promptly;

(2) the Secretary may permit any repairs to be made at a place most convenient to the owner, charterer, or managing operator when the Secretary decides the repairs can be made with safety to those on board and the vessel;

(3) the vessel may be required to cease operating at once; and

(4) if necessary, the certificate shall be suspended or revoked.

(c) The vessel's certificate of inspection shall be revoked if a condition unsafe to life that is ordered to be corrected under this section is not corrected at once.

(d) The owner, charterer, managing operator, agent, master, or individual in charge of a vessel whose certificate has been suspended or revoked shall be given written notice immediately of the suspension or revocation. The owner or master may appeal to the Secretary the suspension or revocation within 30 days of receiving the notice, as provided by regulations prescribed by the Secretary.

(Pub. L. 98–89, Aug. 26, 1983, 97 Stat. 515.)

§3314. EXPIRATION OF CERTIFICATE OF INSPECTION

(a) If the certificate of inspection of a vessel expires when the vessel is on a foreign voyage, the vessel may complete the voyage to a port of the United States within 30 days of the expiration of the certificate without incurring the penalties for operating without a certificate of inspection.

(b) If the certificate of inspection would expire within 15 days of sailing on a foreign voyage from a United States port, the vessel shall secure a new certificate of inspection before sailing, unless the voyage is scheduled to be completed prior to the expiration date of the certificate. If a voyage scheduled to be completed in that time is not so completed, the applicable penalties may be enforced unless the failure to meet the schedule was beyond the control of the owner, charterer, managing operator, agent, master, or individual in charge of the vessel.

(c) When the certificate of inspection of a foreign vessel carrying passengers, operated on a regularly established line, expires at sea after leaving the country to which it belongs or when the vessel is in the United States, the Secretary may permit the vessel to sail on its regular route without further inspection than would have been required had the certificate not expired. This permission applies only when the vessel will be regularly inspected and issued a certificate before the vessel's next return to the United States.

(Pub. L. 98–89, Aug. 26, 1983, 97 Stat. 516.)

§3315. DISCLOSURE OF DEFECTS AND PROTECTION OF INFORMANTS

(a) Each individual licensed under part E of this subtitle shall assist in the inspection or examination under this part of the vessel on which the individual is serving, and shall point out defects and imperfections known to the individual in matters subject to regulations and inspection. The individual also shall make known to officials designated to enforce this part, at the earliest opportunity, any marine casualty producing serious injury to the vessel, its equipment, or individuals on the vessel.

(b) An official may not disclose the name of an individual providing information under this section, or the source of the information, to a person except a person authorized by the Secretary. An official violating this subsection is liable to disciplinary action under applicable law.

(Pub. L. 98–89, Aug. 26, 1983, 97 Stat. 516.)

§3316. CLASSIFICATION SOCIETIES

(a) Each department, agency, and instrumentality of the United States Government shall recognize the American Bureau of Shipping as its agent in classifying vessels owned by the Government and in matters related to classification, as long as the Bureau is maintained as an organization having no capital stock and paying no dividends. The Secretary and the Secretary of Transportation each shall appoint one representative (except when the Secretary is the Secretary of Transportation, in which case the Secretary shall appoint both representatives) who shall represent the Government on the executive committee of the Bureau. The Bureau shall agree that the representatives shall be accepted by it as active members of the committee. The representatives shall serve without compensation, except for necessary traveling expenses.

(b)(1) The Secretary may delegate to the American Bureau of Shipping or another classification society recognized by the Secretary as meeting acceptable standards for such a society, for a vessel documented or to be documented under chapter 121 of this title, the authority to—

(A) review and approve plans required for issuing a certificate of inspection required by this part;

(B) conduct inspections and examinations; and

(C) issue a certificate of inspection required by this part and other related documents.

(2) The Secretary may make a delegation under paragraph (1) to a foreign classification society only—

(A) to the extent that the government of the foreign country in which the society is headquartered delegates authority and provides access to the American Bureau of Shipping to inspect, certify, and provide related services to vessels documented in that country;

(B) if the foreign classification society has offices and maintains records in the United States; and

(C) if the Secretary of State determines that the foreign classification society does not provide comparable services in or for a state sponsor of terrorism.

(3) When an inspection or examination has been delegated under this subsection, the Secretary's delegate—

(A) shall maintain in the United States complete files of all information derived from or necessarily connected with the inspection or examination for at least 2 years after the vessel ceases to be certified; and

(B) shall permit access to those files at all reasonable times to any officer, employee, or member of the Coast Guard designated—

(i) as a marine inspector and serving in a position as a marine inspector; or

(ii) in writing by the Secretary to have access to those files.

(c)(1) A classification society (including an employee or agent of that society) may not review, examine, survey, or certify the construction, repair, or alteration of a vessel in the United States unless the society has applied for approval under this subsection and the Secretary has reviewed and approved that society with respect to the conduct of that society under paragraph (2).

(2) The Secretary may approve a person for purposes of paragraph (1) only if the Secretary determines that—

(A) the vessels surveyed by the person while acting as a classification society have an adequate safety record; and

(B) the person has an adequate program to—

(i) develop and implement safety standards for vessels surveyed by the person;

(ii) make the safety records of the person available to the Secretary in an electronic format;

(iii) provide the safety records of a vessel surveyed by the person to any other classification society that requests those records for the purpose of conducting a survey of the vessel; and

(iv) request the safety records of a vessel the person will survey from any classification society that previously surveyed the vessel.

(d)(1) The Secretary may delegate to the American Bureau of Shipping or another classification society recognized by the Secretary as meeting acceptable standards for such a society, for a United States offshore facility, the authority to—

(A) review and approve plans required for issuing a certificate of inspection, a certificate of compliance, or any other certification and related documents issued by the Coast Guard pursuant to regulations issued under section 30 of the Outer Continental Shelf Lands Act (43 U.S.C. 1356); and

(B) conduct inspections and examinations.

(2) The Secretary may make a delegation under paragraph (1) to a foreign classification society only if—

(A) the foreign society has offices and maintains records in the United States;

(B)(i) the government of the foreign country in which the foreign society is headquartered delegates that authority to the American Bureau of Shipping; or

(ii) the Secretary has entered into an agreement with the government of the foreign country in which the foreign society is headquartered that—

(I) ensures the government of the foreign country will accept plan review, inspections, or examinations conducted by the American Bureau of Shipping and provide equivalent access to inspect, certify, and provide related services to offshore facilities located in that country or operating under the authority of that country; and

(II) is in full accord with principles of reciprocity in regards to any delegation contemplated by the Secretary under paragraph (1); and

(C) the Secretary of State determines that the foreign classification society does not provide comparable services in or for a state sponsor of terrorism.

(3) If an inspection or examination is conducted under authority delegated under this subsection, the person to which the authority was delegated—

(A) shall maintain in the United States complete files of all information derived from or necessarily connected with the inspection or examination for at least 2 years after the United States offshore facility ceases to be certified; and

(B) shall permit access to those files at all reasonable times to any officer, employee, or member of the Coast Guard designated—

(i) as a marine inspector and serving in a position as a marine inspector; or

(ii) in writing by the Secretary to have access to those files.

(4) For purposes of this subsection—

(A) the term "offshore facility" means any installation, structure, or other device (including any vessel not documented under chapter 121 of this title or the laws of another country), fixed or floating, that dynamically holds position or is temporarily or permanently attached to the seabed or subsoil under the sea; and

(B) the term "United States offshore facility" means any offshore facility, fixed or floating, that dynamically holds position or is temporarily or permanently attached to the seabed or subsoil under the territorial sea of the United States or the outer Continental Shelf (as that term is defined in section 2 of the Outer Continental Shelf Lands Act (43 U.S.C. 1331)), including any vessel, rig, platform, or other vehicle or structure subject to regulation under section 30 of the Outer Continental Shelf Lands Act (43 U.S.C. 1356).

(e) The Secretary shall revoke a delegation made to a classification society under subsection (b) or (d) if the Secretary of State determines that the classification society provides comparable services in or for a state sponsor of terrorism.

(f)(1) Upon request of an owner or operator of an offshore supply vessel, the Secretary shall delegate the authorities set forth in paragraph (1) of subsection (b) with respect to such vessel to a classification society to which a delegation is authorized under that paragraph. A delegation by the Secretary under this subsection shall be used for any vessel inspection and examination function carried out by the Secretary, including the issuance of certificates of inspection and all other related documents.

(2) If the Secretary determines that a certificate of inspection or related document issued under authority delegated under paragraph (1) of this subsection with respect to a vessel has reduced the operational safety of that vessel, the Secretary may terminate the certificate or document, respectively.

(3) Not later than 2 years after the date of the enactment of the Howard Coble Coast Guard and Maritime Transportation Act of 2014, and for each year of the subsequent 2-year period, the Secretary shall provide to the Committee on Transportation and Infrastructure of the House of Representatives and the Committee on Commerce, Science, and Transportation of the Senate a report describing—

(A) the number of vessels for which a delegation was made under paragraph (1);

(B) any savings in personnel and operational costs incurred by the Coast Guard that resulted from the delegations; and

(C) based on measurable marine casualty and other data, any impacts of the delegations on the operational safety of vessels for which the delegations were made, and on the crew on those vessels.

(g)(1) There shall be within the Coast Guard an office that conducts comprehensive and targeted oversight of all recognized organizations that act on behalf of the Coast Guard.

(2) The staff of the office shall include subject matter experts, including inspectors, investigators, and auditors, who possess the capability and authority to audit all aspects of such recognized organizations.

(3) In this subsection the term "recognized organization" has the meaning given that term in section 2.45–1 of title 46, Code of Federal Regulations, as in effect on the date of the enactment of the Hamm Alert Maritime Safety Act of 2018.

(h) In this section, the term "state sponsor of terrorism" means any country the government of which the Secretary of State has determined has repeatedly provided support for acts of international terrorism pursuant to section 6(j) [1] of the Export Administration Act of 1979 (as continued in effect under the International Emergency Economic Powers Act), section 620A of the Foreign Assistance Act of 1961, section 40 of the Arms Export Control Act, or any other provision of law.

(Pub. L. 98–89, Aug. 26, 1983, 97 Stat. 516; Pub. L. 104–324, title VI, §607(a), (b)(1), Oct. 19, 1996, 110 Stat. 3931, 3932; Pub. L. 108–293, title IV, §413(a), Aug. 9, 2004, 118 Stat. 1046; Pub. L. 111–281, title VI, §622, Oct. 15, 2010, 124 Stat. 2978; Pub. L. 112–213, title III, §304, Dec. 20, 2012, 126 Stat. 1563; Pub. L. 113–281, title III, §315, Dec. 18, 2014, 128 Stat. 3050; Pub. L. 115–265, title II, §215(a), Oct. 11, 2018, 132 Stat. 3751.)

[1] *See References in Text note below.*

§3317. FEES

(a) The Secretary may prescribe by regulation fees for inspecting or examining a small passenger vessel or a sailing school vessel.

(b) When an inspection or examination under this part of a documented vessel or a foreign vessel is conducted at a foreign port or place at the request of the owner or managing operator of the vessel, the owner or operator shall reimburse the Secretary for the travel and subsistence expenses incurred by the personnel assigned to perform the inspection or examination. Amounts received as reimbursement for these expenses shall be credited to the appropriation for operations and support of the Coast Guard.

(Pub. L. 98–89, Aug. 26, 1983, 97 Stat. 517; Pub. L. 102–587, title V, §5211, Nov. 4, 1992, 106 Stat. 5076; Pub. L. 116–283, div. G, title LVXXXV [LXXXV], §8513(b), Jan. 1, 2021, 134 Stat. 4761.)

§3318. Penalties

(a) Except as otherwise provided in this part, the owner, charterer, managing operator, agent, master, or individual in charge of a vessel operated in violation of this part or a regulation prescribed under this part, and a person violating a regulation that applies to a small passenger vessel, freight vessel of less than 100 gross tons as measured under section 14502 of this title, or an alternate tonnage measured under section 14302 of this title as prescribed by the Secretary under section 14104 of this title, or sailing school vessel, are liable to the United States Government for a civil penalty of not more than $5,000. The vessel also is liable in rem for the penalty.

(b)(1) A person that knowingly manufactures, sells, offers for sale, or possesses with intent to sell, any equipment subject to this part, and the equipment is so defective as to be insufficient to accomplish the purpose for which it is intended, commits a class D felony.

(2) A person commits a class D felony if the person—

(A) alters or services lifesaving, fire safety, or any other equipment subject to this part for compensation; and

(B) by that alteration or servicing, intentionally renders that equipment unsafe and unfit for the purpose for which it is intended.

(c) A person that employs a means or device whereby a boiler may be subjected to a pressure greater than allowed by the terms of the vessel's certificate of inspection commits a class D felony.

(d) A person that deranges or hinders the operation of any machinery or device employed on a vessel to denote the state of steam or water in any boiler or to give warning of approaching danger, or permits the water level of any boiler when in operation of a vessel to fall below its prescribed low-water line, commits a class D felony.

(e) A person that alters, defaces, obliterates, removes, or destroys any plans or specifications required by and approved under a regulation prescribed under section 3306 of this title, with intent to deceive or impede any official of the United States in carrying out that official's duties, commits a class A misdemeanor.

(f) A person commits a class D felony if the person—

(1) forges or counterfeits with intent to make it appear genuine any mark or stamp prescribed for material to be tested and approved under section 3306 of this title or a regulation prescribed under section 3306;

(2) knowingly uses, affixes, or causes to be used or affixed, any such forged or counterfeited mark or stamp to or on material of any description;

(3) with fraudulent intent, possesses any such mark, stamp, or other device knowing it to be forged or counterfeited; or

(4) with fraudulent intent, marks or causes to be marked with the trademark or name of another, material required to be tested and approved under section 3306 of this title or a regulation prescribed under section 3306.

(g) A person is liable to the Government for a civil penalty of not more than $5,000, if the person—

(1) interferes with the inspection of a nautical school vessel;

(2) violates a regulation prescribed for a nautical school vessel;

(3) is an owner of a nautical school vessel operated in violation of this part; or

(4) is an officer or member of the board of directors of a school, organization, association, partnership, or corporation owning a nautical school vessel operated in violation of a regulation prescribed for a nautical school vessel.

(h) An owner, charterer, managing operator, agent, master, or individual in charge of a vessel that fails to give the notice required by section 3304(b) of this title is liable to the Government for a civil penalty of not more than $1,000. The vessel also is liable in rem for the penalty.

(i) A person violating section 3309(c) of this title is liable to the Government for a civil penalty of not more than $1,000.

(j)(1) An owner, charterer, managing operator, agent, master, or individual in charge of a vessel required to be inspected under this chapter operating the vessel without the certificate of inspection is liable to the Government for a civil penalty of not more than $10,000 for each day during which the violation occurs, except when the violation involves operation of a vessel of less than 1,600 gross tons as measured under section 14502 of this title, or an alternate tonnage measured under section 14302 of this title as prescribed by the Secretary under section 14104 of this title, the penalty is not more than $2,000 for each day during which the violation occurs. The vessel also is liable in rem for the penalty.

(2) A person is not liable for a penalty under this subsection if—

(A) the owner, charterer, managing operator, agent, master, or individual in charge of the vessel has notified the Secretary under section 3309(c) of this title;

(B) the owner, charterer, managing operator, agent, master, or individual in charge of the vessel has complied with all other directions and requirements for obtaining an inspection under this part; and

(C) the Secretary believes that unforeseen circumstances exist so that it is not feasible to conduct a scheduled inspection before the expiration of the certificate of inspection.

(k) The owner, charterer, managing operator, agent, master, or individual in charge of a vessel failing to comply with a direction issued by the Secretary under section 3311(b) of this title is liable to the Government for a civil penalty of not more than $10,000 for each day during which the violation occurs. The vessel also is liable in rem for the penalty.

(l) A person committing an act described by subsections (b)–(f) of this section is liable to the Government for a civil penalty of not more than $5,000. If the violation involves the operation of a vessel, the vessel also is liable in rem for the penalty.

(Pub. L. 98–89, Aug. 26, 1983, 97 Stat. 517; Pub. L. 98–498, title II, §211(c), Oct. 19, 1984, 98 Stat. 2304; Pub. L. 99–307, §1(6), May 19, 1986, 100 Stat. 445; Pub. L. 101–380, title IV, §4302(b), Aug. 18, 1990, 104 Stat. 538; Pub. L. 104–324, title III, §310, title VII, §713, Oct. 19, 1996, 110 Stat. 3919, 3936; Pub. L. 109–304, §15(13), Oct. 6, 2006, 120 Stat. 1703.)

CHAPTER 35—CARRIAGE OF PASSENGERS

§3501. NUMBER OF PASSENGERS

(a) Each certificate of inspection issued to a vessel carrying passengers (except a ferry) shall include a statement on the number of passengers that the vessel is permitted to carry.

(b) The owner, charterer, managing operator, agent, master, or individual in charge of a vessel is liable to a person suing them for carrying more passengers than the number of passengers permitted by the certificate of inspection in an amount equal to—

(1) passage money; and

(2) $100 for each passenger in excess of the number of passengers permitted.

(c) An owner, charterer, managing operator, agent, master, or individual in charge of a vessel that knowingly carries more passengers than the number of passengers permitted by the certificate of inspection also shall be fined not more than $100, imprisoned for not more than 30 days, or both.

(d) The vessel also is liable in rem for a penalty under this section.

(e) An offshore supply vessel may not carry passengers except in an emergency.

(Pub. L. 98–89, Aug. 26, 1983, 97 Stat. 519; Pub. L. 99–36, §1(a)(2), May 15, 1985, 99 Stat. 67.)

§3502. LIST OR COUNT OF PASSENGERS

(a) The owner, charterer, managing operator, master, or individual in charge of the following categories of vessels carrying passengers shall keep a correct list of passengers received and delivered from day to day:

(1) vessels arriving from foreign ports (except at United States Great Lakes ports from Canadian Great Lakes ports).

(2) seagoing vessels in the coastwise trade.

(3) passenger vessels making voyages of more than 300 miles on the Great Lakes except from a Canadian to a United States port.

(b) The master of a vessel carrying passengers (except a vessel listed in subsection (a) of this section) shall keep a correct count of all passengers received and delivered.

(c) Lists and counts required under this section shall be open to the inspection of designated officials of the Coast Guard and the Customs Service at all times. The total number of passengers shall be provided to the Coast Guard when requested.

(d) This section applies to a foreign vessel arriving at a United States port.

(e) The owner, charterer, managing operator, master, or individual in charge of a passenger vessel failing to make a list or count of passengers as required by this section is liable to the United States Government for a civil penalty of $100. The vessel also is liable in rem for the penalty.

(Pub. L. 98–89, Aug. 26, 1983, 97 Stat. 519.)

§3503. FIRE-RETARDANT MATERIALS

(a)(1) A passenger vessel of the United States having berth or stateroom accommodations for at least 50 passengers shall be granted a certificate of inspection only if—

(A) the vessel is constructed of fire-retardant materials; and

(B) the vessel—

(i) is operating engines, boilers, main electrical distribution panels, fuel tanks, oil tanks, and generators that meet current Coast Guard regulations; and

(ii) is operating boilers and main electrical generators that are contained within noncombustible enclosures equipped with fire suppression systems.

(2) Before December 1, 2028, this subsection does not apply to any vessel in operation before January 1, 1968, and operating only within the Boundary Line.

(b)(1) The owner or managing operator of an exempted vessel described in subsection (a)(2) shall—

(A) notify in writing prospective passengers, prior to purchase, and each crew member that the vessel does not comply with applicable fire safety standards due primarily to the wooden construction of passenger berthing areas;

(B) display in clearly legible font prominently throughout the vessel, including in each state room the following: "THIS VESSEL FAILS TO COMPLY WITH SAFETY RULES AND REGULATIONS OF THE U.S. COAST GUARD.";

(C) acquire prior to the vessel entering service, and maintain, liability insurance in an amount to be prescribed by the Federal Maritime Commission;

(D) make annual structural alteration to not less than 10 percent of the areas of the vessel that are not constructed of fire retardant materials;

(E) prioritize alterations in galleys, engineering areas of the vessel, including all spaces and compartments containing, or adjacent to spaces and compartments containing, engines, boilers, main electrical distribution panels, fuel tanks, oil tanks, and generators;

(F) ensure, to the satisfaction of the Secretary, that the combustible fire-load has been reduced pursuant to subparagraph (D) during each annual inspection for certification;

(G) ensure the vessel has multiple forms of egress off the vessel's bow and stern;

(H) provide advance notice to the Coast Guard regarding the structural alterations made pursuant to subparagraph (D) and comply with any noncombustible material requirements prescribed by the Coast Guard;

(I) annually notify all ports of call and State emergency management offices of jurisdiction that the vessel does not comply with the requirement under subsection (a)(1);
(J) provide crewmembers manning such vessel shipboard training that—
(i) is specialized for exempted vessels;
(ii) exceeds requirements related to standards for firefighting training under chapter I of title 46, Code of Federal Regulations, as in effect on October 1, 2017; and
(iii) is approved by the Coast Guard; and

(K) to the extent practicable, take all steps to retain previously trained crew knowledgeable of such vessel or to hire crew trained in operations aboard exempted vessels.

(2) The owner or managing operator of an exempted vessel described in subsection (a)(2) may not disclaim liability to a passenger or crew member of such vessel for death, injury, or any other loss caused by fire due to the negligence of the owner or managing operator.
(3) The Secretary shall—
(A) conduct an annual audit and inspection of each exempted vessel described in subsection (a)(2);
(B) in implementing subparagraph (b)(1)(F), consider, to the extent practicable, the goal of preservation of the historic integrity of such vessel in areas carrying or accessible to passengers or generally visible to the public; and
(C) prescribe regulations to carry out this section, including to prescribe the manner in which prospective passengers are to be notified under paragraph (1)(A).

(4) The penalties provided in section 3504(c) of this title shall apply to a violation of this subsection.
(c) In addition to otherwise applicable penalties, the Secretary may immediately withdraw a certificate of inspection for an exempted vessel described in subsection (a)(2) that does not comply with any requirement under subsection (b).

(Pub. L. 98–89, Aug. 26, 1983, 97 Stat. 519; Pub. L. 99–307, §1(7)(A), May 19, 1986, 100 Stat. 445; Pub. L. 102–241, §20, Dec. 19, 1991, 105 Stat. 2216; Pub. L. 104–324, title XI, §1133, Oct. 19, 1996, 110 Stat. 3985; Pub. L. 115–282, title VIII, §834, Dec. 4, 2018, 132 Stat. 4318.)

§3504. NOTIFICATION TO PASSENGERS

(a) A person selling passage on a foreign or domestic passenger vessel having berth or stateroom accommodations for at least 50 passengers and embarking passengers at United States ports for a coastwise or an international voyage shall notify each prospective passenger of the safety standards applicable to the vessel in a manner prescribed by regulation.
(b) All promotional literature or advertising through any medium of communication in the United States offering passage or soliciting passengers for ocean voyages anywhere in the world shall include information similar to the information described in subsection (a) of this section, and shall specify the registry of each vessel named, as a part of the advertisement or description of the voyage. Except for the inclusion of the country of registry of the vessel, this subsection does not apply to voyages by vessels meeting the

safety standards described in section 3505 of this title.

(c) A person violating this section or a regulation prescribed under this section is liable to the United States Government for a civil penalty of not more than $10,000. If the violation involves the sale of tickets for passage, the owner, charterer, managing operator, agent, master, individual in charge, or any other person involved in each violation also is liable to the Government for a civil penalty of $500 for each ticket sold. The vessel on which passage is sold also is liable in rem for a violation of this section or a regulation prescribed under this section.

(Pub. L. 98–89, Aug. 26, 1983, 97 Stat. 519.)

§3505. PREVENTION OF DEPARTURE

Notwithstanding section 3303 of this title, a foreign vessel carrying a citizen of the United States as a passenger or embarking passengers from a United States port may not depart from a United States port if the Secretary finds that the vessel does not comply with the standards stated in the International Convention for the Safety of Life at Sea to which the United States Government is currently a party.

(Pub. L. 98–89, Aug. 26, 1983, 97 Stat. 520; Pub. L. 102–587, title V, §5210(b), Nov. 4, 1992, 106 Stat. 5076; Pub. L. 108–293, title IV, §411(a), Aug. 9, 2004, 118 Stat. 1045.)

§3506. COPIES OF LAWS

A master of a passenger vessel shall keep on board a copy of this subtitle, to be provided by the Secretary at reasonable cost. If the master fails to do so, the master is liable to the United States Government for a civil penalty of $200.

(Pub. L. 98–89, Aug. 26, 1983, 97 Stat. 520.)

§3507. PASSENGER VESSEL SECURITY AND SAFETY REQUIREMENTS

(a) VESSEL DESIGN, EQUIPMENT, CONSTRUCTION, AND RETROFITTING REQUIREMENTS.—

(1) IN GENERAL.—Each vessel to which this subsection applies shall comply with the following design and construction standards:

(A) The vessel shall be equipped with ship rails that are located not less than 42 inches above the cabin deck.

(B) Each passenger stateroom and crew cabin shall be equipped with entry doors that include peep holes or other means of visual identification.

(C) For any vessel the keel of which is laid after the date of enactment of the Cruise Vessel Security and Safety Act of 2010, each passenger stateroom and crew cabin shall be equipped with—

(i) security latches; and

(ii) time-sensitive key technology.

(D) The vessel shall integrate technology that can be used for capturing images of passengers or detecting passengers who have fallen overboard, to the extent that such technology is available.

(E) The vessel shall be equipped with a sufficient number of operable acoustic hailing or other such warning devices to provide communication capability around the entire vessel when operating in high risk areas (as defined by the United States Coast Guard).

(2) FIRE SAFETY CODES.—In administering the requirements of paragraph (1)(C), the Secretary shall take into consideration fire safety and other applicable emergency requirements established by the U.S. Coast Guard and under international law, as appropriate.

(b) VIDEO RECORDING.—
    (1) REQUIREMENT TO MAINTAIN SURVEILLANCE.—
        (A) IN GENERAL.—The owner of a vessel to which this section applies shall maintain a video surveillance system to assist in documenting crimes on the vessel and in providing evidence for the prosecution of such crimes.
        (B) PLACEMENT OF VIDEO SURVEILLANCE EQUIPMENT.—
            (i) IN GENERAL.—Not later than 18 months after the date of the enactment of the Elijah E. Cummings Coast Guard Authorization Act of 2020, the Commandant in consultation with other relevant Federal agencies or entities as determined by the Commandant, shall establish guidance for performance of the risk assessment described in paragraph (2) regarding the appropriate placement of video surveillance equipment in passenger and crew common areas where there is no reasonable expectation of privacy.
            (ii) RISK ASSESSMENT.—Not later than 1 year after the Commandant establishes the guidance described in paragraph (1), the owner shall conduct the risk assessment required under paragraph (1) and shall—
                (I) evaluate the placement of video surveillance equipment to deter, prevent, and record a sexual assault aboard the vessel considering factors such as: ship layout and design, itinerary, crew complement, number of passengers, passenger demographics, and historical data on the type and location of prior sexual assault incident allegations;
                (II) incorporate to the maximum extent practicable the video surveillance guidance established by the Commandant regarding the appropriate placement of video surveillance equipment;
                (III) arrange for the risk assessment to be conducted by an independent third party with expertise in the use and placement of camera surveillance to deter, prevent and record criminal behavior; and
                (IV) the independent third party referred to in paragraph (C) shall be a company that has been accepted by a classification society that is a member of the International Association of Classification Societies (hereinafter referred to as "IACS") or another classification society recognized by the Secretary as meeting acceptable standards for such a society pursuant to section 3316(b).

        (C) SURVEILLANCE PLAN.—Not later than 180 days after completion of the risk assessment conducted under subparagraph (B)(ii), the owner of a vessel shall develop a plan to install video surveillance equipment in places determined to be appropriate in accordance with the results of the risk assessment conducted under subparagraph

(B)(ii), except in areas where a person has a reasonable expectation of privacy. Such plan shall be evaluated and approved by an independent third party with expertise in the use and placement of camera surveillance to deter, prevent and record criminal behavior that has been accepted as set forth in paragraph (2)(D).

(D) INSTALLATION.—The owner of a vessel to which this section applies shall, consistent with the surveillance plan approved under subparagraph (C), install appropriate video surveillance equipment aboard the vessel not later than 2 years after approval of the plan, or during the next scheduled drydock, whichever is later.

(E) ATTESTATION.—At the time of initial installation under subparagraph (D), the vessel owner shall obtain written attestations from—

(i) an IACS classification society that the video surveillance equipment is installed in accordance with the surveillance plan required under subparagraph (C); and

(ii) the company security officer that the surveillance equipment and associated systems are operational, which attestation shall be obtained each year thereafter.

(F) UPDATES.—The vessel owner shall ensure the risk assessment described in subparagraph (B)(ii) and installation plan in subparagraph (C) are updated not later than 5 years after the initial installation conducted under subparagraph (D), and every 5 years thereafter. The updated assessment and plan shall be approved by an independent third party with expertise in the use and placement of camera surveillance to deter, prevent, and record criminal behavior that has been accepted by an IACS classification society. The vessel owner shall implement the updated installation plan not later than 180 days after approval.

(G) AVAILABILITY.—Each risk assessment, installation plan and attestation shall be protected from disclosure under the Freedom of Information Act, section 552 of title 5 but shall be available to the Coast Guard—

(i) upon request, and

(ii) at the time of the certificate of compliance or certificate of inspection examination.

(H) DEFINITIONS.—For purposes of this section a "ship security officer" is an individual that, with the master's approval, has full responsibility for vessel security consistent with the International Ship and Port Facility Security Code.

(2) NOTICE OF VIDEO SURVEILLANCE.—The owner of a vessel to which this section applies shall provide clear and conspicuous signs on board the vessel notifying the public of the presence of video surveillance equipment.

(3) ACCESS TO VIDEO RECORDS.—

(A) LAW ENFORCEMENT.—The owner of a vessel to which this section applies shall provide to any law enforcement official performing official duties in the course and scope of an investigation, upon request, a copy of all records of video surveillance that the official believes may provide evidence of a crime reported to law enforcement officials.

(B) CIVIL ACTIONS.—Except as proscribed by law enforcement authorities or court

order, the owner of a vessel to which this section applies shall, upon written request, provide to any individual or the individual's legal representative a copy of all records of video surveillance—
    (i) in which the individual is a subject of the video surveillance; and
    (ii) that may provide evidence of any sexual assault incident in a civil action.

    (C) LIMITED ACCESS.—The owner of a vessel to which this section applies shall ensure that access to records of video surveillance is limited to the purposes described in this paragraph.

    (4) RETENTION REQUIREMENTS.—The owner of a vessel to which this section applies shall retain all records of video surveillance for not less than 20 days after the footage is obtained. The vessel owner shall include a statement in the security guide required by subsection (c)(1)(A) that the vessel owner is required by law to retain video surveillance footage for the period specified in this paragraph. If an incident described in subsection (g)(3)(A)(i) is alleged and reported to law enforcement, all records of video surveillance from the voyage that the Federal Bureau of Investigation determines are relevant shall—
    (A) be provided to the Federal Bureau of Investigation; and
    (B) be preserved by the vessel owner for not less than 4 years from the date of the alleged incident.

(c) SAFETY INFORMATION.—
    (1) CRIMINAL ACTIVITY PREVENTION AND RESPONSE GUIDE.—The owner of a vessel to which this section applies (or the owner's designee) shall—
    (A) have available for each passenger a guide (referred to in this subsection as the "security guide"), written in commonly understood English, which—
    (i) provides a description of medical and security personnel designated on board to prevent and respond to criminal and medical situations with 24 hour contact instructions;
    (ii) describes the jurisdictional authority applicable, and the law enforcement processes available, with respect to the reporting of homicide, suspicious death, a missing United States national, kidnapping, assault with serious bodily injury, any offense to which section 2241, 2242, 2243, or 2244(a) or (c) of title 18 applies, firing or tampering with the vessel, or theft of money or property in excess of $10,000, together with contact information for the appropriate law enforcement authorities for missing persons or reportable crimes which arise—
    (I) in the territorial waters of the United States;
    (II) on the high seas; or
    (III) in any country to be visited on the voyage;

    (B) provide a copy of the security guide to the Federal Bureau of Investigation for comment; and
    (C) publicize the security guide on the website of the vessel owner.

    (2) EMBASSY AND CONSULATE LOCATIONS.—The owner of a vessel to which this section

applies shall provide in each passenger stateroom, and post in a location readily accessible to all crew and in other places specified by the Secretary, information regarding the locations of the United States embassy and each consulate of the United States for each country the vessel will visit during the course of the voyage.

(d) SEXUAL ASSAULT.—The owner of a vessel to which this section applies shall—

(1) maintain on the vessel adequate, in-date supplies of anti-retroviral medications and other medications designed to prevent sexually transmitted diseases after a sexual assault;

(2) maintain on the vessel equipment and materials for performing a medical examination in sexual assault cases to evaluate the patient for trauma, provide medical care, and preserve relevant medical evidence;

(3) make available on the vessel at all times medical staff who have undergone a credentialing process to verify that he or she—

(A) possesses a current physician's or registered nurse's license and—

(i) has at least 3 years of post-graduate or post-registration clinical practice in general and emergency medicine; or

(ii) holds board certification in emergency medicine, family practice medicine, or internal medicine;

(B) is able to provide assistance in the event of an alleged sexual assault, has received training in conducting forensic sexual assault examination, and is able to promptly perform such an examination upon request and provide proper medical treatment of a victim, including administration of anti-retroviral medications and other medications that may prevent the transmission of human immunodeficiency virus and other sexually transmitted diseases; and

(C) meets guidelines established by the American College of Emergency Physicians relating to the treatment and care of victims of sexual assault;

(4) prepare, provide to the patient, and maintain written documentation of the findings of such examination that is signed by the patient; and

(5) provide the patient free and immediate access to—

(A) contact information for local law enforcement, the Federal Bureau of Investigation, the United States Coast Guard, the nearest United States consulate or embassy, and the National Sexual Assault Hotline program or other third party victim advocacy hotline service; and

(B) a private telephone line and Internet-accessible computer terminal by which the individual may confidentially access law enforcement officials, an attorney, and the information and support services available through the National Sexual Assault Hotline program or other third party victim advocacy hotline service.

(e) CONFIDENTIALITY OF SEXUAL ASSAULT EXAMINATION AND SUPPORT INFORMATION.—The master or other individual in charge of a vessel to which this section applies shall—

(1) treat all information concerning an examination under subsection (d) confidential,

so that no medical information may be released to the cruise line or other owner of the vessel or any legal representative thereof without the prior knowledge and approval in writing of the patient, or, if the patient is unable to provide written authorization, the patient's next-of-kin, except that nothing in this paragraph prohibits the release of—

(A) information, other than medical findings, necessary for the owner or master of the vessel to comply with the provisions of subsection (g) or other applicable incident reporting laws;

(B) information to secure the safety of passengers or crew on board the vessel; or

(C) any information to law enforcement officials performing official duties in the course and scope of an investigation; and

(2) treat any information derived from, or obtained in connection with, post-assault counseling or other supportive services as confidential, so no such information may be released to the cruise line or any legal representative thereof without the prior knowledge and approval in writing of the patient, or, if the patient is unable to provide written authorization, the patient's next-of-kin.

(f) CREW ACCESS TO PASSENGER STATEROOMS.—The owner of a vessel to which this section applies shall—

(1) establish and implement procedures and restrictions concerning—

(A) which crewmembers have access to passenger staterooms; and

(B) the periods during which they have that access; and

(2) ensure that the procedures and restrictions are fully and properly implemented and periodically reviewed.

(g) LOG BOOK AND REPORTING REQUIREMENTS.—

(1) IN GENERAL.—The owner of a vessel to which this section applies shall—

(A) record in a log book, either electronically or otherwise, in a centralized location readily accessible to law enforcement personnel, a report on—

(i) all complaints of crimes described in paragraph (3)(A)(i),

(ii) all complaints of theft of property valued in excess of $1,000, and

(iii) all complaints of other crimes,

committed on any voyage that embarks or disembarks passengers in the United States; and

(B) make such log book available upon request to any agent of the Federal Bureau of Investigation, any member of the United States Coast Guard, and any law enforcement officer performing official duties in the course and scope of an investigation.

(2) DETAILS REQUIRED.—The information recorded under paragraph (1) shall include, at a minimum—

(A) the vessel operator;

(B) the name of the cruise line;

(C) the flag under which the vessel was operating at the time the reported incident occurred;

(D) the age and gender of the victim and the accused assailant;

(E) the nature of the alleged crime or complaint, as applicable, including whether the alleged perpetrator was a passenger or a crewmember;

(F) the vessel's position at the time of the incident, if known, or the position of the vessel at the time of the initial report;

(G) the time, date, and method of the initial report and the law enforcement authority to which the initial report was made;

(H) the time and date the incident occurred, if known;

(I) the total number of passengers and the total number of crew members on the voyage; and

(J) the case number or other identifier provided by the law enforcement authority to which the initial report was made.

(3) REQUIREMENT TO REPORT CRIMES AND OTHER INFORMATION.—

(A) IN GENERAL.—The owner of a vessel to which this section applies (or the owner's designee)—

(i) shall contact the nearest Federal Bureau of Investigation Field Office or Legal Attache by telephone as soon as possible after the occurrence on board the vessel of an incident involving homicide, suspicious death, a missing United States national, kidnapping, assault with serious bodily injury, any offense to which section 2241, 2242, 2243, or 2244(a) or (c) of title 18 applies, firing or tampering with the vessel, or theft of money or property in excess of $10,000 to report the incident;

(ii) shall furnish a written report of each incident specified in clause (i) to the Internet website maintained by the Secretary of Transportation under paragraph (4)(A);

(iii) may report any serious incident that does not meet the reporting requirements of clause (i) and that does not require immediate attention by the Federal Bureau of Investigation via the Internet website maintained by the Secretary of Transportation under paragraph (4)(A); and

(iv) may report any other criminal incident involving passengers or crewmembers, or both, to the proper State or local government law enforcement authority.

(B) INCIDENTS TO WHICH SUBPARAGRAPH (A) APPLIES.—Subparagraph (A) applies to an incident involving criminal activity if—

(i) the vessel, regardless of registry, is owned, in whole or in part, by a United States person, regardless of the nationality of the victim or perpetrator, and the incident occurs when the vessel is within the admiralty and maritime jurisdiction of the United States and outside the jurisdiction of any State;

(ii) the incident concerns an offense by or against a United States national committed outside the jurisdiction of any nation;

(iii) the incident occurs in the Territorial Sea of the United States, regardless of the nationality of the vessel, the victim, or the perpetrator; or

(iv) the incident concerns a victim or perpetrator who is a United States national on a vessel during a voyage that departed from or will arrive at a United States port.

(4) AVAILABILITY OF INCIDENT DATA VIA INTERNET.—

(A) WEBSITE.—

(i) IN GENERAL.—The Secretary of Transportation shall maintain a statistical compilation of all incidents on board a cruise vessel specified in paragraph (3)(A)(i) on an Internet website that provides a numerical accounting of the missing persons and alleged crimes reported under that paragraph without regard to the investigative status of the incident.

(ii) UPDATES AND OTHER REQUIREMENTS.—The compilation under clause (i) shall—

(I) be updated not less frequently than quarterly;

(II) be able to be sorted by cruise line;

(III) identify each cruise line by name;

(IV) identify each crime or alleged crime committed or allegedly committed by a passenger or crewmember;

(V) identify the number of individuals alleged overboard; and

(VI) include the approximate number of passengers and crew carried by each cruise line during each quarterly reporting period.

(iii) USER-FRIENDLY FORMAT.—The Secretary of Transportation shall ensure that the compilation, data, and any other information provided on the Internet website maintained under this subparagraph are in a user-friendly format. The Secretary shall, to the greatest extent practicable, use existing commercial off the shelf technology to transfer and establish the website, and shall not independently develop software, or acquire new hardware in operating the site.

(B) ACCESS TO WEBSITE.—Each cruise line taking on or discharging passengers in the United States shall include a link on its Internet website to the website maintained by the Secretary of Transportation under subparagraph (A).

(h) ENFORCEMENT.—

(1) PENALTIES.—

(A) CIVIL PENALTY.—Any person that violates this section or a regulation under this section shall be liable for a civil penalty of not more than $25,000 for each day during which the violation continues, except that the maximum penalty for a continuing violation is $50,000.

(B) CRIMINAL PENALTY.—Any person that willfully violates this section or a regulation under this section shall be fined not more than $250,000 or imprisoned not more than 1 year, or both.

(2) DENIAL OF ENTRY.—The Secretary may deny entry into the United States to a vessel to which this section applies if the owner of the vessel—

(A) commits an act or omission for which a penalty may be imposed under this subsection; or

(B) fails to pay a penalty imposed on the owner under this subsection.

(i) PROCEDURES.—The Secretary shall maintain guidelines, training curricula, and inspection and certification procedures necessary to carry out the requirements of this section.

(j) REGULATIONS.—The Secretary and the Commandant shall each issue such regulations as are necessary to implement this section.

(k) APPLICATION.—

(1) IN GENERAL.—This section and section 3508 apply to a passenger vessel (as defined in section 2101(31)) that—

(A) is authorized to carry 250 or more passengers;

(B) has overnight accommodations for 250 or more passengers; and

(C) is on a voyage that embarks or disembarks passengers in the United States.

(2) FEDERAL AND STATE VESSELS.—This section and section 3508 do not apply to a vessel of the United States operated by the Federal Government or a vessel owned and operated by a State.

(l) DEFINITION.—In this section and section 3508, the term "owner" means the owner, charterer, managing operator, master, or other individual in charge of a vessel.

(Added Pub. L. 111–207, §3(a), July 27, 2010, 124 Stat. 2244; amended Pub. L. 113–281, title III, §321, Dec. 18, 2014, 128 Stat. 3054; Pub. L. 115–232, div. C, title XXXV, §§3541(b)(9), 3543(a), Aug. 13, 2018, 132 Stat. 2323, 2324; Pub. L. 116–283, div. G, title LVXXXIII [LXXXIII], §8311, div. G, title LVXXXIV [LXXXIV], §8440(a)–(c)(1), Jan. 1, 2021, 134 Stat. 4697, 4739–4741; Pub. L. 117–263, div. K, title CXVIII, §11802, Dec. 23, 2022, 136 Stat. 4163.)

§3508. CRIME SCENE PRESERVATION TRAINING FOR PASSENGER VESSEL CREWMEMBERS

(a) IN GENERAL.—The Secretary, in consultation with the Director of the Federal Bureau of Investigation and the Maritime Administration, shall maintain training standards and curricula to allow for the certification of passenger vessel security personnel, crewmembers, and law enforcement officials on the appropriate methods for prevention, detection, evidence preservation, and reporting of criminal activities in the international maritime environment. The Administrator of the Maritime Administration may certify organizations in the United States and abroad that offer the curriculum for training and certification under subsection (c).

(b) MINIMUM STANDARDS.—The standards established by the Secretary under subsection (a) shall include—

(1) the training and certification of vessel security personnel, crewmembers, and law enforcement officials in accordance with accepted law enforcement and security guidelines, policies, and procedures, including recommendations for incorporating a background check process for personnel trained and certified in foreign ports;

(2) the training of students and instructors in all aspects of prevention, detection,

evidence preservation, and reporting of criminal activities in the international maritime environment; and

(3) the provision or recognition of off-site training and certification courses in the United States and foreign countries to develop and provide the required training and certification described in subsection (a) and to enhance security awareness and security practices related to the preservation of evidence in response to crimes on board passenger vessels.

(c) CERTIFICATION REQUIREMENT.—No vessel to which this section applies may enter a United States port on a voyage (or voyage segment) on which a United States citizen is a passenger unless there is at least 1 crewmember onboard who is certified as having successfully completed training in the prevention, detection, evidence preservation, and reporting of criminal activities in the international maritime environment on passenger vessels under subsection (a).

(d) CIVIL PENALTY.—Any person that violates this section or a regulation under this section shall be liable for a civil penalty of not more than $50,000.

(e) DENIAL OF ENTRY.—The Secretary may deny entry into the United States to a vessel to which this section applies if the owner of the vessel—

(1) commits an act or omission for which a penalty may be imposed under subsection (d); or

(2) fails to pay a penalty imposed on the owner under subsection (d).

(Added Pub. L. 111–207, §3(a), July 27, 2010, 124 Stat. 2250; amended Pub. L. 115–232, div. C, title XXXV, §3543(b), Aug. 13, 2018, 132 Stat. 2324.)

§3509. MEDICAL STANDARDS

The owner of a vessel to which section 3507 applies shall ensure that—

(1) a physician is always present and available to treat any passengers who may be on board the vessel in the event of an emergency situation;

(2) the vessel is in compliance with the Health Care Guidelines for Cruise Ship Medical Facilities established by the American College of Emergency Physicians; and

(3) the initial safety briefing given to the passengers on board the vessel includes—

(A) the location of the vessel's medical facilities; and

(B) the appropriate steps passengers should follow during a medical emergency.

(Added Pub. L. 116–283, div. G, title LVXXXIII [LXXXIII], §8322(a), Jan. 1, 2021, 134 Stat. 4702.)

§3510. ADDITIONAL MEDICAL AND SAFETY STANDARDS

(a) AUTOMATED EXTERNAL DEFIBRILLATORS.—Not later than 1 year after the date of enactment of this section, the Secretary, in consultation with the Secretary of Health and Human Services and other appropriate Federal agencies, shall promulgate regulations to—

(1) require that the owner of a vessel to which section 3507 applies install, and maintain in working order, automated external defibrillators on such vessel;

(2) require that such defibrillators be placed throughout such vessel in clearly designated locations;

(3) require that such defibrillators are available for passenger and crew access in the event of an emergency; and

(4) require that automated external defibrillators, or adjacent equipment, allow passengers and crew to easily contact medical staff of the vessel.

(b) DEFINITION OF OWNER.—In this section, the term "owner" has the meaning given such term in section 3507.

(Added Pub. L. 117–14, §3(a), May 24, 2021, 135 Stat. 275.)

CHAPTER 37—CARRIAGE OF LIQUID BULK DANGEROUS CARGOES

§3701. DEFINITIONS

In this chapter—

(1) "existing", when referring to a type of vessel to which this chapter applies, means a vessel that is not a new vessel.

(2) "new", when referring to a type of vessel to which this chapter applies, means a vessel—

(A) for which the building contract is placed after June 1, 1979;

(B) in the absence of a building contract, the keel of which is laid, or which is at a similar stage of construction, after January 1, 1980;

(C) the delivery of which is after June 1, 1982; or

(D) that has undergone a major conversion under a contract made after June 1, 1979, or construction work that began after January 1, 1980, or was completed after June 1, 1982.

(3) "person" means an individual (even if not a citizen or national of the United States), a corporation, partnership, association, or other entity (even if not organized or existing under the laws of a State), the United States Government, a State or local government, a government of a foreign country, or an entity of one of those governments.

(Pub. L. 98–89, Aug. 26, 1983, 97 Stat. 521; Pub. L. 99–509, title V, §5102(b)(5), Oct. 21, 1986, 100 Stat. 1927; Pub. L. 100–424, §8(c)(2), Sept. 9, 1988, 102 Stat. 1593; Pub. L. 115–232, div. C, title XXXV, §3541(a)(2), Aug. 13, 2018, 132 Stat. 2323.)

§3702. APPLICATION

(a) Subject to subsections (b)–(e) of this section, this chapter applies to a tank vessel.

(b) This chapter does not apply to a documented vessel that would be subject to this chapter only because of the transfer of fuel from the fuel supply tanks of the vessel to offshore drilling or production facilities in the oil industry if the vessel is—

(1) not a tanker; and

(2) in the service of oil exploitation.

(c) This chapter does not apply to a fishing or fish tender vessel of not more than 500 gross tons as measured under section 14502 of this title, or an alternate tonnage measured under section 14302 of this title as prescribed by the Secretary under section 14104 of this title when engaged only in the fishing industry.

(d) This chapter does not apply to a fish processing vessel of not more than 5,000 gross tons as measured under section 14502 of this title, or an alternate tonnage measured under section 14302 of this title as prescribed by the Secretary under section 14104 of this title. However, the vessel is subject to regulation by the Secretary when carrying flammable or combustible liquid cargo in bulk.

(e) This chapter does not apply to a foreign vessel on innocent passage on the navigable waters of the United States.

(f) This chapter does not apply to an oil spill response vessel if—

(1) the vessel is used only in response-related activities; or

(2) the vessel is—

(A) not more than 500 gross tons as measured under section 14502 of this title, or an alternate tonnage measured under section 14302 of this title as prescribed by the Secretary under section 14104 of this title;

(B) designated in its certificate of inspection as an oil spill response vessel; and

(C) engaged in response-related activities.

(Pub. L. 98–89, Aug. 26, 1983, 97 Stat. 521; Pub. L. 98–364, title IV, §402(6), July 17, 1984, 98 Stat. 446; Pub. L. 104–324, title VII, §714, title XI, §1104(b), Oct. 19, 1996, 110 Stat. 3936, 3966; Pub. L. 111–281, title VI, §617(a)(2), Oct. 15, 2010, 124 Stat. 2973.)

§3703. REGULATIONS

(a) The Secretary shall prescribe regulations for the design, construction, alteration, repair, maintenance, operation, equipping, personnel qualification, and manning of vessels to which this chapter applies, that may be necessary for increased protection against hazards to life and property, for navigation and vessel safety, and for enhanced protection of the marine environment. The Secretary may prescribe different regulations applicable to vessels engaged in the domestic trade, and also may prescribe regulations that exceed standards set internationally. Regulations prescribed by the Secretary under this subsection are in addition to regulations prescribed under other laws that may apply to any of those vessels. Regulations prescribed under this subsection shall include requirements about—

(1) superstructures, hulls, cargo holds or tanks, fittings, equipment, appliances, propulsion machinery, auxiliary machinery, and boilers;

(2) the handling or stowage of cargo, the manner of handling or stowage of cargo, and the machinery and appliances used in the handling or stowage;

(3) equipment and appliances for lifesaving, fire protection, and prevention and mitigation of damage to the marine environment;

(4) the manning of vessels and the duties, qualifications, and training of the officers and crew;

(5) improvements in vessel maneuvering and stopping ability and other features that reduce the possibility of marine casualties;

(6) the reduction of cargo loss if a marine casualty occurs; and

(7) the reduction or elimination of discharges during ballasting, deballasting, tank cleaning, cargo handling, or other such activity.

(b) In prescribing regulations under subsection (a) of this section, the Secretary shall consider the types and grades of cargo permitted to be on board a tank vessel.

(c) In prescribing regulations under subsection (a) of this section, the Secretary shall establish procedures for consulting with, and receiving and considering the views of—

(1) interested departments, agencies, and instrumentalities of the United States Government;

(2) officials of State and local governments;

(3) representatives of port and harbor authorities and associations;

(4) representatives of environmental groups; and

(5) other interested parties knowledgeable or experienced in dealing with problems involving vessel safety, port and waterways safety, and protection of the marine environment.

(Pub. L. 98–89, Aug. 26, 1983, 97 Stat. 522.)

§3703A. TANK VESSEL CONSTRUCTION STANDARDS

(a) Except as otherwise provided in this section, a vessel to which this chapter applies shall be equipped with a double hull—

(1) if it is constructed or adapted to carry, or carries, oil in bulk as cargo or cargo residue; and

(2) when operating on the waters subject to the jurisdiction of the United States, including the Exclusive Economic Zone.

(b) This section does not apply to—

(1) a vessel used only to respond to a discharge of oil or a hazardous substance;

(2) a vessel of less than 5,000 gross tons as measured under section 14502 of this title, or an alternate tonnage measured under section 14302 of this title as prescribed by the Secretary under section 14104 of this title equipped with a double containment system determined by the Secretary to be as effective as a double hull for the prevention of a discharge of oil;

(3) a vessel documented under chapter 121 of this title that was equipped with a double hull before August 12, 1992;

(4) a barge of less than 1,500 gross tons (as measured under chapter 145 of this title) carrying refined petroleum product in bulk as cargo in or adjacent to waters of the Bering Sea, Chukchi Sea, and Arctic Ocean and waters tributary thereto and in the waters of the Aleutian Islands and the Alaskan Peninsula west of 155 degrees west longitude; or

(5) a vessel in the National Defense Reserve Fleet pursuant to section 57100.

(c)(1) In this subsection, the age of a vessel is determined from the later of the date on which the vessel—

(A) is delivered after original construction;

(B) is delivered after completion of a major conversion; or

(C) had its appraised salvage value determined by the Coast Guard and is qualified for documentation as a wrecked vessel under section 12112 of this title.

(2) A vessel of less than 5,000 gross tons as measured under section 14502 of this title, or an alternate tonnage measured under section 14302 of this title as prescribed by the Secretary under section 14104 of this title for which a building contract or contract for major conversion was placed before June 30, 1990, and that was delivered under that contract before January 1, 1994, and a vessel of less than 5,000 gross tons as measured under section 14502 of this title, or an alternate tonnage measured under section 14302 of this title as prescribed by the Secretary under section 14104 of this title that had its appraised salvage value determined by the Coast Guard before June 30, 1990, and that qualified for documentation as a wrecked vessel under section 12112 of this title before January 1, 1994, may not operate in the navigable waters or the Exclusive Economic Zone of the United States unless the vessel is equipped with a double hull or with a double containment system determined by the Secretary to be as effective as a double hull for the prevention of a discharge of oil.

(3) A vessel for which a building contract or contract for major conversion was placed before June 30, 1990, and that was delivered under that contract before January 1, 1994, and a vessel that had its appraised salvage value determined by the Coast Guard before June 30, 1990, and that qualified for documentation as a wrecked vessel under section 12112 of this title before January 1, 1994, may not operate in the navigable waters or Exclusive Economic Zone of the United States unless equipped with a double hull—

(A) in the case of a vessel of at least 5,000 gross tons but less than 15,000 gross tons as measured under section 14502, or an alternate tonnage measured under section 14302 as prescribed by the Secretary under section 14104, if the vessel is 25 years old or older and has a single hull, or is 30 years old or older and has a double bottom or double sides;

(B) in the case of a vessel of at least 15,000 gross tons but less than 30,000 gross tons as measured under section 14502, or an alternate tonnage measured under section 14302 as prescribed by the Secretary under section 14104, if the vessel is 25 years old or older and has a single hull, or is 30 years old or older and has a double bottom or double sides; and

(C) in the case of a vessel of at least 30,000 gross tons as measured under section 14502, or an alternate tonnage measured under section 14302 as prescribed by the Secretary under section 14104, if the vessel is 23 years old or older and has a single hull, or is 28 years old or older and has a double bottom or double sides.

(4) Except as provided in subsection (b) of this section—

(A) a vessel that has a single hull may not operate after January 1, 2010; and

(B) a vessel that has a double bottom or double sides may not operate after January 1, 2015.

(d) The operation of barges described in subsection (b)(5) outside waters described in that subsection shall be on any conditions as the Secretary may require.

(e)(1) For the purposes of this section, the gross tonnage of a vessel shall be the gross tonnage that would have been recognized by the Secretary on July 1, 1997, as the tonnage measured under section 14502 of this title, or as an alternate tonnage measured under section 14302 of this title as prescribed by the Secretary under section 14104 of this title.

(2) This subsection does not apply to a tank vessel that, before July 1, 1997, had undergone, or was the subject of a contract for, alterations that reduce the gross tonnage of the tank vessel, as shown by reliable evidence acceptable to the Secretary.

(Added Pub. L. 101–380, title IV, §4115(a), Aug. 18, 1990, 104 Stat. 517; amended Pub. L. 104–324, title VII, §715, title XI, §1103, Oct. 19, 1996, 110 Stat. 3937, 3966; Pub. L. 105–85, div. C, title XXXVI, §3606, Nov. 18, 1997, 111 Stat. 2077; Pub. L. 109–304, §15(15), Oct. 6, 2006, 120 Stat. 1703; Pub. L. 115–91, div. C, title XXXV, §3502(b)(3), Dec. 12, 2017, 131 Stat. 1910; Pub. L. 115–232, div. C, title XXXV, §3544(a), Aug. 13, 2018, 132 Stat. 2324.)

§3704. Coastwise trade vessels

A segregated ballast tank, a crude oil washing system, or an inert gas system, required by this chapter or a regulation prescribed under this chapter, on a vessel entitled to engage in the coastwise trade under chapter 551 of this title shall be installed in the United States (except the trust territories). A vessel failing to comply with this section may not engage in the coastwise trade.

(Pub. L. 98–89, Aug. 26, 1983, 97 Stat. 522; Pub. L. 109–304, §15(16), Oct. 6, 2006, 120 Stat. 1703.)

§3705. Crude oil tanker minimum standards

(a) A new crude oil tanker of at least 20,000 deadweight tons shall be equipped with—

(1) protectively located segregated ballast tanks;

(2) a crude oil washing system; and

(3) a cargo tank protection system consisting of a fixed deck froth system and a fixed inert gas system.

(b) An existing crude oil tanker of at least 40,000 deadweight tons shall be equipped with—

(1) segregated ballast tanks; or

(2) a crude oil washing system.

(c) An existing crude oil tanker of at least 20,000 deadweight tons but less than 40,000 deadweight tons, and at least 15 years of age, shall be equipped with segregated ballast tanks or a crude oil washing system.

(d) An existing crude oil tanker of at least 20,000 deadweight tons shall be equipped with an inert gas system. However, for a crude oil tanker of less than 40,000 deadweight tons not fitted with high capacity tank washing machines, the Secretary may grant an exemption if the vessel's owner can show clearly that compliance would be unreasonable and impracticable due to the vessel's design characteristics.

(e) A crude oil tanker engaged in transferring oil from an offshore oil exploitation or production facility on the Outer Continental Shelf of the United States shall be equipped with segregated ballast tanks, or may operate with dedicated clean ballast tanks or special ballast arrangements. However, the tanker shall comply with other applicable minimum standards of this section.

(Pub. L. 98–89, Aug. 26, 1983, 97 Stat. 523; Pub. L. 115–232, div. C, title XXXV, §3544(b), Aug. 13, 2018, 132 Stat. 2325.)

§3706. PRODUCT CARRIER MINIMUM STANDARDS

(a) A new product carrier of at least 30,000 deadweight tons shall be equipped with protectively located segregated ballast tanks.

(b) A new product carrier of at least 20,000 deadweight tons shall be equipped with a cargo tank protection system consisting of a fixed deck froth system and a fixed inert gas system or, if the product carrier carries dedicated products incompatible with the cargo tank protection system, an alternate protection system authorized by the Secretary.

(c) An existing product carrier of at least 40,000 deadweight tons shall be equipped with segregated ballast tanks or may operate with dedicated clean ballast tanks.

(d) An existing product carrier of at least 20,000 deadweight tons but less than 40,000 deadweight tons, and at least 15 years of age, shall be equipped with segregated ballast tanks or may operate with dedicated clean ballast tanks.

(e) An existing product carrier of at least 40,000 deadweight tons, or an existing product carrier of at least 20,000 deadweight tons but less than 40,000 deadweight tons that is fitted with high-capacity tank washing machines, shall be equipped with an inert gas system.

(Pub. L. 98–89, Aug. 26, 1983, 97 Stat. 523; Pub. L. 115–232, div. C, title XXXV, §3544(c), Aug. 13, 2018, 132 Stat. 2325.)

§3707. TANKER MINIMUM STANDARDS

(a) A new tanker of at least 10,000 gross tons as measured under section 14502 of this title, or an alternate tonnage measured under section 14302 of this title as prescribed by the Secretary under section 14104 of this title shall be equipped with—

(1) 2 remote steering gear control systems operable separately from the navigating bridge;

(2) the main steering gear control in the steering gear compartment;

(3) means of communications and rudder angle indicators on the navigating bridge, a remote steering gear control station, and the steering gear compartment;

(4) at least 2 identical and adequate power units for the main steering gear;

(5) an alternative and adequate power supply, either from an emergency source of electrical power or from another independent source of power located in the steering gear compartment; and

(6) means of automatic starting and stopping of power units with attendant alarms at

all steering stations.

(b) An existing tanker of at least 10,000 gross tons as measured under section 14502 of this title, or an alternate tonnage measured under section 14302 of this title as prescribed by the Secretary under section 14104 of this title shall be equipped with—

(1) 2 remote steering gear control systems operable separately from the navigating bridge;

(2) the main steering gear control in the steering gear compartment; and

(3) means of communications and rudder angle indicators on the navigating bridge, a remote steering gear control station, and the steering gear compartment.

(Pub. L. 98–89, Aug. 26, 1983, 97 Stat. 524; Pub. L. 104–324, title VII, §716, Oct. 19, 1996, 110 Stat. 3937.)

§3708. SELF-PROPELLED TANK VESSEL MINIMUM STANDARDS

A self-propelled tank vessel of at least 10,000 gross tons as measured under section 14502 of this title, or an alternate tonnage measured under section 14302 of this title as prescribed by the Secretary under section 14104 of this title shall be equipped with—

(1) a dual radar system with short-range and long-range capabilities, each with true-north features;

(2) an electronic relative motion analyzer that is at least functionally equivalent to equipment complying with specifications established by the Secretary of Transportation;

(3) an electronic position-fixing device;

(4) adequate communications equipment;

(5) a sonic depth finder;

(6) a gyrocompass; and

(7) up-to-date charts.

(Pub. L. 98–89, Aug. 26, 1983, 97 Stat. 524; Pub. L. 104–324, title VII, §717, Oct. 19, 1996, 110 Stat. 3937.)

§3709. EXEMPTIONS

The Secretary may exempt a vessel from the minimum requirements established by sections 3704–3706 of this title for segregated ballast, crude oil washing, and dedicated clean ballast if the Secretary decides that shore-based reception facilities are a preferred method of handling ballast and that adequate facilities are readily available.

(Pub. L. 98–89, Aug. 26, 1983, 97 Stat. 524.)

§3710. EVIDENCE OF COMPLIANCE BY VESSELS OF THE UNITED STATES

(a) A vessel of the United States to which this chapter applies that has on board oil or hazardous material in bulk as cargo or cargo residue must have a certificate of inspection issued under this part, endorsed to indicate that the vessel complies with regulations prescribed under this chapter.

(b) Each certificate endorsed under this section is valid for not more than 5 years and may be renewed as specified by the Secretary. In appropriate circumstances, the Secretary may issue a temporary certificate valid for not more than 30 days. A certificate shall be suspended or revoked if the Secretary finds that the vessel does not comply with the conditions under which the certificate was issued.

(Pub. L. 98–89, Aug. 26, 1983, 97 Stat. 524; Pub. L. 104–324, title VI, §605(b), Oct. 19, 1996, 110 Stat. 3931.)

§3711. EVIDENCE OF COMPLIANCE BY FOREIGN VESSELS

(a) A foreign vessel to which this chapter applies may operate on the navigable waters of the United States, or transfer oil or hazardous material in a port or place under the jurisdiction of the United States, only if the vessel has been issued a certificate of compliance by the Secretary. The Secretary may issue the certificate only after the vessel has been examined and found to be in compliance with this chapter and regulations prescribed under this chapter. The Secretary may accept any part of a certificate, endorsement, or document, issued by the government of a foreign country under a treaty, convention, or other international agreement to which the United States is a party, as a basis for issuing a certificate of compliance.

(b) A certificate issued under this section is valid for not more than 24 months and may be renewed as specified by the Secretary. In appropriate circumstances, the Secretary may issue a temporary certificate valid for not more than 30 days.

(c) A certificate shall be suspended or revoked if the Secretary finds that the vessel does not comply with the conditions under which the certificate was issued.

(Pub. L. 98–89, Aug. 26, 1983, 97 Stat. 525.)

§3712. NOTIFICATION OF NONCOMPLIANCE

The Secretary shall notify the owner, charterer, managing operator, agent, master, or individual in charge of a vessel found not to be in compliance with a regulation prescribed under this part and state how compliance may be achieved.

(Pub. L. 98–89, Aug. 26, 1983, 97 Stat. 525.)

§3713. PROHIBITED ACTS

(a) A person may not—

(1) violate this chapter or a regulation prescribed under this chapter;

(2) refuse to permit any official, authorized by the Secretary to enforce this chapter, to board a vessel or to enter a shore area, place, or premises, under a person's control to make an inspection under this chapter; or

(3) refuse to obey a lawful directive issued under this chapter.

(b) A vessel to which this chapter applies may not—

(1) operate on the navigable waters of the United States or use a port or place subject to the jurisdiction of the United States when not in compliance with this chapter or a regulation prescribed under this chapter;

(2) fail to comply with a lawful directive issued under this chapter; or

(3) carry a type or grade of oil or hazardous material in bulk as cargo or cargo residue unless its certificate is endorsed to allow that carriage.

(Pub. L. 98–89, Aug. 26, 1983, 97 Stat. 525.)

§3714. INSPECTION AND EXAMINATION

(a)(1) The Secretary shall have each vessel to which this chapter applies inspected or examined at least once each year.

(2) Each of those vessels that is more than 10 years of age shall undergo a special and detailed inspection of structural strength and hull integrity as specified by the Secretary.

(3) The Secretary may make contracts for conducting inspections or examinations in the United States and in foreign countries. An inspector conducting an inspection or examination under contract may not issue a certificate of inspection or a certificate of compliance, but the inspector may issue a temporary certificate.

(4) The Secretary shall prescribe by regulation reasonable fees for an inspection or examination conducted under this section outside the United States, or which, when involving a foreign vessel, is conducted under a contract authorized by paragraph (3) of this subsection. The owner, charterer, or managing operator of a vessel inspected or examined by the Secretary is liable for the fees. Amounts received as fees shall be deposited in the Treasury.

(5) The Secretary may allow provisional entry of a vessel to conduct an inspection or examination under this chapter.

(b) Each vessel to which this chapter applies shall have on board those documents the Secretary considers necessary for inspection and enforcement, including documents listing—

(1) the type, grade, and approximate quantities of cargo on board;

(2) the shipper and consignee of the cargo;

(3) the places of origin and destination of the vessel; and

(4) the name of an agent in the United States authorized to accept service of legal process.

(c) Each vessel to which this chapter applies that operates in the United States shall have a person designated as authorized to accept service of legal process for the vessel.

(Pub. L. 98–89, Aug. 26, 1983, 97 Stat. 526; Pub. L. 99–307, §1(8), May 19, 1986, 100 Stat. 445.)

§3715. LIGHTERING

(a) A vessel may transfer oil or hazardous material in a port or place subject to the jurisdiction of the United States, when the cargo has been transferred from another vessel on the navigable waters of the United States or in the marine environment, only if—

(1) the transfer was conducted consistent with regulations prescribed by the Secretary;

(2) both the delivering and receiving vessels had on board, at the time of transfer, a certificate of inspection or a certificate of compliance, as would have been required under section 3710 or 3711 of this title, had the transfer taken place in a port or place subject to the jurisdiction of the United States;

(3) the delivering and the receiving vessel had on board at the time of transfer, a certificate of financial responsibility as would have been required under section 1016 of the Oil Pollution Act of 1990, had the transfer taken place in a place subject to the jurisdiction of the United States;

(4) the delivering and the receiving vessel had on board at the time of transfer,

evidence that each vessel is operating in compliance with section 311(j) of the Federal Water Pollution Control Act (33 U.S.C. 1321(j)); and

(5) the delivering and the receiving vessel are operating in compliance with section 3703a of this title.

(b) The Secretary shall prescribe regulations to carry out subsection (a) of this section. The regulations shall include provisions on—

(1) minimum safe operating conditions, including sea state, wave height, weather, proximity to channels or shipping lanes, and other similar factors;

(2) the prevention of spills;

(3) equipment for responding to a spill;

(4) the prevention of any unreasonable interference with navigation or other reasonable uses of the high seas, as those uses are defined by treaty, convention, or customary international law;

(5) the establishment of lightering zones; and

(6) requirements for communication and prearrival messages.

(Pub. L. 98–89, Aug. 26, 1983, 97 Stat. 526; Pub. L. 101–380, title IV, §4115(d), Aug. 18, 1990, 104 Stat. 520; Pub. L. 114–120, title III, §306(a)(4), Feb. 8, 2016, 130 Stat. 54.)

§3716. TANK WASHINGS

(a) A vessel may not transfer cargo in a port or place subject to the jurisdiction of the United States if, before arriving, the vessel has discharged tank washings containing oil or hazardous material in preparation for loading at that port or place in violation of the laws of the United States or in a manner or quantities inconsistent with a treaty to which the United States is a party.

(b) The Secretary shall establish effective control and supervisory measures to carry out this section.

(Pub. L. 98–89, Aug. 26, 1983, 97 Stat. 527.)

§3717. MARINE SAFETY INFORMATION SYSTEM

(a) The Secretary shall establish a marine safety information system that shall contain information about each vessel to which this chapter applies that operates on the navigable waters of the United States, or that transfers oil or hazardous material in a port or place under the jurisdiction of the United States. In acquiring this information, the Secretary shall make full use of publicly available information. The Secretary may by regulation require the vessel to provide information that the Secretary considers necessary to carry out this subsection, including—

(1) the name of each person with an ownership interest in the vessel;

(2) details of compliance with the financial responsibility requirements of applicable laws or regulations;

(3) registration information, including all changes in the name of the vessel;

(4) the history of marine casualties and serious repair problems of the vessel; and

(5) a record of all inspections and examinations of a vessel conducted under section 3714 of this title.

(b) On written request from the Secretary, the head of each department, agency, or instrumentality of the United States Government shall provide available information that the Secretary considers necessary to confirm the information received under subsection (a) of this section.

(Pub. L. 98–89, Aug. 26, 1983, 97 Stat. 527.)

§3718. Penalties

(a)(1) A person violating this chapter or a regulation prescribed under this chapter is liable to the United States Government for a civil penalty of not more than $25,000. Each day of a continuing violation is a separate violation.

(2) Each vessel to which this chapter applies that is operated in violation of this chapter or a regulation prescribed under this chapter is liable in rem for a civil penalty under this subsection.

(b) A person willfully and knowingly violating this chapter or a regulation prescribed under this chapter commits a class D felony.

(c) Instead of the penalties provided by subsection (b) of this section, a person willfully and knowingly violating this chapter or a regulation prescribed under this chapter, and using a dangerous weapon, or engaging in conduct that causes bodily injury or fear of imminent bodily injury to an official authorized to enforce this chapter or a regulation prescribed under this chapter, commits a class C felony.

(d) The district courts of the United States have jurisdiction to restrain a violation of this chapter or a regulation prescribed under this chapter.

(e)(1) If any owner, operator, or individual in charge of a vessel is liable for any penalty or fine under this section, or if reasonable cause exists to believe that the owner, operator, or individual in charge may be subject to any penalty or fine under this section, the Secretary of Homeland Security, upon the request of the Secretary, shall with respect to such vessel refuse or revoke any clearance required by section 60105 of this title.

(2) Clearance or a permit refused or revoked under this subsection may be granted upon filing of a bond or other surety satisfactory to the Secretary.

(Pub. L. 98–89, Aug. 26, 1983, 97 Stat. 527; Pub. L. 101–380, title IV, §4302(c), Aug. 18, 1990, 104 Stat. 538; Pub. L. 104–324, title III, §312(d), Oct. 19, 1996, 110 Stat. 3921; Pub. L. 109–304, §15(17), Oct. 6, 2006, 120 Stat. 1703.)

§3719. Reduction of Oil Spills From Single Hull Non-Self-Propelled Tank Vessels

The Secretary shall, in consultation with the National Towing Safety Advisory Committee and taking into consideration the characteristics, methods of operation, and the size and nature of service of single hull non-self-propelled tank vessels and towing vessels, prescribe regulations requiring a single hull non-self-propelled tank vessel that operates in the open ocean or coastal waters, or the vessel towing it, to have at least one of the following:

(1) A crew member and an operable anchor on board the tank vessel that together are capable of arresting the tank vessel without additional assistance under reasonably foreseeable sea conditions.

(2) An emergency system on the tank vessel or towing vessel that without additional

assistance under reasonably foreseeable sea conditions will allow the tank vessel to be retrieved by the towing vessel if the tow line ruptures.

(3) Any other measure or combination of measures that the Secretary determines will provide protection against grounding of the tank vessel comparable to that provided by the measures described in paragraph (1) or (2).

(Added Pub. L. 104–324, title IX, §901(a), Oct. 19, 1996, 110 Stat. 3946; amended Pub. L. 115–282, title VI, §601(c)(6)(B)(i), Dec. 4, 2018, 132 Stat. 4290.)

[CHAPTER 39—REPEALED]

[§§3901, 3902. REPEALED. PUB. L. 107–171, TITLE X, §10418(A)(20), MAY 13, 2002, 116 STAT. 508]

Section 3901, Pub. L. 98–89, Aug. 26, 1983, 97 Stat. 528, related to regulations for accommodations for export animals.

Section 3902, Pub. L. 98–89, Aug. 26, 1983, 97 Stat. 528, related to penalties.

CHAPTER 41—UNINSPECTED VESSELS GENERALLY

§4101. APPLICATION

This chapter applies to an uninspected vessel not subject to chapter 45 of this title—
  (1) on the navigable waters of the United States; or
  (2) owned in the United States and operating on the high seas.

(Pub. L. 98–89, Aug. 26, 1983, 97 Stat. 528; Pub. L. 100–424, §8(b), Sept. 9, 1988, 102 Stat. 1593.)

§4102. SAFETY EQUIPMENT

(a) Each uninspected vessel propelled by machinery shall be provided with the number, type, and size of fire extinguishers, capable of promptly and effectively extinguishing burning liquid fuel, that may be prescribed by regulation. The fire extinguishers shall be kept in condition for immediate and effective use and so placed as to be readily accessible.

(b) The Secretary shall prescribe regulations requiring the installation, maintenance, and use of life preservers and other lifesaving devices for individuals on board uninspected vessels.

(c) Each uninspected vessel shall have the carburetors of each engine of the vessel (except an outboard motor) using gasoline as fuel, equipped with an efficient flame arrestor, backfire trap, or other similar device prescribed by regulation.

(d) Each uninspected vessel using a volatile liquid as fuel shall be provided with the means prescribed by regulation for properly and efficiently ventilating the bilges of the engine and fuel tank compartments, so as to remove any explosive or flammable gases.

(e) Each manned uninspected vessel owned in the United States and operating beyond 3 nautical miles from the baselines from which the territorial sea of the United States is measured or beyond three nautical miles from the coastline of the Great Lakes shall be equipped with the number and type of alerting and locating equipment, including emergency position indicating radio beacons, prescribed by the Secretary.

(f)(1) The Secretary, in consultation with the National Towing Safety Advisory Committee and taking into consideration the characteristics, methods of operation, and nature of service of towing vessels, may require the installation, maintenance, and use of a fire suppression system or other measures to provide adequate assurance that fires on board towing vessels can be suppressed under reasonably foreseeable circumstances.

(2) The Secretary shall require under paragraph (1) the use of a fire suppression system or other measures to provide adequate assurance that a fire on board a towing vessel that is towing a non-self-propelled tank vessel can be suppressed under reasonably foreseeable

circumstances.

(Pub. L. 98–89, Aug. 26, 1983, 97 Stat. 528; Pub. L. 99–640, §16, Nov. 10, 1986, 100 Stat. 3552; Pub. L. 100–424, §2(c), Sept. 9, 1988, 102 Stat. 1590; Pub. L. 100–540, §1(a), Oct. 28, 1988, 102 Stat. 2719; Pub. L. 104–324, title IX, §902(a), Oct. 19, 1996, 110 Stat. 3947; Pub. L. 105–383, title III, §301(b)(3), Nov. 13, 1998, 112 Stat. 3417; Pub. L. 111–281, title VI, §619, Oct. 15, 2010, 124 Stat. 2975; Pub. L. 115–282, title VI, §601(c)(6)(B)(ii), Dec. 4, 2018, 132 Stat. 4290.)

§4103. EXEMPTIONS

(a) The Secretary may exempt a vessel from any part of this chapter if, under regulations prescribed by the Secretary (including regulations on special operating conditions), the Secretary finds that—

(1) good cause exists for granting an exemption; and

(2) the safety of the vessel and individuals on board will not be adversely affected.

(b) Section 4102(a) of this title does not apply to a vessel propelled by outboard motors when competing in a race previously arranged and announced or, if the vessel is designed and intended only for racing, when operated incidental to tuning up the vessel and its engines for the race.

(Pub. L. 98–89, Aug. 26, 1983, 97 Stat. 529; Pub. L. 100–540, §2, Oct. 28, 1988, 102 Stat. 2719.)

[§4104. REPEALED. PUB. L. 101–595, TITLE VI, §603(3)(A), NOV. 16, 1990, 104 STAT. 2993]

Section, Pub. L. 98–89, Aug. 26, 1983, 97 Stat. 529, required Secretary to prescribe regulations to carry out provisions of this chapter.

§4105. UNINSPECTED PASSENGER VESSELS

(a) Chapter 43 of this title applies to an uninspected passenger vessel.

(b)(1) In applying this title with respect to an uninspected vessel of less than 24 meters overall in length that carries passengers to or from a port in the United States Virgin Islands, the Secretary shall substitute "12 passengers" for "6 passengers" each place it appears in section 2101 if the Secretary determines that the vessel complies with, as applicable to the vessel—

(A) the Code of Practice for the Safety of Small Commercial Motor Vessels (commonly referred to as the "Yellow Code"), as published by the U.K. Maritime and Coastguard Agency and in effect on January 1, 2014; or

(B) the Code of Practice for the Safety of Small Commercial Sailing Vessels (commonly referred to as the "Blue Code"), as published by such agency and in effect on such date.

(2) If the Secretary establishes standards to carry out this subsection—

(A) such standards shall be identical to those established in the Codes of Practice referred to in paragraph (1); and

(B) on any dates before the date on which such standards are in effect, the Codes of Practice referred to in paragraph (1) shall apply with respect to the vessels referred to in paragraph (1).

(c) In applying this title with respect to an uninspected vessel of less than 25 feet overall in length that carries passengers on Crane Lake or waters contiguous to such lake in St. Louis County, Minnesota, the Secretary shall substitute "12 passengers" for "6 passengers" each place it appears in section 2101.

(d) The Secretary shall, by regulation, require certain additional equipment which may include liferafts or other lifesaving equipment, construction standards, or specify additional operating standards for those uninspected passenger vessels defined in section 2101(53)(A) of this title.

(Pub. L. 98–89, Aug. 26, 1983, 97 Stat. 529; Pub. L. 103–206, title V, §511(b), Dec. 20, 1993, 107 Stat. 2442; Pub. L. 113–281, title III, §319, Dec. 18, 2014, 128 Stat. 3051; Pub. L. 115–232, div. C, title XXXV, §3541(b)(10), Aug. 13, 2018, 132 Stat. 2323; Pub. L. 115–282, title V, §502, Dec. 4, 2018, 132 Stat. 4269; Pub. L. 117–263, div. K, title CXVI, §11601(c)(2), Dec. 23, 2022, 136 Stat. 4146.)

§4106. PENALTIES

If a vessel to which this chapter applies is operated in violation of this chapter or a regulation prescribed under this chapter, the owner, charterer, managing operator, agent, master, and individual in charge are each liable to the United States Government for a civil penalty of not more than $5,000. The vessel also is liable in rem for the penalty.

(Pub. L. 98–89, Aug. 26, 1983, 97 Stat. 529; Pub. L. 100–540, §3, Oct. 28, 1988, 102 Stat. 2719.)

CHAPTER 43—RECREATIONAL VESSELS

§4301. APPLICATION

(a) This chapter applies to a recreational vessel and associated equipment carried in the vessel on waters subject to the jurisdiction of the United States (including the territorial sea of the United States as described in Presidential Proclamation No. 5928 of December 27, 1988) and, for a vessel owned in the United States, on the high seas.

(b) Except when expressly otherwise provided, this chapter does not apply to a foreign vessel temporarily operating on waters subject to the jurisdiction of the United States.

(c) Until there is a final judicial decision that they are navigable waters of the United States, the following waters lying entirely in New Hampshire are declared not to be waters subject to the jurisdiction of the United States within the meaning of this section: Lake Winnisquam, Lake Winnipesaukee, parts of the Merrimack River, and their tributary and connecting waters.

(Pub. L. 98–89, Aug. 26, 1983, 97 Stat. 529; Pub. L. 105–383, title III, §301(b)(4), Nov. 13, 1998, 112 Stat. 3417.)

§4302. REGULATIONS

(a) The Secretary may prescribe regulations—

(1) establishing minimum safety standards for recreational vessels and associated equipment, and establishing procedures and tests required to measure conformance with those standards, with each standard—

(A) meeting the need for recreational vessel safety; and

(B) being stated, insofar as practicable, in terms of performance;

(2) requiring the installation, carrying, or use of associated equipment (including fuel systems, ventilation systems, electrical systems, sound-producing devices, firefighting equipment, lifesaving devices, signaling devices, ground tackle, life- and grab-rails, and navigational equipment) on recreational vessels and classes of recreational vessels subject to this chapter, and prohibiting the installation, carrying, or use of associated

equipment that does not conform with safety standards established under this section; and

(3) requiring or permitting the display of seals, labels, plates, insignia, or other devices for certifying or evidencing compliance with safety regulations and standards of the United States Government for recreational vessels and associated equipment.

(b) Each regulation prescribed under this section shall specify an effective date that is not earlier than 180 days from the date the regulation was published, unless the Secretary finds that there exists a recreational vessel safety hazard so critical as to require an earlier effective date. However, this period may not be more than 24 months for cases involving, in the discretion of the Secretary, major product design, retooling, or major changes in the manufacturing process.

(c) In prescribing regulations under this section, the Secretary shall, among other things—

(1) consider the need for and the extent to which the regulations will contribute to recreational vessel safety;

(2) consider relevant available recreational vessel safety standards, statistics, and data, including public and private research, development, testing, and evaluation;

(3) not compel substantial alteration of a recreational vessel or item of associated equipment that is in existence, or the construction or manufacture of which is begun before the effective date of the regulation, but subject to that limitation may require compliance or performance, to avoid a substantial risk of personal injury to the public, that the Secretary considers appropriate in relation to the degree of hazard that the compliance will correct; and

(4) consult with the National Boating Safety Advisory Committee established under section 15105 of this title about the considerations referred to in clauses (1)–(3) of this subsection.

(d) Section 8903 of this title does not apply to a vessel being operated for bona fide dealer demonstrations provided without fee to business invitees. However, if on the basis of substantial evidence, the Secretary decides under this section that requiring vessels so operated to be under the control of licensed individuals is necessary for boating safety, then the Secretary may prescribe regulations requiring the licensing of individuals controlling these vessels in the same manner as provided in chapter 89 of this title for individuals in control of vessels carrying passengers for hire.

(e)(1) Under this section, a model year for recreational vessels and associated equipment shall, except as provided in paragraph (2)—

(A) begin on June 1 of a year and end on July 31 of the following year; and

(B) be designated by the year in which it ends.

(2) Upon the request of a recreational vessel manufacturer to which this chapter applies, the Secretary may alter a model year for a model of recreational vessel of the manufacturer and associated equipment, by no more than 6 months from the model year described in paragraph (1).

(Pub. L. 98–89, Aug. 26, 1983, 97 Stat. 530; Pub. L. 114–120, title III, §303(a), Feb. 8, 2016, 130 Stat. 53;

Pub. L. 115–282, title VI, §601(c)(4)(B)(i), Dec. 4, 2018, 132 Stat. 4290.)

§4303. INSPECTION AND TESTING

(a) Subject to regulations, supervision, and reviews that the Secretary may prescribe, the Secretary may delegate to a person, private or public agency, or organization, or to an officer or employee under the supervision of that person or agency, any work, business, or function related to the testing, inspection, and examination necessary for compliance enforcement and for the development of data to enable the Secretary to prescribe regulations under section 4302 of this title.

(b) The Secretary may—

(1) conduct research, testing, and development necessary to carry out this chapter, including the procurement by negotiation or otherwise of experimental and other recreational vessels or associated equipment for research and testing purposes; and

(2) subsequently sell those vessels.

(Pub. L. 98–89, Aug. 26, 1983, 97 Stat. 531.)

§4304. IMPORTATION OF NONCONFORMING VESSELS AND EQUIPMENT

The Secretary and the Secretary of the Treasury may authorize by joint regulations the importation of any nonconforming recreational vessel or associated equipment on conditions, including providing a bond, that will ensure that the recreational vessel or associated equipment will be brought into conformity with applicable safety regulations and standards of the Government before the vessel or equipment is operated on waters subject to the jurisdiction of the United States.

(Pub. L. 98–89, Aug. 26, 1983, 97 Stat. 531.)

§4305. EXEMPTIONS AND EQUIVALENTS

(a) EXEMPTIONS.—If the Secretary considers that recreational vessel safety will not be adversely affected, the Secretary may issue an exemption from this chapter or a regulation prescribed under this chapter.

(b) EQUIVALENTS.—The Secretary may accept a substitution for associated equipment performance or other safety standards for a recreational vessel if the substitution provides an equivalent level of safety.

(Pub. L. 98–89, Aug. 26, 1983, 97 Stat. 531; Pub. L. 116–283, div. G, title LVXXXIII [LXXXIII], §8318(a), Jan. 1, 2021, 134 Stat. 4700.)

§4306. FEDERAL PREEMPTION

Unless permitted by the Secretary under section 4305 of this title, a State or political subdivision of a State may not establish, continue in effect, or enforce a law or regulation establishing a recreational vessel or associated equipment performance or other safety standard or imposing a requirement for associated equipment (except insofar as the State or political subdivision may, in the absence of the Secretary's disapproval, regulate the carrying or use of marine safety articles to meet uniquely hazardous conditions or circumstances within the State) that is not identical to a regulation prescribed under section 4302 of this title.

(Pub. L. 98–89, Aug. 26, 1983, 97 Stat. 531.)

§4307. PROHIBITED ACTS

(a) A person may not—

(1) manufacture, construct, assemble, sell or offer for sale, introduce or deliver for introduction into interstate commerce, or import into the United States, a recreational vessel, associated equipment, or component of the vessel or equipment unless—

(A)(i) it conforms with this chapter or a regulation prescribed under this chapter; and

(ii) it does not contain a defect which has been identified, in any communication to such person by the Secretary or the manufacturer of that vessel, equipment or component, as creating a substantial risk of personal injury to the public; or

(B) it is intended only for export and is so labeled, tagged, or marked on the recreational vessel or equipment, including any markings on the outside of the container in which it is to be exported;

(2) affix, attach, or display a seal, document, label, plate, insignia, or other device indicating or suggesting compliance with standards of the United States Government on, in, or in connection with, a recreational vessel or item of associated equipment that is false or misleading; or

(3) fail to provide a notification as required by this chapter or fail to exercise reasonable diligence in carrying out the notification and reporting requirements of this chapter.

(b) A person may not operate a vessel in violation of this chapter or a regulation prescribed under this chapter.

(Pub. L. 98–89, Aug. 26, 1983, 97 Stat. 531; Pub. L. 98–557, §8(a), Oct. 30, 1984, 98 Stat. 2862.)

§4308. TERMINATION OF UNSAFE OPERATION

If an official charged with the enforcement of this chapter observes a recreational vessel being operated without sufficient lifesaving or firefighting devices or in an overloaded or other unsafe condition (as defined in regulations prescribed under this chapter) and, in the judgment of the official, the operation creates an especially hazardous condition, the official may direct the individual in charge of the recreational vessel to take immediate and reasonable steps necessary for the safety of individuals on board the vessel, including directing the individual in charge to return to a mooring and to remain there until the situation creating the hazard is corrected or ended.

(Pub. L. 98–89, Aug. 26, 1983, 97 Stat. 532; Pub. L. 99–307, §1(9), May 19, 1986, 100 Stat. 445.)

§4309. INVESTIGATION AND REPORTING

(a) A recreational vessel manufacturer to whom this chapter applies shall establish and maintain records and reports and provide information the Secretary may require to enable the Secretary to decide whether the manufacturer has acted or is acting in compliance with this chapter and regulations prescribed under this chapter. On request of an officer, employee, or agent authorized by the Secretary, a recreational vessel manufacturer shall permit the officer, employee, or agent to inspect, at reasonable times, factories or other facilities, and records related to deciding whether the manufacturer has acted or is acting in compliance with this chapter and regulations prescribed under this chapter.

(b) Information reported to or otherwise obtained by the Secretary or the representative of the Secretary under this section containing or related to a trade secret or other matter referred to in section 1905 of title 18, or authorized to be exempt from public disclosure by section 552(b) of title 5, is confidential under section 1905. However, on approval of the Secretary, the information may be disclosed to other officers, employees, or agents concerned with carrying out this chapter or when it is relevant in a proceeding under this chapter.

(Pub. L. 98–89, Aug. 26, 1983, 97 Stat. 532.)

§4310. Repair and replacement of defects

(a) In this section, "associated equipment" includes only items or classes of associated equipment that the Secretary shall prescribe by regulation after deciding that the application of the requirements of this section to those items or classes of associated equipment is reasonable and in furtherance of this chapter.

(b) If a recreational vessel or associated equipment has left the place of manufacture and the recreational vessel manufacturer discovers or acquires information that the manufacturer decides, in the exercise of reasonable and prudent judgment, indicates that a recreational vessel or associated equipment subject to an applicable regulation prescribed under section 4302 of this title either fails to comply with the regulation, or contains a defect that creates a substantial risk of personal injury to the public, the manufacturer shall provide notification of the defect or failure of compliance as provided by subsections (c) and (d) of this section within a reasonable time after the manufacturer has discovered the defect.

(c)(1) The notification required by subsection (b) of this section shall be given to the following persons in the following manner:

(A) by first class mail or by certified mail to the first purchaser for other than resale, except that the requirement for notification of the first purchaser shall be satisfied if the recreational vessel manufacturer exercises reasonable diligence in establishing and maintaining a list of those purchasers and their current addresses, and sends the required notice to each person on that list at the address appearing on the list.

(B) by first class mail or by certified mail to subsequent purchasers if known to the manufacturer.

(C) by first class mail or by certified mail or other more expeditious means to the dealers and distributors of the recreational vessels or associated equipment.

(2) The notification required by subsection (b) of this section is required to be given only for a defect or failure of compliance discovered by the recreational vessel manufacturer within a reasonable time after the manufacturer has discovered the defect or failure, except that the manufacturer's duty of notification under paragraph (1)(A) and (B) of this subsection applies only to a defect or failure of compliance discovered by the manufacturer within one of the following appropriate periods:

(A) if a recreational vessel or associated equipment required by regulation to have a date of certification affixed, 10 years from the date of certification.

(B) if a recreational vessel or associated equipment not required by regulation to have a date of certification affixed, 10 years from the date of manufacture.

(d) The notification required by subsection (b) of this section shall contain a clear description of the defect or failure to comply, an evaluation of the hazard reasonably related to the defect or failure, a statement of the measures to correct the defect or failure, and an undertaking by the recreational vessel manufacturer to take those measures only at the manufacturer's cost and expense.

(e) Each recreational vessel manufacturer shall provide the Secretary with a copy of all notices, bulletins, and other communications to dealers and distributors of that manufacturer, and to purchasers of recreational vessels or associated equipment of that manufacturer, about a defect related to safety in the recreational vessels or associated equipment, and any failure to comply with the regulation or order applicable to the recreational vessels or associated equipment. The Secretary may publish or otherwise disclose to the public information in the notices or other information the Secretary has that the Secretary considers will assist in carrying out this chapter. However, the Secretary may disclose any information that contains or relates to a trade secret only if the Secretary decides that the information is necessary to carry out this chapter.

(f) If, through testing, inspection, investigation, or examination of reports, the Secretary decides that a recreational vessel or associated equipment to which this chapter applies contains a defect related to safety or fails to comply with an applicable regulation prescribed under this chapter and notification under this chapter is appropriate, the Secretary shall notify the recreational vessel manufacturer of the defect or failure. The notice shall contain the findings of the Secretary and shall include a synopsis of the information on which they are based. The manufacturer may then provide the notification required by this chapter to the persons designated in this chapter or dispute the Secretary's decision. If disputed, the Secretary shall provide the manufacturer with an opportunity to present views and establish that there is no such defect or failure. When the Secretary considers it to be in the public interest, the Secretary may publish notice of the proceeding in the Federal Register and provide interested persons, including the National Boating Safety Advisory Committee, with an opportunity to comment. If, after presentation by the manufacturer, the Secretary decides that the recreational vessel or associated equipment contains a defect related to safety or fails to comply with an applicable regulation, the Secretary may direct the manufacturer to provide the notifications specified in this chapter.

(g) The Secretary may prescribe regulations to carry out this section, including the establishment of procedures that require dealers and distributors to assist manufacturers in obtaining information required by this section. A regulation prescribed under this subsection does not relieve a manufacturer of any obligation imposed by this section.

(Pub. L. 98–89, Aug. 26, 1983, 97 Stat. 532; Pub. L. 107–295, title IV, §433, Nov. 25, 2002, 116 Stat. 2129; Pub. L. 115–282, title VI, §601(c)(4)(B)(ii), Dec. 4, 2018, 132 Stat. 4290.)

§4311. PENALTIES AND INJUNCTIONS

(a) A person willfully operating a recreational vessel in violation of this chapter or a regulation prescribed under this chapter shall be fined not more than $5,000, imprisoned for not more than one year, or both.

(b)(1) A person violating section 4307(a) of this title is liable to the United States Government for a civil penalty of not more than $5,000, except that the maximum civil penalty may be not more than $250,000 for a related series of violations.

(2) If the Secretary decides under section 4310(f) that a recreational vessel or associated equipment contains a defect related to safety or fails to comply with an applicable regulation and directs the manufacturer to provide the notifications specified in this chapter, any person, including a director, officer or executive employee of a corporation, who knowingly and willfully fails to comply with that order, may be fined not more than $10,000, imprisoned for not more than one year, or both.

(3) When a corporation violates section 4307(a), or fails to comply with the Secretary's decision under section 4310(f), any director, officer, or executive employee of the corporation who knowingly and willfully ordered, or knowingly and willfully authorized, a violation is individually liable to the Government for a penalty under paragraphs (1) or (2) in addition to the corporation. However, the director, officer, or executive employee is not liable individually under this subsection if the director, officer, or executive employee can demonstrate by a preponderance of the evidence that—

(A) the order or authorization was issued on the basis of a decision, in exercising reasonable and prudent judgment, that the defect or the nonconformity with standards and regulations constituting the violation would not cause or constitute a substantial risk of personal injury to the public; and

(B) at the time of the order or authorization, the director, officer, or executive employee advised the Secretary in writing of acting under this subparagraph and subparagraph (A).

(c) A person violating section 4312(b) of this title is liable to the United States Government for a civil penalty of not more than—

(1) $100 for the first offense;

(2) $250 for the second offense; and

(3) $500 for any subsequent offense.

(d) A person violating any other provision of this chapter or other regulation prescribed under this chapter is liable to the Government for a civil penalty of not more than $1,000. If the violation involves the operation of a vessel, the vessel also is liable in rem for the penalty.

(e) When a civil penalty of not more than $200 has been assessed under this chapter, the Secretary may refer the matter of collection of the penalty directly to the United States magistrate judge of the jurisdiction in which the person liable may be found for collection procedures under supervision of the district court and under an order issued by the court delegating this authority under section 636(b) of title 28.

(f) The district courts of the United States have jurisdiction to restrain a violation of this chapter, or to restrain the sale, offer for sale, introduction or delivery for introduction into interstate commerce, or importation into the United States, of a recreational vessel or associated equipment that the court decides does not conform to safety standards of the

Government. A civil action under this subsection shall be brought by filing a petition by the Attorney General for the Government. When practicable, the Secretary shall give notice to a person against whom an action for injunctive relief is contemplated and provide the person with an opportunity to present views and, except for a knowing and willful violation, shall provide the person with a reasonable opportunity to achieve compliance. The failure to give notice and provide the opportunity does not preclude the granting of appropriate relief by the district court.

(g) A person is not subject to a penalty under this chapter if the person—

(1) establishes that the person did not have reason to know, in exercising reasonable care, that a recreational vessel or associated equipment does not conform with the applicable safety standards of the Government or that the person was not advised by the Secretary or the manufacturer of that vessel, equipment or component that the vessel, equipment or component contains a defect which creates a substantial risk of personal injury to the public; or

(2) holds a certificate issued by the manufacturer of that recreational vessel or associated equipment to the effect that the recreational vessel or associated equipment conforms to all applicable recreational vessel safety standards of the Government, unless the person knows or reasonably should have known that the recreational vessel or associated equipment does not so conform.

(h) Compliance with this chapter or standards, regulations, or orders prescribed under this chapter does not relieve a person from liability at common law or under State law.

(Pub. L. 98–89, Aug. 26, 1983, 97 Stat. 534; Pub. L. 98–557, §8(b), (c), Oct. 30, 1984, 98 Stat. 2862; Pub. L. 101–650, title III, §321, Dec. 1, 1990, 104 Stat. 5117; Pub. L. 108–293, title IV, §406, Aug. 9, 2004, 118 Stat. 1043; Pub. L. 109–241, title IX, §901(e), July 11, 2006, 120 Stat. 564; Pub. L. 116–283, div. G, title LVXXXIII [LXXXIII], §8316(b), Jan. 1, 2021, 134 Stat. 4699.)

§4312. ENGINE CUT-OFF SWITCHES

(a) INSTALLATION REQUIREMENT.—A manufacturer, distributor, or dealer that installs propulsion machinery and associated starting controls on a covered recreational vessel shall equip such vessel with an engine cut-off switch and engine cut-off switch link that meet American Boat and Yacht Council Standard A–33, as in effect on the date of the enactment of the Frank LoBiondo Coast Guard Authorization Act of 2018 (Public Law 115–282).

(b) USE REQUIREMENT.—

(1) IN GENERAL.—An individual operating a covered recreational vessel shall use an engine cut-off switch link while operating on plane or above displacement speed.

(2) EXCEPTIONS.—The requirement under paragraph (1) shall not apply if—

(A) the main helm of the covered vessel is installed within an enclosed cabin; or

(B) the vessel does not have an engine cut-off switch and is not required to have one under subsection (a).

(c) EDUCATION ON CUT-OFF SWITCHES.—The Commandant of the Coast Guard, through the National Boating Safety Advisory Committee established under section 15105, may initiate a boating safety program on the use and benefits of cut-off switches for recreational vessels.

(d) Availability of Standard for Inspection.—

(1) In general.—Not later than 90 days after the date of the enactment of this section, the Commandant shall transmit American Boat and Yacht Council Standard A–33, as in effect on the date of enactment of the Frank LoBiondo Coast Guard Authorization Act of 2018 (Public Law 115–282), to—

(A) the Committee on Transportation and Infrastructure of the House of Representatives;

(B) the Committee on Commerce, Science, and Transportation of the Senate; and

(C) the Coast Guard Office of Design and Engineering Standards; and

(D) the National Archives and Records Administration.

(2) Availability.—The standard submitted under paragraph (1) shall be kept on file and available for public inspection at such Coast Guard office and the National Archives and Records Administration.

(e) Definitions.—In this section:

(1) Covered recreational vessel.—The term "covered recreational vessel" means a recreational vessel that is—

(A) less than 26 feet overall in length; and

(B) capable of developing 115 pounds or more of static thrust.

(2) Dealer.—The term "dealer" means any person who is engaged in the sale and distribution of recreational vessels or associated equipment to purchasers whom the seller in good faith believes to be purchasing any such vessel or associated equipment for purposes other than resale.

(3) Distributor.—The term "distributor" means any person engaged in the sale and distribution of recreational vessels and associated equipment for the purposes of resale.

(4) Manufacturer.—The term "equipment manufacturer" means any person engaged in the manufacture, construction, or assembly of recreational vessels or associated equipment, or the importation of recreational vessels into the United States for subsequent sale.

(5) Propulsion machinery.—The term "propulsion machinery" means a self-contained propulsion system, and includes, but is not limited to, inboard engines, outboard motors, and sterndrive engines.

(6) Static thrust.—The term "static thrust" means the forward or backwards thrust developed by propulsion machinery while stationary.

(Added Pub. L. 115–282, title V, §503(a), Dec. 4, 2018, 132 Stat. 4270; amended Pub. L. 116–283, div. G, title LVXXXIII [LXXXIII], §8316(a), title LVXXXV [LXXXV], §8507(a)(2), Jan. 1, 2021, 134 Stat. 4699, 4752.)

CHAPTER 45—UNINSPECTED COMMERCIAL FISHING INDUSTRY VESSELS

§4501. APPLICATION

(a) This chapter applies to an uninspected vessel which is a fishing vessel, fish processing vessel, or fish tender vessel.

(b) This chapter does not apply to the carriage of bulk dangerous cargoes regulated under chapter 37 of this title.

(Added Pub. L. 98–364, title IV, §402(7)(C), July 17, 1984, 98 Stat. 446; amended Pub. L. 100–424, §2(a), Sept. 9, 1988, 102 Stat. 1585.)

§4502. SAFETY STANDARDS

(a) The Secretary shall prescribe regulations which require that each vessel to which this chapter applies shall be equipped with—

(1) readily accessible fire extinguishers capable of promptly and effectively extinguishing a flammable or combustible liquid fuel fire;

(2) at least one readily accessible life preserver or other lifesaving device for each individual on board;

(3) an efficient flame arrestor, backfire trap, or other similar device on the carburetors of each inboard engine which uses gasoline as fuel;

(4) the means to properly and efficiently ventilate enclosed spaces, including engine and fuel tank compartments, so as to remove explosive or flammable gases;

(5) visual distress signals;

(6) other equipment required to minimize the risk of injury to the crew during vessel operations, if the Secretary determines that a risk of serious injury exists that can be eliminated or mitigated by that equipment; and

(7) a placard as required by regulations prescribed under section 10603(b) of this title.

(b)(1) In addition to the requirements of subsection (a) of this section, the Secretary shall prescribe regulations requiring the installation, maintenance, and use of the equipment in paragraph (2) of this subsection for vessels to which this chapter applies that—

(A) operate beyond 3 nautical miles from the baseline from which the territorial sea of the United States is measured or beyond 3 nautical miles from the coastline of the Great Lakes;

(B) operate with more than 16 individuals on board; or

(C) in the case of a fish tender vessel, engage in the Aleutian trade.

(2) The equipment to be required is as follows:

(A) alerting and locating equipment, including emergency position indicating radio beacons;

(B) subject to paragraph (3), a survival craft that ensures that no part of an individual is immersed in water sufficient to accommodate all individuals on board;

(C) at least one readily accessible immersion suit for each individual on board that vessel when operating on the waters described in section 3102 of this title;

(D) marine radio communications equipment sufficient to effectively communicate with land-based search and rescue facilities;

(E) navigation equipment, including compasses, nautical charts, and publications;

(F) first aid equipment and medical supplies sufficient for the size and area of operation of the vessel; and

(G) ground tackle sufficient for the vessel.

(3) Except for a nonapplicable vessel, an auxiliary craft shall satisfy the equipment requirement under paragraph (2)(B) if such craft is—

(A) necessary for normal fishing operations;

(B) readily accessible during an emergency; and

(C) capable, in accordance with the Coast Guard capacity rating, when applicable, of safely holding all individuals on board the vessel to which the craft functions as an auxiliary.

(c)(1) In addition to the requirements described in subsections (a) and (b) of this section, the Secretary may prescribe regulations establishing the standards in paragraph (2) of this subsection for vessels to which this chapter applies that—

(A)(i) were built after December 31, 1988, or undergo a major conversion completed after that date; and

(ii) operate with more than 16 individuals on board; or

(B) in the case of a fish tender vessel, engage in the Aleutian trade.

(2) The standards shall be minimum safety standards, including standards relating to—

(A) navigation equipment, including radars and fathometers;

(B) lifesaving equipment, immersion suits, signaling devices, bilge pumps, bilge alarms, life rails, and grab rails;

(C) fire protection and firefighting equipment, including fire alarms and portable and semiportable fire extinguishing equipment;

(D) use and installation of insulation material;

(E) storage methods for flammable or combustible material; and

(F) fuel, ventilation, and electrical systems.

426

(d)(1) The Secretary shall prescribe regulations for the operating stability of a vessel to which this chapter applies—

(A) that was built after December 31, 1989; or

(B) the physical characteristics of which are substantially altered after December 31, 1989, in a manner that affects the vessel's operating stability.

(2) The Secretary may accept, as evidence of compliance with this subsection, a certification of compliance issued by the person providing insurance for the vessel or by another qualified person approved by the Secretary.

(e) In prescribing regulations under this chapter, the Secretary—

(1) shall consider the specialized nature and economics of the operations and the character, design, and construction of the vessel; and

(2) may not require the alteration of a vessel or associated equipment that was constructed or manufactured before the effective date of the regulation.

(f) To ensure compliance with the requirements of this chapter, the Secretary—

(1) shall require the individual in charge of a vessel described in subsection (b) to keep a record of equipment maintenance, and required instruction and drills;

(2) shall examine at dockside a vessel described in subsection (b) at least once every 5 years, but may require an exam at dockside every 2 years for vessels described in subsection (b) if—

(A) requested by an owner or operator; or

(B) the vessel is—

(i) at least 50 feet overall in length;

(ii) built before July 1, 2013; and

(iii) 25 years of age or older; and

(3) shall issue a certificate of compliance to a vessel meeting the requirements of this chapter and satisfying the requirements in paragraph (2).

(g)(1) The individual in charge of a vessel described in subsection (b) must pass a training program approved by the Secretary that meets the requirements in paragraph (2) of this subsection and hold a valid certificate issued under that program.

(2) The training program shall—

(A) be based on professional knowledge and skill obtained through sea service and hands-on training, including training in seamanship, stability, collision prevention, navigation, fire fighting and prevention, damage control, personal survival, emergency medical care, emergency drills, and weather;

(B) require an individual to demonstrate ability to communicate in an emergency situation and understand information found in navigation publications;

(C) recognize and give credit for recent past experience in fishing vessel operation; and

(D) provide for issuance of a certificate to an individual that has successfully completed the program.

(3) The Secretary shall prescribe regulations implementing this subsection. The regulations shall require that individuals who are issued a certificate under paragraph (2)(D) must complete refresher training at least once every 5 years as a condition of maintaining the validity of the certificate.

(4) The Secretary shall establish an electronic database listing the names of individuals who have participated in and received a certificate confirming successful completion of a training program approved by the Secretary under this section.

(h) A vessel to which this chapter applies shall be constructed in a manner that provides a level of safety equivalent to the minimum safety standards the Secretary may establish for recreational vessels under section 4302, if—

(1) subsection (b) of this section applies to the vessel;

(2) the vessel is less than 50 feet overall in length; and

(3) the vessel is built after January 1, 2010.

(i)(1) The Secretary of Health and Human Services shall establish a Fishing Safety Training Grants Program to provide funding to municipalities, port authorities, other appropriate public entities, not-for-profit organizations, and other qualified persons that provide commercial fishing safety training—

(A) to conduct fishing vessel safety training for vessel operators and crewmembers that—

(i) in the case of vessel operators, meets the requirements of subsection (g); and

(ii) in the case of crewmembers, meets the requirements of subsection (g)(2)(A), such requirements of subsection (g)(2)(B) as are appropriate for crewmembers, and the requirements of subsections (g)(2)(D), (g)(3), and (g)(4); and

(B) for purchase of safety equipment and training aids for use in those fishing vessel safety training programs.

(2) The Secretary of Health and Human Services, in consultation with and based on criteria established by the Commandant of the Coast Guard [1] shall award grants under this subsection on a competitive basis.

(3) The Federal share of the cost of any activity carried out with a grant under this subsection shall not exceed 75 percent.

(4) There is authorized to be appropriated $3,000,000 for fiscal year 2023 for grants under this subsection.

(j)(1) The Secretary of Health and Human Services shall establish a Fishing Safety Research Grant Program to provide funding to individuals in academia, members of non-profit organizations and businesses involved in fishing and maritime matters, and other persons with expertise in fishing safety, to conduct research on methods of improving the safety of the commercial fishing industry, including vessel design, emergency and survival equipment, enhancement of vessel monitoring systems, communications devices, de-icing technology, and severe weather detection.

(2) The Secretary of Health and Human Services, in consultation with and based on criteria established by the Commandant of the Coast Guard, shall award grants under this

subsection on a competitive basis.

(3) The Federal share of the cost of any activity carried out with a grant under this subsection shall not exceed 75 percent.

(4) There is authorized to be appropriated $3,000,000 for fiscal year 2023 for activities under this subsection.

(k) For the purposes of this section, the term "auxiliary craft" means a vessel that is carried onboard a fishing vessel and is normally used to support fishing operations.

(Added Pub. L. 98–364, title IV, §402(7)(C), July 17, 1984, 98 Stat. 447; amended Pub. L. 98–557, §33(a), Oct. 30, 1984, 98 Stat. 2876; Pub. L. 100–424, §2(a), Sept. 9, 1988, 102 Stat. 1585; Pub. L. 101–595, title VI, §602(c), Nov. 16, 1990, 104 Stat. 2990; Pub. L. 104–324, title III, §307, Oct. 19, 1996, 110 Stat. 3918; Pub. L. 105–383, title III, §301(b)(5), Nov. 13, 1998, 112 Stat. 3417; Pub. L. 111–281, title VI, §604(a), Oct. 15, 2010, 124 Stat. 2962; Pub. L. 112–213, title III, §305(a), (b), Dec. 20, 2012, 126 Stat. 1564; Pub. L. 113–281, title III, §309, Dec. 18, 2014, 128 Stat. 3045; Pub. L. 115–282, title V, §§504–506, Dec. 4, 2018, 132 Stat. 4271; Pub. L. 116–283, div. G, title LVXXXIII [LXXXIII], §8321(a), (b), Jan. 1, 2021, 134 Stat. 4701; Pub. L. 117–263, div. K, title CXIII, §11328(a), title CXV, §11509(a)(1), Dec. 23, 2022, 136 Stat. 4098, 4137.)

---

[1] *So in original. Probably should be followed by a comma.*

§4503. Fishing, fish tender, and fish processing vessel certification

(a) A vessel to which this subsection applies may not be operated unless the vessel—

(1) meets all survey and classification requirements prescribed by the American Bureau of Shipping or another similarly qualified organization approved by the Secretary; and

(2) has on board a certificate issued by the American Bureau of Shipping or that other organization evidencing compliance with this subsection.

(b) Subsection (a) applies to a fish processing vessel to which this chapter applies that—

(1) is built after July 27, 1990; or

(2) undergoes a major conversion completed after that date.

(c)(1) Except as provided in paragraph (2), subsection (a) applies to a vessel to which section 4502(b) of this title applies that is at least 50 feet overall in length and is built after July 1, 2013.

(2) Subsection (a) does not apply to a fishing vessel or fish tender vessel to which section 4502(b) of this title applies, if the vessel—

(A) is at least 50 feet overall in length, and not more than 180 feet overall in length as listed on the vessel's certificate of documentation or certificate of number; and

(B)(i) is built after the date of the enactment of the Coast Guard Authorization Act of 2016; and

(ii) complies with—

(I) the requirements described in subsection (d); or

(II) the alternative requirements established by the Secretary under subsection (e).

(d) The requirements referred to in subsection (c)(2)(B)(ii)(I) are the following:

(1) The vessel is designed by an individual licensed by a State as a naval architect or marine engineer, and the design incorporates standards equivalent to those prescribed by a classification society to which the Secretary has delegated authority under section 3316 or another qualified organization approved by the Secretary for purposes of this paragraph.

(2) Construction of the vessel is overseen and certified as being in accordance with its design by a marine surveyor of an organization accepted by the Secretary.

(3) The vessel—

(A) completes a stability test performed by a qualified individual;

(B) has written stability and loading instructions from a qualified individual that are provided to the owner or operator; and

(C) has an assigned loading mark.

(4) The vessel is not substantially altered without the review and approval of an individual licensed by a State as a naval architect or marine engineer before the beginning of such substantial alteration.

(5) The vessel undergoes a condition survey at least twice in 5 years, not to exceed 3 years between surveys, to the satisfaction of a marine surveyor of an organization accepted by the Secretary.

(6) The vessel undergoes an out-of-water survey at least once every 5 years to the satisfaction of a certified marine surveyor of an organization accepted by the Secretary.

(7) Once every 5 years and at the time of a substantial alteration to such vessel, compliance of the vessel with the requirements of paragraph (3) is reviewed and updated as necessary.

(8) For the life of the vessel, the owner of the vessel maintains records to demonstrate compliance with this subsection and makes such records readily available for inspection by an official authorized to enforce this chapter.

(e)(1) Not later than 10 years after the date of the enactment of the Coast Guard Authorization Act of 2016, the Secretary shall submit to the Committee on Transportation and Infrastructure of the House of Representatives and the Committee on Commerce, Science, and Transportation of the Senate a report that provides an analysis of the adequacy of the requirements under subsection (d) in maintaining the safety of the fishing vessels and fish tender vessels which are described in subsection (c)(2) and which comply with the requirements of subsection (d).

(2) If the report required under this subsection includes a determination that the safety requirements under subsection (d) are not adequate or that additional safety measures are necessary, then the Secretary may establish an alternative safety compliance program for fishing vessels or fish tender vessels (or both) which are described in subsection (c)(2) and which comply with the requirements of subsection (d).

(3) The alternative safety compliance program established under this subsection shall include requirements for—

(A) vessel construction;

(B) a vessel stability test;

(C) vessel stability and loading instructions;

4503a. Repealed. Pub. L. 117–263, div. K, title XV, §11509(a)(3), Dec. 23, 2022, 136 Stat. 4137]

CHAPTER 45—UNINSPECTED
COMMERCIAL FISHING INDUSTRY

(D) an assigned vessel loading mark;

(E) a vessel condition survey at least twice in 5 years, not to exceed 3 years between surveys;

(F) an out-of-water vessel survey at least once every 5 years;

(G) maintenance of records to demonstrate compliance with the program, and the availability of such records for inspection; and

(H) such other aspects of vessel safety as the Secretary considers appropriate.

(f)(1) For purposes of this section and section 4503a, the term "built" means, with respect to a vessel, that the vessel's construction has reached any of the following stages:

(A) The vessel's keel is laid.

(B) Construction identifiable with the vessel has begun and assembly of that vessel has commenced comprising of at least 50 metric tons or one percent of the estimated mass of all structural material, whichever is less.

(2) In the case of a vessel greater than 79 feet overall in length, for purposes of paragraph (1)(A) a keel is deemed to be laid when a marine surveyor affirms that a structure adequate for serving as a keel for such vessel is in place and identified for use in the construction of such vessel.

(Added Pub. L. 98–364, title IV, §402(7)(C), July 17, 1984, 98 Stat. 447; amended Pub. L. 98–557, §33(b), Oct. 30, 1984, 98 Stat. 2876; Pub. L. 100–424, §2(a), Sept. 9, 1988, 102 Stat. 1587; Pub. L. 111–281, title VI, §604(e)(1), Oct. 15, 2010, 124 Stat. 2966; Pub. L. 112–213, title III, §305(c), Dec. 20, 2012, 126 Stat. 1564; Pub. L. 114–120, title III, §318(a), Feb. 8, 2016, 130 Stat. 63; Pub. L. 114–328, div. C, title XXXV, §3503(a), (b)(2), Dec. 23, 2016, 130 Stat. 2775; Pub. L. 115–282, title V, §§507, 508(a), (b), Dec. 4, 2018, 132 Stat. 4272; Pub. L. 117–263, div. K, title CXV, §11509(a)(2), Dec. 23, 2022, 136 Stat. 4137.)

[§4503A. REPEALED. PUB. L. 117–263, DIV. K, TITLE CXV, §11509(A)(3), DEC. 23, 2022, 136 STAT. 4137]

Section, added and amended Pub. L. 115–282, title V, §508(a), (c), Dec. 4, 2018, 132 Stat. 4272, provided for an alternate safety compliance program for certain fishing vessels.

§4504. PROHIBITED ACTS

A person may not operate a vessel in violation of this chapter or a regulation prescribed under this chapter.

(Added Pub. L. 98–364, title IV, §402(7)(C), July 17, 1984, 98 Stat. 447; amended Pub. L. 100–424, §2(a), Sept. 9, 1988, 102 Stat. 1587.)

§4505. TERMINATION OF UNSAFE OPERATIONS

An official authorized to enforce this chapter—

(1) may direct the individual in charge of a vessel to which this chapter applies to immediately take reasonable steps necessary for the safety of individuals on board the vessel if the official observes the vessel being operated in an unsafe condition that

431

the official believes creates an especially hazardous condition, including ordering the individual in charge to return the vessel to a mooring and to remain there until the situation creating the hazard is corrected or ended; and

(2) may order the individual in charge of an uninspected fish processing vessel that does not have on board the certificate required under section 4503(a)(2) of this title to return the vessel to a mooring and to remain there until the vessel is in compliance with that section, except that this paragraph shall not apply with respect to a vessel to which section 4503a [1] applies.

(Added Pub. L. 100–424, §2(a), Sept. 9, 1988, 102 Stat. 1587; amended Pub. L. 115–282, title V, §509, Dec. 4, 2018, 132 Stat. 4274.)

[1] See References in Text note below.

§4506. EXEMPTIONS

The Secretary may exempt a vessel from any part of this chapter if, under regulations prescribed by the Secretary (including regulations on special operating conditions), the Secretary finds that—

(1) good cause exists for granting an exemption; and

(2) the safety of the vessel and those on board will not be adversely affected.

(Added Pub. L. 100–424, §2(a), Sept. 9, 1988, 102 Stat. 1587; amended Pub. L. 102–587, title V, §5222, Nov. 4, 1992, 106 Stat. 5081; Pub. L. 105–383, title III, §301(b)(6), Nov. 13, 1998, 112 Stat. 3417; Pub. L. 111–281, title VI, §604(b), Oct. 15, 2010, 124 Stat. 2964; Pub. L. 114–120, title III, §306(a)(5), Feb. 8, 2016, 130 Stat. 54.)

§4507. PENALTIES

(a) The owner, charterer, managing operator, agent, master, and individual in charge of a vessel to which this chapter applies which is operated in violation of this chapter or a regulation prescribed under this chapter may each be assessed a civil penalty by the Secretary of not more than $5,000. Any vessel with respect to which a penalty is assessed under this subsection is liable in rem for the penalty.

(b) A person willfully violating this chapter or a regulation prescribed under this chapter shall be fined not more than $5,000, imprisoned for not more than one year, or both.

(Added Pub. L. 100–424, §2(a), Sept. 9, 1988, 102 Stat. 1588.)

[§4508. REPEALED. PUB. L. 115–282, TITLE VI, §601(C)(1), DEC. 4, 2018, 132 STAT. 4289]

Section, added Pub. L. 100–424, §2(a), Sept. 9, 1988, 102 Stat. 1588; amended Pub. L. 101–225, title I, §106, Dec. 12, 1989, 103 Stat. 1910; Pub. L. 102–241, §25, Dec. 19, 1991, 105 Stat. 2217; Pub. L. 104–324, title III, §304(b), Oct. 19, 1996, 110 Stat. 3917; Pub. L. 107–295, title III, §331(a), Nov. 25, 2002, 116 Stat. 2105; Pub. L. 108–293, title IV, §418(a), Aug. 9, 2004, 118 Stat. 1049; Pub. L. 109–241, title IX, §901(g), July 11, 2006, 120 Stat. 564; Pub. L. 111–281, title VI, §604(c)(1)–(3), Oct. 15, 2010, 124 Stat. 2964, 2965, established the Commercial Fishing Safety Advisory Committee. See section 15102

§4508. Repealed. Pub. L. 115–282, title VI,
601(c)(1), Dec. 4, 2018, 132 Stat. 4289]

CHAPTER 45—UNINSPECTED
COMMERCIAL FISHING INDUSTRY

of this title.

CHAPTER 47—ABANDONMENT OF BARGES

Sec.
4701.   Definitions.
4702.   Abandonment of barge prohibited.
4703.   Penalty for unlawful abandonment of barge.
4704.   Removal of abandoned barges.
4705.   Liability of barge removal contractors.

§4701. DEFINITIONS

In this chapter—

(1) "abandon" means to moor, strand, wreck, sink, or leave a barge of more than 100 gross tons as measured under section 14502 of this title, or an alternate tonnage measured under section 14302 of this title as prescribed by the Secretary under section 14104 of this title unattended for longer than forty-five days.

(2) "barge removal contractor" means a person that enters into a contract with the United States to remove an abandoned barge under this chapter.

(3) "navigable waters of the United States" means waters of the United States, including the territorial sea.

(4) "removal" or "remove" means relocation, sale, scrapping, or other method of disposal.

(Added Pub. L. 102–587, title V, §5302, Nov. 4, 1992, 106 Stat. 5081; amended Pub. L. 104–324, title VII, §718, Oct. 19, 1996, 110 Stat. 3937.)

§4702. ABANDONMENT OF BARGE PROHIBITED

An owner or operator of a barge may not abandon it on the navigable waters of the United States. A barge is deemed not to be abandoned if—

(1) it is located at a Federally- or State-approved mooring area;

(2) it is on private property with the permission of the owner of the property; or

(3) the owner or operator notifies the Secretary that the barge is not abandoned and the location of the barge.

(Added Pub. L. 102–587, title V, §5302, Nov. 4, 1992, 106 Stat. 5082; amended Pub. L. 109–304, §15(18), Oct. 6, 2006, 120 Stat. 1703.)

§4703. PENALTY FOR UNLAWFUL ABANDONMENT OF BARGE

Thirty days after the notification procedures under section 4704(a)(1) are completed, the Secretary may assess a civil penalty of not more than $1,000 for each day of the violation against an owner or operator that violates section 4702. A vessel with respect to which a penalty is assessed under this chapter is liable in rem for the penalty.

(Added Pub. L. 102–587, title V, §5302, Nov. 4, 1992, 106 Stat. 5082.)

§4704. REMOVAL OF ABANDONED BARGES

(a)(1) The Secretary may remove a barge that is abandoned after complying with the following procedures:

(A) If the identity of the owner or operator can be determined, the Secretary shall notify the owner or operator by certified mail—

(i) that if the barge is not removed it will be removed at the owner's or operator's expense; and

(ii) of the penalty under section 4703.

(B) If the identity of the owner or operator cannot be determined, the Secretary shall publish an announcement in—

(i) a notice to mariners; and

(ii) an official journal of the county in which the barge is located

that if the barge is not removed it will be removed at the owner's or operator's expense.

(2) The United States, and any officer or employee of the United States is not liable to an owner or operator for damages resulting from removal of an abandoned barge under this chapter.

(b) The owner or operator of an abandoned barge is liable, and an abandoned barge is liable in rem, for all expenses that the United States incurs in removing an abandoned barge under this chapter.

(c)(1) The Secretary may, after providing notice under subsection (a)(1), solicit by public advertisement sealed bids for the removal of an abandoned barge.

(2) After solicitation under paragraph (1) the Secretary may award a contract. The contract—

(A) may be subject to the condition that the barge and all property on the barge is the property of the barge removal contractor; and

(B) must require the barge removal contractor to submit to the Secretary a plan for the removal.

(3) Removal of an abandoned barge may begin thirty days after the Secretary completes the procedures under subsection (a)(1).

(Added Pub. L. 102–587, title V, §5302, Nov. 4, 1992, 106 Stat. 5082.)

§4705. LIABILITY OF BARGE REMOVAL CONTRACTORS

(a) A barge removal contractor and its subcontractor are not liable for damages that result from actions taken or omitted to be taken in the course of removing a barge under this chapter.

(b) Subsection (a) does not apply—

(1) with respect to personal injury or wrongful death; or

(2) if the contractor or subcontractor is grossly negligent or engages in willful misconduct.

(Added Pub. L. 102–587, title V, §5302, Nov. 4, 1992, 106 Stat. 5083; amended Pub. L. 109–304, §15(19),

Oct. 6, 2006, 120 Stat. 1703.)

CHAPTER 49—OCEANGOING NON-PASSENGER COMMERCIAL VESSELS

Sec.

4901.   Surveillance requirements.

§4901. Surveillance requirements

(a) In General.—A vessel engaged in commercial service that does not carry passengers, shall maintain a video surveillance system.

(b) Applicability.—The requirements in this section shall apply to—

(1) documented vessels with overnight accommodations for at least 10 individuals on board that are—

(A) on a voyage of at least 600 miles and crosses seaward of the Boundary Line; or

(B) at least 24 meters (79 feet) in overall length and required to have a load line under chapter 51;

(2) documented vessels of at least 500 gross tons as measured under section 14502, or an alternate tonnage measured under section 14302 as prescribed by the Secretary under section 14104 on an international voyage; and

(3) vessels with overnight accommodations for at least 10 individuals on board that are operating for no less than 72 hours on waters superjacent to the outer Continental Shelf (as defined in section 2(a) of the Outer Continental Shelf Lands Act (43 U.S.C. 1331(a)).[1]

(c) Placement of Video and Audio Surveillance Equipment.—

(1) In general.—The owner of a vessel to which this section applies shall install video and audio surveillance equipment aboard the vessel not later than 2 years after enactment of the Don Young Coast Guard Authorization Act of 2022, or during the next scheduled drydock, whichever is later.

(2) Locations.—Video and audio surveillance equipment shall be placed in passageways on to which doors from staterooms open. Such equipment shall be placed in a manner ensuring the visibility of every door in each such passageway.

(d) Notice of Video and Audio Surveillance.—The owner of a vessel to which this section applies shall provide clear and conspicuous signs on board the vessel notifying the crew of the presence of video and audio surveillance equipment.

(e) Access to Video and Audio Records.—The owner of a vessel to which this section applies shall ensure that access to records of video and audio surveillance is not used as part of a labor action against a crew member or employment dispute unless used in a criminal or civil action.

(f) Retention Requirements.—The owner of a vessel to which this section applies shall retain all records of audio and video surveillance for not less than 1 year after the footage is obtained. Any video and audio surveillance found to be associated with an alleged incident should be preserved for not less than 5 years from the date of the alleged incident.

(g) PERSONNEL TRAINING.—A vessel owner or employer of a seafarer shall provide training for all individuals employed by the owner or employer for the purpose of responding to incidents of sexual assault or sexual harassment, including—

(1) such training to ensure the individuals—

(A) retain audio and visual records and other evidence objectively; and

(B) act impartially without influence from the company or others; and

(2) training on applicable Federal, State, Tribal, and local laws and regulations regarding sexual assault and sexual harassment investigations and reporting requirements.

(g) DEFINITION OF OWNER.—In this section, the term "owner" means the owner, charterer, managing operator, master, or other individual in charge of a vessel.

(h) EXEMPTION.—Fishing vessels, fish processing vessels, and fish tender vessels are exempt from this section.

(Added Pub. L. 117–263, div. K, title CXVI, §11607(a), Dec. 23, 2022, 136 Stat. 4150.)

[1] *So in original. Another closing parenthesis probably should precede the period.*

PART C—LOAD LINES OF VESSELS

CHAPTER 51—LOAD LINES

§5101. DEFINITIONS

In this chapter—

(1) "domestic voyage" means movement of a vessel between places in, or subject to the jurisdiction of, the United States, except movement between—

(A) a place in a territory or possession of the United States or the Trust Territory of the Pacific Islands; and

(B) a place outside that territory, possession, or Trust Territory.

(2) "economic benefit of the overloading" means the amount obtained by multiplying the weight of the overload (in tons) by the lesser of—

(A) the average freight rate value of a ton of the vessel's cargo for the voyage; or

(B) $50.

(3) "existing vessel" means—

(A) a vessel on a domestic voyage, the keel of which was laid, or that was at a similar stage of construction, before January 1, 1986; and

(B) a vessel on a foreign voyage, the keel of which was laid, or that was at a similar stage of construction, before July 21, 1968.

(4) "freeboard" means the distance from the mark of the load line assigned under this chapter to the freeboard deck.

(5) "freeboard deck" means the deck or other structure the Secretary prescribes by regulation.

(6) "minimum safe freeboard" means the freeboard that the Secretary decides cannot

441

be reduced safely without limiting the operation of the vessel.

(7) "weight of the overload" means the amount obtained by multiplying the number of inches that the vessel is submerged below the applicable assigned freeboard by the tons-an-inch immersion factor for the vessel at the assigned minimum safe freeboard.

(Pub. L. 99–509, title V, §5101(2), Oct. 21, 1986, 100 Stat. 1913.)

§5102. APPLICATION

(a) Except as provided in subsection (b) of this section, this chapter applies to the following:

(1) a vessel of the United States.

(2) a vessel on the navigable waters of the United States.

(3) a vessel—

(A) owned by a citizen of the United States or a corporation established by or under the laws of the United States or a State; and

(B) not registered in a foreign country.

(4) a public vessel of the United States.

(5) a vessel otherwise subject to the jurisdiction of the United States.

(b) This chapter does not apply to the following:

(1) a vessel of war.

(2) a recreational vessel when operated only for pleasure.

(3) a fishing vessel, unless the vessel is built after July 1, 2013.

(4) a fish processing vessel of not more than 5,000 gross tons as measured under section 14502 of this title, or an alternate tonnage measured under section 14302 of this title as prescribed by the Secretary under section 14104 of this title that—

(A)(i) was constructed as a fish processing vessel before August 16, 1974; or

(ii) was converted for use as a fish processing vessel before January 1, 1983; and

(B) is not on a foreign voyage.

(5) a fish tender vessel of not more than 500 gross tons as measured under section 14502 of this title, or an alternate tonnage measured under section 14302 of this title as prescribed by the Secretary under section 14104 of this title that—

(A)(i) was constructed, under construction, or under contract to be constructed as a fish tender vessel before January 1, 1980; or

(ii) was converted for use as a fish tender vessel before January 1, 1983; and

(B)(i) is not on a foreign voyage; or

(ii) is not engaged in the Aleutian trade (except a vessel in that trade assigned a load line at any time before June 1, 1992).

(6) a vessel of the United States on a domestic voyage that does not cross the Boundary Line, except a voyage on the Great Lakes.

(7) a vessel of less than 24 meters (79 feet) overall in length.

(8) a public vessel of the United States on a domestic voyage.

(9) a vessel excluded from the application of this chapter by an international

agreement to which the United States Government is a party.

(10) an existing vessel of not more than 150 gross tons as measured under section 14502 of this title, or an alternate tonnage measured under section 14302 of this title as prescribed by the Secretary under section 14104 of this title that is on a domestic voyage.

(11) a small passenger vessel on a domestic voyage.

(12) a vessel of the working fleet of the Panama Canal Commission not on a foreign voyage.

(13) a vessel of the United States on a domestic voyage that is within the Gulf of Mexico and operating not more than 15 nautical miles seaward of the base line from which the territorial sea of the United States is measured between Crystal Bay, Florida and Hudson Creek, Florida.

(c) On application by the owner and after a survey under section 5105 of this title, the Secretary may assign load lines for a vessel excluded from the application of this chapter under subsection (b) of this section. A vessel assigned load lines under this subsection is subject to this chapter until the surrender of its load line certificate and the removal of its load line marks.

(d) This chapter does not affect an international agreement to which the Government is a party that is not in conflict with the International Convention on Load Lines currently in force for the United States.

(Pub. L. 99–509, title V, §5101(2), Oct. 21, 1986, 100 Stat. 1914; Pub. L. 101–595, title VI, §602(d), Nov. 16, 1990, 104 Stat. 2991; Pub. L. 104–324, title VII, §719, Oct. 19, 1996, 110 Stat. 3938; Pub. L. 107–295, title IV, §436(a), Nov. 25, 2002, 116 Stat. 2129; Pub. L. 111–281, title VI, §604(d)(1), Oct. 15, 2010, 124 Stat. 2965; Pub. L. 112–213, title III, §305(d)(1), Dec. 20, 2012, 126 Stat. 1565; Pub. L. 114–120, title VI, §612, Feb. 8, 2016, 130 Stat. 85.)

§5103. LOAD LINE REQUIREMENTS

(a) A vessel may be operated only if the vessel has been assigned load lines.

(b) The owner, charterer, managing operator, agent, master, and individual in charge of a vessel shall mark and maintain the load lines permanently and conspicuously in the way prescribed by the Secretary.

(c) A fishing vessel built on or before July 1, 2013, that undergoes a major conversion completed after the later of July 1, 2013, or the date the Secretary establishes standards for an alternate loadline compliance program, shall comply with such an alternative loadline compliance program that is developed in cooperation with the commercial fishing industry and prescribed by the Secretary.

(Pub. L. 99–509, title V, §5101(2), Oct. 21, 1986, 100 Stat. 1915; Pub. L. 111–281, title VI, §604(d)(2), Oct. 15, 2010, 124 Stat. 2965; Pub. L. 112–213, title III, §305(d)(2), Dec. 20, 2012, 126 Stat. 1565.)

§5104. ASSIGNMENT OF LOAD LINES

(a) The Secretary shall assign load lines for a vessel so that they indicate the minimum safe freeboard to which the vessel may be loaded. However, if the owner requests, the Secretary may assign load lines that result in greater freeboard than the minimum safe freeboard.

(b) In assigning load lines for a vessel, the Secretary shall consider—

(1) the service, type, and character of the vessel;

(2) the geographic area in which the vessel will operate; and

(3) applicable international agreements to which the United States Government is a party.

(c) An existing vessel may retain its load lines assigned before January 1, 1986, unless the Secretary decides that a substantial change in the vessel after those load lines were assigned requires that new load lines be assigned under this chapter.

(d) The minimum freeboard of an existing vessel may be reduced only if the vessel complies with every applicable provision of this chapter.

(e) The Secretary may designate by regulation specific geographic areas that have less severe weather or sea conditions and from which there is adequate time to return to available safe harbors. The Secretary may reduce the minimum freeboard of a vessel operating in these areas.

(Pub. L. 99–509, title V, §5101(2), Oct. 21, 1986, 100 Stat. 1915.)

§5105. LOAD LINE SURVEYS

(a) The Secretary may provide for annual, renewal, and other load line surveys.

(b) In conducting a load line survey, the Secretary shall consider whether—

(1) the hull and fittings of the vessel—

(A) are adequate to protect the vessel from the sea; and

(B) meet other requirements the Secretary may prescribe by regulation;

(2) the strength of the hull is adequate for all loading conditions;

(3) the stability of the vessel is adequate for all loading conditions;

(4) the topsides of the vessel are arranged and constructed to allow rapid overboard drainage of deck water in heavy weather; and

(5) the topsides of the vessel are adequate in design, arrangement, and equipment to protect crewmembers performing outside tasks necessary for safe operation of the vessel.

(Pub. L. 99–509, title V, §5101(2), Oct. 21, 1986, 100 Stat. 1916.)

§5106. LOAD LINE CERTIFICATE

(a) On finding that a load line survey of a vessel under this chapter is satisfactory and that the vessel's load lines are marked correctly, the Secretary shall issue the vessel a load line certificate and deliver it to the owner, master, or individual in charge of the vessel.

(b) The certificate shall be maintained as required by the Secretary.

(Pub. L. 99–509, title V, §5101(2), Oct. 21, 1986, 100 Stat. 1916.)

§5107. DELEGATION OF AUTHORITY

(a) The Secretary shall delegate to the American Bureau of Shipping or other similarly qualified organizations the authority to assign load lines, survey vessels, determine that load lines are marked correctly, and issue load line certificates under this chapter.

(b) Under regulations prescribed by the Secretary, a decision of an organization delegated authority under subsection (a) of this section related to the assignment of a load line may be appealed to the Secretary.

(c) For a vessel intended to be engaged on a foreign voyage, the Secretary may delegate to another country that is a party to the International Convention on Load Lines, 1966, the authority to assign load lines, survey vessels, determine that the load lines are marked correctly, and issue an International Load Line Certificate (1966).

(d) The Secretary may terminate a delegation made under this section after giving written notice to the organization.

(Pub. L. 99–509, title V, §5101(2), Oct. 21, 1986, 100 Stat. 1916.)

§5108. Special exemptions

(a) The Secretary may exempt a vessel from any part of this chapter when—

(1) the vessel is entitled to an exemption under an international agreement to which the United States Government is a party; or

(2) under regulations (including regulations on special operations conditions) prescribed by the Secretary, the Secretary finds that good cause exists for granting an exemption.

(b) When the Secretary grants an exemption under this section, the Secretary may issue a certificate of exemption stating the extent of the exemption.

(c) A certificate of exemption issued under subsection (b) of this section shall be maintained as required by the Secretary.

(Pub. L. 99–509, title V, §5101(2), Oct. 21, 1986, 100 Stat. 1916.)

§5109. Reciprocity for foreign vessels

(a) When the Secretary finds that the laws and regulations of a foreign country related to load lines are similar to those of this chapter and the regulations prescribed under this chapter, or when a foreign country is a party to an international load line agreement to which the United States Government is a party, the Secretary shall accept the load line marks and certificate of a vessel of that foreign country as complying with this chapter and the regulations prescribed under this chapter. The Secretary may control the vessel as provided for in the applicable international agreement.

(b) Subsection (a) of this section does not apply to a vessel of a foreign country that does not recognize load lines assigned under this chapter.

(Pub. L. 99–509, title V, §5101(2), Oct. 21, 1986, 100 Stat. 1917.)

§5110. Submersible vessels

Notwithstanding sections 5103–5105 of this title, the Secretary may prescribe regulations for submersible vessels to provide a minimum level of safety. In developing the regulations, the Secretary shall consider factors relevant to submersible vessels, including the structure, stability, and watertight integrity of those vessels.

(Pub. L. 99–509, title V, §5101(2), Oct. 21, 1986, 100 Stat. 1917.)

§5111. Providing loading information

The Secretary may prescribe regulations requiring the owner, charterer, managing operator, and agent of a vessel to provide loading information (including information on loading distribution, stability, and margin of strength) to the master or individual in charge of the vessel in a language the master or individual understands.

(Pub. L. 99–509, title V, §5101(2), Oct. 21, 1986, 100 Stat. 1917.)

§5112. LOADING RESTRICTIONS

(a) A vessel may not be loaded in a way that submerges the assigned load line or the place at which the load line is required to be marked on the vessel.

(b) If the loading or stability conditions of a vessel change, the master or individual in charge of the vessel, before moving the vessel, shall record in the official logbook or other permanent record of the vessel—

(1) the position of the assigned load line relative to the water surface; and
(2) the draft of the vessel fore and aft.

(c) A vessel may be operated only if the loading distribution, stability, and margin of strength are adequate for the voyage or movement intended.

(d) Subsections (a) and (b) of this section do not apply to a submersible vessel.

(Pub. L. 99–509, title V, §5101(2), Oct. 21, 1986, 100 Stat. 1917.)

§5113. DETENTION OF VESSELS

(a) When the Secretary believes that a vessel is about to leave a place in the United States in violation of this chapter or a regulation prescribed under this chapter, the Secretary may detain the vessel by giving notice to the owner, charterer, managing operator, agent, master, or individual in charge of the vessel.

(b) A detained vessel may be cleared under section 60105 of this title only after the violation has been corrected. If the vessel was cleared before being detained, the clearance shall be withdrawn.

(c) Under regulations prescribed by the Secretary, the owner, charterer, managing operator, agent, master, or individual in charge of a detained vessel may petition the Secretary to review the detention order.

(d) After reviewing a petition, the Secretary may affirm, withdraw, or change the detention order. Before acting on the petition, the Secretary may require any independent survey that may be necessary to determine the condition of the vessel.

(e) The owner of a vessel is liable for the cost incident to a petition for review and any required survey if the vessel is found to be in violation of this chapter or a regulation prescribed under this chapter.

(Pub. L. 99–509, title V, §5101(2), Oct. 21, 1986, 100 Stat. 1918; Pub. L. 109–304, §15(20), Oct. 6, 2006, 120 Stat. 1703.)

§5114. USE OF CUSTOMS SERVICE OFFICERS AND EMPLOYEES FOR ENFORCEMENT

(a) With the approval of the Secretary of the Treasury, the Secretary may use an officer or employee of the United States Customs Service to enforce this chapter and the regulations prescribed under this chapter.

§5115. Repealed. Pub. L. 101–595, title VI, 603(5)(A), Nov. 16, 1990, 104 Stat. 2993]

CHAPTER 51—LOAD LINES

(b) The Secretary shall consult with the Secretary of the Treasury before prescribing a regulation that affects the enforcement responsibilities of an officer or employee of the Customs Service.

(Pub. L. 99–509, title V, §5101(2), Oct. 21, 1986, 100 Stat. 1918; Pub. L. 101–595, title VI, §603(4), Nov. 16, 1990, 104 Stat. 2993.)

[§5115. Repealed. Pub. L. 101–595, title VI, §603(5)(A), Nov. 16, 1990, 104 Stat. 2993]

Section, Pub. L. 99–509, title V, §5101(2), Oct. 21, 1986, 100 Stat. 1918, authorized Secretary to prescribe regulations to carry out this chapter.

§5116. Penalties

(a) Except as otherwise provided in this section, the owner, charterer, managing operator, agent, master, and individual in charge of a vessel violating this chapter or a regulation prescribed under this chapter are each liable to the United States Government for a civil penalty of not more than $5,000. Each day of a continuing violation is a separate violation. The vessel also is liable in rem for the penalty.

(b) The owner, charterer, managing operator, agent, master, and individual in charge of a vessel allowing, causing, attempting to cause, or failing to take reasonable care to prevent a violation of section 5112(a) of this title are each liable to the Government for a civil penalty of not more than $10,000 plus an additional amount equal to twice the economic benefit of the overloading. The vessel also is liable in rem for the penalty.

(c) The master or individual in charge of a vessel violating section 5112(b) of this title is liable to the Government for a civil penalty of not more than $5,000. The vessel also is liable in rem for the penalty.

(d) A person causing or allowing the departure of a vessel from a place within the jurisdiction of the United States in violation of a detention order issued under section 5113 of this title commits a class A misdemeanor.

(e) A person causing or allowing the alteration, concealment, or removal of a mark placed on a vessel under section 5103(b) of this title and the regulations prescribed under this chapter, except to make a lawful change or to escape enemy capture in time of war, commits a class A misdemeanor.

(Pub. L. 99–509, title V, §5101(2), Oct. 21, 1986, 100 Stat. 1918; Pub. L. 101–380, title IV, §4302(d), Aug. 18, 1990, 104 Stat. 538.)

§6101. Marine casualties and reporting

(a) The Secretary shall prescribe regulations on the marine casualties to be reported and the manner of reporting. The regulations shall require reporting the following marine casualties:

(1) death of an individual.

(2) serious injury to an individual.

(3) material loss of property.

(4) material damage affecting the seaworthiness or efficiency of the vessel.

(5) significant harm to the environment.

(b) A marine casualty shall be reported within 5 days as provided in this part and regulations prescribed under this part. Each report filed under this section shall include information as to whether the use of alcohol contributed to the casualty.

(c) Notice to State and Tribal Governments.—Not later than 24 hours after receiving a notice of a major marine casualty under this section, the Secretary shall notify each State or federally recognized Indian tribe that is, or may reasonably be expected to be, affected by such marine casualty.

(d)(1) This part applies to a foreign vessel when involved in a marine casualty on the navigable waters of the United States.

(2) This part applies, to the extent consistent with generally recognized principles of international law, to a foreign vessel constructed or adapted to carry, or that carries, oil in bulk as cargo or cargo residue involved in a marine casualty described under subsection (a)(4) or (5) in waters subject to the jurisdiction of the United States, including the Exclusive Economic Zone.

(e) A marine casualty not resulting in the death of an individual shall be classified according to the gravity of the casualty, as prescribed by regulation, giving consideration to the extent of injuries to individuals, the extent of property damage, the dangers that the casualty creates, and the size, occupation, and means of propulsion of each vessel involved.

(f)(1) This chapter applies to a marine casualty involving a United States citizen on a foreign passenger vessel operating south of 75 degrees north latitude, west of 35 degrees west longitude, and east of the International Date Line; or operating in the area south of 60 degrees south latitude that—

(A) embarks or disembarks passengers in the United States; or

(B) transports passengers traveling under any form of air and sea ticket package marketed in the United States.

(2) When there is a marine casualty described in paragraph (1) of this subsection and an investigation is conducted, the Secretary shall ensure that the investigation—
  (A) is thorough and timely; and
  (B) produces findings and recommendations to improve safety on passenger vessels.

(3) When there is a marine casualty described in paragraph (1) of this subsection, the Secretary may—
  (A) seek a multinational investigation of the casualty under auspices of the International Maritime Organization; or
  (B) conduct an investigation of the casualty under chapter 63 of this title.

(g) To the extent consistent with generally recognized practices and procedures of international law, this part applies to a foreign vessel involved in a marine casualty or incident, as defined in the International Maritime Organization Code for the Investigation of Marine Casualties and Incidents, where the United States is a Substantially Interested State and is, or has the consent of, the Lead Investigating State under the Code.

(h) The Secretary shall publish all major marine casualty reports prepared in accordance with this section in an electronic form, and shall provide information electronically regarding how other marine casualty reports can be obtained.

(i) For purposes of this section, the term "major marine casualty" means a casualty involving a vessel, other than a public vessel, that results in—
  (1) the loss of 6 or more lives;
  (2) the loss of a mechanically propelled vessel of 100 or more gross tons;
  (3) property damage initially estimated at $2,000,000 or more; or
  (4) serious threat, as determined by the Commandant with concurrence by the Chairman of the National Transportation Safety Board, to life, property, or the environment by hazardous materials.

(j) The Secretary shall publish all marine casualty reports prepared in accordance with this section in an electronic form.

(Pub. L. 98–89, Aug. 26, 1983, 97 Stat. 536; Pub. L. 98–498, title II, §212(b)(1), Oct. 19, 1984, 98 Stat. 2306; Pub. L. 98–557, §7(b)(1), Oct. 30, 1984, 98 Stat. 2862; Pub. L. 101–380, title IV, §4106(b), Aug. 18, 1990, 104 Stat. 513; Pub. L. 102–241, §33, Dec. 19, 1991, 105 Stat. 2222; Pub. L. 107–295, title IV, §§423, 442(a), Nov. 25, 2002, 116 Stat. 2125, 2132; Pub. L. 109–241, title IX, §901(o), July 11, 2006, 120 Stat. 565; Pub. L. 109–304, §15(21), Oct. 6, 2006, 120 Stat. 1704; Pub. L. 110–181, div. C, title XXXV, §3529(c)(1), Jan. 28, 2008, 122 Stat. 603; Pub. L. 113–281, title III, §312, Dec. 18, 2014, 128 Stat. 3048; Pub. L. 115–232, div. C, title XXXV, §§3541(b)(11), 3546(d), Aug. 13, 2018, 132 Stat. 2323, 2326; Pub. L. 115–265, title II, §211, Oct. 11, 2018, 132 Stat. 3749.)

§6102. STATE MARINE CASUALTY REPORTING SYSTEM

(a) The Secretary shall prescribe regulations for a uniform State marine casualty reporting system for vessels. Regulations shall prescribe the casualties to be reported and the manner of reporting. A State shall compile and submit to the Secretary reports, information, and statistics on casualties reported to the State, including information and statistics concerning the number of casualties in which the use of alcohol contributed to the casualty.

(b) The Secretary shall collect, analyze, and publish reports, information, and statistics on marine casualties together with findings and recommendations the Secretary considers appropriate. If a State marine casualty reporting system provides that information derived from casualty reports (except statistical information) may not be publicly disclosed, or otherwise prohibits use by the State or any person in any action or proceeding against a person, the Secretary may use the information provided by the State only in the same way that the State may use the information.

(Pub. L. 98–89, Aug. 26, 1983, 97 Stat. 536; Pub. L. 98–557, §7(b)(2), Oct. 30, 1984, 98 Stat. 2862.)

§6103. Penalty

(a) An owner, charterer, managing operator, agent, master, or individual in charge of a vessel failing to report a casualty as required under section 6101 of this title or a regulation prescribed under section 6101 or 6102 is liable to the United States Government for a civil penalty of not more than $25,000.

(b) A person failing to comply with section 6104 of this title or a regulation prescribed under that section is liable to the Government for a civil penalty of not more than $5,000.

(Pub. L. 98–89, Aug. 26, 1983, 97 Stat. 536; Pub. L. 98–498, title II, §212(b)(2), Oct. 19, 1984, 98 Stat. 2306; Pub. L. 100–424, §4(b), Sept. 9, 1988, 102 Stat. 1590; Pub. L. 104–324, title III, §§306(a), 314(b), Oct. 19, 1996, 110 Stat. 3918, 3922.)

§6104. Commercial fishing industry vessel casualty statistics

(a) The Secretary shall compile statistics concerning marine casualties from data compiled from insurers of fishing vessels, fish processing vessels, and fish tender vessels.

(b) A person underwriting primary insurance for a fishing vessel, fish processing vessel, or fish tender vessel shall submit periodically to the Secretary data concerning marine casualties that is required by regulations prescribed by the Secretary.

(c) After consulting with the insurance industry, the Secretary shall prescribe regulations under this section to gather a statistical base for analyzing vessel risks.

(d) The Secretary may delegate to a qualified person that has knowledge and experience in the collection of statistical insurance data the authority of the Secretary under this section to compile statistics from insurers.

(Added Pub. L. 100–424, §4(a), Sept. 9, 1988, 102 Stat. 1590.)

CHAPTER 63—INVESTIGATING MARINE CASUALTIES

§6301. INVESTIGATION OF MARINE CASUALTIES

The Secretary shall prescribe regulations for the immediate investigation of marine casualties under this part to decide, as closely as possible—

(1) the cause of the casualty, including the cause of any death;

(2) whether an act of misconduct, incompetence, negligence, unskillfulness, or willful violation of law committed by any individual licensed, certificated, or documented under part E of this subtitle has contributed to the cause of the casualty, or to a death involved in the casualty, so that appropriate remedial action under chapter 77 of this title may be taken;

(3) whether an act of misconduct, incompetence, negligence, unskillfulness, or willful violation of law committed by any person, including an officer, employee, or member of the Coast Guard, contributed to the cause of the casualty, or to a death involved in the casualty;

(4) whether there is evidence that an act subjecting the offender to a civil penalty under the laws of the United States has been committed, so that appropriate action may be undertaken to collect the penalty;

(5) whether there is evidence that a criminal act under the laws of the United States has been committed, so that the matter may be referred to appropriate authorities for prosecution; and

(6) whether there is need for new laws or regulations, or amendment or repeal of existing laws or regulations, to prevent the recurrence of the casualty.

(Pub. L. 98–89, Aug. 26, 1983, 97 Stat. 537.)

§6302. PUBLIC INVESTIGATIONS

Each investigation conducted under this chapter and regulations prescribed under this chapter shall be open to the public, except when evidence affecting the national security is to be received.

(Pub. L. 98–89, Aug. 26, 1983, 97 Stat. 537.)

§6303. RIGHTS OF PARTIES IN INTEREST

In an investigation conducted under this chapter, the following shall be allowed to be represented by counsel, to cross-examine witnesses, and to call witnesses:

(1) an owner,

(2) any holder of a license or certificate of registry,

(3) any holder of a merchant mariner's document,

(4) any other person whose conduct is under investigation, and

(5) any other party in interest.

(Pub. L. 98–89, Aug. 26, 1983, 97 Stat. 537.)

§6304. SUBPOENA AUTHORITY

(a) In an investigation under this chapter, the attendance and testimony of witnesses, including parties in interest, and the production of any evidence may be compelled by subpoena. The subpoena authority granted by this section is coextensive with that of a district court of the United States, in civil matters, for the district in which the investigation is conducted.

(b) When a person fails to obey a subpoena issued under this section, the district court of the United States for the district in which the investigation is conducted or in which the person failing to obey is found, shall on proper application issue an order directing that person to comply with the subpoena. The court may punish as contempt any disobedience of its order.

(c) A witness complying with a subpoena issued under this section may be paid for actual travel and attendance at the rate provided for witnesses in the district courts of the United States.

(d) An official designated to conduct an investigation under this part may issue subpoenas as provided in this section and administer oaths to witnesses.

(Pub. L. 98–89, Aug. 26, 1983, 97 Stat. 538; Pub. L. 117–263, div. K, title CXVIII, §11807(a), Dec. 23, 2022, 136 Stat. 4165.)

§6305. REPORTS OF INVESTIGATIONS

(a) The Secretary shall prescribe regulations about the form and manner of reports of investigations conducted under this part.

(b) Reports of investigations conducted under this part shall be made available to the public. This subsection does not require the release of information described by section 552(b) of title 5 or protected from disclosure by another law of the United States.

(Pub. L. 98–89, Aug. 26, 1983, 97 Stat. 538; Pub. L. 105–383, title III, §305, Nov. 13, 1998, 112 Stat. 3420.)

§6306. PENALTY

A person attempting to coerce a witness, or to induce a witness, to testify falsely in connection with a marine casualty, or to induce a witness to leave the jurisdiction of the United States, shall be fined $5,000, imprisoned for one year, or both.

(Pub. L. 98–89, Aug. 26, 1983, 97 Stat. 538.)

§6307. NOTIFICATIONS TO CONGRESS

(a) The Secretary shall notify the Committee on Commerce, Science, and Transportation of the Senate and the Committee on Transportation and Infrastructure of the House of Representatives of any hearing, before the hearing occurs, investigating a major marine casualty involving a death under section 6301 of this title.

(b) The Secretary shall submit to a committee referred to in subsection (a) of this section information on a major marine casualty that is requested by that committee or the chairman of the committee if the submission of that information is not prohibited by a law of the United States.

(c) The Secretary shall submit annually to Congress a summary of the marine casualties reported during the prior fiscal year, together with a brief statement of action taken concerning those casualties.

(Pub. L. 98–89, Aug. 26, 1983, 97 Stat. 538; Pub. L. 107–295, title IV, §408(c)(1), Nov. 25, 2002, 116 Stat. 2117.)

§6308. INFORMATION BARRED IN LEGAL PROCEEDINGS

(a) Notwithstanding any other provision of law, no part of a report of a marine casualty investigation conducted under section 6301 of this title, including findings of fact, opinions, recommendations, deliberations, or conclusions, shall be admissible as evidence or subject to discovery in any civil or administrative proceedings, other than an administrative proceeding initiated by the United States.

(b) Any member or employee of the Coast Guard investigating a marine casualty pursuant to section 6301 of this title shall not be subject to deposition or other discovery, or otherwise testify in such proceedings relevant to a marine casualty investigation, without the permission of the Secretary. The Secretary shall not withhold permission for such employee or member to testify, either orally or upon written questions, on solely factual matters at a time and place and in a manner acceptable to the Secretary if the information is not available elsewhere or is not obtainable by other means.

(c) Nothing in this section prohibits the United States from calling the employee or member as an expert witness to testify on its behalf. Further, nothing in this section prohibits the employee or member from being called as a fact witness in any case in which the United States is a party. If the employee or member is called as an expert or fact witness, the applicable Federal Rules of Civil Procedure govern discovery. If the employee or member is called as a witness, the report of a marine casualty investigation conducted under section 6301 of this title shall not be admissible, as provided in subsections (a) and (b), and shall not be considered the report of an expert under the Federal Rules of Civil Procedure.

(d) The information referred to in subsections (a), (b), and (c) of this section shall not be considered an admission of liability by the United States or by any person referred to in those conclusions and statements.

(Added Pub. L. 104–324, title III, §313(a), Oct. 19, 1996, 110 Stat. 3921; amended Pub. L. 109–241, title IX, §902(e)(2), formerly §902(e)(2)–(4), July 11, 2006, 120 Stat. 567, renumbered §902(e)(2) and amended Pub. L. 111–281, title IX, §903(a)(5)(B)–(7), Oct. 15, 2010, 124 Stat. 3010.)

§6309. VOYAGE DATA RECORDER ACCESS

Notwithstanding any other provision of law, the Coast Guard shall have full, concurrent, and timely access to and ability to use voyage data recorder data and audio held by any Federal agency in all marine casualty investigations, regardless of which agency is the investigative lead.

(Added Pub. L. 115–265, title II, §207(a), Oct. 11, 2018, 132 Stat. 3747.)

PART E—MERCHANT SEAMEN LICENSES, CERTIFICATES, AND DOCUMENTS

CHAPTER 71—LICENSES AND CERTIFICATES OF REGISTRY

Sec.

§7101. ISSUING AND CLASSIFYING LICENSES AND CERTIFICATES OF REGISTRY

(a) Licenses and certificates of registry are established for individuals who are required to hold licenses or certificates under this subtitle.

(b) Under regulations prescribed by the Secretary, the Secretary—

(1) issues the licenses and certificates of registry; and

(2) may classify the licenses and certificates of registry as provided in subsections (c) and (f) of this section, based on—

(A) the tonnage, means of propulsion, and horsepower of machine-propelled vessels;

(B) the waters on which vessels are to be operated; or

(C) other reasonable standards.

(c) The Secretary may issue licenses in the following classes to applicants found qualified as to age, character, habits of life, experience, professional qualifications, and physical fitness:

(1) masters, mates, and engineers.

(2) pilots.

(3) operators.

(4) radio officers.

(d) In classifying individuals under subsection (c)(1) of this section, the Secretary shall establish, when possible, suitable career patterns and service and other qualifying requirements appropriate to the particular service or industry in which the individuals are engaged.

(e) An individual may be issued a license under subsection (c)(2) of this section only if the applicant—

(1) is at least 21 years of age;

(2) is of sound health and has no physical limitations that would hinder or prevent the performance of a pilot's duties;

(3) has a thorough physical examination each year while holding the license, except that this requirement does not apply to an individual who will serve as a pilot only on a vessel of less than 1,600 gross tons as measured under section 14502 of this title, or an alternate tonnage measured under section 14302 of this title as prescribed by the Secretary under section 14104 of this title;

(4) demonstrates, to the satisfaction of the Secretary, that the applicant has the requisite general knowledge and skill to hold the license;

(5) demonstrates proficiency in the use of electronic aids to navigation;

(6) maintains adequate knowledge of the waters to be navigated and knowledge of regulations for the prevention of collisions in those waters;

(7) has sufficient experience, as decided by the Secretary, to evidence ability to handle any vessel of the type and size which the applicant may be authorized to pilot; and

(8) meets any other requirement the Secretary considers reasonable and necessary.

(f) The Secretary may issue certificates of registry in the following classes to applicants found qualified as to character, knowledge, skill, and experience:

(1) pursers.

(2) medical doctors.

(3) professional nurses.

(g) The Secretary may not issue a license or certificate of registry under this section unless an individual applying for the license or certificate makes available to the Secretary, under section 206(b)(7) of the National Driver Register Act of 1982 (23 U.S.C. 401 note), any information contained in the National Driver Register related to an offense described in section 205(a)(3)(A) or (B) of that Act committed by the individual.

(h) The Secretary may review the criminal record of an individual who applies for a license or certificate of registry under this section.

(i) The Secretary shall require the testing of an individual who applies for issuance or renewal of a license or certificate of registry under this chapter for use of a dangerous drug in violation of law or Federal regulation.

(j) The Secretary may issue a license under this section in a class under subsection (c) to an applicant that—

(1) has at least 3 months of qualifying service on vessels of the uniformed services (as that term is defined in section 101(a) of title 10) of appropriate tonnage or horsepower within the 7-year period immediately preceding the date of application; and

(2) satisfies all other requirements for such a license.

(Pub. L. 98–89, Aug. 26, 1983, 97 Stat. 539; Pub. L. 98–557, §29(a), Oct. 30, 1984, 98 Stat. 2873; Pub. L. 101–380, title IV, §4101(a), Aug. 18, 1990, 104 Stat. 509; Pub. L. 104–324, title VII, §720, Oct. 19, 1996,

110 Stat. 3938; Pub. L. 113–281, title III, §305(a), Dec. 18, 2014, 128 Stat. 3043.)

§7102. CITIZENSHIP

Licenses and certificates of registry for individuals on documented vessels may be issued only to citizens of the United States.

(Pub. L. 98–89, Aug. 26, 1983, 97 Stat. 540.)

§7103. LICENSES FOR RADIO OFFICERS

(a) A license as radio officer may be issued only to an applicant who has a first-class or second-class radiotelegraph operator license issued by the Federal Communications Commission.

(b) Except as provided in section 7318 of this title, this part does not affect the status of radiotelegraph operators serving on board vessels operating only on the Great Lakes.

(Pub. L. 98–89, Aug. 26, 1983, 97 Stat. 540.)

§7104. CERTIFICATES FOR MEDICAL DOCTORS AND NURSES

A certificate of registry as a medical doctor or professional nurse may be issued only to an applicant who has a license as a medical doctor or registered nurse, respectively, issued by a State.

(Pub. L. 98–89, Aug. 26, 1983, 97 Stat. 540.)

§7105. OATHS

An applicant for a license or certificate of registry shall take, before the issuance of the license or certificate, an oath, without concealment or reservation, that the applicant will perform faithfully and honestly, according to the best skill and judgment of the applicant, all the duties required by law.

(Pub. L. 98–89, Aug. 26, 1983, 97 Stat. 540; Pub. L. 111–281, title VI, §613, Oct. 15, 2010, 124 Stat. 2970.)

§7106. DURATION OF LICENSES

(a) IN GENERAL.—A license issued under this part is valid for a 5-year period and may be renewed for additional 5-year periods; except that the validity of a license issued to a radio officer is conditioned on the continuous possession by the holder of a first-class or second-class radiotelegraph operator license issued by the Federal Communications Commission.

(b) ADVANCE RENEWALS.—A renewed license issued under this part may be issued up to 8 months in advance but is not effective until the date that the previously issued license expires or until the completion of any active suspension or revocation of that previously issued license, whichever is later.

(Pub. L. 98–89, Aug. 26, 1983, 97 Stat. 540; Pub. L. 101–380, title IV, §4102(a), Aug. 18, 1990, 104 Stat. 509; Pub. L. 111–281, title VI, §614(b), Oct. 15, 2010, 124 Stat. 2970; Pub. L. 115–282, title V, §510(1), Dec. 4, 2018, 132 Stat. 4274.)

§7107. DURATION OF CERTIFICATES OF REGISTRY

(a) IN GENERAL.—A certificate of registry issued under this part is valid for a 5-year period and may be renewed for additional 5-year periods; except that the validity of a certificate issued to a medical doctor or professional nurse is conditioned on the continuous possession by the holder of a license as a medical doctor or registered nurse, respectively, issued by a State.

(b) ADVANCE RENEWALS.—A renewed certificate of registry issued under this part may be issued up to 8 months in advance but is not effective until the date that the previously issued certificate of registry expires or until the completion of any active suspension or revocation of that previously issued certificate of registry, whichever is later.

(Pub. L. 98–89, Aug. 26, 1983, 97 Stat. 540; Pub. L. 101–380, title IV, §4102(b), Aug. 18, 1990, 104 Stat. 509; Pub. L. 111–281, title VI, §614(c), Oct. 15, 2010, 124 Stat. 2971; Pub. L. 115–282, title V, §510(2), Dec. 4, 2018, 132 Stat. 4274.)

§7108. TERMINATION OF LICENSES AND CERTIFICATES OF REGISTRY

When the holder of a license or certificate of registry, the duration of which is conditioned under section 7106 or 7107 of this title, fails to hold the license required as a condition, the license or certificate of registry issued under this part is terminated.

(Pub. L. 98–89, Aug. 26, 1983, 97 Stat. 540.)

§7109. REVIEW OF CRIMINAL RECORDS

The Secretary may review the criminal record of each holder of a license or certificate of registry issued under this part who applies for renewal of that license or certificate of registry.

(Pub. L. 98–89, Aug. 26, 1983, 97 Stat. 540; Pub. L. 101–380, title IV, §4102(e)(1), Aug. 18, 1990, 104 Stat. 510.)

§7110. EXHIBITING LICENSES

Each holder of a license issued under this part shall display, within 48 hours after employment on a vessel for which that license is required, the license in a conspicuous place on the vessel.

(Pub. L. 98–89, Aug. 26, 1983, 97 Stat. 541.)

§7111. ORAL EXAMINATIONS FOR LICENSES

An individual may take an oral examination for a license to serve on a fishing, fish processing, or fish tender vessel not required to be inspected under part B of this subtitle.

(Pub. L. 98–89, Aug. 26, 1983, 97 Stat. 541; Pub. L. 98–364, title IV, §402(8)(B), July 17, 1984, 98 Stat. 447; Pub. L. 99–307, §1(10), May 19, 1986, 100 Stat. 445.)

§7112. LICENSES OF MASTERS OR MATES AS PILOTS

A master or mate licensed under this part who also qualifies as a pilot is not required to hold 2 licenses. Instead, the qualification of the master or mate as pilot shall be endorsed on the master's or mate's license.

(Pub. L. 98–89, Aug. 26, 1983, 97 Stat. 541.)

§7113. EXEMPTION FROM DRAFT

A licensed master, mate, pilot, or engineer of a vessel inspected under part B of this subtitle, propelled by machinery or carrying hazardous liquid cargoes in bulk, is not liable to draft in time of war, except for performing duties authorized by the license. When performing those duties in the service of the United States Government, the master, mate, pilot, or engineer is entitled to the highest rate of wages paid in the merchant marine of the United States for similar services. If killed or wounded when performing those duties, the master, mate, pilot, or engineer, or the heirs or legal representatives of the master, mate, pilot, or engineer, are entitled to all the privileges under the pension laws of the United States provided to members of the Armed Forces.

(Pub. L. 98–89, Aug. 26, 1983, 97 Stat. 541.)

§7114. Fees

The Secretary may prescribe by regulation reasonable fees for the inspection of and the issuance of a certificate, license, or permit related to small passenger vessels and sailing school vessels.

(Pub. L. 98–89, Aug. 26, 1983, 97 Stat. 541.)

[§7115. Repealed. Pub. L. 115–282, title VI, §601(c)(2), Dec. 4, 2018, 132 Stat. 4289]

Section, added Pub. L. 111–281, title II, §210(a), Oct. 15, 2010, 124 Stat. 2913, established the Merchant Mariner Medical Advisory Committee. See section 15104 of this title.

§7116. Examinations for merchant mariner credentials

(a) Requirement for Sample Exams.—The Secretary shall develop a sample merchant mariner credential examination and outline of merchant mariner examination topics on an annual basis.

(b) Public Availability.—Each sample examination and outline of topics developed under subsection (a) shall be readily available to the public.

(c) Merchant Mariner Credential Defined.—In this section, the term "merchant mariner credential" has the meaning that term has in section 7510.

(Added Pub. L. 114–120, title III, §315(b)(1), Feb. 8, 2016, 130 Stat. 62.)

CHAPTER 73—MERCHANT MARINERS' DOCUMENTS

§7301. GENERAL

(a) In this chapter—

(1) "service on deck" means service in the deck department in work related to the work usually performed on board vessels by able seamen and may include service on fishing, fish processing, fish tender vessels and on public vessels of the United States;

(2) 360 days is equal to one year's service; and

(3) a day is equal to 8 hours of labor or duty.

(b) The Secretary may prescribe regulations to carry out this chapter.

(Pub. L. 98–89, Aug. 26, 1983, 97 Stat. 541; Pub. L. 98–364, title IV, §402(9)(B), July 17, 1984, 98 Stat. 448.)

§7302. ISSUING MERCHANT MARINERS' DOCUMENTS AND CONTINUOUS DISCHARGE BOOKS

(a) The Secretary shall issue a merchant mariner's document to an individual required to have that document under part F of this subtitle if the individual satisfies the requirements of this part. The document serves as a certificate of identification and as a certificate of service, specifying each rating in which the holder is qualified to serve on board vessels on which that document is required under part F.

(b) The Secretary also may issue a continuous discharge book to an individual issued a merchant mariner's document if the individual requests.

(c) The Secretary may not issue a merchant mariner's document under this chapter unless the individual applying for the document makes available to the Secretary, under section 30305(b)(5) of title 49, any information contained in the National Driver Register related to an offense described in section 30304(a)(3)(A) or (B) of title 49 committed by the individual.

(d) The Secretary may review the criminal record of an individual who applies for a merchant mariner's document under this section.

(e) The Secretary shall require the testing of an individual applying for issuance or renewal of a merchant mariner's document under this chapter for the use of a dangerous drug in violation of law or Federal regulation.

(f) PERIODS OF VALIDITY AND RENEWAL OF MERCHANT MARINERS' DOCUMENTS.—

(1) IN GENERAL.—Except as provided in subsection (g), a merchant mariner's

document issued under this chapter is valid for a 5-year period and may be renewed for additional 5-year periods.

(2) ADVANCE RENEWALS.—A renewed merchant mariner's document may be issued under this chapter up to 8 months in advance but is not effective until the date that the previously issued merchant mariner's document expires or until the completion of any active suspension or revocation of that previously issued merchant mariner's document, whichever is later.

(g)(1) The Secretary may, pending receipt and review of information required under subsections (c) and (d), immediately issue an interim merchant mariner's document valid for a period not to exceed 120 days, to—

(A) an individual to be employed as gaming personnel, entertainment personnel, wait staff, or other service personnel on board a passenger vessel not engaged in foreign service, with no duties, including emergency duties, related to the navigation of the vessel or the safety of the vessel, its crew, cargo or passengers; or

(B) an individual seeking renewal of, or qualifying for a supplemental endorsement to, a valid merchant mariner's document issued under this section.

(2) No more than one interim document may be issued to an individual under paragraph (1)(A) of this subsection.

(Pub. L. 98–89, Aug. 26, 1983, 97 Stat. 542; Pub. L. 101–380, title IV, §§4101(b), 4102(c), Aug. 18, 1990, 104 Stat. 509; Pub. L. 107–295, title III, §324(a), Nov. 25, 2002, 116 Stat. 2104; Pub. L. 108–293, title VI, §609(1), Aug. 9, 2004, 118 Stat. 1058; Pub. L. 109–241, title IX, §901(h)(1), (2), July 11, 2006, 120 Stat. 564; Pub. L. 111–281, title VI, §614(a), Oct. 15, 2010, 124 Stat. 2970.)

§7303. POSSESSION AND DESCRIPTION OF MERCHANT MARINERS' DOCUMENTS

A merchant mariner's document shall be retained by the individual to whom issued. The document shall contain the signature, notations of nationality, age, and physical description, the photograph, and the home address of the individual. In addition, the document shall specify the rate or ratings in which the individual is qualified to serve.

(Pub. L. 98–89, Aug. 26, 1983, 97 Stat. 542; Pub. L. 107–295, title IV, §421, Nov. 25, 2002, 116 Stat. 2125; Pub. L. 116–283, div. G, title LVXXXV [LXXXV], §8505(b)(3), Jan. 1, 2021, 134 Stat. 4751.)

§7304. CITIZENSHIP NOTATION ON MERCHANT MARINERS' DOCUMENTS

An individual applying for a merchant mariner's document shall provide satisfactory proof that the individual is a citizen of the United States before that notation is made on the document.

(Pub. L. 98–89, Aug. 26, 1983, 97 Stat. 542.)

§7305. OATHS FOR HOLDERS OF MERCHANT MARINERS' DOCUMENTS

An applicant for a merchant mariner's document shall take, before issuance of the document, an oath that the applicant will perform faithfully and honestly all the duties required by law, and will carry out the lawful orders of superior officers.

(Pub. L. 98–89, Aug. 26, 1983, 97 Stat. 542.)

§7306. GENERAL REQUIREMENTS AND CLASSIFICATIONS FOR ABLE SEAMEN

(a) To qualify for an endorsement as able seaman authorized by this section, an applicant must provide satisfactory proof that the applicant—

(1) is at least 18 years of age;

(2) has the service required by the applicable section of this part;

(3) is qualified professionally as demonstrated by an applicable examination or educational requirements; and

(4) is qualified as to sight, hearing, and physical condition to perform the seaman's duties.

(b) The classifications authorized for endorsement as able seaman are the following:

(1) able seaman—unlimited.

(2) able seaman—limited.

(3) able seaman—special.

(4) able seaman—offshore supply vessels.

(5) able seaman—sail.

(6) able seaman—fishing industry.

(Pub. L. 98–89, Aug. 26, 1983, 97 Stat. 542; Pub. L. 98–364, title IV, §402(9)(C), July 17, 1984, 98 Stat. 448.)

§7307. ABLE SEAMEN—UNLIMITED

The required service for the endorsement of able seaman—unlimited, qualified for unlimited service on a vessel on any waters, is at least 3 years'[1] service on deck on board vessels operating at sea or on the Great Lakes.

(Pub. L. 98–89, Aug. 26, 1983, 97 Stat. 543.)

[1] *See Temporary Reduction of Lengths of Certain Periods of Service note below.*

§7308. ABLE SEAMEN—LIMITED

The required service for the endorsement of able seaman—limited, qualified for limited service on a vessel on any waters, is at least 18 months'[1] service on deck on board vessels of at least 100 gross tons as measured under section 14502 of this title, or an alternate tonnage measured under section 14302 of this title as prescribed by the Secretary under section 14104 of this title operating on the oceans or navigable waters of the United States (including the Great Lakes).

(Pub. L. 98–89, Aug. 26, 1983, 97 Stat. 543; Pub. L. 104–324, title VII, §721, Oct. 19, 1996, 110 Stat. 3938.)

[1] *See Temporary Reduction of Lengths of Certain Periods of Service note below.*

§7309. ABLE SEAMEN—SPECIAL

The required service for the endorsement of able seaman—special, qualified for special service on a vessel on any waters, is at least 12 months'[1] service on deck on board vessels operating on the oceans or the navigable waters of the United States (including the Great Lakes).

(Pub. L. 98–89, Aug. 26, 1983, 97 Stat. 543.)

1 See Temporary Reduction of Lengths of Certain Periods of Service note below.

§7310. ABLE SEAMEN—OFFSHORE SUPPLY VESSELS

For service on a vessel of less than 500 gross tons as measured under section 14502 of this title, or an alternate tonnage measured under section 14302 of this title as prescribed by the Secretary under section 14104 of this title engaged in support of exploration, exploitation, or production of offshore mineral or energy resources, an individual may be rated as able seaman—offshore supply vessels if the individual has at least 6 months' service on deck on board vessels operating on the oceans or the navigable waters of the United States (including the Great Lakes).

(Pub. L. 98–89, Aug. 26, 1983, 97 Stat. 543; Pub. L. 104–324, title VII, §722, Oct. 19, 1996, 110 Stat. 3938.)

§7311. ABLE SEAMEN—SAIL

For service on a sailing school vessel on any waters, an individual may be rated as able seaman—sail if the individual has at least 6 months' service on deck on sailing school vessels, oceanographic research vessels powered primarily by sail, or equivalent sailing vessels operating on the oceans or navigable waters of the United States (including the Great Lakes).

(Pub. L. 98–89, Aug. 26, 1983, 97 Stat. 543.)

§7311A. ABLE SEAMEN—FISHING INDUSTRY

For service on a fish processing vessel, an individual may be rated as able seaman—fishing industry if the individual has at least 6 months' service on deck on board vessels operating on the oceans or the navigable waters of the United States (including the Great Lakes).

(Added Pub. L. 98–364, title IV, §402(9)(D), July 17, 1984, 98 Stat. 448.)

§7312. SCALE OF EMPLOYMENT

(a) Individuals qualified as able seamen—unlimited under section 7307 of this title may constitute all of the able seamen required on a vessel.

(b) Individuals qualified as able seamen—limited under section 7308 of this title may constitute all of the able seamen required on a vessel of less than 1,600 gross tons as measured under section 14502 of this title, or an alternate tonnage measured under section 14302 of this title as prescribed by the Secretary under section 14104 of this title or on a vessel operating on the Great Lakes and the Saint Lawrence River as far east as Sept Iles. Individuals qualified as able seamen—limited may constitute not more than 50 percent of the number of able seamen required on board other vessels.

(c) Individuals qualified as able seamen—special under section 7309 of this title may constitute—

(1) all of the able seamen required on a vessel of not more than 500 gross tons as measured under section 14502 of this title, or an alternate tonnage measured under section 14302 of this title as prescribed by the Secretary under section 14104 of this title

or on a seagoing barge or towing vessel; and

(2) not more than 50 percent of the number of able seamen required on board other vessels.

(d) Individuals qualified as able seamen—offshore. supply vessel under section 7310 of this title may constitute all of the able seamen required on board a vessel of less than 500 gross tons as measured under section 14502 of this title or 6,000 gross tons as measured under section 14302 of this title engaged in support of exploration, exploitation, or production of offshore mineral or energy resources. Individuals qualified as able seamen—limited under section 7308 of this title may constitute all of the able seamen required on board a vessel of at least 500 gross tons as measured under section 14502 of this title or 6,000 gross tons as measured under section as measured under section 14302 of this title as prescribed by the Secretary under section 14104 of this title engaged in support of exploration, exploitation, or production of offshore mineral or energy resources.

(e) When the service of able seamen—limited or able seamen—special is authorized for only a part of the required number of able seamen on board a vessel, the combined percentage of those individuals so qualified may not be greater than 50 percent of the required number.

(f) Individuals qualified as able seamen—fishing industry under section 7311a of this title may constitute—

(1) all of the able seamen required on a fish processing vessel entered into service before January 1, 1988, and of more than 1,600 gross tons but not more than 5,000 gross tons as measured under section 14502 of this title, or an alternate tonnage measured under section 14302 of this title as prescribed by the Secretary under section 14104 of this title; and

(2) all of the able seamen required on a fish processing vessel entered into service after December 31, 1987, and having more than 16 individuals on board primarily employed in the preparation of fish or fish products but of not more than 5,000 gross tons as measured under section 14502 of this title, or an alternate tonnage measured under section 14302 of this title as prescribed by the Secretary under section 14104 of this title.

(Pub. L. 98–89, Aug. 26, 1983, 97 Stat. 543; Pub. L. 98–364, title IV, §402(9)(E), July 17, 1984, 98 Stat. 448; Pub. L. 99–307, §1(11), May 19, 1986, 100 Stat. 445; Pub. L. 104–324, title VII, §723, Oct. 19, 1996, 110 Stat. 3938; Pub. L. 111–281, title VI, §617(b), Oct. 15, 2010, 124 Stat. 2973.)

§7313. GENERAL REQUIREMENTS FOR MEMBERS OF ENGINE DEPARTMENTS

(a) Classes of endorsement as qualified members of the engine department on vessels of at least 100 gross tons as measured under section 14502 of this title, or an alternate tonnage measured under section 14302 of this title as prescribed by the Secretary under section 14104 of this title (except vessels operating on rivers or lakes (except the Great Lakes)) may be prescribed by regulation.

(b) The ratings of wiper and coal passer are entry ratings and are not ratings as qualified members of the engine department.

(c) An applicant for an endorsement as qualified member of the engine department must provide satisfactory proof that the applicant—

(1) has the service required by section 7314 of this title;

(2) is qualified professionally as demonstrated by an applicable examination; and

(3) is qualified as to sight, hearing, and physical condition to perform the member's duties.

(Pub. L. 98–89, Aug. 26, 1983, 97 Stat. 544; Pub. L. 104–324, title VII, §724, Oct. 19, 1996, 110 Stat. 3939.)

§7314. SERVICE REQUIREMENTS FOR QUALIFIED MEMBERS OF ENGINE DEPARTMENTS

To qualify for an endorsement as qualified member of the engine department, an applicant must provide proof that the applicant has 6 months' service in the related entry rating as described in section 7313(b) of this title.

(Pub. L. 98–89, Aug. 26, 1983, 97 Stat. 544.)

§7315. TRAINING

(a) Graduation from a nautical school vessel approved under law and regulation may be substituted for the service requirements under section 7307 or 7314 of this title.

(b) The satisfactory completion of other courses of instruction approved by the Secretary may be substituted for not more than one-third of the required service on deck at sea under sections 7307–7311 of this title.

(c) The satisfactory completion of other courses of instruction approved by the Secretary may be substituted for not more than one-half of the required service at sea under section 7314 of this title.

(Pub. L. 98–89, Aug. 26, 1983, 97 Stat. 544.)

§7316. LIFEBOATMEN

To qualify for an endorsement as lifeboatman, an applicant must provide satisfactory proof that the applicant—

(1) has the service or training required by regulation;

(2) is qualified professionally as demonstrated by examination; and

(3) is qualified professionally by actual demonstration.

(Pub. L. 98–89, Aug. 26, 1983, 97 Stat. 544.)

§7317. TANKERMEN

(a) The Secretary shall prescribe procedures, standards, and qualifications for the issuance of certificates or endorsements as tankerman, stating the types of oil or hazardous material that can be handled with safety to the vessel and the marine environment.

(b) An endorsement as tankerman shall indicate the grades or types of cargo the holder is qualified and authorized to handle with safety on board vessels.

(Pub. L. 98–89, Aug. 26, 1983, 97 Stat. 545.)

§7318. RADIOTELEGRAPH OPERATORS ON GREAT LAKES

(a) A radiotelegraph operator on the Great Lakes only shall have a first-class or second-class radiotelegraph operator's license issued by the Federal Communications Commission.

(b) An endorsement as radiotelegraph operator on the Great Lakes only ends if the holder ceases to hold the license issued by the Commission.

(Pub. L. 98–89, Aug. 26, 1983, 97 Stat. 545.)

§7319. RECORDS OF MERCHANT MARINERS' DOCUMENTS

The Secretary shall maintain records on each merchant mariner's document issued, including the name and address of the individual to whom issued and the next of kin of the individual.

(Pub. L. 98–89, Aug. 26, 1983, 97 Stat. 545; Pub. L. 108–293, title IV, §403, Aug. 9, 2004, 118 Stat. 1043; Pub. L. 116–283, div. G, title LVXXXV [LXXXV], §8505(b)(4), Jan. 1, 2021, 134 Stat. 4751.)

CHAPTER 75—GENERAL PROCEDURES FOR LICENSING, CERTIFICATION, AND DOCUMENTATION

§7501. DUPLICATES

(a) If a license, certificate of registry, or merchant mariner's document issued under this part is lost as a result of a marine casualty, the holder shall be supplied with a duplicate without cost.

(b) For any other loss, the holder may obtain a duplicate on payment of reasonable costs prescribed by regulation by the Secretary.

(Pub. L. 98–89, Aug. 26, 1983, 97 Stat. 545; Pub. L. 99–36, §1(a)(9)(C), May 15, 1985, 99 Stat. 68; Pub. L. 116–283, div. G, title LVXXXV [LXXXV], §8505(b)(5), Jan. 1, 2021, 134 Stat. 4751.)

§7502. RECORDS

(a) The Secretary shall maintain records, including electronic records, on the issuances, denials, suspensions, and revocations of licenses, certificates of registry, merchant mariners' documents, and endorsements on those licenses, certificates, and documents.

(b) The Secretary may prescribe regulations requiring a vessel owner or managing operator of a commercial vessel, or the employer of a seaman on that vessel, to maintain records of each individual engaged on the vessel subject to inspection under chapter 33 on matters of engagement, discharge, and service for not less than 5 years after the date of the completion of the service of that individual on the vessel. The regulations may require that a vessel owner, managing operator, or employer shall make these records available to the individual and the Coast Guard on request.

(c) A person violating this section, or a regulation prescribed under this section, is liable to the United States Government for a civil penalty of not more than $5,000.

(Pub. L. 98–89, Aug. 26, 1983, 97 Stat. 545; Pub. L. 101–380, title IV, §4114(e), Aug. 18, 1990, 104 Stat. 517; Pub. L. 111–281, title VI, §605, Oct. 15, 2010, 124 Stat. 2967.)

§7503. DANGEROUS DRUGS AS GROUNDS FOR DENIAL

A license, certificate of registry, or merchant mariner's document authorized to be issued under this part may be denied to an individual who—

(1) within 10 years before applying for the license, certificate, or document, has been convicted of violating a dangerous drug law of the United States or of a State; or

(2) when applying, has ever been a user of, or addicted to, a dangerous drug unless the individual provides satisfactory proof that the individual is cured.

(Pub. L. 98–89, Aug. 26, 1983, 97 Stat. 545; Pub. L. 99–36, §1(a)(9)(D), May 15, 1985, 99 Stat. 68; Pub. L. 101–380, title IV, §4103(a)(2)(B), Aug. 18, 1990, 104 Stat. 511; Pub. L. 115–232, div. C, title XXXV, §3545(a), Aug. 13, 2018, 132 Stat. 2326.)

§7504. TRAVEL AND EXPENSE REIMBURSEMENT

When a requirement to qualify for the issuance of, or endorsement on, a certificate, license, or document under this part is administered at a place at the request of an applicant or an applicant's representative, the applicant or representative may reimburse the Secretary for the travel and subsistence expenses incurred by the personnel assigned to perform the administration of the requirement. Amounts received as reimbursement under this section shall be credited to the appropriation for operations and support of the Coast Guard.

(Added Pub. L. 99–640, §10(b)(2)(A), Nov. 10, 1986, 100 Stat. 3549; amended Pub. L. 116–283, div. G, title LVXXXV [LXXXV], §8513(b), Jan. 1, 2021, 134 Stat. 4761.)

§7505. REVIEW OF INFORMATION IN NATIONAL DRIVER REGISTER

The Secretary shall make information received from the National Driver Register under section 30305(b)(7) of title 49 available to an individual for review and written comment before denying, suspending, revoking, or taking any other action relating to a license, certificate of registry, or merchant mariner's document authorized to be issued for that individual under this part, based on that information.

(Added Pub. L. 101–380, title IV, §4105(b)(1), Aug. 18, 1990, 104 Stat. 512; amended Pub. L. 115–232, div. C, title XXXV, §3546(e), Aug. 13, 2018, 132 Stat. 2326.)

§7506. CONVENTION TONNAGE FOR LICENSES, CERTIFICATES, AND DOCUMENTS

Notwithstanding any provision of section 14302(c) or 14305 of this title, the Secretary may—

(1) evaluate the service of an individual who is applying for a license, a certificate of registry, or a merchant mariner's document by using the tonnage as measured under chapter 143 of this title for the vessels on which that service was acquired, and

(2) issue the license, certificate, or document based on that service.

(Added Pub. L. 104–324, title VII, §745(a), Oct. 19, 1996, 110 Stat. 3942.)

§7507. AUTHORITY TO EXTEND THE DURATION OF LICENSES, CERTIFICATES OF REGISTRY, AND MERCHANT MARINER DOCUMENTS

(a) LICENSES AND CERTIFICATES OF REGISTRY.—Notwithstanding sections 7106 and 7107, the Secretary of the department in which the Coast Guard is operating may—

(1) extend for not more than one year an expiring license or certificate of registry issued for an individual under chapter 71 if the Secretary determines that the extension is required to enable the Coast Guard to eliminate a backlog in processing applications for those licenses or certificates of registry or in response to a national emergency or natural disaster, as deemed necessary by the Secretary; or

(2) issue for not more than five years an expiring license or certificate of registry issued for an individual under chapter 71 for the exclusive purpose of aligning the expiration date of such license or certificate of registry with the expiration date of a merchant mariner's document.

(b) MERCHANT MARINER DOCUMENTS.—Notwithstanding section 7302(g), the Secretary may—

(1) extend for not more than one year an expiring merchant mariner's document issued for an individual under chapter 73 if the Secretary determines that the extension is required to enable the Coast Guard to eliminate a backlog in processing applications for those merchant mariner documents or in response to a national emergency or natural disaster, as deemed necessary by the Secretary; or

(2) issue for not more than five years an expiring merchant mariner's document issued for an individual under chapter 73 for the exclusive purpose of aligning the expiration date of such merchant mariner's document with the expiration date of a license or certificate of registry.

(c) MANNER OF EXTENSION.—Any extensions granted under this section may be granted to individual seamen or a specifically identified group of seamen.

(Added Pub. L. 111–281, title VI, §615(a), Oct. 15, 2010, 124 Stat. 2971; amended Pub. L. 112–213, title III, §311, Dec. 20, 2012, 126 Stat. 1569; Pub. L. 115–282, title V, §510(3), (4), Dec. 4, 2018, 132 Stat. 4274.)

§7508. AUTHORITY TO EXTEND THE DURATION OF MEDICAL CERTIFICATES

(a) GRANTING OF EXTENSIONS.—Notwithstanding any other provision of law, the Secretary may extend for not more than one year a medical certificate issued to an individual holding a license, merchant mariner's document, or certificate of registry issued under chapter 71 or 73 if the Secretary determines that the extension is required to enable the Coast Guard to eliminate a backlog in processing applications for medical certificates or is in response to a national emergency or natural disaster.

(b) MANNER OF EXTENSION.—An extension under this section may be granted to an individual or a specifically identified group of individuals.

(Added Pub. L. 112–213, title III, §306(a), Dec. 20, 2012, 126 Stat. 1565; amended Pub. L. 116–283, div. G, title LVXXXV [LXXXV], §8505(b)(6), Jan. 1, 2021, 134 Stat. 4751.)

§7509. MEDICAL CERTIFICATION BY TRUSTED AGENTS

(a) IN GENERAL.—Notwithstanding any other provision of law and pursuant to regulations prescribed by the Secretary, a trusted agent may issue a medical certificate to an individual who—

(1) must hold such certificate to qualify for a license, certificate of registry, or merchant mariner's document, or endorsement thereto under this part; and

(2) is qualified as to sight, hearing, and physical condition to perform the duties of such license, certificate, document, or endorsement, as determined by the trusted agent.

(b) PROCESS FOR ISSUANCE OF CERTIFICATES BY SECRETARY.—A final rule implementing this section shall include a process for—

(1) the Secretary of the department in which the Coast Guard is operating to issue medical certificates to mariners who submit applications for such certificates to the Secretary; and

(2) a trusted agent to defer to the Secretary the issuance of a medical certificate.

(c) TRUSTED AGENT DEFINED.—In this section the term "trusted agent" means a medical practitioner certified by the Secretary to perform physical examinations of an individual for purposes of a license, certificate of registry, or merchant mariner's document under this part.

(Added Pub. L. 114–120, title III, §309(a), Feb. 8, 2016, 130 Stat. 56.)

§7510. EXAMINATIONS FOR MERCHANT MARINER CREDENTIALS

(a) DISCLOSURE NOT REQUIRED.—Notwithstanding any other provision of law, the Secretary is not required to disclose to the public—

(1) a question from any examination for a merchant mariner credential;

(2) the answer to such a question, including any correct or incorrect answer that may be presented with such question; and

(3) any quality or characteristic of such a question, including—

(A) the manner in which such question has been, is, or may be selected for an examination;

(B) the frequency of such selection; and

(C) the frequency that an examinee correctly or incorrectly answered such question.

(b) EXCEPTION FOR CERTAIN QUESTIONS.—Notwithstanding subsection (a), the Secretary may, for the purpose of preparation by the general public for examinations required for merchant mariner credentials, release an examination question and answer that the Secretary has retired or is not presently on or part of an examination, or that the Secretary determines is appropriate for release.

(c) EXAM REVIEW.—

(1) IN GENERAL.—Not later than 90 days after the date of the enactment of the Coast Guard Authorization Act of 2016, and once every two years thereafter, the Commandant shall commission a working group to review new questions for inclusion in examinations

required for merchant mariner credentials, composed of—

(A) 1 subject matter expert from the Coast Guard;

(B) representatives from training facilities and the maritime industry, of whom—

(i) one-half shall be representatives from approved training facilities; and

(ii) one-half shall be representatives from the appropriate maritime industry;

(C) at least 1 representative from the National Merchant Marine Personnel Advisory Committee;

(D) at least 2 representatives from the State maritime academies, of whom one shall be a representative from the deck training track and one shall be a representative of the engineer license track;

(E) representatives from other Coast Guard Federal advisory committees, as appropriate, for the industry segment associated with the subject examinations;

(F) at least 1 subject matter expert from the Maritime Administration; and

(G) at least 1 human performance technology representative.

(2) INCLUSION OF PERSONS KNOWLEDGEABLE ABOUT EXAMINATION TYPE.—The working group shall include representatives knowledgeable about the examination type under review.

(3) LIMITATION.—The requirement to convene a working group under paragraph (1) does not apply unless there are new examination questions to review.

(4) BASELINE REVIEW.—

(A) IN GENERAL.—Within 1 year after the date of the enactment of the Coast Guard Authorization Act of 2016, the Secretary shall convene the working group to complete a baseline review of the Coast Guard's Merchant Mariner Credentialing Examination, including review of—

(i) the accuracy of examination questions;

(ii) the accuracy and availability of examination references;

(iii) the length of merchant mariner examinations; and

(iv) the use of standard technologies in administering, scoring, and analyzing the examinations.

(B) PROGRESS REPORT.—The Coast Guard shall provide a progress report to the appropriate congressional committees on the review under this paragraph.

(5) FULL MEMBERSHIP NOT REQUIRED.—The Coast Guard may convene the working group without all members present if any non-Coast-Guard representative is present.

(6) NONDISCLOSURE AGREEMENT.—The Secretary shall require all members of the working group to sign a nondisclosure agreement with the Secretary.

(7) TREATMENT OF MEMBERS AS FEDERAL EMPLOYEES.—A member of the working group who is not a Federal Government employee shall not be considered a Federal employee in the service or the employment of the Federal Government, except that such a member shall be considered a special government employee, as defined in section 202(a) of title 18 for purposes of sections 203, 205, 207, 208, and 209 of such title and shall be subject to any administrative standards of conduct applicable to an employee of the department

in which the Coast Guard is operating.

(8) FORMAL EXAM REVIEW.—The Secretary shall ensure that the Coast Guard Performance Technology Center—

(A) prioritizes the review of examinations required for merchant mariner credentials; and

(B) not later than 3 years after the date of enactment of the Coast Guard Authorization Act of 2016, completes a formal review, including an appropriate analysis, of the topics and testing methodology employed by the National Maritime Center for merchant mariner licensing.

(9) CHAPTER 10 OF TITLE 5.—Chapter 10 of title 5 shall not apply to any working group created under this section to review the Coast Guard's merchant mariner credentialing examinations.

(d) MERCHANT MARINER CREDENTIAL DEFINED.—In this section, the term "merchant mariner credential" means a merchant mariner license, certificate, or document that the Secretary is authorized to issue pursuant to this title.

(Added Pub. L. 114–120, title III, §315(a)(1), Feb. 8, 2016, 130 Stat. 60; amended Pub. L. 114–328, div. C, title XXXV, §3503(a), (b)(1), Dec. 23, 2016, 130 Stat. 2775; Pub. L. 115–232, div. C, title XXXV, §3541(b)(12), Aug. 13, 2018, 132 Stat. 2323; Pub. L. 115–282, title VI, §601(c)(3)(B), Dec. 4, 2018, 132 Stat. 4289; Pub. L. 116–283, div. G, title LVXXXV [LXXXV], §8505(b)(7), Jan. 1, 2021, 134 Stat. 4751; Pub. L. 117–286, §4(a)(290), Dec. 27, 2022, 136 Stat. 4337.)

§7511. CONVICTED SEX OFFENDER AS GROUNDS FOR DENIAL

(a) SEXUAL ABUSE.—A license, certificate of registry, or merchant mariner's document authorized to be issued under this part shall be denied to an individual who has been convicted of a sexual offense prohibited under—

(1) chapter 109A of title 18, except for subsection (b) of section 2244 of title 18; or

(2) a substantially similar offense under State, local, or Tribal law.

(b) ABUSIVE SEXUAL CONTACT.—A license, certificate of registry, or merchant mariner's document authorized to be issued under this part may be denied to an individual who within 5 years before applying for the license, certificate, or document, has been convicted of a sexual offense prohibited under subsection (b) of section 2244 of title 18, or a substantially similar offense under State, local, or Tribal law.

(Added Pub. L. 117–263, div. K, title CXVI, §11602(a), Dec. 23, 2022, 136 Stat. 4147.)

CHAPTER 77—SUSPENSION AND REVOCATION

Sec.

§7701. GENERAL

(a) The purpose of suspension and revocation proceedings is to promote safety at sea.

(b) Licenses, certificates of registry, and merchant mariners' documents may be suspended or revoked for acts described in section 7703 of this title.

(c) When a license, certificate of registry, or merchant mariner's document has been revoked under this chapter, the former holder may be issued a new license, certificate of registry, or merchant mariner's document only after—

(1) the Secretary decides, under regulations prescribed by the Secretary, that the issuance is compatible with the requirement of good discipline and safety at sea; and

(2) the former holder provides satisfactory proof that the bases for revocation are no longer valid.

(d) The Secretary may prescribe regulations to carry out this chapter.

(Pub. L. 98–89, Aug. 26, 1983, 97 Stat. 546; Pub. L. 101–380, title IV, §4103(c), Aug. 18, 1990, 104 Stat. 511.)

§7702. ADMINISTRATIVE PROCEDURE

(a) Sections 551–559 of title 5 apply to each hearing under this chapter about suspending or revoking a license, certificate of registry, or merchant mariner's document.

(b) The individual whose license, certificate of registry, or merchant mariner's document has been suspended or revoked under this chapter may appeal, within 30 days, the suspension or revocation to the Secretary.

(c)(1) The Secretary shall request a holder of a license, certificate of registry, or merchant mariner's document to make available to the Secretary, under section 30305(b)(7) of title 49, all information contained in the National Driver Register related to an offense described in section 205(a)(3)(A) or (B) of that Act [1] committed by the individual.

(2) The Secretary shall require the testing of the holder of a license, certificate of registry, or merchant mariner's document for use of alcohol and dangerous drugs in violation of law or Federal regulation. The testing may include preemployment (with respect to dangerous drugs only), periodic, random, and reasonable cause testing, and shall include post-accident testing.

(d)(1) The Secretary may temporarily, for not more than 45 days, suspend and take possession of the license, certificate of registry, or merchant mariner's document held by an individual if—

(A) that individual performs a safety sensitive function on a vessel, as determined by the Secretary; and

(B) there is probable cause to believe that the individual—

(i) has, while acting under the authority of that license, certificate, or document, performed the safety sensitive function in violation of law or Federal regulation regarding use of alcohol or a dangerous drug;

(ii) has been convicted of an offense that would prevent the issuance or renewal of the license, certificate, or document;

(iii) within the 3-year period preceding the initiation of a suspension proceeding, has been convicted of an offense described in section 30304(a)(3)(A) or (B) of title 49; or

(iv) is a security risk that poses a threat to the safety or security of a vessel or a public or commercial structure located within or adjacent to the marine environment.

(2) If a license, certificate, or document is temporarily suspended under this section, an expedited hearing under subsection (a) of this section shall be held within 30 days after the temporary suspension.

(Pub. L. 98–89, Aug. 26, 1983, 97 Stat. 546; Pub. L. 99–36, §1(a)(3), May 15, 1985, 99 Stat. 67; Pub. L. 101–380, title IV, §4103(a)(1), Aug. 18, 1990, 104 Stat. 510; Pub. L. 105–383, title III, §304(a), Nov. 13, 1998, 112 Stat. 3419; Pub. L. 108–293, title IV, §407, title VI, §609(2), Aug. 9, 2004, 118 Stat. 1044, 1058; Pub. L. 115–232, div. C, title XXXV, §3546(f), Aug. 13, 2018, 132 Stat. 2326.)

[1] See References in Text note below.

§7703. BASES FOR SUSPENSION OR REVOCATION

A license, certificate of registry, or merchant mariner's document issued by the Secretary may be suspended or revoked if the holder—

(1) when acting under the authority of that license, certificate, or document—

(A) has violated or fails to comply with this subtitle, a regulation prescribed under this subtitle, or any other law or regulation intended to promote marine safety or to protect navigable waters; or

(B) has committed an act of misconduct or negligence;

(2) is convicted of an offense that would prevent the issuance or renewal of a license, certificate of registry, or merchant mariner's document;

(3) within the 3-year period preceding the initiation of the suspension or revocation proceeding is convicted of an offense described in section 30304(a)(3)(A) or (B) of title 49;

(4) has committed an act of incompetence relating to the operation of a vessel; or

(5) is a security risk that poses a threat to the safety or security of a vessel or a public or commercial structure located within or adjacent to the marine environment.

(Pub. L. 98–89, Aug. 26, 1983, 97 Stat. 546; Pub. L. 99–36, §1(a)(9)(E), May 15, 1985, 99 Stat. 68; Pub. L. 101–380, title IV, §4103(b), Aug. 18, 1990, 104 Stat. 511; Pub. L. 108–293, title IV, §408, title VI, §609(3), Aug. 9, 2004, 118 Stat. 1044, 1058; Pub. L. 109–241, title IX, §901(h)(3), July 11, 2006, 120 Stat. 564.)

§7704. DANGEROUS DRUGS AS GROUNDS FOR REVOCATION

(a) If it is shown at a hearing under this chapter that a holder of a license, certificate of registry, or merchant mariner's document issued under this part, within 10 years before the beginning of the proceedings, has been convicted of violating a dangerous drug law of the United States or of a State, the license, certificate, or document shall be suspended or revoked.

(b) If it is shown that a holder has been a user of, or addicted to, a dangerous drug, the license, certificate of registry, or merchant mariner's document shall be revoked unless the holder provides satisfactory proof that the holder is cured.

(Pub. L. 98–89, Aug. 26, 1983, 97 Stat. 546; Pub. L. 99–36, §1(a)(9)(F), (G), May 15, 1985, 99 Stat. 68; Pub. L. 101–380, title IV, §4103(a)(2)(B), Aug. 18, 1990, 104 Stat. 511; Pub. L. 108–293, title IV, §402, Aug. 9, 2004, 118 Stat. 1043; Pub. L. 115–232, div. C, title XXXV, §3545(b), Aug. 13, 2018, 132 Stat. 2326.)

§7704A. SEXUAL HARASSMENT OR SEXUAL ASSAULT AS GROUNDS FOR SUSPENSION OR REVOCATION

(a) SEXUAL HARASSMENT.—If it is shown at a hearing under this chapter that a holder of a license, certificate of registry, or merchant mariner's document issued under this part, within 5 years before the beginning of the suspension and revocation proceedings, is the subject of an official finding of sexual harassment, then the license, certificate of registry, or merchant mariner's document may be suspended or revoked.

(b) SEXUAL ASSAULT.—If it is shown at a hearing under this chapter that a holder of a license, certificate of registry, or merchant mariner's document issued under this part, within 10 years before the beginning of the suspension and revocation proceedings, is the subject of an official finding of sexual assault, then the license, certificate of registry, or merchant mariner's document shall be revoked.

(c) OFFICIAL FINDING.—

(1) IN GENERAL.—In this section, the term "official finding" means—

(A) a legal proceeding or agency finding or decision that determines the individual committed sexual harassment or sexual assault in violation of any Federal, State, local, or Tribal law or regulation; or

(B) a determination after an investigation by the Coast Guard that, by a preponderance of the evidence, the individual committed sexual harassment or sexual assault if the investigation affords appropriate due process rights to the subject of the investigation.

(2) ADMINISTRATIVE LAW JUDGE REVIEW.—

(A) COAST GUARD INVESTIGATION.—A determination under paragraph (1)(B) shall be reviewed and affirmed by an administrative law judge within the same proceeding as any suspension or revocation of a license, certificate of registry, or merchant mariner's document under subsection (a) or (b).

(B) LEGAL PROCEEDING.—A determination under paragraph (1)(A) that an individual committed sexual harassment or sexual assault is conclusive in suspension and revocation proceedings.

(Added Pub. L. 117–263, div. K, title CXVI, §11603(a), Dec. 23, 2022, 136 Stat. 4147.)

§7705. Subpenas and oaths

(a) An official designated to investigate or preside at a hearing on matters that are grounds for suspension or revocation of licenses, certificates of registry, and merchant mariners' documents may administer oaths and issue subpenas to compel the attendance and testimony of witnesses and the production of records or other evidence during investigations and at hearings.

(b) The jurisdictional limits of a subpena issued under this section are the same as, and are enforceable in the same manner as, subpenas issued under chapter 63 of this title.

(Pub. L. 98–89, Aug. 26, 1983, 97 Stat. 547; Pub. L. 99–36, §1(a)(9)(H), May 15, 1985, 99 Stat. 68.)

§7706. Drug testing reporting

(a) Release of Drug Test Results to Coast Guard.—Not later than 2 weeks after receiving from a Medical Review Officer a report of a verified positive drug test or verified test violation by a civilian employee of a Federal agency, an applicant for employment by a Federal agency, an officer in the Public Health Services, or an officer in the National Oceanic and Atmospheric Administration Commissioned Officer Corps, who is employed in any capacity on board a vessel operated by the agency, the head of the agency shall release to the Commandant the report.

(b) Standards, Procedures, and Regulations.—The head of a Federal agency shall carry out a release under subsection (a) in accordance with the standards, procedures, and regulations applicable to the disclosure and reporting to the Coast Guard of drug tests results and drug test records of individuals employed on vessels documented under the laws of the United States.

(c) Waiver.—Notwithstanding section 503(e) of the Supplemental Appropriations Act, 1987 (5 U.S.C. 7301 note), the report of a drug test of an employee or an applicant for employment by a Federal agency may be released under this section without the prior written consent of the employee or the applicant.

(Added Pub. L. 108–293, title IV, §414(a), Aug. 9, 2004, 118 Stat. 1046; amended Pub. L. 113–281, title III, §304, Dec. 18, 2014, 128 Stat. 3043; Pub. L. 115–232, div. C, title XXXV, §3541(b)(13), Aug. 13, 2018, 132 Stat. 2323.)

PART F—MANNING OF VESSELS

CHAPTER 81—GENERAL

§8101. COMPLEMENT OF INSPECTED VESSELS

(a) The certificate of inspection issued to a vessel under part B of this subtitle shall state the complement of licensed individuals and crew (including lifeboatmen) considered by the Secretary to be necessary for safe operation. A manning requirement imposed on—

(1) a sailing school vessel shall consider the participation of sailing school instructors and sailing school students in the operation of that vessel;

(2) a mobile offshore drilling unit shall consider the specialized nature of the unit; and

(3) a tank vessel shall consider the navigation, cargo handling, and maintenance functions of that vessel for protection of life, property, and the environment.

(b) The Secretary may modify the complement, by endorsement on the certificate, for reasons of changed conditions or employment.

(c) A requirement made under this section by an authorized official may be appealed to the Secretary under prescribed regulations.

(d) A vessel to which this section applies may not be operated without having in its service the complement required in the certificate of inspection.

(e) When a vessel is deprived of the service of a member of its complement without the consent, fault, or collusion of the owner, charterer, managing operator, agent, master, or individual in charge of the vessel, the master shall engage, if obtainable, a number of members equal to the number of those of whose services the master has been deprived. The replacements must be of the same or a higher grade or rating than those whose places they fill. If the master finds the vessel is sufficiently manned for the voyage, and replacements are not available to fill all the vacancies, the vessel may proceed on its voyage. Within 12 hours after the vessel arrives at its destination, the master shall report in writing to the Secretary the cause of each deficiency in the complement. A master failing to make the report is liable to the United States Government for a civil penalty of $1,000 for each deficiency.

(f) The owner, charterer, or managing operator of a vessel not manned as required by this section is liable to the Government for a civil penalty of $10,000.

(g) A person may not employ an individual as, and an individual may not serve as, a master, mate, engineer, radio officer, or pilot of a vessel to which this part applies or which is subject to inspection under chapter 33 of this title if the individual is not licensed by the Secretary. A person (including an individual) violating this subsection is liable to the Government for a civil penalty of not more than $10,000. Each day of a continuing violation is a separate offense.

(h) The owner, charterer, or managing operator of a freight vessel of less than 100 gross tons as measured under section 14502 of this title, or an alternate tonnage measured under section 14302 of this title as prescribed by the Secretary under section 14104 of this title, a small passenger vessel, or a sailing school vessel not manned as required by this section is liable to the Government for a civil penalty of $1,000. The vessel also is liable in rem for the penalty.

(i) When the 2 next most senior licensed officers on a vessel reasonably believe that the master or individual in charge of the vessel is under the influence of alcohol or a dangerous drug and is incapable of commanding the vessel, the next most senior master, mate, or operator licensed under section 7101(c)(1) or (3) of this title shall—

(1) temporarily relieve the master or individual in charge;

(2) temporarily take command of the vessel;

(3) in the case of a vessel required to have a log under chapter 113 of this title, immediately enter the details of the incident in the log; and

(4) report those details to the Secretary—

(A) by the most expeditious means available; and

(B) in written form transmitted within 12 hours after the vessel arrives at its next port.

(Pub. L. 98–89, Aug. 26, 1983, 97 Stat. 547; Pub. L. 98–557, §29(b), Oct. 30, 1984, 98 Stat. 2873; Pub. L. 99–640, §11(b), Nov. 10, 1986, 100 Stat. 3550; Pub. L. 101–380, title IV, §§4104, 4114(c), 4302(e), Aug. 18, 1990, 104 Stat. 511, 517, 538; Pub. L. 104–324, title VII, §725, Oct. 19, 1996, 110 Stat. 3939.)

§8102. WATCHMEN

(a) The owner, charterer, or managing operator of a vessel carrying passengers during the nighttime shall keep a suitable number of watchmen in the vicinity of the cabins or staterooms and on each deck to guard against and give alarm in case of a fire or other danger. An owner, charterer, or managing operator failing to provide watchmen required by this section is liable to the United States Government for a civil penalty of $1,000.

(b) The owner, charterer, managing operator, agent, master, or individual in charge of a fish processing vessel of more than 100 gross tons as measured under section 14502 of this title, or an alternate tonnage measured under section 14302 of this title as prescribed by the Secretary under section 14104 of this title shall keep a suitable number of watchmen trained in firefighting on board when hotwork is being done to guard against and give alarm in case of a fire.

(Pub. L. 98–89, Aug. 26, 1983, 97 Stat. 548; Pub. L. 98–364, title IV, §402(10), July 17, 1984, 98 Stat. 448; Pub. L. 104–324, title VII, §726, Oct. 19, 1996, 110 Stat. 3939.)

§8103. CITIZENSHIP AND NAVY RESERVE REQUIREMENTS

(a) Except as otherwise provided in this title, only a citizen of the United States may serve as master, chief engineer, radio officer, or officer in charge of a deck watch or engineering watch on a documented vessel.

(b)(1) Except as otherwise provided in this section, on a documented vessel—

(A) each unlicensed seaman must be—

(i) a citizen of the United States;

(ii) an alien lawfully admitted to the United States for permanent residence; or

(iii) a foreign national who is enrolled in the United States Merchant Marine Academy; and

(B) not more than 25 percent of the total number of unlicensed seamen on the vessel may be aliens lawfully admitted to the United States for permanent residence.

(2) Paragraph (1) of this subsection does not apply to—

(A) a yacht;

(B) a fishing vessel fishing exclusively for highly migratory species (as that term is defined in section 3 of the Magnuson-Stevens Fishery Conservation and Management Act (16 U.S.C. 1802)); and

(C) a fishing vessel fishing outside of the exclusive economic zone.

(3) The Secretary may waive a citizenship requirement under this section, other than a requirement that applies to the master of a documented vessel, with respect to—

(A) an offshore supply vessel or other similarly engaged vessel of less than 1,600 gross tons as measured under section 14502 of this title, or an alternate tonnage measured under section 14302 of this title as prescribed by the Secretary under section 14104 of this title that operates from a foreign port;

(B) a mobile offshore drilling unit or other vessel engaged in support of exploration, exploitation, or production of offshore mineral energy resources operating beyond the water above the outer Continental Shelf (as that term is defined in section 2(a) of the Outer Continental Shelf Lands Act (43 U.S.C. 1331(a)); and

(C) any other vessel if the Secretary determines, after an investigation, that qualified seamen who are citizens of the United States are not available.

(c) On each departure of a vessel (except a passenger vessel) for which a construction differential subsidy has been granted, all of the seamen of the vessel must be citizens of the United States.

(d)(1) On each departure of a passenger vessel for which a construction differential subsidy has been granted, at least 90 percent of the entire complement (including licensed individuals) must be citizens of the United States.

(2) An individual not required by this subsection to be a citizen of the United States may be engaged only if the individual has a declaration of intention to become a citizen of the United States or other evidence of admission to the United States for permanent residence. An alien may be employed only in the steward's department of the passenger vessel.

(e) If a documented vessel is deprived for any reason of the services of an individual (except the master and the radio officer) when on a foreign voyage and a vacancy consequently occurs, until the vessel's return to a port at which in the most expeditious manner a replacement who is a citizen of the United States can be obtained, an individual not a citizen of the United States may serve in—

(1) the vacancy; or

(2) a vacancy resulting from the promotion of another individual to fill the original vacancy.

(f) A person employing an individual in violation of this section or a regulation prescribed under this section is liable to the United States Government for a civil penalty of $500 for each individual so employed.

(g) A deck or engineer officer employed on a vessel on which an operating differential subsidy is paid, or employed on a vessel (except a vessel of the Coast Guard or Great Lakes St. Lawrence Seaway Development Corporation) owned or operated by the Department of Transportation or by a corporation organized or controlled by the Department, if eligible, shall be a member of the Navy Reserve.

(h) The President may—

(1) suspend any part of this section during a proclaimed national emergency; and

(2) when the needs of commerce require, suspend as far and for a period the President considers desirable, subsection (a) of this section for crews of vessels of the United States documented for foreign trade.

(i)(1) Except as provided in paragraph (3) of this subsection, each unlicensed seaman on a fishing, fish processing, or fish tender vessel that is engaged in the fisheries in the navigable waters of the United States or the exclusive economic zone must be—

(A) a citizen of the United States;

(B) an alien lawfully admitted to the United States for permanent residence;

(C) any other alien allowed to be employed under the Immigration and Nationality Act (8 U.S.C. 1101 et seq.); or

(D) an alien allowed to be employed under the immigration laws of the Commonwealth of the Northern Mariana Islands if the vessel is permanently stationed at a port within the Commonwealth and the vessel is engaged in the fisheries within the exclusive economic zone surrounding the Commonwealth or another United States territory or possession.

(2) Not more than 25 percent of the unlicensed seamen on a vessel subject to paragraph (1) of this subsection may be aliens referred to in clause (C) of that paragraph.

(3) This subsection does not apply to a fishing vessel fishing exclusively for highly migratory species (as that term is defined in section 3 of the Magnuson-Stevens Fishery Conservation and Management Act (16 U.S.C. 1802)).

(j) RIDING GANG MEMBER.—This section does not apply to an individual who is a riding gang member.

(k) CREW REQUIREMENTS FOR LARGE PASSENGER VESSELS.—

(1) CITIZENSHIP AND NATIONALITY.—Each unlicensed seaman on a large passenger vessel shall be—

(A) a citizen of the United States;

(B) an alien lawfully admitted to the United States for permanent residence;

(C) an alien allowed to be employed in the United States under the Immigration and Nationality Act (8 U.S.C. 1101 et seq.), including an alien crewman described in section 101(a)(15)(D)(i) of that Act (8 U.S.C. 1101(a)(15)(D)(i)), who meets the requirements of paragraph (3)(A) of this subsection; or

(D) a foreign national who is enrolled in the United States Merchant Marine Academy.

(2) PERCENTAGE LIMITATION FOR ALIEN SEAMEN.—Not more than 25 percent of the unlicensed seamen on a vessel described in paragraph (1) of this subsection may be aliens referred to in subparagraph (B) or (C) of that paragraph.

(3) SPECIAL RULES FOR CERTAIN UNLICENSED SEAMEN.—

(A) QUALIFICATIONS.—An unlicensed seaman described in paragraph (1)(C) of this subsection—

(i) shall have been employed, for a period of not less than 1 year, on a passenger vessel under the same common ownership or control as the vessel described in paragraph (1) of this subsection, as certified by the owner or managing operator of such vessel to the Secretary;

(ii) shall have no record of material disciplinary actions during such employment, as verified in writing by the owner or managing operator of such vessel to the Secretary;

(iii) shall have successfully completed a United States Government security check of the relevant domestic and international databases, as appropriate, or any other national security-related information or database;

(iv) shall have successfully undergone an employer background check—

(I) for which the owner or managing operator provides a signed report to the Secretary that describes the background checks undertaken that are reasonably and legally available to the owner or managing operator including personnel file information obtained from such seaman and from databases available to the public with respect to the seaman;

(II) that consisted of a search of all information reasonably available to the owner or managing operator in the seaman's country of citizenship and any other country in which the seaman receives employment referrals, or resides;

(III) that is kept on the vessel and available for inspection by the Secretary; and

(IV) the information derived from which is made available to the Secretary upon request; and

(v) may not be a citizen or temporary or permanent resident of a country designated by the United States as a sponsor of terrorism or any other country that the Secretary, in consultation with the Secretary of State and the heads of other appropriate United States agencies, determines to be a security threat to the United States.

(B) RESTRICTIONS.—An unlicensed seaman described in paragraph (1)(C) of this subsection—

(i) may be employed only in the steward's department of the vessel; and

(ii) may not perform watchstanding, automated engine room duty watch, or vessel navigation functions.

(C) STATUS, DOCUMENTATION, AND EMPLOYMENT.—An unlicensed seaman described in subparagraph (C) or (D) of paragraph (1) of this subsection—

(i) is deemed to meet the nationality requirements necessary to qualify for a merchant mariner's document notwithstanding the requirements of part 12 of title 46, Code of Federal Regulations;

(ii) is deemed to meet the proof-of-identity requirements necessary to qualify for a merchant mariner's document, as prescribed under regulations promulgated by the Secretary, if the seaman possesses—

(I) an unexpired passport issued by the government of the country of which the seaman is a citizen or subject; and

(II) an unexpired visa issued to the seaman, as described in paragraph (1)(C);

(iii) shall, if eligible, be issued a merchant mariner's document with an appropriate annotation reflecting the restrictions of subparagraph (B) of this paragraph; and

(iv) may be employed for a period of service on board not to exceed 36 months in the aggregate as a nonimmigrant crewman described in section 101(a)(15)(D)(i) of the Immigration and Nationality Act (8 U.S.C. 1101(a)(15)(D)(i)) on vessels engaged in domestic voyages notwithstanding the departure requirements and time limitations of such section and section 252 of the Immigration and Nationality Act (8 U.S.C. 1282) and the regulations and rules promulgated thereunder.

(4) MERCHANT MARINER'S DOCUMENT REQUIREMENTS NOT AFFECTED.—This subsection shall not be construed to affect any requirement under Federal law that an individual must hold a merchant mariner's document.

(5) DEFINITIONS.—In this subsection:

(A) STEWARD'S DEPARTMENT.—The term "steward's department" means the department that includes entertainment personnel and all service personnel, including wait staff, housekeeping staff, and galley workers, as defined in the vessel security plan approved by the Secretary pursuant to section 70103(c) of this title.

(B) LARGE PASSENGER VESSEL.—The term "large passenger vessel" means a vessel of more than 70,000 gross tons, as measured under section 14302 of this title, with capacity for at least 2,000 passengers and documented with a coastwise endorsement under chapter 121 of this title.

(Pub. L. 98–89, Aug. 26, 1983, 97 Stat. 548; Pub. L. 100–239, §§5(a)(1), (2), (b)–(d)(1), Jan. 11, 1988, 101 Stat. 1780; Pub. L. 100–255, Mar. 4, 1988, 102 Stat. 23; Pub. L. 101–595, title VI, §603(6), title VII, §711, Nov. 16, 1990, 104 Stat. 2993, 2997; Pub. L. 104–208, div. A, title I, §101(a) [title II, §211(b)], Sept. 30, 1996, 110 Stat. 3009, 3009–41; Pub. L. 104–324, title VII, §727, title XI, §1123, Oct. 19, 1996, 110 Stat. 3939, 3980; Pub. L. 108–293, title IV, §412, Aug. 9, 2004, 118 Stat. 1046; Pub. L. 109–163, div. A, title V, §515(f)(3)(A), (B), Jan. 6, 2006, 119 Stat. 3236; Pub. L. 109–241, title III, §312(c)(1), July 11, 2006, 120 Stat. 533; Pub. L. 109–304, §15(22), Oct. 6, 2006, 120 Stat. 1704; Pub. L. 109–364, div. C, title XXXV, §3509, Oct. 17, 2006, 120 Stat. 2518; Pub. L. 110–181, div. C, title XXXV, §3529(d), Jan. 28, 2008, 122 Stat. 604; Pub. L. 114–120, title III, §§306(a)(6), 313(d), Feb. 8, 2016, 130 Stat. 54, 59; Pub. L. 116–260, div. AA, title V, §512(c)(6)(B), Dec. 27, 2020, 134 Stat. 2757; Pub. L. 116–283, div. G, title LVXXXV [LXXXV], §8505(b)(8), Jan. 1, 2021, 134 Stat. 4751.)

§8104. WATCHES

(a) An owner, charterer, managing operator, master, individual in charge, or other person having authority may permit an officer to take charge of the deck watch on a vessel when leaving or immediately after leaving port only if the officer has been off duty for at least 6 hours within the 12 hours immediately before the time of leaving.

(b) On an oceangoing or coastwise vessel of not more than 100 gross tons as measured under section 14502 of this title, or an alternate tonnage measured under section 14302 of this title as prescribed by the Secretary under section 14104 of this title (except a fishing, fish processing, or fish tender vessel), a licensed individual may not be required to work more than 9 of 24 hours when in port, including the date of arrival, or more than 12 of 24 hours at sea, except in an emergency when life or property are endangered.

(c) On a towing vessel (except a towing vessel operated only for fishing, fish processing, fish tender, or engaged in salvage operations) operating on the Great Lakes, harbors of the Great Lakes, and connecting or tributary waters between Gary, Indiana, Duluth, Minnesota, Niagara Falls, New York, and Ogdensburg, New York, an individual in the deck or engine department may not be required to work more than 8 hours in one day or permitted to work more than 15 hours in any 24-hour period, or more than 36 hours in any 72-hour period, except in an emergency when life or property are endangered.

(d) On a merchant vessel of more than 100 gross tons as measured under section 14502 of this title, or an alternate tonnage measured under section 14302 of this title as prescribed by the Secretary under section 14104 of this title (except a vessel only operating on rivers, harbors, lakes (except the Great Lakes), bays, sounds, bayous, and canals, a fishing, fish tender, or whaling vessel, a fish processing vessel of not more than 5,000 gross tons as measured under section 14502 of this title, or an alternate tonnage measured under section 14302 of this title as prescribed by the Secretary under section 14104 of this title, yacht, or vessel engaged in salvage operations), the licensed individuals, sailors, and oilers shall be divided, when at sea, into at least 3 watches, and shall be kept on duty successively to perform ordinary work incident to the operation and management of the vessel. The requirement of this subsection applies to radio officers only when at least 3 radio officers are employed. An individual in the deck or engine department may not be required to work more than 8 hours in one day.

(e) On a vessel designated by subsection (d) of this section—

    (1) an individual may not be—

        (A) engaged to work alternately in the deck and engine departments; or

        (B) required to work in the engine department if engaged for deck department duty or required to work in the deck department if engaged for engine department duty;

    (2) an individual may not be required to do unnecessary work on Sundays, New Year's Day, July 4th, Labor Day, Thanksgiving Day, or Christmas Day, when the vessel is in a safe harbor, but this clause does not prevent dispatch of a vessel on a voyage; and

    (3) when the vessel is in a safe harbor, 8 hours (including anchor watch) is a day's work.

(f) Subsections (d) and (e) of this section do not limit the authority of the master or other officer or the obedience of the seamen when, in the judgment of the master or other officer, any part of the crew is needed for—

    (1) maneuvering, shifting the berth of, mooring, or unmooring, the vessel;

    (2) performing work necessary for the safety of the vessel, or the vessel's passengers, crew, or cargo;

    (3) saving life on board another vessel in jeopardy; or

    (4) performing fire, lifeboat, or other drills in port or at sea.

(g)(1) On a towing vessel, an offshore supply vessel, or a barge to which this section applies, that is engaged on a voyage of less than 600 miles, the licensed individuals and crewmembers may be divided, when at sea, into at least 2 watches.

(2) Paragraph (1) applies to an offshore supply vessel of at least 6,000 gross tons as measured under section 14302 of this title if the individuals engaged on the vessel are in compliance with hours of service requirements (including recording and recordkeeping of that service) as prescribed by the Secretary.

(h) On a vessel to which section 8904 of this title applies, an individual licensed to operate a towing vessel may not work for more than 12 hours in a consecutive 24-hour period except in an emergency.

(i) A person violating subsection (a) or (b) of this section is liable to the United States Government for a civil penalty of $10,000.

(j) The owner, charterer, or managing operator of a vessel on which a violation of subsection (c), (d), (e), or (h) of this section occurs is liable to the Government for a civil penalty of $10,000. The individual is entitled to discharge from the vessel and receipt of wages earned.

(k) On a fish processing vessel subject to inspection under part B of this subtitle, the licensed individuals and deck crew shall be divided, when at sea, into at least 3 watches.

(l) Except as provided in subsection (k) of this section, on a fish processing vessel, the licensed individuals and deck crew shall be divided, when at sea, into at least 2 watches if the vessel—

    (1) entered into service before January 1, 1988, and is more than 1,600 gross tons as measured under section 14502 of this title, or an alternate tonnage measured under section 14302 of this title as prescribed by the Secretary under section 14104 of this title; or

    (2) entered into service after December 31, 1987, and has more than 16 individuals on board primarily employed in the preparation of fish or fish products.

(m) This section does not apply to a fish processing vessel—

    (1) entered into service before January 1, 1988, and not more than 1,600 gross tons as measured under section 14502 of this title, or an alternate tonnage measured under section 14302 of this title as prescribed by the Secretary under section 14104 of this title; or

    (2) entered into service after December 31, 1987, and having not more than 16 individuals on board primarily employed in the preparation of fish or fish products.

(n) On a tanker, a licensed individual or seaman may not be permitted to work more than 15 hours in any 24-hour period, or more than 36 hours in any 72-hour period, except in an emergency or a drill. In this subsection, "work" includes any administrative duties associated with the vessel whether performed on board the vessel or onshore.

(o)(1) Except as provided in paragraph (2) of this subsection, on a fish tender vessel of not more than 500 gross tons as measured under section 14502 of this title, or less than 500 gross tons as measured under section 14502 of this title, or is less than 2,500 gross tons as measured under section 14302 of this title engaged in the Aleutian trade, the licensed individuals and crewmembers shall be divided, when at sea, into at least 3 watches.

(2) On a fish tender vessel of not more than 500 gross tons as measured under section 14502 of this title, or less than 500 gross tons as measured under section 14502 of this title, or is less than 2,500 gross tons as measured under section 14302 of this title engaged in the Aleutian trade, the licensed individuals and crewmembers shall be divided, when at sea, into at least 2 watches, if the vessel—

(A) before September 8, 1990, operated in that trade; or

(B)(i) before September 8, 1990, was purchased to be used in that trade; and

(ii) before June 1, 1992, entered into service in that trade.

(p) The Secretary may prescribe the watchstanding and work hours requirements for an oil spill response vessel.

(Pub. L. 98–89, Aug. 26, 1983, 97 Stat. 549; Pub. L. 98–364, title IV, §402(11), July 17, 1984, 98 Stat. 448; Pub. L. 98–557, §33(c), Oct. 30, 1984, 98 Stat. 2876; Pub. L. 99–307, §1(12), May 19, 1986, 100 Stat. 445; Pub. L. 101–380, title IV, §§4114(b), 4302(f), Aug. 18, 1990, 104 Stat. 517, 538; Pub. L. 101–595, title VI, §602(e)(1), Nov. 16, 1990, 104 Stat. 2991; Pub. L. 102–587, title V, §5212, Nov. 4, 1992, 106 Stat. 5077; Pub. L. 103–206, title III, §322(a), Dec. 20, 1993, 107 Stat. 2428; Pub. L. 104–324, title VII, §728, title XI, §§1104(c), 1114, Oct. 19, 1996, 110 Stat. 3939, 3967, 3971; Pub. L. 109–241, title III, §311(b), July 11, 2006, 120 Stat. 530; Pub. L. 111–281, title VI, §617(d), title IX, §903(a)(1), Oct. 15, 2010, 124 Stat. 2973, 3010; Pub. L. 113–281, title III, §316, Dec. 18, 2014, 128 Stat. 3050; Pub. L. 116–283, div. G, title LVXXXV [LXXXV], §8505(b)(9), Jan. 1, 2021, 134 Stat. 4751.)

§8105. Fishing vessel exemption

Notwithstanding any other provision of law, neither the International Convention on Standards of Training, Certification and Watchkeeping for Seafarers, 1978, nor any amendment to such convention, shall apply to a fishing vessel, including a fishing vessel used as a fish tender vessel.

(Added Pub. L. 104–324, title XI, §1146(a), Oct. 19, 1996, 110 Stat. 3992.)

§8106. Riding gangs

(a) In General.—The owner or managing operator of a freight vessel of the United States on voyages covered by the International Convention for Safety of Life at Sea, 1974 (32 UST 47m) shall—

(1) ensure that—

(A) subject to subsection (d), each riding gang member on the vessel—

(i) is a United States citizen or an alien lawfully admitted to the United States for permanent residence; or

(ii) possesses a United States nonimmigrant visa for individuals desiring to enter the United States temporarily for business, employment-related and personal identifying information, and any other documentation required by the Secretary;

(B) all required documentation for such member is kept on the vessel and available for inspection by the Secretary; and

(C) each riding gang member is identified on the vessel's crew list;

(2) ensure that—

(A) the owner or managing operator attests in a certificate that the background of each riding gang member has been examined and found to be free of any credible information indicating a material risk to the security of the vessel, the vessel's cargo, the ports the vessel visits, or other individuals onboard the vessel;

(B) the background check consisted of a search of all information reasonably available to the owner or managing operator in the riding gang member's country of citizenship and any other country in which the riding gang member works, receives employment referrals, or resides;

(C) the certificate required under subparagraph (A) is kept on the vessel and available for inspection by the Secretary; and

(D) the information derived from any such background check is made available to the Secretary upon request;

(3) ensure that each riding gang member, while on board the vessel, is subject to the same random chemical testing and reporting regimes as crew members;

(4) ensure that each such riding gang member receives basic safety familiarization and basic safety training approved by the Coast Guard as satisfying the requirements for such training under the International Convention of Training, Certification, and Watchkeeping for Seafarers, 1978;

(5) prevent from boarding the vessel, or cause the removal from the vessel at the first available port, and disqualify from future service on board any other vessel owned or operated by that owner or operator, any riding gang member—

(A) who has been convicted in any jurisdiction of an offense described in paragraph (2) or (3) of section 7703;

(B) whose license, certificate of registry, or merchant mariner's document has been suspended or revoked under section 7704; or

(C) who otherwise constitutes a threat to the safety of the vessel;

(6) ensure and certify to the Secretary that the sum of—

(A) the number of riding gang members on board a freight vessel, and

(B) the number of individuals in addition to crew permitted under section 3304,

does not exceed 12;

(7) ensure that every riding gang member is employed on board the vessel under conditions that meet or exceed the minimum international standards of all applicable international labor conventions to which the United States is a party, including all of the merchant seamen protection and relief provided under United States law; and

(8) ensure that each riding gang member—

(A) is supervised by an individual who holds a license issued under chapter 71; and

(B) only performs work in conjunction with individuals who hold merchant mariners documents issued under chapter 73 and who are part of the vessel's crew.

(b) PERMITTED WORK.—Subject to subsection (f), a riding gang member on board a vessel to which subsection (a) applies who is neither a United States citizen nor an alien lawfully admitted to the United States for permanent residence may not perform any work on board the vessel other than—

(1) work in preparation of a vessel entering a shipyard located outside of the United States;

(2) completion of the residual repairs after departing a shipyard located outside of the United States; or

(3) technical in-voyage repairs, in excess of any repairs that can be performed by the vessel's crew, in order to advance the vessel's useful life without having to actually enter a shipyard.

(c) WORKDAY LIMIT.—

(1) IN GENERAL.—The maximum number of days in any calendar year that the owner or operator of a vessel to which subsection (a) applies may employ on board riding gang members who are neither United States citizens nor aliens lawfully admitted to the United States for permanent residence for work on board that vessel is 60 days. If the vessel is at sea on the 60th day, each riding gang member shall be discharged from the vessel at the next port of call reached by the vessel after the date on which the 60-workday limit is reached.

(2) CALCULATION.—For the purpose of calculating the 60-workday limit under this subsection, each day worked by a riding gang member who is neither a United States citizen nor an alien lawfully admitted to the United States for permanent residence shall be counted against the limitation.

(d) EXCEPTIONS FOR WARRANTY WORK.—

(1) IN GENERAL.—Subsections (b), (c), (e), and (f) do not apply to a riding gang member employed exclusively to perform, and who performs only, work that is—

(A) customarily performed by original equipment manufacturers' technical representatives;

(B) required by a manufacturer's warranty on specific machinery and equipment; or

(C) required by a contractual guarantee or warranty on actual repairs performed in a shipyard located outside of the United States.

(2) CITIZENSHIP REQUIREMENT.—Subsection (a)(1)(A) applies only to a riding gang member described in paragraph (1) who is on the vessel when it calls at a United States port.

(e) RECORDKEEPING.—In addition to the requirements of subsection (a), the owner or managing operator of a vessel to which subsection (a) applies shall ensure that all information necessary to ensure compliance with this section, as determined by the

Secretary, is entered into the vessel's official logbook required by chapter 113.

(f) FAILURE TO EMPLOY QUALIFIED AVAILABLE U.S. CITIZENS OR RESIDENTS.—

(1) IN GENERAL.—The owner or operator of a vessel to which subsection (a) applies may not employ a riding gang member who is neither a United States citizen nor an alien lawfully admitted to the United States for permanent residence to perform work described in subsection (b) unless the owner or operator determines, in accordance with procedures established by the Secretary to carry out section 8103(b)(3)(C), that there is not a sufficient number of United States citizens or individuals lawfully admitted to the United States for permanent residence who are qualified and available for the work for which the riding gang member is to be employed.

(2) CIVIL PENALTY.—A violation of paragraph (1) is punishable by a civil penalty of not more than $10,000 for each day during which the violation continues.

(3) CONTINUING VIOLATIONS.—The maximum amount of a civil penalty for a violation under this subsection shall be $100,000.

(4) DETERMINATION OF AMOUNT.—In determining the amount of the penalty, the Secretary shall take into account the nature, circumstances, extent, and gravity of the violation committed and, with respect to the violator, the degree of culpability, the history of prior offenses, the ability to pay, and such other matters as justice may require.

(5) COMPROMISE, MODIFICATION, AND REMITTAL.—The Secretary may compromise, modify, or remit, with or without conditions, any civil penalty imposed under this section.

(Added Pub. L. 109–241, title III, §312(a), July 11, 2006, 120 Stat. 530; amended Pub. L. 115–232, div. C, title XXXV, §3546(g), Aug. 13, 2018, 132 Stat. 2326.)

§8107. USE OF FORCE AGAINST PIRACY

(a) LIMITATION ON LIABILITY.—An owner, operator, time charterer, master, mariner, or individual who uses force or authorizes the use of force to defend a vessel of the United States against an act of piracy shall not be liable for monetary damages for any injury or death caused by such force to any person engaging in an act of piracy if such force was in accordance with standard rules for the use of force in self-defense of vessels prescribed by the Secretary.

(b) PROMOTION OF COORDINATED ACTION.—To carry out the purpose of this section, the Secretary of the department in which the Coast Guard is operating shall work through the International Maritime Organization to establish agreements to promote coordinated action among flag- and port-states to deter, protect against, and rapidly respond to piracy against the vessels of, and in the waters under the jurisdiction of, those nations, and to ensure limitations on liability similar to those established by subsection (a).

(c) DEFINITION.—For the purpose of this section, the term "act of piracy" means any act of aggression, search, restraint, depredation, or seizure attempted against a vessel of the United States by an individual not authorized by the United States, a foreign government, or an international organization recognized by the United States to enforce law on the high seas.

(Added Pub. L. 111–281, title IX, §912(a), Oct. 15, 2010, 124 Stat. 3016.)

8108. Repealed. Pub. L. 115–282, title VI,
601(c)(3)(A), Dec. 4, 2018, 132 Stat. 4289]

CHAPTER 81—GENERAL

[§8108. REPEALED. PUB. L. 115–282, TITLE VI, §601(C)(3)(A), DEC. 4, 2018, 132 STAT. 4289]

Section, added Pub. L. 113–281, title III, §310(a), Dec. 18, 2014, 128 Stat. 3045; amended Pub. L. 115–232, div. C, title XXXV, §3541(b)(14), Aug. 13, 2018, 132 Stat. 2323, established the Merchant Marine Personnel Advisory Committee. See section 15103 of this title.

CHAPTER 83—MASTERS AND OFFICERS

Sec.
8301.   Minimum number of licensed individuals.
8302.   Staff department.
[8303.   Repealed.]
8304.   Implementing the Officers' Competency Certificates Convention, 1936.

§8301. MINIMUM NUMBER OF LICENSED INDIVIDUALS

(a) Except as provided in chapter 89 of this title and except for a vessel operating only on rivers, harbors, lakes (except the Great Lakes), bays, sounds, bayous, and canals, a vessel subject to inspection under chapter 33 of this title shall engage a minimum of licensed individuals as follows:

(1) Each of those vessels propelled by machinery or carrying passengers shall have a licensed master.

(2) A vessel of at least 1,000 gross tons as measured under section 14502 of this title, or an alternate tonnage measured under section 14302 of this title as prescribed by the Secretary under section 14104 of this title and propelled by machinery shall have 3 licensed mates, except—

(A) in the case of a vessel other than a mobile offshore drilling unit, if on a voyage of less than 400 miles from port of departure to port of final destination, the vessel shall have 2 licensed mates; and

(B) in the case of a mobile offshore drilling unit, the vessel shall have licensed individuals as provided by regulations prescribed by the Secretary under section 8101 of this title.

(3) A vessel of at least 200 gross tons but less than 1,000 gross tons as measured under section 14502 of this title, or an alternate tonnage measured under section 14302 of this title as prescribed by the Secretary under section 14104 of this title and propelled by machinery shall have 2 licensed mates.

(4) A vessel of at least 100 gross tons but less than 200 gross tons as measured under section 14502 of this title, or an alternate tonnage measured under section 14302 of this title as prescribed by the Secretary under section 14104 of this title and propelled by machinery shall have one licensed mate. However, if the vessel is on a voyage of more than 24 hours, it shall have 2 licensed mates.

(5) A freight vessel or a passenger vessel of at least 300 gross tons as measured under section 14502 of this title, or an alternate tonnage measured under section 14302 of this title as prescribed by the Secretary under section 14104 of this title and propelled by machinery shall have a licensed engineer.

(b)(1) An offshore supply vessel of less than 500 gross tons as measured under section 14502 of this title or 6,000 gross tons as measured under section 14302 of this title on a voyage of less than 600 miles shall have a licensed mate. If the vessel is on a voyage of at least 600 miles, however, the vessel shall have 2 licensed mates.

(2) An offshore supply vessel of at least 6,000 gross tons as measured under section 14302 of this title on a voyage of less than 600 miles shall have at least two licensed mates, provided the offshore supply vessel meets the requirements of section 8104(g)(2). An offshore supply vessel of at least 6,000 gross tons as measured under section 14302 of this title on a voyage of at least 600 miles shall have three licensed mates.

(3) An offshore supply vessel of more than 200 gross tons as measured under section 14502 of this title, or an alternate tonnage measured under section 14302 of this title as prescribed by the Secretary under section 14104 of this title, may not be operated without a licensed engineer.

(c) Subsection (a) of this section does not apply to a fishing or whaling vessel, a mobile offshore drilling unit when on location, or a yacht.

(d) The Secretary may—

(1) suspend any part of this chapter during a national emergency proclaimed by the President; and

(2) increase the number of licensed individuals on a vessel to which this chapter applies if, in the Secretary's judgment, the vessel is not sufficiently manned for safe operation.

(e) The Secretary may prescribe the minimum number of licensed individuals for an oil spill response vessel.

(Pub. L. 98–89, Aug. 26, 1983, 97 Stat. 550; Pub. L. 98–557, §29(c), (d), Oct. 30, 1984, 98 Stat. 2873, 2874; Pub. L. 99–640, §11(d), Nov. 10, 1986, 100 Stat. 3550; Pub. L. 100–448, §7, Sept. 28, 1988, 102 Stat. 1842; Pub. L. 103–206, title III, §322(b), Dec. 20, 1993, 107 Stat. 2428; Pub. L. 104–324, title VII, §729, title XI, §1104(d), Oct. 19, 1996, 110 Stat. 3940, 3967; Pub. L. 111–281, title VI, §617(c), Oct. 15, 2010, 124 Stat. 2973.)

§8302. STAFF DEPARTMENT

(a) This section applies to a vessel of the United States except—

(1) a fishing or whaling vessel or a yacht;

(2) a vessel operated only on bays, sounds, inland waters, and lakes (except the Great Lakes); and

(3) a vessel ferrying passengers and cars on the Great Lakes.

(b) The staff department on a vessel is a separate and independent department. It consists of individuals registered under section 7101 of this title, clerks, and individuals assigned to the senior registered medical doctor.

(c) The staff department is composed of a medical division and a purser's division. The officer in charge of each division is responsible only to the master. The senior registered medical doctor is in charge of the medical division. The senior registered purser is in charge of the purser's division.

(d) The officer in charge of the purser's division of the staff department on an oceangoing passenger vessel licensed to carry more than 100 passengers shall be a registered chief purser. When more than 3 individuals are employed in the purser's division of that vessel, there also shall be at least one registered senior assistant purser and one registered junior assistant purser.

(e) A person may not employ an individual to serve in, and an individual may not serve in, a grade of staff officer on a vessel, when that staff officer is required by this section to be registered, if the individual does not have a certificate of registry as staff officer in that grade. A person (including an individual) violating this subsection is liable to the United States Government for a civil penalty of $100. However, if a registered staff officer is not available at the time of sailing, the vessel may sail with an unregistered staff officer or without a staff officer.

(f) A staff officer may not be included in a vessel's certificate of inspection.

(g) A registered staff officer serving under this section who is a member of the Navy Reserve may wear on the officer's uniform special distinguishing insignia prescribed by the Secretary of the Navy.

(h) The uniform stripes, decoration, or other insignia worn by a staff officer shall be of gold braid or woven gold or silver material. A crewmember (except a staff officer) may not wear any uniform with a staff officer's identifying insignia.

(Pub. L. 98–89, Aug. 26, 1983, 97 Stat. 551; Pub. L. 99–36, §1(a)(4), May 15, 1985, 99 Stat. 67; Pub. L. 109–163, div. A, title V, §515(f)(3)(A), Jan. 6, 2006, 119 Stat. 3236; Pub. L. 116–283, div. G, title LVXXXV [LXXXV], §8505(b)(10), Jan. 1, 2021, 134 Stat. 4751.)

[§8303. Repealed. Pub. L. 116–283, div. G, title LVXXXV [LXXXV], §8503(a)(1), Jan. 1, 2021, 134 Stat. 4747]

Section, Pub. L. 98–89, Aug. 26, 1983, 97 Stat. 552, related to individuals issued a license without examination before Oct. 29, 1941.

§8304. Implementing the Officers' Competency Certificates Convention, 1936

(a) In this section, "high seas" means waters seaward of the Boundary Line.

(b) The Officers' Competency Certificates Convention, 1936 (International Labor Organization Draft Convention Numbered 53, on the minimum requirement of professional capacity for masters and officers on board merchant vessels), as ratified by the President on September 1, 1938, with understandings appended, and this section apply to a documented vessel operating on the high seas except—

(1) a public vessel;

(2) a wooden vessel of primitive build, such as a dhow or junk;

(3) a barge; and

(4) a vessel of less than 200 gross tons as measured under section 14502 of this title, or an alternate tonnage measured under section 14302 of this title as prescribed by the Secretary under section 14104 of this title.

(c) A person may not engage or employ an individual to serve as, and an individual may not serve as, a master, mate, or engineer on a vessel to which this section applies, if the individual does not have a license issued under section 7101 of this title authorizing service in the capacity in which the individual is to be engaged or employed.

(d) A person (including an individual) violating this section is liable to the United States Government for a civil penalty of $100.

(e) A license issued to an individual to whom this section applies is a certificate of competency.

(f) A designated official may detain a vessel to which this section applies (by written order served on the owner, charterer, managing operator, agent, master, or individual in charge of the vessel) when there is reason to believe that the vessel is about to proceed from a port of the United States to the high seas in violation of this section or a provision of the convention described in subsection (b) of this section. The vessel may be detained until the vessel complies with this section. Clearance may not be granted to a vessel ordered detained under this section.

(g) A foreign vessel to which the convention described in subsection (b) of this section applies, on the navigable waters of the United States, is subject to detention under subsection (f) of this section, and to an examination that may be necessary to decide if there is compliance with the convention.

(h) The owner, charterer, managing operator, agent, master, or individual in charge of a vessel detained under subsection (f) or (g) of this section may appeal the order within 5 days as provided by regulation.

(i) An officer or employee of the Customs Service may be designated to enforce this section.

(Pub. L. 98–89, Aug. 26, 1983, 97 Stat. 552; Pub. L. 104–324, title VII, §730, Oct. 19, 1996, 110 Stat. 3940.)

CHAPTER 85—PILOTS

Sec.
8501.   State regulation of pilots.
8502.   Federal pilots required.
8503.   Federal pilots authorized.

§8501. STATE REGULATION OF PILOTS

(a) Except as otherwise provided in this subtitle, pilots in the bays, rivers, harbors, and ports of the United States shall be regulated only in conformity with the laws of the States.

(b) The master of a vessel entering or leaving a port on waters that are a boundary between 2 States, and that is required to have a pilot under this section, may employ a pilot licensed or authorized by the laws of either of the 2 States.

(c) A State may not adopt a regulation or provision that discriminates in the rate of pilotage or half-pilotage between vessels sailing between the ports of one State and vessels sailing between the ports of different States, or against vessels because of their means of propulsion, or against public vessels of the United States.

(d) A State may not adopt a regulation or provision that requires a coastwise vessel to take a pilot licensed or authorized by the laws of a State if the vessel—

(1) is propelled by machinery and subject to inspection under part B of this subtitle; or

(2) is subject to inspection under chapter 37 of this title.

(e) Any regulation or provision violating this section is void.

(Pub. L. 98–89, Aug. 26, 1983, 97 Stat. 553; Pub. L. 98–557, §29(e), Oct. 30, 1984, 98 Stat. 2874.)

§8502. FEDERAL PILOTS REQUIRED

(a) Except as provided in subsections (g) and (i) of this section, a coastwise seagoing vessel shall be under the direction and control of a pilot licensed under section 7101 of this title if the vessel is—

(1) not sailing on register;

(2) underway;

(3) not beyond 3 nautical miles from the baselines from which the territorial sea of the United States is measured; and

(4)(A) propelled by machinery and subject to inspection under part B of this subtitle; or

(B) subject to inspection under chapter 37 of this title.

(b) The fees charged for pilotage by pilots required under this section may not be more than the customary or legally established rates in the States in which the pilotage is performed.

(c) A State or political subdivision of a State may not impose on a pilot licensed under this subtitle an obligation to procure a State or other license, or adopt any other regulation that will impede the pilot in the performance of the pilot's duties under the laws of the

United States.

(d) A State or political subdivision of a State may not levy pilot charges on a vessel lawfully piloted by a pilot required under this section.

(e) The owner, charterer, managing operator, agent, master, or individual in charge of a vessel operated in violation of this section or a regulation prescribed under this section is liable to the United States Government for a civil penalty of $10,000. The vessel also is liable in rem for the penalty.

(f) An individual serving as a pilot without having a license required by this section or a regulation prescribed under this section is liable to the Government for a civil penalty of $10,000.

(g)(1) The Secretary shall designate by regulation the areas of the approaches to and waters of Prince William Sound, Alaska, if any, on which a vessel subject to this section is not required to be under the direction and control of a pilot licensed under section 7101 of this title.

(2) In any area of Prince William Sound, Alaska, where a vessel subject to this section is required to be under the direction and control of a pilot licensed under section 7101 of this title, the pilot may not be a member of the crew of that vessel and shall be a pilot licensed by the State of Alaska who is operating under a Federal license, when the vessel is navigating waters between 60°49' North latitude and the Port of Valdez, Alaska.

(h) The Secretary shall designate waters on which tankers over 1,600 gross tons subject to this section shall have on the bridge a master or mate licensed to direct and control the vessel under section 7101(c)(1) of this title who is separate and distinct from the pilot required under subsection (a) of this section.

(i)(1) Except as provided in paragraph (2), a dredge to which this section would otherwise apply is exempt from the requirements of this section.

(2) If the Secretary determines, after notice and comment, that the exemption under paragraph (1) creates a hazard to navigational safety in a specified area, the Secretary may require that a dredge exempted by paragraph (1) which is operating in that area shall comply with this section.

(Pub. L. 98–89, Aug. 26, 1983, 97 Stat. 553; Pub. L. 98–557, §29(f)(1), (2), Oct. 30, 1984, 98 Stat. 2874; Pub. L. 99–307, §1(13), May 19, 1986, 100 Stat. 446; Pub. L. 101–380, title IV, §§4116(a), (b), 4302(g), Aug. 18, 1990, 104 Stat. 522, 539; Pub. L. 101–595, title III, §307, Nov. 16, 1990, 104 Stat. 2985; Pub. L. 105–383, title III, §301(b)(7), Nov. 13, 1998, 112 Stat. 3417.)

§8503. Federal pilots authorized

(a) The Secretary may require a pilot licensed under section 7101 of this title on a self-propelled vessel when a pilot is not required by State law and the vessel is—

(1) engaged in foreign commerce; and

(2) operating—

(A) in internal waters of the United States; or

(B) within 3 nautical miles from the baselines from which the territorial sea of the United States is measured.

(b) A requirement prescribed under subsection (a) of this section is terminated when the State having jurisdiction over the area involved—

498

(1) establishes a requirement for a State licensed pilot; and

(2) notifies the Secretary of that fact.

(c) For the Saint Lawrence Seaway, the Secretary may not delegate the authority under this section to an agency except the Great Lakes St. Lawrence Seaway Development Corporation.

(d) A person violating this section or a regulation prescribed under this section is liable to the United States Government for a civil penalty of not more than $25,000. Each day of a continuing violation is a separate violation. The vessel also is liable in rem for the penalty.

(e) A person that knowingly violates this section or a regulation prescribed under this section commits a class D felony.

(Added Pub. L. 98–557, §29(f)(3)(A), Oct. 30, 1984, 98 Stat. 2874; amended Pub. L. 101–380, title IV, §4302(h), Aug. 18, 1990, 104 Stat. 539; Pub. L. 105–383, title III, §301(b)(8), Nov. 13, 1998, 112 Stat. 3417; Pub. L. 116–260, div. AA, title V, §512(c)(6)(C), Dec. 27, 2020, 134 Stat. 2757.)

CHAPTER 87—UNLICENSED PERSONNEL

Sec.

§8701. MERCHANT MARINERS' DOCUMENTS REQUIRED

(a) This section applies to a merchant vessel of at least 100 gross tons as measured under section 14502 of this title, or an alternate tonnage measured under section 14302 of this title as prescribed by the Secretary under section 14104 of this title except—

(1) a vessel operating only on rivers and lakes (except the Great Lakes);

(2) a barge (except a seagoing barge or a barge to which chapter 37 of this title applies);

(3) a fishing, fish tender, or whaling vessel or a yacht;

(4) a sailing school vessel with respect to sailing school instructors and sailing school students;

(5) an oceanographic research vessel with respect to scientific personnel;

(6) a fish processing vessel entered into service before January 1, 1988, and not more than 1,600 gross tons as measured under section 14502 of this title, or an alternate tonnage measured under section 14302 of this title as prescribed by the Secretary under section 14104 of this title or entered into service after December 31, 1987, and having not more than 16 individuals on board primarily employed in the preparation of fish or fish products;

(7) a fish processing vessel (except a vessel to which clause (6) of this subsection applies) with respect to individuals on board primarily employed in the preparation of fish or fish products or in a support position not related to navigation;

(8) a mobile offshore drilling unit with respect to individuals, other than crew members required by the certificate of inspection, engaged on board the unit for the sole purpose of carrying out the industrial business or function of the unit;

(9) a passenger vessel not engaged in a foreign voyage with respect to individuals on board employed for a period of not more than 30 service days within a 12 month period as entertainment personnel, with no duties, including emergency duties, related to the navigation of the vessel or the safety of the vessel, its crew, cargo or passengers; and

(10) the Secretary may prescribe the individuals required to hold a merchant mariner's document serving onboard an oil spill response vessel.

(b) A person may not engage or employ an individual, and an individual may not serve, on board a vessel to which this section applies if the individual does not have a merchant mariner's document issued to the individual under section 7302 of this title. Except for an individual required to be licensed or registered under this part, the document must authorize service in the capacity for which the holder of the document is engaged or employed.

(c) On a vessel to which section 10306 or 10503 of this title does not apply, an individual required by this section to hold a merchant mariner's document must exhibit it to the master of the vessel before the individual may be employed.

(d) A person (including an individual) violating this section is liable to the United States Government for a civil penalty of $500.

(Pub. L. 98–89, Aug. 26, 1983, 97 Stat. 554; Pub. L. 98–364, title IV, §402(12)(A), July 17, 1984, 98 Stat. 449; Pub. L. 99–640, §11(c), Nov. 10, 1986, 100 Stat. 3550; Pub. L. 104–324, title VII, §731, title XI, §1104(e), Oct. 19, 1996, 110 Stat. 3940, 3967; Pub. L. 107–295, title III, §324(b), Nov. 25, 2002, 116 Stat. 2104.)

§8702. CERTAIN CREW REQUIREMENTS

(a) This section applies to a vessel of at least 100 gross tons as measured under section 14502 of this title, or an alternate tonnage measured under section 14302 of this title as prescribed by the Secretary under section 14104 of this title except—

(1) a vessel operating only on rivers and lakes (except the Great Lakes);

(2) a barge (except a seagoing barge or a barge to which chapter 37 of this title applies);

(3) a fishing, fish tender, or whaling vessel (except a fish tender vessel engaged in the Aleutian trade) or a yacht;

(4) a sailing school vessel with respect to sailing school instructors and sailing school students;

(5) an oceanographic research vessel with respect to scientific personnel;

(6) a fish processing vessel entered into service before January 1, 1988, and not more than 1,600 gross tons as measured under section 14502 of this title, or an alternate tonnage measured under section 14302 of this title as prescribed by the Secretary under section 14104 of this title or entered into service after December 31, 1987, and having not more than 16 individuals on board primarily employed in the preparation of fish or fish products; and

(7) a fish processing vessel (except a vessel to which clause (6) of this subsection applies) with respect to individuals on board primarily employed in the preparation of fish or fish products or in a support position not related to navigation.

(b) A vessel may operate only if at least—

(1) 75 percent of the crew in each department on board is able to understand any order spoken by the officers, and

(2) 65 percent of the deck crew (excluding licensed individuals) have merchant mariners' documents endorsed for a rating of at least able seaman, except that this percentage may be reduced to 50 percent—

(i) on a vessel permitted under section 8104 of this title to maintain a 2-watch system; or

(ii) on a fish tender vessel engaged in the Aleutian trade.

(c) An able seaman is not required on a towing vessel operating on bays and sounds connected directly with the seas.

(d) An individual having a rating of less than able seaman may not be permitted at the wheel in ports, harbors, and other waters subject to congested vessel traffic, or under conditions of reduced visibility, adverse weather, or other hazardous circumstances.

(e) The owner, charterer, managing operator, agent, master, or individual in charge of a vessel operated in violation of this section or a regulation prescribed under this section is liable to the United States Government for a civil penalty of $10,000.

(Pub. L. 98–89, Aug. 26, 1983, 97 Stat. 554; Pub. L. 98–364, title IV, §402(12)(B), July 17, 1984, 98 Stat. 449; Pub. L. 100–239, §5(e), Jan. 11, 1988, 101 Stat. 1781; Pub. L. 101–380, title IV, §4302(i), Aug. 18, 1990, 104 Stat. 539; Pub. L. 101–595, title VI, §602(e)(2), Nov. 16, 1990, 104 Stat. 2992; Pub. L. 104–324, title VII, §732, Oct. 19, 1996, 110 Stat. 3941.)

§8703. Tankermen on tank vessels

(a) A vessel of the United States to which chapter 37 of this title applies, that has on board oil or hazardous material in bulk as cargo or cargo residue, shall have a specified number of the crew certified as tankermen as required by the Secretary. This requirement shall be noted on the certificate of inspection issued to the vessel.

(b) A vessel to which section 3702(b) of this title applies shall have on board as a crewmember in charge of the transfer operation an individual certified as a tankerman (qualified for the grade of fuel transferred), unless a master, mate, pilot, engineer, or operator licensed under section 7101 of this title is present in charge of the transfer. If the vessel does not have that individual on board, chapter 37 of this title applies to the vessel.

(Pub. L. 98–89, Aug. 26, 1983, 97 Stat. 555; Pub. L. 98–557, §18, Oct. 30, 1984, 98 Stat. 2869; Pub. L. 115–232, div. C, title XXXV, §3546(h), Aug. 13, 2018, 132 Stat. 2326.)

§8704. Alien deemed to be employed in the United States

An alien is deemed to be employed in the United States for purposes of section 274A of the Immigration and Nationality Act (8 U.S.C. 1324a) if the alien is an unlicensed individual employed on a fishing, fish processing, or fish tender vessel that—

(1) is a vessel of the United States engaged in the fisheries in the navigable waters of the United States or the exclusive economic zone; and

(2) is not engaged in fishing exclusively for highly migratory species (as that term is defined in section 3 of the Magnuson-Stevens Fishery Conservation and Management Act (16 U.S.C. 1802).

(Added Pub. L. 100–239, §5(f)(1), Jan. 11, 1988, 101 Stat. 1781; amended Pub. L. 104–208, div. A, title I, §101(a) [title II, §211(b)], Sept. 30, 1996, 110 Stat. 3009, 3009–41.)

CHAPTER 89—SMALL VESSEL MANNING

Sec.
8901. Freight vessels.
8902. Small passenger vessels.
8903. Self-propelled, uninspected passenger vessels.
8904. Towing vessels.
8905. Exemptions.
8906. Penalty.

§8901. FREIGHT VESSELS

A freight vessel of less than 100 gross tons as measured under section 14502 of this title, or an alternate tonnage measured under section 14302 of this title as prescribed by the Secretary under section 14104 of this title shall be operated by an individual licensed by the Secretary to operate that type of vessel in the particular geographic area, under prescribed regulations.

(Pub. L. 98–89, Aug. 26, 1983, 97 Stat. 555; Pub. L. 104–324, title VII, §733, Oct. 19, 1996, 110 Stat. 3941.)

§8902. SMALL PASSENGER VESSELS

A small passenger vessel shall be operated by an individual licensed by the Secretary to operate that type of vessel in the particular geographic area, under prescribed regulations.

(Pub. L. 98–89, Aug. 26, 1983, 97 Stat. 555.)

§8903. SELF-PROPELLED, UNINSPECTED PASSENGER VESSELS

A self-propelled, uninspected passenger vessel shall be operated by an individual licensed by the Secretary to operate that type of vessel, under prescribed regulations.

(Pub. L. 98–89, Aug. 26, 1983, 97 Stat. 555; Pub. L. 99–307, §1(14)(B), (C), May 19, 1986, 100 Stat. 446.)

§8904. TOWING VESSELS

(a) A towing vessel that is at least 26 feet in length measured from end to end over the deck (excluding sheer), shall be operated by an individual licensed by the Secretary to operate that type of vessel in the particular geographic area, under prescribed regulations.

(b) A vessel that tows a disabled vessel for consideration shall be operated by an individual licensed by the Secretary to operate that type of vessel in the particular geographic area, under prescribed regulations.

(c) The Secretary may prescribe by regulation requirements for maximum hours of service (including recording and recordkeeping of that service) of individuals engaged on a towing vessel that is at least 26 feet in length measured from end to end over the deck (excluding the sheer).

(Pub. L. 98–89, Aug. 26, 1983, 97 Stat. 555; Pub. L. 99–640, §12(a), Nov. 10, 1986, 100 Stat. 3550; Pub. L. 108–293, title IV, §409(a), Aug. 9, 2004, 118 Stat. 1044.)

§8905. Exemptions

(a) Section 8903 of this title applies to a recreational vessel operated in dealer demonstrations only if the Secretary decides that the application of section 8903 is necessary for recreational vessel safety under section 4302(d) of this title.

(b) Section 8904 of this title does not apply to an oil spill response vessel while engaged in oil spill response or training activities.

(c) After consultation with the Governor of Alaska and the State boating law administrator of Alaska, the Secretary may exempt an individual operating a self-propelled uninspected passenger vessel from the requirements of section 8903 of this title, if—

(1) the individual only operates such vessel wholly within waters located in Alaska; and

(2) such vessel is—

(A) 26 feet or less in length; and

(B) carrying not more than 6 passengers.

(Pub. L. 98–89, Aug. 26, 1983, 97 Stat. 556; Pub. L. 104–324, title VII, §734, title XI, §1104(f), Oct. 19, 1996, 110 Stat. 3941, 3967; Pub. L. 111–281, title VI, §606, Oct. 15, 2010, 124 Stat. 2967; Pub. L. 116–283, div. G, title LVXXXIII [LXXXIII], §8317, Jan. 1, 2021, 134 Stat. 4700.)

§8906. Penalty

An owner, charterer, managing operator, agent, master, or individual in charge of a vessel operated in violation of this chapter or a regulation prescribed under this chapter is liable to the United States Government for a civil penalty of not more than $25,000. The vessel also is liable in rem for the penalty.

(Pub. L. 98–89, Aug. 26, 1983, 97 Stat. 556; Pub. L. 104–324, title III, §306(b), Oct. 19, 1996, 110 Stat. 3918.)

CHAPTER 91—TANK VESSEL MANNING STANDARDS

§9101. STANDARDS FOR FOREIGN TANK VESSELS

(a)(1) The Secretary shall evaluate the manning, training, qualification, and watchkeeping standards of a foreign country that issues documentation for any vessel to which chapter 37 of this title applies—

(A) on a periodic basis; and

(B) when the vessel is involved in a marine casualty required to be reported under section 6101(a)(4) or (5) of this title.

(2) After each evaluation made under paragraph (1) of this subsection, the Secretary shall determine whether—

(A) the foreign country has standards for licensing and certification of seamen that are at least equivalent to United States law or international standards accepted by the United States; and

(B) those standards are being enforced.

(3) If the Secretary determines under this subsection that a country has failed to maintain or enforce standards at least equivalent to United States law or international standards accepted by the United States, the Secretary shall prohibit vessels issued documentation by that country from entering the United States until the Secretary determines those standards have been established and are being enforced.

(4) The Secretary may allow provisional entry of a vessel prohibited from entering the United States under paragraph (3) of this subsection if—

(A) the owner or operator of the vessel establishes, to the satisfaction of the Secretary, that the vessel is not unsafe or a threat to the marine environment; or

(B) the entry is necessary for the safety of the vessel or individuals on the vessel.

(b) A foreign vessel to which chapter 37 of this title applies that has on board oil or hazardous material in bulk as cargo or cargo residue shall have a specified number of personnel certified as tankerman or equivalent, as required by the Secretary, when the vessel transfers oil or hazardous material in a port or place subject to the jurisdiction of the United States. The requirement of this subsection shall be noted in applicable terminal operating procedures. A transfer operation may take place only if the crewmember in charge is capable of clearly understanding instructions in English.

(Pub. L. 98–89, Aug. 26, 1983, 97 Stat. 556; Pub. L. 101–380, title IV, §4106(a), Aug. 18, 1990, 104 Stat. 513.)

§9102. STANDARDS FOR TANK VESSELS OF THE UNITED STATES

The Secretary shall prescribe standards for the manning of each vessel of the United

States to which chapter 37 of this title applies, related to the duties, qualifications, and training of the officers and crew of the vessel, including standards related to—

(1) instruction in vessel and cargo handling and vessel navigation under normal operating conditions in coastal and confined waters and on the high seas;

(2) instruction in vessel and cargo handling and vessel navigation in emergency situations and under marine casualty or potential casualty conditions;

(3) qualifications for licenses by specific type and size of vessels;

(4) qualifications for licenses by use of simulators for the practice or demonstration of marine-oriented skills;

(5) minimum health and physical fitness criteria for various grades of licenses and certificates;

(6) periodic retraining and special training for upgrading positions, changing vessel type or size, or assuming new responsibilities;

(7) decisions about licenses and certificates, conditions of licensing or certification, and periods of licensing or certification by reference to experience, amount of training completed, and regular performance testing; and

(8) instruction in vessel maintenance functions.

(Pub. L. 98–89, Aug. 26, 1983, 97 Stat. 556; Pub. L. 101–380, title IV, §4114(d), Aug. 18, 1990, 104 Stat. 517; Pub. L. 116–283, div. G, title LVXXXV [LXXXV], §8503(b), Jan. 1, 2021, 134 Stat. 4747.)

CHAPTER 93—GREAT LAKES PILOTAGE

§9301. DEFINITIONS

In this chapter—

(1) "Canadian registered pilot" means an individual (except a regular crewmember of a vessel) who is registered by Canada on the same basis as an individual registered under section 9303 of this title.

(2) "Great Lakes" means Lakes Superior, Michigan, Huron, Erie, and Ontario, their connecting and tributary waters, the Saint Lawrence River as far east as Saint Regis, and adjacent port areas.

(3) "United States registered pilot" means an individual (except a regular crewmember of a vessel) who is registered under section 9303 of this title.

(Pub. L. 98–89, Aug. 26, 1983, 97 Stat. 557.)

§9302. GREAT LAKES PILOTS REQUIRED

(a)(1) Except as provided in subsections (d), (e), and (f) of this section, each vessel of the United States operating on register and each foreign vessel shall engage a United States or Canadian registered pilot for the route being navigated who shall—

(A) in waters of the Great Lakes designated by the President, direct the navigation of the vessel subject to the customary authority of the master; and

(B) in waters of the Great Lakes not designated by the President, be on board and available to direct the navigation of the vessel at the discretion of and subject to the customary authority of the master.

(2) The President shall make water designations under this subsection with regard to the public interest, the effective use of navigable waters, marine safety, and the foreign relations of the United States.

(b) A member of the complement of a vessel of the United States operating on register or of a vessel of Canada may serve as the pilot required on waters not designated by the President if the member is licensed under section 7101 of this title, or under equivalent provisions of Canadian law, to direct the navigation of the vessel on the waters being navigated.

(c) The authority extended under subsections (a) and (b) of this section to a Canadian registered pilot or other Canadian licensed officer to serve on certain vessels in United States waters of the Great Lakes shall continue as long as Canada extends reciprocity to United States registered pilots and other individuals licensed by the United States for pilotage service in Canadian waters of the Great Lakes.

(d) A vessel may be operated on the United States waters of the Great Lakes without a United States or Canadian registered pilot when—

(1) the Secretary notifies the master that a registered pilot is not available; or

(2) the vessel or its cargo is in distress or jeopardy.

(e) A Canadian vessel regularly operating on the Great Lakes or between ports on the Great Lakes and the Saint Lawrence River, with only an occasional voyage to ports in the maritime provinces of Canada in the Canadian coastal trade, is exempt from subsection (a) of this section as long as Canada permits enrolled vessels of the United States to be operated on Canadian waters of the Great Lakes under the direction of individuals licensed under section 7101 of this title.

(f) A documented vessel regularly operating on the Great Lakes or between ports on the Great Lakes and the St. Lawrence River is exempt from the requirements of subsection (a) of this section.

(Pub. L. 98–89, Aug. 26, 1983, 97 Stat. 557; Pub. L. 101–380, title IV, §4108(a), Aug. 18, 1990, 104 Stat. 514; Pub. L. 104–324, title XI, §1115(b)(5)–(7), Oct. 19, 1996, 110 Stat. 3972.)

§9303. UNITED STATES REGISTERED PILOT SERVICE

(a) The Secretary shall prescribe by regulation standards of competency to be met by each applicant for registration under this chapter. An applicant must—

(1) have a license as master, mate, or pilot issued under section 7101 of this title;

(2) have acquired at least 24 months licensed service or equivalent experience on vessels or integrated towing vessels and tows of at least 4,000 gross tons as measured under section 14502 of this title, or an alternate tonnage measured under section 14302 of this title as prescribed by the Secretary under section 14104 of this title, operating on the Great Lakes or oceans, with a minimum of 6 months of that service or experience having been on the Great Lakes; and

(3) agree that, if appointed as a United States registered pilot, the applicant will be available for service when required.

(b) The Secretary shall issue to each registered pilot under this chapter a certificate of registration describing the areas within which the pilot may serve. The pilot shall carry the certificate when in the service of a vessel.

(c) The Secretary shall prescribe by regulation the duration of validity of registration.

(d) The Secretary may prescribe by regulation the conditions for service by United States registered pilots, including availability for service.

(e) Subject to sections 551–559 of title 5, the Secretary may suspend or revoke a certificate of registration issued under this section if the holder fails to comply with a regulation prescribed under this chapter. Suspension or revocation of the holder's license under chapter 77 of this title includes the holder's certificate of registration.

(f) The Secretary shall prescribe by regulation rates and charges for pilotage services, giving consideration to the public interest and the costs of providing the services. The Secretary shall establish new pilotage rates by March 1 of each year. The Secretary shall establish base pilotage rates by a full ratemaking at least once every 5 years and shall conduct annual reviews of such base pilotage rates, and make adjustments to such base rates, in each intervening year.

(g) The Secretary shall ensure that a sufficient number of individuals are assigned to carrying out subsection (f).

(Pub. L. 98–89, Aug. 26, 1983, 97 Stat. 558; Pub. L. 104–324, title VII, §735, Oct. 19, 1996, 110 Stat. 3941; Pub. L. 109–241, title III, §302, July 11, 2006, 120 Stat. 527.)

§9304. Pilotage pools

(a) The Secretary may authorize the formation of a pool by a voluntary association of United States registered pilots to provide for efficient dispatching of vessels and rendering of pilotage services.

(b) For pilotage pools, the Secretary may—

(1) limit the number of the pools;

(2) prescribe regulations for their operation and administration;

(3) prescribe a uniform system of accounts;

(4) perform audits and inspections; and

(5) require coordination on a reciprocal basis with similar pool arrangements authorized by the appropriate agency of Canada.

(Pub. L. 98–89, Aug. 26, 1983, 97 Stat. 559.)

§9305. Agreements with Canada

To provide for a coordinated system of pilotage service on the Great Lakes, the Secretary, subject to the concurrence of the Secretary of State, may make agreements with the appropriate agency of Canada to—

(1) fix the number of pilots to be registered in each country;

(2) provide for participation on an equitable basis;

(3) prescribe joint or identical rates and charges;

(4) coordinate pool operations; and

(5) establish conditions for services by registered pilots.

(Pub. L. 98–89, Aug. 26, 1983, 97 Stat. 559.)

§9306. State regulation prohibited

A State or political subdivision of a State may not regulate or impose any requirement on pilotage on the Great Lakes.

(Pub. L. 98–89, Aug. 26, 1983, 97 Stat. 559.)

§9307. Great Lakes Pilotage Advisory Committee

(a) The Secretary shall establish a Great Lakes Pilotage Advisory Committee. The Committee—

(1) may review proposed Great Lakes pilotage regulations and policies and make recommendations to the Secretary that the Committee considers appropriate;

(2) may advise, consult with, report to, and make recommendations to the Secretary on matters relating to Great Lakes pilotage;

(3) may make available to the Congress recommendations that the Committee makes to the Secretary; and

(4) shall meet at the call of—

(A) the Secretary, who shall call such a meeting at least once during each calendar year; or

(B) a majority of the Committee.

(b)(1) The Committee shall consist of 8 members appointed by the Secretary in accordance with this subsection, each of whom has at least 5 years practical experience in maritime operations. The term of each member is for a period of not more than 5 years, specified by the Secretary. Before filling a position on the Committee, the Secretary shall publish a notice in the Federal Register soliciting nominations for membership on the Committee.

(2) The membership of the Committee shall include—

(A) the President of each of the 3 Great Lakes pilotage districts, or the President's representative;

(B) one member chosen from among nominations made by vessel operators that contract for Great Lakes pilotage services;

(C) one member chosen from among nominations made by Great Lakes port authorities and marine terminals;

(D) one member chosen from among nominations made by shippers whose cargoes are transported through Great Lakes ports;

(E) one member chosen from among nominations made by Great Lakes maritime labor organizations; and

(F) a member who—

(i) must have been recommended to the Secretary by a unanimous vote of the other members of the Committee, and

(ii) may be appointed without regard to requirement in paragraph (1) that each member have 5 years of practical experience in maritime operations.

(c)(1) The Committee shall elect one of its members as the Chairman and one of its members as the Vice Chairman. The Vice Chairman shall act as Chairman in the absence or incapacity of the Chairman, or in the event of a vacancy in the office of the Chairman.

(2) The Secretary shall, and any other interested agency may, designate a representative to participate as an observer with the Committee. The Secretary's designated representative shall act as the executive secretary of the Committee and shall perform the duties set forth in section 1009(c) of title 5.

(d)(1) The Secretary shall, whenever practicable, consult with the Committee before taking any significant action relating to Great Lakes pilotage.

(2) The Secretary shall consider the information, advice, and recommendations of the Committee in formulating policy regarding matters affecting Great Lakes pilotage.

(3) Any recommendations to the Secretary under subsection (a)(2) must have been approved by at least all but one of the members then serving on the committee.

(e)(1) A member of the Committee, when attending meetings of the Committee or when otherwise engaged in the business of the Committee, is entitled to receive—

    (A) compensation at a rate fixed by the Secretary, not exceeding the daily equivalent of the current rate of basic pay in effect for GS–18 of the General Schedule under section 5332 of title 5 including travel time; and

    (B) travel or transportation expenses under section 5703 of title 5, United States Code.

(2) A member of the Committee shall not be considered to be an officer or employee of the United States for any purpose based on their receipt of any payment under this subsection.

(f)(1) Chapter 10 of title 5 applies to the Committee, except that the Committee terminates on September 30, 2030.

(2) 2 years before the termination date set forth in paragraph (1) of this subsection, the Committee shall submit to the Congress its recommendation regarding whether the Committee should be renewed and continued beyond the termination date.

(Pub. L. 98–89, Aug. 26, 1983, 97 Stat. 559; Pub. L. 105–383, title III, §303, Nov. 13, 1998, 112 Stat. 3418; Pub. L. 106–554, §1(a)(4) [div. A, §1118], Dec. 21, 2000, 114 Stat. 2763, 2763A–209; Pub. L. 108–293, title IV, §418(d), Aug. 9, 2004, 118 Stat. 1049; Pub. L. 109–304, §15(23), Oct. 6, 2006, 120 Stat. 1704; Pub. L. 111–281, title VI, §621(a), Oct. 15, 2010, 124 Stat. 2976; Pub. L. 116–283, div. G, title LVXXXIII [LXXXIII], §8334(a), Jan. 1, 2021, 134 Stat. 4705; Pub. L. 117–286, §4(a)(291), Dec. 27, 2022, 136 Stat. 4337.)

§9308. Penalties

(a) An owner, charterer, managing operator, agent, master, or individual in charge of a vessel knowingly allowing the vessel to be operated in violation of section 9302 of this title is liable to the United States Government for a civil penalty of no more than $10,000 for each day during which the vessel is in violation. The vessel also is liable in rem for the penalty.

(b) An individual who directs the navigation of a vessel in violation of section 9302 of this title is liable to the Government for a civil penalty of no more than $10,000 for each day during which the violation occurs.

(c) A person violating a regulation prescribed under section 9303 of this title is liable to the Government for a civil penalty of no more than $10,000.

(Pub. L. 98–89, Aug. 26, 1983, 97 Stat. 560; Pub. L. 101–380, title IV, §4108(b), Aug. 18, 1990, 104 Stat. 515.)

PART G—MERCHANT SEAMEN PROTECTION AND RELIEF

CHAPTER 101—GENERAL

§10101. DEFINITIONS

In this part—

(1) "master" means the individual having command of a vessel.

(2) "owner" means the person to whom the vessel belongs.

(3) "seaman" means an individual (except scientific personnel, a sailing school instructor, or a sailing school student) engaged or employed in any capacity on board a vessel.

(4) "fishing vessel" includes—

(A) a fish tender vessel; or

(B) a fish processing vessel entered into service before January 1, 1988, and not more than 1,600 gross tons as measured under section 14502 of this title, or an alternate tonnage measured under section 14302 of this title as prescribed by the Secretary under section 14104 of this title or entered into service after December 31, 1987, and having not more than 16 individuals on board primarily employed in the preparation of fish or fish products.

(Pub. L. 98–89, Aug. 26, 1983, 97 Stat. 560; Pub. L. 98–364, title IV, §402(13), July 17, 1984, 98 Stat. 449; Pub. L. 98–557, §33(d), Oct. 30, 1984, 98 Stat. 2876; Pub. L. 99–640, §10(b)(3), Nov. 10, 1986, 100 Stat. 3550; Pub. L. 104–324, title VII, §736, Oct. 19, 1996, 110 Stat. 3941.)

[§10102. REPEALED. PUB. L. 103–206, TITLE IV, §422(C)(1), DEC. 20, 1993, 107 STAT. 2439]

Section, Pub. L. 98–89, Aug. 26, 1983, 97 Stat. 560, related to designations and duties of shipping commissioners.

§10103. REPORTS

(a) A master of a vessel to which section 8701(a) of this title applies, who engages or discharges a seaman, shall submit reports to the vessel owner in the form, content, and manner of filing as prescribed by regulation, to ensure compliance with laws related to manning and the engagement and discharge of seamen.

(b) This section does not apply to a ferry or towing vessel operated in connection with a ferry operation, employed only in trades other than with foreign ports, lakes, bays, sounds, bayous, canals, or harbors.

(Pub. L. 98–89, Aug. 26, 1983, 97 Stat. 560; Pub. L. 103–206, title IV, §417, Dec. 20, 1993, 107 Stat. 2438.)

§10104. REQUIREMENT TO REPORT SEXUAL OFFENSES

(a) MANDATORY REPORTING BY RESPONSIBLE ENTITY OF A VESSEL.—

(1) IN GENERAL.—The responsible entity of a vessel shall report to the Commandant any complaint or incident of harassment, sexual harassment, or sexual assault in violation of employer policy or law, of which such entity is made aware.

(2) PENALTY.—A responsible entity of a vessel who knowingly fails to report in compliance with paragraph (1) is liable to the United States Government for a civil penalty of not more than $50,000.

(b) REPORTING PROCEDURES.—

(1) RESPONSIBLE ENTITY OF A VESSEL REPORTING.—A report required under subsection (a) shall be made immediately after the responsible entity of a vessel gains knowledge of a sexual assault or sexual harassment incident by the fastest telecommunication channel available to—

(A) a single entity in the Coast Guard designated by the Commandant to receive such reports; and

(B) the appropriate officer or agency of the government of the country in whose waters the incident occurs.

(2) CONTENTS.—Such shall include, to the best of the knowledge of the individual making the report—

(A) the name, official position or role in relation to the vessel, and contact information of such individual;

(B) the name and official number of the documented vessel;

(C) the time and date of the incident;

(D) the geographic position or location of the vessel when the incident occurred; and

(E) a brief description of the alleged sexual harassment or sexual assault being reported.

(3) RECEIVING REPORTS; COLLECTION OF INFORMATION.—

(A) RECEIVING REPORTS.—With respect to reports submitted under subsection (a), the Commandant—

(i) may establish additional reporting procedures, including procedures for receiving reports through—

(I) a single telephone number that is continuously manned at all times; and

(II) a single email address that is continuously monitored; and

(ii) shall use procedures that include preserving evidence in such reports and providing emergency service referrals.

(B) COLLECTION OF INFORMATION.—After receipt of the report made under subsection (a), the Coast Guard shall collect information related to the identity of each alleged victim, alleged perpetrator, and any witnesses identified in the report through means designed to protect, to the extent practicable, the personal identifiable information of such individuals.

(c) SUBPOENA AUTHORITY.—

(1) IN GENERAL.—The Commandant may compel the testimony of witnesses and the production of any evidence by subpoena to determine compliance with this section.

(2) JURISDICTIONAL LIMITS.—The jurisdictional limits of a subpoena issued under this section are the same as, and are enforceable in the same manner as, subpoenas issued under chapter 63 of this title.

(d) COMPANY AFTER-ACTION SUMMARY.—

(1) A responsible entity of a vessel that makes a report under subsection (a) shall—

(A) submit to the Commandant a document with detailed information to describe the actions taken by such entity after becoming aware of the sexual assault or sexual harassment incident, including the results of any investigation into the complaint or incident and any action taken against the offending individual; and

(B) make such submission not later than 10 days after such entity made the report under subsection (a).

(2) CIVIL PENALTY.—A responsible entity of a vessel that fails to comply with paragraph (1) is liable to the United States Government for a civil penalty of $25,000 and $500 shall be added for each day of noncompliance, except that the total amount of a penalty with respect to a complaint or incident shall not exceed $50,000 per violation.

(e) INVESTIGATORY AUDIT.—The Commandant shall periodically perform an audit or other systematic review of the submissions made under this section to determine if there were any failures to comply with the requirements of this section.

(f) APPLICABILITY; REGULATIONS.—

(1) REGULATIONS.— The Secretary may issue regulations to implement the requirements of this section.

(2) INTERIM REPORTS.—Any report required to be made to the Commandant under this section shall be made to the Coast Guard National Command Center, until regulations implementing the procedures required by this section are issued.

(g) DEFINITION OF RESPONSIBLE ENTITY OF A VESSEL.—In this section, the term "responsible entity of a vessel" means—

(1) the owner, master, or managing operator of a documented vessel engaged in commercial service; or

(2) the employer of a seafarer on such a vessel.

(Added Pub. L. 101–225, title II, §214(a)(2), Dec. 12, 1989, 103 Stat. 1914; amended Pub. L. 117–263, div. K, title CXVI, §11609, Dec. 23, 2022, 136 Stat. 4152.)

§10105. REPORTS TO CONGRESS

(a) IN GENERAL.—Not later than 1 year after the date of enactment of the Don Young Coast Guard Authorization Act of 2022, and on an annual basis thereafter, the Commandant shall submit to the Committee on Commerce, Science, and Transportation of the Senate and the Committee on Transportation and Infrastructure of the House of Representatives a report that includes—

(1) the number of reports received under section 10104;

(2) the number of penalties issued under such section;

(3) the number of open investigations under such section, completed investigations under such section, and the outcomes of such open or completed investigations;

(4) the number of assessments or audits conducted under section 3203 and the outcome of those assessments or audits;

(5) a statistical analysis of compliance with the safety management system criteria under section 3203;

(6) the number of credentials denied or revoked due to sexual harassment, sexual assault, or related offenses; and

(7) recommendations to support efforts of the Coast Guard to improve investigations and oversight of sexual harassment and sexual assault in the maritime sector, including funding requirements and legislative change proposals necessary to ensure compliance with title CXVI of the Don Young Coast Guard Authorization Act of 2022 and the amendments made by such title.

(b) PRIVACY.—In collecting the information required under subsection (a), the Commandant shall collect such information in a manner that protects the privacy rights of individuals who are subjects of such information.

(Added Pub. L. 117–263, div. K, title CXVI, §11611(a), Dec. 23, 2022, 136 Stat. 4155.)

CHAPTER 103—FOREIGN AND INTERCOASTAL VOYAGES

§10301. APPLICATION

(a) Except as otherwise specifically provided, this chapter applies to a vessel of the United States—

(1) on a voyage between a port in the United States and a port in a foreign country (except a port in Canada, Mexico, or the West Indies); or

(2) of at least 75 gross tons as measured under section 14502 of this title, or an alternate tonnage measured under section 14302 of this title as prescribed by the Secretary under section 14104 of this title on a voyage between a port of the United States on the Atlantic Ocean and a port of the United States on the Pacific Ocean.

(b) This chapter does not apply to a vessel on which the seamen are entitled by custom or agreement to share in the profit or result of a voyage or to riding gang members.

(c) Unless otherwise provided, this chapter does not apply to a foreign vessel.

(Pub. L. 98–89, Aug. 26, 1983, 97 Stat. 561; Pub. L. 104–324, title VII, §737, Oct. 19, 1996, 110 Stat. 3941; Pub. L. 109–241, title III, §312(c)(2), July 11, 2006, 120 Stat. 533.)

§10302. SHIPPING ARTICLES AGREEMENTS

(a) The owner, charterer, managing operator, master, or individual in charge shall make a shipping agreement in writing with each seaman before the seaman commences employment.

(b) The agreement shall contain the following:

(1) the nature, and, as far as practicable, the duration of the intended voyage, and the port or country in which the voyage is to end.

(2) the number and description of the crew and the capacity in which each seaman is to be engaged.

(3) the time at which each seaman is to be on board to begin work.

(4) the amount of wages each seaman is to receive.

(5) regulations about conduct on board, and information on fines, short allowance of provisions, and other punishment for misconduct provided by law.

(6) a scale of the provisions that are to be provided each seaman.

(7) any stipulation in reference to advances and allotments of wages.

(8) other matters not contrary to law.

(c) Each shipping agreement must be signed by the master or individual in charge or a representative of the owner, charterer, or managing operator, and by each seaman employed.

(d) The owner, charterer, managing operator, master, or individual in charge shall maintain the shipping agreement and make the shipping agreement available to the seaman.

(Pub. L. 98–89, Aug. 26, 1983, 97 Stat. 561; Pub. L. 103–206, title IV, §401, Dec. 20, 1993, 107 Stat. 2435.)

§10303. PROVISIONS

(a) A seaman shall be served at least 3 meals a day that total at least 3,100 calories, including adequate water and adequate protein, vitamins, and minerals in accordance with the United States Recommended Daily Allowances.

(b) The text of subsection (a) of this section shall be included in the agreement required by section 10302 of this title. A copy of the text also shall be posted in a conspicuous place in the galley and forecastle of each vessel.

(c) This section does not apply to a fishing or whaling vessel or a yacht.

(Pub. L. 98–89, Aug. 26, 1983, 97 Stat. 562.)

§10304. FORM OF AGREEMENT

The form of the agreement required by section 10302 of this title shall be in substance as follows:

UNITED STATES OF AMERICA

(Date and place of first signature of agreement):

It is agreed between the master and seamen of the   , of which   is at present master, or whoever shall go for master, now bound from the port of   to   (here the voyage is to be described, and the places named at which the vessel is to touch, or if that cannot be done, the general nature and probable length of the voyage is to be stated).

The seamen agree to conduct themselves in an orderly, faithful, honest, and sober manner, and to be at all times diligent in their respective duties, and to be obedient to the lawful commands of the master, or of an individual who lawfully succeeds the master, and of their superior officers in everything related to the vessel, and the stores and cargo of the vessel, whether on board, in boats, or on shore. In consideration of this service by the seamen to be performed, the master agrees to pay the crew, as wages, the amounts beside their names respectively expressed, and to supply them with provisions according to the annexed scale.

It is agreed that any embezzlement, or willful or negligent destruction of any part of the vessel's cargo or stores, shall be made good to the owner out of the wages of the person guilty of the embezzlement or destruction.

If an individual holds himself or herself out as qualified for a duty which the individual proves incompetent to perform, the individual's wages shall be reduced in proportion to the incompetency.

It also is agreed that if a seaman considers himself or herself to be aggrieved by any breach of this agreement or otherwise, the seaman shall present the complaint to the master or officer in charge of the vessel, in a quiet and orderly manner, who shall take steps that the case requires.

It also is agreed that (here any other stipulations may be inserted to which the parties agree, and that are not contrary to law).

In witness whereof, the parties have subscribed their names to this agreement, on the dates beside their respective signatures.

Signed by   , master, on the   day of   , nineteen hundred and   .

Signature of seaman   Time of service:
Birthplace   Months
Age   Days
Height: Hospital money
   Feet   Whole wages
   Inches   Wages due
Description: Place and time of entry
   Complexion   Time at which seaman is to
   Hair   be on board
Wages each month   In what capacity
Wages each voyage   Allotment payable to
Advance wages   Conduct qualifications
Amount of monthly allotment

NOTE.—In the place for signature and descriptions of individuals engaged after the first departure of the vessel, the entries are to be made as above, except that the signature of the consul or vice consul, customs officer, or witness before whom the individual is engaged, is to be entered.

(Pub. L. 98–89, Aug. 26, 1983, 97 Stat. 562; Pub. L. 103–206, title IV, §402, Dec. 20, 1993, 107 Stat. 2436.)

§10305. MANNER OF SIGNING AGREEMENT

The agreement required by section 10302 of this title shall be signed—
   (1) first by the master and dated at that time, after which each seaman shall sign; and
   (2) in the presence of the master or individual in charge.

(Pub. L. 98–89, Aug. 26, 1983, 97 Stat. 563; Pub. L. 103–206, title IV, §403, Dec. 20, 1993, 107 Stat. 2436.)

§10306. Exhibiting merchant mariners' documents

Before signing the agreement required by section 10302 of this title, each individual required by section 8701 of this title to have a merchant mariner's document shall exhibit to the master or individual in charge a document issued to the individual, appropriately endorsed for the capacity in which the individual is to serve.

(Pub. L. 98–89, Aug. 26, 1983, 97 Stat. 564; Pub. L. 103–206, title IV, §404, Dec. 20, 1993, 107 Stat. 2436.)

§10307. Posting agreements

At the beginning of a voyage, the master shall have a legible copy of the agreement required by section 10302 of this title, omitting signatures, exhibited in a part of the vessel accessible to the crew.

(Pub. L. 98–89, Aug. 26, 1983, 97 Stat. 564; Pub. L. 103–206, title IV, §405, Dec. 20, 1993, 107 Stat. 2436.)

§10308. Foreign engagements

When a seaman is engaged outside the United States, the agreement required by section 10302 of this title shall be signed in the presence of a consular officer. If a consular officer is not available at the port of engagement, the seaman may be engaged, and the agreement shall be signed in the next port at which a consular officer is available.

(Pub. L. 98–89, Aug. 26, 1983, 97 Stat. 564; Pub. L. 103–206, title IV, §406, Dec. 20, 1993, 107 Stat. 2436.)

§10309. Engaging seamen to replace those lost by desertion or casualty

(a) If a desertion or casualty results in the loss of at least one seaman, the master shall engage, if obtainable, a number equal to the number of seamen of whose services the master has been deprived. The new seaman must have at least the same grade or rating as the seaman whose place the new seaman fills. The master shall report the loss and replacement to a consular officer at the first port at which the master arrives.

(b) This section does not apply to a fishing or whaling vessel or a yacht.

(Pub. L. 98–89, Aug. 26, 1983, 97 Stat. 564; Pub. L. 103–206, title IV, §407, Dec. 20, 1993, 107 Stat. 2436.)

§10310. Discharge

A master shall deliver to a seaman a full and true account of the seaman's wages and all deductions at least 48 hours before paying off or discharging the seaman.

(Pub. L. 98–89, Aug. 26, 1983, 97 Stat. 564; Pub. L. 103–206, title IV, §408, Dec. 20, 1993, 107 Stat. 2436.)

§10311. Certificates of discharge

(a) On discharging a seaman and paying the seaman's wages, the master or individual in charge shall provide the seaman with a certificate of discharge. The form of the certificate shall be prescribed by regulation. It shall contain—

(1) the name of the seaman;
(2) the citizenship or nationality of the seaman;

(3) the number of the seaman's merchant mariner's document;

(4) the name and official number of the vessel;

(5) the nature of the voyage (foreign, intercoastal, or coastwise);

(6) the propulsion class of the vessel;

(7) the date and place of engagement;

(8) the date and place of discharge; and

(9) the seaman's capacity on the voyage.

(b) The certificate of discharge may not contain a reference about the character or ability of the seaman. The certificate shall be signed by the master and the seaman.

(c) A certificate of discharge may not be issued if the seaman holds a continuous discharge book. The entries shall be made in the discharge book in the same manner as the entries required by subsection (a) of this section.

(d)(1) A record of each discharge shall be maintained by the owner, charterer, managing operator, master, or individual in charge in the manner and location prescribed by regulation. The records may not be open for general or public use or inspection.

(2) A duplicate of a record of discharge shall be issued to a seaman at the request of the seaman.

(e) This section does not apply to a fishing or whaling vessel or a yacht.

(Pub. L. 98–89, Aug. 26, 1983, 97 Stat. 564; Pub. L. 103–206, title IV, §409, Dec. 20, 1993, 107 Stat. 2436.)

§10312. SETTLEMENTS ON DISCHARGE

When discharge and settlement are completed, the master, individual in charge, or owner and each seaman shall sign the agreement required by section 10302 of this title.

(Pub. L. 98–89, Aug. 26, 1983, 97 Stat. 565; Pub. L. 103–206, title IV, §410, Dec. 20, 1993, 107 Stat. 2437.)

§10313. WAGES

(a) A seaman's entitlement to wages and provisions begins when the seaman begins work or when specified in the agreement required by section 10302 of this title for the seaman to begin work or be present on board, whichever is earlier.

(b) Wages are not dependent on the earning of freight by the vessel. When the loss or wreck of the vessel ends the service of a seaman before the end of the period contemplated in the agreement, the seaman is entitled to wages for the period of time actually served. The seaman shall be deemed a destitute seaman under section 11104 of this title. This subsection applies to a fishing or whaling vessel but not a yacht.

(c) When a seaman who has signed an agreement is discharged improperly before the beginning of the voyage or before one month's wages are earned, without the seaman's consent and without the seaman's fault justifying discharge, the seaman is entitled to receive from the master or owner, in addition to wages earned, one month's wages as compensation.

(d) A seaman is not entitled to wages for a period during which the seaman—

(1) unlawfully failed to work when required, after the time fixed by the agreement for the seaman to begin work; or

(2) lawfully was imprisoned for an offense, unless a court hearing the case otherwise

directs.

(e) After the beginning of the voyage, a seaman is entitled to receive from the master, on demand, one-half of the balance of wages earned and unpaid at each port at which the vessel loads or delivers cargo during the voyage. A demand may not be made before the expiration of 5 days from the beginning of the voyage, not more than once in 5 days, and not more than once in the same port on the same entry. If a master does not comply with this subsection, the seaman is released from the agreement and is entitled to payment of all wages earned. Notwithstanding a release signed by a seaman under section 10312 of this title, a court having jurisdiction may set aside, for good cause shown, the release and take action that justice requires. This subsection does not apply to a fishing or whaling vessel or a yacht.

(f) At the end of a voyage, the master shall pay each seaman the balance of wages due the seaman within 24 hours after the cargo has been discharged or within 4 days after the seaman is discharged, whichever is earlier. When a seaman is discharged and final payment of wages is delayed for the period permitted by this subsection, the seaman is entitled at the time of discharge to one-third of the wages due the seaman.

(g)(1) Subject to paragraph (2), when payment is not made as provided under subsection (f) of this section without sufficient cause, the master or owner shall pay to the seaman 2 days' wages for each day payment is delayed.

(2) The total amount required to be paid under paragraph (1) with respect to all claims in a class action suit by seamen on a passenger vessel capable of carrying more than 500 passengers for wages under this section against a vessel master, owner, or operator or the employer of the seamen shall not exceed ten times the unpaid wages that are the subject of the claims.

(3) A class action suit for wages under this subsection must be commenced within three years after the later of—

(A) the date of the end of the last voyage for which the wages are claimed; or

(B) the receipt, by a seaman who is a claimant in the suit, of a payment of wages that are the subject of the suit that is made in the ordinary course of employment.

(h) Subsections (f) and (g) of this section do not apply to a fishing or whaling vessel or a yacht.

(i) This section applies to a seaman on a foreign vessel when in a harbor of the United States. The courts are available to the seaman for the enforcement of this section.

(Pub. L. 98–89, Aug. 26, 1983, 97 Stat. 566; Pub. L. 99–640, §10(b)(4), Nov. 10, 1986, 100 Stat. 3550; Pub. L. 111–281, title IX, §902(a)(1), Oct. 15, 2010, 124 Stat. 3008.)

§10314. ADVANCES

(a)(1) A person may not—

(A) pay a seaman wages in advance of the time when the seaman has earned the wages;

(B) pay advance wages of the seaman to another person; or

(C) make to another person an order, note, or other evidence of indebtedness of the wages, or pay another person, for the engagement of seamen when payment is deducted or to be deducted from the seaman's wage.

(2) A person violating this subsection is liable to the United States Government for a civil penalty of not more than $500. A payment made in violation of this subsection does not relieve the vessel or the master from the duty to pay all wages after they have been earned.

(b) A person demanding or receiving from a seaman or an individual seeking employment as a seaman, remuneration for providing the seaman or individual with employment, is liable to the Government for a civil penalty of not more than $500.

(c) This section applies to a foreign vessel when in waters of the United States. An owner, charterer, managing operator, agent, or master of a foreign vessel violating this section is liable to the Government for the same penalty as an owner, charterer, managing operator, agent, or master of a vessel of the United States for the same violation.

(d) The owner, charterer, managing operator, agent, or master of a vessel seeking clearance from a port of the United States shall present the agreement required by section 10302 of this title at the office of clearance. Clearance may be granted to a vessel only if this section has been complied with.

(e) This section does not apply to a fishing or whaling vessel or a yacht.

(Pub. L. 98–89, Aug. 26, 1983, 97 Stat. 567; Pub. L. 99–640, §10(b)(4), Nov. 10, 1986, 100 Stat. 3550.)

§10315. ALLOTMENTS

(a) Under prescribed regulations, a seaman may stipulate as follows in the agreement required by section 10302 of this title for an allotment of any part of the wages the seaman may earn:

(1) to the seaman's grandparents, parents, spouse, sister, brother, or children;

(2) to an agency designated by the Secretary of the Treasury to handle applications for United States savings bonds, to purchase bonds for the seaman; and

(3) for deposits to be made in an account for savings or investment opened by the seaman and maintained in the seaman's name at a savings bank or a savings institution in which the accounts are insured by the Federal Deposit Insurance Corporation or the Federal Savings and Loan Insurance Corporation.

(b) An allotment is valid only if made in writing and signed by and approved by a shipping commissioner. The shipping commissioner shall examine allotments and the parties to them to enforce compliance with the law. Stipulations for allotments made at the beginning of a voyage shall be included in the agreement and shall state the amounts and times of payment and the person to whom payments are to be made.

(c) Only an allotment complying with this section is lawful. A person falsely claiming qualification as an allottee under this section is liable to the United States Government for a civil penalty of not more than $500.

(d) The owner, charterer, managing operator, agent, or master of a vessel seeking clearance from a port of the United States shall present the agreement at the office of clearance. Clearance may be granted to a vessel only if this section has been complied with.

(e) This section applies to a foreign vessel when in waters of the United States. An owner, charterer, managing operator, agent, or master of a foreign vessel violating this section is liable to the Government for the same penalty as an owner, charterer, managing operator, agent, or master of a vessel of the United States for the same violation.

(f) DEPOSITS IN SEAMAN ACCOUNT.—By written request signed by the seaman, a seaman employed on a passenger vessel capable of carrying more than 500 passengers may authorize the master, owner, or operator of the vessel, or the employer of the seaman, to make deposits of wages of the seaman into a checking, savings, investment, or retirement account, or other account to secure a payroll or debit card for the seaman if—

(1) the wages designated by the seaman for such deposit are deposited in a United States or international financial institution designated by the seaman;

(2) such deposits in the financial institution are fully guaranteed under commonly accepted international standards by the government of the country in which the financial institution is licensed;

(3) a written wage statement or pay stub, including an accounting of any direct deposit, is delivered to the seaman no less often than monthly; and

(4) while on board the vessel on which the seaman is employed, the seaman is able to arrange for withdrawal of all funds on deposit in the account in which the wages are deposited.

(Pub. L. 98–89, Aug. 26, 1983, 97 Stat. 567; Pub. L. 111–281, title IX, §902(a)(2), Oct. 15, 2010, 124 Stat. 3009.)

§10316. TRUSTS

Sections 10314 and 10315 of this title do not prevent an employer from making deductions from the wages of a seaman, with the written consent of the seaman, if—

(1) the deductions are paid into a trust fund established only for the benefit of seamen employed by that employer, and the families and dependents of those seamen (or of those seamen, families, and dependents jointly with other seamen employed by other employers, and the families and dependents of the other seamen); and

(2) the payments are held in trust to provide, from principal or interest, or both, any of the following benefits for those seamen and their families and dependents:

(A) medical or hospital care, or both.

(B) pensions on retirement or death of the seaman.

(C) life insurance.

(D) unemployment benefits.

(E) compensation for illness or injuries resulting from occupational activity.

(F) sickness, accident, and disability compensation.

(G) purchasing insurance to provide any of the benefits specified in this section.

(Pub. L. 98–89, Aug. 26, 1983, 97 Stat. 568.)

§10317. LOSS OF LIEN AND RIGHT TO WAGES

A master or seaman by any agreement other than one provided for in this chapter may not forfeit the master's or seaman's lien on the vessel or be deprived of a remedy to which the master or seaman otherwise would be entitled for the recovery of wages. A stipulation in an agreement inconsistent with this chapter, or a stipulation by which a seaman consents to abandon a right to wages if the vessel is lost, or to abandon a right the seaman may have or obtain in the nature of salvage, is void.

(Pub. L. 98–89, Aug. 26, 1983, 97 Stat. 568.)

§10318. WAGES ON DISCHARGE IN FOREIGN PORTS

(a) When a master or seaman applies to a consular officer for the discharge of the seaman, the consular officer shall require the master to pay the seaman's wages if it appears that the seaman has carried out the agreement required by section 10302 of this title or otherwise is entitled to be discharged. Then the consular officer shall discharge the seaman. A consular officer shall require the payment of extra wages only as provided in this section or in chapter 109 of this title.

(b) When discharging a seaman, a consular officer who fails to require the payment of the wages due a seaman at the time, and of the extra wages due under subsection (a) of this section, is accountable to the United States Government for the total amount.

(c) A seaman discharged under this section with the consent of the seaman is entitled to wages up to the time of discharge, but not for any additional period.

(d) If the seaman is discharged involuntarily, and it appears that the discharge was not because of neglect of duty, incompetency, or injury incurred on the vessel, the master shall provide the seaman with employment on a vessel agreed to by the seaman or shall provide the seaman with one month's extra wages.

(e) Expenses for the maintenance and return of an ill or injured seaman to the United States shall be paid by the Secretary of State. If a seaman is incapacitated by illness or injury and prompt discharge is necessary, but a personal appearance of the master before a consular officer is impracticable, the master may provide transportation to the seaman to the nearest consular officer for discharge.

(f) A deduction from wages of the seaman is permitted only if the deduction appears in the account of the seaman required to be delivered under section 10310 of this title, except for matters arising after delivery of the account, in which case a supplementary account is required. During a voyage, the master shall record in the official logbook the matters about which deductions are to be made with the amounts of the deductions. The entries shall be made as the matters occur. The master shall produce the official logbook at the time of payment of wages, and also before a competent authority on the hearing of any complaint or question about the payment of wages.

(Pub. L. 98–89, Aug. 26, 1983, 97 Stat. 568.)

§10319. COSTS OF A CRIMINAL CONVICTION

In a proceeding about a seaman's wages, if it is shown that the seaman was convicted during the voyage of an offense by a competent tribunal and sentenced by the tribunal, the court hearing the case may direct that a part of the wages due the seaman, but not more than $15, be applied to reimburse the master for costs properly incurred in procuring the conviction and sentence.

(Pub. L. 98–89, Aug. 26, 1983, 97 Stat. 569.)

§10320. RECORDS OF SEAMEN

The Secretary shall prescribe regulations requiring vessel owners to maintain records of seamen on matters of engagement, discharge, and service. A vessel owner shall make these records available to the seaman and the Coast Guard on request.

(Pub. L. 98–89, Aug. 26, 1983, 97 Stat. 569; Pub. L. 103–206, title IV, §411, Dec. 20, 1993, 107 Stat. 2437.)

§10321. GENERAL PENALTY

(a) A person violating any provision of this chapter or a regulation prescribed under this chapter is liable to the United States Government for a civil penalty of not more than $5,000.

(b) The vessel is liable in rem for any penalty assessed under this section.

(Pub. L. 98–89, Aug. 26, 1983, 97 Stat. 569; Pub. L. 103–206, title IV, §412, Dec. 20, 1993, 107 Stat. 2437.)

CHAPTER 105—COASTWISE VOYAGES

§10501. APPLICATION

(a) Except for a vessel to which chapter 103 of this title applies, this chapter applies to a vessel of at least 50 gross tons as measured under section 14502 of this title, or an alternate tonnage measured under section 14302 of this title as prescribed by the Secretary under section 14104 of this title on a voyage between a port in one State and a port in another State (except an adjoining State).

(b) This chapter does not apply to a vessel on which the seamen are entitled by custom or agreement to share in the profit or result of a voyage.

(c) Unless otherwise provided, this chapter does not apply to a foreign vessel.

(Pub. L. 98–89, Aug. 26, 1983, 97 Stat. 570; Pub. L. 104–324, title VII, §738, Oct. 19, 1996, 110 Stat. 3941.)

§10502. SHIPPING ARTICLES AGREEMENTS

(a) The owner, charterer, managing operator, master, or individual in charge shall make a shipping agreement in writing with each seaman before the seaman commences employment.

(b) The agreement shall include the date and hour on which the seaman must be on board to begin the voyage.

(c) The agreement may not contain a provision on the allotment of wages or a scale of provisions.

(d) Each shipping agreement must be signed by the master or individual in charge or a representative of the owner, charterer, or managing operator, and by each seaman employed.

(e) The owner, charterer, managing operator, master, or individual in charge shall maintain the shipping agreement and make the shipping agreement available to the seaman.

(f) The Secretary shall prescribe regulations requiring shipping companies to maintain records of seamen on matters of engagement, discharge, and service. The shipping companies shall make these records available to the seaman and the Coast Guard on request.

(Pub. L. 98–89, Aug. 26, 1983, 97 Stat. 570; Pub. L. 103–206, title IV, §413, Dec. 20, 1993, 107 Stat. 2437.)

§10503. Exhibiting merchant mariners' documents

Before signing the agreement required by section 10502 of this title, a seaman required by section 8701 of this title to have a merchant mariner's document shall exhibit to the master a document issued to the seaman and appropriately endorsed for the capacity in which the seaman is to serve.

(Pub. L. 98–89, Aug. 26, 1983, 97 Stat. 570.)

§10504. Wages

(a) After the beginning of a voyage, a seaman is entitled to receive from the master, on demand, one-half of the balance of wages earned and unpaid at each port at which the vessel loads or delivers cargo during the voyage. A demand may not be made before the expiration of 5 days from the beginning of the voyage, not more than once in 5 days, and not more than once in the same port on the same entry. If a master does not comply with this subsection, the seaman is released from the agreement required by section 10502 of this title and is entitled to payment of all wages earned. Notwithstanding a release signed by a seaman under section 10312 of this title, a court having jurisdiction may set aside, for good cause shown, the release and take action that justice requires. This subsection does not apply to a fishing or whaling vessel or a yacht.

(b) The master shall pay a seaman the balance of wages due the seaman within 2 days after the termination of the agreement required by section 10502 of this title or when the seaman is discharged, whichever is earlier.

(c)(1) Subject to subsection (d), and except as provided in paragraph (2), when payment is not made as provided under subsection (b) of this section without sufficient cause, the master or owner shall pay to the seaman 2 days' wages for each day payment is delayed.

(2) The total amount required to be paid under paragraph (1) with respect to all claims in a class action suit by seamen on a passenger vessel capable of carrying more than 500 passengers for wages under this section against a vessel master, owner, or operator or the employer of the seamen shall not exceed ten times the unpaid wages that are the subject of the claims.

(3) A class action suit for wages under this subsection must be commenced within three years after the later of—

(A) the date of the end of the last voyage for which the wages are claimed; or

(B) the receipt, by a seaman who is a claimant in the suit, of a payment of wages that are the subject of the suit that is made in the ordinary course of employment.

(d) Subsections (b) and (c) of this section do not apply to:
(1) a vessel engaged in coastwise commerce.
(2) a yacht.
(3) a fishing vessel.
(4) a whaling vessel.

(e) This section applies to a seaman on a foreign vessel when in harbor of the United States. The courts are available to the seaman for the enforcement of this section.

(f) Deposits in Seaman Account.—On written request signed by the seaman, a seaman employed on a passenger vessel capable of carrying more than 500 passengers may authorize, the master, owner, or operator of the vessel, or the employer of the seaman, to make deposits of wages of the seaman into a checking, savings, investment, or retirement account, or other account to secure a payroll or debit card for the seaman if—

(1) the wages designated by the seaman for such deposit are deposited in a United States or international financial institution designated by the seaman;

(2) such deposits in the financial institution are fully guaranteed under commonly accepted international standards by the government of the country in which the financial institution is licensed;

(3) a written wage statement or pay stub, including an accounting of any direct deposit, is delivered to the seaman no less often than monthly; and

(4) while on board the vessel on which the seaman is employed, the seaman is able to arrange for withdrawal of all funds on deposit in the account in which the wages are deposited.

(Pub. L. 98–89, Aug. 26, 1983, 97 Stat. 570; Pub. L. 99–36, §1(a)(5), May 15, 1985, 99 Stat. 67; Pub. L. 99–640, §10(b)(4), (5), Nov. 10, 1986, 100 Stat. 3550; Pub. L. 111–281, title IX, §902(b), Oct. 15, 2010, 124 Stat. 3009.)

§10505. ADVANCES

(a)(1) A person may not—

(A) pay a seaman wages in advance of the time when the seaman has earned the wages;

(B) pay advance wages of the seaman to another person; or

(C) make to another person an order, note, or other evidence of indebtedness of the wages, or pay another person, for the engagement of seamen when payment is deducted or to be deducted from the seaman's wage.

(2) A person violating this subsection is liable to the United States Government for a civil penalty of not more than $5,000. A payment made in violation of this subsection does not relieve the vessel or the master from the duty to pay all wages after they have been earned.

(b) A person demanding or receiving from a seaman or an individual seeking employment as a seaman, remuneration for providing the seaman or individual with employment, is liable to the Government for a civil penalty of not more than $5,000.

(c) The owner, charterer, managing operator, agent, or master of a vessel seeking clearance from a port of the United States shall present the agreement required by section 10502 of this title at the office of clearance. Clearance may be granted to a vessel only if this section has been complied with.

(d) This section does not apply to a fishing or whaling vessel or a yacht.

(Pub. L. 98–89, Aug. 26, 1983, 97 Stat. 571; Pub. L. 99–640, §10(b)(4), Nov. 10, 1986, 100 Stat. 3550; Pub. L. 103–206, title IV, §414, Dec. 20, 1993, 107 Stat. 2437.)

§10506. TRUSTS

Section 10505 of this title does not prevent an employer from making deductions from the wages of a seaman, with the written consent of the seaman, if—

(1) the deductions are paid into a trust fund established only for the benefit of seamen

employed by that employer, and the families and dependents of those seamen (or of those seamen, families, and dependents jointly with other seamen employed by other employers, and the families and dependents of the other seamen); and

(2) the payments are held in trust to provide, from principal or interest, or both, any of the following benefits for those seamen and their families and dependents:

(A) medical or hospital care, or both.

(B) pensions on retirement or death of the seaman.

(C) life insurance.

(D) unemployment benefits.

(E) compensation for illness or injuries resulting from occupational activity.

(F) sickness, accident, and disability compensation.

(G) purchasing insurance to provide any of the benefits specified in this section.

(Pub. L. 98–89, Aug. 26, 1983, 97 Stat. 571.)

[§10507. Repealed. Pub. L. 103–206, title IV, §415(a), Dec. 20, 1993, 107 Stat. 2438]

Section, Pub. L. 98–89, Aug. 26, 1983, 97 Stat. 571, related to duties of shipping commissioners.

§10508. General penalties

(a) A master who carries a seaman on a voyage without first making the agreement required by section 10502 of this title shall pay to the seaman the highest wage that was paid for a similar voyage within the 3 months before the time of engagement at the port or place at which the seaman was engaged. A seaman who has not signed an agreement is not bound by the applicable regulations, penalties, or forfeitures.

(b) A master engaging a seaman in violation of this chapter or a regulation prescribed under this chapter is liable to the United States Government for a civil penalty of not more than $5,000. The vessel also is liable in rem for the penalty.

(Pub. L. 98–89, Aug. 26, 1983, 97 Stat. 572; Pub. L. 103–206, title IV, §416, Dec. 20, 1993, 107 Stat. 2438.)

§10509. Penalty for failing to begin voyage

(a) A seaman who fails to be on board at the time contained in the agreement required by section 10502 of this title, without having given 24 hours' notice of inability to do so, shall forfeit, for each hour's lateness, one-half of one day's pay to be deducted from the seaman's wages if the lateness is recorded in the official logbook on the date of the violation.

(b) A seaman who does not report at all or subsequently deserts forfeits all wages.

(c) This section does not apply to a fishing or whaling vessel or a yacht.

(Pub. L. 98–89, Aug. 26, 1983, 97 Stat. 572.)

CHAPTER 106—FISHING VOYAGES

Sec.

§10601. FISHING AGREEMENTS

(a) Before proceeding on a voyage, the owner, charterer, or managing operator, or a representative thereof, including the master or individual in charge, of a fishing vessel, fish processing vessel, or fish tender vessel shall make a fishing agreement in writing with each seaman employed on board if the vessel is—

(1) at least 20 gross tons as measured under section 14502 of this title, or an alternate tonnage measured under section 14302 of this title as prescribed by the Secretary under section 14104 of this title; and

(2) on a voyage from a port in the United States.

(b) The agreement shall—

(1) state the period of effectiveness of the agreement;

(2) include the terms of any wage, share, or other compensation arrangement peculiar to the fishery in which the vessel will be engaged during the period of the agreement;

(3) in the case of a seaman employed on a vessel that is a catcher processor or fish processing vessel that employs more than 25 crewmembers, include a requirement that each crewmember shall be served not less than three meals a day that—

(A) total not less than 3,100 calories; and

(B) include adequate water and minerals in accordance with the United States Recommended Daily Allowances; and

(4) include other agreed terms.

(Pub. L. 100–424, §6(a), Sept. 9, 1988, 102 Stat. 1591; Pub. L. 104–324, title VII, §739, Oct. 19, 1996, 110 Stat. 3942; Pub. L. 107–295, title IV, §441(a), (b), Nov. 25, 2002, 116 Stat. 2131; Pub. L. 117–263, div. K, title CXV, §11526, Dec. 23, 2022, 136 Stat. 4145.)

§10602. RECOVERY OF WAGES AND SHARES OF FISH UNDER AGREEMENT

(a) When fish caught under an agreement under section 10601 of this title are delivered to the owner of the vessel for processing and are sold, the vessel is liable in rem for the wages and shares of the proceeds of the seamen. An action under this section must be brought within six months after the sale of the fish.

(b)(1) In an action under this section, the owner shall produce an accounting of the sale and division of proceeds under the agreement. If the owner fails to produce the accounting, the vessel is liable for the highest value alleged for the shares.

(2) The owner may offset the value of general supplies provided for the voyage and other supplies provided the seaman bringing the action.

(c) This section does not affect a common law right of a seaman to bring an action to recover the seaman's share of the fish or proceeds.

(Pub. L. 100–424, §6(a), Sept. 9, 1988, 102 Stat. 1592.)

§10603. SEAMAN'S DUTY TO NOTIFY EMPLOYER REGARDING ILLNESS, DISABILITY, AND INJURY

(a) A seaman on a fishing vessel, fish processing vessel, or fish tender vessel shall notify the master or individual in charge of the vessel or other agent of the employer regarding any illness, disability, or injury suffered by the seaman when in service to the vessel not later than seven days after the date on which the illness, disability, or injury arose.

(b) The Secretary shall prescribe regulations requiring that each fishing vessel, fish processing vessel, and fish tender vessel shall have on board a placard displayed in a prominent location accessible to the crew describing the seaman's duty under subsection (a) of this section.

(Pub. L. 100–424, §6(a), Sept. 9, 1988, 102 Stat. 1592.)

CHAPTER 107—EFFECTS OF DECEASED SEAMEN

Sec.
10701.   Application.
10702.   Duties of masters.
10703.   Procedures of masters.
10704.   Duties of consular officers.
10705.   Disposition of money, property, and wages by consular officers.
10706.   Seamen dying in the United States.
[10707.   Repealed.]
10708.   Sale of property.
10709.   Distribution.
10710.   Unclaimed money, property, and wages.
10711.   Penalties.

§10701. APPLICATION

(a) Except as otherwise specifically provided, this chapter applies to a vessel on a voyage between—

(1) a port of the United States and a port in a foreign country (except a port in Canada, Mexico, and the West Indies); and

(2) a port of the United States on the Atlantic Ocean and a port of the United States on the Pacific Ocean.

(b) This chapter does not apply to a vessel on which a seaman by custom or agreement is entitled to share in the profit or result of a voyage.

(c) This chapter does not apply to a foreign vessel.

(Pub. L. 98–89, Aug. 26, 1983, 97 Stat. 572.)

§10702. DUTIES OF MASTERS

(a) When a seaman dies during a voyage, the master shall take charge of the seaman's money and property. An entry shall be made in the official logbook, signed by the master, the chief mate, and an unlicensed crewmember containing an inventory of the money and property and a statement of the wages due the seaman, with the total of the deductions to be made.

(b) On compliance with this chapter, the master shall obtain a written certificate of compliance from the consular officer or court clerk. Clearance may be granted to a foreign-bound vessel only when the certificate is received at the office of customs.

(Pub. L. 98–89, Aug. 26, 1983, 97 Stat. 572; Pub. L. 103–206, title IV, §422(a), Dec. 20, 1993, 107 Stat. 2438.)

§10703. PROCEDURES OF MASTERS

(a) If the vessel is proceeding to the United States when a seaman dies, the master shall deliver the seaman's money, property, and wages when the agreement required by this part

535

is ended, as provided in section 10706 of this title.

(b) If the vessel touches at a foreign port after the death of the seaman, the master shall report to the first available consular officer. The consular officer may require the master to deliver to the officer the money, property, and wages of the seaman. The consular officer shall give the master a receipt for the matters delivered and certify on the agreement the particulars of the delivery. When the agreement ends, the master shall deliver the receipt to a district court of the United States.

(c) If the consular officer does not require the master to deliver the seaman's money, property, and wages, the officer shall so certify on the agreement, and the master shall dispose of the money, property, and wages as provided under section 10706 of this title.

(d) A deduction from the account of a deceased seaman is valid only if certified by a proper entry in the official logbook.

(Pub. L. 98–89, Aug. 26, 1983, 97 Stat. 573; Pub. L. 103–206, title IV, §418, Dec. 20, 1993, 107 Stat. 2438.)

§10704. DUTIES OF CONSULAR OFFICERS

When a seaman dies outside the United States leaving money or property not on board a vessel, the consular officer nearest the place at which the money and property is located shall claim and take charge of it.

(Pub. L. 98–89, Aug. 26, 1983, 97 Stat. 573.)

§10705. DISPOSITION OF MONEY, PROPERTY, AND WAGES BY CONSULAR OFFICERS

When money, property, or wages of a deceased seaman comes into possession of a consular officer, the officer may—

(1) sell the property and remit the proceeds and other money or wages of the seaman the officer has received, to the district court of the United States for the district in which the voyage begins or ends; or

(2) deliver the money, property, and wages to the district court.

(Pub. L. 98–89, Aug. 26, 1983, 97 Stat. 573.)

§10706. SEAMEN DYING IN THE UNITED STATES

When a seaman dies in the United States and is entitled at death to claim money, property, or wages from the master or owner of a vessel on which the seaman served, the master or owner shall deliver the money, property, and wages to a district court of the United States within one week of the seaman's death. If the seaman's death occurs at sea, such money, property, or wages shall be delivered to a district court or a consular officer within one week of the vessel's arrival at the first port call after the seaman's death.

(Pub. L. 98–89, Aug. 26, 1983, 97 Stat. 573; Pub. L. 103–206, title IV, §419, Dec. 20, 1993, 107 Stat. 2438.)

[§10707. REPEALED. PUB. L. 103–206, TITLE IV, §420(A), DEC. 20, 1993, 107 STAT. 2438]

Section, Pub. L. 98–89, Aug. 26, 1983, 97 Stat. 573, related to delivery to district court of money, property, and wages of a deceased seaman.

§10708. SALE OF PROPERTY

A district court of the United States may direct the sale of any part of the property of a deceased seaman. Proceeds of the sale shall be held as wages of the seaman are held.

(Pub. L. 98–89, Aug. 26, 1983, 97 Stat. 574.)

§10709. DISTRIBUTION

(a)(1) If the money, property, and wages of a seaman, including proceeds from the sale of property, are not more than $1,500 in value, the court, subject to deductions it allows for expenses and at least 60 days after receiving the money, property, and wages, may deliver the money, property, and wages to a claimant proving to be—

(A) the seaman's surviving spouse or child;

(B) entitled to the money, property, and wages under the seaman's will or under a law or at common law; or

(C) entitled to secure probate, or take out letters of administration, although no probate or letters of administration have been issued.

(2) The court is released from further liability for the money, property, and wages distributed under paragraph (1) of this subsection.

(3) Instead of acting under paragraphs (1) and (2) of this subsection, the court may require probate or letters of administration to be taken out, and then deliver the money, property, and wages to the legal representative of the seaman.

(b) If the money, property, and wages are more than $1,500 in value, the court, subject to deductions for expenses, shall deliver the money, property, and wages to the legal representative of the seaman.

(Pub. L. 98–89, Aug. 26, 1983, 97 Stat. 574; Pub. L. 99–307, §1(15), May 19, 1986, 100 Stat. 446.)

§10710. UNCLAIMED MONEY, PROPERTY, AND WAGES

(a) When a claim for the money, property, or wages of a deceased seaman held by a district court of the United States has not been substantiated within 6 years after their receipt by the court, the court, if a subsequent claim is made, may allow or refuse the claim.

(b) If, after money, property, and wages have been held by the court for 6 years, it appears to the court that no claim will have to be satisfied, the property shall be sold. The money and wages and the proceeds from the sale shall be deposited in the Treasury trust fund receipt account "Unclaimed Moneys of Individuals Whose Whereabouts are Unknown".

(Pub. L. 98–89, Aug. 26, 1983, 97 Stat. 574.)

§10711. PENALTIES

An owner or master violating this chapter are each liable to the United States Government for a civil penalty of 3 times the value of the seaman's money, property, and wages involved or, if the value is not determined, of $200.

(Pub. L. 98–89, Aug. 26, 1983, 97 Stat. 574.)

§ 10,702. Sale of property.

§ 10,703. Disposition.

CHAPTER 109—PROCEEDINGS ON UNSEAWORTHINESS

§10901. APPLICATION

This chapter applies to a vessel of the United States except a fishing or whaling vessel or a yacht.

(Pub. L. 98–89, Aug. 26, 1983, 97 Stat. 575.)

§10902. COMPLAINTS OF UNFITNESS

(a)(1) If the chief and second mates or a majority of the crew of a vessel ready to begin a voyage discover, before the vessel leaves harbor, that the vessel is unfit as to crew, hull, equipment, tackle, machinery, apparel, furniture, provisions of food or water, or stores to proceed on the intended voyage and require the unfitness to be inquired into, the master immediately shall apply to the district court of the United States at the place at which the vessel is located, or, if no court is being held at the place at which the vessel is located, to a judge or justice of the peace, for the appointment of surveyors. At least 2 complaining seamen shall accompany the master to the judge or justice of the peace.

(2) A master failing to comply with this subsection is liable to the United States Government for a civil penalty of $500.

(b)(1) Any 3 seamen of a vessel may complain that the provisions of food or water for the crew are, at any time, of bad quality, unfit for use, or deficient in quantity. The complaint may be made to the Secretary, commanding officer of a United States naval vessel, consular officer, or chief official of the Customs Service.

(2) The Secretary, officer, or official shall examine, or have examined, the provisions of food or water. If the provisions are found to be of bad quality, unfit for use, or deficient in quantity, the person making the findings shall certify to the master of the vessel which provisions are of bad quality, unfit for use, or deficient.

(3) The Secretary, officer, or official to whom the complaint was made shall—

(A) make an entry in the official logbook of the vessel on the results of the examination; and

(B) submit a report on the examination to the district court of the United States at which the vessel is to arrive, with the report being admissible into evidence in any legal proceeding.

(4) The master is liable to the Government for a civil penalty of not more than $100 each time the master, on receiving the certification referred to in paragraph (2) of this subsection—

(A) does not provide other proper provisions of food or water, when available, in place of the provisions certified as of bad quality or unfit for use;

(B) does not obtain sufficient provisions when the certification includes a finding of a deficiency in quantity; or

(C) uses provisions certified to be of bad quality or unfit for use.

(Pub. L. 98–89, Aug. 26, 1983, 97 Stat. 575; Pub. L. 103–206, title IV, §422(b), Dec. 20, 1993, 107 Stat. 2439.)

§10903. PROCEEDINGS ON EXAMINATION OF VESSEL

(a) On application made under section 10902(a) of this title, the judge or justice of the peace shall appoint 3 experienced and skilled marine surveyors to examine the vessel for the defects or insufficiencies complained of. The surveyors have the authority to receive and consider evidence necessary to evaluate the complaint. When the complaint involves provisions of food or water, one of the surveyors shall be a medical officer of the Public Health Service, if available. The surveyors shall make a report in writing, signed by at least 2 of them, stating whether the vessel is fit to proceed to sea or, if not, in what respect it is unfit, making appropriate recommendations about additional seamen, provisions, or stores, or about physical repairs, alterations, or additions necessary to make the vessel fit.

(b) On receiving the report, the judge or justice of the peace shall endorse on the report the judgment of the judge or justice on whether the vessel is fit to proceed on the voyage, and, if not, whether the vessel may proceed to another port at which the deficiencies can be corrected. The master and the crew shall comply with the judgment.

(c) The master shall pay all costs of the survey, report, and judgment. However, if the complaint of the crew appears in the report and judgment to have been without foundation, or if the complaint involved provisions of food or water, without reasonable grounds, the master or owner may deduct the amount of the costs and reasonable damages for the detention of the vessel, as determined by the judge or justice of the peace, from the wages of the complaining seamen.

(d) A master of a vessel violating this section who refuses to pay the costs and wages is liable to the United States Government for a civil penalty of $100 and is liable in damages to each person injured by the refusal.

(Pub. L. 98–89, Aug. 26, 1983, 97 Stat. 575.)

§10904. REFUSAL TO PROCEED

After a judgment under section 10903 of this title that a vessel is fit to proceed on the intended voyage, or after the order of a judgment to make up deficiencies is complied with, if a seaman does not proceed on the voyage, the unpaid wages of the seaman are forfeited.

(Pub. L. 98–89, Aug. 26, 1983, 97 Stat. 576.)

§10905. COMPLAINTS IN FOREIGN PORTS

(a) When a complaint under section 10902(a) of this title is made in a foreign port, the procedures of this chapter shall be followed, with a consular officer performing the duties of the judge or justice of the peace.

(b) On review of the marine surveyors' report, the consular officer may approve and must certify any part of the report with which the officer agrees. If the consular officer dissents from any part of the report, the officer shall certify reasons for dissenting from that part.

(Pub. L. 98–89, Aug. 26, 1983, 97 Stat. 576.)

§10906. DISCHARGE OF CREW FOR UNSUITABILITY

When a survey is made at a foreign port, the surveyors shall state in the report whether, in their opinion, the vessel had been sent to sea unsuitably provided in any important particular, by neglect or design or through mistake or accident. If by neglect or design, and the consular officer approves the finding, the officer shall discharge a seaman requesting discharge and shall require the master to pay one month's wages to that seaman in addition to wages then due, or sufficient money for the return of the seaman to the nearest and most convenient port of the United States, whichever is the greater amount.

(Pub. L. 98–89, Aug. 26, 1983, 97 Stat. 576.)

§10907. PERMISSION TO MAKE COMPLAINT

(a) A master may not refuse to permit, deny the opportunity to, or hinder a seaman who wishes to make a complaint authorized by this chapter.

(b) A master violating this section is liable to the United States Government for civil penalty of $500.

(Pub. L. 98–89, Aug. 26, 1983, 97 Stat. 577.)

§10908. PENALTY FOR SENDING UNSEAWORTHY VESSEL TO SEA

A person that knowingly sends or attempts to send, or that is a party to sending or attempting to send, a vessel of the United States to sea, in an unseaworthy state that is likely to endanger the life of an individual, shall be fined not more than $1,000, imprisoned for not more than 5 years, or both.

(Pub. L. 98–89, Aug. 26, 1983, 97 Stat. 577.)

CHAPTER 111—PROTECTION AND RELIEF

§11101. ACCOMMODATIONS FOR SEAMEN

(a) On a merchant vessel of the United States the construction of which began after March 4, 1915 (except a yacht, pilot vessel, or vessel of less than 100 gross tons as measured under section 14502 of this title, or an alternate tonnage measured under section 14302 of this title as prescribed by the Secretary under section 14104 of this title)—

(1) each place appropriated to the crew of the vessel shall have a space of at least 120 cubic feet and at least 16 square feet, measured on the floor or deck of that place, for each seaman or apprentice lodged in the vessel;

(2) each seaman shall have a separate berth and not more than one berth shall be placed one above another;

(3) the place or berth shall be securely constructed, properly lighted, drained, heated, and ventilated, properly protected from weather and sea, and, as far as practicable, properly shut off and protected from the effluvium of cargo or bilge water;

(4) crew space shall be kept free from goods or stores that are not the personal property of the crew occupying the place in use during the voyage; and

(5) each crew berthing area shall be equipped with information regarding—

(A) vessel owner or company policies prohibiting sexual assault and sexual harassment, retaliation, and drug and alcohol usage; and

(B) procedures and resources to report crimes, including sexual assault and sexual harassment, including information—

(i) on the telephone number, website address, and email address for reporting allegations of sexual assault and sexual harassment to the Coast Guard;

(ii) on vessel owner or company procedures to report violations of company policy and access resources;

(iii) on resources provided by outside organizations such as sexual assault hotlines and counseling;

(iv) on the retention period for surveillance video recording after an incident of sexual harassment or sexual assault is reported; and

(v) additional items specified in regulations issued by, and at the discretion of, the Secretary of the department in which the Coast Guard is operating.

(b) In addition to the requirements of subsection (a) of this section, a merchant vessel of the United States that in the ordinary course of trade makes a voyage of more than 3 days' duration between ports and carries a crew of at least 12 seamen shall have a hospital compartment, suitably separated from other spaces. The compartment shall have at least one bunk for each 12 seamen constituting the crew (but not more than 6 bunks may be required).

(c) A steam vessel of the United States operating on the Mississippi River or its tributaries shall provide, under the direction and approval of the Secretary, an appropriate place for the crew that shall conform to the requirements of this section, as far as they apply to the steam vessel, by providing a properly heated sleeping room in the engineroom of the steam vessel properly protected from the cold, wind, and rain by means of suitable awnings or screens on either side of the guards or sides and forward, reaching from the boiler deck to the lower or main deck.

(d) A merchant vessel of the United States, the construction of which began after March 4, 1915, having more than 10 seamen on deck, shall have at least one lighted, clean, and properly heated and ventilated washing place. There shall be provided at least one washing outfit for each 2 seamen of the watch. A separate washing place shall be provided for the fireroom and engineroom seamen, if their number is more than 10, that shall be large enough to accommodate at least one-sixth of them at the same time, and have a hot and cold water supply and a sufficient number of washbasins, sinks, and shower baths. In each washing space in a visible location there shall be information regarding procedures and resources to report crimes upon the vessel, including sexual assault and sexual harassment, and vessel owner or company policies prohibiting sexual assault and sexual harassment, retaliation, and drug and alcohol usage.

(e) Forecastles shall be fumigated at intervals provided by regulations prescribed by the Secretary of Health and Human Services, with the approval of the Secretary, and shall have at least 2 exits, one of which may be used in emergencies.

(f) The owner, charterer, managing operator, agent, master, or licensed individual of a vessel not complying with this section is liable to the United States Government for a civil penalty of at least $50 but not more than $500.

(Pub. L. 98–89, Aug. 26, 1983, 97 Stat. 577; Pub. L. 99–36, §1(a)(6), May 15, 1985, 99 Stat. 67; Pub. L. 104–324, title VII, §740, Oct. 19, 1996, 110 Stat. 3942; Pub. L. 117–263, div. K, title CXVI, §11604, Dec. 23, 2022, 136 Stat. 4148.)

§11102. MEDICINE CHESTS

(a) A vessel of the United States on a voyage from a port in the United States to a foreign port (except to a Canadian port), and a vessel of the United States of at least 75 gross tons as measured under section 14502 of this title, or an alternate tonnage measured under section 14302 of this title as prescribed by the Secretary under section 14104 of this title on a voyage between a port of the United States on the Atlantic Ocean and Pacific Ocean, shall be provided with a medicine chest.

(b) The owner and master of a vessel not equipped as required by subsection (a) of this section or a regulation prescribed under subsection (a) are liable to the United States Government for a civil penalty of $500. If the offense was due to the fault of the owner, a master penalized under this section has the right to recover the penalty and costs from the owner.

(Pub. L. 98–89, Aug. 26, 1983, 97 Stat. 578; Pub. L. 104–324, title VII, §741, Oct. 19, 1996, 110 Stat. 3942.)

§11103. SLOP CHESTS

(a) A vessel to which section 11102 of this title applies shall be provided with a slop chest containing sufficient clothing for the intended voyage for each seaman, including—
    (1) boots or shoes;
    (2) hats or caps;
    (3) underclothing;
    (4) outer clothing;
    (5) foul weather clothing;
    (6) everything necessary for the wear of a seaman; and
    (7) a complete supply of tobacco and blankets.

(b) Merchandise in the slop chest shall be sold to a seaman desiring it, for the use of the seaman, at a profit of not more than 10 percent of the reasonable wholesale value of the merchandise at the port at which the voyage began.

(c) This section does not apply to a vessel on a voyage to Canada, Bermuda, the West Indies, Mexico, or Central America, or a fishing or whaling vessel.

(Pub. L. 98–89, Aug. 26, 1983, 97 Stat. 578.)

§11104. DESTITUTE SEAMEN

(a) A consular officer shall provide, for a destitute seaman of the United States, subsistence and passage to a port of the United States in the most reasonable manner, at the expense of the United States Government and subject to regulations prescribed by the Secretary of State. A seaman, if able, shall be required to perform duties on the vessel giving the seaman passage, in accordance with the seaman's rating.

(b) A master of a vessel of the United States bound to a port of the United States shall take a destitute seaman on board at the request of a consular officer and transport the seaman to the United States. A master refusing to transport a destitute seaman when requested is liable to the United States Government for a civil penalty of $100. The certificate signed and sealed by a consular officer is prima facie evidence of refusal. A master is not required to carry a destitute seaman if the seaman's presence would cause the number of individuals on board to exceed the number permitted in the certificate of inspection or if the seaman has a contagious disease.

(c) Compensation for the transportation of destitute seamen to the United States who are unable to work shall be agreed on by the master and the consular officer, under regulations prescribed by the Secretary of State. However, the compensation may be not more than the lowest passenger rate of the vessel, or 2 cents a mile, whichever is less.

(d) When a master of a vessel of the United States takes on board a destitute seaman unable to work, from a port or place not having a consular officer, for transportation to the United States or to a port at which there is a consular officer, the master or owner of the vessel shall be compensated reasonably under regulations prescribed by the Secretary of State.

(Pub. L. 98–89, Aug. 26, 1983, 97 Stat. 578.)

§11105. WAGES ON DISCHARGE WHEN VESSEL SOLD

(a) When a vessel of the United States is sold in a foreign country, the master shall deliver to the consular officer a certified crew list and the agreement required by this part. The master shall pay each seaman the wages due the seaman and provide the seaman with employment on board another vessel of the United States bound for the port of original engagement of the seaman or to another port agreed on. If employment cannot be provided, the master shall—

(1) provide the seaman with the means to return to the port of original engagement;

(2) provide the seaman passage to the port of original engagement; or

(3) deposit with the consular officer an amount of money considered sufficient by the officer to provide the seaman with maintenance and passage home.

(b) The consular officer shall endorse on the agreement the particulars of the payment, provision, or deposit made under this section.

(c) An owner of a vessel is liable to the United States Government for a civil penalty of $500 if the master does not comply with this section.

(Pub. L. 98–89, Aug. 26, 1983, 97 Stat. 579.)

§11106. WAGES ON JUSTIFIABLE COMPLAINT OF SEAMEN

(a) Before a seaman on a vessel of the United States is discharged in a foreign country by a consular officer on the seaman's complaint that the agreement required by this part has been breached because the vessel is badly provisioned or unseaworthy, or against the officers for cruel treatment, the officer shall inquire about the complaint. If satisfied of the justice of the complaint, the consular officer shall require the master to pay the wages due the seaman plus one month's additional wages and shall discharge the seaman. The master shall provide the seaman with employment on another vessel or provide the seaman with passage on another vessel to the port of original engagement, to the most convenient port of the United States, or to some port agreeable to the seaman.

(b) When a vessel does not have sufficient provisions for the intended voyage, and the seaman has been forced to accept a reduced ration or provisions that are bad in quality or unfit for use, the seaman is entitled to recover from the master or owner an allowance, as additional wages, that the court hearing the case considers reasonable.

(c) Subsection (b) of this section does not apply when the reduction in rations was for a period during which the seaman willfully and without sufficient cause failed to perform duties or was lawfully under confinement on board or on shore for misconduct, unless that reduction can be shown to have been unreasonable.

(d) Subsection (b) of this section does not apply to a fishing or whaling vessel or a yacht.

(Pub. L. 98–89, Aug. 26, 1983, 97 Stat. 579.)

§11107. Unlawful engagements void

An engagement of a seaman contrary to a law of the United States is void. A seaman so engaged may leave the service of the vessel at any time and is entitled to recover the highest rate of wages at the port from which the seaman was engaged or the amount agreed to be given the seaman at the time of engagement, whichever is higher.

(Pub. L. 98–89, Aug. 26, 1983, 97 Stat. 580.)

§11108. Taxes

(a) Withholding.—Wages due or accruing to a master or seaman on a vessel in the foreign, coastwise, intercoastal, interstate, or noncontiguous trade or an individual employed on a fishing vessel or any fish processing vessel may not be withheld under the tax laws of a State or a political subdivision of a State. However, this section does not prohibit withholding wages of a seaman on a vessel in the coastwise trade between ports in the same State if the withholding is under a voluntary agreement between the seaman and the employer of the seaman.

(b) Liability.—

(1) Limitation on jurisdiction to tax.—An individual to whom this subsection applies is not subject to the income tax laws of a State or political subdivision of a State, other than the State and political subdivision in which the individual resides, with respect to compensation for the performance of duties described in paragraph (2).

(2) Application.—This subsection applies to an individual—

(A) engaged on a vessel to perform assigned duties in more than one State as a pilot licensed under section 7101 of this title or licensed or authorized under the laws of a State; or

(B) who performs regularly assigned duties while engaged as a master, officer, or crewman on a vessel operating on navigable waters in 2 or more States.

(Pub. L. 98–89, Aug. 26, 1983, 97 Stat. 580; Pub. L. 98–364, title IV, §402(14), July 17, 1984, 98 Stat. 450; Pub. L. 106–489, §1, Nov. 9, 2000, 114 Stat. 2207; Pub. L. 111–281, title IX, §906, Oct. 15, 2010, 124 Stat. 3012.)

§11109. Attachment of wages

(a) Wages due or accruing to a master or seaman are not subject to attachment or arrestment from any court, except for an order of a court about the payment by a master or seaman of any part of the master's or seaman's wages for the support and maintenance of the spouse or minor children of the master or seaman, or both. A payment of wages to a master or seaman is valid, notwithstanding any prior sale or assignment of wages or any attachment, encumbrance, or arrestment of the wages.

(b) An assignment or sale of wages or salvage made before the payment of wages does not bind the party making it, except allotments authorized by section 10315 of this title.

(c) This section applies to an individual employed on a fishing vessel or any fish processing vessel.

(Pub. L. 98–89, Aug. 26, 1983, 97 Stat. 580; Pub. L. 98–364, title IV, §402(15), July 17, 1984, 98 Stat. 450.)

§11110. Seamen's clothing

The clothing of a seaman is exempt from attachments and liens. A person detaining a seaman's clothing shall be fined not more than $500, imprisoned for not more than 6 months, or both.

(Pub. L. 98–89, Aug. 26, 1983, 97 Stat. 580.)

§11111. Limit on amount recoverable on voyage

When a seaman is on a voyage on which a written agreement is required under this part, not more than $1 is recoverable from the seaman by a person for a debt incurred by the seaman during the voyage for which the seaman is signed on until the voyage is ended.

(Pub. L. 98–89, Aug. 26, 1983, 97 Stat. 581.)

§11112. Master's lien for wages

The master of a documented vessel has the same lien against the vessel for the master's wages and the same priority as any other seaman serving on the vessel.

(Added Pub. L. 99–307, §1(19)(B), May 19, 1986, 100 Stat. 446.)

§11113. Treatment of abandoned seafarers

(a) Abandoned Seafarers Fund.—

(1) Establishment.—There is established in the Treasury a separate account to be known as the Abandoned Seafarers Fund.

(2) Authorized uses.—Amounts in the Fund may be appropriated to the Secretary for use—

(A) to pay necessary support of a seafarer—

(i) who—

(I) was paroled into the United States under section 212(d)(5) of the Immigration and Nationality Act (8 U.S.C. 1182(d)(5)), or for whom the Secretary has requested parole under such section; and

(II) is involved in an investigation, reporting, documentation, or adjudication of any matter that is related to the administration or enforcement of law by the Coast Guard; or

(ii) who—

(I) is physically present in the United States;

(II) the Secretary determines was abandoned in the United States; and

(III) has not applied for asylum under the Immigration and Nationality Act (8 U.S.C. 1101 et seq.); and

(B) to reimburse a vessel owner or operator for the costs of necessary support of a seafarer who has been paroled into the United States to facilitate an investigation, reporting, documentation, or adjudication of any matter that is related to the administration or enforcement of law by the Coast Guard, if—

(i) the vessel owner or operator is not convicted of a criminal offense related to such matter; or

(ii) the Secretary determines that reimbursement is appropriate.

(3) CREDITING OF AMOUNTS TO FUND.—

(A) IN GENERAL.—Except as provided in subparagraph (B), there shall be credited to the Fund the following:

(i) Penalties deposited in the Fund under section 9 of the Act to Prevent Pollution from Ships (33 U.S.C. 1908).

(ii) Amounts reimbursed or recovered under subsection (c).

(B) LIMITATION.—Amounts may be credited to the Fund under subparagraph (A) only if the unobligated balance of the Fund is less than $5,000,000.

(4) REPORT REQUIRED.—Except as provided in paragraph (5), on the date on which the President submits each budget for a fiscal year pursuant to section 1105 of title 31, the Secretary shall submit to the Committee on Transportation and Infrastructure of the House of Representatives and the Committee on Commerce, Science, and Transportation of the Senate a report that describes—

(A) the amounts credited to the Fund under paragraph (3) for the preceding fiscal year; and

(B) amounts in the Fund that were expended for the preceding fiscal year.

(5) NO REPORT REQUIRED.—A report under paragraph (4) shall not be required if there were no expenditures from the Fund in the preceding fiscal year. The Commandant shall notify Congress in the event a report is not required under paragraph (4) by reason of this paragraph.

(b) LIMITATION.—Nothing in this section shall be construed—

(1) to create a private right of action or any other right, benefit, or entitlement to necessary support for any person; or

(2) to compel the Secretary to pay or reimburse the cost of necessary support.

(c) REIMBURSEMENT; RECOVERY.—

(1) IN GENERAL.—A vessel owner or operator shall reimburse the Fund an amount equal to the total amount paid from the Fund for necessary support of a seafarer, if—

(A) the vessel owner or operator—

(i) during the course of an investigation, reporting, documentation, or adjudication of any matter that the Coast Guard referred to a United States attorney or the Attorney General, fails to provide necessary support of a seafarer who was paroled into the United States to facilitate the investigation, reporting, documentation, or adjudication; and

(ii) subsequently is—

(I) convicted of a criminal offense related to such matter; or

(II) required to reimburse the Fund pursuant to a court order or negotiated settlement related to such matter; or

(B) the vessel owner or operator abandons a seafarer in the United States, as determined by the Secretary based on substantial evidence.

(2) ENFORCEMENT.—If a vessel owner or operator fails to reimburse the Fund under paragraph (1) within 60 days after receiving a written, itemized description of reimbursable expenses and a demand for payment, the Secretary may—

(A) proceed in rem against the vessel on which the seafarer served in the Federal district court for the district in which the vessel is found; and

(B) withhold or revoke the clearance required under section 60105 for the vessel and any other vessel operated by the same operator (as that term is defined in section 2(a)(9)(A) [1] of the Act to Prevent Pollution from Ships (33 U.S.C. 1901(a)(9)(A)) [2] as the vessel on which the seafarer served.

(3) OBTAINING CLEARANCE.—A vessel may obtain clearance from the Secretary after it is withheld or revoked under paragraph (2)(B) if the vessel owner or operator—

(A) reimburses the Fund the amount required under paragraph (1); or

(B) provides a bond, or other evidence of financial responsibility, sufficient to meet the amount required to be reimbursed under paragraph (1).

(4) NOTIFICATION REQUIRED.—The Secretary shall notify the vessel at least 72 hours before taking any action under paragraph (2)(B).

(d) DEFINITIONS.—In this section:

(1) ABANDONS; ABANDONED.—Each of the terms "abandons" and "abandoned" means—

(A) a vessel owner's or operator's unilateral severance of ties with a seafarer; or

(B) a vessel owner's or operator's failure to provide necessary support of a seafarer.

(2) FUND.—The term "Fund" means the Abandoned Seafarers Fund established under this section.

(3) NECESSARY SUPPORT.—The term "necessary support" means normal wages and expenses the Secretary considers reasonable for lodging, subsistence, clothing, medical care (including hospitalization), repatriation, and any other support the Secretary considers to be appropriate.

(4) SEAFARER.—The term "seafarer" means an alien crew member who is employed or engaged in any capacity on board a vessel subject to the jurisdiction of the United States.

(5) VESSEL SUBJECT TO THE JURISDICTION OF THE UNITED STATES.—The term "vessel subject to the jurisdiction of the United States" has the meaning given that term in section 70502(c), except that it does not include a vessel that is—

(A) owned, or operated under a bareboat charter, by the United States, a State or political subdivision thereof, or a foreign nation; and

(B) not engaged in commerce.

(Added Pub. L. 113–281, title III, §320(a), Dec. 18, 2014, 128 Stat. 3051; amended Pub. L. 114–120, title III, §306(a)(7), Feb. 8, 2016, 130 Stat. 54; Pub. L. 115–232, div. C, title XXXV, §3546(i), Aug. 13, 2018, 132 Stat. 2326; Pub. L. 116–283, div. G, title LVXXXII [LXXXII], §8240(d), Jan. 1, 2021, 134 Stat. 4667.)

[1] *So in original. Probably should be "2(a)(9)(a)".*

[2] *So in original. Probably should be "33 U.S.C. 1901(a)(9)(a)))".*

CHAPTER 112—MERCHANT MARINER BENEFITS

§11201. ELIGIBILITY FOR VETERANS' BURIAL AND CEMETERY BENEFITS

(a) ELIGIBILITY.—

(1) IN GENERAL.—The qualified service of an individual referred to in paragraph (2) shall be considered to be active duty in the Armed Forces during a period of war for purposes of eligibility for benefits under the following provisions of title 38:

(A) Chapter 23 (relating to burial benefits).

(B) Chapter 24 (relating to interment in national cemeteries).

(2) COVERED INDIVIDUALS.—Paragraph (1) applies to an individual who—

(A) receives an honorable service certificate under section 11203 of this title; and

(B) is not eligible under any other provision of law for benefits under laws administered by the Secretary of Veterans Affairs.

(b) REIMBURSEMENT FOR BENEFITS PROVIDED.—The Secretary shall reimburse the Secretary of Veterans Affairs for the value of benefits that the Secretary of Veterans Affairs provides for an individual by reason of eligibility under this section.

(c) APPLICABILITY.—

(1) GENERAL RULE.—Benefits may be provided under the provisions of law referred to in subsection (a)(1) by reason of this chapter only for deaths occurring after the date of the enactment of this chapter.

(2) BURIALS, ETC. IN NATIONAL CEMETERIES.—Notwithstanding paragraph (1), in the case of an initial burial or columbarium placement after the date of the enactment of this chapter, benefits may be provided under chapter 24 of title 38 by reason of this chapter (regardless of the date of death), and in such a case benefits may be provided under section 2306 of such title.

(Added Pub. L. 105–368, title IV, §402(a), Nov. 11, 1998, 112 Stat. 3336; amended Pub. L. 116–283, div. G, title LVXXXV [LXXXV], §8505(b)(11), Jan. 1, 2021, 134 Stat. 4751.)

§11202. QUALIFIED SERVICE

For purposes of this chapter, an individual shall be considered to have engaged in qualified service if, between August 16, 1945, and December 31, 1946, the individual—

(1) was a member of the United States merchant marine (including the Army Transport Service and the Naval Transport Service) serving as a crewmember of a vessel that was—

(A) operated by the War Shipping Administration or the Office of Defense

Transportation (or an agent of the Administration or Office);

(B) operated in waters other than inland waters, the Great Lakes, and other lakes, bays, and harbors of the United States;

(C) under contract or charter to, or property of, the Government of the United States; and

(D) serving the Armed Forces; and

(2) while so serving, was licensed or otherwise documented for service as a crewmember of such a vessel by an officer or employee of the United States authorized to license or document the individual for such service.

(Added Pub. L. 105–368, title IV, §402(a), Nov. 11, 1998, 112 Stat. 3336; amended Pub. L. 116–283, div. G, title LVXXXV [LXXXV], §8505(b)(12), Jan. 1, 2021, 134 Stat. 4752.)

§11203. DOCUMENTATION OF QUALIFIED SERVICE

(a) RECORD OF SERVICE.—The Secretary, or in the case of personnel of the Army Transport Service or the Naval Transport Service, the Secretary of Defense, shall, upon application—

(1) issue a certificate of honorable service to an individual who, as determined by that Secretary, engaged in qualified service of a nature and duration that warrants issuance of the certificate; and

(2) correct, or request the appropriate official of the Federal Government to correct, the service records of that individual to the extent necessary to reflect the qualified service and the issuance of the certificate of honorable service.

(b) TIMING OF DOCUMENTATION.—A Secretary receiving an application under subsection (a) shall act on the application not later than 1 year after the date of that receipt.

(c) STANDARDS RELATING TO SERVICE.—In making a determination under subsection (a)(1), the Secretary acting on the application shall apply the same standards relating to the nature and duration of service that apply to the issuance of honorable discharges under section 401(a)(1)(B) of the GI Bill Improvement Act of 1977 (38 U.S.C. 106 note).

(d) CORRECTION OF RECORDS.—An official who is requested under subsection (a)(2) to correct the service records of an individual shall make such correction.

(Added Pub. L. 105–368, title IV, §402(a), Nov. 11, 1998, 112 Stat. 3337; amended Pub. L. 116–283, div. G, title LVXXXV [LXXXV], §8505(b)(13), Jan. 1, 2021, 134 Stat. 4752.)

§11204. PROCESSING FEES

(a) COLLECTION OF FEES.—The Secretary, or in the case of personnel of the Army Transport Service or the Naval Transport Service, the Secretary of Defense, shall collect a fee of $30 from each applicant for processing an application submitted under section 11203(a) of this title.

(b) TREATMENT OF FEES COLLECTED.—Amounts received by the Secretary under this section shall be deposited in the General Fund of the Treasury as offsetting receipts of the department in which the Coast Guard is operating and ascribed to Coast Guard activities.

Amounts received by the Secretary of Defense under this section shall be deposited in the General Fund of the Treasury as offsetting receipts of the Department of Defense. In either case, such amounts shall be available, subject to appropriation, for the administrative costs of processing applications under section 11203 of this title.

(Added Pub. L. 105–368, title IV, §402(a), Nov. 11, 1998, 112 Stat. 3337.)

CHAPTER 113—OFFICIAL LOGBOOKS

Sec.

§11301. LOGBOOK AND ENTRY REQUIREMENTS

(a) Except a vessel on a voyage from a port in the United States to a port in Canada, a vessel of the United States shall have an official logbook if the vessel is—

(1) on a voyage from a port in the United States to a foreign port; or

(2) of at least 100 gross tons as measured under section 14502 of this title, or an alternate tonnage measured under section 14302 of this title as prescribed by the Secretary under section 14104 of this title and is on a voyage between a port of the United States on the Atlantic Ocean and on the Pacific Ocean.

(b) The master of the vessel shall make or have made in the official logbook the following entries:

(1) each legal conviction of a seaman of the vessel and the punishment inflicted.

(2) each offense committed by a seaman of the vessel for which it is intended to prosecute or to enforce under a forfeiture, together with statements about reading the entry and the reply made to the charge as required by section 11502 of this title.

(3) each offense for which punishment is inflicted on board and the punishment inflicted.

(4) a statement of the conduct, character, and qualifications of each seaman of the vessel or a statement that the master declines to give an opinion about that conduct, character, and qualifications.

(5) each illness of or injury to a seaman of the vessel, the nature of the illness or injury, and the medical treatment.

(6) each death on board, with the cause of death, and if a seaman, the information required by section 10702 of this title.

(7) each birth on board, with the sex of the infant and name of the parents.

(8) each marriage on board, with the names and ages of the parties.

(9) the name of each seaman who ceases to be a crewmember (except by death), with the place, time, manner, and the cause why the seaman ceased to be a crewmember.

(10) the wages due to a seaman who dies during the voyage and the gross amount of all deductions to be made from the wages.

(11) the sale of the property of a seaman who dies during the voyage, including a statement of each article sold and the amount received for the property.

(12) when a marine casualty occurs, a statement about the casualty and the circumstances under which it occurred, made immediately after the casualty when practicable to do so.

(13) when a vessel fails to carry out ballast water management requirements as

applicable and pursuant to regulations promulgated by the Secretary, including when the vessel fails to carry out ballast water management requirements due to an allowed safety exemption, a statement regarding the failure to comply and the circumstances under which the failure occurred, made immediately after the failure, when practicable to do so.

(Pub. L. 98–89, Aug. 26, 1983, 97 Stat. 581; Pub. L. 98–557, §30, Oct. 30, 1984, 98 Stat. 2875; Pub. L. 104–324, title VII, §742, Oct. 19, 1996, 110 Stat. 3942; Pub. L. 115–282, title IX, §903(d), Dec. 4, 2018, 132 Stat. 4357.)

§11302. MANNER OF MAKING ENTRIES

Each entry made in the official logbook—

(1) shall be made as soon as possible after the occurrence;

(2) if not made on the day of the occurrence, shall be dated and state the date of the occurrence;

(3) if the entry is about an occurrence happening before the vessel's arrival at the final port of discharge, shall be made not later than 24 hours after the arrival;

(4) shall be signed by the master; and

(5) shall be signed by the chief mate or another seaman.

(Pub. L. 98–89, Aug. 26, 1983, 97 Stat. 581.)

§11303. PENALTIES

(a) A master failing to maintain an official logbook as required by this part is liable to the United States Government for a civil penalty of $200.

(b) A master failing to make an entry in the vessel's official logbook as required by this part is liable to the Government for a civil penalty of $200.

(c) A person is liable to the Government for a civil penalty of $150 when the person makes, procures to be made, or assists in making, an entry in the vessel's official logbook—

(1) later than 24 hours after the vessel's arrival at the final port of discharge; and

(2) that is about an occurrence that happened before that arrival.

(Pub. L. 98–89, Aug. 26, 1983, 97 Stat. 582.)

§11304. ADDITIONAL LOGBOOK AND ENTRY REQUIREMENTS

(a) A vessel of the United States that is subject to inspection under section 3301 of this title, except a vessel on a voyage from a port in the United States to a port in Canada, shall have a logbook, which may be in any form, including electronic, and shall be kept available for review by the Secretary on request.

(b) The logbook required by subsection (a) shall include the following entries:

(1) The time when each seaman and each officer assumed or relieved the watch.

(2) The number of hours in service to the vessels of each seaman and each officer.

(3) Each illness of, and injury to, a seaman of the vessel, the nature of the illness or injury, and the medical treatment provided for the injury or illness.

(Added Pub. L. 111–281, title VI, §607(a), Oct. 15, 2010, 124 Stat. 2967; amended Pub. L. 115–282, title V, §511, Dec. 4, 2018, 132 Stat. 4274.)

CHAPTER 115—OFFENSES AND PENALTIES

Sec.

§11501. PENALTIES FOR SPECIFIED OFFENSES

When a seaman lawfully engaged commits any of the following offenses, the seaman shall be punished as specified:

(1) For desertion, the seaman forfeits any part of the money or property the seaman leaves on board and any part of earned wages.

(2) For neglecting or refusing without reasonable cause to join the seaman's vessel or to proceed to sea in the vessel, for absence without leave within 24 hours of the vessel's sailing from a port (at the beginning or during the voyage), or for absence without leave from duties and without sufficient reason, the seaman forfeits from the seaman's wages not more than 2 days' pay or a sufficient amount to defray expenses incurred in hiring a substitute.

(3) For quitting the vessel without leave after the vessel's arrival at the port of delivery and before the vessel is placed in security, the seaman forfeits from the seaman's wages not more than one month's pay.

(4) For willful disobedience to a lawful command at sea, the seaman, at the discretion of the master, may be confined until the disobedience ends, and on arrival in port forfeits from the seaman's wages not more than 4 days' pay or, at the discretion of the court, may be imprisoned for not more than one month.

(5) For continued willful disobedience to lawful command or continued willful neglect of duty at sea, the seaman, at the discretion of the master, may be confined, on water and 1,000 calories, with full rations every 5th day, until the disobedience ends, and on arrival in port forfeits, for each 24 hours' continuance of the disobedience or neglect, not more than 12 days' pay or, at the discretion of the court, may be imprisoned for not more than 3 months.

(6) For assaulting a master, mate, pilot, engineer, or staff officer, the seaman shall be imprisoned for not more than 2 years.

(7) For willfully damaging the vessel, or embezzling or willfully damaging any of the stores or cargo, the seaman forfeits from the seaman's wages the amount of the loss sustained and, at the discretion of the court, may be imprisoned for not more than 12 months.

(8) For smuggling for which a seaman is convicted causing loss or damage to the owner or master, the seaman is liable to the owner or master for the loss or damage, and any part of the seaman's wages may be retained to satisfy the liability. The seaman also

may be imprisoned for not more than 12 months.

(Pub. L. 98–89, Aug. 26, 1983, 97 Stat. 582.)

§11502. ENTRY OF OFFENSES IN LOGBOOK

(a) When an offense listed in section 11501 of this title is committed, an entry shall be made in the vessel's official logbook—

(1) on the day of the offense;

(2) stating the details;

(3) signed by the master; and

(4) signed by the chief mate or another seaman.

(b) Before arrival in port if the offense was committed at sea, or before departure if the offense was committed in port and the offender is still on the vessel—

(1) the entry shall be read to the offender;

(2) the offender shall be given a copy; and

(3) the offender shall be given the opportunity to reply.

(c) After subsection (b) of this section has been complied with, an entry shall be made in the official logbook—

(1) stating that the entry about the offense was read and a copy provided to the offender;

(2) stating the offender's reply;

(3) signed by the master; and

(4) signed by the chief mate or another seaman.

(d) In a subsequent legal proceeding, if the entries required by this section are not produced or proved, the court may refuse to receive evidence of the offense.

(Pub. L. 98–89, Aug. 26, 1983, 97 Stat. 583.)

§11503. DUTIES OF CONSULAR OFFICERS RELATED TO INSUBORDINATION

(a) A consular officer shall use every means to discountenance insubordination on vessels of the United States, including employing the aid of local authorities.

(b) When a seaman is accused of insubordination, a consular officer shall inquire into the facts and proceed as provided in section 11106 of this title. If the consular officer discharges the seaman, the officer shall endorse the agreement required by this part and enter in the vessel's official logbook the cause and particulars of the discharge.

(Pub. L. 98–89, Aug. 26, 1983, 97 Stat. 583.)

§11504. ENFORCEMENT OF FORFEITURES

When an offense by a seaman also is a criminal violation, it is not necessary that a criminal proceeding be brought to enforce a forfeiture.

(Pub. L. 98–89, Aug. 26, 1983, 97 Stat. 584.)

§11505. Disposal of forfeitures

(a) Money, property, and wages forfeited under this chapter for desertion may be applied to compensate the owner or master of the vessel for expenses caused by the desertion. The balance shall be transferred to the appropriate district court of the United States when the voyage is completed.

(b) If it appears to the district court that the forfeiture was imposed properly, the property transferred may be sold in the same manner prescribed for the disposition of the property of deceased seamen. The court shall deposit in the Treasury as miscellaneous receipts the proceeds of the sale and any money and wages transferred to the court.

(c) When an owner or master fails to transfer the balance as required under subsection (a) of this section, the owner or master is liable to the United States Government for a civil penalty of 2 times the amount of the balance, recoverable by the Secretary in the same manner that seaman's wages are recovered.

(d) In all other cases of forfeiture of wages, the forfeiture shall be for the benefit of the owner of the vessel.

(Pub. L. 98–89, Aug. 26, 1983, 97 Stat. 584; Pub. L. 103–206, title IV, §421, Dec. 20, 1993, 107 Stat. 2438.)

§11506. Carrying sheath knives

A seaman in the merchant marine may not wear a sheath knife on board a vessel without the consent of the master. The master of a vessel of the United States shall inform each seaman of this prohibition before engagement. A master failing to advise a seaman is liable to the United States Government for a civil penalty of $50.

(Pub. L. 98–89, Aug. 26, 1983, 97 Stat. 584.)

§11507. Surrender of offending officers

When an officer of a vessel of the United States (except the master) has violated section 2191 of title 18, and the master has actual knowledge of the offense or if complaint is made within 3 days after reaching port, the master shall surrender the offending officer to the proper authorities. If the master fails to use diligence to comply with this section and the offender escapes, the owner, the master, and the vessel are liable for damages to the individual unlawfully punished.

(Pub. L. 98–89, Aug. 26, 1983, 97 Stat. 584.)

PART H—IDENTIFICATION OF VESSELS

CHAPTER 121—DOCUMENTATION OF VESSELS

SUBCHAPTER I—GENERAL

SUBCHAPTER II—ENDORSEMENTS AND SPECIAL DOCUMENTATION

SUBCHAPTER III—MISCELLANEOUS

SUBCHAPTER IV—PENALTIES

SUBCHAPTER I—GENERAL

§12101. Definitions

(a) Rebuilt in the United States.—In this chapter, a vessel is deemed to have been rebuilt in the United States only if the entire rebuilding, including the construction of any major component of the hull or superstructure, was done in the United States.

(b) Related Terms in Other Laws.—When the following terms are used in a law, regulation, document, ruling, or other official act referring to the documentation of a vessel, the following definitions apply:

(1) Registry endorsement.—The terms "certificate of registry", "register", and "registry" mean a certificate of documentation with a registry endorsement issued under this chapter.

(2) Coastwise endorsement.—The terms "license", "enrollment and license", "license for the coastwise (or coasting) trade", and "enrollment and license for the coastwise (or coasting) trade" mean a certificate of documentation with a coastwise endorsement issued under this chapter.

(3) Yacht.—The term "yacht" means a recreational vessel even if not documented.

(Pub. L. 109–304, §5, Oct. 6, 2006, 120 Stat. 1491.)

§12102. Vessels requiring documentation

(a) In General.—Except as otherwise provided, a vessel may engage in a trade only if the vessel has been issued a certificate of documentation with an endorsement for that trade under this chapter.

(b) Vessels Less Than 5 Net Tons.—A vessel of less than 5 net tons may engage in a trade without being documented if the vessel otherwise satisfies the requirements to engage in the particular trade.

(c) Barges.—A barge qualified to engage in the coastwise trade may engage in the coastwise trade, without being documented, on rivers, harbors, lakes (except the Great Lakes), canals, and inland waters.

(d) Aquaculture Waiver.—

(1) Permitting of nonqualified vessels to perform certain aquaculture support operations.—Notwithstanding section 12113 and any other law, the Secretary of Transportation may issue a waiver allowing a documented vessel with a registry endorsement or a foreign flag vessel to be used in operations that treat aquaculture fish for or protect aquaculture fish from disease, parasitic infestation, or other threats to their health if the Secretary finds, after publishing a notice in the Federal Register, that a suitable vessel of the United States is not available that could perform those services.

(2) Prohibition.—Vessels operating under a waiver issued under this subsection may not engage in any coastwise transportation.

(Pub. L. 109–304, §5, Oct. 6, 2006, 120 Stat. 1492; Pub. L. 111–281, title IX, §901(c)(1), Oct. 15, 2010, 124 Stat. 3008.)

§12103. GENERAL ELIGIBILITY REQUIREMENTS

(a) IN GENERAL.—Except as otherwise provided, a certificate of documentation for a vessel may be issued under this chapter only if the vessel is—

(1) wholly owned by one or more individuals or entities described in subsection (b);

(2) at least 5 net tons as measured under part J of this subtitle; and

(3) not documented under the laws of a foreign country.

(b) ELIGIBLE OWNERS.—For purposes of subsection (a)(1), the following are eligible owners:

(1) An individual who is a citizen of the United States.

(2) An association, trust, joint venture, or other entity if—

(A) each of its members is a citizen of the United States; and

(B) it is capable of holding title to a vessel under the laws of the United States or a State.

(3) A partnership if—

(A) each general partner is a citizen of the United States; and

(B) the controlling interest in the partnership is owned by citizens of the United States.

(4) A corporation if—

(A) it is incorporated under the laws of the United States or a State;

(B) its chief executive officer, by whatever title, and the chairman of its board of directors are citizens of the United States; and

(C) no more of its directors are noncitizens than a minority of the number necessary to constitute a quorum.

(5) The United States Government.

(6) The government of a State.

(c) TEMPORARY CERTIFICATES PRIOR TO MEASUREMENT.—Notwithstanding subsection (a)(2), the Secretary may issue a temporary certificate of documentation for a vessel before it is measured.

(Pub. L. 109–304, §5, Oct. 6, 2006, 120 Stat. 1492.)

§12104. APPLICATIONS FOR DOCUMENTATION

(a) IN GENERAL.—An application for a certificate of documentation or endorsement under this chapter must be filed by the owner of the vessel. The application must be filed in the manner, be in the form, and contain the information prescribed by the Secretary.

(b) APPLICANT'S IDENTIFYING INFORMATION.—The Secretary shall require the applicant to provide—

(1) if the applicant is an individual, the individual's social security number; or

(2) if the applicant is an entity—

(A) the entity's taxpayer identification number; or

(B) if the entity does not have a taxpayer identification number, the social security number of an individual who is a corporate officer, general partner, or individual trustee of the entity and who signs the application.

(Pub. L. 109–304, §5, Oct. 6, 2006, 120 Stat. 1493.)

§12105. ISSUANCE OF DOCUMENTATION

(a) IN GENERAL.—Except as provided in section 12152 of this title, the Secretary, on receipt of a proper application, shall issue a certificate of documentation or a temporary certificate of documentation for a vessel satisfying the requirements of section 12103 of this title. The certificate shall contain each endorsement under subchapter II of this chapter for which the owner applies and the vessel is eligible.

(b) TEMPORARY CERTIFICATES FOR RECREATIONAL VESSELS.—The Secretary may delegate, subject to the supervision and control of the Secretary and under terms prescribed by regulation, to private entities determined and certified by the Secretary to be qualified, the authority to issue a temporary certificate of documentation for a recreational vessel eligible under section 12103 of this title. A temporary certificate issued under this subsection is valid for not more than 30 days.

(c) INFORMATION TO BE INCLUDED IN CERTIFICATE.—A certificate of documentation shall—

(1) identify and describe the vessel;

(2) identify the owner of the vessel; and

(3) contain additional information prescribed by the Secretary.

(d) PROCEDURES TO ENSURE INTEGRITY AND ACCURACY.—The Secretary shall prescribe procedures to ensure the integrity of, and the accuracy of information contained in, certificates of documentation.

(e) EFFECTIVE PERIOD.—

(1) IN GENERAL.—Except as provided in paragraphs (2) and (3), a certificate of documentation issued under this part is valid for a 1-year period and may be renewed for additional 1-year periods.

(2) RECREATIONAL VESSELS.—

(A) IN GENERAL.—The owner or operator of a recreational vessel may choose a period of effectiveness of between 1 and 5 years for a certificate of documentation for a recreational vessel or the renewal thereof.

(B) FEES.—

(i) REQUIREMENT.—The Secretary shall assess and collect a fee—

(I) for the issuance of a certificate of documentation for a recreational vessel that is equivalent to the fee established for the issuance of a certificate of documentation under section 2110; and

(II) for the renewal of a certificate of documentation for a recreational vessel that is equivalent to the number of years of effectiveness of the certificate of documentation multiplied by the fee established for the renewal of a certificate of documentation under section 2110.

(ii) TREATMENT.—Fees collected under this subsection—

(I) shall be credited to the account from which the costs of such issuance or renewal were paid; and

(II) may remain available until expended.

(3) NOTICE OF CHANGE IN INFORMATION.—

(A) REQUIREMENT.—The owner of a vessel shall notify the Coast Guard of each change in the information on which the issuance of the certificate of documentation for the vessel is based that occurs before the expiration of the certificate under this subsection, by not later than 30 days after such change.

(B) TERMINATION OF CERTIFICATE.—The certificate of documentation for a vessel shall terminate upon the expiration of such 30-day period if the owner has not notified the Coast Guard of such change before the end of such period.

(4) STATE AND LOCAL AUTHORITY TO REMOVE ABANDONED AND DERELICT VESSELS.—Nothing in this section shall be construed to limit the authority of a State or local authority from taking action to remove an abandoned or derelict vessel.

(Pub. L. 109–304, §5, Oct. 6, 2006, 120 Stat. 1493; Pub. L. 115–282, title V, §512, Dec. 4, 2018, 132 Stat. 4275; Pub. L. 117–81, div. C, title XXXV, §3511, Dec. 27, 2021, 135 Stat. 2238.)

§12106. SURRENDER OF TITLE AND NUMBER

(a) IN GENERAL.—A documented vessel may not be titled by a State or required to display numbers under chapter 123 of this title, and any certificate of title issued by a State for a documented vessel shall be surrendered as provided by regulations prescribed by the Secretary.

(b) VESSELS COVERED BY PREFERRED MORTGAGE.—The Secretary may approve the surrender under subsection (a) of a certificate of title for a vessel covered by a preferred mortgage under section 31322(d) of this title only if the mortgagee consents.

(Pub. L. 109–304, §5, Oct. 6, 2006, 120 Stat. 1494.)

§12107. WRECKED VESSELS

(a) REQUIREMENTS.—A vessel is a wrecked vessel under this chapter if it—

(1) was wrecked on a coast of the United States or adjacent waters; and

(2) has undergone repairs in a shipyard in the United States equal to at least 3 times the appraised salvage value of the vessel.

(b) APPRAISALS.—The Secretary may appoint a board of three appraisers to determine whether a vessel satisfies subsection (a)(2). The costs of the appraisal shall be paid by the owner of the vessel.

(Pub. L. 109–304, §5, Oct. 6, 2006, 120 Stat. 1494.)

§12108. AUTHORITY TO EXTEND DURATION OF VESSEL CERTIFICATES

(a) CERTIFICATES.—Provided a vessel is in compliance with inspection requirements in section 3313, the Secretary of the department in which in the Coast Guard is operating may, if the Secretary makes the determination described in subsection (b), extend, for a period of not more than 1 year, an expiring certificate of documentation issued for a vessel under chapter 121.

(b) DETERMINATION.—The determination referred to in subsection (a) is a determination that such extension is required to enable the Coast Guard to—

(1) eliminate a backlog in processing applications for such certificates; or

(2) act in response to a national emergency or natural disaster.

(c) MANNER OF EXTENSION.—Any extension granted under this section may be granted to individual vessels or to a specifically identified group of vessels.

(Added Pub. L. 116–283, div. G, title LVXXXIII [LXXXIII], §8320(a), Jan. 1, 2021, 134 Stat. 4701.)

SUBCHAPTER II—ENDORSEMENTS AND SPECIAL DOCUMENTATION

§12111. REGISTRY ENDORSEMENT

(a) REQUIREMENTS.—A registry endorsement may be issued for a vessel that satisfies the requirements of section 12103 of this title.

(b) AUTHORIZED ACTIVITY.—A vessel for which a registry endorsement is issued may engage in foreign trade or trade with Guam, American Samoa, Wake, Midway, or Kingman Reef.

(c) CERTAIN VESSELS OWNED BY TRUSTS.—

(1) NONAPPLICATION OF BENEFICIARY CITIZENSHIP REQUIREMENT.—For the issuance of a certificate of documentation with only a registry endorsement, the beneficiaries of a trust are not required to be citizens of the United States if the trust qualifies under paragraph (2) and the vessel is subject to a charter to a citizen of the United States.

(2) REQUIREMENTS FOR TRUST TO QUALIFY.—

(A) IN GENERAL.—Subject to subparagraph (B), a trust qualifies under this paragraph with respect to a vessel only if—

(i) each trustee is a citizen of the United States; and

(ii) the application for documentation of the vessel includes the affidavit of each trustee stating that the trustee is not aware of any reason involving a beneficiary of the trust that is not a citizen of the United States, or involving any other person that is not a citizen of the United States, as a result of which the beneficiary or other person would hold more than 25 percent of the aggregate power to influence or limit the exercise of the authority of the trustee with respect to matters involving any ownership or operation of the vessel that may adversely affect the interests of the United States.

(B) AUTHORITY OF NON-CITIZENS.—If any person that is not a citizen of the United States has authority to direct or participate in directing a trustee for a trust in matters involving any ownership or operation of the vessel that may adversely affect the interests of the United States or in removing a trustee for a trust without cause, either directly or indirectly through the control of another person, the trust is not qualified under this paragraph unless the trust instrument provides that persons who are not citizens of the United States may not hold more than 25 percent of the aggregate authority to so direct or remove a trustee.

(C) OWNERSHIP BY NON-CITIZENS.—Subparagraphs (A) and (B) do not prohibit a person that is not a citizen of the United States from holding more than 25 percent of the beneficial interest in a trust.

(3) CITIZENSHIP OF PERSON CHARTERING VESSEL.—If a person chartering a vessel from a trust that qualifies under paragraph (2) is a citizen of the United States under section 50501 of this title, the vessel is deemed to be owned by a citizen of the United States for purposes of that section and related laws, except chapter 531 of this title.

(d) ACTIVITIES INVOLVING MOBILE OFFSHORE DRILLING UNITS.—

(1) IN GENERAL.—Only a vessel for which a certificate of documentation with a registry endorsement is issued may engage in—

(A) the setting, relocation, or recovery of the anchors or other mooring equipment of a mobile offshore drilling unit that is located over the outer Continental Shelf (as defined in section 2(a) of the Outer Continental Shelf Lands Act (43 U.S.C. 1331(a))); or

(B) the transportation of merchandise or personnel to or from a point in the United States from or to a mobile offshore drilling unit located over the outer Continental Shelf that is not attached to the seabed.

(2) COASTWISE TRADE NOT AUTHORIZED.—Nothing in paragraph (1) authorizes the employment in the coastwise trade of a vessel that does not meet the requirements of section 12112 of this title.

(Pub. L. 109–304, §5, Oct. 6, 2006, 120 Stat. 1494; Pub. L. 109–241, title III, §310, July 11, 2006, 120 Stat. 529; Pub. L. 110–181, div. C, title XXXV, §3525(a)(1), (b), Jan. 28, 2008, 122 Stat. 600, 601.)

§12112. COASTWISE ENDORSEMENT

(a) REQUIREMENTS.—A coastwise endorsement may be issued for a vessel that—

(1) satisfies the requirements of section 12103 of this title;

(2)(A) was built in the United States; or

(B) if not built in the United States—

(i) was captured in war by citizens of the United States and lawfully condemned as prize;

(ii) was adjudged to be forfeited for a breach of the laws of the United States; or

(iii) qualifies as a wrecked vessel under section 12107 of this title; and

(3) otherwise qualifies under the laws of the United States to engage in the coastwise trade.

(b) AUTHORIZED ACTIVITY.—Subject to the laws of the United States regulating the coastwise trade, a vessel for which a coastwise endorsement is issued may engage in the coastwise trade.

(Pub. L. 109–304, §5, Oct. 6, 2006, 120 Stat. 1495.)

§12113. FISHERY ENDORSEMENT

(a) REQUIREMENTS.—A fishery endorsement may be issued for a vessel that—

(1) satisfies the requirements of section 12103 of this title and, if owned by an entity, the entity satisfies the ownership requirements in subsection (c);

(2) was built in the United States;

(3) if rebuilt, was rebuilt in the United States;

(4) was not forfeited to the United States Government after July 1, 2001, for a breach of the laws of the United States; and

(5) otherwise qualifies under the laws of the United States to engage in the fisheries.

(b) AUTHORIZED ACTIVITY.—

(1) IN GENERAL.—Subject to the laws of the United States regulating the fisheries, a vessel for which a fishery endorsement is issued may engage in the fisheries.

(2) USE BY PROHIBITED PERSONS.—A fishery endorsement is invalid immediately if the vessel for which it is issued is used as a fishing vessel while it is chartered or leased to an individual who is not a citizen of the United States or to an entity that is not eligible to own a vessel with a fishery endorsement.

(c) OWNERSHIP REQUIREMENTS FOR ENTITIES.—

(1) IN GENERAL.—A vessel owned by an entity is eligible for a fishery endorsement only if at least 75 percent of the interest in the entity, at each tier of ownership and in the aggregate, is owned and controlled by citizens of the United States.

(2) DETERMINING 75 PERCENT INTEREST.—In determining whether at least 75 percent of the interest in the entity is owned and controlled by citizens of the United States under paragraph (1), the Secretary shall apply section 50501(d) of this title, except that for this purpose the terms "control" or "controlled"—

(A) include the right to—

(i) direct the business of the entity;

(ii) limit the actions of or replace the chief executive officer, a majority of the board of directors, any general partner, or any person serving in a management capacity of the entity; or

(iii) direct the transfer, operation, or manning of a vessel with a fishery endorsement; but

(B) do not include the right to simply participate in the activities under subparagraph (A), or the exercise of rights under loan or mortgage covenants by a mortgagee eligible to be a preferred mortgagee under section 31322(a) of this title, except that a mortgagee not eligible to own a vessel with a fishery endorsement may only operate such a vessel to the extent necessary for the immediate safety of the vessel or for repairs, drydocking, or berthing changes.

(3) EXCEPTIONS.—This subsection does not apply to a vessel when it is engaged in the fisheries in the exclusive economic zone under the authority of the Western Pacific Fishery Management Council established under section 302(a)(1)(H) of the Magnuson-Stevens Fishery Conservation and Management Act (16 U.S.C. 1852(a)(1)(H)) or to a purse seine vessel when it is engaged in tuna fishing in the Pacific Ocean outside the exclusive economic zone or pursuant to the South Pacific Regional Fisheries Treaty, provided that the owner of the vessel continues to comply with the eligibility requirements for a fishery endorsement under the Federal law that was in effect on October 1, 1998. A fishery endorsement issued pursuant to this paragraph is valid for engaging only in the activities described in this paragraph.

(d) REQUIREMENTS BASED ON LENGTH, TONNAGE, OR HORSEPOWER.—

(1) APPLICATION.—This subsection applies to a vessel that—

(A) is greater than 165 feet in registered length;

(B) is more than 750 gross registered tons as measured under chapter 145 of this title or 1,900 gross registered tons as measured under chapter 143 of this title; or

(C) has an engine or engines capable of producing a total of more than 3,000 shaft horsepower.

(2) REQUIREMENTS.—A vessel subject to this subsection is not eligible for a fishery endorsement unless—

(A)(i) a certificate of documentation was issued for the vessel and endorsed with a fishery endorsement that was effective on September 25, 1997; and

(ii) the vessel is not placed under foreign registry after October 21, 1998;

(B) the owner of the vessel demonstrates to the Secretary that—

(i) the regional fishery management council of jurisdiction established under section 302(a)(1) of the Magnuson-Stevens Fishery Conservation and Management Act (16 U.S.C. 1852(a)(1)) has recommended after October 21, 1998, and the Secretary of Commerce has approved, conservation and management measures in accordance with the American Fisheries Act (Public Law 105–277, div. C, title II) (16 U.S.C. 1851 note) [1] to allow the vessel to be used in fisheries under the council's authority; and

(ii) in the case of a vessel listed in paragraphs (1) through (20) of section 208(e) of the American Fisheries Act (title II of division C of Public Law 105–277; 112 Stat. 2681–625 et seq.), the vessel is neither participating in nor eligible to participate in the non-AFA trawl catcher processor subsector (as that term is defined under section 219(a)(7) of the Department of Commerce and Related Agencies Appropriations Act, 2005 (Public Law 108–447; 118 Stat. 2887));

(C) the vessel—

(i) is either a rebuilt vessel or replacement vessel under section 208(g) of the American Fisheries Act (title II of division C of Public Law 105–277; 112 Stat. 2681–627);

(ii) is eligible for a fishery endorsement under this section; and

(iii) in the case of a vessel listed in paragraphs (1) through (20) of section 208(e) of the American Fisheries Act (title II of division C of Public Law 105–277; 112 Stat. 2681–625 et seq.), is neither participating in nor eligible to participate in the non-AFA trawl catcher processor subsector (as that term is defined under section 219(a)(7) of the Department of Commerce and Related Agencies Appropriations Act, 2005 (Public Law 108–447; 118 Stat. 2887)); or

(D) the vessel is a fish tender vessel that is not engaged in the harvesting or processing of fish.

(e) VESSELS MEASURING 100 FEET OR GREATER.—

(1) IN GENERAL.—The Administrator of the Maritime Administration shall administer subsections (c) and (d) with respect to vessels 100 feet or greater in registered length. The owner of each such vessel shall file a statement of citizenship setting forth all relevant facts regarding vessel ownership and control with the Administrator on an annual basis

to demonstrate compliance with those provisions.

(2) REGULATIONS.—Regulations to implement this subsection shall conform to the extent practicable with the regulations establishing the form of citizenship affidavit set forth in part 355 of title 46, Code of Federal Regulations, as in effect on September 25, 1997, except that the form of the statement shall be written in a manner to allow the owner of the vessel to satisfy any annual renewal requirements for a certificate of documentation for the vessel and to comply with this subsection and subsections (c) and (d), and shall not be required to be notarized.

(3) TRANSFER OF OWNERSHIP.—Transfers of ownership and control of vessels subject to subsection (c) or (d), which are 100 feet or greater in registered length, shall be rigorously scrutinized for violations of those provisions, with particular attention given to—

(A) leases, charters, mortgages, financing, and similar arrangements;

(B) the control of persons not eligible to own a vessel with a fishery endorsement under subsection (c) or (d), over the management, sales, financing, or other operations of an entity; and

(C) contracts involving the purchase over extended periods of time of all, or substantially all, of the living marine resources harvested by a fishing vessel.

(f) VESSELS MEASURING LESS THAN 100 FEET.—The Secretary shall establish reasonable and necessary requirements to demonstrate compliance with subsections (c) and (d), with respect to vessels measuring less than 100 feet in registered length, and shall seek to minimize the administrative burden on individuals who own and operate those vessels.

(g) VESSELS PURCHASED THROUGH FISHING CAPACITY REDUCTION PROGRAM.—A vessel purchased by the Secretary of Commerce through a fishing capacity reduction program under the Magnuson-Stevens Fishery Conservation and Management Act (16 U.S.C. 1801 et seq.) or section 308 [2] of the Interjurisdictional Fisheries Act of 1986 (16 U.S.C. 4107) is not eligible for a fishery endorsement, and any fishery endorsement issued for that vessel is invalid.

(h) REVOCATION OF ENDORSEMENTS.—The Secretary shall revoke the fishery endorsement of any vessel subject to subsection (c) or (d) whose owner does not comply with those provisions.

(i) REGULATIONS.—Regulations to implement subsections (c) and (d) and sections 12151(c) and 31322(b) of this title shall prohibit impermissible transfers of ownership or control, specify any transactions that require prior approval of an implementing agency, identify transactions that do not require prior agency approval, and to the extent practicable, minimize disruptions to the commercial fishing industry, to the traditional financing arrangements of that industry, and to the opportunity to form fishery cooperatives.

(Pub. L. 109–304, §5, Oct. 6, 2006, 120 Stat. 1495; Pub. L. 110–181, div. C, title XXXV, §3529(a)(2), Jan. 28, 2008, 122 Stat. 603; Pub. L. 111–281, title VI, §602(a), Oct. 15, 2010, 124 Stat. 2959; Pub. L. 112–213, title III, §307, Dec. 20, 2012, 126 Stat. 1565; Pub. L. 115–232, div. C, title XXXV, §3546(j), Aug. 13, 2018, 132 Stat. 2326.)

[1] See References in Text note below.

[2] See References in Text note below.

§12114. Recreational endorsement

(a) REQUIREMENTS.—A recreational endorsement may be issued for a vessel that satisfies the requirements of section 12103 of this title.

(b) AUTHORIZED ACTIVITY.—A vessel operating under a recreational endorsement may be operated only for pleasure.

(c) APPLICATION OF CUSTOMS LAWS.—A vessel for which a recreational endorsement is issued may proceed between a port of the United States and a port of a foreign country without entering or clearing with the Secretary of Homeland Security. However, a recreational vessel is subject to the requirements for reporting arrivals under section 433 of the Tariff Act of 1930 (19 U.S.C. 1433), and individuals on the vessel are subject to applicable customs regulations.

(Pub. L. 109–304, §5, Oct. 6, 2006, 120 Stat. 1498.)

§12115. Temporary endorsement for vessels procured outside the United States

(a) GENERAL AUTHORITY.—The Secretary and the Secretary of State, acting jointly, may provide for the issuance of a certificate of documentation with an appropriate endorsement for a vessel procured outside the United States and meeting the ownership requirements of section 12103 of this title.

(b) AUTHORIZED ACTIVITY.—Subject to limitations the Secretary may prescribe, a vessel documented under this section may proceed to the United States and engage en route in foreign trade or trade with Guam, American Samoa, Wake, Midway, or Kingman Reef.

(c) APPLICATION OF UNITED STATES JURISDICTION AND LAWS.—A vessel documented under this section is subject to the jurisdiction and laws of the United States. However, if the Secretary considers it to be in the public interest, the Secretary may suspend for a period of not more than 6 months the application of a vessel inspection law carried out by the Secretary or regulations prescribed under that law.

(d) SURRENDER OF CERTIFICATE.—On the vessel's arrival in the United States, the certificate of documentation shall be surrendered as provided by regulations prescribed by the Secretary.

(Pub. L. 109–304, §5, Oct. 6, 2006, 120 Stat. 1498.)

§12116. Limited endorsements for Guam, American Samoa, and Northern Mariana Islands

(a) ENDORSEMENTS.—A vessel satisfying the requirements of subsection (b) may be issued—

(1) a coastwise endorsement to engage in the coastwise trade of fisheries products between places in Guam, American Samoa, and the Northern Mariana Islands; or

(2) a fishery endorsement to engage in fishing in the territorial sea and fishery conservation zone adjacent to Guam, American Samoa, and the Northern Mariana Islands.

(b) REQUIREMENTS.—An endorsement may be issued under subsection (a) for a vessel that—

(1) satisfies the requirements of section 12103 of this title;

(2) was not built in the United States, except that for an endorsement under subsection (a)(2), the vessel must not have been built or rebuilt in the United States;

(3) is less than 200 gross tons as measured under section 14502 of this title, or an alternate tonnage as measured under section 14302 of this title as prescribed by the Secretary under section 14104 of this title; and

(4) otherwise qualifies under the laws of the United States to engage in the coastwise trade or the fisheries, as the case may be.

(Pub. L. 109–304, §5, Oct. 6, 2006, 120 Stat. 1499.)

§12117. OIL SPILL RESPONSE VESSELS

(a) REQUIREMENTS.—A coastwise endorsement may be issued for a vessel that—

(1) satisfies the requirements for a coastwise endorsement, except for the ownership requirement otherwise applicable without regard to this section;

(2) is owned by a not-for-profit oil spill response cooperative or by members of such a cooperative that dedicate the vessel to use by the cooperative;

(3) is at least 50 percent owned by individuals or entities described in section 12103(b) of this title; and

(4) is to be used only for—

(i) deploying equipment, supplies, and personnel to recover, contain, or transport oil discharged into the navigable waters of the United States or the exclusive economic zone; or

(ii) training exercises to prepare to respond to such a discharge.

(b) DEEMED OWNED BY CITIZENS.—A vessel satisfying subsection (a) is deemed to be owned only by citizens of the United States under sections 12103, 12132, and 50501 of this title.

(Pub. L. 109–304, §5, Oct. 6, 2006, 120 Stat. 1499.)

§12118. OWNERS ENGAGED PRIMARILY IN MANUFACTURING OR MINERAL INDUSTRY

(a) DEFINITIONS.—In this section:

(1) BOWATERS CORPORATION.—The term "Bowaters corporation" means a corporation that has filed a certificate under oath with the Secretary, in the form and at the times prescribed by the Secretary, establishing that—

(A) the corporation is incorporated under the laws of the United States or a State;

(B) a majority of the officers and directors of the corporation are individuals who are citizens of the United States;

(C) at least 90 percent of the employees of the corporation are residents of the United States;

(D) the corporation is engaged primarily in a manufacturing or mineral industry in the United States;

(E) the total book value of the vessels owned by the corporation is not more than 10 percent of the total book value of the assets of the corporation; and

(F) the corporation buys or produces in the United States at least 75 percent of the raw materials used or sold in its operations.

(2) PARENT.—The term "parent" means a corporation that has filed a certificate under oath with the Secretary, in the form and at the times prescribed by the Secretary, establishing that the corporation—

(A) is incorporated under the laws of the United States or a State; and

(B) controls, directly or indirectly, at least 50 percent of the voting stock of a Bowaters corporation.

(3) SUBSIDIARY.—The term "subsidiary" means a corporation that has filed a certificate under oath with the Secretary, in the form and at the times prescribed by the Secretary, establishing that the corporation—

(A) is incorporated under the laws of the United States or a State; and

(B) has at least 50 percent of its voting stock controlled, directly or indirectly, by a Bowaters corporation or its parent.

(b) DEEMED CITIZEN.—A Bowaters corporation is deemed to be a citizen of the United States for purposes of chapters 121, 551, and 561 and section 80104 of this title.

(c) ISSUANCE OF DOCUMENTATION.—A certificate of documentation and appropriate endorsement may be issued for a vessel that—

(1) is owned by a Bowaters corporation;

(2) was built in the United States; and

(3)(A) is self-propelled and less than 500 gross tons as measured under section 14502 of this title, or an alternate tonnage as measured under section 14302 of this title as prescribed by the Secretary under section 14104 of this title; or

(B) is not self-propelled.

(d) EFFECTS OF DOCUMENTATION.—

(1) IN GENERAL.—Subject to paragraph (2)—

(A) a vessel documented under this section may engage in the coastwise trade; and

(B) the vessel and its owner and master are entitled to the same benefits and are subject to the same requirements and penalties as if the vessel were otherwise documented or exempt from documentation under this chapter.

(2) TRANSPORTATION OF PASSENGERS OR MERCHANDISE.—A vessel documented under this section may transport passengers or merchandise for hire in the coastwise trade only—

(A) as a service for a parent or subsidiary of the corporation owning the vessel; or

(B) when under a demise or bareboat charter, at prevailing rates for use not in the domestic noncontiguous trades, from the corporation owning the vessel to a carrier that—

(i) is subject to jurisdiction under subchapter II of chapter 135 of title 49;

(ii) otherwise qualifies as a citizen of the United States under section 50501 of this title; and

(iii) is not owned or controlled, directly or indirectly, by the corporation owning the vessel.

(e) VALIDITY OF CORPORATE CERTIFICATE.—A certificate filed by a corporation under this section remains valid only as long as the corporation continues to satisfy the conditions required of the corporation by this section. When a corporation no longer satisfies those conditions, the corporation loses its status under this section and immediately shall surrender to the Secretary any documents issued to it based on that status.

(f) PENALTIES.—

(1) FALSIFYING MATERIAL FACT.—If a corporation knowingly falsifies a material fact in a certificate filed under subsection (a), the vessel (or its value) documented or operated under this section shall be forfeited.

(2) TRANSPORTING MERCHANDISE.—If a vessel transports merchandise for hire in violation of this section, the merchandise shall be forfeited to the United States Government.

(3) TRANSPORTING PASSENGERS.—If a vessel transports passengers for hire in violation of this section, the vessel is liable for a penalty of $200 for each passenger so transported.

(4) REMISSION OR MITIGATION.—A penalty or forfeiture incurred under this subsection may be remitted or mitigated under section 2107(b) of this title.

(Pub. L. 109–304, §5, Oct. 6, 2006, 120 Stat. 1500.)

§12119. OWNERS ENGAGED PRIMARILY IN LEASING OR FINANCING TRANSACTIONS

(a) DEFINITIONS.—In this section:

(1) AFFILIATE.—The term "affiliate" means, with respect to any person, any other person that is—

(i) directly or indirectly controlled by, under common control with, or controlling that person; or

(ii) named as being part of the same consolidated group in any report or other document submitted to the United States Securities and Exchange Commission or the Internal Revenue Service.

(2) CARGO.—The term "cargo" does not include cargo to which title is held for non-commercial reasons and primarily for the purpose of evading the requirements of subsection (c)(3).

(3) OIL.—The term "oil" has the meaning given that term in section 2101(26) of this title.

(4) PASSIVE INVESTMENT.—The term "passive investment" means an investment in which neither the investor nor any affiliate of the investor is involved in, or has the power to be involved in, the formulation, determination, or direction of any activity or function concerning the management, use, or operation of the asset that is the subject of the investment.

(5) QUALIFIED PROPRIETARY CARGO.—The term "qualified proprietary cargo" means—

(A) oil, petroleum products, petrochemicals, or liquefied natural gas cargo that is beneficially owned by the person that submits to the Secretary an application or annual certification under subsection (c)(3), or by an affiliate of that person, immediately before, during, or immediately after the cargo is carried in coastwise trade on a vessel owned by that person;

(B) oil, petroleum products, petrochemicals, or liquefied natural gas cargo not beneficially owned by the person that submits to the Secretary an application or an annual certification under subsection (c)(3), or by an affiliate of that person, but which is carried in coastwise trade by a vessel owned by that person and which is part of an arrangement in which vessels owned by that person and at least one other person are operated collectively as one fleet, to the extent that an equal amount of oil, petroleum products, petrochemicals, or liquefied natural gas cargo beneficially owned by that person, or by an affiliate of that person, is carried in coastwise trade on one or more other vessels, not owned by that person, or by an affiliate of that person, if the other vessel or vessels are also part of the same arrangement;

(C) in the case of a towing vessel associated with a non-self-propelled tank vessel where both vessels function as a single self-propelled vessel, oil, petroleum products, petrochemicals, or liquefied natural gas cargo that is beneficially owned by the person that owns both the towing vessel and the non-self-propelled tank vessel, or any United States affiliate of that person, immediately before, during, or immediately after the cargo is carried in coastwise trade on either of those vessels; or

(D) any oil, petroleum products, petrochemicals, or liquefied natural gas cargo carried on any vessel that is either a self-propelled tank vessel having a length of at least 210 meters or a tank vessel that is a liquefied natural gas carrier that—

(i) was delivered by the builder of the vessel to the owner of the vessel after December 31, 1999; and

(ii) was purchased by a person for the purpose, and with the reasonable expectation, of transporting on the vessel liquefied natural gas or unrefined petroleum beneficially owned by the owner of the vessel, or an affiliate of the owner, from Alaska to the continental United States.

(6) UNITED STATES AFFILIATE.—The term "United States affiliate" means, with respect to any person, an affiliate the principal place of business of which is located in the United States.

(b) REQUIREMENTS.—A coastwise endorsement may be issued for a vessel if—

(1) the vessel satisfies the requirements for a coastwise endorsement, except for the ownership requirement otherwise applicable without regard to this section;

(2) the person that owns the vessel (or, if the vessel is owned by a trust or similar arrangement, the beneficiary of the trust or similar arrangement) meets the requirements of subsection (c);

(3) the vessel is under a demise charter to a person that certifies to the Secretary that the person is a citizen of the United States under section 50501 of this title for engaging in the coastwise trade; and

(4) the demise charter is for a period of at least 3 years or a shorter period as may be prescribed by the Secretary.

(c) OWNERSHIP CERTIFICATION.—

(1) IN GENERAL.—A person meets the requirements of this subsection if the person transmits to the Secretary each year the certification required by paragraph (2) or (3) with respect to a vessel.

(2) INVESTMENT CERTIFICATION.—To meet the certification requirement of this paragraph, a person shall certify that it—

(A) is a leasing company, bank, or financial institution;

(B) owns, or holds the beneficial interest in, the vessel solely as a passive investment;

(C) does not operate any vessel for hire and is not an affiliate of any person that operates any vessel for hire; and

(D) is independent from, and not an affiliate of, any charterer of the vessel or any other person that has the right, directly or indirectly, to control or direct the movement or use of the vessel.

(3) CERTAIN TANK VESSELS.—

(A) IN GENERAL.—To meet the certification requirement of this paragraph, a person shall certify that—

(i) the aggregate book value of the vessels owned by the person and United States affiliates of the person does not exceed 10 percent of the aggregate book value of all assets owned by the person and its United States affiliates;

(ii) not more than 10 percent of the aggregate revenues of the person and its United States affiliates is derived from the ownership, operation, or management of vessels;

(iii) at least 70 percent of the aggregate tonnage of all cargo carried by all vessels owned by the person and its United States affiliates and documented with a coastwise endorsement is qualified proprietary cargo;

(iv) any cargo other than qualified proprietary cargo carried by all vessels owned by the person and its United States affiliates and documented with a coastwise endorsement consists of oil, petroleum products, petrochemicals, or liquified natural gas;

(v) no vessel owned by the person or any of its United States affiliates and documented with a coastwise endorsement carries molten sulphur; and

(vi) the person owned one or more vessels documented under this section as of August 9, 2004.

(B) APPLICATION ONLY TO CERTAIN VESSELS.—A person may make a certification under this paragraph only with respect to—

(i) a tank vessel having a tonnage of at least 6,000 gross tons, as measured under section 14502 of this title (or an alternative tonnage measured under section 14302 of this title as prescribed by the Secretary under section 14104 of this title); or

(ii) a towing vessel associated with a non-self-propelled tank vessel that meets the requirements of clause (i), where both vessels function as a single self-propelled vessel.

(d) Filing of Demise Charter.—The demise charter and any amendments to the charter shall be filed with the certification required by subsection (b)(3) or within 10 days after filing an amendment to the charter. The charter and amendments shall be made available to the public.

(e) Continuation of Endorsement After Termination of Charter.—When a charter required by subsection (b)(3) is terminated for default by the charterer, the Secretary may continue the coastwise endorsement for not more than 6 months on terms and conditions the Secretary may prescribe.

(f) Deemed Owned by Citizens.—A vessel satisfying the requirements of this section is deemed to be owned only by citizens of the United States under sections 12103 and 50501 of this title.

(Pub. L. 109–304, §5, Oct. 6, 2006, 120 Stat. 1501; Pub. L. 115–232, div. C, title XXXV, §3541(b)(15), Aug. 13, 2018, 132 Stat. 2324.)

§12120. Liquified gas tankers

Notwithstanding any agreement with the United States Government, the Secretary may issue a certificate of documentation with a coastwise endorsement for a vessel to transport liquified natural gas or liquified petroleum gas to Puerto Rico from other ports in the United States, if the vessel—

(1) is a foreign built vessel that was built before October 19, 1996; or

(2) was documented under this chapter before that date, even if the vessel is placed under a foreign registry and subsequently redocumented under this chapter for operation under this section.

(Pub. L. 109–304, §5, Oct. 6, 2006, 120 Stat. 1504.)

§12121. Small passenger vessels and uninspected passenger vessels

(a) Definitions.—In this section:

(1) Eligible vessel.—The term "eligible vessel" means a vessel that—
(A) was built in the United States;
(B) was not built in the United States and is at least 3 years old; or
(C) if rebuilt, was rebuilt—
(i) in the United States; or
(ii) outside the United States at least 3 years before the certificate requested under subsection (b) would take effect.

(2) Small passenger vessel; uninspected passenger vessel; passenger for hire.—The terms "small passenger vessel", "uninspected passenger vessel", and "passenger for hire" have the meaning given those terms in section 2101 of this title.

(b) Issuance of Certificate and Endorsement.—Notwithstanding sections 12112, 12113, 12132, 55102, and 55103 of this title, the Secretary may issue a certificate of documentation with an appropriate endorsement for employment in the coastwise trade as a small passenger vessel or an uninspected passenger vessel in the case of an eligible vessel authorized to carry no more than 12 passengers for hire if the Secretary of Transportation, after notice and an opportunity for public comment, determines that the employment of the vessel in the coastwise trade will not adversely affect—

(1) United States vessel builders; or

(2) the coastwise trade business of any person that employs vessels built in the United States in that business.

(c) REVOCATION.—

(1) FOR FRAUD.—The Secretary shall revoke a certificate or endorsement issued under subsection (b) if the Secretary of Transportation, after notice and an opportunity for a hearing, determines that the certificate or endorsement was obtained by fraud.

(2) OTHER PROVISIONS NOT AFFECTED.—Paragraph (1) does not affect—

(A) the criminal prohibition on fraud and false statements in section 1001 of title 18; or

(B) any other authority of the Secretary to revoke a certificate or endorsement issued under subsection (b).

(Pub. L. 109–304, §5, Oct. 6, 2006, 120 Stat. 1504; Pub. L. 116–283, div. G, title LVXXXIII [LXXXIII], §8312, Jan. 1, 2021, 134 Stat. 4697.)

SUBCHAPTER III—MISCELLANEOUS

§12131. Command of documented vessels

(a) IN GENERAL.—Except as provided in subsection (b), a documented vessel may be placed under the command only of a citizen of the United States.

(b) EXCEPTIONS.—Subsection (a) does not apply to—

(1) a vessel with only a recreational endorsement; or

(2) an unmanned barge operating outside of the territorial waters of the United States.

(Pub. L. 109–304, §5, Oct. 6, 2006, 120 Stat. 1505; Pub. L. 110–181, div. C, title XXXV, §3529(a)(3), Jan. 28, 2008, 122 Stat. 603.)

§12132. Loss of coastwise trade privileges

(a) SOLD FOREIGN OR PLACED UNDER FOREIGN REGISTRY.—A vessel of more than 200 gross tons (as measured under chapter 143 of this title), eligible to engage in the coastwise trade, and later sold foreign in whole or in part or placed under foreign registry may not thereafter engage in the coastwise trade.

(b) REBUILT OUTSIDE THE UNITED STATES.—A vessel eligible to engage in the coastwise trade and later rebuilt outside the United States may not thereafter engage in the coastwise trade.

(Pub. L. 109–304, §5, Oct. 6, 2006, 120 Stat. 1505.)

§12133. Duty to carry certificate on vessel and allow examination

(a) DUTY TO CARRY.—The certificate of documentation of a vessel shall be carried on the vessel unless the vessel is exempt by regulation from carrying the certificate.

(b) AVAILABILITY.—The owner or individual in charge of a vessel required to carry its certificate of documentation shall make the certificate available for examination at the request of an officer enforcing the revenue laws or as otherwise required by law or regulation.

(c) CRIMINAL PENALTY.—A person willfully violating subsection (b) shall be fined under title 18, imprisoned for not more than one year, or both.

(Pub. L. 109–304, §5, Oct. 6, 2006, 120 Stat. 1505.)

§12134. Evidentiary uses of documentation

A certificate of documentation is—

(1) conclusive evidence of nationality for international purposes, but not in a proceeding conducted under the laws of the United States;

(2) conclusive evidence of qualification to engage in a specified trade; and

(3) not conclusive evidence of ownership in a proceeding in which ownership is in issue.

(Pub. L. 109–304, §5, Oct. 6, 2006, 120 Stat. 1506.)

§12135. Invalidation of certificates of documentation

A certificate of documentation or an endorsement on the certificate is invalid if the vessel for which it is issued—

(1) no longer meets the requirements of this chapter and regulations prescribed under this chapter applicable to the certificate or endorsement; or

(2) is placed under the command of an individual not a citizen of the United States in violation of section 12131 of this title.

(Pub. L. 109–304, §5, Oct. 6, 2006, 120 Stat. 1506.)

§12136. SURRENDER OF CERTIFICATES OF DOCUMENTATION

(a) SURRENDER.—An invalid certificate of documentation, or a certificate with an invalid endorsement, shall be surrendered as provided by regulations prescribed by the Secretary.

(b) CONDITIONS FOR SURRENDER.—

(1) VESSELS OVER 1,000 TONS.—The Secretary may condition approval of the surrender of the certificate of documentation for a vessel over 1,000 gross tons.

(2) VESSELS COVERED BY MORTGAGE.—The Secretary may approve the surrender of the certificate of documentation of a vessel covered by a mortgage filed or recorded under section 31321 of this title only if the mortgagee consents.

(3) NOTICE OF LIEN.—The Secretary may not refuse to approve the surrender of the certificate of documentation for a vessel solely on the basis that a notice of a claim of a lien on the vessel has been recorded under section 31343(a) of this title.

(c) CONTINUED APPLICATION OF CERTAIN LAWS.—

(1) IN GENERAL.—Notwithstanding subsection (a), until the certificate of documentation is surrendered with the approval of the Secretary, a documented vessel is deemed to continue to be documented under this chapter for purposes of—

(A) chapter 313 of this title for an instrument filed or recorded before the date of invalidation and an assignment after that date;

(B) sections 56101 and 56102(a)(2) and chapter 563 of this title; and

(C) any other law of the United States identified by the Secretary by regulation as a law to which the Secretary applies this subsection.

(2) EXCEPTION.—This subsection does not apply when a vessel is forfeited or sold by order of a district court of the United States.

(Pub. L. 109–304, §5, Oct. 6, 2006, 120 Stat. 1506.)

§12137. RECORDING OF VESSELS BUILT IN THE UNITED STATES

The Secretary may provide for recording and certifying information about vessels built in the United States that the Secretary considers to be in the public interest.

(Pub. L. 109–304, §5, Oct. 6, 2006, 120 Stat. 1507.)

§12138. LIST OF DOCUMENTED VESSELS

(a) IN GENERAL.—The Secretary shall publish periodically a list of all documented vessels and information about those vessels that the Secretary considers pertinent or useful. The list shall contain a notation clearly indicating all vessels classed by the American Bureau of Shipping.

(b) VESSELS FOR CABLE LAYING, MAINTENANCE, AND REPAIR.—

(1) IN GENERAL.—The Secretary of Transportation shall develop, maintain, and periodically update an inventory of vessels that are documented under this chapter, are at least 200 feet in length, and have the capability to lay, maintain, or repair a submarine cable, without regard to whether a particular vessel is classed as a cable ship or cable vessel.

(2) INFORMATION TO BE INCLUDED.—For each vessel listed in the inventory, the Secretary of Transportation shall include in the inventory—

(A) the name, length, beam, depth, and other distinguishing characteristics of the vessel;

(B) the abilities and limitations of the vessel with respect to laying, maintaining, and repairing a submarine cable; and

(C) the name and address of the person to whom inquiries regarding the vessel may be made.

(3) PUBLICATION.—The Secretary of Transportation shall publish in the Federal Register an updated inventory every 6 months.

(Pub. L. 109–304, §5, Oct. 6, 2006, 120 Stat. 1507.)

§12139. REPORTS

(a) IN GENERAL.—To ensure compliance with this chapter and laws governing the qualifications of vessels to engage in the coastwise trade and the fisheries, the Secretary may require owners, masters, charterers, and mortgagees of documented vessels to submit reports in any reasonable form and manner the Secretary may prescribe.

(b) VESSELS REBUILT OUTSIDE UNITED STATES.—

(1) IN GENERAL.—Under regulations prescribed by the Secretary, if a vessel exceeding the tonnage specified in paragraph (2) and documented or last documented under the laws of the United States is rebuilt outside the United States, the owner or master shall submit a report of the rebuilding to the Secretary.

(2) TONNAGE.—The tonnage referred to in paragraph (1) is—

(A) 500 gross tons as measured under section 14502 of this title; or

(B) an alternate tonnage as measured under section 14302 of this title as prescribed by the Secretary under section 14104 of this title.

(3) TIMING OF SUBMISSION.—If the rebuilding is completed in the United States, the report shall be submitted when the rebuilding is completed. If the rebuilding is completed outside the United States, the report shall be submitted when the vessel first arrives at a port in the customs territory of the United States.

(Pub. L. 109–304, §5, Oct. 6, 2006, 120 Stat. 1507; Pub. L. 109–241, title III, §308, July 11, 2006, 120 Stat. 528; Pub. L. 110–181, div. C, title XXXV, §3525(a)(2), (b), Jan. 28, 2008, 122 Stat. 600, 601.)

§12140. INVESTIGATIONS BY SECRETARY

(a) IN GENERAL.—The Secretary may conduct investigations and inspections regarding compliance with this chapter and regulations prescribed under this chapter.

(b) AUTHORITY TO OBTAIN EVIDENCE.—

(1) IN GENERAL.—For the purposes of any investigation conducted under this section, the Secretary may issue a subpoena to require the attendance of a witness or the production of documents or other evidence relevant to the matter under investigation if—

(A) before the issuance of the subpoena, the Secretary requests a determination by the Attorney General as to whether the subpoena—

(i) is reasonable; and

(ii) will interfere with a criminal investigation; and

(B) the Attorney General—

(i) determines that the subpoena is reasonable and will not interfere with a criminal investigation; or

(ii) fails to make a determination with respect to the subpoena before the date that is 30 days after the date on which the Secretary makes a request under subparagraph (A) with respect to the subpoena.

(2) ENFORCEMENT.—In the case of a refusal to obey a subpoena issued to any person under this section, the Secretary may invoke the aid of the appropriate district court of the United States to compel compliance.

(Added Pub. L. 112–213, title III, §308(a), Dec. 20, 2012, 126 Stat. 1566.)

SUBCHAPTER IV—PENALTIES

§12151. Penalties

(a) In General.—

(1) Civil penalties.—Except as provided in paragraph (2), a person that violates this chapter or a regulation prescribed under this chapter is liable to the United States Government for a civil penalty of not more than $15,000. Each day of a continuing violation is a separate violation.

(2) Activities involving mobile offshore drilling units.—A person that violates section 12111(d) or a regulation prescribed under that section is liable to the United States Government for a civil penalty in an amount that is $25,000 or twice the charter rate of the vessel involved in the violation (as determined by the Secretary), whichever is greater. Each day of a continuing violation is a separate violation.

(b) Seizure and Forfeiture of Vessels.—A vessel and its equipment are liable to seizure by and forfeiture to the Government if—

(1) the owner of the vessel or the representative or agent of the owner knowingly falsifies or conceals a material fact, or knowingly makes a false statement or representation, about the documentation of the vessel or in applying for documentation of the vessel;

(2) a certificate of documentation is knowingly and fraudulently used for the vessel;

(3) the vessel is operated after its endorsement has been denied or revoked under section 12152 of this title;

(4) the vessel is employed in a trade without an appropriate endorsement;

(5) the vessel has only a recreational endorsement and is operated other than for pleasure;

(6) the vessel is a documented vessel and is placed under the command of a person not a citizen of the United States, except as authorized by section 12131(b) of this title; or

(7) the vessel is rebuilt outside the United States and a report of the rebuilding is not submitted as required by section 12139(b) of this title.

(c) Engaging in Fishing After Falsifying Eligibility.—In addition to other penalties under this section, the owner of a documented vessel for which a fishery endorsement has been issued is liable to the Government for a civil penalty of not more than $100,000 for each day the vessel engages in fishing (as defined in section 3 of the Magnuson-Stevens Fishery Conservation and Management Act (16 U.S.C. 1802)) within the exclusive economic zone, if the owner or the representative or agent of the owner knowingly falsified or concealed a material fact, or knowingly made a false statement or representation, about the eligibility of the vessel under section 12113(c) or (d) of this title in applying for or applying to renew the fishery endorsement.

(Pub. L. 109–304, §5, Oct. 6, 2006, 120 Stat. 1508; Pub. L. 112–213, title III, §309, Dec. 20, 2012, 126 Stat. 1566.)

§12152. Denial or revocation of endorsement for non-payment of

CIVIL PENALTY

If the owner of a vessel fails to pay a civil penalty imposed by the Secretary, the Secretary may deny the issuance or renewal of an endorsement, or revoke the endorsement, on a certificate of documentation issued for the vessel under this chapter.

(Pub. L. 109–304, §5, Oct. 6, 2006, 120 Stat. 1508.)

CHAPTER 123—NUMBERING UNDOCUMENTED VESSELS

§12301. NUMBERING VESSELS

(a) An undocumented vessel equipped with propulsion machinery of any kind shall have a number issued by the proper issuing authority in the State in which the vessel principally is operated.

(b) The Secretary may require an undocumented barge of more than 100 gross tons operating on the navigable waters of the United States to be numbered.

(Pub. L. 98–89, Aug. 26, 1983, 97 Stat. 590; Pub. L. 102–587, title V, §5305, Nov. 4, 1992, 106 Stat. 5083; Pub. L. 115–282, title V, §513, Dec. 4, 2018, 132 Stat. 4276.)

§12302. STANDARD NUMBERING SYSTEM

(a) The Secretary shall prescribe by regulation a standard numbering system for vessels to which this chapter applies. On application by a State, the Secretary shall approve a State numbering system that is consistent with the standard numbering system. In carrying out its numbering system, a State shall adopt any definitions of relevant terms prescribed by regulations of the Secretary.

(b) A State with an approved numbering system is the issuing authority within the meaning of this chapter. The Secretary is the issuing authority in a State in which a State numbering system has not been approved.

(c) When a vessel is numbered in a State, it is deemed in compliance with the numbering system of a State in which it temporarily is operated.

(d) When a vessel is removed to a new State of principal operation, the issuing authority of that State shall recognize the validity of the number issued by the original State for 60 days.

(e) If a State has a numbering system approved after the Secretary issues a number, the State shall recognize the validity of the number issued by the Secretary for one year.

(f) When the Secretary decides that a State numbering system is not being carried out consistent with the standard numbering system or the State has changed the system without the Secretary's approval, the Secretary may withdraw approval after giving notice to the State, in writing, stating the reasons for the withdrawal.

(Pub. L. 98–89, Aug. 26, 1983, 97 Stat. 590.)

§12303. EXEMPTION FROM NUMBERING REQUIREMENTS

(a) When the Secretary is the authority issuing a number under this chapter, the Secretary may exempt a vessel or class of vessels from the numbering requirements of this chapter under conditions the Secretary may prescribe.

(b) When a State is the issuing authority, it may exempt from the numbering requirements of this chapter a vessel or class of vessels exempted under subsection (a) of this section or otherwise as permitted by the Secretary.

(Pub. L. 98–89, Aug. 26, 1983, 97 Stat. 591.)

§12304. CERTIFICATES OF NUMBERS

(a) A certificate of number is granted for a number issued under this chapter. The certificate shall be at all times available for inspection on the vessel for which issued when the vessel is in operation, and may be in hard copy or digital form. Any certificate issued in hard copy under this section shall be pocketsized. The certificate shall be valid for not more than 3 years. The certificate of number for a vessel less than 26 feet in length and leased or rented to another for the latter's noncommercial operation of less than 7 days may be retained on shore by the vessel's owner or representative at the place from which the vessel departs or returns to the possession of the owner or the owner's representative. A vessel that does not have the certificate of number on board shall be identified when in operation, and comply with requirements, as the issuing authority prescribes.

(b) The owner of a vessel numbered under this chapter shall provide—

(1) the issuing authority notice of the transfer of any part of the owner's interest in the vessel or of the destruction or abandonment of the vessel, within a reasonable time after the transfer, destruction, or abandonment; and

(2) notice of a change of address within a reasonable time of the change, as prescribed by regulation.

(Pub. L. 98–89, Aug. 26, 1983, 97 Stat. 591; Pub. L. 117–263, div. K, title CXV, §11506, Dec. 23, 2022, 136 Stat. 4136.)

§12305. DISPLAYING NUMBERS

A number required by this chapter shall be painted on, or attached to, each side of the forward half of the vessel for which it was issued, and shall be the size, color, and type as may be prescribed by the Secretary. No other number may be carried on the forward half of the vessel.

(Pub. L. 98–89, Aug. 26, 1983, 97 Stat. 591.)

§12306. SAFETY CERTIFICATES

When a State is the authority issuing a number under this chapter, it may require that the individual in charge of a numbered vessel have a valid safety certificate issued under conditions set by the issuing authority, except when the vessel is subject to manning requirements under part F of this subtitle.

(Pub. L. 98–89, Aug. 26, 1983, 97 Stat. 591.)

§12307. REGULATIONS ON NUMBERING AND FEES

The authority issuing a number under this chapter may prescribe regulations and establish fees to carry out the intent of this chapter. The fees shall apply equally to residents and nonresidents of the State. A State issuing authority may impose only conditions for vessel numbering that are—

(1) prescribed by this chapter or regulations of the Secretary about the standard numbering system; or

(2) related to proof of payment of State or local taxes.

(Pub. L. 98–89, Aug. 26, 1983, 97 Stat. 591.)

§12308. PROVIDING VESSEL NUMBERING AND REGISTRATION INFORMATION

A person may request from an authority issuing a number under this chapter the numbering and registration information of a vessel that is retrievable from vessel numbering system records of the issuing authority. When the issuing authority is satisfied that the request is reasonable and related to a boating safety purpose, the information shall be provided on paying the cost of retrieving and providing the information requested.

(Pub. L. 98–89, Aug. 26, 1983, 97 Stat. 592.)

§12309. PENALTIES

(a) A person willfully violating this chapter or a regulation prescribed under this chapter shall be fined not more than $5,000, imprisoned for not more than one year, or both.

(b) A person violating this chapter or a regulation prescribed under this chapter is liable to the United States Government for a civil penalty of not more than $1,000. If the violation involves the operation of a vessel, the vessel also is liable in rem for the penalty.

(c) When a civil penalty of not more than $200 has been assessed under this chapter, the Secretary may refer the matter of collection of the penalty directly to the United States magistrate judge of the jurisdiction in which the person liable may be found for collection procedures under supervision of the district court and under an order issued by the court delegating this authority under section 636(b) of title 28.

(Pub. L. 98–89, Aug. 26, 1983, 97 Stat. 592; Pub. L. 101–650, title III, §321, Dec. 1, 1990, 104 Stat 5117.)

§12310. REGULATIONS ON NUMBERING VESSELS

§12308. PROOF OF VESSEL NUMBERING AND REGISTRATION INFORMATION

§12309. PENALTIES

CHAPTER 125—VESSEL IDENTIFICATION SYSTEM

§12501. ESTABLISHMENT OF A VESSEL IDENTIFICATION SYSTEM

(a) The Secretary of Transportation shall establish a vessel identification system to make available information under section 12503 of this title for use by the public for law enforcement and other purposes relating to—

(1) the ownership of documented vessels;

(2) the ownership of vessels numbered under chapter 123 of this title; and

(3) the ownership of vessels titled under the law of a State.

(b) The vessel identification system shall include information prescribed by the Secretary including—

(1) identifying a vessel;

(2) identifying the owner of the vessel, including—

(A) the owner's social security number or, if that number is not available, other means of identification acceptable to the Secretary; or

(B) for an owner other than an individual—

(i) the owner's taxpayer identification number; or

(ii) if the owner does not have a taxpayer identification number, the social security number of an individual who is a corporate officer, general partner, or individual trustee of the owner and who signed the application for documentation or numbering for the vessel;

(3) identifying the State in which it is titled or numbered;

(4) indicating whether the vessel is numbered or titled, or both;

(5) if titled in a State, indicating where evidence of a lien or other security interest may be found against the vessel in that State; and

(6) information assisting law enforcement officials.

(c) The Secretary may maintain information under this chapter in connection with any other information system maintained by the Secretary.

(Added Pub. L. 100–710, title I, §101(a), Nov. 23, 1988, 102 Stat. 4735; amended Pub. L. 101–225, title III, §302(1), Dec. 12, 1989, 103 Stat. 1922; Pub. L. 101–595, title VI, §603(10), Nov. 16, 1990, 104 Stat. 2993.)

§12502. IDENTIFICATION NUMBERS, SIGNAL LETTERS, AND MARKINGS

(a) For the identification of a vessel of the United States, the Secretary of Transportation—

(1) shall maintain a unique numbering system and assign a number to each vessel of the United States;

(2) may maintain a system of signal letters for a documented vessel;

(3) shall record a name selected by the owner of a documented vessel approved by the Secretary as the vessel's name of record; and

(4) may establish other identification markings.

(b) The manufacturer or owner of a vessel shall affix to the vessel and maintain in the manner prescribed by the Secretary the number assigned and any other markings the Secretary may require.

(c) Once a number is assigned under this section, it may not be used by another vessel.

(d) Once a documented vessel's name is established, the name may not be changed without the approval of the Secretary.

(e) A person may not tamper with or falsify a number or other marking required under this section.

(Added Pub. L. 100–710, title I, §101(a), Nov. 23, 1988, 102 Stat. 4736.)

§12503. INFORMATION AVAILABLE TO THE SYSTEM

(a) Except as provided in subsections (b) and (c) of this section, a State or a State's delegate approved by the Secretary of Transportation may make information available to the Secretary if, in a manner and form prescribed by the Secretary, the State—

(1) identifies the vessel;

(2) identifies the owner of the vessel, including by—

(A) the owner's social security number or, if that number is not available, other means of identification acceptable to the Secretary; or

(B) for an owner other than an individual—

(i) the owner's taxpayer identification number; or

(ii) if the owner does not have a taxpayer identification number, the social security number of an individual who is a corporate officer, general partner, or individual trustee of the owner and who signed the application for documentation or numbering for the vessel;

(3) identifies the State in which it is titled or numbered;

(4) indicates whether the vessel is numbered or titled, or both;

(5) if titled in a State, indicates where evidence of a lien or other security interest may be found against the vessel in that State;

(6) includes information to assist law enforcement; and

(7) includes other information agreed to by the Secretary and the State.

(b) Except as provided in subsection (c) of this section, the Secretary also may accept information under conditions and in a manner and form prescribed by the Secretary.

(c) The Secretary shall—

(1) retain information on a vessel with a preferred mortgage under section 31322(d) of this title that is no longer titled in a State making information available to the Secretary under this chapter until the mortgage is discharged or the vessel is sold; and

(2) accept information under section 31321(h) of this title only if that information cannot be provided to a State.

(Added Pub. L. 100–710, title I, §101(a), Nov. 23, 1988, 102 Stat. 4736; amended Pub. L. 101–225, title III, §302(2), Dec. 12, 1989, 103 Stat. 1922; Pub. L. 101–595, title VI, §603(10), Nov. 16, 1990, 104 Stat. 2993; Pub. L. 109–304, §15(24), Oct. 6, 2006, 120 Stat. 1704.)

§12504. INFORMATION AVAILABLE FROM THE SYSTEM

For law enforcement or other purposes and under conditions prescribed by the Secretary of Transportation, the Secretary—

(1) shall make available information in the vessel identification system to a State making information available under section 12503(a) of this title; and

(2) may make available information in the vessel identification system to others.

(Added Pub. L. 100–710, title I, §101(a), Nov. 23, 1988, 102 Stat. 4736; amended Pub. L. 101–225, title III, §302(3), Dec. 12, 1989, 103 Stat. 1923.)

§12505. FEES

(a) The Secretary of Transportation may charge a fee under section 9701 of title 31 for providing information to or requesting information from the vessel identification system, except to—

(1) an agency; or

(2) a State making information available to the Secretary under section 12503(a) of this title.

(b) The Secretary shall deposit amounts transferred or collected under this section in the general fund of the Treasury as proprietary receipts of the Secretary and ascribed to the vessel identification system.

(Added Pub. L. 100–710, title I, §101(a), Nov. 23, 1988, 102 Stat. 4737; amended Pub. L. 101–595, title VI, §603(11), Nov. 16, 1990, 104 Stat. 2993.)

§12506. DELEGATION OF AUTHORITY

The Secretary of Transportation may delegate to an agency, a State, or a qualified person the authority to—

(1) establish and maintain the vessel identification system; and

(2) charge fees under section 12505 of this title to a person making information available to or requesting information from the vessel identification system.

(Added Pub. L. 100–710, title I, §101(a), Nov. 23, 1988, 102 Stat. 4737.)

§12507. PENALTIES

(a) A person shall be fined under title 18, imprisoned for not more than 2 years, or both, if the person with the intent to defraud—

(1) provides false information to the Secretary of Transportation or a State issuing authority regarding the identification of a vessel under this chapter; or

(2) tampers with, removes, or falsifies the unique vessel identification number assigned to a vessel under section 12502 of this title.

(b) A person is liable to the United States Government for a civil penalty of not more than $10,000 if the person—

(1) provides false information to the Secretary or a State issuing authority regarding the identification of a vessel under this chapter;

(2) violates section 12502 of this title; or

(3) fails to comply with requirements prescribed by the Secretary under section 12505 of this title.

(c) A vessel involved in a violation of this chapter, or regulation under this chapter, and its equipment, may be seized by, and forfeited to, the Government.

(d) If a person, not an individual, is involved in a violation of this chapter, the president or chief executive of the person also is subject to any penalty provided under this section.

(Added Pub. L. 100–710, title I, §101(a), Nov. 23, 1988, 102 Stat. 4737.)

§13101. DEFINITIONS

In this chapter:

(1) ELIGIBLE STATE.—The term "eligible State" means a State that has a State recreational boating safety program accepted by the Secretary.

(2) STATE RECREATIONAL BOATING SAFETY PROGRAM.—The term "State recreational boating safety program" means education, assistance, and enforcement activities conducted for maritime casualty prevention, reduction, and reporting for recreational boating.

(Pub. L. 109–304, §16(b)(2), Oct. 6, 2006, 120 Stat. 1705.)

§13102. STATE RECREATIONAL BOATING SAFETY PROGRAMS

(a) To encourage greater State participation and uniformity in boating safety efforts, and particularly to permit the States to assume the greater share of boating safety education, assistance, and enforcement activities, the Secretary shall carry out a national recreational boating safety program. Under this program, the Secretary shall make contracts with, and allocate and distribute amounts to, eligible States to assist them in developing, carrying out, and financing State recreational boating safety programs.

(b) The Secretary shall establish guidelines and standards for the program. In doing so, the Secretary—

(1) shall consider, among other things, factors affecting recreational boating safety by contributing to overcrowding and congestion of waterways, such as the increasing number of recreational vessels operating on those waterways and their geographic distribution, the availability and geographic distribution of recreational boating facilities in and among applying States, and State marine casualty and fatality statistics for recreational vessels;

(2) shall consult with the Secretary of the Interior to minimize duplication with the purposes and expenditures of chapter 2003 of title 54, United States Code,[1] the Federal

Aid in Sport Fish Restoration Act of 1950 (16 U.S.C. 777–777k), and with the guidelines developed under those Acts; and

(3) shall maintain environmental standards consistent with the Coastal Zone Management Act of 1972 (16 U.S.C. 1451–1464) and other laws and policies of the United States intended to safeguard the ecological and esthetic quality of the waters and wetlands of the United States.

(c) A State whose recreational boating safety program has been approved by the Secretary is eligible for allocation and distribution of amounts under this chapter to assist that State in developing, carrying out, and financing its program. Matching amounts shall be allocated and distributed among eligible States by the Secretary as provided by section 13104 of this title.

(Pub. L. 98–89, Aug. 26, 1983, 97 Stat. 592, §13101; Pub. L. 98–369, div. A, title X, §1011(b), July 18, 1984, 98 Stat. 1013; Pub. L. 101–595, title III, §312(a), Nov. 16, 1990, 104 Stat. 2987; renumbered §13102 and amended Pub. L. 109–304, §16(b)(1), (c)(3), Oct. 6, 2006, 120 Stat. 1705, 1706; Pub. L. 113–287, §5(n), Dec. 19, 2014, 128 Stat. 3272.)

[1] So in original. The words "United States Code," probably should not appear.

§13103. PROGRAM ACCEPTANCE

(a) The Secretary shall make a contract with, and allocate and distribute amounts from the Sport Fish Restoration and Boating Trust Fund established by section 9504 of the Internal Revenue Code of 1986 (26 U.S.C. 9504) to, a State that has an approved State recreational boating safety program, if the State demonstrates to the Secretary's satisfaction that—

(1) the program submitted by that State is consistent with this chapter and chapters 61 and 123 of this title;

(2) amounts distributed will be used to develop and carry out a State recreational boating safety program containing the minimum requirements of subsection (c) of this section;

(3) sufficient State matching amounts are available from general State revenue, undocumented vessel numbering and license fees, State marine fuels taxes, or from a fund constituted from the proceeds of those taxes and established to finance a State recreational boating safety program; and

(4) the program submitted by that State designates a State lead authority or agency that will carry out or coordinate carrying out the State recreational boating safety program supported by financial assistance of the United States Government in that State, including the requirement that the designated State authority or agency submit required reports that are necessary and reasonable to carry out properly and efficiently the program and that are in the form prescribed by the Secretary.

(b) Amounts of the Government (except amounts from sources referred to in subsection (a)(3) of this section) may not be used to provide a State's share of the costs of the program described under this section. State matching amounts committed to a program under this chapter may not be used to constitute the State's share of matching amounts required by another program of the Government.

(c) The Secretary shall approve a State recreational boating safety program, and the program is eligible to receive amounts authorized to be expended under section 13107 of this title, if the program includes—

(1) a vessel numbering system approved or carried out by the Secretary under chapter 123 of this title;

(2) a cooperative boating safety assistance program with the Coast Guard in that State;

(3) sufficient patrol and other activity to ensure adequate enforcement of applicable State boating safety laws and regulations;

(4) an adequate State boating safety education program, that includes the dissemination of information concerning the hazards of operating a vessel when under the influence of alcohol or drugs; and

(5) a system, approved by the Secretary, for reporting marine casualties required under section 6102 of this title.

(d) The Secretary's approval under this section is a contractual obligation of the Government for the payment of a proportionate share of the cost of carrying out the program.

(Pub. L. 98–89, Aug. 26, 1983, 97 Stat. 593, §13102; Pub. L. 98–369, div. A, title X, §1011(c), July 18, 1984, 98 Stat. 1013; Pub. L. 98–557, §7(b)(3), Oct. 30, 1984, 98 Stat. 2862; Pub. L. 99–307, §1(17), May 19, 1986, 100 Stat. 446; Pub. L. 99–626, §4(a), (b), Nov. 7, 1986, 100 Stat. 3505; Pub. L. 100–448, §6(b)(3)–(5), Sept. 28, 1988, 102 Stat. 1840; Pub. L. 101–595, title III, §312(b), Nov. 16, 1990, 104 Stat. 2987; Pub. L. 109–59, title X, §10141, Aug. 10, 2005, 119 Stat. 1931; renumbered §13103 and amended Pub. L. 109–304, §§15(25), 16(b)(1), (c)(4), Oct. 6, 2006, 120 Stat. 1704–1706.)

§13104. ALLOCATIONS

(a) The Secretary shall allocate amounts available for allocation and distribution under this chapter for State recreational boating safety programs as follows:

(1) One-third shall be allocated equally each fiscal year among eligible States.

(2) One-third shall be allocated among eligible States that maintain a State vessel numbering system approved under chapter 123 of this title and a marine casualty reporting system approved under this chapter so that the amount allocated each fiscal year to each eligible State will be in the same ratio as the number of vessels numbered in that State bears to the number of vessels numbered in all eligible States.

(3) One-third shall be allocated so that the amount allocated each fiscal year to each eligible State will be in the same ratio as the amount of State amounts expended by the State for the State recreational boating safety program during the prior fiscal year bears to the total State amounts expended during that fiscal year by all eligible States for State recreational boating safety programs.

(b) The amount received by a State under this section in a fiscal year may be not more than one-half of the total cost incurred by that State in developing, carrying out, and financing that State's recreational boating safety program in that fiscal year.

(c) The Secretary may allocate not more than 5 percent of the amounts available for allocation and distribution in a fiscal year for national boating safety activities of national nonprofit public service organizations.

(Pub. L. 98–89, Aug. 26, 1983, 97 Stat. 594, §13103; Pub. L. 98–369, div. A, title X, §1011(d), July 18, 1984, 98 Stat. 1013; Pub. L. 101–595, title III, §312(c), Nov. 16, 1990, 104 Stat. 2987; renumbered §13104, Pub. L. 109–304, §16(b)(1), Oct. 6, 2006, 120 Stat. 1705.)

§13105. Availability of allocations

(a)(1) Amounts allocated to a State shall be available for obligation by that State for a period of 3 years after the date of allocation.

(2) Amounts allocated to a State that are not obligated at the end of the 3-year period referred to in paragraph (1) shall be withdrawn and allocated by the Secretary in addition to any other amounts available for allocation in the fiscal year in which they are withdrawn or the following fiscal year.

(b) Amounts available to the Secretary for State recreational boating safety programs for a fiscal year that have not been allocated at the end of the fiscal year shall be allocated among States in the next fiscal year in addition to amounts otherwise available for allocation to States for that next fiscal year.

(Pub. L. 98–89, Aug. 26, 1983, 97 Stat. 595, §13104; Pub. L. 99–307, §1(18), May 19, 1986, 100 Stat. 446; Pub. L. 102–587, title V, §5101, Nov. 4, 1992, 106 Stat. 5070; Pub. L. 105–178, title VII, §7405(a), June 9, 1998, 112 Stat. 487; Pub. L. 109–59, title X, §10142, Aug. 10, 2005, 119 Stat. 1931; renumbered §13105, Pub. L. 109–304, §16(b)(1), Oct. 6, 2006, 120 Stat. 1705.)

§13106. Computation decisions about State amounts expended

(a) Consistent with regulations prescribed by the Secretary, the computation by a State of amounts expended for the State recreational boating safety program shall include—

   (1) the acquisition, maintenance, and operating costs of land, facilities, equipment, and supplies;

   (2) personnel salaries and reimbursable expenses;

   (3) the costs of training personnel;

   (4) public boat safety education;

   (5) the costs of carrying out the program; and

   (6) other expenses that the Secretary considers appropriate.

(b) The Secretary shall decide an issue arising out of the computation made under subsection (a) of this section.

(Pub. L. 98–89, Aug. 26, 1983, 97 Stat. 596, §13105; Pub. L. 98–369, div. A, title X, §1011(e), July 18, 1984, 98 Stat. 1013; Pub. L. 101–595, title III, §312(c), Nov. 16, 1990, 104 Stat. 2987; renumbered §13106, Pub. L. 109–304, §16(b)(1), Oct. 6, 2006, 120 Stat. 1705.)

§13107. Authorization of appropriations

(a) Subject to subsection (c), the Secretary shall expend in each fiscal year for State recreational boating safety programs, under contracts with States under this chapter, an amount equal to the amount transferred to the Secretary under subsections (a)(2) and (f) of section 4 of the Dingell-Johnson Sport Fish Restoration Act (16 U.S.C. 777c(a)(2) and (f)). The amount shall be allocated as provided under section 13104 of this title and shall be available for State recreational boating safety programs as provided under the guidelines established under subsection (b) of this section. Amounts authorized to be expended for State recreational boating safety programs shall remain available until expended and are deemed to have been expended only if an amount equal to the total amounts authorized to be expended under this section for the fiscal year in question and all prior fiscal years have been obligated. Amounts previously obligated but released by payment of a final voucher or modification of a program acceptance shall be credited to the balance of unobligated amounts and are immediately available for expenditure.

(b) The Secretary shall establish guidelines prescribing the purposes for which amounts available under this chapter for State recreational boating safety programs may be used. Those purposes shall include—

(1) providing facilities, equipment, and supplies for boating safety education and law enforcement, including purchase, operation, maintenance, and repair;

(2) training personnel in skills related to boating safety and to the enforcement of boating safety laws and regulations;

(3) providing public boating safety education, including educational programs and lectures, to the boating community and the public school system;

(4) acquiring, constructing, or repairing public access sites used primarily by recreational boaters;

(5) conducting boating safety inspections and marine casualty investigations;

(6) establishing and maintaining emergency or search and rescue facilities, and providing emergency or search and rescue assistance;

(7) establishing and maintaining waterway markers and other appropriate aids to navigation; and

(8) providing State recreational vessel numbering and titling programs.

(c)(1)(A) The Secretary may use amounts made available each fiscal year under section 4(b)(2) of the Dingell-Johnson Sport Fish Restoration Act (16 U.S.C. 777c(b)(2)) for payment of expenses of the Coast Guard for investigations, personnel, and activities directly related to—

(i) administering State recreational boating safety programs under this chapter; or

(ii) coordinating or carrying out the national recreational boating safety program under this title.

(B) Of the amounts used by the Secretary each fiscal year under subparagraph (A)—

(i) not less than $2,100,000 is available to ensure compliance with chapter 43 of this title; and

(ii) not more than $1,500,000 is available to conduct by grant or contract a survey of levels of recreational boating participation and related matters in the United States.

(2) On or after October 1, 2024, no funds available to the Secretary under this subsection may be used to replace funding provided through general appropriations, nor for any purposes except those purposes authorized by this section.

(3) Amounts made available by this subsection shall remain available during the 2 succeeding fiscal years. Any amount that is unexpended or unobligated at the end of the 3-year period during which it is available shall be withdrawn by the Secretary and allocated to the States in addition to any other amounts available for allocation in the fiscal year in which they are withdrawn or the following fiscal year.

(4) The Secretary shall publish annually in the Federal Register a detailed accounting of the projects, programs, and activities funded under this subsection.

(Pub. L. 98–89, Aug. 26, 1983, 97 Stat. 596, §13106; Pub. L. 98–369, div. A, title X, §1012, July 18, 1984, 98 Stat. 1013; Pub. L. 99–626, §4(c), Nov. 7, 1986, 100 Stat. 3505; Pub. L. 99–640, §7(b), (c), Nov. 10, 1986, 100 Stat. 3548; Pub. L. 100–448, §6(b)(1)(A), (2), (6), Sept. 28, 1988, 102 Stat. 1839, 1840; Pub. L. 105–178, title VII, §7405(b), (c)(1), June 9, 1998, 112 Stat. 487, 488; Pub. L. 108–88, §9(c), Sept. 30, 2003, 117 Stat. 1126; Pub. L. 108–202, §7(c), Feb. 29, 2004, 118 Stat. 484; Pub. L. 108–224, §6(c), Apr. 30, 2004, 118 Stat. 632; Pub. L. 108–263, §6(c), June 30, 2004, 118 Stat. 704; Pub. L. 108–280, §6(c), July 30, 2004, 118 Stat. 882; Pub. L. 108–310, §9(c), Sept. 30, 2004, 118 Stat. 1159; Pub. L. 109–14, §8(c), May 31, 2005, 119 Stat. 335; Pub. L. 109–20, §8(c), July 1, 2005, 119 Stat. 357; Pub. L. 109–35, §8(c), July 20, 2005, 119 Stat. 390; Pub. L. 109–37, §8(c), July 22, 2005, 119 Stat. 405; Pub. L. 109–40, §8(c), July 28, 2005, 119 Stat. 421; Pub. L. 109–59, title X, §10143, Aug. 10, 2005, 119 Stat. 1931; Pub. L. 109–74, title I, §102, title II, §203, Sept. 29, 2005, 119 Stat. 2030, 2032; renumbered §13107 and amended Pub. L. 109–304, §16(b)(1), (c)(5), Oct. 6, 2006, 120 Stat. 1705, 1706; Pub. L. 114–94, div. A, title X, §10002, Dec. 4, 2015, 129 Stat. 1621; Pub. L. 115–232, div. C, title XXXV, §3546(k), Aug. 13, 2018, 132 Stat. 2327; Pub. L. 117–58, div. B, title VIII, §28001(a)(4), Nov. 15, 2021, 135 Stat. 887.)

§13108. COMPUTING AMOUNTS ALLOCATED TO STATES AND STATE RECORDS REQUIREMENTS

(a) Amounts allocated and distributed under section 13104 of this title shall be computed and paid to the States as follows:

(1) During the second quarter of a fiscal year and on the basis of computations made under section 13106 of this title and submitted by the States for the preceding fiscal year, the Secretary shall determine the percentage of the amounts available to which each eligible State is entitled for the next fiscal year.

(2) Notice of the percentage and of the dollar amount, if it can be determined, for each State shall be provided to the States at the earliest practicable time.

(3) If the Secretary determines that an amount made available to a State for a prior fiscal year is greater or less than the amount that should have been made available to the State for the prior fiscal year, because of later or more accurate State expenditure information, the amount for the current fiscal year may be increased or decreased by the appropriate amount.

(b) The Secretary shall schedule the payment of amounts, consistent with the program purposes and applicable regulations prescribed by the Secretary of the Treasury, to minimize the time elapsing between the transfer of amounts from the Treasury and the subsequent disbursement of the amounts by a State.

(c) The Secretary shall notify a State authority or agency that further payments will be made to the State only when the program complies with the prescribed standards or a failure to comply substantially with standards is corrected if the Secretary, after reasonable notice to the designated State authority or agency, finds that—

(1) the State recreational boating safety program submitted by the State and accepted by the Secretary has been so changed that it no longer complies with this chapter or standards prescribed by regulations; or

(2) in carrying out the State recreational boating safety program, there has been a failure to comply substantially with the standards prescribed by regulations.

(d) The Secretary shall provide for the accounting, budgeting, and other fiscal procedures that are necessary and reasonable to carry out this section properly and efficiently. Records related to amounts allocated under this chapter shall be made available to the Secretary and the Comptroller General to conduct audits.

(Pub. L. 98–89, Aug. 26, 1983, 97 Stat. 596; Pub. L. 98–369, div. A, title X, §1011(f), July 18, 1984, 98 Stat. 1013; Pub. L. 101–595, title III, §312(d), Nov. 16, 1990, 104 Stat. 2987; Pub. L. 104–324, title VII, §746(a)(3), (4), Oct. 19, 1996, 110 Stat. 3943; Pub. L. 109–304, §16(c)(6), Oct. 6, 2006, 120 Stat. 1706.)

§13109. CONSULTATION, COOPERATION, AND REGULATION

(a) In carrying out responsibilities under this chapter, the Secretary may consult with State and local governments, public and private agencies, organizations and committees, private industry, and other persons having an interest in boating safety.

(b) The Secretary may advise, assist, and cooperate with the States and other interested public and private agencies in planning, developing, and carrying out boating safety programs. Acting under section 141 [1] of title 14, the Secretary shall ensure the fullest cooperation between the State and United States Government authorities in promoting boating safety by making agreements and other arrangements with States when possible. Subject to chapter 23 [1] of title 14, the Secretary may make available, on request of a State, the services of members of the Coast Guard Auxiliary to assist the State in promoting boating safety on State waters.

(c) The Secretary may prescribe regulations to carry out this chapter.

(Pub. L. 98–89, Aug. 26, 1983, 97 Stat. 597; Pub. L. 98–369, div. A, title X, §1011(g), July 18, 1984, 98 Stat. 1013.)

[1] *See References in Text note below.*

[§13110. REPEALED. PUB. L. 115–282, TITLE VI, §601(C)(4)(A), DEC. 4, 2018, 132 STAT. 4289]

Section, Pub. L. 98–89, Aug. 26, 1983, 97 Stat. 598; Pub. L. 99–626, §3(a)(1), (b)(1), (2), Nov. 7, 1986, 100 Stat. 3505; Pub. L. 100–448, §20(a), Sept. 28, 1988, 102 Stat. 1846; Pub. L. 102–241, §24, Dec. 19, 1991, 105 Stat. 2217; Pub. L. 104–324, title III, §304(f), Oct. 19, 1996, 110 Stat. 3918; Pub. L. 107–295, title III, §335, Nov. 25, 2002, 116 Stat. 2105; Pub. L. 108–293, title IV, §418(f), Aug. 9, 2004, 118 Stat. 1049; Pub. L. 111–281, title VI, §621(b), Oct. 15, 2010, 124 Stat. 2976, established the National Boating Safety Advisory Council. See section 15105 of this title.

PART J—MEASUREMENT OF VESSELS

CHAPTER 141—GENERAL

§14101. DEFINITIONS

In this part—

(1) "Convention" means the International Convention on Tonnage Measurement of Ships, 1969.

(2) "existing vessel" means a vessel the keel of which was laid or that was at a similar stage of construction before July 18, 1982.

(3) "Great Lakes" means—

(A) the Great Lakes; and

(B) the St. Lawrence River west of—

(i) a rhumb line drawn from Cap des Rosiers to West Point, Anticosti Island; and

(ii) on the north side of Anticosti Island, the meridian of longitude 63 degrees west.

(4) "vessel that engages on a foreign voyage" means a vessel—

(A) that arrives at a place under the jurisdiction of the United States from a place in a foreign country;

(B) that makes a voyage between places outside the United States;

(C) that departs from a place under the jurisdiction of the United States for a place in a foreign country; or

(D) that makes a voyage between a place within a territory or possession of the United States and another place under the jurisdiction of the United States not within that territory or possession.

(Pub. L. 99–509, title V, §5101(3), Oct. 21, 1986, 100 Stat. 1919; Pub. L. 111–281, title III, §303(a), Oct. 15, 2010, 124 Stat. 2923.)

[§14102. REPEALED. PUB. L. 101–595, TITLE VI, §603(12)(A), NOV. 16, 1990, 104 STAT. 2993]

Section, Pub. L. 99–509, title V, §5101(3), Oct. 21, 1986, 100 Stat. 1919, authorized Secretary to prescribe regulations to carry out this part.

§14103. DELEGATION OF AUTHORITY

(a) The Secretary may delegate to a qualified person the authority to measure a vessel and issue an International Tonnage Certificate (1969) or other appropriate certificate of measurement under this part.

(b) Under regulations prescribed by the Secretary, a decision of the person delegated authority under subsection (a) of this section related to measuring a vessel or issuing a certificate may be appealed to the Secretary.

(c) For a vessel that engages on a foreign voyage, the Secretary may delegate to another country that is a party to the Convention the authority to measure the vessel and issue an International Tonnage Certificate (1969) under chapter 143 of this title.

(d) The Secretary may terminate a delegation made under this section after giving written notice to the person.

(Pub. L. 99–509, title V, §5101(3), Oct. 21, 1986, 100 Stat. 1919; Pub. L. 111–281, title III, §303(b), Oct. 15, 2010, 124 Stat. 2924.)

§14104. Measurement to determine application of a law

(a) When the application of a law of the United States to a vessel depends on the vessel's tonnage, the vessel shall be measured under this part.

(b) If a statute allows for an alternate tonnage to be prescribed under this section, the Secretary may prescribe it by regulation. Any such regulation shall be considered to be an interpretive regulation for purposes of section 553 of title 5. Until an alternate tonnage is prescribed, the statutorily established tonnage shall apply to vessels measured under chapter 143 or chapter 145 of this title.

(c) The head of each Federal agency shall ensure that regulations issued by the agency that specify particular tonnages comply with the alternate tonnages implemented by the Secretary.

(Pub. L. 99–509, title V, §5101(3), Oct. 21, 1986, 100 Stat. 1920; Pub. L. 104–324, title VII, §702, Oct. 19, 1996, 110 Stat. 3933.)

CHAPTER 143—CONVENTION MEASUREMENT

Sec.

§14301. APPLICATION

(a) Except as otherwise provided in this section, this chapter applies to any vessel for which the application of an international agreement or other law of the United States to the vessel depends on the vessel's tonnage.

(b) This chapter does not apply to the following:

(1) a vessel of war, unless the government of the country to which the vessel belongs elects to measure the vessel under this chapter.

(2) a vessel of less than 24 meters (79 feet) overall in length.

(3) a vessel of United States or Canadian registry or nationality, or a vessel operated under the authority of the United States or Canada, and that is operating only on the Great Lakes, unless the owner requests.

(4) a vessel of United States registry or nationality, or one operated under the authority of the United States (except a vessel that engages on a foreign voyage) the keel of which was laid or that was at a similar stage of construction before January 1, 1986, unless—

(A) the owner requests; or

(B) the vessel undergoes a change that the Secretary finds substantially affects the vessel's gross tonnage.

(5) a barge of United States registry or nationality, or a barge operated under the authority of the United States (except a barge that engages on a foreign voyage) unless the owner requests.

(c) An existing vessel that has not undergone a change that the Secretary finds substantially affects the vessel's gross tonnage (or a vessel to which IMO Resolutions A.494 (XII) of November 19, 1981, A.540 (XIII) of November 17, 1983, or A.541 (XIII) of November 17, 1983, apply) may retain its tonnages existing on July 18, 1994, for the application of relevant requirements under international agreements (except the Convention) and other laws of the United States. However, if the vessel undergoes a change substantially affecting its tonnage after July 18, 1994, the vessel shall be remeasured under this chapter.

(d) This chapter does not affect an international agreement to which the United States Government is a party that is not in conflict with the Convention or the application of IMO Resolutions A.494 (XII) of November 19, 1981, A.540 (XIII) of November 17, 1983, and

A.541 (XIII) of November 17, 1983.

(Pub. L. 99–509, title V, §5101(3), Oct. 21, 1986, 100 Stat. 1920; Pub. L. 101–595, title III, §305, Nov. 16, 1990, 104 Stat. 2985; Pub. L. 111–281, title III, §303(c), Oct. 15, 2010, 124 Stat. 2924.)

§14302. MEASUREMENT

(a) The Secretary shall measure a vessel to which this chapter applies in the way provided by this chapter and the Convention.

(b) A vessel measured under this chapter may not be required to be measured under another law.

(c) Unless otherwise provided by law, the measurement of a vessel under this chapter applies to a law of the United States whose applicability depends on a vessel's tonnage, if that law—

(1) becomes effective after July 18, 1994; or

(2) is in effect before July 19, 1994, is not enumerated in section 14305 of this title, and is identified by the Secretary by regulation as a law to which this chapter applies.

(Pub. L. 99–509, title V, §5101(3), Oct. 21, 1986, 100 Stat. 1921; Pub. L. 111–281, title III, §303(d), Oct. 15, 2010, 124 Stat. 2924.)

§14303. TONNAGE CERTIFICATE

(a) After measuring a vessel under this chapter, the Secretary shall issue, on request of the owner, an International Tonnage Certificate (1969) and deliver it to the owner or master of the vessel. For a vessel to which the Convention does not apply, the Secretary shall prescribe a certificate to be issued as evidence of a vessel's measurement under this chapter.

(b) The certificate issued under this section shall be maintained as required by the Secretary.

(Pub. L. 99–509, title V, §5101(3), Oct. 21, 1986, 100 Stat. 1921; Pub. L. 111–281, title III, §303(e)(1), Oct. 15, 2010, 124 Stat. 2925.)

§14304. REMEASUREMENT

(a) To the extent necessary, the Secretary shall remeasure a vessel to which this chapter applies if—

(1) the Secretary or the owner alleges an error in its measurement; or

(2) the vessel or the use of its space is changed in a way that substantially affects its tonnage.

(b) Except as provided in this chapter or section 14504 of this title, a vessel that has been measured does not have to be remeasured to obtain another document or endorsement under chapter 121 of this title.

(Pub. L. 99–509, title V, §5101(3), Oct. 21, 1986, 100 Stat. 1921.)

§14305. OPTIONAL REGULATORY MEASUREMENT

(a) On request of the owner of a vessel measured under this chapter that is of United States registry or nationality, or a vessel operated under the authority of the United States, the Secretary also shall measure the vessel under chapter 145 of this title. The tonnages determined under that chapter shall be used in applying—

(1) parts A, B, C, E, F, and G of this subtitle and section 12116 of this title;

(2) section 3(d)(3) of the Longshore and Harbor Workers' Compensation Act (33 U.S.C. 903(d)(3));

(3) section 4 of the Bridge to Bridge Radiotelephone Act (33 U.S.C. 1203(a));

(4) section 4(a)(3) [1] of the Ports and Waterways Safety Act (33 U.S.C. 1223(a)(3));

(5) section 30524 of this title;

(6) sections 12118 and 12132 of this title;

(7) section 12139(b) of this title;

(8) sections 351, 352, 355, and 356 of the Ship Radio Act (47 U.S.C. 351, 352, 354, and 354a);

(9) section 403 of the Commercial Fishing Industry Vessel Act (46 U.S.C. 3302 note);

(10) the Officers' Competency Certificates Convention, 1936, and section 8304 of this title;

(11) the International Convention for the Safety of Life at Sea as provided by IMCO Resolution A.494 (XII) of November 19, 1981;

(12) the International Convention on Standards of Training, Certification, and Watchkeeping for Seafarers, 1978, as provided by IMO Resolution A.540 (XIII) of November 17, 1983;

(13) the International Convention for the Prevention of Pollution from Ships, 1973, as modified by the Protocol of 1978 Relating to the International Convention for the Prevention of Pollution from Ships, 1973, as provided by IMO Resolution A.541 (XIII) of November 17, 1983;

(14) provisions of law establishing the threshold tonnage levels at which evidence of financial responsibility must be demonstrated; or

(15) unless otherwise provided by law, any other law of the United States in effect before July 19, 1994, and not listed by the Secretary under section 14302(c) of this title.

(b) As long as the owner of a vessel has a request in effect under subsection (a) of this section, the tonnages determined under that request shall be used in applying the other provisions of law described in subsection (a) to that vessel.

(Pub. L. 99–509, title V, §5101(3), Oct. 21, 1986, 100 Stat. 1921; Pub. L. 109–304, §15(26), Oct. 6, 2006, 120 Stat. 1704; Pub. L. 111–281, title III, §303(f), Oct. 15, 2010, 124 Stat. 2925; Pub. L. 116–283, div. G, title LVXXXV [LXXXV], §8503(a)(2), Jan. 1, 2021, 134 Stat. 4747; Pub. L. 117–263, div. K, title CXV, §11503(f)(1), Dec. 23, 2022, 136 Stat. 4131.)

[1] *See References in Text note below.*

§14306. RECIPROCITY FOR FOREIGN VESSELS

(a) When the Secretary finds that the laws and regulations of a foreign country related to measurement of vessels are similar to those of this chapter and the regulations prescribed under this chapter, or when a foreign country is a party to the Convention, the Secretary shall accept the measurement and certificate of a vessel of that foreign country as complying with this chapter and the regulations prescribed under this chapter.

(b) Subsection (a) of this section does not apply to a vessel of a foreign country that does not recognize measurements under this chapter. The Secretary may apply measurement standards the Secretary considers appropriate to the vessel, subject to applicable international agreements to which the United States Government is a party.

(Pub. L. 99–509, title V, §5101(3), Oct. 21, 1986, 100 Stat. 1922.)

§14307. INSPECTION OF FOREIGN VESSELS

(a) The Secretary may inspect a vessel of a foreign country to verify that—

(1) the vessel has an International Tonnage Certificate (1969) and the main characteristics of the vessel correspond to the information in the certificate; or

(2) if the vessel is from a country not a party to the Convention, the vessel has been measured under laws and regulations similar to those of this chapter and the regulations prescribed under this chapter.

(b) For a vessel of a country that is a party to the Convention, if the inspection reveals that the vessel does not have an International Tonnage Certificate (1969) or that the main characteristics of the vessel differ from those stated on the certificate or other records in a way that increases the gross or net tonnage of the vessel, the Secretary promptly shall inform the country whose flag the vessel is flying.

(c) For a vessel of a country not a party to the Convention—

(1) if the vessel has been measured under laws and regulations that the Secretary finds are similar to those of this chapter and the regulations prescribed under this chapter, the vessel shall be deemed to have been issued an International Tonnage Certificate (1969); and

(2) if the vessel has not been measured as described in clause (1) of this subsection, the Secretary may measure the vessel.

(d) An inspection under this section shall be conducted in a way that does not delay a vessel of a country that is a party to the Convention.

(Pub. L. 99–509, title V, §5101(3), Oct. 21, 1986, 100 Stat. 1922.)

CHAPTER 145—REGULATORY MEASUREMENT

SUBCHAPTER I—GENERAL

SUBCHAPTER II—FORMAL SYSTEMS

SUBCHAPTER III—SIMPLIFIED SYSTEM

SUBCHAPTER I—GENERAL

§14501. APPLICATION

This chapter applies to the following:

(1) A vessel not measured under chapter 143 of this title if the application of an international agreement or other law of the United States to the vessel depends on the vessel's tonnage.

(2) A vessel measured under chapter 143 of this title if the owner requests that the vessel also be measured under this chapter as provided in section 14305 of this title.

(Pub. L. 99–509, title V, §5101(3), Oct. 21, 1986, 100 Stat. 1923; Pub. L. 111–281, title III, §303(g), Oct. 15, 2010, 124 Stat. 2925.)

§14502. MEASUREMENT

The Secretary shall measure a vessel to which this chapter applies in the way provided by this chapter.

(Pub. L. 99–509, title V, §5101(3), Oct. 21, 1986, 100 Stat. 1923.)

§14503. CERTIFICATE OF MEASUREMENT

(a) The Secretary shall prescribe the certificate to be issued as evidence of a vessel's measurement under this chapter.

(b) The certificate shall be maintained as required by the Secretary.

(Pub. L. 99–509, title V, §5101(3), Oct. 21, 1986, 100 Stat. 1923; Pub. L. 111–281, title III, §303(e)(2), Oct. 15, 2010, 124 Stat. 2925.)

§14504. REMEASUREMENT

(a) To the extent necessary, the Secretary shall remeasure a vessel to which this chapter applies if—

(1) the Secretary or the owner alleges an error in its measurement;

(2) the vessel or the use of its space is changed in a way that substantially affects its tonnage;

(3) after being measured under subchapter III of this chapter, the vessel becomes subject to subchapter II of this chapter because the vessel or its use is changed; or

(4) although not required to be measured under subchapter II of this chapter, the vessel was measured under subchapter II and the owner requests that the vessel be measured under subchapter III of this chapter.

(b) Except as provided in this section and chapter 143 of this title, a vessel that has been measured does not have to be remeasured to obtain another document or endorsement under chapter 121 of this title.

(Pub. L. 99–509, title V, §5101(3), Oct. 21, 1986, 100 Stat. 1923.)

SUBCHAPTER II—FORMAL SYSTEMS

§14511. Application

This subchapter applies to a vessel described in section 14501 of this title if—
(1) the owner requests; or
(2) the vessel is—
(A) self-propelled;
(B) at least 24 meters (79 feet) overall in length; and
(C) not operated only for pleasure.

(Pub. L. 99–509, title V, §5101(3), Oct. 21, 1986, 100 Stat. 1924.)

§14512. Standard tonnage measurement

(a) The Secretary shall prescribe regulations for measuring the gross and net tonnages of a vessel under this subchapter. The regulations shall provide for tonnages comparable to the tonnages that could have been assigned under sections 4151 and 4153 of the Revised Statutes of the United States, as sections 4151 and 4153 existed immediately before the enactment of this section.

(b) On application of the owner or master of a vessel of the United States used in foreign trade, the Secretary may attach an appendix to the vessel's register stating the measurement of spaces that may be deducted from gross tonnage under laws and regulations of other countries but not under those of the United States.

(Pub. L. 99–509, title V, §5101(3), Oct. 21, 1986, 100 Stat. 1924.)

§14513. Dual tonnage measurement

(a) On application by the owner and approval by the Secretary, the tonnage of spaces prescribed by the Secretary may be excluded in measuring under this section the gross tonnage of a vessel measured under section 14512 of this title. The spaces prescribed by the Secretary shall be comparable to the spaces that could have been excluded under section 2 of the Act of September 29, 1965 (Public Law 89–219, 79 Stat. 891), as section 2 existed immediately before the enactment of this section.

(b) The Secretary shall prescribe the design, location, and dimensions of the tonnage mark to be placed on a vessel measured under this section.

(c)(1) If a vessel is assigned two sets of gross and net tonnages under this section, each certificate stating the vessel's tonnages shall state the gross and net tonnages when the vessel's tonnage mark is submerged and when it is not submerged.

(2) Except as provided in paragraph (1) of this subsection, a certificate stating a vessel's tonnages may state only one set of gross and net tonnages as assigned under this section.

(Pub. L. 99–509, title V, §5101(3), Oct. 21, 1986, 100 Stat. 1924; Pub. L. 111–281, title III, §303(h), Oct. 15, 2010, 124 Stat. 2925.)

§14514. Reciprocity for foreign vessels

For a foreign vessel not measured under chapter 143, if the Secretary finds that the laws and regulations of a foreign country related to measurement of vessels are substantially similar to those of this chapter and the regulations prescribed under this chapter, the Secretary may accept the measurement and certificate of a vessel of that foreign country as complying with this chapter and the regulations prescribed under this chapter.

(Added Pub. L. 111–281, title III, §303(i), Oct. 15, 2010, 124 Stat. 2925.)

SUBCHAPTER III—SIMPLIFIED SYSTEM

§14521. APPLICATION

This subchapter applies to a vessel described in section 14501 of this title that is not measured under subchapter II of this chapter.

(Pub. L. 99–509, title V, §5101(3), Oct. 21, 1986, 100 Stat. 1925.)

§14522. MEASUREMENT

(a) In this section, "length" means the horizontal distance of the hull between the foremost part of the stem and the aftermost part of the stern, excluding fittings and attachments.

(b)(1) The Secretary shall assign gross and net tonnages to a vessel based on its length, breadth, depth, other dimensions, and appropriate coefficients.

(2) The Secretary shall prescribe the way dimensions (except length) are measured and which coefficients are appropriate.

(c) The resulting gross tonnages, taken as a group, reasonably shall reflect the relative internal volumes of the vessels measured under this subchapter. The resulting net tonnages shall be in approximately the same ratios to corresponding gross tonnages as are the net and gross tonnages of comparable vessels measured under subchapter II of this chapter.

(d) Under regulations prescribed by the Secretary, the Secretary may determine the gross and net tonnages of a vessel representative of a designated class, model, or type, and then assign those gross and net tonnages to other vessels of the same class, model, or type.

(Pub. L. 99–509, title V, §5101(3), Oct. 21, 1986, 100 Stat. 1925.)

CHAPTER 147—PENALTIES

§14701. GENERAL VIOLATION

The owner, charterer, managing operator, agent, master, and individual in charge of a vessel violating this part or a regulation prescribed under this part are each liable to the United States Government for a civil penalty of not more than $20,000. Each day of a continuing violation is a separate violation. The vessel also is liable in rem for the penalty.

(Pub. L. 99–509, title V, §5101(3), Oct. 21, 1986, 100 Stat. 1925.)

§14702. FALSE STATEMENTS

A person knowingly making a false statement or representation in a matter in which a statement or representation is required by this part or a regulation prescribed under this part is liable to the United States Government for a civil penalty of not more than $20,000 for each false statement or representation. The vessel also is liable in rem for the penalty.

(Pub. L. 99–509, title V, §5101(3), Oct. 21, 1986, 100 Stat. 1925.)

Part K—National Maritime Transportation Advisory Committees

CHAPTER 151—NATIONAL MARITIME TRANSPORTATION ADVISORY COMMITTEES

§15101. National Chemical Transportation Safety Advisory Committee

(a) ESTABLISHMENT.—There is established a National Chemical Transportation Safety Advisory Committee (in this section referred to as the "Committee").

(b) FUNCTION.—The Committee shall advise the Secretary on matters relating to the safe and secure marine transportation of hazardous materials.

(c) MEMBERSHIP.—

(1) IN GENERAL.—The Committee shall consist of not more than 25 members appointed by the Secretary in accordance with this section and section 15109 of this chapter.

(2) EXPERTISE.—Each member of the Committee shall have particular expertise, knowledge, and experience in matters relating to the function of the Committee.

(3) REPRESENTATION.—Each member of the Committee shall represent 1 of the following:

(A) Chemical manufacturing entities.

(B) Entities related to marine handling or transportation of chemicals.

(C) Vessel design and construction entities.

(D) Marine safety or security entities.

(E) Marine environmental protection entities.

(4) DISTRIBUTION.—The Secretary shall, based on the needs of the Coast Guard, determine the number of members of the Committee who represent each entity specified in paragraph (3). Neither this paragraph nor any other provision of law shall be construed to require an equal distribution of members representing each entity specified in paragraph (3).

(Added Pub. L. 115–282, title VI, §601(a), Dec. 4, 2018, 132 Stat. 4280.)

§15102. National Commercial Fishing Safety Advisory Committee

(a) Establishment.—There is established a National Commercial Fishing Safety Advisory Committee (in this section referred to as the "Committee").

(b) Function.—The Committee shall—

(1) advise and provide recommendations in writing to the Secretary on matters relating to the safe operation of vessels to which chapter 45 of this title applies, including the matters of—

(A) navigation safety;

(B) safety equipment and procedures;

(C) marine insurance;

(D) vessel design, construction, maintenance, and operation; and

(E) personnel qualifications and training;

(2) review regulations proposed under chapter 45 of this title (during preparation of the regulations); and

(3) review marine casualties and investigations of vessels covered by chapter 45 of this title and make recommendations to the Secretary to improve safety and reduce vessel casualties.

(c) Membership.—

(1) In general.—The Committee shall consist of 18 members appointed by the Secretary in accordance with this section and section 15109 of this chapter.

(2) Expertise.—Each member of the Committee shall have particular expertise, knowledge, and experience in matters relating to the function of the Committee.

(3) Representation.—Members of the Committee shall be appointed as follows:

(A) 10 members shall represent the commercial fishing industry and—

(i) as a group, shall together reflect a regional and representational balance; and

(ii) as individuals, shall each have experience—

(I) in the operation of vessels to which chapter 45 of this title applies; or

(II) as a crew member or processing line worker on a fish processing vessel.

(B) 1 member shall represent naval architects and marine engineers.

(C) 1 member shall represent manufacturers of equipment for vessels to which chapter 45 of this title applies.

(D) 1 member shall represent education and training professionals related to fishing vessel, fish processing vessel, and fish tender vessel safety and personnel qualifications.

(E) 1 member shall represent underwriters that insure vessels to which chapter 45 of this title applies.

(F) 1 member shall represent owners of vessels to which chapter 45 of this title applies.

(G) 3 members shall represent the general public and, to the extent possible, shall include—

(i) an independent expert or consultant in maritime safety;

(ii) a marine surveyor who provides services to vessels to which chapter 45 of this title applies; and

(iii) a person familiar with issues affecting fishing communities and the families of fishermen.

(d) QUORUM.—A quorum of 10 members is required to send any written recommendations from the Committee to the Secretary.

(e) SAVINGS CLAUSE.—Nothing in this section shall preclude the Secretary from taking emergency action to ensure safety and preservation of life at sea.

(Added Pub. L. 115–282, title VI, §601(a), Dec. 4, 2018, 132 Stat. 4281; amended Pub. L. 116–283, div. G, title LVXXXIII [LXXXIII], §8335(a)(1), Jan. 1, 2021, 134 Stat. 4706.)

§15103. NATIONAL MERCHANT MARINE PERSONNEL ADVISORY COMMITTEE

(a) ESTABLISHMENT.—There is established a National Merchant Marine Personnel Advisory Committee (in this section referred to as the "Committee").

(b) FUNCTION.—The Committee shall advise the Secretary on matters relating to personnel in the United States merchant marine, including the training, qualifications, certification, documentation, and fitness of mariners.

(c) MEMBERSHIP.—

(1) IN GENERAL.—The Committee shall consist of 19 members appointed by the Secretary in accordance with this section and section 15109 of this chapter.

(2) EXPERTISE.—Each member of the Committee shall have particular expertise, knowledge, and experience in matters relating to the function of the Committee.

(3) REPRESENTATION.—Members of the Committee shall be appointed as follows:

(A) 9 members shall represent mariners and, of the 9—

(i) each shall—

(I) be a citizen of the United States; and

(II) hold an active license or certificate issued under chapter 71 of this title or a merchant mariner document issued under chapter 73 of this title;

(ii) 3 shall be deck officers who represent merchant marine deck officers and, of the 3—

(I) 2 shall be licensed for oceans any gross tons;

(II) 1 shall be licensed for inland river route with a limited or unlimited tonnage;

(III) 2 shall have a master's license or a master of towing vessels license;

(IV) 1 shall have significant tanker experience; and

(V) to the extent practicable—

(aa) 1 shall represent labor; and

(bb) 1 shall represent management;

(iii) 3 shall be engineering officers who represent merchant marine engineering officers and, of the 3—

(I) 2 shall be licensed as chief engineer any horsepower;

(II) 1 shall be licensed as either a limited chief engineer or a designated duty

engineer; and
 (III) to the extent practicable—
  (aa) 1 shall represent labor; and
  (bb) 1 shall represent management;

 (iv) 2 shall be unlicensed seamen who represent merchant marine unlicensed seaman and, of the 2—
  (I) 1 shall represent able-bodied seamen; and
  (II) 1 shall represent qualified members of the engine department; and

 (v) 1 shall be a pilot who represents merchant marine pilots.

(B) 6 members shall represent marine educators and, of the 6—
 (i) 3 shall be marine educators who represent maritime academies and, of the 3—
  (I) 2 shall represent State maritime academies (and are jointly recommended by such academies); and
  (II) 1 shall represent either State maritime academies or the United States Merchant Marine Academy; and

 (ii) 3 shall be marine educators who represent other maritime training institutions and, of the 3, 1 shall represent the small vessel industry.

(C) 2 members shall represent shipping companies employed in ship operation management.
(D) 2 members shall represent the general public.
(Added Pub. L. 115–282, title VI, §601(a), Dec. 4, 2018, 132 Stat. 4282.)

§15104. NATIONAL MERCHANT MARINER MEDICAL ADVISORY COMMITTEE

(a) ESTABLISHMENT.—There is established a National Merchant Mariner Medical Advisory Committee (in this section referred to as the "Committee").
(b) FUNCTION.—The Committee shall advise the Secretary on matters relating to—
 (1) medical certification determinations for the issuance of licenses, certification of registry, and merchant mariners' documents with respect to merchant mariners;
 (2) medical standards and guidelines for the physical qualifications of operators of commercial vessels;
 (3) medical examiner education; and
 (4) medical research.

(c) MEMBERSHIP.—
 (1) IN GENERAL.—The Committee shall consist of 14 members appointed by the Secretary in accordance with this section and section 15109 of this chapter.
 (2) EXPERTISE.—Each member of the Committee shall have particular expertise, knowledge, and experience in matters relating to the function of the Committee.
 (3) REPRESENTATION.—Members of the Committee shall be appointed as follows:
  (A) 9 shall represent health-care professionals and have particular expertise,

knowledge, and experience regarding the medical examinations of merchant mariners or occupational medicine.

(B) 5 shall represent professional mariners and have particular expertise, knowledge, and experience in occupational requirements for mariners.

(Added Pub. L. 115–282, title VI, §601(a), Dec. 4, 2018, 132 Stat. 4283.)

§15105. NATIONAL BOATING SAFETY ADVISORY COMMITTEE

(a) ESTABLISHMENT.—There is established a National Boating Safety Advisory Committee (in this section referred to as the "Committee").

(b) FUNCTION.—The Committee shall advise the Secretary on matters relating to national boating safety.

(c) MEMBERSHIP.—

(1) IN GENERAL.—The Committee shall consist of 21 members appointed by the Secretary in accordance with this section and section 15109 of this chapter.

(2) EXPERTISE.—Each member of the Committee shall have particular expertise, knowledge, and experience in matters relating to the function of the Committee.

(3) REPRESENTATION.—Members of the Committee shall be appointed as follows:

(A) 7 members shall represent State officials responsible for State boating safety programs.

(B) 7 members shall represent recreational vessel and associated equipment manufacturers.

(C) 7 members shall represent the general public or national recreational boating organizations and, of the 7, at least 5 shall represent national recreational boating organizations.

(Added Pub. L. 115–282, title VI, §601(a), Dec. 4, 2018, 132 Stat. 4283.)

§15106. NATIONAL OFFSHORE SAFETY ADVISORY COMMITTEE

(a) ESTABLISHMENT.—There is established a National Offshore Safety Advisory Committee (in this section referred to as the "Committee").

(b) FUNCTION.—The Committee shall advise the Secretary on matters relating to activities directly involved with, or in support of, the exploration of offshore mineral and energy resources, to the extent that such matters are within the jurisdiction of the Coast Guard.

(c) MEMBERSHIP.—

(1) IN GENERAL.—The Committee shall consist of 15 members appointed by the Secretary in accordance with this section and section 15109 of this chapter.

(2) EXPERTISE.—Each member of the Committee shall have particular expertise, knowledge, and experience in matters relating to the function of the Committee.

(3) REPRESENTATION.—Members of the Committee shall be appointed as follows:

(A) 2 members shall represent entities engaged in the production of petroleum.

(B) 2 members shall represent entities engaged in offshore drilling.

(C) 2 members shall represent entities engaged in the support, by offshore supply vessels or other vessels, of offshore operations.

(D) 1 member shall represent entities engaged in the construction of offshore facilities.

(E) 1 member shall represent entities providing diving services to the offshore industry.

(F) 1 member shall represent entities providing safety and training services to the offshore industry.

(G) 1 member shall represent entities providing subsea engineering, construction, or remotely operated vehicle support to the offshore industry.

(H) 2 members shall represent individuals employed in offshore operations and, of the 2, 1 shall have recent practical experience on a vessel or offshore unit involved in the offshore industry.

(I) 1 member shall represent national environmental entities and entities providing environmental protection, compliance, or response services to the offshore industry.

(J) 1 member shall represent entities engaged in offshore oil exploration and production on the Outer Continental Shelf adjacent to Alaska.

(K) 1 member shall represent the general public (but not a specific environmental group).

(Added Pub. L. 115–282, title VI, §601(a), Dec. 4, 2018, 132 Stat. 4284; amended Pub. L. 116–283, div. G, title LVXXXIII [LXXXIII], §8331(a), Jan. 1, 2021, 134 Stat. 4702.)

§15107. National Navigation Safety Advisory Committee

(a) ESTABLISHMENT.—There is established a National Navigation Safety Advisory Committee (in this section referred to as the "Committee").

(b) FUNCTION.—The Committee shall advise the Secretary on matters relating to maritime collisions, rammings, and groundings, Inland Rules of the Road, International Rules of the Road, navigation regulations and equipment, routing measures, marine information, and aids to navigation systems.

(c) MEMBERSHIP.—

(1) IN GENERAL.—The Committee shall consist of not more than 21 members appointed by the Secretary in accordance with this section and section 15109 of this chapter.

(2) EXPERTISE.—Each member of the Committee shall have particular expertise, knowledge, and experience in matters relating to the function of the Committee.

(3) REPRESENTATION.—Each member of the Committee shall represent 1 of the following:

(A) Commercial vessel owners or operators.

(B) Professional mariners.

(C) Recreational boaters.

(D) The recreational boating industry.

(E) State agencies responsible for vessel or port safety.

(F) The Maritime Law Association.

(4) DISTRIBUTION.—The Secretary shall, based on the needs of the Coast Guard, determine the number of members of the Committee who represent each entity specified in paragraph (3). Neither this paragraph nor any other provision of law shall be construed

to require an equal distribution of members representing each entity specified in paragraph (3).

(Added Pub. L. 115–282, title VI, §601(a), Dec. 4, 2018, 132 Stat. 4285.)

§15108. NATIONAL TOWING SAFETY ADVISORY COMMITTEE

(a) ESTABLISHMENT.—There is established a National Towing Safety Advisory Committee (in this section referred to as the "Committee").

(b) FUNCTION.—The Committee shall advise the Secretary on matters relating to shallow-draft inland navigation, coastal waterway navigation, and towing safety.

(c) MEMBERSHIP.—

(1) IN GENERAL.—The Committee shall consist of 18 members appointed by the Secretary in accordance with this section and section 15109 of this chapter.

(2) EXPERTISE.—Each member of the Committee shall have particular expertise, knowledge, and experience in matters relating to the function of the Committee.

(3) REPRESENTATION.—Members of the Committee shall be appointed as follows:

(A) 7 members shall represent the barge and towing industry, reflecting a regional geographic balance.

(B) 1 member shall represent the offshore mineral and oil supply vessel industry.

(C) 1 member shall represent masters and pilots of towing vessels who hold active licenses and have experience on the Western Rivers and the Gulf Intracoastal Waterway.

(D) 1 member shall represent masters of towing vessels in offshore service who hold active licenses.

(E) 1 member shall represent masters of active ship-docking or harbor towing vessels.

(F) 1 member shall represent licensed and unlicensed towing vessel engineers with formal training and experience.

(G) 2 members shall represent port districts, authorities, or terminal operators.

(H) 2 members shall represent shippers and, of the 2, 1 shall be engaged in the shipment of oil or hazardous materials by barge.

(I) 2 members shall represent the general public.

(Added Pub. L. 115–282, title VI, §601(a), Dec. 4, 2018, 132 Stat. 4285.)

§15109. ADMINISTRATION

(a) MEETINGS.—

(1) IN GENERAL.—Except as provided in paragraph (2), each committee established under this chapter or to which this chapter applies shall, at least once each year, meet at the call of the Secretary or a majority of the members of the committee.

(2) MINIMUM REQUIREMENTS.—The committee established under section 15102,[1] shall—

(A) meet in-person, not less frequently than twice each year, at the call of the Secretary of a majority of the members of the committee;

(B) hold additional meetings as necessary;

(C) post the minutes of each meeting of the committee on a publicly available website not later than 2 weeks after the date on which a meeting concludes; and

(D) provide reasonable public notice of any meeting of the committee, and publish such notice in the Federal Register and on a publicly available website.

(b) EMPLOYEE STATUS.—A member of a committee established under this chapter or to which this chapter applies shall not be considered an employee of the Federal Government by reason of service on such committee, except for the purposes of the following:

(1) Chapter 81 of title 5.

(2) Chapter 171 of title 28 and any other Federal law relating to tort liability.

(c) COMPENSATION.—Notwithstanding subsection (b), a member of a committee established under this chapter or to which this chapter applies, when actually engaged in the performance of the duties of such committee, may—

(1) receive compensation at a rate established by the Secretary, not to exceed the maximum daily rate payable under section 5376 of title 5; or

(2) if not compensated in accordance with paragraph (1)—

(A) be reimbursed for actual and reasonable expenses incurred in the performance of such duties; or

(B) be allowed travel expenses, including per diem in lieu of subsistence, as authorized by section 5703 of title 5.

(d) ACCEPTANCE OF VOLUNTEER SERVICES.—A member of a committee established under this chapter or to which this chapter applies may serve on such committee on a voluntary basis without pay without regard to section 1342 of title 31 or any other law.

(e) STATUS OF MEMBERS.—

(1) IN GENERAL.—Except as provided in paragraph (2), with respect to a member of a committee established under this chapter or to which this chapter applies whom the Secretary appoints to represent an entity or group—

(A) the member is authorized to represent the interests of the applicable entity or group; and

(B) requirements under Federal law that would interfere with such representation and that apply to a special Government employee (as defined in section 202(a) of title 18), including requirements relating to employee conduct, political activities, ethics, conflicts of interest, and corruption, do not apply to the member.

(2) EXCEPTION.—Notwithstanding subsection (b), a member of a committee established under this chapter or to which this chapter applies shall be treated as a special Government employee for purposes of the committee service of the member if—

(A) the Secretary appointed the member to represent the general public; or

(B) the member, without regard to service on the committee, is a special Government employee.

(f) SERVICE ON COMMITTEE.—

(1) SOLICITATION OF NOMINATIONS.—Before appointing an individual as a member of a committee established under this chapter or to which this chapter applies, the

Secretary shall publish, in the Federal Register, a timely notice soliciting nominations for membership on such committee.

(2) APPOINTMENTS.—

(A) IN GENERAL.—After considering nominations received pursuant to a notice published under paragraph (1), the Secretary may, as necessary, appoint a member to the applicable committee established under this chapter or to which this chapter applies.

(B) PROHIBITION.—The Secretary shall not seek, consider, or otherwise use information concerning the political affiliation of a nominee in making an appointment to any committee established under this chapter or to which this chapter applies.

(3) SERVICE AT PLEASURE OF THE SECRETARY.—

(A) IN GENERAL.—Each member of a committee established under this chapter or to which this chapter applies shall serve at the pleasure of the Secretary.

(B) EXCEPTION.—Notwithstanding subparagraph (A), a member of the committee established under section 15102 may only be removed prior to the end of the term of that member for just cause.

(4) SECURITY BACKGROUND EXAMINATIONS.—The Secretary may require an individual to have passed an appropriate security background examination before appointment to a committee established under this chapter or to which this chapter applies.

(5) PROHIBITION.—

(A) IN GENERAL.—Except as provided in subparagraph (B), a Federal employee may not be appointed as a member of a committee established under this chapter or to which this chapter applies.

(B) SPECIAL RULE FOR NATIONAL MERCHANT MARINE PERSONNEL ADVISORY COMMITTEE.—The Secretary may appoint a Federal employee to serve as a member of the National Merchant Marine Personnel Advisory Committee to represent the interests of the United States Merchant Marine Academy and, notwithstanding paragraphs (1) and (2), may do so without soliciting, receiving, or considering nominations for such appointment.

(6) TERMS.—

(A) IN GENERAL.—The term of each member of a committee established under this chapter or to which this chapter applies shall expire on December 31 of the third full year after the effective date of the appointment.

(B) CONTINUED SERVICE AFTER TERM.—When the term of a member of a committee established under this chapter or to which this chapter applies ends, the member, for a period not to exceed 1 year, may continue to serve as a member until a successor is appointed.

(7) VACANCIES.—A vacancy on a committee established under this chapter or to which this chapter applies shall be filled in the same manner as the original appointment.

(8) SPECIAL RULE FOR REAPPOINTMENTS.—

(A) REAPPOINTMENT.—Notwithstanding paragraphs (1) and (2), the Secretary may reappoint a member of a committee established under this chapter or to which this chapter applies for any term, other than the first term of the member, without soliciting, receiving, or considering nominations for such appointment.

(B) LIMITATION.—With respect to the committee established under section 15102, members may serve not more than 3 terms.

(g) STAFF SERVICES.—The Secretary shall furnish to each committee established under this chapter or to which this chapter applies any staff and services considered by the Secretary to be necessary for the conduct of the committee's functions.

(h) CHAIRMAN; VICE CHAIRMAN.—

(1) IN GENERAL.—Each committee established under this chapter or to which this chapter applies shall elect a Chairman and Vice Chairman from among the committee's members.

(2) VICE CHAIRMAN ACTING AS CHAIRMAN.—The Vice Chairman shall act as Chairman in the absence or incapacity of, or in the event of a vacancy in the office of, the Chairman.

(i) SUBCOMMITTEES AND WORKING GROUPS.—

(1) IN GENERAL.—The Chairman of a committee established under this chapter or to which this chapter applies may establish and disestablish subcommittees and working groups for any purpose consistent with the function of the committee.

(2) PARTICIPANTS.—Subject to conditions imposed by the Chairman, members of a committee established under this chapter or to which this chapter applies and additional individuals drawn from entities or groups designated by this chapter to be represented on the committee or the general public may be assigned to subcommittees and working groups established under paragraph (1).

(3) CHAIR.—Only committee members may chair subcommittees and working groups established under paragraph (1).

(j) CONSULTATION, ADVICE, REPORTS, AND RECOMMENDATIONS.—

(1) CONSULTATION.—

(A) IN GENERAL.—Before taking any significant action, the Secretary shall consult with, and consider the information, advice, and recommendations of, a committee established under this chapter or to which this chapter applies if the function of the committee is to advise the Secretary on matters related to the significant action.

(B) INCLUSION.—For purposes of this paragraph, regulations proposed under chapter 45 of this title are significant actions.

(2) ADVICE, REPORTS, AND RECOMMENDATIONS.—Each committee established under this chapter or to which this chapter applies shall submit, in writing, to the Secretary its advice, reports, and recommendations, in a form and at a frequency determined appropriate by the committee.

(3) EXPLANATION OF ACTIONS TAKEN.—Not later than 60 days after the date on which the Secretary receives recommendations from a committee under paragraph (2), the Secretary shall—

(A) publish the recommendations on a website accessible at no charge to the public;

(B) if the recommendations are from the committee established under section 15102, establish a mechanism for the submission of public comments on the recommendations;

(C) respond, in writing, to the committee regarding the recommendations, including by providing an explanation of actions taken regarding the recommendations; and

(D) make all responses required by subparagraph (C) which are related to recommendations made by the committee established under section 15102 available to the public not later than 30 days after the date of response.

(4) SUBMISSION TO CONGRESS.—

(A) IN GENERAL.—The Secretary shall submit to the Committee on Transportation and Infrastructure of the House of Representatives and the Committee on Commerce, Science, and Transportation of the Senate the advice, reports, and recommendations received from committees under paragraph (2).

(B) ADDITIONAL SUBMISSION.—With respect to a committee established under section 70112 and to which this section applies, the Secretary shall submit the advice, reports, and recommendations received from the committee under paragraph (2) to the Committee on Homeland Security of the House of Representatives in addition to the committees specified in subparagraph (A).

(k) OBSERVERS.—

(1) IN GENERAL.—Any Federal agency with matters under such agency's administrative jurisdiction related to the function of a committee established under this chapter [2] may designate a representative to—

(A) attend any meeting of such committee; and

(B) participate as an observer at meetings of such committee that relate to such a matter.

(2) NATIONAL COMMERCIAL FISHING SAFETY ADVISORY COMMITTEE.—With respect to the committee established under section 15102, the Commandant of the Coast Guard shall designate a representative under paragraph (1).

(l) TECHNICAL ASSISTANCE.—

(1) IN GENERAL.—The Secretary shall provide technical assistance to the Committee if requested by the Chairman.

(2) COMMITTEE CONSULTATION.—With respect to the committee established under section 15102, the Chairman of the committee shall seek expertise from the fishing industry, marine safety experts, the shipbuilding industry, and others as the committee determines appropriate.

(m) TERMINATION.—Each committee established under this chapter or to which this chapter applies shall terminate on September 30, 2029.

(n) SAVINGS CLAUSE.—Nothing in this section shall preclude the Secretary from taking emergency action to ensure safety and preservation of life at sea.

(Added Pub. L. 115–282, title VI, §601(a), Dec. 4, 2018, 132 Stat. 4286; amended Pub. L. 116–283, div. G, title LVXXXIII [LXXXIII], §§8331(b), 8335(a)(2), title LVXXXV [LXXXV], §8505(b)(14), Jan. 1, 2021, 134 Stat. 4703, 4707, 4752.)

[1] *So in original. The comma probably should not appear.*

[2] *So in original. Probably should be followed by "or to which this chapter applies".*

www.ingramcontent.com/pod-product-compliance
Lightning Source LLC
Chambersburg PA
CBHW070046030426
42335CB00016B/1814